PHONIC FOOLERS

PHONIC FOOLERS

A Creative Arts
DICTIONARY OF HOMOPHONES

Gerald I. Manus, Ph.D.
Muriel R. Manus, M.S.

CREATIVE ARTS BOOK COMPANY
Berkeley • 1998

Copyright © 1998 by Gerald and Muriel Manus

No part of this book may be reproduced in any manner without written permission from the publisher, except in brief quotations used in articles or reviews.

For Information contact:
Creative Arts Book Company
833 Bancroft Way
Berkeley, California 94710

ISBN 0-88739-154-0
Library of Congress Catalog Number 97-65995

Printed in the United States of America

DEDICATION

This book is dedicated to Clark, Carol, Edi, Justin, Taylor and Maxine, our loving supportive family, and to innumerable friends who encouraged this "hobby".

                    Jerry and Muriel Manus
                          June 1997

INTRODUCTION

Although words that sound alike but are spelled differently are often called homonyms, it is better to make a distinction between homophones and homonyms. Homonyms are words that sound the same and are spelled the same though the words have different meanings (e.g., bear, bear); homophones are words that also have different meanings, sound alike but are spelled differently (e.g., bear, bare). Homophones are caused by identical or similar pronunciations of letters or combinations of letters. But homophones are also the result of the lack of precision in the sounding of letters or the combinations of letters. These imprecisions are produced by limitations in the speech apparatus of humans and in the variability among individuals in their ability to articulate or enunciate the letters or combinations of letters. Physiological, developmental, cultural and regional variations in the manner of expressing sounds contribute to the similarity in the way sounds are spoken and heard. For example, the words *escalate, escalade* are similar in sounds but in careful pronunciation of the last three letters, a distinction can be heard; however, in the rapid pronunciation of each word, as in our everyday speech, clear distinction is difficult or impossible to hear. As the Morrises[1] point out the English language is imbued with more homophones than other languages because it has acquired so many words from different languages. Thus, *tea* and *tee* come from the Chinese and Scotch languages respectfully.

We have researched and compiled the following list of words that we believe to be the most complete and the most accurate list of homophones yet published in the United States. We have given the name **PHONIC FOOLERS**© to those words which sound alike but are spelled differently and have different meanings. In completing this list, the following sources were reviewed and revised to insure the comprehensiveness and modern usage of the words listed:

1. The Encyclopedia of Homonyms 'sound-alikes'
   Dora Newhouse (Editor). Los Angeles: Newhouse Press, 1976.

---

[1] Morris, William & Morris, Mary. *The Morris Dictionary of Word and Phrase Origins.* New York: Harper & Row, Publishers, 1977.

2. Webster's Treasury of Synonyms, Antonyms and Homonyms
   New York: Avenel Books, Crown Publishers, 1953.

3. American Heritage Dictionary of the English Language
   Boston: Houghton-Mifflin, 1981.

4. Webster's New Universal Unabridged Dictionary, Deluxe 2nd Edition
   New York: Dorset & Baber, 1983.

Corrections and deletions were made in the words listed in the Newhouse "Encyclopedia" (1). Therefore our list differs from this work in many of the entries because of the inclusions and exclusions of many words. For example, the Newhouse "Encyclopedia" includes many of the words excluded by our criteria because the pronunciation given in the "Encyclopedia" does not correspond to the acceptable pronunciations in any American language dictionary we have used in our research. We have as a result excluded, among others, the following homonyms (sic) listed in the "Encyclopedia": *fours, force; Latin, latten; lumbar, lumber; yeld, yelde, yelled; hearse, herse*. The preferred and least colloquial pronunciation was adoped from the Webster's New Universal Unabridged Dictionary. Escept for the word *Sunday*, proper nouns were excluded from our list (e.g., *Wayne, wane*) as were words that are archaic, slang, obsolete, foreign or idiosyncratically pronounced. In addition, poetic expressions (e.g., *o'er*) have been omitted from the list. But included in our list are contractions, plural forms, possessive forms and words of general use as established by the Editors of Webster's New Universal Unabridged Dictionary. The list expands the number of homophones that appear in the Newhouse "Encyclopedia" and the Webster "Treasury of Synonyms, Antonyms and Homonyms".

The definitions provided are not complete definitions but are provided as guides to distinguish between the meanings of the **PHONIC FOOLERS**©. For a complete definition of the words' meanings, it is best to refer to any unabridged English dictionary.

On page iii we have provided a tally of the **PHONIC FOOLERS**© in each letter of the alphabet (there were no **PHONIC FOOLERS**© for the letters "x" and "z"). We have also included a tally of the number of **PHONIC FOOLERS**© groups whose sound is similar (e.g., *air, ere, heir, ere*). We call these groups "families". Our list of individual **PHONIC FOOLERS**© and **PHONIC FOOLERS**© families are listed on page iii.

Among the **PHONIC FOOLERS**© we have also identified 29 reversible **PHONIC FOOLERS**©. These are words in which changes in the position of one or more letters in a word result in a **PHONIC FOOLER**©:

bare, bear	noes, nose	tare, tear
bares, bears	pare, pear	tares, tears
feet, fete	pares, pears	tied, tide
grate, great	pride, pried	tier, tire
grates, greats	rued, rude	tiers, tires
hide, hied	roes, rose	timber, timbre
hoes, hose	sere, seer	timbers, timbres
mantle, mantel	seres, seers	ware, wear
mantles, mantels	stake, steak	wares, wears
meet, mete	stakes, steaks	

In the following pages, certain words are **underlined** to indicate words that have two acceptable pronunciations. Also, some of the words are followed by a **double asterisk** (******). These are words in which the "h" sound occurs. Although precise pronunciation would disqualify these words as homophones, ordinary speech does not make the "h" sound distinction. Thus, the "h" sound, which in precise speech should be an explosive blowing of air through the lips, is not carried out by most speakers. The sound of "h" is therefore blurred in such words as *hue, where,* and other words in which the "h" sound occurs.

Letter	Individual Words	Families
A	137	84
B	278	137
C	277	174
D	94	47
E	77	44
F	144	73
G	95	55
H	93	46
I	84	21
J	21	07
K	32	18
L	117	55

M	142	74
N	30	06
O	23	08
P	210	115
Q	17	01
R	190	109
S	271	105
T	147	73
U	10	03
V	36	16
W	180	67
Y	14	05
TOTAL	**2,719**	**1,343**

We have called words whose initial letters differ from the initial letter of its **PHONIC FOOLERS©**, crossovers (e.g., effect, affect; air, heir, err). Below we have listed the number of crossovers for each letter. The total number of crossovers is 562.

A	47		N	20
B	0		O	7
C	73		P	17
D	0		Q	15
E	76		R	31
F	17		S	64
G	11		T	0
H	33		U	8
I	51		V	0
J	7		W	39
K	36		Y	10
L	0			

PHONIC FOOLERS

A

absence   act of being away or not being present
    absents   *withdraws or stays away from*

absents   withdraws or stays away from
    absence   *act of being away or not being present*

accidence   the essentials of a subject
    accidents   *unplanned events*

accidents   unplanned events
    accidence   *the essentials of a subject*

acclamation   loud expression of approval or joy
    acclimation   *the act of becoming accustomed to a new climate or environment*

acclimation   the act of becoming accustomed to a new climate or environment
    acclamation   *loud expression of approval or joy*

acetic   vinegary or sour
    ascetic   *a person who is self-denying for religious reasons; rigid or severe for religious reasons*

acidic   having a sour taste, like an acid
    ascitic   *fluid accumulation in the body*

ad   short version of advertisement
    add   *to combine or total*

add

add	to combine or total
ad	short version of advertisement
addicts	persons with a compulsive habit
attics	rooms under the roof of a house
adds	combines or totals
ads	short version of advertisements.
adze (adz)	an axe with a curved blade.
adherence	devotion to a cause or belief
adherents	people who are devoted to a cause or belief
adherents	people who are devoted to a cause or belief
adherence	devotion to a cause or belief
adieu	a farewell or goodbye
ado	trouble or fuss
ado	trouble or fuss.
adieu	a farewell or goodbye.
adolescence	the period between puberty and adulthood; "the teen years"
adolescents	individuals in their teen years
adolescents	individuals in their teen years.
adolescence	the period between puberty and adulthood; "the teen years"
ads	short version of advertisements
adds	combines or totals
adze (adz)	an axe with a curved blade
adze (adz)	an axe with a curved blade
adds	combines or totals
ads	short version of advertisements
aerie	a nest or house in a high place
aery	a high place
airy	ventilated

aery   a high place
    aerie   *a nest or house in a high place*
    airy   *ventilated*

affect   to influence or act upon
    effect   *to produce a result or influence; a result*

affected   influenced or acted upon
    effected   *carried out; produced a result*

affective   that which stimulates or influences emotion
    effective   *that which produces a result or outcome*

affectively   stimulated or influenced emotionally
    effectively   *done in a way to produce a result or outcome*

affects   influences or acts upon
    effects   *produces a result or outcome*

aid   help or assistance; to assist
    aide   *a person who provides help or assistance*

aide   a person who provides help or assistance
    aid   *help or assistance; to assist*

aides   people who provide help or assistance
    aids   *helps or assistances; assists*

aids   helps or assistances; assists
    aides   *people who provide help or assistance*

ail   to be ill
    ale   *a femented malt beverage*

ails   is ill
    ales   *fermented malt beverages*

air

air		the gases surrounding the earth; to ventilate or expose to air; to publicize
	ere	before
	<u>err</u>	make a mistake
	heir	a beneficiary of an estate
aired		vented; allowed air to circulate; open to view
	erred	made a mistake
airing		venting; allowing air to circulate; open to view
	erring	making a mistake
airs		allows air to circulate; opens to view
	<u>errs</u>	makes a mistake
	heirs	beneficiaries of an estate
airy		ventilated
	aerie	a nest or house in a high place
	aery	a high place
aisle		a passage between rows of seats
	I'll	contraction of "I will" or "I shall"
	isle	a small island
aisles		passages between rows of seats
	isles	small islands
ait		a small isle in a river
	ate	having taken in food or eaten
	eight	the number between 7 & 9
ale		a fermented malt beverage
	ail	to be ill
ales		fermented malt beverages
	ails	is ill
all		total
	awl	a tool for piercing materials such as leather

Note: Underlined words have two acceptable pronunciations.

allowed	**permitted**
aloud	*spoken or uttered so it can be heard easily*
allude	**refer to indirectly or briefly**
elude	*avoid or escape*
illude	*trick or deceive*
alluded	**referred to indirectly or briefly**
eluded	*avoided or escaped*
illuded	*tricked or deceived*
alludes	**refers to indirectly or briefly**
eludes	*avoids or escapes*
illudes	*tricks or deceives*
alluding	**referring to indirectly or briefly**
eluding	*avoiding or escaping*
illuding	*tricking or deceiving*
allusion	**a reference to something indirectly or briefly**
elusion	*an evasion or escape*
illusion	*deception or false belief or delusion*
allusions	**references to something indirectly or briefly**
elusions	*evasions or escapes*
illusions	*deceptions or false beliefs or delusions*
allusive	**referring to indirectly; suggestive**
elusive	*avoiding or escaping*
illusive	*tricking or deceptive*
allusively	**referring indirectly**
elusively	*acting evasively or escaping*
illusively	*deceptively or in a tricky way*
alms	**money or goods for charity**
arms	*upper body appendages; weapons*
aloud	**spoken or uttered so it can be heard easily**
allowed	*permitted*

altar

altar	**an elevated structure for worship.**
alter	*change or modify*
altars	**elevated structures for worship**
alters	*changes or modifications*
alter	**change or modify**
altar	*an elevated structure of worship*
alters	**changes or modifications**
altars	*elevated structures for worship*
analyst	**one who separates for study**
annalist	*one who keeps a chronological record*
analysts	**those who separate for study**
annalists	*people who keep chronological records*
analyze	**separate for study**
annalize	*record chronologically*
analyzes	**separates for study**
annalizes	*records chronologically*
anele	**anoint**
anneal	*temper through heat to strengthen*
aneled	**anointed**
annealed	*tempered through heat to strengthen*
aneles	**anoints**
anneals	*tempers through heat to strengthen*
aneling	**anointing**
annealing	*tempering through heat to strengthen*
annalist	**one who keeps a chronological record**
analyst	*one who separates for study*
annalists	**people who keep chronological records**
analysts	*those who separate for study*

anti

annalize	record chronologically
analyze	*separate for study.*
annalizes	records chronologically.
analyzes	*separates for study*
anneal	temper through heat to strengthen
anele	*anoint*
annealed	tempered through heat to strengthen
aneled	*anointed*
annealing	tempering through heat to strengthen
aneling	*anointing*
anneals	tempers through heat to strengthen
aneles	*anoints*
ant	a specific class of insects
aunt	*sister of one's parents*
ante	an initial stake in a card game (i.e. poker)
anti	*one who is opposed to a group or policy*
auntie (aunty)	*sister of one's parents*
antecedence	that which precedes
antecedents	*those who or that which precedes*
antecedents	those who or that which precedes
antecedence	*that which precedes*
antes	initial stakes in a card game (i.e. poker)
antis	*persons opposed to a group or policy*
aunties	*sisters of one's parents*
anti	one who is opposed to a group or policy
ante	*an initial stake in a card game (i.e. poker)*
auntie (aunty)	*sister of one's parents*

antis
---

antis	persons opposed to a group or policy
antes	*initial stakes in a card game (i.e. poker)*
aunties (auntys)	*sisters of one's parents*
ants	more than one of a specific kind of insect
aunts	*sisters of one's parents*
arc	a sector of a circle; bow; curve.
ark	*container for Biblical commandments; boat or shelter like ark built by Noah*
arcs	sectors of a circle; bows; curves.
arks	*containers for Biblical commandments; boats or shelters like ark built by Noah*
ark	container for Biblical commandments; boat or shelter like ark built by Noah
arc	*a sector of a circle; bow; curve*
arks	containers for Biblical commandments; boats or shelters like ark built by Noah
arcs	*sectors of a circle; bows; curves*
armer	equipment for battle
armor	*protective or defensive covering*
armor	protective or defensive covering
armer	*equipment for battle*
arms	upper body appendages; weapons
alms	*money or goods for charity*
arrant	blatant; unrestricted
errant	*straying, erring from a standard*
ascent	rise or climb
assent	*agreement; agree*
ascents	rises or climbs
assents	*agreements; agrees*

aspirations

ascetic   a person who is self-denying for religious reasons; rigid or severe for religious reasons
acetic   *vinegary or sour*

ascitic   fluid accumulation in the body.
acidic   *having a sour taste, like an acid*

asperate   make uneven or roughen
aspirate   *pronounce a vowel with a puff of air; remove liquids or gases from a body part by means of air or suction*

asperates   roughens or makes uneven
aspirates   *pronounces a vowel with a puff of air; removes liquids or gases from a body part by means of air or suction*

asperation   the process of roughening
aspiration   *pronunciation of a vowel with a puff of air; the process of removing liquids or gases from a body part by means of air or suction*

asperations   the processes of roughening or making uneven
aspirations   *pronunciations of vowels with a puff of air; the process of removing liquids or gases from a body part by means of air or suction*

aspirate   to pronounce a vowel with a puff of air; to remove liquids or gases from a body part by means of air or suction
asperate   *to make uneven or roughen*

aspirates   pronounces a vowel with a puff of air; removes liquids or gases from a body part by means of air or suction
asperates   *roughens or makes uneven*

aspiration   pronunciation of a vowel with a puff of air; the process of removing liquids or gases from a body part by means of air or suction
asperation   *the process of roughening or making uneven*

aspirations   pronunciations of vowels with a puff of air; the process of removing liquids or gases from a body part by means of air or suction
asperations   *the processes of roughening or making uneven*

assent

assent	**agreement; agree.**
ascent	*rise or climb*
assents	**agreements; agrees**
ascents	*rises or climbs*
assistance	**help or aid**
assistants	*helpers or aides*
assistants	**helpers or aides**
assistance	*help or aid*
ate	**having taken in food or eaten**
ait	*a small isle in a river*
eight	*the number between 7 & 9*
attendance	**act of attending; persons present**
attendants	*those who attend; consequences*
attendants	**those who attend; consequences**
attendance	*act of attending; persons present*
attics	**rooms under the roof of a house**
addicts	*persons with a compulsive habit*
auger	**tool for boring**
augur	*a seer or prophet; to foretell by omens*
augers	**tools for boring.**
augurs	*seers or prophets; foretells by omens*
aught	**in any way or part; cipher**
ought	*that which is obligatory or expected*
aughts	**in any ways or parts; ciphers**
oughts	*those things which are obligatory or expected*
augur	**a seer or prophet; to foretell by omens**
auger	*tool for boring*

augurs	seers or prophets; foretells by omens
augers	*tools for boring*
auntie (aunty)	sister of one's parents
ante	*an initial stake in a card game (i.e., poker)*
anti	*one who is opposed to a group or policy*
aunties (auntys)	sisters of one's parents
antes	*initial stakes in a card game (i.e. poker)*
antis	*persons opposed to a group or policy*
aural	pertaining to the ear
oral	*spoken; pertaining to the mouth*
aureole	a halo
oriole	*a type of bird*
aureoles	halos
orioles	*types of birds*
auricles	external parts of the outer ears.
oracles	*divine utterances; persons or things that express divine utterance*
auricle	external part of the outer ear
oracle	*divine utterance; person or thing that expresses divine utterance*
away	off in another place
aweigh	*free of the bottom of the water (e.g., anchor)*
aweigh	free of the bottom of the water (e.g., anchor)
away	*off in another place*
awful	terrible
offal	*refuse or garbage*

awl

awl   a tool for piercing materials such as leather
   all   *total*

axal   forming an axis
   axil   *angle formed by leaf and stem*
   axle   *means by which wheel rotates*

axes   tools with handles for chopping; bissecting lines; lines around which something turns
   axis   *central bissecting line; line around which something turns*

axil   angle formed by leaf and stem
   axal   *forming an axis*
   axle   *means by which wheel rotates*

axils   angles formed by leaves and stems
   axles   *means by which wheels rotate*

axis   central bissecting line; line around which something turns
   axes   *tools with handles for chopping; bissecting lines; lines around which something turns*

axle   means by which wheels rotate
   axal   *forming an axis*
   axil   *angle formed by leaf and stem*

axles   means by which wheels rotate
   axils   *angles formed by leaves and stems*

aye   yes
   eye   *sensory organ for vision; to see*
   I   *personal pronoun for self*

ayer   one who agrees or affirms
   eyer   *one who views or observes*
   ire   *wrath*

ayes   yesses
   eyes   *sensory organs for vision; sees*
   I's   *referring to oneselves*

B

bad — not good
   bade — ordered; wished; directed; invited

bade — ordered; wished; directed; invited
   bad — not good.

bade — ordered; wished; directed; invited
   bayed — dammed up; barked

bail — property given for security; handle of pail; remove waste from a boat
   bale — a bundle of hay, cord, etc; woe

bailed — removed water from a boat; given bail
   baled — tied in bundles

bailee — a receiver of bail
   bailey — outer protective wall of a castle

bailees — receivers of bail
   baileys — outer protective walls of a castle

bailer — one who bails
   baler — one who bundles

bailers — those who bail
   balers — those who bundle

bailey — outer protective wall of a castle
   bailee — a receiver of bail

baileys — outer protective walls of a castle
   bailees — receivers of bail

Note: Underlined words have two acceptable pronunciations.

bails

bails		providing bail; removing water from a boat
	bales	*bundles*
bait		lure; attract
	bate	*to reduce; lessen*
baize		green soft woolen felt material
	bays	*inlet of water; storage area*
	beys	*provincial governors in ancient Turkey*
bald		absence of hair or other growth
	balled	*shaped into a ball*
	bawled	*cried loudly*
balea		bundle of hay, cord, etc; woe
	bail	*property given for security; handle of pail; remove waste from a boat*
baled		tied in bundles
	bailed	*removed water from a boat; given bail*
baler		one who bundles
	bailer	*one who bails*
balers		those who bundle
	bailers	*those who bail*
bales		bundles
	bails	*providing bail; removing water from a boat*
ball		sphere
	bawl	*cry loudly*
balled		shaped into a ball
	bald	*absence of hair or other growth*
	bawled	*cried loudly*
baller		one who rolls material into a ball
	bawler	*one who cries loudly*

ballers		those who roll material into a ball
	bawlers	*those who cry loudly*
balling		the act of rolling material into a ball
	bawling	*the act of crying loudly*
balls		rolls material into a ball
	bawls	*cries loudly*
balm		an oily soothing substance; sweet smelling material
	bomb	*explosive device; to attack with an explosive device*
balms		oily soothing substances
	bombs	*explosive devices; attacks with an explosive device*
balming		putting an oily soothing substance on the skin
	bombing	*attacking with an explosive device*
band		group of people; (e.g. musicians, troops)
	banned	*forbidden*
banned		forbidden
	band	*group of people; (e.g. musicians, troops)*
banns		public notice of intended marriage
	bans	*forbids*
bans		forbids
	banns	*public notice of intended marriage*
bar		block entrance; that which blocks entrance
	barre	*covering two strings of a musical instrument*
bard		a poet
	barred	*having bars; prevented from entering*
bare		without covering; unfurnished
	bear	*a type of mammal; to carry; to tolerate*
barer		more exposed; more unfurnished
	bearer	*carrier*

bares

bares	**exposes**
bears	*carries; tolerates; gives birth; types of mammal*
baring	**exposing**
bearing	*carrying*
bark	**sharp sound of a dog; outside covering of a tree trunk**
barque	*sailing vessel*
barks	**sharp sounds of a dog; outside coverings of tree trunks**
barques	*sailing vessels*
baron	**lower level of royalty**
barren	*unproductive; dull*
baroness	**wife of a baron**
barrenness	*emptiness; state of unproductivity*
barque	**sailing vessel**
bark	*sharp sound of a dog; outside covering of a tree trunk*
barques	**sailing vessels**
barks	*sharp sounds of a dog; outside coverings of tree trunks*
barre	**covering two strings of a musical instrument**
bar	*block entrance; that which blocks entrance*
barred	**having bars; prevented from entering**
bard	*a poet*
barren	**unproductive; dull**
baron	*lower level of royalty*
barrenness	**emptiness; state of unproductivity**
baroness	*wife of a baron*
barres	**covers two strings of a musical instrument.**
bars	*blocks entrance; that which blocks entrance*
bars	**blocks entrance; that which blocks entrance**
barres	*covers two strings of a musical instrument*

~ 16 ~

base	establish; station; bottom support; fundamental principle; morally low
bass	*lowest range of male voice*
based	established; stationed; resting on
baste	*sew with loose stitches; to moisten meat in cooking; to beat or scold*
bases	establishes; stations; foundations; fundamental principles
basis	*foundation*
basses	*lowest ranges of male voices*
basis	foundation
bases	*establishes; stations; foundations; fundamental principles*
basses	*lowest ranges of male voices*
bask	lie in pleasant warmth; to enjoy
basque	*a tight fitting garment*
basks	lies in a pleasant warmth; enjoys
basques	*tight fitting garments*
basque	a tight fitting garment
bask	*lie in pleasant warmth; to enjoy*
basques	tight fitting garments
basks	*lies in a pleasant warmth; enjoys*
bass	lowest range of male voice
base	*establish; station; foundations; fundamental principle; morally low*
basses	lowest range of male voices
bases	*establishes; stations; foundations; fundamental principles*
basis	*foundation*
baste	sew with loose stitches; to moisten meat in cooking; to beat or scold
based	*established; stationed; resting on*

bat

bat	a wooden club used in baseball
batt	*a sheet of material bunched together*
bate	to reduce; lessen
bait	*lure; attract*
bats	wooden clubs used in baseball
batts	*sheets of material bunched together*
batt	a sheet of material bunched together
bat	*a wooden club used in baseball*
batts	sheets of material bunched together
bats	*wooden clubs used in baseball*
bawl	cry loudly
ball	*sphere*
bawled	cried loudly
bald	*absence of air or other growth*
balled	*shaped into a ball*
bawler	one who cries loudly
baller	*one who rolls material into a ball*
bawlers	those who cry loudly
ballers	*those who roll material into a ball*
bawling	the act of crying loudly
balling	*the act of rolling material into a ball*
bawls	cries loudly
balls	*rolls material into a ball*
bay	inlet of water; storage area
bey	*provincial governor in ancient Turkey*
bayed	dammed up; barked
<u>bade</u>	*ordered; wished; directed; invited*

Note: Underlined words have two acceptable pronunciations.

bays		inlets of water; storage areas
	baize	*green soft woolen felt material*
	beys	*provincial governors in ancient Turkey*

bazaar — marketplace
bizarre — *odd; wierd*

be — exist; take place
bee — *a type of insect; a gathering for an activity*

beach — a sandy shore alongside a sea, rim or lake
beech — *type of tree*

beaches — sandy shores alongside a sea, rim or lake
beeches — *types of trees*

bean — a legume; a kind of vegetable
been — *was (past participle of be)*

been — was (past participle of be)
bean — *a legume; a kind of vegetable*

bear — a type of mammal; to carry; to tolerate
bare — *without covering; unfurnished*

bearer — carrier
barer — *more exposed; more unfurnished*

bearing — carrying
baring — *exposing*

bears — carries; tolerates; gives birth; types of mammal.
bares — *exposes*

beat — strike with a series of blows; defeat; assigned path
beet — *edible root of a certain plant*

beats — strikes with a series of blows; assigned paths
beets — *edible roots of certain plant*

beau

beau	a steady male escort
bow	*a tied piece of ribbon; tool to shoot an arrow*
beaus	steady male escorts
bows	*tied pieces of ribbon; tools to shoot arrows*
bee	a type of insect; a gathering for an activity
be	*exist; take place*
beech	type of tree
beach	*a sandy shore alongside a sea, rim or lake*
beeches	types of trees
beaches	*sandy shores alongside a sea, rim or lake*
been	was (past participle of be)
bean	*a legume; a kind of vegetable*
been	was (past participle of be)
bin	*a storage box*
beer	a brewed alcoholic beverage
bier	*a frame for a coffin*
beers	brewed alcoholic beverages
biers	*frames for coffins*
bees	types of insects; gatherings for activities
bise (bize)	*a cold, north wind*
beet	edible root of a certain plant
beat	*strike with a series of blows; defeat; assigned path*
beets	edible roots of a certain plant
beats	*strikes with a series of blows; defeats; assigned paths*
bell	instrument to produce a ringing sound; sound of a ring
belle	*a beautiful, charming woman*

Note: Underlined words have two acceptable pronunciations.

belle	a beautiful, charming woman
bell	*instrument to produce a ringing sound; sound of a ring*
belles	beautiful charming women
bells	*instruments to produce a ringing sound; ringing sounds*
belligerence	warlike characteristic
belligerents	*those who wage war*
belligerents	those who wage war
belligerence	*warlike characteristic*
bells	instruments to produce a ringing sound; ringing sounds
belles	*beautiful, charming women*
berried	full of berries
buried	*interred*
berries	small juicy fruits
buries	*inters*
berry	a small juicy fruit
bury	*inter*
berth	space to dock ships; sleeping space on a ship; rank
birth	*coming into life; heritage; origination*
berthing	finding a place to dock a ship; finding a space to sleep on a ship; ranking
birthing	*act of being born*
berths	spaces to dock ships; sleeping spaces on a ship; ranks
births	*comings into life; heritages; originations*
better	of superior quality
bettor	*one who bets*
betters	those who are superior; defeats
bettors	*persons who bet*

bettor

bettor	one who bets
better	*of superior quality*
bettors	persons who bet
betters	*those who are superior; defeats*
bey	provincial governor in ancient Turkey
baize	*green soft woolen felt material*
bay	*inlet of water; storage area*
beys	provincial governors in ancient Turkey
bays	*inlets of water; storage areas*
bib	cloth to protect clothing; part of an apron
bibb	*type of faucet*
bibb	type of a faucet
bib	*cloth to protect clothing; part of an apron*
bibbs	types of faucets
bibs	*pieces of cloth to protect clothing; parts of aprons*
bibs	pieces of cloth to protect clothing; parts of aprons
bibbs	*types of faucets*
bier	a frame for a coffin
beer	*a brewed alcoholic beverage*
biers	frames for coffins
beers	*brewed alcoholic beverages*
bight	a bend or coil; a curve in the river
bite	*cut or tear with teeth; eat into*
byte	*a unit of space in computer terminology*
bights	bends or coils; curves in the river
bites	*cuts or tears with teeth; eats into*
bytes	*units of space in computer terminology*
billed	sent a bill; persons name placed on an advertisement
build	*construct*

bin		a storage box
	been	was (past participle of be)
bird		a warm blooded vertebrae with feathers
	birred	made a whirring sound
	burred	made a guttural sound; forming a rough edge
birr		force; power; emphasis in oral communication
	bur	prickly edge of a plant or nut
	burr	a small tool used to cut or deepen; rough edge on metal or paper; rough sound
birred		made a guttural sound; forming a rough edge
	bird	a warm blooded vertebrae with feathers
	burred	made a whirring sound
birth		come into life; heritage; origination
	berth	space to dock ships; sleeping space on a ship; rank
birthing		act of being born
	berthing	finding a place to dock a ship; finding a space to sleep on a ship; ranking
births		comings into life; heritages; originations
	berths	spaces to dock ships; sleeping spaces on a ship; ranks
bise (bize)		a cold, north wind
	bees	types of insects; gatherings for activities
bit		part of a drill that makes a hole
	bitt	deck post of a ship around which rope is wrapped
bite		cut or tear with teeth; eat into
	bight	a bend or coil; a curve in the river
	byte	a unit of space in computer terminology
bites		cuts or tears with teeth; eats into
	bights	bends or coils; curves in the river
	bytes	units of space in computer terminology

Note: Underlined words have two acceptable pronunciations.

bits

bits	parts of drills which make holes; small amounts
bitts	*deck posts of ships around which rope is wrapped*
bitt	deck post of a ship around which rope is wrapped
bit	*part of a drill that makes a hole*
bitts	deck posts of ships around which rope is wrapped
bits	*parts of drills which make hopes; small amounts*
blend	intermix
blende	*zinc ore; certain sulfides*
blende	zinc ore; certain sulfides
blend	*intermix*
blendes	zinc ores; certain sulfides
blends	*intermixes*
blends	intermixes
blendes	*zinc ores; certain sulfides*
blew	made a wind sound; produced a puff of air
blue	*one of the primary colors*
bloc	a political group
block	*obstruct; a three-dimensional square or rectangular form*
block	obstruct; a three-dimensional square or rectangular form
bloc	*a political group*
blocks	obstructs; three-dimensional squares or rectangular forms
blocs	*political groups*
blocs	political groups
blocks	*obstructs; three-dimensional squares or rectangular forms*
blue	one of the primary colors
blew	*made a wind sound; produced a puff of air*
boar	wild pig
bore	*cause to feel dull or tired; those who are dull or tiring; make an opening or hole*

bolled

board	a unit of timber; a panel of executives; food provided for a roomer
bored	made to feel dull or tired; made an opening or hole
boarder	a roomer who is provided meals
border	edge; boundary line
boarders	roomers who are provided meals
borders	edges; boundary lines
boars	wild pigs
bores	causes to feel dull or tired; those who are dull or tiring; makes an opening or hole
bode	predict; foreshadow
<u>*bowed*</u>	bent like a bow
bold	daring; striking or showy
bolled	formed into a pod
bowled	rolled a ball;
bolder	more daring
boulder	large size rock
bole	soft clay
boll	pod of cotton plant
bowl	roll a ball; play a game of tenpins; a dish used to serve liquids
boles	pieces of soft clay
bolls	pods of cotton plants
bowls	plays a game of tenpins; dishes used to serve liquids
boll	pod of cotton plant
bole	soft clay
bowl	roll a ball; play a game of tenpins; a dish used to serve liquids
bolled	formed into a pod
bold	daring; striking or showy
bowled	rolled a ball; played a game of tenpins

Note: Underlined words have two acceptable pronunciations.

bolls

bolls	pods of cotton plants
boles	pieces of soft clay
bowls	plays a game of tenpins; dishes used to serve liquids
bomb	explosive device; to attack with an explosive device
balm	an oily soothing substance; sweet smelling material
bombing	attacking with an explosive device
balming	putting an oily soothing substance on the skin
bombs	explosive devices; attacks with an explosive device
balms	oily soothing substances; sweet smelling materials
boos	to make sounds showing disapproval
booze	liquor; to drink excessively
booze	liquor; to drink excessively
boos	to make sounds showing disapproval
border	edge; boundary line
boarder	a roomer who is provided meals
borders	edges; boundary lines
boarders	roomers who are provided meals
bore	cause to feel dull or tired; those who are dull or tiring; make an opening or hole
boar	a wild pig
bored	made to feel dull or tired; made an opening or hole
board	a unit of timber; a panel of executives; food provided for a roomer
bores	causes to feel dull or tired; those who are dull or tiring; makes an opening or hole
boars	wild pigs
born	coming forth at birth
borne	carried
bourne	a limit or a goal; domain; a brook or a stream

bowed

borne	**carried**
born	*coming forth at birth*
bourne	*a limit or a goal; domain; a brook or a stream*
borough	**a geographical political unit**
burro	*a donkey*
burrow	*shelter, tunnel, retreat*
boroughs	**geographical political units**
burros	*donkeys*
burrows	*shelters, tunnels, retreats*
bough	**limb of a tree**
<u>*bow*</u>	*bend forward as a gesture of appreciation or honor; the act of bending forward*
boughs	**limbs of a tree**
<u>*bows*</u>	*bends forward as a gesture of appreciation or honor; the act of bending forward*
bouillon	**clear broth**
bullions	*bar or mass of gold or silver*
bouillons	**clear broths**
bullions	*bars or masses of gold or silver*
bourne	**a limit or a goal; domain; a brook or a stream**
born	*coming forth at birth*
borne	*carried*
<u>**bow**</u>	**a tied piece of ribbon; tool to shoot an arrow**
beau	*a steady male escort*
<u>**bow**</u>	**bend forward as a gesture of appreciation or honor; the act of bending forward**
bough	*limb of a tree*
bowed	**bent like a bow**
bode	*predict; foreshadow*

Note: Underlined words have two acceptable pronunciations.

bowl

bowl	roll a ball; a game of tenpins; a dish used to serve liquids
bole	*soft clay*
boll	*pod of cotton plant*
bowled	rolled a ball, played a game of tenpins
bold	*daring; striking or showy*
bolled	*formed into a pod*
bowls	plays a game of tenpins; dishes used to serve liquids
boles	*pieces of soft clay*
bolls	*pods of cotton plants*
<u>**bows**</u>	tied pieces of ribbon; tools to shoot arrows
beaus	*steady male escorts*
<u>**bows**</u>	bends forward as a gesture of appreciation or honor; the act of bending forward
boughs	*limbs of a tree*
boy	young male
<u>*buoy*</u>	*float to mark a shipping hazard; encourage*
boys	young males
<u>*buoys*</u>	*floats to mark a shipping hazard; encourages*
braid	ribbon or hair woven together
brayed	*made a loud harsh sound; crush into a powder; to spread thinly*
brail	a line to control sails on a ship
braille	*a form of printing with dots to permit sightless persons to read*
braille	a form of printing with dots to permit sightless persons to read
brail	*a line to control sails on a ship*
braise	cooking meat in small amount of liquid to sear meat
brays	*harsh loud sounds*
braze	*solder, especially with an alloy*

Note: Underlined words have two acceptable pronunciations.

break

braises	**cooks meat in small amount of liquid to sear meat**
brazes	*solders, especially with an alloy*
brake	**an instrument for stopping forward motion; e.g., vehicle or engine**
break	*part; to suddenly or violently tear apart, such as a dish; pause*
brakes	**instruments for stopping forward motion; e.g., vehicles or engines**
breaks	*parts; suddenly or violently tears apart, such as a dish; pauses*
braking	**stopping, as a vehicle or engine**
breaking	*tearing apart suddenly, such as a dish; pausing*
brayed	**made a loud harsh sound; crush into a powder; to spread thinly**
braid	*ribbon or hair woven together*
brays	**makes harsh loud sounds**
braise	*cooking meat in small amount of liquid to sear meat*
braze	*solder, especially with an alloy*
braze	**solder, especially with an alloy**
braise	*cooking meat in small amount of liquid to sear meat*
brays	*makes harsh loud sounds*
brazes	**solders, especially with an alloy**
braises	*cooks meat in small amount of liquid to sear meat*
breach	**break of a rule or regulation**
breech	*part below the waist*
breaches	**breaks a rule or regulation**
breeches	*trousers*
bread	**baked dough**
bred	*produced or raised*
break	**part; to suddenly or violently tear apart such as a dish**
brake	*an instrument for stopping forward motion; e.g., vehicle or engine; pause*

~ 29 ~

breaks

breaks	parts; suddenly or violently tears apart such as a dish; stops
brakes	*instruments for stopping forward motion; e.g., vehicles or engines; pauses*
breaking	tearing apart suddenly, such as a dish; pausing
braking	*stopping as a vehicle or engine*
bred	produced or raised
bread	*baked dough*
breech	part below the waist
breach	*break of a rule or regulation*
breeches	parts below the waist
breaches	*breaks a rule or regulation*
brewed	infused or boiled liquid (e.g., coffee, tea)
brood	*sit as a hen to hatch an egg; group of related family members*
brews	infuses or boils liquids (e.g., coffee, tea)
bruise	*an injury in which skin is not broken*
briar	white heath; pipe made from white heath
brier	*a certain prickly bush*
briars	white heaths; pipes made from white heaths
briers	*certain prickly bushes*
bridal	referring to a bride or wedding
bridle	*a restraining run and bit for a horse; put back the head in displeasure*
bridle	a restraining run and bit for a horse; put back the head in displeasure
bridal	*referring to a bride or wedding*
brier	A certain prickly bush
briar	*white heath; pipe made from white heath*
briers	certain prickly bushes
briars	*white heaths; pipes made from white heaths*

bruise

broach	a spit; an awl; to open a subject or discussion
brooch	an ornamental pin
broaches	spits; awls; opens a subject or discussion
broochs	ornamental pins
brooch	an ornamental pin
broach	a spit; an awl; to open a subject or discussion
broochs	ornamental pins
broaches	spits; awls; opens a subject or discussion
brood	sit as a hen to hatch an egg; group of related family members
brewed	infused or boiled liquid (e.g., coffee, tea)
broom	a device for sweeping
brougham	a closed carriage for two or more people
brume	fog; mist
brooms	devices for sweeping
broughams	closed carriages for two or more people
brumes	fogs; mists
brougham	a closed carriage for two or more people
broom	a device for sweeping
brume	fog; mist
broughams	closed carriages for two or more people
brooms	devices for sweeping
brumes	fogs; mists
brows	areas above the eyes; foreheads
browse	to nibble or graze in a pasture or forest; to scan casually
browse	to nibble or graze in a pasture or forest; to scan casually
brows	areas above the eyes; foreheads
bruise	an injury in which skin is not broken
brews	infuses or boils liquids (e.g., coffee or tea)

Note: Underlined words have two acceptable pronunciations.

bruit

bruit	to voice publicly
brut	dry (as in wine)
brute	a cruel or inhuman person; to shape a diamond
bruits	voices publicly
brutes	cruel or inhuman persons; shapes a diamond
brume	fog; mist
broom	a device for sweeping
brougham	a closed carriage for two or more people
brumes	fogs; mists
brooms	devices for sweeping
broughams	closed carriages for two or more people
brut	dry (as in wine)
bruit	to voice publicly
brute	a cruel or inhuman person; to shape a diamond
brute	a cruel or inhuman person; to shape a diamond
bruit	to voice publicly
brut	dry (as in wine)
brutes	cruel or inhuman persons; shapes a diamond
bruits	voices publicly
build	construct
billed	sent a bill; persons name placed on an advertisement
bullion	bar or mass of gold or silver
bouillon	clear broth
bullions	bars or masses of gold or silver
bouillons	clear broths
buoy	float to mark shipping hazard; encourage
boy	young male
buoys	floats to mark shipping hazard; encourages
boys	young males

Note: Underlined words have two acceptable pronunciations.

burrows

bur — prickly edge of a plant or nut
   birr — force; power; emphasis in oral communication
   burr — a small tool used to cut or deepen; rough edge on metal or paper; rough sound

buried — interred
   berried — full of berries

buries — inters
   berries — small juicy fruits

burley — type of tobacco
   burly — having a large body size; rough

burly — having a large body size; rough
   burley — type of tobacco

burr — A small tool used to cut or deepen; rough edge on metal or paper; rough sound
   birr — force; power; emphasis in oral communication
   bur — prickly edge of a plant or nut

burred — made a whirring sound
   bird — a warm blooded vertebrae with feathers
   birred — made a guttural sound; forming a rough edge

burro — a donkey
   borough — a geographical political unit
   burrow — shelter, tunnel, retreat

burros — donkeys
   boroughs — geographical political units
   burrows — shelters, tunnels, retreats

burrow — shelter, tunnel, retreat
   borough — a geographical political unit
   burro — a donkey

burrows — shelters, tunnels, retreats
   boroughs — geographical political units
   burros — donkeys

bursa

bursa	**a sac in the muscle**
bursar	*a treasurer*
bursar	**a treasurer**
bursa	*a sac in the muscle*
bursars	**treasurers**
bursas	*sacs in the muscles*
bursas	**sacs in the muscles**
bursars	*treasurers*
bury	**inter**
berry	*a small juicy fruit*
bus	**vehicle to carry many passengers; to transport**
buss	*to kiss*
buses	**vehicles to carry many passengers; transports**
busses	*kisses*
buss	**kiss**
bus	*vehicle to carry many passengers; to transport*
bussed	**kissed**
bust	*break*
busses	**kisses**
buses	*vehicles to carry many passengers; transports*
bust	**break**
bussed	*kissed*
but	**except; however**
butt	*end; target of ridicule or joke; place end to end*
butt	**end; target of ridicule or joke; place end to end**
but	*except; however*

buy	**purchase**
by	*near; through*
bye	*advance automatically (in sports)*
buyer	**one who purchases good or materials**
byre	*a cow barn*
buyers	**those who purchase good or materials**
byres	*cow barns*
buys	**purchases; bargains**
byes	*advances automatically (in sports)*
by	**near; through**
bye	*advance automatically (in sports)*
buy	*purchase*
bye	**to advance automatically (in sports)**
buy	*purchase*
by	*near; through*
byes	**advances automatically (in sports)**
buys	*purchases; bargains*
byre	**a cow barn**
buyer	*one who purchases goods or materials*
byres	**cow barns**
buyers	*those who purchase good or materials*
byte	**a unit of space in computer terminology**
bight	*a bend or coil; a curve in the river*
bite	*cut or tear with teeth; eat into*
bytes	**units of space in computer terminology**
bights	*bends or coils; curves in the river*
bites	*cuts or tears with teeth; eats into*

cache

C

cache	hidden treasure
cash	*negotiable money*
cached	hidden, concealed
cashed	*exchanged for negotiable money*
caches	hidden treasures; hides or conceals
cashes	*exchanges for negotiable money*
caching	hiding or concealing
cashing	*exchanging for negotiable money*
calendar	a system for recording days and months of the year
calender	*a machine for pressing smooth paper or cloth*
calendars	systems for recording days and months of the year
calenders	*machines for pressing smooth paper or cloth*
calender	a machine for pressing smooth paper or cloth
calendar	*a system for recording days and months of the year*
calenders	machines for pressing smooth paper or cloth
calendars	*systems for recording days and months of the year*
calk	a spike on a horseshoe to prevent slipping
caulk	*make water-tight with a water-sealing compound*
calks	spikes on a horseshoe to prevent slipping
caulks	*makes water tight with a water-sealing compound*
call	cry out; summon
caul	*a membrane surrounding internal tissue or a fetus*
callous	toughened; lacking in feeling
callus	*thickening of the skin*

~ 36 ~

calls	cries out; summons
cauls	*membranes surrounding internal tissues or a fetus*
<u>canape</u>	a cracker or bread spread with cheese or meat
canopy	*a covering over a doorway or person*
cannon	a large heavy firearm
canon	*a law or standard*
cannons	large heavy firearms
canons	*laws or standards*
canon	a law or standard
cannon	*a large heavy firearm*
canons	laws or standards
cannons	*large heavy firearms*
canopy	a covering over a doorway or person
<u>canape</u>	*a cracker or bread spread with cheese or meat*
cant	upsetting motion; jargon; insincere speech
can't	*contraction for "can not"*
can't	contraction for "can not"
cant	*upsetting motion; jargon; insincere speech*
canter	a medium-paced gallop; to run at a medium-paced gallop
cantor	*chief singer in a synagogue*
canters	medium-paced gallops; runs at a medium-paced gallop
cantors	*chief singers in synagogues*
cantor	chief singer in a synagogue
canter	*a medium-paced gallop; to run at a medium-paced gallop*
cantors	chief singers in synagogues
canters	*medium-paced gallops; runs at a medium-paced gallop*

Note: Underlined words have two acceptable pronunciations.

canvas

canvas	heavy cotton or other heavy fabric
canvass	*to survey opinion or votes*
canvases	heavy cotton or other heavy fabrics
canvasses	*surveys opinions or votes*
canvass	to survey opinion or votes
canvas	*heavy cotton or other heavy fabric*
canvasses	surveys opinions or votes
canvases	*heavy cotton or other heavy fabrics*
capital	geographical seat of government; wealth
capitol	*building that is the center of the legislative branch*
capitals	geographical seats of government
capitols	*buildings that are the center of the legislative branch*
capitol	building that is the center of the legislative branch
capital	*geographical seat of government; wealth*
capitols	buildings that are the center of the legislative branch
capitals	*geographical seats of government*
carat	unit of measurement for precious stones
caret	*editing symbol to note where a word or punctuation mark is to be inserted*
carrot	*yellow-orange colored root vegetable*
karat	*measure indicating ratio of gold in an alloy*
carats	units of measurement for precious stones
carets	*editorial symbols to note where a word or punctuation mark is to be inserted*
carrots	*yellow-orange colored root vegetables*
karats	*measures indicating ratio of gold in an alloy*
caret	editing symbol to note where a word or punctuation mark is to be inserted
carat	*a unit of measure for precious stones*
carrot	*yellow-orange colored root vegetable*
karat	*measure indicating ratio of gold in an alloy*

~ 38 ~

carets		editorial symbols to note where a word or punctuation mark is to be inserted
	carats	units of measurement for precious stones
	carrots	yellow-orange colored root vegetables
	karats	measures indicating ratio of gold in an alloy
caries		decay especially of teeth
	carries	holds something and moves with it; bears an object
carol		a song of happiness or celebration
	carrel	a cubicle for study in a library
carols		songs of happiness or celebration
	carrels	cubicles for study in libraries
carrel		a cubicle for study in a library
	carol	a song of happiness or celebration
carrels		cubicles for study in libraries
	carols	songs of happiness or celebration
carries		holds something and moves with it; bears an object
	caries	decay especially of teeth
carrot		yellow-orange colored root vegetable
	carat	unit of measurement for precious stones
	caret	an editing symbol to note where a word or punctuation mark is to be inserted
	karat	measure indicating ratio of gold in an alloy
carrots		yellow orange colored root vegetables
	carats	units of measurement for previous stones
	carets	editing symbols to note where a word or punctuation mark is to be inserted
	karats	measures indicating ratio of gold in an alloy
cash		negotiable money
	cache	hidden treasure
cashed		exchanged for negotiable money
	cached	hidden, concealed

cashes

cashes	**exchanges for negotiable money**
caches	*hidden treasures; hides or conceals*
cashing	**exchanging for negotiable money**
caching	*hiding or concealing*
cask	**a large barrel-type container**
casque	*helmet-like head covering*
casks	**large barrel-type containers**
casques	*helmet-like coverings*
casque	**helmet-like head covering**
cask	*a large barrel-type container*
casques	**helmet-like head coverings**
casks	*large barrel-type containers*
cast	**throw; an impression or mold**
caste	*an acquired or inherited social status*
caste	**an acquired or inherited social status**
cast	*throw; an impression or mold*
caster	**that which casts; a wheel under a board that can rotate to move furniture**
castor	*a kind of bean used in emetics or as a lubricant*
castes	**acquired or inherited social statuses**
casts	*throws; impressions or molds*
castor	**a kind of bean used in emetics or as a lubricant**
caster	*that which casts; a wheel under a board that can rotate to move furniture*
casts	**throws; impressions or molds**
castes	*acquired or inherited social statuses*
caudal	**referring to the tail**
caudle	*a warm spiced drink*

ceded

caudle	**a warm spiced drink**
caudal	*referring to the tail*
caul	**membrame surrounding internal tissue or a fetus**
call	*cry out; summon*
caulk	**to make water-tight with a water-sealing compound**
calk	*a spike on a horseshoe to prevent slipping*
caulks	**makes water right with a water-sealing compound**
calks	*spikes on a horseshoe to prevent slipping*
cauls	**membranes surrounding internal tissues or a fetus**
calls	*cries out; summons*
cause	**that which acts to produce an effect, result or outcome**
caws	*deep base sounds of birds such as crows*
caws	**deep base sounds of birds such as crows**
cause	*that which acts to produce an effect, result or outcome*
<u>**cay**</u>	**small island**
key	*metal tool to open a lock; symbol of explanation*
cedar	**a specific kind of tree; wood from a cedar tree**
ceder	*one who yields*
seeder	*a tool or device for spreading seed*
cedars	**specific kind of trees; wood from cedar trees**
ceders	*people who yield*
seeders	*tools or devices for spreading seed*
cede	**yield**
seed	*fertile part of a flowering plant; rank (in sports)*
ceded	**yielded**
seeded	*sowed; ranked (in sports)*

Note: Underlined words have two acceptable pronunciations.

cedes

cedes		yields
	seeds	*fertile parts of a flowering plant; ranks (in sports)*
ceding		yielding
	seeding	*the act of spreading seed; ranking (in sports)*
ceil		seal; to enclose with a ceiling
	seal	*seal; to close tightly; to mark with an official stamp or emblem*
ceiled		sealed; enclosed with a ceiling
	sealed	*closed tightly; marked with an official stamp or emblem*
ceiling		the top of a room
	sealing	*closing a box or envelope tightly*
ceils		seals; encloses with a ceiling
	seals	*closes tightly; marks with an official stamp or emblem*
cell		a small restricted space; a minute unit of a biological organism
	sell	*to give to a buyer for purchase*
cellar		the area beneath a building
	seller	*one who offers for purchase*
cellars		areas beneath buildings
	sellers	*those who offer for purchase*
cells		small restricted spaces; minute units of biological organisms
	sells	*offers for purchase*
cense		spread with incense
	cents	*pennies*
	scents	*odors*
	sense	*feel or know through one of the 5 senses; one of the 5 ways of knowing the world*
censer		container for burning incense
	censor	*regulate or sift the contents of written or oral material*
	senser	*one who feels or knows through one of the 5 ways of knowing the world*
	sensor	*a detection device for sight, sound, etc.*

censers	**containers for burning incense**
censors	*regulates or sifts the contents of written or oral material*
sensers	*those who feel or know through one of the 5 ways of knowing the world*
sensors	*detection devices for sight, sound, etc.*
censes	**spreads with incense**
census	*a survey or count of a population*
senses	*feels or knows through one of the 5 senses; the 5 means of knowing the world*
censor	**regulate or sift the contents of written or oral material**
censer	*container for burning incense*
senser	*one who feels or knows through one of the 5 ways of knowing the world*
sensor	*a detection device for sight, sound, etc.*
censors	**regulates or sifts the contents of written or oral material**
censers	*containers for burning incense*
sensers	*those who feel or know through one of the 5 ways of knowing the world*
sensors	*detection devices for sight, sound, etc.*
census	**a survey or count of a population**
censes	*spreads with incense*
senses	*feels or knows through one of the 5 senses; the 5 means of knowing the world*
cent	**a penny**
scent	*smell; odor; detect a smell or odor*
sent	*forwarded, mailed, transmitted*
cents	**pennies**
cense	*spread with incense*
scents	*smells; odors; detects smells or odors*
sense	*feel or know through one of the 5 ways of knowing the world; one of the 5 ways of knowing the world*

cere

cere	**a wax-like covering of certain birds' beaks**
sear	*burn or scorch*
seer	*prophet*
sere	*dry; change in cycle of a plant*
cereal	**a grain especially that used as breakfast food**
serial	*a publication issued at various intervals; anything arranged in a series*
cereals	**grains especially used as breakfast food**
serials	*publications issued at various intervals; things arranged in a series*
ceres	**wax-like coverings of certain birds' beaks**
sears	*burns or scorches*
seers	*prophets*
seres	*changes in cycles of plants*
cession	**ceding; yielding as by treaty or agreement**
session	*period; specific interval of time for meeting*
cessions	**cedings; yieldings as by treaty or agreement**
sessions	*periods; specific intervals of time for meeting*
cetaceous	**pertaining to marine mammals**
setaceous	*with bristles*
chance	**opportunity; luck; risk**
chants	*songs; sings*
chard	**leafy vegetable related to the beet**
charred	*burned; scorched*
charred	**burned; scorched**
chard	*leafy vegetable related to the beet*
chased	**followed; pursued; ornamented by engraving**
chaste	*pure; undefiled*
chaste	**pure; undefiled**
chased	*followed; pursued; ornamented by engraving*

chauffeur	person employed as a driver; to work as a chauffeur
shofar	*a ram's horn sounded at Rosh Hoshanna & Yom Kippur*
chauffeurs	persons employed as drivers; works as chauffeurs
shofars	*rams' horns sounded at Rosh Hoshanna & Yom Kippur*
cheap	inexpensive; low in cost relative to other prices; low in value; stingy
cheep	*to make a sound like a small bird; peep*
censor	make a sound like a small bird; peep
cheap	*inexpensive; low in cost relative to other prices; low in value; stingy*
chews	crushes or grinds as with the teeth
choose	*select; pick*
chic	fashionable; stylish
<u>sheik</u>	*chief; head (among Arabs)*
chili	a hot pepper
chilly	*cool*
chilly	cool
chili	*a hot pepper*
chock	a wedge or block to fill in a space or hold back an object
chuck	*pat or touch lightly; toss; a block*
chocks	wedges or blocks to fill spaces or hold back objects
chucks	*pats or touches lightly; tosses; blocks*
choir	a group of singers
quire	*24 or 25 sheets of equal size paper*
choirs	groups of singers
quires	*sets of 24 or 25 sheets of equal size paper*
choler	anger; irritability
collar	*part of clothing that covers the neck; restraining device around the neck*

Note: Underlined words have two acceptable pronunciations.

cholers

cholers — angers; irritabilities
collars — parts of clothing that cover the neck; restraining devices around the neck

choose — select; pick
chews — crushes or grinds as with the teeth

choral — referring to a chorus
coral — remains of the skeleton of certain sea animals; yellow/red color
corol — a corolla; inner leaves of a flower

chorale — a hymn; singing group
corral — an enclosure or pen for animals (especially horses or cattle)

chorales — hymns; singing groups
corrals — enclosures or pens for animals (especially horses or cattle)

chorals — referring to choruses
corals — remains of skeletons of certain sea animals; yellow/red colors
corols — corollas; inner leaves of flowers

chord — segment of a circle; combination of different notes played together
cord — string; 128 cubic feet of wood
cored — removed the center of an object

chords — segments of a circle; combinations of different notes played
cords — strings; stacks of wood measuring 128 cubic feet

chough — a type of crow with red legs
chuff — a coarse man; boor

choughs — types of crows with red legs
chuffs — coarse men; boors

chute (shute) — deep incline; move down a chute
shoot — fire as a gun; discharge a weapon

chutes (shutes) — deep inclines; moves down a chute
shoots — fires a gun; discharges a weapon

chuting (shuting)		deep incline; moving down a chute
	shooting	*firing as a gun; discharging a weapon*
cider		juice of an apple
	sider	*siderite; one who takes a side*
cingle		girth; belt
	single	*one; unmarried person; one-base hit in baseball*
cingles		girths; belts
	singles	*ones; unmarried persons; one base hits in baseball*
cinque		five markings on a card or die
	sink	*fall to a lower level; collapse; a bathroom or kitchen fixture used for washing*
cinques		five markings on cards or dice
	sinks	*falls to a lower level; collapses; bathroom or kitchen fixtures used for washing*
cirrhosis		disease of the liver; chronic liver damage
	sorosis	*fleshy, complex fruit; women's association or club*
cirrhoses		diseases of the liver; chronic liver damage
	soroses	*fleshy, complex fuits; women's associations or clubs*
cirrus		a slender filament or tentacle; a thin narrow cloud formation
	serous	*watery, like serum*
cite		refer to (a book, a passage in a text)
	sight	*seeing; a view; a notable or shocking view*
	site	*place or location; locate*
cited		referred to (a book or passage in a text)
	sited	*placed or located*
	sighted	*having vision; viewed*
cites		refers to (a book or passage in a text)
	sights	*views; notable or shocking views*
	sites	*places or locations; locates*

clause

clause	a section of a sentence that can stand alone; part of a legal document
claws	*sharp nails on an animal's paws; heads of hammers*
claws	sharp nails on an animal's paws; heads of hammers
clause	*a section of a sentence that can stand alone; part of a legal document*
cleek	a type of golf club
<u>clique</u>	*a closed group or association*
cleft	space caused by splitting; fissure
klepht	*a brigand*
clefts	spaces caused by splitting; fissures
klepht	*brigands*
clew	a ball of yarn or thread
clue	*a guide to a solution or mystery; hint*
click	a sharp sound
<u>clique</u>	*a closed group or association*
climb	to go up; ascend; crawl up
clime	*poetic form of "climate"*
climbs	goes up; ascends; crawls up
climes	*poetic form of "climates"*
<u>clique</u>	a closed group or association
cleek	*a type of golf club*
<u>clique</u>	a closed group or association
click	*a sharp sound*
close	shut
clothes	*apparel*
clothes	apparel
close	*shut*

Note: Underlined words have two acceptable pronunciations.

clue	a guide to a solution or mystery; hint
clew	*a ball of yarn or thread*
coal	a kind of fuel
cole	*a vegetable of the cabbage family*
coarse	rough; unrefined; a substance made up of large parts
course	*a direction or path; part of a meal*
coarser	rougher; less refined; made of larger parts
courser	*a pursuer*
coat	an outer covering
cote	*a shelter for birds*
coats	outer coverings
cotes	*shelters for birds*
coax	gently urge or persuade
cokes	*forms of coal; certain soft drinks (slang)*
cocky	aggressively self-confident
<u>khaki</u>	*yellow-brown color; a heavy twilled fabric*
coddling	cooking gently; treating with extreme care
codling	*young cod*
codling	young cod
coddling	*cooking gently; treating with extreme care*
coif	hoodlike cap; to arrange the style of hair
quaff	*to drink (especially liquor) with enthusiasm*
coiffed	arranged the style of hair
quaffed	*drank (especially liquor) with enthusiasm*
coiffing	arranging the style of hair
quaffing	*drinking (especially liquor) with enthusiasm*
coifs	hoodlike caps; arranges the style of hair
quaffs	*drinks (especially liquor) with enthusiasm*

Note: Underlined words have two acceptable pronunciations.

coign

coign (coigne)
   (quoin)   a wedge used in typesetting; a cornerstone
   coin   a metal piece used for money; to make money, terms or phases

coigne (coign)
   (quoin)   a wedge used in typesetting; a cornerstone
   coin   a metal piece used for money; to make money, terms or phrases

coignes (coigns)
   (quoins)   wedges used in typesetting; cornerstones
   coins   metal pieces used for money; makes money, terms or phrases

coigns (coignes)
   (quoins)   wedges used in typesetting; cornerstones
   coins   metal pieces used for money; makes money, terms or phrases

coin   a metal piece used for money; to make money, terms or phases
   coign (coigne)
   (quoin)   a wedge used in typesetting; a cornerstone

coining   making coins; making money, terms or phrases
   quoining   wedging used in typesetting
   (coigning)

coins   metal pieces used for money; makes money, terms or phrases
   coignes (coigns)   wedges used in typesetting; cornerstones
   (quoins)

cokes   forms of coal; certain soft drinks (slang)
   coax   gently urge or persuade

cole   a vegetable of the cabbage family
   coal   a kind of fuel

collar   part of clothing that covers the neck; restraining device around the neck
   choler   anger; irritability

collard   a kind of cabbage; kale
   collared   having a collar

complementing

collared	**having a collar**
collard	*a kind of cabbage; kale*
collars	**parts of clothing that cover the neck; restraining devices around the neck**
cholers	*angers; irritabilities*
colonel	**a high ranking officer below brigadier general**
kernel	*seed within the shell of a fruit or nut; core*
colonels	**high ranking officers below brigadier generals**
kernels	*seeds within the shell of fruits or nuts; cores*
color	**tint; hue; shade**
culler	*one who chooses, picks or collects*
colors	**tints; hues; shades**
cullers	*those who choose, pick or collect*
complacent	**satisfied; content**
<u>*complaisant*</u>	*seeking to please*
complacence	**characteristic of being satisfied**
complaisance	*characteristic of being pleasing*
complaisance	**characteristic of being pleasing**
complacence	*characteristic of being satisfied*
<u>**complaisant**</u>	**seeking to please**
complacent	*satisfied; content*
complement	**that which makes it complete or full**
compliment	*praise*
complemented	**made complete or full**
complimented	*praised*
complementing	**making complete or full**
complimenting	*praising*

Note: Underlined words have two acceptable pronunciations.

complements

complements   makes complete or full
compliments   *praises*

compliment   praise
complement   *that which makes it complete or full*

complimented   praised
complemented   *made complete or full*

complimenting   praising
complementing   *making complete or full*

compliments   praises
complements   *makes complete or full*

concenter   bring to a common place
consenter   *one who agrees or consents*

concenters   brings to a common place
consenters   *those who agree or consent*

consenter   one who agrees or consents
concenter   *bring to a common place*

consenters   those who agree or consent
concenters   *brings to a common place*

consequence   effect or result; importance
consequents   *effects or results*

consequents   effects or results
consequence   *effect or result; importance*

consonance   agreement; correspondence
consonants   *letter sounds such as p, t, n, etc. formed from blocking of air*

consonants   letter sounds such as p, t, n, etc. formed from blocking of air
consonance   *agreement; correspondence*

coo   sound of a pigeon or dove; to make loving sounds
coup   *successful action*

coolie	unskilled Asian laborer
coolly	*in a cool manner*
coolly	in a cool manner
coolie	*unskilled Asian laborer*
coop	an enclosure for foul or mammals
<u>coupe</u>	*2-door shortened sedan*
coos	sounds of pigeons or doves; makes loving sounds
coups	*successful actions*
coral	remains of the skeleton of cetain sea animals; yellow/red color
choral	*referring to a chorus*
corol	*a corolla; inner leaves of a flower*
cord	string; 128 cubic feet of wood
chord	*segment of a circle; combination of different notes played together*
cored	*removed the center of an object*
cords	strings; stacks of wood measuring 128 cubic feet
chords	*segments of a circle; combinations of different notes played*
core	center of a fruit; remove the core
corp	*a military unit; a group united for some action*
cored	removed the center of an object
chord	*segment of a circle; combination of different notes played together*
cord	*string; 128 cubic feet of wood*
cores	centers of fruits; removes the core
corps	*military units; groups united for some action*
corol	a corolla; inner leaves of a flower
choral	*referring to a chorus*
coral	*remains of the skeleton of certain sea animals; yellow/red color*
corols	corollas; inner leaves of flowers
chorals	*referring to choruses*
corals	*remains of skeletons of certain sea animals; yellow/red colors*

Note: Underlined words have two acceptable pronunciations.

corp

corp	a military unit; a group united for some action
core	*center of a fruit; remove the core*
corps	military units; groups united for some action
cores	*centers of fruits; removes the core*
corral	an enclosure or pen for animals (especially horses or cattle)
chorale	*a hymn; singing group*
corrals	enclosures or pens for animals (especially horses or cattle)
chorales	*hymns; singing groups*
correspondence	communication by writing; similarity
correspondents	*those who communicate with letters or reports*
correspondents	those who communicate with letters or reports
correspondence	*communication by writing; similarity*
co-sign	to sign a promissory note with another person to guarantee repayment
cosine	*the sine of the complement of the angle*
co-signs	signs a promissory note with another person to guarantee repayment
cosines	*sines of the complements of the angles*
cosine	the sine of the complement of the angle
co-sign	*to sign a promissory note with another person to guarantee repayment*
cosines	sines of the complements of the angles
co-signs	*signs a promissory note with another person to guarantee repayment*
cote	a shelter for birds
coat	*an outer covering*
cotes	shelters for birds
coats	*outer coverings*
council	an administrative, legislative or advisory group
counsel	*advice or advise*

councilor	council member
counselor	*advisor; lawyer; embassy official*
councilors	council members
counselors	*advisors; lawyers; embassy officials*
councils	administrative, legislative or advisory groups
counsels	*gives advice or advises*
counsel	advice or advise
council	*an administrative, legislative or advisory group*
counselor	advisor; lawyer; embassy official
councilor	*council member*
counselors	advisors; lawyers; embassy officials
councilors	*council members*
counsels	gives advice or advises
councils	*administrative, legislative or advisory groups*
<u>**coupe**</u>	2-door shortened sedan
coop	*an enclosure for foul or mammals*
coups	successful actions
coos	*sounds of pigeons or doves; makes loving sounds*
course	a direction or path; part of a meal
coarse	*rough; unrefined; a substance made up of large parts*
courser	a pursuer
coarser	*rougher; less refined; made of larger parts*
cousin	child of uncle or aunt
cozen	*trick*
cousins	children of uncles or aunts
cozens	*tricks*
coward	one who is lacking in courage
cowered	*hid or crouched out of fear*

Note: Underlined words have two acceptable pronunciations.

cozen

cozen	trick
cousin	*child of uncle or aunt*
cozens	tricks
cousins	*children of uncles or aunts*
creak	make a squeaky noise
creek	*a small area of running water*
creaks	makes squeaky noises
creeks	*small areas of running water*
crease	a fold
creese (kris)	*a Malay dagger*
creases	folds
creeses (krises)	*Malay daggers*
creek	a small area of running water
creak	*make a squeaky noise*
creeks	small areas of running water
creaks	*makes squeaky noises*
creese (kris)	a Malay dagger
crease	*a fold*
creeses (krises)	Malay daggers
creases	*folds*
crewel	yarn for embroidering
cruel	*mean; inflicting pain*
crewelist	a person who does embroidery
cruelest	*most mean; inflicting the most pain*
crews	ship's staffs; groups of workers
cruise	*sail without a specific direction*
cruel	mean; inflicting pain
crewel	*yarn for embroidering*

cruelest	most mean; inflicting the most pain
crewelist	*a person who does embroidery*
cruise	sail without a specific direction
crews	*ship's staffs; groups of workers*
cubical	referring to the volume of a cube
cubicle	*small room or section of a room*
cubicle	small room or section of a room
cubical	*referring to the volume of a cube*
cue	a hint or prompt; a stick used to play the game of pool
queue	*a long braid of hair; a line or order of people or events*
cued	hinted or prompted
queued	*lined up; placed in order*
cues	hints or prompts; sticks used to play the game of pool
queues	*long braids of hair; lines or orders of people or events*
cuing	hinting or prompting
queuing	*lining up in order*
culler	one who chooses, picks or collects
color	*tint; hue; shade*
cullers	those who choose, pick or collect
colors	*tints; hues; shades*
currant	a kind of fruit related to a raisin
current	*present; a flow of water*
currants	kinds of fruit related to raisins
currents	*flows of water*
current	present; a flow of water
currant	*a kind of fruit related to a raisin*
currents	flows of water
currants	*kinds of fruit related to raisins*

curser		one who expresses evil or profanity
	cursor	*a guide*
cursers		those who express evil or profanity
	cursors	*guides*
cursor		a guide
	curser	*one who expresses evil or profanity*
cursors		guides
	cursers	*those who express evil or profanity*
cygnet		a young swan
	signet	*a small seal*
cygnets		young swans
	signets	*small seals*
cymbal		metallic percussion instrument
	symbol	*a mark to represent an idea, place or action*
cymbals		metallic percussion instruments
	symbols	*marks to represent ideas, places or actions*

D

dam		a barrier to obstruct the flow o of of water; a female parent (especially a dog or cat)
	damn	*declare something to be evil or loathsome*
dammed		obstructed by a barrier; stopped the flow of water
	damned	*condemned or doomed; evil or loathsome*
damming		obstructing; stopping the flow of water
	damning	*declaring something to be evil or loathsome*

damn	**declare something to be evil or loathsome**
dam	*a barrier to obstruct the flow of water; a female parent (especially a dog or cat)*
damned	**condemned or doomed; evil or loathsome**
dammed	*obstructed by a barrier; stopped the flow of water*
damning	**declaring something to be evil or loathsome**
damming	*obstructing; stopping the flow of water*
damns	**declares something to be evil or loathsome**
dams	*barriers to obstruct the flow of water; female parents (especially dogs or cats)*
dams	**barriers to obstruct the flow of water; female parents (especially dogs or cats)**
damns	*declares something to be evil or loathsome*
days	**periods of time between sunrise and sunset**
daze	*to stun or stupefy with a blow or shock; to confuse*
daze	**stun or stupefy with a blow or shock; to confuse**
days	*periods of time between sunrise and sunset*
dear	**beloved or loved; high-priced, expensive**
deer	*a four-footed antlered animal*
decadence	**falling into an inferior condition or state; decay**
decadents	*those people who fall into decay*
decadents	**those people who fall into decay**
decadence	*falling into an inferior condition or state; decay*
deer	**a four-footed antlered animal**
dear	*beloved or loved; high priced, expensive*
defuse	**remove the fuse from a bomb, mine; to reduce the threat of explosion (e.g., between conflicting parties)**
diffuse	*pour out and spread as a liquid; disseminate*

defused

defused	removed the fuse from a bomb, mine; reduced the threat of explosion (e.g., between conflicting parties)
diffused	*poured out and spread as a liquid; disseminated*
defuser	one who removes the fuse from a bomb, mine; one who reduces the threat of explosion or conflict
diffuser	*one who pours out and spreads a liquid; an instrument that pours out or spreads a liquid*
defuses	removes the fuse from a bomb, mine; reduces the threat of explosion or conflict
diffuses	*pours out and spreads as a liquid; disseminates*
defusing	removing fuses from bombs, mines; reducing the threat of explosion or conflict
diffusing	*pouring out and spreading liquids; disseminating*
demean	degrade; lower; behave oneself
demesne	*possession; domain*
demeans	degrades; lowers; behaves oneself
demesnes	*possessions; domains*
demesne	possession; domain
demean	*degrade; lower; behave oneself*
demesnes	possessions; domains
demeans	*degrades; lowers; behaves oneself*
dense	having parts close together, crowded, compact; stupid; slow-witted; dull
dents	*hollows or depressions in a surface from a blow*
dents	hollows or depressions in a surface from a blow
dense	*having parts close together, crowded, compact; stupid; slow-witted; dull*
dependence	needing aid or support
dependents	*people needing someone or something for aid or support*
dependents	people needing someone or something for aid or support
dependence	*needing aid or support*

depravation	the act of making something bad or worse; corruption
deprivation	*the act of removing or withholding something that is needed or wanted*
depravations	the acts of making something bad or worse; corruptions
deprivations	*the acts of removing or withholding something that is needed or wanted*
deprivation	the act of removing or withholding something that is needed or wanted
depravation	*the act of making something bad or worse; corruption*
deprivations	the acts of removing or withholding something that is needed or wanted
depravations	*the acts of making something bad or worse; corruptions*
descent	the act of going down an incline or slope
dissent	*differ in sentiment or opinion; disagree*
descents	the acts of going down an incline or slope
dissents	*differs in sentiment or opinion; disagreements*
<u>desert</u>	abandon, forsake
dessert	*fruit, pudding or cake served at the end of a meal*
<u>deserts</u>	abandons, forsakes
desserts	*fruits, puddings or cakes served at the end of a meal*
dessert	fruit, pudding or cake served at the end of a meal
<u>desert</u>	*abandon, for sake*
desserts	fruits, puddings or cakes served at the end of a meal
<u>deserts</u>	*abandons, forsakes*
deterrence	the process of restraining or discouraging
deterrents	*things which discourage or restrain*
deterrents	things which discourage or restrain
deterrence	*the process of restraining or discouraging*

Note: Underlined words have two acceptable pronunciations.

deviser

deviser	one who contrives or plans
divisor	*in math, the number by which another number is divided*
devisers	contrivers or planners
divisors	*in math, the numbers by which other numbers are divided*
dew	moisture condensed from the atmosphere at night
<u>*do*</u>	*to perform an act or duty*
due	*immediately owed; rightful; proper*
die	cease to live; expire; singular of dice; a device for shaping a form
dye	*coloring matter; color*
died	ceased to live; expired
dyed	*colored*
dies	ceases to live; expires; devices for shaping forms
dyes	*coloring matters; colors*
diffuse	pour out and spread as a liquid; disseminate
defuse	*remove the fuse from a bomb, mine; to reduce the threat of explosion or conflict*
diffused	poured out and spread as a liquid; disseminated
defused	*removed the fuse from a bomb, mine; reduced the threat of explosion (e.g., between conflicting parties)*
diffuser	one who pours out and spreads a liquid; an instrument that pours out or spreads a liquid
defuser	*one who removes the fuse from a bomb, mine; one who reduced the threat of explosion or conflict*
diffuses	pours out and spreads as a liquid; disseminates
defuses	*removes the fuse from a bomb, mine; reduces the threat of explosion or conflict*
diffusing	pouring out and spreading liquids; disseminating
defusing	*removing fuses from bombs, mines; reducing the threat of explosion or conflict*

Note: Underlined words have two acceptable pronunciations.

dine	**to eat the principle meal of the day; to entertain at dinner**
dyne	*a unit of force in physics*
dines	**eats the principle meal of the day; entertains at dinner**
dynes	*units of force in physics*
dire	**causing or involving great fear or suffering; dreadful**
dyer	*a person who uses coloring matter*
discous	**shaped like a disk**
discus	*disk used in Olympic games*
discreet	**maintaining silence about something of a delicate nature**
discrete	*detached from others; separate; distinct*
discreetly	**in a discreet way; showing caution and restraint about something of a delicate nature**
discretely	*in a discrete way; being detached from others or separated or distinct*
discreetness	**that which is silent about something of a delicate nature**
discreteness	*that which is detached from others; separation; distinction*
discrete	**detached from others; separate; distinct**
discreet	*maintaining silence about something of a delicate nature*
discretely	**in a discrete way; being detached from others or separated or distinct**
discreetly	*in a discreet way; showing caution and restraint about something of a delicate nature*
discreteness	**that which is detached from others; separation; distinction**
discreetness	*that which is silent about something of a delicate nature*
discus	**disk used in Olympic games**
discous	*shaped like a disk*
dissent	**differ in sentiment or opinion; disagree**
descent	*the act of going down an incline or slope*

dissents

dissents	differs in sentiment or opinion; disagreements
descents	the acts of going down an incline or slope
dissidence	disagreement
dissidents	people who disagree in opinions or attitudes
dissidents	people who disagree in opinions or attitudes
dissidence	disagreement
divisor	in math, the number by which another number is divided
deviser	one who contrives or plans
divisors	in math, the numbers by which other numbers are divided
devisers	contrivers or planners
<u>do</u> (music)	the syllable used for the first tone or keynote of a scale
doe	a female deer, antelope, goat, rabbit
dough	flour or meal combined with water or milk to bake bread or cake
<u>do</u>	perform an act or duty
dew	moisture condensed from the atmosphere at night
due	immediately owed; rightful; proper
doe	a female deer, antelope, goat, rabbit
<u>do</u> (music)	the syllable used for the first tone or keynote of a scale
dough	flour or meal combined with water or milk to bake bread or cake
does	female deer, antelopes, goats, rabbits
doze	to sleep lightly, fitfully or for a brief period
done	completed
dun	make repeated demands for payment of a debt
dough	flour or meal combined with water or milk in a mass to bake bread or cake
<u>do</u> (music)	the syllable used for the first tone or keynote of a scale
doe	a female deer, antelope, goat, rabbit
dour	sullen; gloomy
dower	a wife's inheritance

Note: Underlined words have two acceptable pronunciations.

dower	**a wife's inheritance**
dour	*sullen; gloomy*
doze	**sleep lightly, fitfully or for a brief period**
<u>*does*</u>	*female deer, antelopes, goats, rabbits*
draft	**drawing; first copy of a paper; flow of air; a means of selecting people for service**
draught	*drinking or taking in a drink*
drafts	**drawings; first copies of a paper; flows of air; means of selecting people for service**
draughts	*drinking or taking of drinks*
draught	**drinking or taking in a drink**
draft	*drawing; first copy of a paper; flow of air; a means of selecting people for service*
draughts	**drinking or taking of drinks**
drafts	*drawings; first copies of a paper; flows of air; means of selecting people for service*
drawers	**a space (in a chest or under a desk) that slides in and out; one who draws**
draws	*pulls; makes a drawing*
draws	**pulls; makes a drawing**
drawers	*a space (in a chest or under a desk) that slides in and out; one who draws*
dual	**composed of two; double**
duel	*a combat between 2 people with or without physical weapons*
dualist	**a believer in the separation of body and soul or body and mind**
duelist	*one who duels*
ducked	**moved the head or body to escape; avoided physical contact**
duct	*a channel for flow of water, gas or electricity*

Note: Underlined words have two acceptable pronunciations.

duct

duct	a channel for flow of water, gas or electricity
ducked	*moved the head or body to escape; avoided physical contact*
due	immediately owed; rightful; proper
dew	*moisture condensed from the atmosphere at night*
<u>do</u>	*perform an act or duty*
duel	a combat between 2 people with or without physical weapons
dual	*compose of two; double*
duelist	one who duels
dualist	*a believer in the separations of body and soul or body and mind*
dun	make repeated demands for payment of a debt
done	*completed*
dye	coloring matter; color
die	*to cease to live; expire; singular of dice; a device for shaping a form*
dyed	colored
died	*ceased to live; expired*
dyer	a person who uses coloring matter
dire	*causing or involving great fear or suffering; dreadful*
dyes	coloring matters; colors
dies	*ceases to live; expires; devices for shaping forms*
dyne	a unit of force in physics
dine	*to eat the principle meal of the day; to entertain at dinner*
dynes	units of force in physics
dines	*eats the principle meal of the day; entertains at dinner*

Note: Underlined words have two acceptable pronunciations.

E

earn	merit; to obtain through effort
ern(e)	variety of eagle that lives near water
urn	type of vase
earns	merits; obtains through effort
ern(e)s	varieties of eagles that live near water
urns	types of vases
eave	edge of a roof
eve	night before a holiday
eaves	edges of roofs
eves	nights before holidays
effect	produce a result or influence; a result
affect	influence or act upon
effected	carried out; produced a result
affected	be influenced or acted upon
effective	done in a way to produce a result or outcome
affective	stimulated or influenced emotionally
effects	produces a result or outcome
affects	influences or acts upon
effluence	flowing out
effluents	materials that flow out of a lake or sewer
effluents	materials that flow out of a lake or sewer
effluence	flowing out
eight	the number between 7 & 9
ait	a small isle in a river
ate	having taken in food or eaten

elicit

elicit	**bring out**
illicit	*illegal and/or immoral; against the law*
elude	**avoid or escape**
allude	*refer to indirectly or briefly*
illude	*trick or deceive*
eluded	**avoided or escaped**
alluded	*referred to indirectly or briefly*
illuded	*tricked or deceived*
eludes	**avoids or escapes**
alludes	*refers to indirectly or briefly*
illudes	*tricks or deceives*
elusion	**an evasion or escape**
allusion	*a reference to something indirectly or briefly*
illusion	*deception or false belief or delusion*
elusions	**evasions or escapes**
allusions	*references to something indirectly or briefly*
illusions	*deceptions or false beliefs or delusions*
elusive	**avoiding or escaping**
illusive	*tricking or deceiving*
allusive	*referring to especially indirectly; suggestive*
elusively	**acting evasively or escaping**
allusively	*referring indirectly*
illusively	*deceptively or in a tricky way*
emerge	**come out (of water or hidden view)**
immerge	*to plunge into*
emerged	**came out (of water or hidden view)**
immerged	*plunged into*
emerges	**comes out (of water or hidden view)**
immerges	*plunges into*
emerging	**coming out (of water or of hidden view)**
immerging	*plunging into*

emersion	act of coming out
immersion	*act of plunging into*
emersions	acts of coming out (of water or hidden view)
immersions	*acts of plunging into*
empyreal	referring to the sky; made up of fire
imperial	*referring to empire, emperor or empress*
enervate	deprive of energy or power
innervate	*energize; give life to*
enervated	deprived of energy or power
innervated	*energized; gave life to*
enervates	deprives of energy or power
innervates	*energizes; gives life to*
enervation	the act of depriving of energy or power
innervation	*the act of energizing; the act of giving life to*
enervations	acts of depriving of energy or power
innervations	*acts of energizing; acts of giving life to*
enervator	one who deprives of energy or power
innervator	*one who energizes; one who gives life to*
enervators	those who deprive of energy or power
innervators	*those who energize; those who give life to*
entrance	coming in; an entry point
entrants	*those who are entered (e.g., race, contest or organization)*
entrants	those who are entered (e.g., race, contest or organization)
entrance	*coming in; an entry point*
epic	a poetic tale of a hero; of great size
epoch	*era*
epics	poetic tales of heroes
epochs	*eras*

epoch

epoch   **era**
   epic   *a poetic tale of a hero; of great size*

epochs   **eras**
   epics   *poetic tales of heroes*

ere   **before**
   air   *the gases surrounding the earth*
   err   *make a mistake*
   heir   *a beneficiary of an estate*

ern(e)   **variety of eagle that lives near water**
   earn   *merit; to obtain through effort*
   urn   *type of vase*

ern(e)s   **variety of eagles that live near water**
   earns   *merits; obtains through effort*
   urns   *types of vases*

err   **make a mistake**
   air   *the gases surrounding the earth*
   ere   *before*
   heir   *a beneficiary of an estate*

errant   **straying; erring from a standard**
   arrant   *blatant; unrestricted*

erred   **made a mistake**
   aired   *vented; allowed air to circulate*

erring   **making a mistake**
   airing   *venting; allowing air to circuate*

errs   **makes a mistake**
   airs   *allows air to circulate; opens to view*
   heirs   *beneficiaries of an estate*

erupt   **break out; explode**
   irrupt   *show violent activity*

errupted   **broken out; exploded**
   irrupted   *showed violent activity*

Note: Underlined words have two acceptable pronunciations.

erupting		**breaking out; exploding**
	irrupting	*violently active*
eruption		**the act of breaking out or exploding**
	irruption	*the act of showing violent activity*
eruptive		**characteristic of breaking out or exploding**
	irruptive	*characteristic of violent activity*
erupts		**breaks out; explodes**
	irrupts	*shows violent activity*
escaladed		**scaled by means of ladders**
	escalated	*increased; raised*
escalading		**scaling by means of ladders**
	escalating	*increasing; raising*
escalated		**increased; raised**
	escaladed	*scaled by means of ladders*
escalating		**increasing; raising**
	escalading	*scaling by means of ladders*
eve		**night before a holiday**
	eave	*edge of a roof*
eves		**nights before holidays**
	eaves	*edges of roofs*
ewe		**a female sheep**
	*hew***	*cut; sever; cut down*
	*hue***	*color; tint*
	yew	*a type of evergreen tree*
	you	*personal pronoun referring to another person*
ewer		**pitcher**
	*hewer***	*one who axes; that which cuts*
	*huer***	*colorer; tinter*

** Although precise pronunciation would disqualify these words as homophones, ordinary speech does not make the distinction clear to most listeners. Thus the "h" sound which should be an explosive blowing of the lips is not carried out by most speakers. This sound is therefore blurred in such words as *hue, where* and other words where the "h" sound occurs.

ewers

ewers	pitchers
*hewers***	*cutters*
*huers***	*colorers; tinters*
ewes	female sheep
*hews***	*cuts; severs; cuts down*
*hues***	*colors; tints*
use	*employ*
yews	*type of evergreen trees*
ex-checker	a former checker
exchequer	*state or national treasury*
ex-checkers	former checkers
exchequers	*state or national treasuries*
exercise	to engage in physical or mental activity
exorcise	*expel an evil spirit*
exercised	engaged in physical or mental activity
exorcised	*expelled an evil spirit*
exercises	engages in physical or mental activity
exorcises	*expels evil spirits*
exercising	engaging in physical or mental activity
exorcising	*expelling evil spirits*
exorcised	expelled an evil spirit
exercised	*engaged in physical or mental activity*
exorcises	expels evil spirits
exercises	*engages in physical or mental acitivity*
exorcising	engaging in physical or mental activity
exercising	*expelling evil spirits*

** Although precise pronunciation would disqualify these words as homophones, ordinary speech does not make the distinction clear to most listeners. Thus the "h" sound which should be an explosive blowing of the lips is not carried out by most speakers. This sound is therefore blurred in such words as *hue, where* and other words where the "h" sound occurs.

exorcise	expel an evil spirit
exercise	*engage in physical or mental activity*
expedience	a process of promoting a result
expedients	*means to promote a result*
expedients	means to promote a result
expedience	*a process of promoting a result*
eye	sensory organ for vision; to see
aye	*yes*
I	*personal pronoun for self*
eyed	viewed
I'd	*contraction for "I would", or "I should"*
eyelet	a small hole for lacing
islet	*a very small isle*
eyelets	small holes for lacing
islets	*small isles*
eyer	one who views or observes
ayer	*one who agrees or affirms*
ire	*wrath*
eyes	sensory organs for vision; sees
ayes	*yesses*
I's	*referring to oneselves*

F

fade	become dim or recede into the background
fayed	*fitted closely together*

fail

fail	**unable to perform, succeed or behave effectively**
faille	*woven, ribbed fabric*
faille	**woven, ribbed fabric**
file	*classify; arrange in order; a tool for shaping or smoothing; to shape or smooth*
phial	*a small container of liquid (especially medicine)*
faille	**woven, ribbed fabric**
fail	*unable to perform, succeed or behave effectively*
failles	**woven ribbed cloths**
files	*arranges in order; classifies; tools for shaping or smoothing; shapes or smoothes*
phials	*small containers of liquid (especially medicine)*
fain	**gladly**
feign	*pretend*
faint	**less bright in illumination; to become weak and nearly lose consciousness**
feint	*to make a deceptive motion*
fainted	**became weak and nearly lost consciousness**
feinted	*made a deceptive motion*
fainter	**one who becomes weak and nearly loses consciousness**
feinter	*one who makes a deceptive motion*
fainting	**the act of becoming weak and losing consciousness**
feinting	*the act of making a deceptive motion*
faints	**becomes weak and nearly loses consciousness**
feints	*makes a deceptive motion*
fair	**just; equitable; gathering for an exhibition and sale**
fare	*cost of transportation*
fairs	**gatherings for exhibitions and sales**
fares	*costs of transportation*

Note: Underlined words have two acceptable pronunciations.

faker	one who fakes, deceives
fakir	Indian religious mystic
fakers	people who fake, deceive
fakirs	Indian religious mystic
<u>**fakir**</u>	Indian religious mystic
faker	one who fakes, deceives
<u>**fakirs**</u>	Indian religious mystics
fakers	people who fake, deceive
fare	cost of transportation
fair	just; equitable; gathering for an exhibition and sale
fares	costs of transportation
fairs	gatherings for exhibitions and sales
farther	a greater distance or degree
father	sire; male parent
fate	destiny; an inevitable result
<u>fete</u>	a feast or festival
fated	destined; characteristic of an inevitable result
<u>feted</u>	carried out as a feast or festival
fates	destinies; inevitable results
<u>fetes</u>	feasts or festivals
father	sire; male parent
farther	a greater distance or degree
faun	a mythical creature, half human, half goat
fawn	a young deer; color of a fawn; grovel
fauns	mythical creatures, half human, half goat
fawns	young deer; grovels
fawn	a young deer; color of a fawn; grovel
faun	a mythical creature, half human, half goat

Note: Underlined words have two acceptable pronunciations.

fawns

fawns — young deer; grovels
fauns — mythical creatures, half human, half goat

fay — closely fit together
fey — unnatural; unreal

fayed — fitted closely together
fade — become dim or recede into the back ground

fays — fits together closely
faze — disturb
phase — a stage or cycle

faze — disturb
fays — fits together closely
phase — a stage or cycle

fazed — disturbed
phased — staged or cycled

fazes — disturbs
phases — stages or cycles

fazing — disturbing
phasing — staging or cycling

feat — exceptional act or achievement
feet — lower portions of legs; measurements equal to 12 inches

feet — lower portions of legs; measurements equal to 12 inches
feat — exceptional act or achievement

feign — pretend
fain — gladly

feint — deceptive motion; to made a deceptive motion
faint — less bright in illumination; to become weak and nearly lose consciousness

feinted — made a deceptive motion
fainted — became weak and nearly lost consciousness

feinter	one who makes a deceptive motion	
fainter	*one who becomes weak and nearly loses consciousness*	
feinting	the act of making a deceptive motion	
fainting	*the act of becoming weak and nearly losing consciousness*	
feints	makes a deceptive motion	
faints	*becomes weak and nearly loses consciousness*	
felloe	rim of a wheel	
fellow	*man or boy*	
felloes	rims of wheels	
fellows	*men or boys*	
fellow	man or boy	
felloe	*rim of a wheel*	
fellows	men or boys	
felloes	*rims of wheels*	
ferrule	a ring to reinforce a pole or post	
ferule	*a cane or rod for punishment*	
ferrules	rings to reinforce poles or posts	
ferules	*canes or rods for punishment*	
ferule	a cane or rod for punishment	
ferrule	*a ring to reinforce a pole or post*	
ferules	canes or rods for punishment	
ferrules	*rings to reinforce poles or posts*	
<u>**fete**</u>	a feast or festival	
fate	*destiny; an inevitable result*	
<u>**feted**</u>	carried out as a feast or festival	
fated	*destined; characteristic of an inevitable result*	
<u>**fetes**</u>	feasts or festivals	
fates	*destinies; inevitable results*	

Note: Underlined words have two acceptable pronunciations.

fey

fey	**unnatural; unreal**
fay	*closely fit together*
fila	**thread-like structures**
phylla	*classifications of plants or languages*
file	**classify; arrange in order; a tool for shaping or smoothing; to shape or smooth**
faille	*woven, ribbed fabric*
phial	*a small container of liquid (especially medicine)*
files	**arranges in order; classifies; tools for shaping or smoothing; shapes or smooths**
<u>*failles*</u>	*woven ribbed cloths*
phials	*small containers of liquid (especially medicine)*
filter	**a device to screen out impurities; to screen out impurities**
philter	*a magic dose of a liquid*
filters	**devices to screen out impurities; screens out impurities**
philters	*magic doses of liquids*
filum	**thread-like structure**
phyllum	*classification of plants or languages*
find	**to locate something lost or searched for**
fined	*paid money for a legal infraction*
fined	**paid money for a legal infraction**
find	*locate something lost or searched for*
fir	**a type of evergreen tree**
fur	*soft outer skin of animals*
firs	**types of evergreen trees**
furs	*soft outer skins of animals*
furze	*beanlike plants*
fisher	**a person or animal that fishes; a type of animal (a marten)**
fissure	*a separation. natural or induced*

Note: Underlined words have two acceptable pronunciations.

flee

fissure	**a separation, natural or induced**
fisher	*a person or animal that fishes; a type of animal (a marten)*
flair	**talent; knack**
flare	*a flaming torchlike fire; appear suddenly as a rash or fever*
flairs	**talents; knacks**
flares	*flaming torchlike fires; appears suddenly like a rash or fever*
flaks	**criticisms; anti-aircraft attacks**
flax	*a plant that is used to produce linen*
flare	**a flaming torchlike fire; appear suddenly as a rash or fever**
flair	*talent; knack*
flares	**flaming torchlike fires; appears suddenly like a rash or fever**
flairs	*talents; knacks*
flaw	**failing; defect**
floor	*lower, horizontal surface of a room*
flawed	**made an error or defect; that which has an error or defect**
floored	*made with a floor; to surprise; to knock down*
flaws	**failings; defects**
floors	*lower, horizontal surfaces in rooms*
flax	**a plant that is used to produce linen**
flaks	*criticisms; anti-aircraft attacks*
flea	**a small, wingless insect**
flee	*run from; speed away*
fleas	**small, wingless insects**
flees	*runs from; speeds away*
flecks	**specks**
flex	*bend*
flee	**run from; speed away**
flea	*a small, wingless insect*

~ 79 ~

flew

flew	**took flight; soared**
flu	*influenza*
flue	*fishing net; smoke duct in a chimney*
flews	**sides of lips of some dogs**
flues	*fishing nets; smoke ducts in chimneys*
flex	**bend**
flecks	*speck*
flocks	**pieces of material (especially for upholstery); groups of animals or birds or people**
phlox	*a type of herb with varied colored flowers*
floe	**a floating ice sheet**
flow	*move along as a stream of air*
floes	**floating ice sheets**
flows	*moves along as a stream of air*
floor	**lower, horizontal surface of a room**
flaw	*failing; defect*
floored	**made with a floor; to surprise; to knock down**
flawed	*made an error or defect; that which has an error or defect*
floors	**lower, horizontal surfaces in rooms**
flaws	*failings; defects*
flour	**fine soft powdery meal of grains**
flower	*plant blossom; to bloom*
flours	**fine soft powdery meals of grains**
flowers	*plant blossoms; blooms*
flow	**move along as a stream or air**
floe	*a floating ice sheet*
flower	**plant blossom; to bloom**
flour	*fine soft powdery meal of grains*

forego

flowers	**plant blossoms; blooms**
flours	*fine soft powdery meals of grains*
flows	**moves along as a stream or air**
floes	*floating ice sheets*
flu	**influenza**
flew	*took flight; soared*
flue	*fishing net; smoke duct in chimney*
flue	**fishing net; smoke duct in chimney**
flew	*took flight; soared*
flu	*influenza*
flues	**fishing nets; smoke ducts in chimneys**
flews	*sides of lips of some dogs*
foaled	**gave birth to a horse**
fold	*bend something (a piece of paper, sheet, etc.) over itself*
fold	**bend something (a piece of paper, sheet, etc.) over itself**
foaled	*gave birth to a horse*
for	**toward; in favor of**
fore	*before; in front of; the front end of a ship*
four	*the cardinal number following 3*
forbear	**hold back; abstain**
forebear	*ancestor*
fore	**before; in front of; the front end of a ship**
for	*toward; in favor of*
four	*the cardinal number following 3*
forebear	**ancestor**
forbear	*hold back; abstain*
forego	**go before**
forgo	*abstain; refrain from*

foreward

foreward	preface to any written work
forward	*ahead; assertive*
forgo	abstain; refrain from
forego	*go before*
fort	a defensive fortified place
forte	*notably strong feature or characteristic*
forte	notably strong feature or characteristic
fort	*a defensive fortified place*
forts	defensive fortified places
fortes	*notably strong features or characteristics*
fortes	notably strong features or characteristics
forts	*defensive fortified places*
forth	forward; onward
fourth	*following the third in order*
foul	offensive; not fair
fowl	*any of a number of domestic birds (e.g., chicken, turkey, duck)*
fouled	soiled; did something that is not fair (especially in sports)
fowled	*hunted fowl*
fouler	one who fouls; one who produces offensive utterances
fowler	*a hunter of fowl*
fouling	defiling; doing something that is not fair (especially in sports)
fowling	*hunting for fowl*
fouls	defiles; does something that is not fair (especially in sports)
fowls	*domestic birds (e.g., chicken, turkey, duck)*
forward	ahead; assertive
foreward	*preface to any written work*

Note: Underlined words have two acceptable pronunciations.

freeze

fowl	any of a number of domestic birds (e.g., chicken, turkey, duck)
foul	*offensive; not fair*
fowled	hunted fowl
fouled	*soiled; did something that is not fair (especially in sports)*
fowler	a hunter of fowl
fouler	*one who fouls; one who produces offensive utterances*
fowling	hunting for fowl
fouling	*defiling; doing something that is not fair (especially in sports)*
fowls	domestic birds (e.g., chicken, turkey, duck)
fouls	*defiles; does something that is not fair (especially in sports*
fraise	fortress of sharply pointed rods
frays	*fights; battles*
phrase	*part of a sentence in speech or writing*
franc	a coin of France
frank	*sincere; give the right of sending something free*
francs	coins of France
franks	*gives the right of sending something free*
frank	sincere; give the right of sending something free
franc	*a coin of France*
franks	gives the right of sending something free
francs	*coins of France*
frays	fights; battles
fraise	*fortress of sharply pointed rods*
phrase	*part of a sentence in speech or writing*
frees	lets go; releases
freeze	*place at temperature below the freezing point*
frieze	*a three-dimensional design over a mantel or upper part of a wall*
freeze	place at temperature below the freezing point
frees	*lets go; releases*
frieze	*a three-dimensional design over a mantel or upper part of a wall*

~ 83 ~

freezes

freezes   places at temperature below the freezing point
   friezes   *three-dimensional designs over mantels or upper part of walls*

friar   a member of a religious order
   frier (fryer)   *that which fries food; a young chicken used for frying*

frier (fryer)   that which fries food; a young chicken used for frying
   friar   *a member of a religious order*

frieze   a three-dimensional design over a mantel or upper part of a wall
   freeze   *place at temperature below the freezing point*
   frees   *lets go; releases*

friezes   three-dimensional designs over mantels or upper part of walls
   freezes   *places at temperatures below the freezing point*

fro   back (e.g., to and fro)
   frow (froe)   *a cleaving tool with right angle handle*

frow (froe)   a cleaving tool with right angle handle
   fro   *back (e.g., to and fro)*

frows   cleavage tools with right angle handles
   froze   *placed or having reached the state of being below the freezing point*

froze   placed or having reached the state of being below the freezing point
   frows   *cleavage tools with right angle handles*

fryer (frier)   that which fries food; a young chicken used for frying
   friar   *a member of a religious order*

fungous   relating to fungus
   fungus   *plant without chlorophyll (e.g., mushrooms)*

fungus   plant without chlorophyll (e.g., mushrooms)
   fungous   *relating to fungus*

furs	**soft outer skins of animals**
firs	*type of evergreen trees*
furze	*beanlike plants*
furze	**beanlike plants**
furs	*soft outer skins of animals*
firs	*type of evergreen trees*

G

gaff	**a hook for fishing or climbing**
gaffe	*a blunder*
gaffe	**a blunder**
gaff	*a hook for fishing or climbing*
gaffes	**blunders**
gaffs	*hooks for fishing or hooks for climbing*
gaffs	**hooks for fishing or hooks for climbing**
gaffes	*blunders*
gage	**variety of plum; a challenge**
gauge	*to measure, evaluate or judge; a device for measuring or judging*
gaged	**challenged**
gauged	*measured or estimated*
gages	**varieties of plums; challenges**
gauges	*measures or judges; devices for measuring or judging*
gaging	**challenging**
gauging	*measuring or estimating*
gait	**step or pace**
gate	*a barrier or enclosure (e.g., a fence)*

gaited

gaited	**having a specific step or pace**
gated	*having a barrier or enclosure (e.g., a fence)*
gaiting	**teaching a gait to a horse**
gating	*enclosing in a barrier (e.g., a fence)*
gaits	**steps or paces**
gates	*barriers or enclosures*
gamble	**risk or chance**
gambol	*to move playfully*
gambled	**risked or took a chance**
gamboled	*moved playfully*
gambles	**risks or takes a chance**
gambols	*moves playfully*
gambling	**risking or taking a chance**
gamboling	*moving playfully*
gambol	**to move playfully**
gamble	*risk or chance*
gamboled	**moved playfully**
gambled	*risked or took a chance*
gamboling	**moving playfully**
gambling	*risking or taking a chance*
gambols	**moves playfully**
gambles	*risks or takes a chance*
gang	**a group of people (e.g., a crew)**
gangue	*material mixed with ore*
gangs	**groups of people (e.g., crews)**
gangues	*materials mixed with ore*
gangue	**material mixed with ore**
gang	*a group of people (e.g., a crew)*

gangues   materials mixed with ore
gangs   *groups of people (e.g., crews)*

gate   a barrier or enclosure (e.g., a fence)
gait   *step or pace*

gated   having a barrier or enclosure (e.g., a fence)
gaited   *having a specific step or pace*

gates   barriers or enclosures
gaits   *steps or paces*

gating   enclosing in a barrier (e.g., a fence)
gaiting   *teaching a gait to a horse*

gauge   to measure, evaluate or judge; a device for measuring or judging
gage   *variety of plum; a challenge*

gauged   measured or estimated
gaged   *challenged*

gauges   measures or judges; devices for measuring or judging
gages   *varieties of plums; challenges*

gauging   measuring or estimating
gaging   *challenging*

gays   male homosexuals
gaze   *stare*

gaze   stare
gays   *male homosexuals*

gel   chemical suspension in liquid
jell   *to crystallize or become clear*

gels   chemical suspensions in liquid
jells   *crystallizes or becomes clear*

genes   hereditary units
jeans   *slacks made of heavy cotton material*

gibe

gibe	tease or ridicule
jibe	shifting direction in the wind
gibed	teased or ridiculed
jibed	shifted direction in the wind
gibes	teases or ridicules
jibes	shifts direction in the wind
gibing	teasing or ridiculing
jibing	shifting directions in the wind
gild	coat with gold
guild	a craft association
gilled	having gills
gilled	having gills
gild	coat with gold
guild	a craft association
gilt	gold covered; a female pig who has not borne young
guilt	state of having committed a crime; a feeling of having done a wrong or failure to do what was right
glair	white part of an egg
glare	an extremely bright light; an angry look
glairs	white parts of eggs
glares	extremely bright lights; angry looks
glare	an extremely bright light; an angry look
glair	white part of an egg
glares	extremely bright lights; angry looks
glairs	white parts of eggs
glows	exudes brightness
gloze	shine; alibi
gloze	shine; alibi
glows	exudes brightness

graphed

gneiss	a multi-layered rock of different minerals
nice	*pleasant*
gnu	a type of antelope
knew	*was aware of*
new	*having just occurred; recent*
gnus	types of antelopes
news	*information; report(s) of event(s)*
gored	made up of triangular pieces of fabric or land; pierced through by an animal's horns
gourd	*a melon-like plant*
gorilla	largest ape
guerrilla	*surprise tactic of attack*
gorillas	largest apes
guerrillas	*surprise tactics of attack*
gourd	a melon-like plant
gored	*made up of triangular pieces of fabric or land; pierced through by an animal's horns*
grade	rating; angle of incline
grayed (greyed)	*made or became gray*
graft	transfer of tissue
graphed	*depicted by a graph*
grander	greater; higher in status
grandeur	*greatness*
grandeur	greatness
grander	*greater; higher in status*
graphed	depicted by a graph
graft	*transfer of tissue*

grate

grate		metal frame (e.g., for fire wood); scrape food into small parts; noisy sound
	great	*very large; exceptionally superior*
grater		that which grates; a device to scrape food into small parts
	greater	*larger of two things*
grates		metal frames (e.g., for fire wood); scrapes food into small parts; noisy sounds
	greats	*superior persons*
grayed (grayed)		made or became gray
	grade	*rating; angle of incline*
grays		colors of grey
	graze	*eat off growth*
graze		eat off growth
	grays	*colors of grey*
great		very large; exceptionally superior
	grate	*metal frame (e.g.,, for fire wood); scrape food into small parts; noisy sound*
greater		larger of two things
	grater	*that which grates; a device to scrape food into small parts*
greats		superior persons
	grates	*metal frames (e.g., for fire wood); scrapes food into small parts; noisy sounds*
grill		a utensil to broil food; broil
	grille	*a screen of metal or cloth*
grille		a screen of metal or cloth
	grill	*a utensil to broil food; broil*
grilles		screens of metal or cloth
	grills	*utensils to broil food; broils*

guild

grills		utensils to broil food; broils
	grilles	*screens of metal or cloth*
grip		grasp; a device for holding onto
	grippe	*influenza*
grippe		influenza
	grip	*grasp; a device for holding onto*
grisly		gruesome or horrible
	grizzly	*grayish*
grizzly		grayish
	grisly	*gruesome or horrible*
groan		a low sound of complaint, pain or disapproval
	grown	*having been raised or matured*
grown		having been raised or matured
	groan	*a low sound of complaint, pain or disapproval*
guerrilla		surprise tactic of attack
	gorilla	*largest ape*
guerrillas		surprise tactics of attack
	gorillas	*largest apes*
guessed		estimated or played a hunch
	guest	*a person who stays in another person's home; a lodger in a hotel or motel*
guest		a person who stays in another person's home; a lodger in a hotel or motel
	guessed	*estimated or played a hunch*
guide		direct or channel
	guyed	*steadied with rope or wire*
guild		a craft association
	gild	*coat with gold*
	gilled	*having gills*

guile

guile	deceptive way
gyle	*vat especially for beer or vinegar*
guiles	deceptive ways
gyles	*vats especially for beer or vinegar*
guilt	state of having committed a crime; a feeling of having done a wrong or failure to do what was right
gilt	*gold covered; a female pig who has not borne young*
guise	superficial appearance
guys	*ropes or wires to steady an object*
guyed	steadied with rope or wire
guide	*direct or channel*
guys	ropes or wires to steady an object
guise	*superficial appearance*
gyle	vat especially for beer or vinegar
guile	*deceptive way*
gyles	vats especially for beer or vinegar
guiles	*deceptive ways*

H

haik	outer clothing worn by Arabs
hake	*sea fish related to cod*
haik	outer clothing worn by Arabs
hike	*walk a long distance*
haiks	outer clothing worn by Arabs
hakes	*sea fish related to cod*

Note: Underlined words have two acceptable pronunciations.

<u>haiks</u>	outer clothing worn by Arabs	
hikes	*walks a long distance*	
hail	salute; greet	
hale	*force along; healthy*	
hails	salutes; greets	
hales	*forces along*	
hair	fine soft tissue covering the skin	
hare	*rabbit*	
hairs	fine soft tissues covering the skin	
hares	*rabbits*	
hake	sea fish related to cod	
<u>*haik*</u>	*outer clothing worn by Arabs*	
hale	force along; healthy	
hail	*salute; greet*	
hales	forces along	
hails	*salutes; greets*	
hall	corridor; walkway in a building	
haul	*drag; pull; carry*	
halled	having a hall	
hauled	*dragged; pulled; carried*	
halls	corridors; walkways in buildings	
hauls	*drags; pulls; carries*	
halve	divide in two	
have	*possess*	
halves	divides in two	
haves	*possessors of wealth, power or status*	
handsome	good looking	
hansom	*a two-passenger horse-drawn carriage*	

Note: Underlined words have two acceptable pronunciations.

hangar

hangar	housing for an airplane
hanger	*a device for hanging clothing*
hanger	a device for hanging clothing
hangar	*housing for an airplane*
hansom	a two-passenger horse-drawn carriage
handsome	*good looking*
hardy	durable
hearty	*cordial; vigorous; large*
hare	rabbit
hair	*fine soft tissue covering the skin*
hares	rabbits
hairs	*fine soft tissues covering the skin*
hart	male deer
heart	*organ of the body that pumps blood; core of anything*
hartin	fossil resin in lignite rock
hearten	*encourage*
harts	male deer
hearts	*organs of bodies that pump blood; cores of anything*
haul	drag; pull; carry
hall	*corridor; walk in a building*
hauled	dragged; pulled; carried
halled	*having a hall*
hauls	drags; pulls; carries
halls	*corridors; walks in buildings*
have	possess
halve	*divide in two*
haves	possessors of wealth, power or status
halves	*divides in two*

hays	dried grasses
haze	*a filmy appearance; to subject newcomers to ridicule or abuse*
haze	a filmy appearance; to subject newcomers to ridicule or abuse
hays	*dried grasses*
heal	mend; cure
heel	*back part of the foot; back part of anything*
healed	mended; cured
heeled	*having a heel; having wealth*
heals	mends; cures
heels	*back parts of feet; back parts of anything*
hear	perceive the sound
here	*now; present*
heard	perceived the sound
herd	*a group of animals*
heart	organ of the body that pumps blood; core of anything
hart	*male deer*
hearten	encourage
hartin	*fossil resin in lignite rock*
hearty	cordial; vigorous; large
hardy	*durable*
heated	warmed
heeded	*paid attention to*
he'd	contraction for "he had" or "he would"
heed	*pay attention to*
heed	pay attention to
he'd	*contraction for "he had" or "he would"*
heeded	paid attention to
heated	*warmed*

heel

heel	back part of the foot; back part of anything
heal	*mend; cure*
heir	a beneficiary of an estate
ere	*before*
air	*the gases surrounding the earth; ventilate or expose to air; to publicize*
<u>*err*</u>	*make a mistake*
heirs	beneficiaries of an estate
airs	*allows air to circulate; opens to view*
<u>*errs*</u>	*makes a mistake*
herd	a group of animals
heard	*perceived the sound*
here	now; present
hear	*perceive the sound*
heroin	a narcotic derived from opium
heroine	*female who shows bravery or daring*
heroine	female who shows bravery or daring
heroin	*a narcotic derived from opium*
hertz	a measure of frequency
hurts	*pains; causes pain*
hew**	cut; sever; cut down
ewe	*a female sheep*
hue**	*color; tint*
yew	*a type of evergreen tree*
you	*personal pronoun referring to another person*
hewer**	one who axes; that which cuts
ewer	*pitcher*
huer**	*colorer; tinter*

Note: Underlined words have two acceptable pronunciations.

** Although precise pronunciation would disqualify these words as homophones, ordinary speech does not make the distinction clear to most listeners. Thus the "h" sound which should be an explosive blowing of the lips is not carried out by most speakers. This sound is therefore blurred in such words as *hue, where* and other words where the "h" sound occurs.

hewers**	**cutters**
ewers	*pitchers*
huers**	*colorers; tinters*
hews**	**cuts; severs; cuts down**
hues**	*colors; tints*
ewers	*female sheep*
use	*employ; utilize*
yews	*type of evergreen trees*
hide	**conceal; cover up; secrete; an animal skin**
hied	*hastened*
hie	**hasten**
high	*lofty place; peak; intoxicated state*
hied	**hastened**
hide	*conceal; cover up; secrete; an animal skin*
hies	**hastens**
highs	*lofty places; peaks; intoxicated states*
high	**lofty place; peak; intoxicated state**
hie	*hasten*
higher	**beyond a certain level; above**
hire	*employ*
highs	**lofty places; peaks; intoxicated states**
hies	*hastens*
hike	**walk a long distance**
<u>*haik*</u>	*outer clothing worn by Arabs*
hikes	**walks a long distance**
<u>*haiks*</u>	*outer clothing worn by Arabs*

Note: Underlined words have two acceptable pronunciations.

** Although precise pronunciation would disqualify these words as homophones, ordinary speech does not make the distinction clear to most listeners. Thus the "h" sound which should be an explosive blowing of the lips is not carried out by most speakers. This sound is therefore blurred in such words as *hue, where* and other words where the "h" sound occurs.

him

him — objective pronoun for "he"
    hymn — a song in praise

hire — employ
    higher — beyond a certain level; above

hoar — an aged appearance
    whore — prostitute; someone who sells himself or herself

hoard — collect supplies secretly
    horde — a very large number of people
    whored — prostituted; sold oneself

hoarse — a voice sound that is soft and raspy
    horse — a 4-legged hoofed animal used for travel or for pulling a load

hoes — hand tools for turning the soil
    hose — stockings

hold — have in one's arm or hands; maintain
    holed — having holes

hole — a perforation or opening
    whole — total; all

holed — having holes
    hold — have in one's arm or hands; maintain

holes — perforations or openings
    wholes — totals

holey — having holes
    holy — sacred; religiously meaningful
    wholly — fully; totally

holy — sacred; religiously meaningful
    holey — having holes
    wholly — fully; totally

horde — a very large number of people
    hoard — collect supplies secretly
    whored — prostituted; sold oneself

horse		a 4-legged hoofed animal used for travel or for pulling a load
	hoarse	*a voice sound that is soft and raspy*
hose		stockings
	hoes	*hand tools for turning the soil*
hostel		an inn or guest residence
	hostile	*showing or feeling enmity*
hostile		showing or feeling enmity
	hostel	*an inn or guest residence*
hour		1/24th part of a day; a unit of 60 minutes
	our	*belong to "us"*
hours		1/24th parts of a day; units of 60 minutes
	ours	*belonging to "us"*
hue**		color; tint
	ewe	*a female sheep*
	hew**	*cut; sever; cut down*
	yew	*a type of evergreen trees*
	you	*personal pronoun referring to another person*
huer**		colorer; tinter
	ewer	*pitcher*
	hewer**	*one who axes; that which cuts*
huers**		colorers; tinters
	ewers	*pitchers*
	hewers**	*cutters*
hues**		colors; tints
	ewes	*female sheep*
	hews**	*cuts; severs; cuts down*
	use	*employ; utilize*
	yews	*type of evergreen trees*

** Although precise pronunciation would disqualify these words as homophones, ordinary speech does not make the distinction clear to most listeners. Thus the "h" sound which should be an explosive blowing of the lips is not carried out by most speakers. This sound is therefore blurred in such words as *hue, where* and other words where the "h" sound occurs.

humerus

humerus   human bone from shoulder to elbow
    humorous   witty; funny

humorous   witty; funny
    humerus   human bone from shoulder to elbow

hurts   pains; causes pain
    hertz   a measure of frequency

hymn   a song in praise
    him   objective pronoun for "he"

I

I   personal pronoun for self
    aye   yes
    eye   sensory organ for vision; to see

I'd   contraction for "I would"
    eyed   viewed

idle   remain inactive
    idol   object or person of adoration, worship or admiration
    idyl (idyll)   a poem about a place of country-like attractiveness

idles   remains inactive
    idols   objects or persons of adoration, worship or admiration
    idyls   places of country-like attractiveness

idol   object or person of adoration, worship or admiration
    idle   remain inactive
    idyl (idyll)   a poem about a place of country-like attractiveness

idols   objects or persons of adoration, worship or admiration
    idles   remains inactive
    idyls   poems about places of country-like attractiveness

idyl (idyll)	**A poem about a place of country-like attractiveness**
idle	*remain inactive*
idol	*object or person of adoration, worship or admiration*
idyls (idylls)	**poems about places of country-like attractiveness**
idles	*remains inactive*
idols	*objects or persons of adoration, worship or admiration*
I'll	**contraction for "I will" or "I shall."**
aisle	*a passage between rows of seats*
isle	*a small island*
illicit	**illegal and/or immoral; against the law**
elicit	*bring out*
illude	**trick or deceive**
allude	*refer to indirectly or briefly*
elude	*avoid or escape*
illuded	**tricked or deceived**
alluded	*referred to indirectly or briefly*
eluded	*avoided or escaped*
illudes	**tricks or deceives**
alludes	*refers to indirectly or briefly*
eludes	*avoids or escapes*
illuding	**tricking or deceiving**
alluding	*referring to indirectly or briefly*
eluding	*avoiding or escaping*
illusion	**deception or false belief or delusion**
allusion	*indirect or brief reference*
elusion	*an evasion or escape*
illusions	**deceptions or false beliefs or delusions**
allusions	*direct or brief references*
elusions	*evasions or escapes*

illusive

illusive — **tricking or deceiving**
   allusive — *referring to indirectly or briefly; suggestive*
   elusive — *avoiding or escaping*

illusively — **deceptively or in a tricky way**
   allusively — *referring to indirectly or briefly; suggestively*
   elusively — *acting evasively or escaping*

immanence — **incorporated; internal**
   imminence — *about to happen*

immanent — **incorporated; internal**
   imminent — *that which is about to happen*

immerge — **to plunge into**
   emerge — *come out (of water or of hidden view)*

immerged — **plunged into**
   emerged — *came out (of water or hidden view)*

immerges — **plunges into**
   emerges — *comes out (of water or hidden view)*

immerging — **plunging into**
   emerging — *coming out (of water or hidden view)*

immersed — **plunged into**
   emersed — *came out (of water or hidden view)*

immersion — **act of plunging into**
   emersion — *act of coming out (of water or hidden view)*

immersions — **acts of plunging into**
   emersions — *acts of coming out (of water or hidden view)*

imminence — **about to happen**
   immanence — *incorporated; internal*

imminent — **that which is about to happen**
   immanent — *incorporated; internal*

impassable	not able to be crossed	
impassible	*not able to feel pain or suffering*	

impassible	not able to feel pain or suffering	
impassable	*not able to be crossed*	

imperial	referring to the empire, emperor or empress	
empyreal	*referring to the sky; made up of fire; the heaven*	

in	included	
inn	*motel or hotel for guests*	

incidence	an event	
incidents	*occurrences*	

incidents	occurrences	
incidence	*an event*	

incipit	beginning of a composition	
insipid	*not interesting or tasteful*	

independence	free of dependency or control	
independents	*those who are free of dependency; those who are not connected to a specific person or group*	

independents	those who are free of dependency; those who are not connected to a specific person or group	
independence	*free of dependency or control*	

indict	charge with a crime; accuse	
indite	*compose*	

indicter (indictor)	one who accuses	
inditer	*a composer*	

indicting	charging with a crime; accusing	
inditing	*composing*	

indictment	a charge (with a crime); accusation	
inditement	*composition*	

indictor

indictor
(indicter)   one who accuses
   inditer   *a composer*

indicts   charges for a crime
   indites   *composes*

indiscreet   not showing good judgment
   indiscrete   *not separated into sections*

indiscrete   not separated into sections
   indiscreet   *not showing good judgment*

indite   compose
   indict   *charge with a crime; accuse*

inditement   composition
   indictment   *a charge (with a crime); accusation*

inditer   a composer
   indictor
   (indicter)   *one who accuses*

indites   composes
   indicts   *charges with a crime*

inditing   composing
   indicting   *charging with a crime; accusing*

inn   motel or hotel for guests
   in   *included*

innervate   show energy
   enervate   *weaken*

innervated   showed energy
   enervated   *weakened*

innervates   shows energy
   enervates   *weakens*

innervation   the act of showing energy
   enervation   *the act of weakening*

innervator	one who shows energy
enervator	one who weakens
innervators	those who show energy
enervators	that which or those who weaken
innocence	state of being free of sin or fault; lacking sophistication
innocents	those who are free of sin or fault; those who lack sophistication
innocents	those who are free of sin or fault; those who lack sophistication
innocence	state of being free of sin or fault; lacking sophistication
insipid	not interesting or tasteful
incipit	beginning of a composition
instance	a single time or event
instants	those single events or times
instants	those single events or times
instance	a single time or event
intense	strong feeling or emotion; powerful
intents	purposes
intension	state of being intense
intention	purpose or goal
intensions	states of being intense
intentions	purposes or goals
intention	purpose or goal
intension	state of being intense
intentions	purposes or goals
intensions	states of being intense
intents	purposes
intense	strong feeling or emotion; powerful
invade	encroach upon or attack the territory of another
inveighed	complained against; protested

inveighed

inveighed	complained against; protested
invade	encroach upon or attack the territory of another
ire	wrath
ayer	one who agrees or affirms
eyer	one who views or observes
irrupt	to show violent activity
erupt	break out; explode
irrupted	showed violent activity
erupted	broken out; exploded
irrupting	violently active
erupting	breaking out; exploding
irruption	the act of showing violent activity
eruption	the act of breaking out or exploding
irruptive	characteristic of violent activity
eruptive	characteristic of breaking out or exploding
irruptively	in a way that shows violent activity
eruptively	in an exploding way
irrupts	shows violent activity
erupts	breaks out; explodes
I's	referring to oneselves
ayes	yesses
eyes	sensory organs for vision; sees
isle	a small island
aisle	a passage between rows of seats
I'll	contraction of "I will" or "I shall"
isles	small islands
aisles	passages between rows of seats
islet	a very small isle
eyelet	a small hole for lacing
islets	small isles
eyelets	small holes for lacing

it's   contraction of "it is"
     its   *signifying possessive (e.g., the house lost its roof in the storm)*

its   signifying possessive (e.g., the house lost its roof in the storm)
     it's   *contraction of "it is"*

J

jam   press into a tight space; crushed fruit and sug
     jamb   *side support for a door; door frame*

jamb   side support for a door; door frame
     jam   *press into a tight space; crushed fruit and sugar*

jambs   side supports for a door; door frames
     jams   *crushed fruits and sugars*

jams   crushed fruits and sugars
     jambs   *side supports for a door; door frames*

jeans   slacks made of heavy cotton material
     genes   *hereditary units*

jell   crystallize or become clear
     gel   *chemical suspension in liquid*

jells   crystallizes or becomes clear
     gels   *chemical suspensions in liquid*

jewel   a highly valuable stone; anything highly valuable
     <u>*joule*</u>   *a unit of energy*

jewels   highly valuable stones; things highly valuable
     <u>*joules*</u>   *units of energy*

Note: Underlined words have two acceptable pronunciations.

jibe

jibe	shifting direction in the wind; shift from side to side
gibe	teased or ridiculed
jibed	shifted direction in the wind; shifted from side to side
gibed	teased or ridiculed
jibes	shifts direction in the wind; shifts from side to side
gibes	teases or ridicules
jibing	shifting directions in the wind; shifting from side to side
gibing	teasing or ridiculing
<u>**joule**</u>	a unit of energy
jewel	a highly valuable stone; anyting highly valuable
<u>**joule**</u>	a unit of energy
jowl	a fleshy part hanging from the jaw or neck; lower jaw
<u>**joules**</u>	units of energy
jewels	highly valuable stones; things highly valuable
<u>**joules**</u>	units of energy
jowls	fleshy parts hanging from the jaw or neck; lower jaws
<u>**joust**</u>	combat on horseback by knights using swords
just	merely; fair; even
jowl	a fleshy part hanging from the jaw or neck; lower jaw
<u>*joule*</u>	a unit of energy
jowls	fleshy parts hanging from the jaw or neck; lower jaws
<u>*joules*</u>	units of energy
just	merely; fair; even
joust	combat on horseback by knights using swords

Note: Underlined words have two acceptable pronunciations.

K

karat	measure indicating ratio of gold in an alloy
carat	unit of measurement for precious stones
caret	an editing symbol to note where a word or punctuation mark is to be inserted
carrot	yellow-orange colored root vegetable
karats	measures indicating ratio of gold in an alloy
carats	units of measurement for precious stones
carets	editing symbols to note where a word or punctuation mark is to be inserted
carrots	yellow-orange colored root vegetables
kernel	seed within the shell of a fruit or nut; core
colonel	a high ranking officer below brigadier general
kernels	seeds within the shell of fruits or nuts; cores
colonels	high ranking officers below brigadier generals
key	metal tool to open a lock; symbol of explanation
<u>*cay*</u>	small island
key	metal tool to open a lock; symbol of explanation
quay	landing place for boats
keys	metal tools to open locks; symbols of explanation
cays	small islands
keys	metal tools to open locks; symbols of explanation
quays	landing places for boats
<u>**khaki**</u>	yellow-brown color; a heavy twilled fabric
cocky	aggressively self-confident
kissed	touched with the lips
kist	a money container

Note: Underlined words have two acceptable pronunciations.

kist

kist	**a money container**
kissed	*touched with the lips*
klepht	**a brigand**
cleft	*space caused by splitting; fissure*
klephts	**brigands**
clefts	*spaces caused by splitting; fissures*
knave	**someone who is without principles**
nave	*central area of a church*
knaves	**those without principles**
naves	*central areas of churches*
knead	**to mold (dough, clay)**
kneed	*struck with the knee*
need	*require; necessitate*
kneaded	**molded dough or clay**
needed	*required; necessitated*
kneading	**molding dough or clay**
needing	*requiring; necessitating*
kneads	**molds dough or clay**
needs	*requires; necessitates*
kneed	**struck with the knee**
knead	*to mold (dough, clay)*
need	*require; necessitate*
knew	**was aware of; understood**
gnu	*a type of antelope*
new	*having just occurred; recent; unused*
knight	**one who has the rank of the medieval soldier given for chivalrous deeds**
night	*the part of the day when the sun is down; darkness*
knights	**those who have the rank of the medieval soldiers given for chivalrous deeds**
nights	*parts of days when the sun is down; darkness*

knit		join yarn by loops
	nit	*insect egg or newborn insect*
knits		joins yarn by loops
	nits	*insect eggs or newborn insects*
knock		to tap to make a sound
	nock	*notch on an arrow for the bowstring to fit*
knocks		taps to make sounds
	nocks	*notches on arrows for bowstring to fit*
knot		intertwined material (e.g., lace, cord, rope)
	not	*denial or refusal of an action (e.g., "I do not choose to run")*
know		to be aware of; to understand
	no	*an expression of denial or refusal*
knows		is aware of; understands
	noes	*expressions of denial or refusal*
	nose	*human and animal sensory organ that detects odor*
kris (creese)		a Malay dagger
	crease	*a fold*
krises (creeses)		Malay daggers
	creases	*folds*

L

lacks		deficient; that which is missing
	lax	*not strict; loose*
lade		load
	laid	*placed down*
ladder		a device of metal or wood for climbing
	latter	*the most recent or last mentioned*

lager

lager	**a well-seasoned beer**
logger	*someone who cuts trees; one who records travels*
lagers	**well-seasoned beers**
loggers	*persons who cut trees; persons who record travels*
laid	**placed down**
lade	*load*
lain	**placed in supine or prostrate position**
lane	*a narrow path; section of a highway*
lair	**a resting place for an animal; den**
<u>layer</u>	*tier; one who lays*
laired	**made into a lair; provided with a den**
<u>layered</u>	*tiered*
lairs	**resting places for animals; dens**
<u>layers</u>	*tiers; those who lay*
lam	**escape**
lamb	*young sheep*
lama	**a priest of a Buddhist sect**
llama	*a type of animal related to the camel*
lamas	**priests of a Buddhist sect**
llamas	*types of animal related to the camel*
lamb	**young sheep**
lam	*escape*
lambs	**young sheep**
lams	*escapes*
lams	**escapes**
lambs	*young sheep*

Note: Underlined words have two acceptable pronunciations.

lane	**a narrow path; section of a highway**
lain	*placed in supine or prostrate position*
laps	**folds; parts that fold over; turns around a track**
lapse	*a slip or gap*
lapse	**a slip or gap**
laps	*folds; parts that fold over; turns around a track*
latter	**the most recent or last mentioned**
ladder	*a device of metal or wood for climbing*
lax	**not strict; loose**
lacks	*deficient; that which is missing*
lay	**place at rest; deposit (as eggs of a hen); non-professional**
lei	*Hawaiian wreath*
<u>**layer**</u>	**tier; one who lays**
lair	*a resting place for an animal; den*
<u>**layered**</u>	**tiered**
laired	*made into a lair; provided with a den*
<u>**layers**</u>	**tiers; those who lay**
lairs	*resting paces for animals; dens*
lays	**deposits of hen's eggs**
laze	*idle; loaf*
leis	*Hawaiian wreaths*
laze	**idle; loaf**
lays	*deposits of eggs of hens*
leis	*Hawaiian wreaths*
lea	**a meadow**
lee	*shelter*
leach	**remove liquid**
leech	*blood sucking worm; parasite*

Note: Underlined words have two acceptable pronunciations.

leaches

leaches	removes liquid
leechs	*blood sucking worms; parasites*
leachy	porous
lichee (litchi)	*fruit of a chinese soapberry tree*
lead	type of metal
led	*went ahead of others; took an advance position*
lead	go in front of; take an advance position
lied	*a German ballad*
leader	one who is ahead of others
liter	*a measure of capacity equal to 1.06 liquid quarts*
leaders	those who are ahead of others
liters	*measures of capacity equal to 1.06 liquid quarts*
leaf	green or colored part of a plant that grows out of a stem
lief	*gladly*
leak	seepage of liquid or information
leek	*a vegetable related to an onion*
leaks	seepages of liquid or information
leeks	*vegetables related to onions*
lean	bend or tilt; thin; devoid of fat
lien	*property claim against money owed*
leans	bends or tilts
liens	*property claims against money owed*
leas	meadows
lees	*shelters*
leased	rented out
least	*smallest amount*
led	went ahead of others; took an advance position
lead	*type of metal*

Note: Underlined words have two acceptable pronunciations.

lee		**shelter**
	lea	*meadow*
leech		**blood sucking worm; parasite**
	leach	*remove liquid*
leechs		**blood sucking worms; parasites**
	leaches	*removes liquid*
leek		**a vegetable related to an onion**
	leak	*seepage of liquid or information*
leeks		**vegetables related to onions**
	leaks	*seepages of liquid or information*
lees		**shelters**
	leas	*meadows*
lei		**Hawaiian wreath**
	lay	*place at rest; deposit (as eggs of a hen); non-professional*
leis		**Hawaiian wreaths**
	lays	*deposits of hen's eggs*
	laze	*idle; loaf*
lends		**gives use of something temporarily**
	lens	*glass that transmits light for magnification*
lens		**glass that transmits light for magnification**
	lends	*gives use of something temporarily*
lessen		**reduce**
	lesson	*a section of a subject taught*
lessens		**reduces**
	lessons	*sections of a subject to be taught*
lesser		**the smaller of two things**
	lessor	*one who leases to another*
lesson		**a section of a subject taught**
	lessen	*reduce*

lessons

lessons	sections of a subject to be taught)
lessens	reduces
lessor	one who leases to another
lesser	the smaller of two things
levee	a raised area to hold back water; an official reception
levy	tax
levees	raised areas to hold back water; official receptions
levies	taxes
levies	taxes
levees	raised areas to hold back water; official receptions
levy	tax
levee	a raised area to hold back water; an official reception
liable	morally or legally responsible; a contingency; likely to happen
libel	defame in writing or print
liar	one who does not tell the truth
lier	one who lies down
lyre	small stringed instrument similar to a harp
liars	those who do not tell the truth
liers	those who lie down
lyres	small stringed instruments similar to a harp
libel	defame in writing or print
liable	morally or legally responsible; a contingency; likely to happen
lichen	a growth of fungus and algae that live off each other
liken	compare as similar something to another
lichens	growths of fungi and algae that live off each other
likens	compares as similar something to another
licker	one who licks with the tongue
liquor	alcoholic beverage

limbed

lie		be prone or supine; be quiet; to knowingly say something untrue
	lye	a strong antiseptic
lied		a German ballad
	lead	go in front of; take an advance position
lief		gladly
	leaf	green or colored part of a plant that grows out of a stem
lien		property claim against money owed
	lean	bend or tilt; thin; devoid of fat
liens		property claims against money owed
	leans	bends or tilts
lier		one who lies down
	liar	one who does not tell the truth
	lyre	small stringed instrument similar to a harp
liers		those who lie down
	liars	those who do not tell the truth
	lyres	small stringed instruments similar to a harp
lightening		reducing the weight
	lightning	a flash of light especially from a storm cloud
liken		compare as similar something to another
	lichen	a growth of fungus and algae that live off each other
likens		compares as similar something to another
	lichens	growths of fungi and algae that live off each other
limb		part of a body that extends from the trunk (e.g., leg, arm)
	limn	describe or picture in words
limbed		having limbs
	limned	described or pictured in words

Note: Underlined words have two acceptable pronunciations.

limbs

limbs	**parts of a body that extend from the trunk (e.g., legs, arms)**
limns	*describes or pictures in words*
limn	**describe or picture in words**
limb	*part of a body that extends from the trunk (e.g., leg, arm)*
limned	**described or pictured in words**
limbed	*having limbs*
limns	**describes or pictures in words**
limbs	*parts of a body that extend from the trunk (e.g., legs, arms)*
links	**connections; a golf course; sausages**
lynx	*a type of feline*
liquor	**alcohol beverage**
licker	*one who licks with the tongue*
liter	**a measure of capacity equal to 1.06 liquid quarts**
leader	*one who is ahead of others*
liters	**measures of capacity equal to 1.06 liquid quarts**
leaders	*those who are ahead of others*
literal	**strict interpretation; word for word (i.e., not paraphrased)**
littoral	*referring to the shore of a body of water*
littoral	**referring to the shore of a body of water**
literal	*strict interpretation; word for word (i.e., not paraphrased)*
llama	**a type of animal related to the camel**
lama	*a priest of the Buddhist sect*
llamas	**types of animal related to the camel**
lamas	*priests of the Buddhist sect*
load	**a weight or quantity; a limit in weight**
lode	*a metal deposit of ore*
lowed	*made a low sound*
loads	**weights or quantities; limits in weight**
lodes	*metal deposits of ore*

loop

loan	provide something to someone on a temporary basis
lone	*solo; isolated*
loaner	that which is provided to someone on a temporary basis; that which is lent
loner	*someone who is alone*
locks	devices for securing doors, boxes, windows
lox	*smoked salmon; liquid oxygen*
lode	a metal deposit of ore
load	*a weight or quantity; a limit in weight*
lowed	*made a low sound*
lodes	metal deposits of ore
loads	*weights or quantities; limits in weight*
logger	someone who cuts trees; one who records travels
lager	*a well seasoned beer*
loggers	persons who cut trees; persons who record travels
lagers	*well seasoned beers*
lone	solo; isolated
loan	*provide something to someone on a temporary basis*
loner	someone who is alone
loaner	*that which is provided to someone on a temporary basis; that which is lent*
loon	a type of fish-eating diving bird
lune	*the shape of a half moon*
loons	types of fish-eating diving birds
lunes	*the shapes of a half moon*
loop	a twist or turn of material in the form of a circle; a circle of a path
loupe	*a magnifying glass used by a jeweler*

loops

loops		twists or turns of material in the form of a circle; circles of a path
	loupes	*magnifying glasses used by a jeweler*
loose		slack; not tied
	luce	*a full grown pike (fish)*
loot		stolen goods; to steal
	lute	*a stringed instrument*
loupe		a magnifying glass used by a jeweler
	loop	*a twist or turn of material in the form of a circle; a circle of a path*
loupes		magnifying glasses used by a jeweler
	loops	*twists or turns of material in the form of a circle; circles of a path*
lowed		made a low sound
	load	*a weight or quantity; a limit in weight*
	lode	*a metal deposit of ore*
lox		smoked salmon; liquid oxygen
	locks	*devices for securing doors, boxes, windows*
luce		a full grown pike (fish)
	loose	*slack; not tied*
lune		the shape of a half moon
	loon	*a type of fish-eating diving bird*
lunes		the shapes of a half moon
	loons	*types of fish-eating diving birds*
lute		a stringed instrument
	loot	*stolen goods; to steal*
lye		a strong antiseptic
	lie	*be prone or supine; be quiet; to knowingly say something untrue*
lynx		a type of feline
	links	*connections; a golf course; sausages*

lyre	small stringed instrument similar to a harp
liar	*one who does not tell the truth*
lier	*one who lies down*
lyres	small stringed instruments similar to a harp
liars	*those who do not tell the truth*
liers	*those who lie down*

M

madam	respectful address for a woman; woman in charge of a house of prostitution
madame	*address of respect for a married woman*
madame	address of respect for a married woman
madam	*respectful address for a woman; woman in charge of a house of prostitution*
made	produced; activated
maid	*a young woman; a woman servant*
magnate	an influential person, especially in industry or business
magnet	*that which attracts*
magnet	that which attracts
magnate	*an influential person, especially in industry or business*
maid	a young woman; a woman servant
made	*produced; activated*
mail	letters or similar communication transmitted via a postal service
male	*masculine sex; a person of masculine sex*
mails	letters or similar communications transmitted via a postal service
males	*masculine sex; persons of masculine sex*

main

main		chief; principal
	mane	hair of the neck of a horse or some large felines
maize		the color of corn; yellow
	maze	interconnected path, often confusing
maizes		the colors of corn
	mazes	interconnected paths, often confusing
male		masculine sex; a person of masculine sex
	mail	letters or similar communication transmitted via a postal service
males		masculine sex; persons of masculine sex
	mails	letters or similar communications transmitted via a postal service
mall		a group of retail shops; an open tree-covered area
	maul	handle roughly so as to injure
malled		built like a mall; retail shops enclosed into one center of commerce
	mauled	handled roughly so as to injure
malls		groups of retail shops; open-tree-covered areas
	mauls	handles roughly so as to injure
mane		hair of the neck of a horse or some large felines
	main	chief; principal
manner		a way of behavior or happening
	manor	estate or mansion
manners		ways of behavior or happening
	manors	estates or mansions
manor		estate or mansion
	manner	a way of behavior or happening
manors		estates or mansions
	manners	ways of behavior or happening
man's		owned by or belonging to a man
	manse	a minister's house

martial

manse	a minister's house	
man's	*owned by or belonging to a man*	
mantel	a structure above a fireplace forming a shelf	
mantle	*loose, sleeveless coat*	
mantels	structures above fireplaces forming a shelf	
mantles	*loose, sleeveless coats*	
mantle	loose, sleeveless coat	
mantel	*a structure above a fireplace forming a shelf*	
mantles	loose, sleeveless coats	
mantels	*structures above fireplaces forming a shelf*	
mare	female horse	
mayor	*chief elected official of a city*	
mares	female horses	
mayors	*chief elected officials of cities*	
marine	pertaining to the sea or navigation	
moreen	*a heavy woolen or cotton fabric*	
marquees	protective shelters above doors; protective shelters for signs above a theater	
marquise	*wife or widow of a nobleman*	
marquise	wife or widow of a nobleman	
marquees	*protective shelters above doors; protective shelters for signs above a theater*	
marshal	military officer or public police officer	
martial	*war-like*	
marten	certain carnivorous animals	
martin	*a kind of swallow*	
martial	war-like	
marshal	*military officer or public police officer*	

~ 123 ~

martin

martin	**a kind of swallow**
marten	*certain carnivorous animals*
mask	**a covering for hiding the face; disguise**
masque	*dramatic entertainment*
masks	**coverings for hiding faces; disguises**
masques	*dramatic entertainments*
masque	**dramatic entertainment**
mask	*a covering for hiding the face; disguise*
masques	**dramatic entertainments**
masks	*coverings for hiding faces; disguises*
massed	**gathered; combined**
mast	*support for sails*
mast	**support for sails**
massed	*gathered; combined*
maul	**handle roughly so as to injure**
mall	*a group of retail shops; an open tree-covered area*
mauled	**handled roughly so as to injure**
malled	*built like a mall; retail shops enclosed into one center of commerce*
mauls	**handles roughly so as to injure**
malls	*groups of retail shops; open tree covered areas*
mayor	**chief elected official of a city**
mare	*female horse*
mayors	**chief elected officials of cities**
mares	*female horses*
maze	**interconnected paths, ofen confusing**
maize	*the color of corn; yellow*
mazes	**interconnected paths, often confusing**
maizes	*the colors of corn*

meet

mead		type of alcoholic beverage
	meed	*a reward (poetic)*
mean		average; intend; inferior character
	mien	*appearance*
means		averages; ways; intentions
	miens	*appearances*
meats		animal or plant flesh (plural), especially for food
	meets	*contacts; encounters*
	metes	*allots; doles; limits*
medal		an award for an exceptional act or performance
	meddle	*enter into another's affairs without permission*
medaled		awarded for an exceptional act or performance
	meddled	*entered into another's affairs without permission*
medals		awards for exceptional acts or performances
	meddles	*enters into another's affairs without permission*
meddle		enter into another's affairs without permission
	medal	*an award for an exceptional act or performance*
meddled		entered into another's affairs without permission
	medaled	*awarded for an exceptional act or performance*
meddles		enters into another's affairs without permission
	medals	*awards for exceptional acts or performances*
meddlesome		having the characteristic of meddling
	mettlesome	*spirited*
meed		a reward (poetic)
	mead	*type of alcoholic beverage*
meet		contact; encounter
	meat	*animal or plant flesh, especially for food*
	mete	*allot; dole; a limit*

~ 125 ~

meeter

meeter	one who meets
meter	an instrument for measurement; a unit of length; unit of measurement in poetry and music
meeting	the act of coming together, contacting or encountering
meting	the act of allotting or doling
meets	contacts; encounters
meats	animal or plant flesh (plural), especially for food
metes	allots; doles; limits
metal	basic natural or alloyed substances (e.g. gold, silver, etc)
mettle	character; courageousness
metals	basic natural or alloyed substances (e.g. gold, silver, etc)
mettles	courageous traits
mettle	character; courageousness
metal	basic natural or alloyed substance (e.g. gold, silver, etc.)
mettles	courageous traits
metals	basic natural or alloyed substances (e.g. gold, silver, etc.)
mettlesome	spirited
meddlesome	having the characteristic of meddling
mewl	soft cry as of a young child
mule	an animal that is a cross between a male donkey and a female horse; type of shoe-like slipper
mewls	soft cries as of a young child
mules	animals that are a cross between male donkeys and female horses; types of shoe-like slippers
mews	sounds made by cats; an enclosure; residence designed around a courtyard
muse	think about something to oneself
mho	a measure of electrical conduction; reciprocal of ohm
mot	a saying or succinct comment
mow	cut grass or grain

mhos	**measures of electrical conduction; reciprocals of ohm**
mots	*sayings or succinct comments*
mows	*cuts grass or grain*
mien	**appearance**
mean	*average; intend; inferior character*
miens	**appearances**
means	*averages; ways; intensions*
might	**strength; perhaps; possibly**
mite	*a type of very small aphid-like insect; anything very small*
mil	**a wire measurement (1/1000 of an inch)**
mill	*a factory; anywhere materials are processed; where flour is ground*
mill	**a factory; anywhere materials are processed; where flour is ground**
mil	*a wire measurement (1/1000 of an inch)*
mills	**factories; anywhere materials are processed; places where flour is ground**
mils	*measurements of wire (1/000 of an inch)*
mils	**measurements of wire (1/1000 of an inch)**
mills	*factories; anywhere materials are processed; places where flour is ground*
mince	**cut into small bits; to modify one's speech for propriety**
mints	*after-dinner candy; any candy flavored with mint; places where money is coined or printed*
mind	**the part of the human being that thinks and feels**
mined	*extracted from ore*
mined	**extracted from ore**
mind	*the part of the human being that thinks and feels*
miner	**one who extracts from ore**
minor	*one under a legal age; the less important or less significant thing*

miners

miners	those who extract from ores
minors	*those who are under the legal age; less important or less significant things*
minks	animals similar to weasels
minx	*a perky, forward-type of woman*
minor	one under a legal age; the less important or less significant thing
miner	*one who extracts from ore*
minors	those who are the legal age; less important or less significant things
miners	*those who extract from ores*
mints	after-dinner candy; any candy flavored with mint; places where money is coined or printed
mince	*cut into small bits; to modify one's speech for propriety*
minx	a perky, forward-type of woman
minks	*animals similar to weasels*
missal	a volume of prayers or rituals
missile	*a propelled object*
missals	volumes of prayers or rituals
missiles	*propelled objects*
missed	having failed to reach a goal or an appointment; be aware of the absence of someone or something
mist	*a foggy atmosphere; to produce a light spray of moisture (as for plants)*
missile	a propelled object
missal	*a volume of prayers or rituals*
missiles	propelled objects
missals	*volumes of prayers or rituals*
mite	a type of very small aphid-like insect; anything very small
might	*strength; perhaps; possibly*

moan	a low extended plaintive sound	
mown	*cut grass or grain; destroy*	
moat	a trench filled with water around a fortress	
mote	*a speck*	
moats	trenches filled with water around fortresses	
motes	*specks*	
mode	style or method	
mowed	*cut grass or grain*	
moire	having a watery pattern	
moray	*type of eel*	
mol	a chemical measure equal to one gram	
mole	*a dark colored mark on the body*	
mole	a dark colored mark on the body	
mol	*a chemical measure equal to one gram*	
moles	dark colored marks on the body	
mols	*chemical measures equal to one gram*	
mols	chemical measures equal to one gram	
moles	*dark colored marks on the body*	
monachal	pertaining to monkeys	
monocle	*eyeglass for one eye*	
monocle	eyeglass for one eye	
monachal	*pertaining to monkeys*	
mood	disposition; emotional state	
mooed	*made a sound like a cow*	
mooed	made a sound like a cow	
mood	*disposition; emotional state*	
moor	tie to the dock	
more	*in addition; additional amount*	

moose

moose	a large deer-like animal
mousse	a sweet dessert of gelatin and whipped cream
moray	type of eel
moire	having a watery pattern
morays	types of eel
mores	customs or habits of a people
mordant	biting (remark, comment); an acid or caustic substance to stabilize dyes
mordent	a sharp change of tone in music
mordent	a sharp change of tone in music
mordant	biting (remark, comment); an acid or caustic substance to stabilize dyes
more	in addition; additional
moor	tie to the dock
moreen	a heavy woolen or cotton fabric
marine	pertaining to the sea or navigation
mores	customs or habits of a people
morays	eels
morn	morning (in poetry)
mourn	to express sorrow at a loss
morning	early part of the day (before noon)
mourning	expressing sorrow at a loss
morns	mornings (in poetry)
mourns	expresses sorrow at a loss
mot	a saying or succinct comment
mho	a measure of electrical conduction; reciprocal of ohm
mow	cut grass or grain
mots	sayings or succinct comments
mhos	measures of electrical conduction; reciprocals of ohm
mows	cuts grass or grain

mousse	a sweet dessert of gelatin and whipped cream
moose	*a large deer-like animal*
mow	cut grass or grain
mho	*a measure of electrical conduction; reciprocal of ohm*
mot	*a saying or succinct comment*
mowed	cut grass or grain
mode	*style or method*
mown	cut grass or grain; destroy
moan	*a low, extended plaintive sound*
mows	cuts grass or grain
mhos	*measures of electrical conduction; reciprocals of ohm*
mots	*sayings or succinct comments*
mucous	related to mucus; mucus-like
mucus	*a thick secretion of the membrane of the lungs, intestine or genital systems*
mucus	a thick secretion of the membrane of the lungs, intestine or genital systems
mucous	*related to mucus; mucus-like*
mule	an animal that is a cross between a male donkey and a female horse; type of shoe-like slipper
mewl	*soft cry as of a young child*
mules	animals that are a cross between male donkeys and female horses; types of shoe-like slippers
mewls	*soft cries as of a young child*
muscle	a tissue that contracts for motion
mussel	*a type of mollusk*
muscles	tissues that contract for motion
mussels	*types of mollusks*

muse

muse	think about something to oneself
mews	*sounds made by cats; an enclosure; residence designed around a courtyard*
mussel	a type of mollusk
muscle	*a tissue that contracts for motion*
mussels	types of mollusks
muscles	*tissues that contract for motion*
mustard	a condiment made from the seed of the mustard plant
mustered	*assembled; gathered (especially troops)*
mustered	assembled; gathered (especially troops)
mustard	*a condiment made from the seed of the mustard plant*

N

nap	light or brief period of sleep
nappe	*surface of a cone*
nappe	surface of a cone
nap	*light or brief period of sleep*
nappes	surfaces of cones
naps	*light or brief periods of sleep*
naps	light or brief periods of sleep
nappes	*surfaces of cones*
naval	referring to the Navy or to ships
navel	*referring to the middle or umbilical point*
nave	center area of a church
knave	*someone who is without principles*

navel	**referring to the middle or umbilical point**
naval	*referring to the Navy or to ships*
naves	**central areas of churches**
knaves	*those without principles*
nay	**no; refusing agreement**
nee	*born; maiden name*
neigh	*sound made by a horse*
nays	**noes; refusing agreements**
neighs	*sounds of horses*
nee	**born; maiden name**
nay	*no; refusing agreement*
neigh	*sound made by a horse*
need	**require; necessitate**
knead	*to mold (dough, clay)*
kneed	*struck with the knee*
needed	**required; necessitated**
kneaded	*molded dough or clay*
needing	**requiring; necessitating**
kneading	*molding dough or clay*
needs	**requires; necessitates**
kneads	*molds dough or clay*
neigh	**sound made by a horse**
nay	*no; refusing agreement*
nee	*born; maiden name*
new	**having just occurred; recent; unused**
gnu	*a type of antelope*
knew	*was aware of; understood*
news	**information; report(s) of event(s)**
gnus	*types of antelopes*

nice

nice	pleasant
gneiss	a multi-layered rock of different minerals
night	the part of the day when the sun is down; darkness
knight	one who has the rank of the medieval soldier given for chivalrous deeds
nights	parts of days when the sun is down; darkness
knights	those who have the rank of the medieval soldiers given for chivalrous deeds
nit	insect egg or newborn insect
knit	join yarn by loops
nits	insect eggs or newborn insects
knits	joins yarn by loops
no	an expression of denial or refusal
know	to be aware of; to understand
noes	expressions of denial or refusal
nose	human and animal sensory organ that detects odor
knows	is aware of; understands
nock	notch on an arrow for the bowstring to fit
knock	to tap to make a sound
nocks	notches on arrows for bowstring to fit
knocks	taps to make sounds
none	not any; nobody
nun	woman in a religious order
nose	human and animal sensory organ that detects odor
noes	expressions of denial or refusal
knows	is aware of; understands
nun	woman in a religious order
none	not any; nobody

O

oar — a tool for rowing
    or — used to show alternatives (e.g., this or that)
    ore — rock containing mineral

oars — tools for rowing
    ores — rocks containing mineral

ode — a poem of praise
    owed — was indebted to

offal — refuse or garbage
    awful — terrible

oh — an expression (of surprise, fear, etc.)
    owe — be indebted to

oleo — abbreviation for oleomargarine
    olio — potpourri; hodgepodge

olio — potpourri; hodgepodge
    oleo — abbreviation for oleomargarine

one — single; the first number in the cardinal series
    won — defeated; overcame

or — used to show alternatives (e.g., this or that)
    oar — a tool for rowing
    ore — rock containing mineral

oracle — divine utterance; person or thing that expresses divine utterance
    auricle — external part of the outer ear

oracles

oracles	**divine utterances; persons or things that express divine utterance**
auricles	*external parts of the outer ears*
oral	**spoken; pertaining to the mouth**
aural	*pertaining to the ear*
ordinance	**statute**
ordnance	*military weapon and ammunition*
ordinances	**statutes**
ordnances	*military weapons and ammunition*
ordnance	**military weapon and ammunition**
ordinance	*statute*
ordnances	**military weapons and ammunition**
ordinances	*statutes*
ore	**rock containing mineral**
oar	*a tool for rowing*
or	*used to show alternatives (e.g., this or that)*
ores	**rocks containing mineral**
oars	*tools for rowing*
oriole	**a type of bird**
aureole	*a halo*
orioles	**types of birds**
aureoles	*halos*
our	**belong to "us"**
hour	*1\24th part of a day; a unit of 60 minutes*
owe	**be indebted to**
oh	*an expression (of surprise, fear, etc.)*
owed	**was indebted to**
ode	*a poem of praise*

P

paced   set a rate of movement
paste   adhere to a surface; a substance used to adhere something to a surface

packed   put goods together in a smaller space
pact   a treaty or agreement

pact   a treaty or agreement
packed   put goods together in a smaller space

paean   a song of praise or joy
paeon   a type of verse in poetry
peon   an attendant or servant

paeons   types of verse in poetry
paeans   songs of verse in poetry
peons   attendants or servants

pail   a container for liquids; bucket
pale   dim; faint; devoid of color; stake or enclosure

pails   containers for liquids; buckets
pales   fades

pain   discomfort or suffering
pane   a section or plate of glass

pained   expressed or showed discomfort or suffering
paned   had sections or plates of glass

paining   that which induces or causes discomfort or suffering
paning   having sections or plates of glass

painless   without discomfort or suffering
paneless   without sections or plates of glass

Note: Underlined words have two acceptable pronunciations.

pains

pains	expresses or shows discomfort or suffering
panes	sections or plates of glass
pair	two matching parts; a couple
pare	peel the skin (of a fruit or vegetable)
pear	a specific type of fruit
paired	matched or coupled
pared	peeled the skin (e.g., of a fruit or vegetable)
pairing	matching or coupling
paring	peeling the skin (e.g., of a fruit or vegetable)
pairs	matches or couples
pares	peels the skin (e.g., of a fruit or vegetable)
pears	specific types of fruit
palate	roof of the mouth; taste
pallet	a board to support ceramic objects
palette	a board to hold paints for an artist
palates	roofs of the mouth
pallets	boards to support ceramic objects
palettes	boards to hold paints for an artist
pale	dim; faint; devoid of color; stake or enclosure
pail	a container for liquids; bucket
pales	fades
pails	containers for liquids; buckets
palette	a board to hold paints for an artist
palate	roof of the mouth; taste
pallet	a board to support ceramic objects
palettes	boards to hold paints for an artist
palates	roofs of the mouth
pallets	boards to support ceramic objects
pall	to lose strength; a dark, gloomy setting
pawl	a device for restricting rotation to one direction

pallet	**a board to support ceramic objects**
palette	*a board to hold paints for an artist*
palate	*roof of the mouth; taste*
palls	**loses strength; dark, gloomy settings**
pawls	*devices for restricting rotation to one direction*
palmar	**relating to the inner part of the hand**
palmer	*one who palms or hides something in the palm*
pane	**section or plate of glass**
pain	*discomfort or suffering*
paned	**having sections or plates of glass**
pained	*expressed or showed discomfort or suffering*
paneless	**without sections or plates of glass**
painless	*without discomfort or suffering*
panes	**sections or plates of glass**
pains	*expresses discomfort or suffering*
paning	**sections or plates of glass**
paining	*that which induces or causes discomfort or suffering*
pare	**peel the skin (e.g., of a fruit or vegetable)**
pair	*two matching parts; a couple*
pear	*a specific type of fruit*
pared	**peeled the skin (e.g., of a fruit or vegetable)**
paired	*matched or coupled*
pares	**peels the skin (of a fruit or vegetable)**
pairs	*matches or couples*
pears	*specific types of fruit*
paring	**peeling the skin (of a fruit or vegetable)**
pairing	*matching or coupling*
pars	**equalities or averages**
parse	*analyze by parts of speech*

parse

parse	**analyze by parts of speech**
pars	*equalities or averages*
passable	**acceptable**
passible	*able to feel emotion*
passableness	**characteristic of acceptability**
passibleness	*characteristic of feeling emotion*
passed	**went beyond**
past	*ago; time gone by*
passible	**able to feel emotion**
passable	*acceptable*
passibleness	**characteristic of feeling emotion**
passableness	*characteristic of acceptability*
past	**ago; time gone by**
passed	*went beyond*
paste	**adhere to a surface; a substance used to adhere something to a surface**
paced	*set a rate of movement*
patience	**tolerance of delay, frustration, etc.**
patients	*persons being cared for by health care provider*
patients	**persons being cared for by health care provider**
patience	*tolerance of delay, frustration, etc.*
pause	**a delay, interruption, halt**
paws	*feet of animals; scratches or scrapes with the paw*
pawl	**a device for restricting rotation to one direction**
pall	*to lose strength; a dark, glowing setting*
pawls	**devices for restricting rotation to one direction**
palls	*loses strength; dark, gloomy settings*

pealings

paws	feet of animals; scratches or scrapes with the paw
pause	*a delay, interruption, halt*
peace	quiet, absence of hostility
piece	*part of a whole; a unit*
peak	high point
peek	*glance quickly; brief look*
pique	*irritate; offend; arouse, stimulate*
peaked	at a high point; shaped to a high point
peeked	*glanced quickly; looked briefly*
piqued	*irritated; offended; aroused; stimulated*
peaking	coming to a high point; shaping to a high point
peeking	*glancing quickly; looking briefly*
piquing	*irritating; offending; arousing; stimulating*
peaks	high points
peeks	*glances quickly; looks briefly*
piques	*irritations; irritates; arouses; stimulates*
peal	a sharp, ringing sound
peel	*pare; a tool for moving food in or out of the oven*
pealed	made a sharp ringing sound
peeled	*pared*
pealer	one who makes a sharp ringing sound
peeler	*parer*
pealers	those who make a sharp, ringing sound
peelers	*parers*
pealing	a sharp, ringing sound
peeling	*paring*
pealings	sharp, ringing sounds
peelings	*parings*

peals

peals	sharp, ringing sounds
peels	*pares*
pear	a specific type of fruit
pair	*two matching parts; a couple*
pare	*peel the skin (e.g., of a fruit or vegetable)*
pearl	a gem produced by an oyster or other mollusk
purl	*a looped knitting stitch; liquid flowing with a low sound*
pearled	covered with pearls
purled	*knitted with a looped stitch; liquid that flowed with a low sound*
pearls	gems produced by oysters or other mollusks
purls	*looped, knitting stitches; liquid that flows with a low sound*
pedal	a part operated by the foot
peddle	*sell goods in different places*
pedaled	moved a part with the foot
peddled	*sold goods in different places*
pedaler	one who moves a part with the foot
peddler	*one who sells goods in different places*
pedaling	moving a part with the foot
peddling	*selling goods in different places*
pedals	moves parts with the foot
peddles	*sells goods in different places*
peddle	sell goods in different places
pedal	*a part operated by the foot*
peddled	sold goods in different places
pedaled	*moved a part with the foot*
peddler	one who sells goods in different places
pedaler	*one who moves a part with the foot*

peelings

peddles	sells goods in different places
pedals	moves parts with the foot
peddling	selling goods in different places
pedaling	moving a part with the foot
peek	glance quickly; brief look
peak	high point
pique	irritate; offend; arouse; stimulate
peeked	glanced quickly; looked briefly
peaked	at a high point; shaped to a high point
piqued	irritated; offended; aroused; stimulated
peeking	glancing quickly; looking briefly
piquing	irritating; offending; arousing; stimulating
peaking	coming to a high point; shaping to a high point
peeks	glances quickly; looks briefly
peaks	high point
piques	irritations; irritates; arouses; stimulates
peel	pare; a tool for moving food in or out of the oven
peal	a sharp, ringing sound
peeled	pared
pealed	made a sharp, ringing round
peeler	parer
pealer	one who makes a sharp, ringing sound
peelers	parers
pealers	those who make a sharp, ringing sound
peeling	paring
pealing	the act of sound a sharp, ringing sound
peelings	parings
pealings	sharp, ringing sounds

peels

peels	**pares**
peals	sharp ringing, sounds
peer	**an equal in rank; look intensively**
pier	a dock
peers	**equals in rank; looks intensively**
piers	docks
pelisse	**a fur-lined long, outer coat**
police	an organization to maintain law and order
penance	**punishment for sin**
pennants	flags
pencil	**a writing tool made of graphite**
<u>pensile</u>	hanging (as nests)
pend	**hang; await action or completion**
penned	written; confined to a small area
pendant	**something that hangs**
pendent	hanging or remaining pending
pends	**hangs, awaits action or completion**
pens	writing tools that use ink
pendent	**hanging or remaining pending**
pendant	something that hangs
pennants	**flags**
penance	punishment for sin
penned	**written; confined to a small area**
pend	hang; await action or completion
<u>**pensile**</u>	**hanging (as nests)**
pencil	a writing tool made of graphite

Note: Underlined words have two acceptable pronunciations.

philter

peon	an attendant or servant
paean	*a song of praise or joy*
paeon	*type of verse in poetry*
peons	attendants or servants
paeans	*songs of praise or joy*
paeons	*types of verse in poetry*
per	each; by
purr	*a low, murmuring sound (especially of pleasure)*
perse	gray-blue
purse	*a small bag to carry personal articles; to shape or fold the lips or brow; a sum of money as a prize or reward*
phase	a stage or cycle
fays	*closely fit together*
faze	*to disturb*
phased	staged or cycled
fazed	*disturbed*
phases	stages or cycles
fazes	*disturbs*
phasing	staging or cycling
fazing	*disturbing*
phial	a small container of liquid (especially medicine)
faille	*woven, ribbed fabric*
file	*classify; arrange in order; a tool for shaping or smoothing; to shape or smooth*
phials	small containers of liquid (especially medicine)
<u>*failles*</u>	*woven ribbed cloths*
files	*arranges in order; classifies; tools for shaping or smoothing; shapes or smooths*
philter	a magic dose of a liquid
filter	*a device to screen out impurities; to screen out impurities*

Note: Underlined words have two acceptable pronunciations.

philters

philters   magic doses of liquids
    filters   *devices to screen out impurities; screens out impurities*

phlox   a type of herb with varied colored flowers
    flocks   *pieces of material (especially for upholstery); groups of animals or birds or people*

phrase   part of a sentence in speech or writing
    fraise   *fortress of sharply pointed rods*
    frays   *fights; battles*

phylla   classifications of plants or languages
    fila   *thread-like structures*

phyllum   classification of plants or languages
    filum   *thread-like structure*

pi   a mixed collection of printing type; a mathematical symbol equal to 3.141
    pie   *a deep dish pastry crust filled with fruit, pudding or meat and vegetables*

pie   a deep dish pastry crust filled with fruit, pudding or meat and vegetables
    pi   *a mixed collection of printing types; a mathematical symbol equal to 3.141*

piece   part of a whole; a unit
    peace   *quiet, absence of hostility*

pier   a dock
    peer   *an equal in rank; look intensively*

piers   docks
    peers   *equals in rank; looks intensively*

pies   deep dish pastry crusts filled with fruit, pudding or meat and vegetables
    pis   *mixed collections of printing types; mathematical symbols equal to 3.141*

pistol

pillar   a stone or wood vertical structure shaped like a post
   piller   *one who makes pills*

pillars   stone or wood vertical structures shaped like posts
   pillers   *those who make pills*

piller   one who makes pills
   pillar   *a stone or wood vertical structure shaped like a post*

pillers   those who make pills
   pillars   *stone or wood vertical structures shaped like posts*

pique   irritate; offend; arouse; stimulate
   peak   *high point*
   peek   *glance quickly; brief look*

piqued   irritated; offended; aroused; stimulated
   peaked   *at a high point; shaped to a high point*
   peeked   *glanced quickly; looked briefly*

piques   irritations; irritates; arouses; stimulates
   peaks   *high points*
   peeks   *glances quickly; looks briefly*

piquing   irritating; offending; arousing; stimulating
   peaking   *coming to a high point; shaping to a high point*
   peeking   *glancing quickly; looking briefly*

pis   mixed collections of printing types; mathematical symbols equal to 3.141
   pies   *deep dish pastry crusts filled with fruit, pudding or meat and vegetables*

pistil   part of the flower that bears seeds
   pistol   *hand gun*

pistils   parts of the flowers that bear seeds
   pistols   *hand guns*

pistol   hand gun
   pistil   *part of the flower that bears seeds*

pistols

pistols	**hand guns**
pistils	*parts of the flowers that bear seeds*
plain	**simple; without adornment; clear, lucid; land that is level**
plane	*a flat surface; level; tool for smoothing a surface*
plains	**lands that are level**
planes	*flat surfaces; tools for smoothing surfaces*
plait	**braid (of hair or rope)**
plate	*a flat dish; a sheet of metal*
plaited	**braided (hair or rope)**
plated	*covered with metal (especially gold, silver, bronze)*
plaiting	**braiding (of hair or rope)**
plating	*covering with metal (especially gold, silver, bronze)*
plane	**a flat surface; level; tool for smoothing a surface**
plain	*simple; without adornment; clear, lucid; land that is level*
planes	**flat surfaces; tools for smoothing surfaces**
plains	*lands that are level*
platan	**plane tree**
platen	*the roller in a typewriter; a plate that rolls paper in a printing press*
platans	**plane trees**
platens	*rollers in a typewriter; plates that roll paper in printing presses*
plate	**a flat dish; a sheet of metal**
plait	*braid (of hair or rope)*
plated	**covered with metal (especially gold, silver, bronze)**
plaited	*braided (hair or rope)*
platen	**the roller in a typewriter; a plate that rolls paper in a printing press**
platan	*plane tree*

platens	rollers in a typewiter; plates that roll paper in printing presses
platans	*plane trees*
plating	covering with metal (especially gold, silver, bronze)
plaiting	*braiding (of hair or rope)*
pleas	beggings; responses to a legal charge
please	*satisfy; an expression of request*
please	satisfy; an expression of request
pleas	*beggings; responses to a legal charge*
plum	particular type of fruit
plumb	*metal material to measure water depth or determine a perpendicular line*
plumb	metal material to measure water depth or determine a perpendicular line
plum	*particular type of fruit*
plumbs	measures with or tests with a plumb
plums	*particular type of fruits*
plums	particular type of fruits
plumbs	*measures with or tests with a plumb*
polar	referring to one side or extreme
poler	*one who uses a pole*
poller	*one who surveys opinions*
pole	a long wood or metal object; an extreme of an object, topic or view; one of two electric faces of a battery
poll	*vote; survey of opinions*
poled	having a pole
polled	*surveyed opinions*
poler	one who uses a pole
polar	*referring to one side or extreme*
poller	*one who surveys opinions*

poles

poles	long wood or metal objects; the extremes of an object, topic or view; the electric faces of batteries
polls	*votes; surveys of opinions*
police	an organization to maintain law and order
pelisse	*a fur-lined long, outer coat*
poll	vote; survey of opinions
pole	*a long wood or metal object, an extreme of an object, topic or view; one of two electric faces of a battery*
polled	surveyed opinions
poled	*having a pole*
poller	one who surveys opinions
polar	*referring to one side or extreme*
poler	*one who uses a pole*
polls	votes; surveys of opinions
poles	*long wood or metal objects; the extremes of an object, topic or view; the electric faces of batteries*
poor	impoverished; lacking material or other resources
pore	*an opening in the skin or surface; to concentrate attention*
pour	*dispense liquid from a container*
populace	inhabitants (especially the lesser social classes)
populous	*crowded; well populated*
populous	crowded; well populated
populace	*inhabitants (especially the lesser social classes)*
pore	an opening in the skin or surface; to concentrate attention
poor	*impoverished; lacking material or other resources*
pour	*dispense liquid from a container*
pored	had openings in the skin or surface; concentrated attention
poured	*dispensed liquid from a container*
pores	openings in the skin or surface; concentrates attention
pours	*dispenses liquid from a container*

premiere

poring   concentrating attention
pouring   *dispensing liquid from a container*

pour   dispense liquid from a container
poor   *impoverished; lacking material or other resources*
pore   *an opening in the skin or surface; to concentrate attention*

poured   dispensed liquid from a container
pored   *had openings in the skin or surface; concentrated attention*

pouring   dispensing liquid from a container
poring   *concentrating attention*

pours   dispenses liquid from a container
pores   *openings in the skin or surface; concentrates attention*

praise   approval; applause
prays   *expresses a deep felt hope or request; addresses a Superior Being or other object of worship*
preys   *victims; animals sought for food; preoccupies one's thoughts in a negative way*

pray   express a deep felt hope or request; address a Superior Being or other object of worship
prey   *a victim; any animal sought for food; to preoccupy one's thoughts in a negative way*

prayed   expressed a deep felt hope or request; addressed a Superior Being or other object of worship
preyed   *victimized*

prays   expresses a deep felt hope or request; addresses a Superior Being or other object of worship
praise   *approval; applause*
preys   *victims; animals sought for food; preoccupies one's thoughts in a negative way*

premier   chief officer of a country equivalent to Prime Minister
premiere   *earliest initial appearance; initial; first*

premiere   earliest initial appearance; initial; first
premier   *chief officer of a country equivalent to Prime Minister*

premieres

premieres   initial appearances
premiers   chief officers of a country equivalent to Prime Ministers

premiers   chief officers of a country equivalent to Prime Ministers
premieres   initial appearances

presence   attendance
presents   gifts

prey   a victim; any animal sought for food; to preoccupy one's thoughts in a negative way
pray   express a deep felt hope or request; address a Superior Being or other object of worship

preyed   victimized
prayed   expressed a deep felt hope or request; addressed a Superior Being or other object of worship

preys   victims; animals sought for food; preoccupies one's thoughts in a negative way
praise   approval; applause
prays   expresses a deep felt hope or request; addresses a Superior Being or other object of worship

pride   self-respect; exaggerated self-admiration
pried   forced open; investigated private matters

pried   forced open; investigated private matters
pride   self-respect; exaggerated self-admiration

prier (pryer)   someone who investigates secret or personal areas
prior   before; a high official in a monastery or religious order

pries   pulls apart
prize   award

primer   basic book for teaching reading
primmer   more exaggerated proper behavior

primmer   more exaggerated proper behavior
primer   basic book for teaching reading

prose

prince — son of the king or queen
prints — reproduces letters, designs or pictures on paper; publishes

principal — headmaster of the school
principle — chief; primary; guide

principals — headmasters of schools
principles — chiefs; guides

principle — chief; primary; guide
principal — headmaster of the school

principles — chiefs; guides
principals — headmasters of schools

prints — reproduces letters, designs or pictures on paper; publishes
prince — son of the king or queen

prior — before; a high official in a monastery or religious order
prier (pryer) — someone who investigates secret or personal areas

prize — award
pries — pulls apart

profit — gain; surplus in excess of costs
prophet — predictor; specially endowed person of vision

profits — gains; surpluses in excess of costs
prophets — predictors; specially endowed people of vision

prophet — predictor; specially endowed person of vision
profit — gain; surplus in excess of costs

prophets — predictors; specially endowed people of vision
profits — gains; surpluses in excess of costs

pros — those in favor of; professionals
prose — non-poetic speech or writing

prose — non-poetic speech or writing
pros — those in favor of; professionals

pryer

pryer (prier)	someone who investigates secret or personal areas
prior	*before; a high official in a monastery or religious order*
psychosis	a type of functional or organic mental disorder
sycosis	*staphyloccic infection of the beard*
psychoses	types of functional or organic mental disorders
sycoses	*staphyloccic infections of beards*
puisne	junior in rank
puny	*inferior in power or size*
puny	inferior in power or size
puisne	*junior in rank*
purest	most free of impurity, defect or deficiency
purist	*one who is strict in adherence to rules or style*
purist	one who is strict in adherence to rules or style
purest	*most free of impurity, defect or deficiency*
purl	a looped knitting stitch; liquid flowing with a low sound
pearl	*a gem produced by an oyster or other mollusk*
purled	knitted with a looped stitch; liquid that flowed with a low sound
pearled	*covered with pearls*
purls	looped, knitting stitches; liquid that flows with a low sound
pearls	*gems produced by oysters or other mollusks*
purr	a low, murmuring sound (especially of pleasure)
per	*each; by*
purse	a small bag to carry personal articles; to shape or fold the lips or brow; a sum of money as a prize or reward
perse	*gray-blue*

Q

quaff	to drink (especially liquor) with enthusiasm
coif	*hoodlike cap; to arrange the style of hair*
quaffed	drank (especially liquor) with enthusiasm
coiffed	*arranged the style of hair*
quaffing	drinking (especially liquor) with enthusiasm
coiffing	*arranging the style of hair*
quaffs	drinks (especially liquor) with enthusiasm
coifs	*hoodlike caps; arranges the style of hair*
quarts	measures of 32 oz. capacity
quartz	*a common metal, silicon dioxide*
quartz	a common metal, silicon dioxide
quarts	*measures of 32 oz. capacity*
quay	landing place for boats
key	*metal tool to open a lock; symbol of explanation*
quays	landing places for boats
keys	*metal tools to open locks; symbols of explanation*
queue	a long braid of hair; a line or order of people or events
cue	*a hint or prompt; a stick used to play the game of pool*
queued	hair made into a long braid; people lined up or events placed in order
cued	*hinted or prompted*
queuing	making hair into a long braid; lining people up or placing events in order
cuing	*hinting or prompting*

queues

queues	**long braids of hair; lines or orders of people or events**
cues	*hints or prompts; sticks used to play the game of pool*
quire	**24 or 25 sheets of equal size paper**
choir	*a group of singers*
quires	**sets of 24 or 25 sheets of equal size paper**
choirs	*groups of singers*
quoin **(coign)** **(coigne)**	**a wedge used in typesetting; a cornerstone**
coin	*a metal piece used for money; to make money, terms or phrases*
quoins **(coigns)** **(coignes)**	**wedges used in typesetting; cornerstones**
coins	*metal pieces used for money; makes money, terms or phrases*
quoining	**wedging used in typesetting**
coining	*making coins; making money, terms or phrases*

R

rabbet	**a carpentry joint to connect two boards**
rabbit	*a species of mammal of the rodent family*
rabbets	**carpentry joints to connect two boards**
rabbits	*species of mammals of the rodent family*
rabbit	**a species of mammal of the rodent family**
rabbet	*a carpentry joint to connect two boards*
rabbits	**species of mammals of the rodent family**
rabbets	*carpentry joints to connect two boards*

rained

rack	**a metal or wood frame on which objects are hung**
wrack	*destroy; remains of a destroyed object*
racket	**a loud noise; an illegal or predatory activity**
racquet	*equipment used for tennis*
rackets	**loud noises; illegal or predatory activities**
racquets	*equipment used for tennis*
racks	**metal or wood frames on which objects are hung**
wracks	*destroys; remains of a destroyed object*
racquet	**equipment used for tennis**
racket	*a loud noise; an illegal or predatory activity*
racquets	**equipment used for tennis**
rackets	*loud noises; illegal or predatory activities*
radical	**from the root or source; one who believes in basic reform**
radicle	*root-like beginning in nerves or veins*
radicals	**from the roots or sources; those who believe in basic reform**
radicles	*root-like beginnings in nerves or veins*
radicle	**root-like beginning in nerves or veins**
radical	*from the root or source; one who believes in basic reform*
radicles	**root-like beginnings in nerves or veins**
radicals	*from the roots or sources; those who believe in basic reform*
raid	**attack; invade**
rayed	*having rays, beams or extensions from a center*
rain	**precipitation; falling moisture**
reign	*a ruler or ruling period*
rein	*a strap tied to an animal to guide its movement; control*
rained	**moisture fell**
reigned	*ruled*
reined	*controlled; held back by straps*

~ 157 ~

raining

raining	moisture that is falling
reigning	ruling
reining	controlling; holding back by straps
rains	moisture that falls; times when moisture falls
reigns	rules
reins	controls; holds back by straps
raise	lift; increase
rays	beams; extensions from a center
raze	tear down to ground level
raised	lifted; increased
razed	torn down to ground level
raiser	lifter; one who causes an increase
razer	one who tears down to ground level
razor	sharp instrument for shaving hair
raisers	lifters; those who cause an increase
razers	those who tear down to ground level
razors	sharp instruments for shaving hair
raising	lifting; increasing
razing	tearing down to ground level
rancor	bitter feelings
ranker	more offensive
ranker	more offensive
rancor	bitter feelings
rap	tap; strike lightly
wrap	enclose in paper; wind tightly
rapped	tapped lightly; stroked lightly
rapt	intensively absorbed in thought
wrapped	enclosed in paper; wound tightly
rappel	descend by means of rope
repel	push back; resist

rays

rappeled	**descended by means of ropes**
repelled	*pushed back; resisted*
rappeler	**one who descends by means of ropes**
repeller	*one who pushes back; resists*
rapelling	**descending by means of ropes**
repelling	*pushing back; resisting*
rapper	**one who taps lightly; one who strikes lightly**
wrapper	*one who encloses items in paper; one who winds tightly*
rappers	**those who tap lightly; those who strike lightly**
wrappers	*those who enclose items in paper; those who wind tightly*
rapping	**the act of tapping lighly; the act of striking lightly**
wrapping	*enclosing items in paper or cloth; the material used to enclose an object or person; winding tightly*
raps	**taps lightly; strikes lightly**
wraps	*encloses items in paper or cloth; the materials used to enclose objects or persons; winds tightly*
rapt	**intensively absorbed in thought**
rapped	*tapped lighly; stroked lightly*
wrapped	*enclosed in paper or cloth; wound tightly*
raven	**large glossy colored black bird**
ravin	*violent plundering*
ravin	**violent plundering**
raven	*large glossy colored black bird*
rayed	**having rays, beams or extensions from a center**
raid	*attack; invade*
rays	**beams; extensions from a center**
raise	*lift; increase*
raze	*tear down to ground level*

raze

raze		tear down to ground level
	raise	*lift; increase*
	rays	*beams; extensions from a center*
razed		torn down to ground level
	raised	*lifted; increased*
razer		one who tears down to ground level
	raiser	*lifter; one who causes an increase*
	razor	*sharp instrument for shaving hair*
razers		those who tear down to ground level
	raisers	*lifters; those who cause an increase*
	razors	*sharp instruments for shaving hair*
razing		tearing down to ground level
	raising	*lifting; increasing*
razor		sharp instrument for shaving hair
	raiser	*lifter; one who causes an increase*
	razer	*one who tears down to ground level*
razors		sharp instruments for shaving hair
	raisers	*lifters; those who cause an increase*
	razers	*those who tear down to ground level*
<u>**read**</u>		had understood the words or gone over the writing
	red	*one of the primary colors*
<u>**read**</u>		to understand the words; go over writing
	reed	*a thin flexible piece of wood or metal*
reader		one who reads; one who goes over writing
	reeder	*one who thatches with a reed; also one who grooves metal*
reading		the act of understanding the words; perusing the writing
	reeding	*the act of thatching with a reed; the act of grooving metal*
reads		understands the words or goes over the writing
	reeds	*thin flexible pieces of wood or metal*

Note: Underlined words have two acceptable pronunciations.

real		actual; true
	reel	to sway; a circular object that revolves to hold tape, wire, etc; a spool
rebait		bait again; to again set food to attract fish or animal
	rebate	deduction; deduct
recede		to go back; ebb
	reseed	to sow seed again
receded		went back; ebbed
	reseeded	sowed seed again
recedes		goes back; ebbs
	reseeds	sows seed again
receding		going back; ebbing
	reseeding	sowing seed again
receipt		evidence of payment
	reseat	to seat again
receipted		gave evidence of payment
	reseated	was seated again
receipts		evidences of payment
	reseats	seats again
reck		take or show care
	wreck	ruin; destroy completely
red		one of the primary colors
	read	had understood the words or gone over the writing
reed		a thin, flexible piece of wood or metal
	read	to understand the words; peruse the writing
reeder		one who thatches with a reed; also one who grooves metal
	reader	one who reads; one who peruses writing

Note: Underlined words have two acceptable pronunciations.

reeding

reeding	the act of thatching with a reed; the act of grooving metal
reading	*the act of understanding the words; perusing the writing*
reeds	thin, flexible pieces of wood or metal
reads	*understands the words or goes over the writing*
reek	strong smell; smell of smoke
wreak	*inflict, vent onto (punishment or anger, etc.)*
reeked	smelled strongly; smelled of smoke
wreaked	*inflicted, vented onto (punishment or anger, etc.)*
reeks	smells strongly; smells of smoke
wreaks	*inflicts, vents onto (punishment or anger, etc.)*
reel	to sway; a circular object that revolves to hold tape, wire, etc; a spool
real	*actual; true*
reign	a ruler or ruling period
rain	*precipitation; falling moisture*
rein	*a strap tied to an animal to guide its movement; control*
reigned	ruled
rained	*moisture that fell*
reined	*controlled; held back by straps*
reigning	ruling
raining	*moisture that is falling*
reining	*controlling; holding back by straps*
reigns	rules
rains	*moisture that falls; times when moisture falls*
reins	*controls; holds back by straps*
rein	a strap tied to an animal to guide its movement; control
reign	*a ruler or ruling period*
rain	*precipitation; falling moisture*

reined   controlled; held back by straps
   rained   *moisture that fell*
   reigned   *ruled*

reining   controlling; holding back by straps
   raining   *moisture that is falling*
   reigning   *ruling*

reins   controls; holds back by straps
   rains   *moisture that falls; times when moisture falls*
   reigns   *rules*

remand   send back; order to go back
   remanned   *staffed again*

remanned   staffed again
   remand   *send back; order to go back*

remark   notice; observe; comment
   remarque   *a proof mark to identify the proof*

remarks   notices; observes; comments
   remarques   *proof marks to identify the proofs*

remarque   a proof mark to identify the proof
   remark   *notice; observe; comment*

remarques   proof marks to identify the proofs
   remarks   *notices; observes; comments*

reseat   to seat again
   receipt   *evidence of payment*

reseated   was seated again
   receipted   *gave evidence of payment*

reseats   seats again
   receipts   *evidences of payment*

reseed   to sow seed again
   recede   *to go back; ebb*

reseeded

reseeded   sowed seed again
receded   went back; ebbed

reseeding   sowing seed again
receding   going back; ebbing

reseeds   sows seed again
recedes   goes back; ebbs

residence   place where one lives
residents   persons who live at a particular place

residents   persons who live at a particular place
residence   place where one lives

resister   one who resists or opposes
resistor   a device for resisting electrical current

resisters   those who resist or oppose
resistors   devices for resisting electrical current

resistor   a device for reisting electrical current
resister   one who resists or opposes

resistors   devices for resisting electrical current
resisters   those who resist or oppose

resold   sold again
resoled   soled again

resoled   soled again
resold   sold again

rest   remainder; to be at ease
wrest   to take away from by force; force from one's group

retch   to vomit
wretch   a miserably unlucky or unhappy person

retches   vomits
wretches   miserably unlucky or unhappy persons

review	evaluation of written or oral material
revue	*theatrical event of music and dance*
reviews	evaluations of written or oral material
revues	*theatrical events of music and dances*
revue	theatrical event of music and dance
review	*evaluation of written or oral material*
revues	theatrical events of music and dances
reviews	*evaluations of written or oral material*
rheum	a mucous discharge
room	*space marked by four walls*
rheums	mucous discharges
rooms	*spaces marked by four walls*
rhumb	a constant path line of a ship
rum	*liquor derived from sugar cane*
rhumbs	constant path lines of ships
rums	*liquors derived from sugar cane*
rhyme	two words whose final sounds agree
rime	*ice particle formed by rapid freezing*
rhymed	having two words whose final sounds agree
rimed	*having an ice particle formed by rapid freezing*
rhymes	two words whose final sounds agree
rimes	*ice particles formed by rapid freezing*
rhyming	two words which have the final sounds agreeing
riming	*making ice particles formed by rapid freezing*
rial	a coin of Iran
rile	*irk; anger*
rials	coins of Iran
riles	*irks; angers*

rigger

rigger	**one who rigs**
rigor	*rigidity; strictness*
riggers	**those who rig**
rigors	*rigidities; strictnesses*
right	**correct; the opposite of left; an entitlement of law or custom**
rite	*ceremony*
wright	*one of different kinds of construction workers*
write	*record by pen, pencil, etc.*
righting	**putting into upright or correct position**
writing	*recording by pen, pencil, etc.*
rights	**puts into upright or correct position; entitlements of law or custom**
rites	*ceremonies*
wrights	*any of different kinds of construction workers*
writes	*records by pen, pencil, etc.*
rigors	**rigidities; strictnesses**
riggers	*those who rig*
rile	**irk; anger**
rial	*a coin of Iran*
riles	**irks; angers**
rials	*coins of Iran*
rime	**ice particle formed by rapid freezing**
rhyme	*two words whose final sounds agree*
rimed	**having ice particles formed by rapid freezing**
rhymed	*having two words whose final sounds agree*
rimes	**ice particles formed by rapid freezing**
rhymes	*two words whose final sounds agree*
riming	**making ice particles formed by rapid freezing**
rhyming	*two words which have the final sounds agreeing*

rode

ring	**a circular piece of material (e.g., wedding ring); a circular mark**
wring	*to twist; to twist so as to squeeze out water*
ringer	**that which circles or rings**
wringer	*one who twists so as to squeeze out water*
rings	**circles; circular pieces of material (e.g., wedding rings)**
wrings	*twists so as to squeeze out water*
rise	**to get up (e.g., from a bed or chair)**
ryes	*types of cereal grains*
rite	**ceremony**
right	*correct; the opposite of left; an entitlement of law or custom*
wright	*one of different kinds of construction workers*
write	*record by pen, pencil, etc.*
rites	**ceremonies**
rights	*puts into upright or correct position; entitlements of law or custom*
wrights	*any of different kinds of construction workers*
writes	*records by pen, pencil, etc.*
road	**a path for motor vehicles**
rode	*was a passenger or driver in a vehicle or on an animal*
rowed	*moved oars or paddles to propel a vessel in the water*
roc	**a fabled bird of prey**
rock	*a large stone; to sway back and forth*
rock	**a large stone; to sway back and forth**
roc	*a fabled bird of prey*
rocks	**large stones; sways back and forth**
rocs	*fabled birds of prey*
rocs	**fabled birds of prey**
rocks	*large stones; sways back and forth*
rode	**was a passenger or driver in a vehicle or on an animal**
road	*a path for motor vehicles*
rowed	*moved oars or paddles to propel a vessel in the water*

absroeence

roe		fish egg; "caviar"
	row	move oars or paddles to propel a vessel in the water; an array of objects

roes — fish eggs
    rose — got up; moved up; a type of flower
    rows — moves oars or paddles to propel a vessel in the water; arrays of objects

roil — stir up so as to make something less calm
    royal — associated with a king, queen

role — a part taken in a social group; a part played in a play, movie or TV program
    roll — a bread dough shaped into an individual portion; to turn over and over

roles — parts taken in social groups; parts played in a play, movie or TV program
    rolls — bread dough shaped into individual portions; turns over and over

roll — a bread dough shaped into an individual portion; to turn over and over
    role — a part taken in a social group; a part played in a play, movie or TV program

rolls — bread dough shaped into individual portions; turns over and over
    roles — parts taken in social groups; parts played in a play, movie or TV program

rood — a measurement equal to 1/4 of an acre; a cross at the entrance to a church
    rude — impolite
    rued — regretted

room — space marked by four walls
    rheum — a mucous discharge

Note: Underlined words have two acceptable pronunciations.

rouse

roomer	person who is renting a room
rumor	*an unconfirmed report*
roomers	persons who are renting rooms
rumors	*unconfirmed reports*
rooms	spaces marked by four walls
rheums	*mucous discharges*
root	part of a plant below the ground; to dig out; to cheer
route	*a path or regular course*
rooted	developed roots; dug out; cheered
routed	*directed on a path or regular course*
rooting	forming a root system; digging out; cheering; encouraging or favoring
routing	*directing to a path or regular course*
roots	parts of plants below the ground; digs out; cheers
routes	*paths or regular courses*
rose	got up; moved up; a type of flower
roes	*fish eggs*
rows	*moves oars or paddles to propel a vessel in the water; arrays of objects*
rote	routine, mechanically repetitive
wrote	*recorded with pen or pencil, etc.*
rough	uneven; coarse
ruff	*collar*
roughed	coarsened; injured
ruffed	*having a collar*
roughs	makes uneven; injures
ruffs	*collars*
rouse	stir; awaken
rows	*fights; quarrels*

Note: Underlined words have two acceptable pronunciations.

rout

rout	defeat and chase; to dig up
route	a path or regular course
route	a path or regular course
root	part of a plant below the ground; to dig out; to cheer
route	a path or regular course
rout	defeat and chase; to dig up
routed	directed to a path or regular course
rooted	developed roots; dug up; cheered
routes	paths or regular courses
routs	defeats and chases; digs up
routes	paths or regular courses
roots	parts of plants below the ground; digs out; cheers
routing	directing to a path or regular course
rooting	forming a root system; cheering; encouraging or favoring
routs	defeats and chases; digs up
routes	paths or regular courses
row	move oars or paddles to propel a vessel in the water; an array of objects
roe	fish egg; "caviar"
rowed	moved oars or paddles to propel a vessel in the water
road	a path for motor vehicles
rode	was a passenger or driver in a vehicle or on an animal
rows	moves oars or paddles to propel a vessel in the water; arrays of objects
roes	fish eggs; caviars
rose	got up; moved up; a type of flower
rows	fights; quarrels
rouse	stir; awaken

Note: Underlined words have two acceptable pronunciations.

royal	associated with a king, queen
roil	*stir up so as to make something less calm*
rude	impolite
rued	*regretted*
rood	*a measurement equal to 1/4 of an acre; a cross at the entrance to a church*
ruff	collar
rough	*uneven; coarse*
ruffed	having a collar
roughed	*coarsened; injured*
ruffs	collars
roughs	*makes uneven; injures*
ruin	destroy (e.g. structurally or financially
rune	*marking of an ancient alphabet*
ruins	destroys (e.g. structurally or financially)
runes	*markings of an ancient alphabet*
rum	liquor derived from sugar cane
rhumb	*a constant path line of a ship*
rumor	an unconfirmed report
roomer	*person who is renting a room*
rumors	unconfirmed reports
roomers	*persons who are renting rooms*
rums	liquors derived from sugar cane
rhumbs	*constant path lines of ships*
rune	marking of an ancient alphabet
ruin	*destroy (e.g. structurally or financially)*
runes	markings of an ancient alphabet
ruins	*destroys (e.g. structurally or financially)*

rung

rung	a step on a ladder
wrung	*twisted; twisted to squeeze out water*
rye	a type of cereal grain
wry	*twisted or distorted*
ryes	types of cereal grains
rise	*to get up (e.g., from a bed or chair)*

S

sac	a pouch in humans, animals or plants
sack	*a bag of paper or cloth; to attack and steal*
sack	a bag of paper or cloth; to attack and steal
sac	*a pouch in humans, animals or plants*
sacs	pouches in humans, animals or plants
sacks	*bags of paper or cloth; attacks and steals*
sacks	bags of paper or cloth; attacks and steals
sacs	*pouches in humans, animals or plants*
sail	a cloth material on a ship's mast; move on water or air
sale	*the selling of goods; an event in which goods are specially priced*
sailer	a ship that moves by means of sails
sailor	*one who sails on a ship; a crewman of a ship*
sailers	ships that move by means of sails
sailors	*those who sail on ships; crew of ships*
sailor	one who sails on a ship; a crewman of a ship
sailer	*a ship that moves by means of sails*

sailors	**those who sail on ships; crew of ships**
sailers	*ships that move by means of sails*
sails	**cloth materials on a ship's mast; moves on water or air**
sales	*selling of goods; events in which goods are specially priced*
sale	**the selling of goods; an event in which goods are specially priced**
sail	*a cloth material on a ship's mast; move on water or air*
sales	**selling of goods; events in which goods are specially priced**
sails	*cloth materials on a ship's mast; moves on water or air*
sane	**rational; of sound mind**
seine	*a net used in fishing*
sari	**a silk scarf worn by Hindu women**
sorry	*to regret; poorer in material or moral characteristics*
satiric	**characterized by ridicule or caricature**
satyric	*characteristic of satyrs (woodland creatures in mythology that were part human and part goat)*
satyric	**characteristic of satyrs (woodland creatures in mythology that were part human and part goat)**
satiric	*characterized by ridicule or caricature*
saurel	**a type of salt water fish**
sorel	*a small, male deer*
sorrel	*tan-reddish brown color; a type of plant*
saurels	**types of salt water fish**
sorels	*small, male deer*
sorrels	*types of plants*
saver	**one who saves**
savor	*taste; to enjoy the taste*
savers	**those who save**
savors	*tastes; enjoys the taste*

savor

savor	taste; to enjoy the taste
saver	one who saves
savors	tastes; enjoys the taste
savers	those who save
scalar	that which has size but no direction
scaler	that which or one who scales
scaler	that which or one who scales
scalar	that which has size but no direction
scene	a picture, view, place of action; segment of an act in a play or movie
seen	viewed; understood
scent	smell; odor; detect a smell or odor
cent	a penny
sent	forwarded, mailed, transmitted
scents	smells; odors; detects smells or odors
cense	spread with incense
cents	pennies
sense	feel or know through one of the 5 ways of knowing the world; one of the 5 ways of knowing the world
scull	on oar to propel a small boat; a small boat used for racing
skull	bony part of the head; cranium
sculls	oars to propel small boats; small boats used for racing
skulls	bony parts of the head; craniums
sea	ocean
see	view; know something through vision
seal	to close tightly
ceil	enclose with a ceiling
sealed	closed tightly; marked with an official stamp or emblem
ceiled	enclosed with a ceiling

seed

sealing	closing a box or envelope tightly
ceiling	the top of a room
seals	closes tightly; marks with an official stamp or emblem
ceils	encloses with a ceiling
seam	connection point of 2 pieces of material
seem	appear; look like
seamed	connected points of 2 pieces of material
seemed	appeared; looked like
seamen	sailors
semen	the liquid produced by male sex glands
seaming	connecting points of 2 pieces of material
seeming	appearing; looking like
seams	connection points of 2 pieces of material
seems	appears; looks like
sear	burn or scorch
cere	a wax-like covering of certain bird's beaks
seer	prophet
sere	dry; change in cycle of a plant
sears	burns or scorches
ceres	wax-like coverings of certain birds' beaks
seers	prophets
seres	changes in cycles of plants
seas	oceans
sees	views; knows something through vision
seize	grab; grasp
see	view; know something through vision
sea	ocean
seed	fertile part of a flowering plant
cede	yield

~ 175 ~

seeded

seeded	sowed; ranked (in sports)
ceded	*yielded*
seeder	a tool or device for spreading seed
cedar	*a specific kind of tree; wood from a cedar tree*
ceder	*one who yields*
seeders	tools or devices for spreading seed
cedars	*specific kind of trees; wood from cedar trees*
ceders	*people who yield*
seeding	the act of spreading seed; ranking (in sports)
ceding	*yielding*
seeds	fertile parts of a flowering plant; ranks (in sports)
cedes	*yields*
seem	appear; look like
seam	*connection point of 2 pieces of material*
seemed	appearing; looking like
seaming	*connecting 2 pieces of material*
seems	appears; looks like
seams	*connections of 2 pieces of material*
seen	viewed; understood
scene	*a picture, view, place of action; segment of an act in a play or movie*
seer	prophet
cere	*a wax-like covering of certain bird's beaks*
sear	*burn or scorch*
sere	*dry; change in cycle of a plant*
seers	prophets
ceres	*wax-like coverings of certain birds's beaks*
sears	*burns or scorches*
seres	*changes in cycles of plants*

sees		views; knows something through vision
	seas	oceans
	seize	grab; grasp
seine		a net used in fishing
	sane	rational; of sound mind
seize		grab; grasp
	seas	oceans
	sees	views; knows something through vision
sell		to give to a buyer for purchase
	cell	a small restricted space; a minute unit of a biological organism
seller		one who offers for purchase
	cellar	the area beneath a building
sellers		those who offer for purchase
	cellars	areas beneath buildings
sells		offers for purchase
	cells	small restricted spaces; minute units of biological organisms
semen		the liquid produced by male sex glands
	seamen	sailors
senate		one of the legislative bodies in government
	sennet	notes to signify entrance or exit in Elizabethan plays
	sennit	braided straw or rope
sense		feel or know through one of the 5 ways of knowing the world; one of the 5 ways of knowing the world
	cense	spread with incense
	cents	pennies
	scents	smells; odors; detects smells or odors
senser		one who feels or knows through one of the 5 ways of knowing the world
	censer	a container for burning incense
	censor	regulate or sift the contents of written or oral material
	sensor	detection device for light, sound, etc.

senses

senses   feels or knows through one of the 5 ways of knowing the world
- *censes* — spread with incense
- *census* — a survey or count of a population

sensors   detection devices for light, sound, etc.
- *sensers* — those who feel or know through one of the 5 ways of knowing the world
- *censers* — containers for burning incense
- *censors* — regulates or sifts the contents of written or oral material

sent   forwarded, mailed, transmitted
- *cent* — a penny
- *scent* — smell; odor; detect a smell or odor

sequence   order of position or place
- *sequents* — things that follow in order

sequents   things that follow in order
- *sequence* — order of position or place

sere   dry; change in cycle of a plant
- *cere* — a wax-like covering of certain bird's beaks
- *sear* — burn or scorch
- *seer* — prophet

seres   changes in cycles of plants
- *ceres* — wax-like coverings of certain bird's beaks
- *sears* — burns or scorches
- *seers* — prophets

serf   slave
- *surf* — breaking place of waves

serfs   slaves
- *surfs* — breaking places of waves

serge   fabric of a twill weave
- *surge* — rush of energy as of a wave

serges   fabrics of twill weaves
- *surges* — rushes of energy as of waves

serial	a publication issued at various intervals; anything arranged in a series
cereal	*a grain especially used as breakfast food*
serials	publications issued at various intervals; things arranged in a series
cereals	*grains especially used as breakfast food*
serous	watery, like serum
cirrus	*a slender filament or tentacle; a thin narrow cloud formation*
session	period; specific interval of time for meeting
cession	*ceding; yielding as by treaty or agreement*
sessions	periods; specific intervals of time for meetings
cessions	*cedings; yieldings as by treaty or agreement*
setaceous	with bristles
cetaceous	*pertaining to marine mammals (e.g., whale, dolphin)*
sew	stitch; connect material using needle and thread
so	*this way; thus*
<u>*sow*</u>	*disperse seed*
sewed	stitched; connected material using needle and thread
<u>*sowed*</u>	*dispersed seed*
<u>**sewer**</u>	one who stitches; one who connects material with needle and thread
sower	*one who disperses seed*
<u>**sewer**</u>	a collection for refuse or waste products
suer	*one who sues; one who begs; one who places a legal claim against another person or group*
<u>**sewers**</u>	collection places for refuse or waste products
suers	*those who sue; those who beg; those who place claims against another person or group*

Note: Underlined words have two acceptable pronunciations.

sewers

sewers		those who stitch; those who connect material with needle and thread
	sowers	*those who disperse seed*
sewing		stitching; connecting material using needle and thread
	sowing	*dispersing seed*
sews		stitches; connects material using needle and thread
	sows	*disperses seed*
shear		cut; separate
	sheer	*transparent fabric; a sharply pitched incline*
sheer		transparent fabric; a sharply pitched incline
	shear	*cut; separate*
sheik		chief; head (among Arabs)
	chic	*fashionable; stylish*
shoal		a shallow part in a body of water
	shole	*a plank to support a docked ship*
shoals		shallow parts in bodies of water
	sholes	*planks to support docked ships*
shoe		a covering for the foot; a metal plate to protect a horse's hoof
	shoo	*go away; to chase*
shofar		a ram's horn sounded at Rosh Hoshanna & Yom Kippur
	chauffeur	*person employed as a driver; to work as a chauffeur*
shofars		ram's horns sounded at Rosh Hoshanna & Yom Kippur
	chauffeurs	*persons employed as drivers; works as chauffeurs*
shole		a plank to support a docked ship
	shoal	*a shallow part in a body of water*
sholes		planks to support docked ships
	shoals	*shallow parts in bodies of water*

Note: Underlined words have two acceptable pronunciations.

shone	**bright; excelled**
shown	*demonstrated; exhibited*
shoo	**go away; to chase**
shoe	*a covering for the foot; a metal plate to protect a horse's hoof*
shoot	**fire a gun; discharge a weapon**
shute	
(chute)	*deep incline; move down a chute*
shooting	**firing a gun; discharging a weapon**
shuting	
(chuting)	*deep incline; moving down a chute*
shoots	**fires a gun; discharges a weapon**
shutes	
(chutes)	*deep inclines; moves down a chute*
shown	**demonstrated; exhibited**
shone	*bright; excelled*
shute	
(chute)	**deep incline; move down a chute**
shoot	*fire a gun; discharge a weapon*
shutes	
(chutes)	**deep inclines; moves down a chute**
shoots	*fires a gun; discharges a weapon*
shuting	
(chuting)	**deep inclines; moving down a chute**
shooting	*firing a gun; discharging a weapon*
sic	**thus; as is; to encourage; to attack**
sick	*ill*
sick	**ill**
sic	*thus; as is; to encourage; to attack*

side

side	left or right part of the human body; a surface of an object; agree with
sighed	*exhaled and made a sound in relief of tension or in sadness or fatigue*
sider	siderite; a mineral containing iron; one who takes a side
cider	*juice of an apple*
sighed	exhaled and made a sound in relief of tension or in sadness or fatigue
side	*left or right part of the human body; a surface of an object; agree with*
sigher	one who sighs
sire	*male parent of a horse; procreate (by male)*
sighers	those who sigh
sires	*male parents of horses; procreates (by males)*
sighs	exhales and makes a sound in relief of tension or in sadness or fatigue
size	*magnitude*
sight	seeing; a view; a notable or shocking view
cite	*refer to (a book, a passage in a text)*
site	*place or location; locate*
sighted	having vision; viewed
cited	*referred to (a book or passage in a text)*
sited	*placed or located*
sights	views; notable or shocking views
cites	*refers to (a book or passage in a text)*
sites	*places or locations; locates*
sign	mark; symbol, signal to communicate
sine	*in trigonometry the ratio of the side opposite an angle to the hypotenuse*
signet	a small seal
cygnet	*a young swan*

site

signets — small seals
   cygnets — young swans

signs — marks; symbols, signals to communicate
   sines — in trigonometry the ratios of the sides opposite an angle to the hypotenuse

sine — in trigonometry the ratio of the side opposite an angle to the hypotenuse
   sign — mark; symbol; signal to communicate

sines — in trigonometry the ratios of the sides opposite an angle to the hypotenuse
   signs — marks; symbols; signals to communicate

single — one; unmarried person; one-base hit in baseball
   cingle — girth; belt

singles — ones; unmarried persons; one-base hits in baseball
   cingles — girths; belts

sink — fall to a lower level; collapse; a bathroom or kitchen fixture used for washing
   cinque — five markings on a card or die

sinks — falls to a lower level; collapses; bathroom or kitchen fixtures used for washing
   cinques — five markings on cards or dice

sire — male parent of a horse; procreate (by male)
   sigher — one who sighs

sires — male parents of horses; procreates (by males)
   sighers — those who sigh

site — place or location; locate
   cite — refer to (a book or a passage in a text)
   sight — seeing; a view; a notable or shocking view

sited

sited	**placed or located**
cited	*referred to (a book or passage in a text)*
sighted	*having vision; viewed*
sites	**places or locations; locates**
cites	*refers to (a book or passage in a text)*
sights	*views; notable or shocking views*
size	**magnitude**
sighs	*exhales and makes a sound in relief of tension or in sadness or fatigue*
skull	**bony part of the head; cranium**
scull	*an oar to propel a small boat; a small boat used for racing*
skulls	**bony parts of the head; craniums**
sculls	*oars to propel small boats; small boats used for racing*
slay	**kill (especially with violence)**
sleigh	*a vehicle for traveling over snow or ice*
slays	**kills (especially with violence)**
sleighs	*vehicles for traveling over snow or ice*
sleave	**an unraveled thread; a tangle**
sleeve	*part of a garment for the arm; a tube*
sleaves	**unraveled threads; tangles**
sleeves	*parts of garments for the arms; tubes*
sleeves	**parts of a garments for the arms; tubes**
sleaves	*unraveled threads; tangles*
sleigh	**a vehicle for traveling over snow or ice**
slay	*kill (especially with violence)*
sleighs	**vehicles for traveling over snow or ice**
slays	*kills (especially with violence)*
sleight	**adeptiveness**
slight	*very little; small in stature*

slew	**killed (especially violently)**
slue (slew)	*turn on the axis; turn*
slight	**very little; small in stature**
sleight	*adeptiveness*
sloe	**nut of black thorn; wild plum**
<u>slough</u>	*deep mire; dejection; moral depth*
slow	*not fast; not bright intellectually*
sloes	**nuts of black thorns; wild plums**
<u>sloughs</u>	*deep mires; dejections; moral depths*
slows	*goes less fast*
<u>slough</u>	**deep mire; dejection; moral depth**
slow	*not fast; not bright intellectually*
sloe	*nut of black thorn; wild plum*
<u>sloughs</u>	**deep mires; dejections; moral depths**
sloes	*nuts of black thorns; wild plums*
slows	*goes less fast*
slow	**not fast; not bright intellectually**
sloe	*nut of black thorn; wild plum*
<u>slough</u>	*deep mire; dejection; moral depth*
slows	**goes less fast**
sloes	*nuts of black thorns; wild plums*
<u>sloughs</u>	*deep mires; dejections; moral depths*
slue (slew)	**turn on the axis; turn**
slew	*killed (especially violently)*
so	**this way; thus**
sew	*stitch; connect material using needle and thread*
sow	*disperse seed*
soar	**rise upward; aspire**
sore	*painful*

Note: Underlined words have two acceptable pronunciations.

soared

soared	**rose upward; aspired**
sword	*a weapon having a long, curved, sharp blade*
soars	**rises upward; aspires**
sores	*places of injury to the body*
sodder	**one who covers the ground with sod**
solder	*a material used to join metals*
sold	**given in exchange for money**
soled	*fitted with a sole*
solder	**a material used to join metals**
sodder	*one who covers the ground with sod*
sole	**only one; lone; also the bottom of a shoe**
soul	*spiritual center of human beings; spirit*
soled	**fitted with a sole**
sold	*given in exchange for money*
soles	**bottoms of shoes**
souls	*spiritual centers of human beings; spirits*
some	**a few; a certain amount**
sum	*total; summary*
son	**male heir; male child**
sun	*center of the solar system which transmits heat and light to the earth*
sons	**male heirs; male children**
suns	*centers of heat and light*
soot	**particles of burned material**
suit	*a pair of pants and a jacket; a set of cards; a legal action; fit*
soots	**covers with particles of burned material**
suits	*sets of pants and jackets; sets of cards; legal actions; fits*

sordid	dirty; base
sorted	*arranged; separated into categories*
sore	painful
soar	*rise upward; aspire*
sorel	a small, male deer
saurel	*a type of salt water fish*
sorrel	*tan-reddish brown color; a type of plant*
sorels	small, male deer
saurels	*types of salt water fish*
sorrels	*types of plants*
sores	places of injury to the body
soars	*rises upward; aspires*
soroses	fleshy, complex fruits; women's associations or clubs
cirrhoses	*diseases of the liver; chronic liver damage*
sorosis	fleshy, complex fruit; women's association or club
cirrhosis	*disease of the liver; chronic liver damage*
sorrel	tan-reddish brown color; a type of plant
saurel	*a type of salt water fish*
sorel	*a small, male deer*
sorrels	types of plants
saurels	*types of salt water fish*
sorels	*small, male deer*
sorry	to regret; poorer in material or moral characteristics
sari	*a silk scarf worn by Hindu women*
soul	spiritual center of human beings; spirit
sole	*only one; lone; also the bottom of a shoe*
souls	spiritual centers of human beings; spirits
soles	*bottoms of shoes*

~ 187 ~

sow

sow	**disperse seed**
sew	*stitch; connect material using needle and thread*
so	*this way; thus*
sowed	**dispersed seed**
sewed	*stitched; connected material using needle and thread*
sower	**one who disperses seed**
sewer	*one who stitches; one who connects material with needle and thread*
sowers	**those who disperse seed**
sewers	*those who stitch; those who connect material with needle and thread*
sowing	**dispersing seed**
sewing	*stitching; connecting material using needle and thread*
sows	**disperses seed**
sews	*stitches; connects material using needle and thread*
spade	**a long handled tool for digging; a symbol on a black playing card**
spayed	*to neuter an animal by removing sexual reproductive organs*
speiss	**product of smelting ores**
spice	*any plant that is aromatic and is used in cooking*
spice	**any plant that is aromatic and is used in cooking**
speiss	*product of smelting ores*
spits	**to release saliva; to spew saliva**
spitz	*a variety of Pomeranian dog*
spitz	**a variety of Pomeranian dog**
spits	*to release saliva; to spew saliva*
stabile	**fixed**
stable	*housing for horses and cattle; durable and reliable overtime*

Note: Underlined words have two acceptable pronunciations.

steak

stable	housing for horses and cattle; durable and reliable overtime
stabile	*fixed*
staid	serious and proper
stayed	*remained; slowed or retarded a process or action*
stair	step
stare	*peer intently*
staired	having steps or stairs
stared	*peered intently*
stairs	steps
stares	*peers intently*
stake	a wooden or metal strip to mark a place or for support of a tree
steak	*a cut of meat or fish for cooking*
stakes	wooden or metal strips to mark a place or for support of a tree
steaks	*cuts of meat or fish for cooking*
stare	peer intently
stair	*step*
stared	peered intently
staired	*having steps or stairs*
stares	peers intently
stairs	*steps*
stationary	fixed and set in one place
stationery	*materials (paper, pens, etc.) for writing*
stationery	materials (paper, pens, etc.) for writing
stationary	*fixed and set in one place*
stayed	remained; slowed or retarded a process or action
staid	*serious and proper*
steak	a cut of meat or fish for cooking
stake	*a wooden or metal strip to mark a place or for support of a tree*

~ 189 ~

steaks

steaks	**cuts of meat or fish for cooking**
stakes	*wooden or metal strips to mark a place or for support of a tree*
steal	**rob; to take the possessions of another person without obtaining permission**
steel	*a metal produced by heating iron in high temperature*
steel	**a metal produced by heating iron in high temperature**
steal	*rob; to take the possessions of another person without obtaining permission*
steer	**to direct or guide; a male, beef cattle; a castrated male calf**
stere	*a cubic meter*
steers	**directs or guides; male, beef cattle; castrated male calves**
steres	*cubic meters*
steppes	**plains; treeless land**
steps	*paces; walks; stages in a process; a series of graded wood, metal or concrete planks to go up a height*
steps	**paces; walks; stages in a process; a series of graded wood, metal or concrete planks to go up a height**
steppes	*plains; treeless land*
stere	**a cubic meter**
steer	*to direct or guide; a male, beef cattle; a castrated male calf*
steres	**cubic meters**
steers	*directs or guides; male, beef cattle; castrated male calves*
stile	**a step for a fence; a device for controlling passage into an area**
style	*fashion*
stiles	**steps for a fence; devices for controlling passage into an area**
styles	*fashions*
stoop	**a porch step; to bend the body downward**
stupe	*a wrung out cloth*

stoops	porch steps; bends the body downward
stupes	*wrung out cloths*
straight	direct; in an unbending line
strait	*water between 2 larger bodies of water; a difficult position*
straighten	make straight
straiten	*to place in a difficult position*
straightened	made straight
straitened	*placed in a difficult position*
straightens	makes straight
straitens	*places in a difficult position*
strait	water between 2 larger bodies of water; a difficult position
straight	*direct; in an unbending line*
straiten	to place in a difficult position
straighten	*make straight*
straitened	placed in a difficult position
straightened	*made straight*
straitens	places in a difficult position
straightens	*makes straight*
stupe	a wrung out cloth
stoop	*a porch step; to bend the body downward*
stupes	wrung out cloths
stoops	*porch steps; bends the body downward*
sty	an enclosed place for a pig
stye	*an inflammation of the eyelid*
stye	an inflammation of the eyelid
sty	*an enclosed place for a pig*
styes	inflammations of the eyelids
stys	*enclosed places for pigs*

style

style	**fashion**
stile	*step for a fence; a device for controlling passage into an area*
styles	**fashions**
stiles	*steps for a fence; devices for controlling passage into an area*
stys	**enclosed places for pigs**
styes	*inflammations of the eyelids*
subtle	**discriminating; delicately skillful**
suttle	*net weight*
succor	**help; relief**
sucker	*that which or one who sucks*
sucker	**that which or one who sucks**
succor	*help; relief*
suede	**a leather with a soft fur-like surface**
swayed	*moved back and forth; went back and forth in one's opinions*
suer	**one who sues; one who begs; one who places a legal claim against another group or person**
<u>sewer</u>	*a collection for refuse or waste products*
suers	**those who sue; those who beg; those who place legal claims against another group or person**
<u>sewers</u>	*collection places for refuse or waste products*
suit	**a pair of pants and a jacket; a set of cards; a legal action; fit**
soot	*particles of burned material*
suits	**sets of pants and jackets; sets of cards; legal actions; fits**
soots	*covers with particles of burned material*
suite	**a set of rooms or servants**
sweet	*a substance flavored like sugar; pleasing*
<u>suites</u>	**a series or sets of rooms or servants**
sweets	*substances flavored like sugar*

Note: Underlined words have two acceptable pronunciations.

sum	**total; summary**
some	*a few; a certain amount*
summary	**a resume; a brief statement of key points**
summery	*like summer*
summery	**like summer**
summary	*a resume; a brief statement of key points*
sun	**center of the solar system which transmits heat and light to the earth**
son	*male heir; male child*
sundae	**an ice cream dish topped with fruit, nuts and/or cream**
Sunday	*first day of the week in the Christian calendar*
sundaes	**ice cream dishes topped with fruits, nuts and/or cream**
Sundays	*the first days of the week in the Christian calendar*
Sunday	**first day of the week in the Christian calendar**
sundae	*an ice cream dish topped with fruit, nuts and/or cream*
Sundays	**the first days of the week in the Christian calendar**
sundaes	*ice cream dishes topped with fruits, nuts and/or cream*
suns	**centers of heat and light**
sons	*male heirs; male children*
surf	**breaking place of waves**
serf	*slave*
surfs	**breaking places of waves**
serfs	*slaves*
surge	**rush of energy as of a wave**
serge	*fabric of a twill weave*
surges	**rushes of energy as of waves**
serges	*fabrics of twill weaves*

suttle

suttle	**net weight**
subtle	*discriminating; delicately skillful*
swayed	**moved back and forth; went back and forth in one's opinions**
suede	*a leather with a soft fur-like surface*
sweet	**a substance flavored like sugar; pleasing**
suite	*a set of rooms or servants*
sweets	**substances flavored like sugar**
suites	*a series or sets of rooms or servants*
sword	**a weapon having a long curved sharp blade**
soared	*rose upward; aspired*
sycosis	**staphyloccic infection of the beard**
psychosis	*a type of functional or organic mental disorder*
sycoses	**staphyloccic infections of beards**
psychoses	*types of functional or organic mental disorders*
symbol	**a mark to represent an idea, place or action**
cymbal	*metallic percussion instrument*
symbols	**marks to represent ideas, places or actions**
cymbals	*metallic percussion instruments*

T

tacked	**fastened**
tact	*sensitiveness to effect on persons or situations*
tacks	**small sharp flat-headed nails**
tax	*levy*

tact	**sensitiveness to effect on persons or situations**
tacked	*fastened*
tail	**back part extending from an animal or bird**
tale	*story; an imaginary story*
tails	**back parts extending from animals or birds**
tales	*stories; imaginary stories*
tale	**story; an imaginary story**
tail	*back part extending from an animal or bird*
tales	**stories; imaginary stories**
tails	*back parts extending from animals or birds*
taper	**become narrower or smaller; a thin candle**
tapir	*a pig-like animal with a long muzzle*
tapers	**narrows or becomes smaller; thin candles**
tapirs	*pig-like animals with long muzzles*
tapir	**a pig-like animal with a long muzzle**
taper	*become narrower or smaller; a thin candle*
tapirs	**pig-like animals with long muzzles**
tapers	*narrows or becomes smaller; thin candles*
tare	**the weight of an empty holder or vehicle**
<u>*tear*</u>	*rip; rend*
tares	**weights of empty holders or vehicles**
<u>*tears*</u>	*rips; rends*
taught	**instructed; shared skill or knowledge**
taut	*tight; tense*
taut	**tight; tense**
taught	*instructed; shared skill or knowledge*

Note: Underlined words have two acceptable pronunciations.

tax

tax	levy
tacks	*small sharp flat-headed nails*
tea	a plant used to make a beverage; any beverage made by immersing the dried leaves in water
tee	*20th letter of the English alphabet; a small support for a golf ball*
team	a group of individuals united for some common action or purpose
teem	*overrun; to overpopulate; pour (rain)*
teamed	united for a common action or purpose
teemed	*overrun; overpopulated; poured (rained)*
teaming	uniting for a common action or purpose
teeming	*overrunning; overpopulating; pouring (raining)*
teams	groups of individuals united for a common action or purpose
teems	*overruns; overpopulates; pours (rains)*
tear	rip; rend
tare	*the weight of an empty holder or vehicle*
tear	moisture coming from the eye
tier	*layer*
teared	showed moisture coming from the eye
tiered	*layered*
tearing	showing moisture coming from the eye
tiering	*layering*
tears	rips; rends
tares	*weights of empty holders or vehicles*
tears	drops of moisture coming from the eye
tiers	*layers*

Note: Underlined words have two acceptable pronunciations.

teas	**plants used to make a beverage; beverages made by immersing dried leaves in water**
tees	*20th letters of the English alphabet; supports for golf balls*
tease	*taunt; separate piece by piece*
tease	**taunt; separate piece by piece**
teas	*plants used to make a beverage; beverages made by immersing dried leaves in water*
tees	*20th letters of the English alphabet; supports for golf balls*
tee	**20th letter of the English alphabet; a small support for a golf ball**
tea	*a plant used to make a beverage; any beverage made by immersing the dried leaves in water*
teem	**overrun; to overpopulate; discharge**
team	*a group of individuals united for some common action or purpose*
teemed	**overrun; overpopulated; poured (rained)**
teamed	*united for a common action or purpose*
teeming	**overrunning; overpopulating; pouring (raining)**
teaming	*uniting for a common action or purpose*
teems	**overruns; overpopulates; pours (rains)**
teams	*groups of individuals united for a common action or purpose*
tees	**20th letters of the English alphabet; small supports for golf balls**
teas	*plants whose dried leaves are used to make a beverage; beverages made by immersing dried leaves in water*
tease	*taunt; separate piece by piece*
tense	**tightly wound; nervous**
tents	*shelters of cloth tied to the ground by ropes*
tenser	**more tightly wound; more nervous**
tensor	*a muscle that stretched or contracts*
tensor	**a muscle that stretched or contracts**
tenser	*more tightly wound; more nervous*

tents

tents	shelters of cloth tied to the ground by ropes
tense	*tightly wound; nervous*
tern	a type of bird related to a sea gull; a set of 3 numbers
turn	*move around; change position*
terns	types of birds related to sea gulls; sets of 3 numbers
turns	*moves around; changes position*
terrene	worldly
tureen	
(terrine)	*a covered dish for serving soup, etc.*
testees	those who are tested
testes	*male reproductive glands*
testes	male reproductive glands
testees	*those who are tested*
their	belonging to them (e.g., their book)
there	*in that place*
they're	*contraction for "they are"*
theirs	belonging to them (e.g., it is theirs)
there's	*contraction for "there is"*
there	in that place
their	*belonging to them (e.g., their book)*
they're	*contraction for "they are"*
they're	contraction for "they are"
their	*belonging to them (e.g., their book)*
there	*in that place*
threw	tossed; hurled
through	*passing between 2 points or over a place (e.g., he went through the park)*
throe	spasm
throw	*toss; hurl*

tied

throes	**spasms; convulsions**
throws	*tosses; hurls*
throne	**a seat of royalty**
thrown	*tossed; hurled*
through	**passing between 2 points or over a place (e.g., he went through the park)**
threw	*tossed; hurled*
throw	**toss; hurl**
throe	*spasm*
thrown	**tossed; hurled**
throne	*a seat of royalty*
throws	**tosses; hurls**
throes	*spasms; convulsions*
thyme	**a garden herb used in cooking**
time	*a method of keeping track of events; keep track of speed*
tic	**an involuntary contraction of a muscle**
tick	*a soft sharp repeated noise; a mark to note work completed*
tick	**a soft sharp repeated noise; a mark to note work completed**
tic	*an involuntary contraction of a muscle*
ticks	**soft sharp repeated noises; marks to note work completed**
tics	*involuntary contractions of muscles*
tics	**involuntary contractions of muscles**
ticks	*soft sharp repeated noises; marks to note work completed*
tide	**the periodic rise and fall of the seas**
tied	*bound or fastened*
tied	**bound or fastened**
tide	*the periodic rise and fall of the seas*

tier

tier	layer	
tear	moisture coming from the eye	
tier	one who ties	
tire	become fatigued; rubber covering for metal wheels	
tiered	layered	
teared	showed moisture coming from the eye	
tiering	layering	
tearing	showing moisture coming from the eye	
tiers	layers	
tears	drops of moisture coming from the eye	
tiers	those who tie	
tires	becomes fatigued; rubber coverings for metal wheels	
tighter	more firm or more taut	
titre (titer)	measure out a standard strength of a solution	
timbal	kettle drum	
timbale	a chicken or fish flavored recipe baked into a custard form	
timbale	a chicken or fish flavored recipe baked into a custard form	
timbal	kettle drum	
timbales	chicken or fish flavored recipes baked into a custard form	
timbals	kettle drums	
timbals	kettle drums	
timbales	chicken or fish flavored recipes baked into a custard form	
timber	the wood used for building	
timbre	the sound that depends on the nature of the frequencies	
timbers	wood pieces used for building	
timbres	the sounds that depend on the nature of the frequencies	

Note: Underlined words have two acceptable pronunciations.

timbre	the sound that depends on the nature of the frequencies
timber	*the wood used for building*
timbres	the sounds that depend on the nature of the frequencies
timbers	*wood pieces used for building*
time	a method of keeping track of events; keep track of speed
thyme	*a garden herb used in cooking*
tire	become fatigued; rubber covering for metal wheels
<u>tier</u>	*one who ties*
titer (titre)	measure out a standard strength of a solution
tighter	*more firm or more taut*
to	in the direction; from one to another
too	*also*
two	*a number between one and three; one plus one*
toad	a frog
towed	*pulled*
toed	*having toes or digits on the foot*
tocsin	a signal, bell or alarm
toxin	*a poison produced by micro-organisms*
tocsins	signals, bells or alarms
toxins	*poisons produced by micro-organisms*
toe	a digit of a foot
tow	*pull*
toed	having toes or digits on the foot
toad	*a frog*
towed	*pulled*
toes	digits of the feet
tows	*pulls*

Note: Underlined words have two acceptable pronunciations.

told

told   related; narrated
   tolled   rang; collected a payment (e.g., for passage over a bridge or for the use of the telephone)

tole   type of lacquered metal product
   toll   ring; a payment (e.g., for passage over a bridge or for the use of the telephone)

toll   ring; a payment (e.g., for passage over a bridge or for the use of the telephone)
   tole   type of lacquered metal product

tolled   rang; collected a payment (e.g., for passage over a bridge or for the use of the telephone)
   told   related; narrated

ton   2,000 pounds (U.S. weight)
   tun   a container for wine; store in a wine container

tongue   the organ of taste that is attached to the floor of the mouth; language
   tung   a species of tree

too   also
   to   in the direction; from one to another
   two   a number between one and three; one plus one

tool   a device for hammering or cutting, etc.
   tulle   a thin, fine material for dresses or hats

toon   wood similar to mahogany
   tune   musical sound; a melody; adjust or adapt

tooter   one who toots with a horn or whistle
   tutor   teacher, instructor

tooters   those who toot using a horn or whistle
   tutors   teachers, instructors

tor   rocky hill
   tore   ripped; rent
   torr   a measure of pressure

tore	ripped; rent
torr	*a measure of pressure*
tor	*rocky hill*
tort	wrongful or harming action in law
torte	*rich cake*
torte	rich cake
tort	*wrongful or harming action in law*
tortes	rich cakes
torts	*wrongful or harming actions in law*
torts	wrongful or harming actions in law
tortes	*rich cakes*
tow	pull
toe	*a digit of a foot*
towed	pulled
toad	*a frog*
toed	*having toes or digits on the foot*
tows	pulls
toes	*digits of the foot*
toxin	a poison produced by micro-organisms
tocsin	*a signal, bell or alarm*
toxins	poisons produced by micro-organisms
tocsins	*signals, bells or alarms*
tracked	followed; plodded; aligned
tract	*an area of land; an essay on a controversial topic*
tract	an area of land; an essay on a controversial topic
tracked	*followed; plodded; aligned*
transcience	lacking permanence or stability; transitory
transients	*those who are not stable or permanent residents*

transients

transients — those who are not stable or permanent residents
  transcience — *lacking permanence or stability; transitory*

tray — a holder to carry objects (e.g., food)
  trey — *a playing card with three markers*

trays — holders to carry objects (e.g. food)
  treys — *playing cards with three markers*

treaties — agreements; pacts
  treatise — *tract; dissertation*

treatise — tract, dissertation
  treaties — *agreements; pacts*

trey — a playing card with three markers
  tray — *a holder to carry objects (e.g., food)*

treys — playing cards with three markers
  trays — *holders to carry objects (e.g. food)*

troche — a medicinal lozenge
  trochee — *a type of poetic measure of one long syllable followed by a short syllable*

trochee — a type of poetic measure of one long syllable followed by a short syllable
  troche — *a medicinal lozenge*

trochees — types of poetic measures of one long syllable followed by a short syllable
  troches — *medicinal lozenges*

troches — medicinal lozenges
  trochees — *types of poetic measures of one long syllable followed by a short syllable*

troop — a band or group (especially of soldiers)
  troupe — *a theater group*

tune

trooper	a member of the police force or a soldier
trouper	*a member of a theater group*
troopers	members of the police force or soldiers
troupers	*members of theater groups*
troops	bands or groups (especially of soldiers)
troupes	*theater groups*
troupe	a theater group
troop	*a band or group (especially of soldiers)*
trouper	a member of a theater group
trooper	*a member of the police force or a soldier*
troupers	members of theater groups
troopers	*members of the police force or soldiers*
troupes	theater groups
troops	*bands or groups (especially of soldiers)*
trussed	tied firmly
trust	*belief, confidence, faith*
trust	belief, confidence, faith
trussed	*tied firmly*
tulle	a thin, fine material for dresses or hats
tool	*a device for hammering or cutting, etc.*
tun	a container for wine; store in a wine container
ton	*2,000 pounds (U.S. weight)*
tuna	salt water fish
tuner	*one who tunes (especially one who adjusts a musical instrument)*
tunas	salt water fish
tuners	*those who tune (especially those who adjust musical instruments)*
tune	musical sound; a melody; adjust or adapt
toon	*wood similar to mahogany*

tuner

tuner	one who tunes (especially one who adjusts a musical instrument)
tuna	salt water fish
tuners	those who tune (especially those who adjust musical instruments)
tunas	salt water fish
tung	a species of tree
tongue	the organ of taste that is attached to the floor of the mouth; language
turn	move around; change position
tern	a type of bird related to a sea gull; a set of 3 numbers
turns	moves around; changes position
terns	types of birds related to sea gulls; sets of 3 numbers
tutor	teacher, instructor
tooter	those who toot with a horn or whistle
tutors	teachers, instructors
tooters	those who toot using a horn or whistle
two	a number between one and three; one plus one
to	in the direction; from one to another
too	also

U

unceded	not ceded
unseated	not seated; standing; deposed from office
unseeded	not sown; unranked (in sports)
undo	cancel; unfasten
undue	not appropriate; not within normal limits

undue not appropriate; not within normal limits
   undo   *cancel; unfasten*

unseeded not sown; unranked (in sports)
   unceded   *not ceded*
   unseated   *not seated; standing; deposed from office*

unseated not seated; standing; deposed from office
   unceded   *not ceded*
   unseeded   *not sown; unranked (in sports)*

uranyl uranium oxide
   urinal   *a place for urinating*

urinal a place for urinating
   uranyl   *uranium oxide*

urn type of vase
   earn   *merit; to obtain through effort*
   ern(e)   *variety of eagle that lives near water*

urns type of vases
   earns   *merits; obtains through effort*
   ern(e)s   *varieties of eagles that live near water*

use employ
   ewes   *female sheep*
   hews**   *cuts; severs; cuts down*
   hues**   *colors; tints*
   yews   *type of evergreen trees*

** Although precise pronunciation would disqualify these words as homophones, ordinary speech does not make the distinction clear to most listeners. Thus the "h" sound which should be an explosive blowing of the lips is not carried out by most speakers. This sound is therefore blurred in such words as *hue, where* and other words where the "h" sound occurs.

V

vail — **to sink or lower**
    vale — *valley*
    veil — *a cloth covering (especially for the face and head); to cover or hide*

vails — **sinks or lowers**
    vales — *valleys*
    veils — *cloth coverings (especially for the face and head); covers or hides*

vain — **unimportant; proud in a haughty way; egotistic**
    vane — *device for determining direction of the wind*
    vein — *a blood vessel that carries blood to the heart;*
    a mark or path in a rock or on the ground

vale — **valley**
    vail — *to sink or lower*
    veil — *a cloth covering (especially for the face and head); to cover or hide*

vales — **valleys**
    vails — *sinks or lowers*
    veils — *cloth coverings (especially for the face and head); covers or hides*

vane — **device for determining direction of the wind**
    vain — *unimportant; proud in a haughty way; egotistic*
    vein — *a blood vessel that carries blood to the heart;*
    a mark or path in a rock or on the ground

vanes — **devices for determining the direction of the wind**
    veins — *blood vessels that carry blood to the heart;*
    markings or paths in a rock or on the ground

veil — **a cloth covering (especially for the face and head); to cover or hide**
    vail — *to sink or lower*
    vale — *valley*

vile

veils		cloth coverings (especially for the face and head); covers or hides
	vails	sinks or lowers
	vales	valleys
vein		a blood vessel that carries blood to the heart; a mark or path in a rock or on the ground
	vain	unimportant; proud in a haughty way; egotistic
	vane	device for determining direction of the wind
veins		blood vessels that carry blood to the heart; markings or paths in a rock or on the ground
	vanes	devices for determining the direction of the wind
veracious		truthful
	voracious	having a large appetite (for food or ideas or information)
veracities		truths; truthfulnesses
	voracities	greeds in eating; ravenousnesses
veracity		truth; truthfulness
	voracity	greed in eating; ravenousness
vial		a small container
	vile	terrible; filthy and/or depraved
	viol	a musical instrument with 6 strings
vials		small containers
	viols	musical instruments with 6 strings
vice		immoral act or behavior
	<u>vise</u>	a clamp for holding articles during carpentry or mechanics
vices		immoral acts or behaviors
	<u>vises</u>	clamps for holding articles during carpentry or mechanics
vile		terrible; filthy and/or depraved
	vial	a small container
	viol	a musical instrument with 6 strings

Note: Underlined words have two acceptable pronunciations.

villain

villain   a mean, evil person
    villein   *feudal serf*

villains   mean, evil people
    villeins   *feudal serfs*

villein   feudal serf
    villain   *a mean, evil person*

villeins   feudal serfs
    villains   *mean, evil people*

villous   having a small nutrition-absorbing fiber
    villus   *a small nutrition-absorbing fiber*

villus   a small nutrition-absorbing fiber
    villous   *having a small nutrition-absorbing fiber*

viol   a musical instrument with 6 strings
    vial   *a small container*
    vile   *terrible; filthy and/or depraved*

viols   musical instruments with 6 strings
    vials   *small containers*

<u>**vise**</u>   a clamp for holding articles during carpentry or mechanics
    vice   *immoral act or behavior*

<u>**vises**</u>   clamps for holding articles during carpentry or mechanics
    vices   *immoral acts or behaviors*

volva   membrane surrounding young mushrooms
    vulva   *external female genital organ*

volvas   membranes surrounding young mushrooms
    vulvas   *external female genital organs*

voracious   having a large appetite (for food or ideas or information)
    veracious   *truthful*

Note: Underlined words have two acceptable pronunciations.

voracities	greeds in eating; ravenousnesses
veracities	*truths; truthfulnesses*
voracity	greed in eating; ravenousness
veracity	*truth; truthfulness*
vulva	external female genital organ
volva	*membrane surrounding young mushrooms*
vulvas	external female genital organs
volvas	*membranes surrounding young mushrooms*

wade	enter shallow water; go through pages, etc with great effort
weighed	*determined the weight of a person or object; mentally measured the consequences of an act*
wail	an extended non-verbal sharp mournful cry
wale	*ridge or mark; weave along the length of fabric*
*whale***	*a large sea mammal; hunt for whales*
wailed	made an extended non-verbal sharp mournful cry
waled	*marked with ridges; having weaves along the length of fabric*
*whaled***	*hunted for whales*
wailer	one who makes an extended, non-verbal mournful cry
waler	*those who make wales*
*whaler***	*one who hunts for whales*

** Although precise pronunciation would disqualify these words as homophones, ordinary speech does not make the distinction clear to most listeners. Thus the "h" sound which should be an explosive blowing of the lips is not carried out by most speakers. This sound is therefore blurred in such words as *hue, where* and other words where the "h" sound occurs.

wailing

wailing	the act of making an extended, non-verbal mournful cry
waling	*making of wales*
*whaling***	*hunting for whales*
wails	extended, non-verbal sharp mournful cries
wales	*ridges or marks; weaves along the length of fabric*
*whales***	*large sea mammals; hunts for whales*
wain	large open wagon
wane	*fade; decrease in size or amount*
waist	circumference of the human body above the hips
waste	*that which is not used or not usable; discards*
waisted	having a waist
wasted	*discarded; part of an object, material goods, etc. lost because of a lack of frugality*
waists	circumferences of the human body above the hips
wastes	*discards; loses part of an object, material goods, etc. because of a lack of frugality*
wait	anticipate an event; hold off action
weight	*the pounds or kilograms of mass of an object or person; burden*
waited	anticipated an event; held off action
weighted	*having weight; burdened*
waiter	one who serves meals to restaurant guests
weighter	*one who weighs objects*
waiting	anticipating an event; holding off action; providing meal service
weighting	*burdening*
waits	anticipates an event; holds off action
weights	*burdens*

** Although precise pronunciation would disqualify these words as homophones, ordinary speech does not make the distinction clear to most listeners. Thus the "h" sound which should be an explosive blowing of the lips is not carried out by most speakers. This sound is therefore blurred in such words as *hue, where* and other words where the "h" sound occurs.

waive		give up a right or privilege
	wave	*a surge of water, electricity, etc; express a greeting or other signal by a motion of one's hand*
waived		gave up a right or privilege
	waved	*expressed a greeting or other signal by a motion of one's hand; felt or showed uncertainty*
waiver		act of giving up a right or privilege
	waver	*one who expresses a greeting or other signal by a motion of one's hand; to feel or show uncertainty*
waivers		acts of giving up a right or privilege
	wavers	*those who express a greeting or other signal by a motion of one's hand; feels or shows uncertainty*
waives		gives up a right or privilege
	waves	*surges of water, electricity, etc; expresses a greeting or other signal by a motion of one's hand*
waiving		giving up a right or privilege
	waving	*the act of expressing a greeting or other signal by a motion of one's hand*
wale		ridge or mark; weave along the length of fabric
	wail	*an extended non-verbal sharp mournful cry*
	*whale***	*a large sea mammal; hunt for whales*
waled		marked with ridges; having weaves along the length of fabric
	wailed	*made an extended non-verbal sharp mournful cry*
	*whaled***	*hunted for whales*
waler		those who make wales
	wailer	*one who makes an extended, non-verbal mournful cry*
	*whaler***	*one who hunts for whales*

** Although precise pronunciation would disqualify these words as homophones, ordinary speech does not make the distinction clear to most listeners. Thus the "h" sound which should be an explosive blowing of the lips is not carried out by most speakers. This sound is therefore blurred in such words as *hue, where* and other words where the "h" sound occurs.

wales

wales   ridges or marks; weaves along the length of fabric
   wails   extended, non-verbal sharp mournful cries
   whales**   large sea mammals; hunts for whales

waling   making of wales
   wailing   the act of making an extended, non-verbal mournful cry
   whaling**   hunting for whales

walled   enclosed by 4 vertical partitions
   wauled
   (wawled)   cried like a cat

walling   enclosing by using 4 vertical partitions
   wauling
   (wawling)   crying of a cat

walls   vertical partitions; separations
   wauls
   (wawls)   cat cries; cries like a cat

wane   fade; decrease in size or amount
   wain   large open wagon

war   conflict, especially with guns or other deadly weapons; hostility
   wore   put on clothes; donned; eroded

ward   a section of a political area; a child in the custody of the state or county; section of a hospital
   warred   in conflict, especially with guns or other deadly weapons

ware   a kind of merchandise
   wear   put on clothes; don; erode
   weir   a dam or screen in a stream or river
   we're   contraction of "we are"
   where**   a description of a location or a question about a location

---

** Although precise pronunciation would disqualify these words as homophones, ordinary speech does not make the distinction clear to most listeners. Thus the "h" sound which should be an explosive blowing of the lips is not carried out by most speakers. This sound is therefore blurred in such words as *hue*, *where* and other words where the "h" sound occurs.

wauling

wares   kinds of merchandise
- *wears*   puts on clothes; dons; erodes
- *weirs*   dams or screens in streams or rivers
- *where's***   contraction of "where is"

warn   to caution; to advise of danger
- *worn*   has put on clothes; donned; eroded

warred   in conflict, especially with guns or other deadly weapons
- *ward*   a section of a political area; a child in the custody of the state or county; section of a hospital

waste   that which is not used or not usable; discards
- *waist*   circumference of the human body part above the hips

wasted   discarded; part of an object, material goods, etc. lost because of a lack of frugality
- *waisted*   having a waist

wastes   discards; loses part of an object, material goods, etc. because of a lack of frugality
- *waists*   circumferences of the human body part above the hips

watt   a unit of electrical power
- *what***   asking a question for general information

watts   units of electrical power
- *what's***   contraction of what is

wauled (wawled)   cried like a cat
- *walled*   enclosed by 4 vertical partitions

wauling (wawling)   crying of a cat
- *walling*   enclosing by using 4 verticial partitions

** Although precise pronunciation would disqualify these words as homophones, ordinary speech does not make the distinction clear to most listeners. Thus the "h" sound which should be an explosive blowing of the lips is not carried out by most speakers. This sound is therefore blurred in such words as *hue, where* and other words where the "h" sound occurs.

wauls

wauls (wawls)	cat cries; cries like a cat
walls	*vertical partitions; separations*
wave	a surge of water, electricity, etc; express a greeting or other signal by a motion of one's hand
waive	*give up a right or privilege*
waved	expressed a greeting or other signal by a motion of one's hand; felt or showed uncertainty
waived	*gave up a right or privilege*
waver	one who expresses a greeting or other signal by a motion of one's hand; to feel or show uncertainty
waiver	*act of giving up a right or privilege*
wavers	those who express a greeting or other signal by a motion of one's hand; feels or shows uncertainty
waivers	*acts of giving up a right or privilege*
waving	the act of expressing a greeting or other signal by a motion of one's hand
waiving	*giving up a right or privilege*
wax	a substance produced by bees to make their honey-combs; increase; grow; enlarge
whacks**	*strikes; a loud blow*
way	path or direction; method
weigh	*determine the amount of pounds or kilograms of a person or object; mentally measure the consequences of an act*
whey**	*the watery part of milk*
ways	paths or directions; methods
weighs	*determines the amount of pounds or kilograms of a person or object; mentally measures the consequences of an act*
wheys**	*watery parts of milk*

** Although precise pronunciation would disqualify these words as homophones, ordinary speech does not make the distinction clear to most listeners. Thus the "h" sound which should be an explosive blowing of the lips is not carried out by most speakers. This sound is therefore blurred in such words as *hue, where* and other words where the "h" sound occurs.

weave

we		plural of the pronoun I
	wee	small; little
weak		frail; not strong
	week	7 days in the calendar
weakly		feebly
	weekly	every 7 days
weal		a ridge on the skin
	we'll	contraction for "we will" or "we shall"
	*wheal***	a swelling of the skin
	*wheel***	a round object that turns on an axis
weaner		one who or that which weans a child or mammal
	wiener	smoked sausage in a case; frankfurter
weaners		those who or that which weans a child or mammal
	wieners	smoked sausages in cases; frankfuters
wear		put on clothes; don; erode
	ware	a kind of merchandise
	weir	a dam or screen in a stream or river
	we're	contraction of "we are"
	*where***	a description of a location or a question about a location
wears		puts on clothes; dons; erodes
	wares	kinds of merchandise
	weirs	dams or screens in streams or rivers
	*where's***	contraction of "where is"
weather		condition of climate (i.e., wind, rain, sun, etc.)
	whether	presenting an alternative (i.e., whether or not)
weave		to make fabric by moving the threads in and out over each other
	we've	contraction for "we have"

** Although precise pronunciation would disqualify these words as homophones, ordinary speech does not make the distinction clear to most listeners. Thus the "h" sound which should be an explosive blowing of the lips is not carried out by most speakers. This sound is therefore blurred in such words as *hue*, *where* and other words where the "h" sound occurs.

we'd

we'd	contraction for "we had" or "we would" or "we should"
weed	uncultivated plant
wee	small; little
we	plural of the pronoun I
weed	uncultivated plant
we'd	contraction for "we had" or "we would" or "we should"
week	7 days in the calendar
weak	frail; not strong
weekly	every 7 days
weakly	feebly
weigh	determine the amount of pounds or kilograms of a person or object; mentally measure the consequences of an act
way	path or direction; method
*whey***	the watery part of milk
weighed	determined the amount of pounds or kilograms of a person or object; mentally measured the consequences of an act
wade	enter shallow water; go through pages, etc with great effort
weighs	determines the amount of pounds or kilograms of a person or object; mentally measures the consequences of an act
ways	paths or directions; methods
*wheys***	watery parts of milk
weight	the pounds or kilograms of mass of an object or person; burden
wait	anticipate an event; hold off action
weighted	having weight; burdened
waited	anticipated an event; held off action
weighter	one who weighs objects
waiter	one who serves meals to restaurant guests

** Although precise pronunciation would disqualify these words as homophones, ordinary speech does not make the distinction clear to most listeners. Thus the "h" sound which should be an explosive blowing of the lips is not carried out by most speakers. This sound is therefore blurred in such words as *hue, where* and other words where the "h" sound occurs.

we're

weighting — burdening
waiting — anticipating an event; holding off action; providing meal service

weights — burdens
waits — anticipates an event; holds off action

weir — a dam or screen in a stream or river
ware — a kind of merchandise
wear — put on clothes; don; erode
we're — contraction of "we are"
*where*** — a description of a location or a question about a location

weirs — dams or screens in streams or rivers
wares — kinds of merchandise
wears — puts on clothes; dons; erodes
*where's*** — contraction of "where is"

weld — to join (e.g., metal) by heat or force
welled — like a well; pushed up from the earth

we'll — contraction for "we will" or "we shall"
weal — a ridge on the skin
*wheal*** — a swelling of the skin
*wheel*** — a round object that turns on an axis

welled — like a well; pushed up from the earth
weld — to join (e.g., metal) by heat or force

wen — a tumor of the hairy follicle
*when*** — at what time

we're — contraction of "we are"
ware — a kind of merchandise
wear — put on clothes; don; erode
weir — a dam or screen in a stream or river
*where*** — a description of a location or a question about a location

---

** Although precise pronunciation would disqualify these words as homophones, ordinary speech does not make the distinction clear to most listeners. Thus the "h" sound which should be an explosive blowing of the lips is not carried out by most speakers. This sound is therefore blurred in such words as *hue*, *where* and other words where the "h" sound occurs.

were

were	**have been**
whir	
*(whirr)***	*a buzzing sound accompanying movement*
wet	**moist**
*whet***	*stimulate (e.g., appetite); to sharpen*
wets	**moistens**
*whets***	*stimulates (e.g., appetites); sharpens*
wetted	**moistened**
*whetted***	*stimulated (e.g., appetites); sharpened*
wetting	**moistening**
*whetting***	*stimulating (e.g., appetites); sharpening*
we've	**contraction for "we have"**
weave	*to make fabric by moving the threads in and out over each other*
whacks**	**strikes; a loud blow**
wax	*a substance produced by bees to make their honey-combs; increase; grow; enlarge*
whale**	**a large sea mammal; hunt for whales**
wail	*extended a non-verbal sharp mournful cry*
wale	*ridge or mark; weave along the length of fabric*
whaled**	**hunted for whales**
wailed	*made an extended non-verbal sharp mournful cry*
waled	*marked with ridges; having weaves along the length of fabric*
whaler**	**one who hunts for whales**
wailer	*one who makes an extended, non-verbal mournful cry*
waler	*those who make wales*
whales**	**large sea mammals: hunts for whales**
wails	*extended, non-verbal sharp mournful cries*
wales	*ridges or marks; weaves along the length of a piece of fabric*

** Although precise pronunciation would disqualify these words as homophones, ordinary speech does not make the distinction clear to most listeners. Thus the "h" sound which should be an explosive blowing of the lips is not carried out by most speakers. This sound is therefore blurred in such words as *hue, where* and other words where the "h" sound occurs.

where's

whaling**	hunting for whales
wailing	the act of making an extended, non-verbal mournful cry
waling	making of wales
what**	asking a question for general information
watt	a unit of electrical power
what's**	contraction of what is
watts	units of electrical power
wheal**	a swelling of the skin
weal	a ridge on the skin
we'll	contraction for "we will" or "we shall"
*wheel****	a round object that turns on an axis
wheel**	a round object that turns on an axis
weal	a ridge on the skin
we'll	contraction for "we will" or "we shall"
*wheal****	a swelling of the skin
wheeled**	on wheels; moved on a device with wheels
wield	use a weapon, power, authority, etc.
when**	at what time
wen	a tumor of the hairy follicle
where**	a description of a location or a question about a location
ware	a kind of merchandise
wear	put on clothes; don; erode
weir	a dam or screen in a stream or river
we're	contraction of "we are"
where's**	contraction of "where is"
wares	kinds of merchandise
wears	puts on clothes; dons; erodes
weirs	dams or screens in streams or rivers

** Although precise pronunciation would disqualify these words as homophones, ordinary speech does not make the distinction clear to most listeners. Thus the "h" sound which should be an explosive blowing of the lips is not carried out by most speakers. This sound is therefore blurred in such words as *hue*, *where* and other words where the "h" sound occurs.

whet

whet**   stimulate (e.g., appetite); to sharpen
    wet   *moist*

whether**   presenting an alternative (i.e., whether or not)
    weather   *condition of climate (i.e., wind, rain, sun, etc.)*

whets**   stimulates (e.g., appetites); sharpens
    wets   *moistens*

whetted**   stimulated (e.g., appetites); sharpened
    wetted   *moistened*

whetting**   stimulating (e.g., appetites); sharpening
    wetting   *moistening*

whey**   the watery part of milk
    way   *path or direction; method*
    weigh   *determine the amount of pounds or kilograms of a person or object; mentally measure the consequences of an act*

wheys**   watery parts of milk
    ways   *paths or directions; methods*
    weighs   *determines the amount of pounds or kilograms of a person or object; mentally measures the consequences of an act*

which**   what thing or person
    witch   *a female who practices magic powers*

while**   in the mean time; during the time
    wile   *entice; enticement*

whiled**   passed time
    wild   *untamed*
    wiled   *enticed*

Note: Underlined words have two acceptable pronunciations.

** Although precise pronunciation would disqualify these words as homophones, ordinary speech does not make the distinction clear to most listeners. Thus the "h" sound which should be an explosive blowing of the lips is not carried out by most speakers. This sound is therefore blurred in such words as *hue, where* and other words where the "h" sound occurs.

whither

whiles**	passes time	
wiles	entices	
whine**	low cry or complaint	
wine	beverage of fermented grapes; give or provide with wine	
whined**	cried or complained	
wined	given or provided with wine	
wind	turn in a circle; coil	
whines**	cries or complains	
wines	beverages of fermented grapes; gives or provides with wine	
whining**	crying or complaining	
wining	giving or providing with wine	
whir (whirr)**	a buzzing sound accompanying rapid movement	
were	have been	
whirl**	turn fast in a circle	
whorl**	arrangement in a coil	
whirled**	turned fast in a circle	
whorled**	arranged in a coil	
world	the universe; all the countries on earth	
whirls**	turns fast in a circle	
whorls**	arrangements in a coil	
whirred**	made a buzzing sound accompanying rapid movement	
word	a group of letters having a specific meaning	
whit**	a small amount; iota	
wit	intellectual sharpness and humor; one who shows humor or sharp awareness	
whither**	where; whereto	
wither	become dry and lifeless; loses vigorous appearance	

** Although precise pronunciation would disqualify these words as homophones, ordinary speech does not make the distinction clear to most listeners. Thus the "h" sound which should be an explosive blowing of the lips is not carried out by most speakers. This sound is therefore blurred in such words as *hue, where* and other words where the "h" sound occurs.

wholly

wholly — **fully; totally**
   holey — *having perforations or openings*
   holy — *sacred; religiously meaningful*

whore — **prostitute; someone who sells himself or herself**
   hoar — *an aged appearance*

whored — **prostituted; sold oneself**
   hoard — *collect supplies secretly*
   horde — *a very large number of people*

whorl** — **arrangement in a coil**
   whirl** — *to turn fast in a circle*

whorled** — **arranged in a coil**
   whirled** — *turned fast in a circle*
   world — *the universe; all the countries on earth*

whorls** — **arrangements in a coil**
   whirls** — *turns fast in a circle*

who's — **contraction for who is or who has**
   whose — *who it belongs to*

whose — **who it belongs to**
   who's — *contraction for who is or who has*

whys — **for what reasons**
   wise — *having great perceptive ability*

wield — **use a weapon, power, authority, etc.**
   wheeled** — *on wheels; moved on a device with wheels*

wiener — **smoked sausage in a case; frankfuter**
   weaner — *one who or that which weans a child or mammal*

wieners — **smoked sausages in cases; frankfuters**
   weaners — *those who or that which weans a child or mammal*

** Although precise pronunciation would disqualify these words as homophones, ordinary speech does not make the distinction clear to most listeners. Thus the "h" sound which should be an explosive blowing of the lips is not carried out by most speakers. This sound is therefore blurred in such words as *hue, where* and other words where the "h" sound occurs.

witch

wild	**untamed**
*whiled***	*passed time*
wiled	*enticed*
wile	**to entice; enticement**
*while***	*in the mean time; during the time*
wiled	**enticed**
*whiled***	*passed time*
wild	*untamed*
wiles	**entices**
*whiles***	*passes time*
wine	**beverage of fermented grapes; give or provide with wine**
*whine***	*low cry or complaint*
wined	**given or provided with wine**
*whined***	*cried or complained*
<u>*wind*</u>	*turn in a circle; coil*
wines	**beverages of fermented grapes; gives or provides with wine**
*whines***	*cries or complains*
wining	**giving or providing with wine**
*whining***	*crying or complaining*
wise	**having great perceptive ability**
whys	*for what reasons*
wit	**intellectual sharpness and humor; one who shows humor or sharp awareness**
*whit***	*a small amount; iota*
witch	**a female who practices magic powers**
*which***	*what thing or person*

Note: Underlined words have two acceptable pronunciations.

** Although precise pronunciation would disqualify these words as homophones, ordinary speech does not make the distinction clear to most listeners. Thus the "h" sound which should be an explosive blowing of the lips is not carried out by most speakers. This sound is therefore blurred in such words as *hue, where* and other words where the "h" sound occurs.

wither

wither	become dry and lifeless; lose vigorous appearance
*whither***	where; whereto
won	defeated; overcame
one	single; the first number in the cardinal series
wood	the core of a tree; lumber
would	is willing to
word	a group of letters having a specific meaning
*whirred***	made a buzzing sound accompanying rapid movement
wore	put on clothes; donned; eroded
war	conflict, especially with guns or other deadly weapons; hostility
world	the universe; all the countries on earth
*whorled***	arranged in a coil
*whirled***	turned fast in a circle
worn	has put on clothes; donned; eroded
warn	caution; advise of danger
would	is willing to
wood	the core of a tree; lumber
wrack	destroy; remains of a destroyed object
rack	a metal or wood frame on which objects are hung
wracks	destroys; remains of destroyed objects
racks	metal or wood frames on which objects are hung
wrap	enclose in paper or cloth; wind tightly
rap	tap; strike lightly
wrapped	enclosed in paper or cloth; wound tightly
rapped	tapped lightly; stroked lightly
rapt	intensively absorbed in thought

** Although precise pronunciation would disqualify these words as homophones, ordinary speech does not make the distinction clear to most listeners. Thus the "h" sound which should be an explosive blowing of the lips is not carried out by most speakers. This sound is therefore blurred in such words as *hue, where* and other words where the "h" sound occurs.

wrapper		one who encloses items in paper or cloth; one who winds tightly
	rapper	*one who taps lightly; one who strikes lightly*
wrappers		those who enclose items in paper or cloth; those who wind tightly
	rappers	*those who tap lightly; those who strike lightly*
wrapping		enclosing items in paper or cloth; the material used to enclose an object or person
	rapping	*the act of tapping lightly; the act of striking lightly*
wraps		encloses items in paper or cloth; winds tightly
	raps	*taps lightly; strikes lightly*
wreak		inflict, vent onto (punishment or anger, etc.)
	reek	*strong smell; smell of smoke*
wreaked		inflicted, vented onto (punishment or anger, etc.)
	reeked	*smelled strongly; smelled of smoke*
wreaks		inflicts, vents onto (punishment or anger, etc.)
	reeks	*smells strongly; smells of smoke*
wrest		to take away from by force; force from one's grasp
	rest	*remainder; cease activity*
wrests		takes away from by force; forces from one's grasp
	rests	*remainders; ceases activity*
wretch		a miserably unlucky or unhappy person
	retch	*to attempt to vomit*
wretches		miserably unlucky or unhappy persons
	retches	*attempts to vomit*
wright		one of different kinds of construction worker
	right	*correct; the opposite of left; an entitlement of law or custom*
	rite	*ceremony*
	write	*record by pen, pencil, etc.*

wrights

wrights — any of different kinds of construction workers
   rights — puts into upright or correct position; entitlements of law or custom
   rites — ceremonies
   writes — records by pen, pencil, etc.

wring — to twist; to twist so as to squeeze out water
   ring — a circular piece of material (e.g., wedding ring); a circular mark

wringer — one who twists so as to squeeze out water
   ringer — that which circles or rings

wrings — twists so as to squeeze out water
   rings — circles; circular pieces of material (e.g., wedding rings)

write — record by pen, pencil, etc.
   right — correct; the opposite of left; an entitlement of law or custom
   rite — ceremony
   wright — one of different kinds of construction worker

writes — records by pen, pencil, etc.
   rights — puts into upright or correct position; entitlements of law or custom
   rites — ceremonies
   wrights — any of different kinds of construction workers

writing — recording by pen, pencil, etc.
   righting — putting into upright or correct position

wrote — recorded with pen or pencil, etc.
   rote — routine, mechanically repetitive

wrung — twisted; twisted to squeeze out water
   rung — a step on a ladder

wry — twisted or distorted
   rye — a type of cereal grain

Y

yew	a type of evergreen tree
ewe	a female sheep
hew**	cut; sever; cut down
hue**	color; tint
you	personal pronoun referring to another person
yews	type of evergreen trees
ewes	female sheep
hews**	cuts; severs; cuts down
hues**	colors; tints
use	employ
yoke	a device for connecting two animals for hauling
yolk	the yellow, embryonic part of an egg
yoked	joined together as horses or cattle
yolked	having yolks (i.e., embryonic parts of an egg)
yokes	devices for connecting two animals for hauling
yolks	the yellow, embryonic parts of eggs
yolk	the yellow, embryonic part of an egg
yoke	a device for connecting two animals for hauling
yolked	having yolks (i.e., embryonic parts of an egg)
yoked	joined together as horses or cattle
yolks	the yellow, embryonic parts of eggs
yokes	devices for connecting two animals for pulling

** Although precise pronunciation would disqualify these words as homophones, ordinary speech does not make the distinction clear to most listeners. Thus the "h" sound which should be an explosive blowing of the lips is not carried out by most speakers. This sound is therefore blurred in such words as *hue, where* and other words where the "h" sound occurs.

yore

yore   **the past**
    your   *that which belongs to you*
    you're   *contraction for "you are"*

you   **personal pronoun referring to another person**
    ewe   *a female sheep*
    hew**   *cut; sever; cut down*
    hue**   *color; tint*
    yew   *a type of evergreen tree*

you'll   **contraction for "you will" or "you shall"**
    yule   *Christmas*

your   **that which belongs to you**
    yore   *the past*
    you're   *contraction for "you are"*

you're   **contraction for "you are"**
    yore   *the past*
    your   *that which belongs to you*

yule   **Christmas**
    you'll   *contraction for "you will" or "you shall"*

** Although precise pronunciation would disqualify these words as homophones, ordinary speech does not make the distinction clear to most listeners. Thus the "h" sound which should be an explosive blowing of the lips is not carried out by most speakers. This sound is therefore blurred in such words as *hue, where* and other words where the "h" sound occurs.

Photo by Clark Manus

Dr. Gerald Manus is a retired Professor of Rehabilitation and Clinical Psychologist, who is involved in local community affairs in Oakland and is currently writing a book on how our society has changed over the past 80 years. Muriel Manus is a semi-retired administrator who does business consultations and edits a local homeowners newsletter in Oakland, CA.

The Screen Music of Trevor Jones

The first significant publication devoted entirely to Trevor Jones's work, *The Screen Music of Trevor Jones: Technology, Process, Production* investigates the key phases of his career within the context of developments in the British and global screen-music industries. This book draws on the direct testimony of the composer and members of his team as well as making use of the full range of archival materials held in the University of Leeds's unique Trevor Jones Archive, which was digitised with support from the Arts and Humanities Research Council.

Through a comprehensive series of chapters covering Jones's early career to his recent projects, this book demonstrates how Jones has been active in an industry that has experienced a prolonged period of major technological change, including the switchover from analogue to digital production and post-production techniques, and developments in computer software for score production and sound recording/editing.

This is a valuable study for scholars, researchers and professionals in the areas of film music, film-score production and audio-visual media.

David Cooper is Emeritus Professor of Music at the University of Leeds. He has published extensively on film music (especially that of Bernard Herrmann, Trevor Jones and Michael Nyman), the music of Béla Bartók and the traditional music of Ireland. His outputs include volumes on Herrmann's scores for the films *Vertigo* and *The Ghost and Mrs Muir*; a major biography of Bartók and a study of the latter's *Concerto for Orchestra*; and the monograph *The Musical Traditions of Northern Ireland and Its Diaspora*. He was principal investigator of the AHRC-funded project 'The Professional Career and Output of Trevor Jones'.

Ian Sapiro is Associate Professor of Music at the University of Leeds. His monograph, *Scoring the Score*, is the first academic study of screen-music orchestration and orchestrators, and he has published on a range of screen-music and musical-theatre subjects. Outputs include a volume on Ilan Eshkeri's score for *Stardust* and publications on John Williams's orchestration, the film adaptations of *Les Misérables* and *Annie*, British 'rock operas' and Michael Nyman's Greenaway scores, and he is currently working on a critical edition of the Gershwin musical *Girl Crazy*. He was co-investigator on the AHRC-funded project 'The Professional Career and Output of Trevor Jones'.

Laura Anderson is an Irish Research Council Post-Doctoral Fellow at Maynooth University, where her project 'Disruptive Soundscapes' offers a new view of avant-garde post-war French film sound design by examining its relationship with wider cultural developments. Between 2013 and 2016, she was the Post-Doctoral Research Fellow on the AHRC-funded project 'The Professional Career and Output of Trevor Jones' at the University of Leeds. Other projects include publications on Jean Cocteau's engagement with music and sound in film; pre-existing music in Jean-Pierre Melville's *Les Enfants terribles*; John Williams's score for *Angela's Ashes*; and Brian Boydell's music for documentary film.

Ashgate Screen Music
Series Editors: James Deaville
Carleton University, Canada
Kathryn Kalinak
Rhode Island College, USA
Ben Winters
Open University, UK

The *Ashgate Screen Music* series publishes monographs and edited collections about music in film, television, video games and in new screening contexts such as the internet from any time and any location. All of these titles share the common dedication to advancing our understanding of how music interacts with moving images, supporting narrative, creating affect, suspending disbelief, and engrossing audiences. The series is not tied to a particular medium or genre but can range from director-composer auteur studies (Hitchcock and Herrmann, Leone and Morricone, Burton and Elfman) through multi-author volumes on music in specific television programmes (Glee, Doctor Who, Lost) to collective explorations of topics that cut across genres and media (music on small screens, non-Western music in Western moving-image representations). As such, the *Ashgate Screen Music* series is intended to make a valuable contribution to the literature about music and moving images.

Re-Locating the Sounds of the Western
Edited by Kendra Preston Leonard and Mariana Whitmer

Recomposing the Past
Representations of Early Music on Stage and Screen
Edited by James Cook, Alexander Kolassa and Adam Whittaker

Reeled In
Pre-existing Music in Narrative Film
Jonathan Godsall

Heavy Metal at the Movies
Gerd Bayer

The Screen Music of Trevor Jones
Technology, Process, Production
David Cooper, Ian Sapiro and Laura Anderson

For more information about this series, please visit: www.routledge.com/music/series/ASM

The Screen Music of Trevor Jones
Technology, Process, Production

David Cooper, Ian Sapiro and Laura Anderson

LONDON AND NEW YORK

First published 2020 by Routledge

2 Park Square, Milton Park, Abingdon, Oxon, OX14 4RN
605 Third Avenue, New York, NY 10017

Routledge is an imprint of the Taylor & Francis Group, an informa business

First issued in paperback 2020

Copyright © 2020 David Cooper, Ian Sapiro and Laura Anderson

The right of David Cooper, Ian Sapiro and Laura Anderson to be identified as the authors has been asserted by them in accordance with sections 77 and 78 of the Copyright, Designs and Patents Act 1988.

All rights reserved. No part of this book may be reprinted or reproduced or utilised in any form or by any electronic, mechanical, or other means, now known or hereafter invented, including photocopying and recording, or in any information storage or retrieval system, without permission in writing from the publishers.

Notice:
Product or corporate names may be trademarks or registered trademarks, and are used only for identification and explanation without intent to infringe.

British Library Cataloguing-in-Publication Data
A catalogue record for this book is available from the British Library

Library of Congress Cataloging-in-Publication Data
A catalog record for this book has been requested

ISBN: 978-1-4724-7317-2 (hbk)
ISBN: 978-0-367-78577-2 (pbk)

Typeset in Times New Roman
by Apex CoVantage, LLC

Contents

List of figures	vii
List of tables	x
Foreword by Trevor Jones	xii
Acknowledgements	xvi
Introduction	1

PART I
Jones's early career (1978–87) — 13

1 Musical education and the National Film School — 15
2 Breaking into the industry — 27

PART II
The 'toolkit' years (1987–93) — 47

3 Alan Parker and the development of the toolkit — 49
4 Towards a mainstream sound — 65

PART III
Mainstream scoring (1993–2004) — 93

5 Hollywood blockbusters part one — 95
6 Hollywood blockbusters part two — 129
7 Music for television — 148

PART IV
Recent projects (2004–) 175

8 A brief foray into video games 177

9 Work in diverse areas of screen programming 189

Conclusions 207

Trevor Jones's filmography 222
Bibliography 227
Index 235

Figures

0.1	Graphical representation of the metadata schema for the Trevor Jones Archive	6
1.1	Track sheet showing the breakdown of instrumentation for each cue of *The Black Angel*	21
1.2	Aural transcription of the main theme from *The Black Angel*	22
1.3	Lady of the Lake theme from *Excalibur*	23
1.4	Extract from a track sheet for *The Dollar Bottom* showing the required instrumentation	24
2.1	Aural transcription of the main theme from *The Last Days of Pompeii*	38
2.2	Main theme from *The Last Place on Earth*	40
2.3	Pitches of the labyrinth motif from *Labyrinth*	44
3.1	Aural transcription of the melody of 'Moving On' from *Runaway Train*	50
3.2	Twenty-four-track breakdown of the toolkit Alex 2 from *Angel Heart*	54
3.3	Twenty-four-track breakdown of TK1 and TK2 from *Just Ask for Diamond*	59
4.1	Twenty-four-track breakdown of the 'Iranian Fiasco/Suspense Master' from *Sea of Love*	68
4.2	Twenty-four-track breakdown of the Iranian Fiasco Toolkit from *Sea of Love*	70
4.3	Twenty-four-track breakdown of toolkit TKM2 from *Sea of Love*	71
4.4	Track sheet for the twenty-four track mix of cue 9M1 'Brother Helps' from *Bad Influence*, showing the level adjustments for sounds drawn from the Atmos Toolkit	73
4.5	Twenty-four-track breakdown of toolkit TK1 from *By Dawn's Early Light*	76
4.6	Track sheet for the recording of 1M2 from *Arachnophobia*	79
4.7	Track sheet for the six-track mix of cue 4M1 from *Freejack*, showing descriptions of the tracks	85
4.8	Track sheet for the eight-track mix of cue 6M1 from *CrissCross*	86

Figures

5.1	Aural transcription of the riff from the title cue from *In the Name of the Father*	104
5.2	'Traditional' fiddle rhythm from cue 14M1 of *In the Name of the Father* as heard on working tape 4/7	105
5.3	The 'Giuseppe' motif from *In the Name of the Father*	106
5.4	Cue list for *Brassed Off*	109
5.5	Seating plan for Grimethorpe Colliery Band	110
5.6	Extract from the lead sheet for Rossini's overture to *William Tell* with editing annotations	112
5.7	Track sheet for multiple cues in *Brassed Off*, showing the breakdown of instrumentation	114
5.8	Acoustic guitar melody from cue 1M2 of *In the Name of the Father*, taken from the Sibelius file 'Notting Hill – Will and Anna edit' in the Trevor Jones Archive	122
5.9	Track sheet for 7M4 'She', with Elvis Costello's vocals	125
6.1	Missiles theme from cue 1M2 from *Thirteen Days*	133
6.2	Aural transcription of the melody at the end of the first phrase of cue 1M2 from *From Hell*. The bracketed pitches are omitted when this material is turned into a slow waltz in cue 4M6	136
6.3	Jones's theme for the league in *The League of Extraordinary Gentlemen*: (a) The initial statement in bars 33–35 of cue 1M6 'Fight in the Britannia Club'; (b) extended by one permutation in cue 2M1; (c) more compact version from cue 2M3; (d) compressed version from cue 2M6	142
6.4	The Quatermain theme from *The League of Extraordinary Gentlemen*	143
7.1	Aural transcription of the main theme from *Joni Jones*	152
7.2	Aural transcription of the main theme from *Those Glory, Glory Days*	152
7.3	Excerpt from the spotting notes for *Detonator*	157
7.4	Aural transcription of the main theme from *Gulliver's Travels*	161
7.5	Main theme from *Merlin*	162
7.6	Aural transcription of the main theme from *Cleopatra*	162
7.7	Aural transcription of the main theme from the *Dinotopia* mini-series	163
7.8	Simplified representation of where commercial bumpers and act-ins/outs lie in a television programme with advert breaks	166
8.1	Complete cue list from *Rise of the Imperfects*	181
8.2	The three main melodic elements of M01 from *Rise of the Imperfects*: (a) The initial ascending melody drawing on the Gypsy/Hungarian scale that bears a similarity to the opening bass theme of *Dark City* (1998); (b) the Imperfects theme; (c) variant bass melody with echoes of Holst's 'Mars'	183
8.3	The three main melodic elements of M03 from *Rise of the Imperfects*: (a) The Superhero theme; (b) angular melody that recalls a second theme from *Dark City* (1998); (c) third melodic idea from M03	183

9.1	Syncopated rhythmic ostinati from different sections of cue 1M2 from *Aegis*	192
9.2	Melody from the first section of cue 1M1 from *Chaos*	193
9.3	Decorated linear descent to the tonic from the final part of cue 1M1 from *Chaos*	194
9.4	Main theme from *We Fight to Be Free*	197
9.5	Melody from cue 6M3 from *Three and Out*	200
10.1	Some of Jones's harmonic fingerprints as heard in cue 1M1A from *Labyrinth*	209
10.2	Main members of Jones's music team across multiple projects	216

Tables

1.1	Student films scored by Jones at the National Film School	19
1.2	Breakdown of audio recordings across the three sixteen-track two-inch tapes for *The Black Angel*	22
2.1	Music used at key plot points in *Excalibur*	30
2.2	Development of the pod dance from *The Dark Crystal* based on audio recordings in the archive	35
3.1	A list of toolkits and descriptions for *Angel Heart* as described in the 'Music Notes'	53
3.2	Construction of passes 1 to 5 of toolkit Alex 2 from *Angel Heart*	55
3.3	Sources and dates (where known) relating to *Dominick and Eugene*	58
4.1	The six Venetian Dances from *Blame It on the Bellboy*	80
4.2	Placement of extracts from the six Venetian Dances in *Blame It on the Bellboy*	81
4.3	Key relationships between the temp score and Jones's early material for *Blame It on the Bellboy*	83
4.4	Temp track information for *The Last of the Mohicans*	88
5.1	Contents of the six two-inch multitrack tapes for *In the Name of the Father* held in the Trevor Jones Archive	101
5.2	Musical cues by Trevor Jones listed in the score and source popular music used in the film *In the Name of the Father*	102
5.3	Use of the 'Giuseppe' and 'Thief of Your Heart' melodies in *In the Name of the Father*	107
5.4	Different structures of 'She' for the closing sequence of *Notting Hill* on the VHS tape from 5 January 1999	126
6.1	Outline of the schedule for the production of the score for *Thirteen Days* from material in the Trevor Jones Archive	131
7.1	Jones's television projects in chronological order, showing era, programme form, industry and broadcaster (asterisked when commercial)	150
7.2	Names and durations of bumpers for *The Last Days of Pompeii*	167
7.3	Names and durations of bumpers for *The Last Place on Earth*	168

7.4	The cues for *Joni Jones*, with the cue numbers indicating the episode to which they belong	170
8.1	Principal Marvel video games produced in the three years leading up to *Rise of the Imperfects*, showing the composers and their screen-composition experience	179
8.2	Summary of Trevor Jones's score for *Marvel Nemesis: Rise of the Imperfects* using Tim Summers's outline 'How to Hear a Video Game' (2016, pp. 208–214) as a structural framework	186
8.3	Hit points in the MIDI file from *Zelda Ruin*	187

Foreword

I am particularly indebted to Professor David Cooper, who initiated the archiving of my work, and the invaluable contributions of Dr Ian Sapiro, Dr Laura Anderson and Sarah Hall at the School of Music in the Faculty of Arts, Humanities and Culture at the University of Leeds; I thank them all most sincerely. Thanks must also go to Hatty Matthews, Ed Cooper and Maddy Stevens, whose cataloguing and capturing of the metadata is greatly appreciated. Special thanks must go to the following people who contributed time, knowledge and general assistance: Neil Stemp, Victoria Seale, Geoff Alexander, Dave Barraclough, Neil Sorrell and the National Film and Television School of Great Britain. Finally I would like to thank the Arts and Humanities Research Council (AHRC) for the funding of this project, which could never have been undertaken without their generous help and support.

My objective as a composer of media music is to provide a score that contributes to and clarifies the director's vision of the narrative while at the same time exploring the potential in combining with conventional instrumentation whatever innovative resources, by way of sound technology, becomes available to me. I also audaciously attempt to break with convention and the accepted styles of music-scoring for each of the genres in which I work – to break the mould and re-invent the wheel, so to speak. Whether or not I have succeeded is debatable, but I am heartened by the fact that some of my past solutions have been adopted by other composers.

In the preparation for my career as a media composer I realised that the orchestra was the standard vehicle for the longevity of music in the media as exemplified by the majority of Disney scores for their various projects. The ongoing development of synthesisers and samplers led to an extension of the sound palette, and the fusion of orchestral and instrumental sounds with synthetic sounds was the way in which one could produce scores that had a longevity and 'shelf-life'. Pure synthetic or re-synthesised sounds were destined to date-mark the era in which they were produced – giving the project a stamp, a sound, which identified it and confined it to its time – making it 'old-fashioned' within a very short period, whereas the use of the symphonic orchestra enabled the scores to transcend their time. With the advent of computation and its rapid development one is now able to use software programs to facilitate the creation of scores, though mercifully as yet they have not overtaken the creative compositional process.

The archive material spans several trends in popular culture including the era of political commentary and narrative – as exemplified by projects such as *In the*

Name of the Father (1993), *Mississippi Burning* (1988), *Brassed Off* (1996) and *Aegis* (2005) – and *The League of Extraordinary Gentlemen* (2003) saw the advent of the superhero and characters from DC comics of the 1930s and 1940s. The archive also covers the era of film and television that saw the technology of music recording transition from the analogue to the digital age, advances that revolutionised the way in which music was created, realised, recorded and produced. The archive currently comprises most of the analogue and early digital tapes and will be expanded further in due course with the inclusion of materials archived in other formats including AIT and Exabyte Backup tapes currently retained at Contemporary Music Media Productions (CMMP).

Apart from the very early scores, the circumstances under which the archived music was produced were by no means ideal. The nature of writing music to order within a given time-frame, to a schedule and (in almost all instances) to a budget that was extremely compromised, was both hectic and stressful. Music is the last creative element to be applied to the film-making process, and the pressure of completion of the film – because of the ongoing financial interest accruing on the investment and costs – becomes acute. The luxury of revision, of circumspection, of the themes and their variants as they pertained to the scenes and the narrative, as well as the director's vision and expectation of the music, was never an indulgence that I experienced, and I regret to say that in most instances I felt that I had had to abandon work on the scores at the deadline for final delivery to the dubbing mix. What survives, in almost all circumstances, are exercises in 'shooting from the hip'. Broadly speaking it occurs to me that there are three factors that impact on and govern the creation of a score: time, money and quality. As a composer one requires more time to produce a low-budget music score of quality, whereas lacking sufficient time but having a substantial budget enables one to throw money at the music production, employ many people and produce an adequate score; this scenario still lacks time for reflection, circumspection and re-writes, however, and invariably results in the quality of the score being compromised.

The process of manipulating the parameters of music and the ongoing discovery of the ways in which they could be combined with images fascinates me and became addictive. I have a passion for scoring to this day and am still in pursuit of realising the ideal music score within a given time-frame. How is it best to realise the potential of a succession of images and to make the narrative clearer in the most lucid and economical way, while aiding the dramatic intent of the screenwriter and director, within a pre-set budget and time-frame? The processes of film-making and the creation of a score for a film are extremely similar, and at film school I realised that rather than defining myself as a composer I was a film-maker working in music. I became aware that the similarities in the realisation of film and the production of music for film are analogous: I compare the screenwriter to the composer, the director to the conductor, the cinematographer to the recording engineer, and so on. The analogy can be continued and comparisons made for both production processes.

My experiences with directors on set and the video projects that I myself had directed at the University of York made me aware that music was one of the most difficult elements of film-making to direct. Unlike the other crafts that contributed to the making of a film, it posed great difficulty in terms of communication between composer and director, and I wanted to find solutions to the way in which a director could more effectively convey his or her ideas and direct a composer. I set out to be as 'user-friendly' as possible and to develop ways in which ideas between composer and director could be conveyed and transmitted. This took the form of examples: by the use of established pieces of music, using synthesiser and sample sketches, and the development of the 'toolkit'. The initial idea of a toolkit was to record a palette of sounds with differing rhythmic patterns that combined to form a piece of music, which could be constructed from the choices made by the director. The toolkits were originally developed to try and give directors like Alan Parker maximum control over the way in which they wanted to combine the sounds of the toolkit to convey their preferences – in the choices they made – while still being contained by the rhythmic and notational choices that I had pre-ordained. In the hands of a 'musical' director this was a positive approach to the construction of particular cues, but I had not anticipated that there would be an intermediary influence in the form of the dubbing mixer. Although I often included an example demo in the form of a 'guide mix' as a note to my personal preference of the combinations and the volumes of each individual sound, the dubbing mixer's choice of sounds, how they related to each other, and the levels at which individual sounds were played often had a more than significant impact on the outcome of the final cues. Over the last three years I have taken to painting in oils and find that I choose my palette of colours in much the same way that I chose my sounds for the toolkits – using only those colours and their combinations best suited to the subject matter of the painting. Similarly, at the start of each project I assembled a 'sound palette', a collection of sounds that I felt inherently conveyed the tone of the subject matter of the project. Later my use of the toolkit became more of a 'palette of sounds' that would enable me to compile specific sounds that had an emotional connotation for me. These combinations could be used in the construction of themes, motifs and melodies when composing cues in a score; these latter toolkits therefore did not perform the same role as those for *Mississippi Burning* and other projects.

If I have succeeded in anything it is in retaining my passion for scoring. I went in search of an approach to writing that broadly encompassed a wide range of styles, in the words of one of my mentors, Liz Lutyens, to 'write what the film needs in an appropriate style': composing and realising musically what the film needed while approaching the underscore on the basis of 're-inventing the wheel' in whatever genre presented itself. I set out to find the musical expression that Liz said would 'bring out the meaning of the scenes in the film', while at the same time being aware of Erik Satie's 'furniture music' – that the music should not overtly draw attention to itself but, as with the other elements of film-making, contribute to the director's vision and the story-telling process. Given the circumstances under which one works – the pressures of time and schedules, very little time for reflection and circumspection (especially in the pre-computational era), inadequate music budgets, and unrealistic expectations of what music can and should contribute to the film (amongst other constraints) – my fascination for the way in which two crafts running parallel in a continuum can interact increased further. The result has been a continuous learning experience, made exciting by the discoveries and revelations experienced when manipulating the parameters of music in the construction of a cue and its combination with a series of images, to make clear to an audience the director's vision of the narrative. This makes for a preoccupation with the craft of scoring, which continues to be a passion and that fuels long working days and sets the commercial and political pressures and the artistically high expectations of the commercial world in their proper perspective. The good fortune of being able to work in the creation of music and its extraordinary chemistry with images incentivised me, and I was excited by and thankful for each commission as it presented itself.

That the body of work as contained in the archive should be examined and scrutinised and that I should become 'a subject' for such investigation in my lifetime continues to surprise me! I consider myself extremely fortunate to have been given the opportunity to work with so many talented people. I am very grateful to all those concerned who have made this possible so that I can continue to indulge my passion for scoring and, more often than not, enjoy the experience very much.

Trevor Jones
January 2018

Acknowledgements

This book is the culmination of a three-year £570,000 research project funded by the Arts and Humanities Research Council (AHRC), 'The Professional Career and Output of Trevor Jones' (reference: AH/K003828/1), that ran in the School of Music at the University of Leeds from October 2013 to September 2016. The fourth member of our small project team was our doctoral researcher, Sarah Hall, who undertook the significant task of exploring Jones's scoring processes when composing music for television. Her work forms the basis for Chapter 7 of this book, which focuses on Jones's televisual output, and we could not have completed the project, let alone this book, without her invaluable contribution to the team. Three undergraduate students from the School of Music – Hatty Matthews, Ed Cooper and Maddy Stevens – worked on the project across its final summer, taking on the arduous task of entering metadata relating to the final batch of digitised materials in the Trevor Jones Archive and assisting with the validation of existing metadata for the audio and textual items that were already logged in the system. Their efforts and irrepressible good humour were much appreciated. Hatty has worked on and with the archival materials over two summers as a Laidlaw Undergraduate Research and Leadership Scholar, and in particular her work with Ian researching the materials and processes for Jones's score for *Dark City* (1998) has informed the discussion of that film in Chapter 5.

Several people were interviewed or otherwise provided information for this book, and thanks must go to Geoff Alexander, Dave Barraclough, Victoria Seale, Neil Sorrell, Neil Stemp, and staff at the National Film and Television School for patiently answering our questions and enabling us to delve into their combined memories of Jones's various scoring projects. The project and its legacy have been well supported by successive heads of the University of Leeds School of Music, Professor Martin Iddon and Professor Karen Burland, and the advice of Tim Banks, Graham Blyth, Rachel Proudfoot and Brenda Philips on matters of research-data management has been and continues to be invaluable. We would also like to thank Heidi Bishop and Annie Vaughan at Routledge and the Ashgate Screen Music Series editors, James Deaville, Kathryn Kalinak and Ben Winters, for their help bringing this book to press.

Finally, and most importantly, we would like to express our sincere thanks to Trevor Jones himself, not only for donating his unique collection of archival screen-music materials to the University of Leeds and for being interviewed numerous times by various members of the project team, but also for his continued engagement with and interest in our work.

David Cooper, Ian Sapiro and Laura Anderson
January 2018

Introduction

Miguel Mera notes that 'film musicologists have been reluctant to engage in the examination of both process and product. [. . .] But this debate is one of the most potentially fertile and fascinating areas for development' (2007, p. 78). This reluctance can partly be ascribed to the lack of available resources for undertaking a sufficiently rigorous evaluation of the development and creation of scores and the film-scoring process. While music is acknowledged by most people working in the industry as an essential component of a successful film, television programme or video game, for the vast majority of productions, session recordings, musical scores and associated paperwork are either not kept at all by studios, or if they are retained are not made readily available for scholarly scrutiny. Whereas cut and alternative scenes are now regularly preserved for DVD and Blu-ray releases, unused, rewritten and rejected musical cues are generally viewed as superfluous by studios and production companies. Similarly, although materials relating to the processes of screen scoring (for example, spotting notes, mix documentation and track sheets) may be retained by the composers themselves, in many cases they are simply disposed of by the studios once a film or game is released or a programme is broadcast. Furthermore, a significant proportion of materials surviving from the analogue era was created using equipment that has largely been rendered redundant by the switch to digital technology. This combination of factors can have the effect of further limiting the availability of such resources to scholars.

The materials that remain from the screen-score production process are generally held in one of four places, at least as far as UK and US productions are concerned. Some resources are held in studio libraries, and others have been retained in or acquired for private collections – notably those of the composers or their estates – but in both circumstances the scale of such collections is very difficult to estimate, especially given that composers and particularly studios can be unaware of the extent of (and gaps in) their own holdings. Collections are held by some university libraries in the United States, with examples being the Warner Brothers' Archives at the University of Southern California, Los Angeles, and the Max Steiner Collection at Brigham Young University, Utah; although such archives offer varying degrees of scholarly access, they generally consist largely of notated scores and represent only a small number of high-profile composers working in the Hollywood studio system. Miguel Mera and Ben Winters's scoping study for the Music

Libraries Trust, 'Film and Television Music Sources in the UK and Ireland' (2009), revealed that the final location in which film-score-production materials are held is in collections of varying sizes at UK higher-education institutions, with one such collection being the Trevor Jones Archive at the University of Leeds.

Trevor Jones was the keynote interviewee at a Film and Music Conference jointly organised by the University of Leeds and Brunel University and hosted at Bradford's National Museum for Photography, Film and Television (now the National Science and Media Museum) in March 2005 as part of the eleventh Bradford Film Festival. Following this event, he offered some of his archival film-music materials to the University of Leeds (which already had an established reputation for film-music study) with an agreement that they should be used exclusively for research and teaching. Little more than two months later, Jones personally delivered to the university a donation of more than 400 multitrack analogue tapes, including session recordings and demonstration mock-ups of cues, as well as associated items of documentation such as spotting notes, mixer settings and other records of communication between members of the music and production teams. In 2010 he made a second substantial donation of archival materials, around 300 individual items including rough and fine cuts for several pictures in a range of video formats, and additional audio materials in the form of demo and multitrack recordings and final stereo mixes for some projects. Two further donations were made in 2013 and 2015, expanding the Trevor Jones Archive to more than 1000 audio-visual items alongside supporting documentation, and Jones has continued to add to the holdings through the provision of digital files for more-recent projects. Furthermore, since artefacts such as the analogue multitrack tapes usually contain recordings of numerous individual cues, the total number of resources from the score-production process held in the collection is over 10,000.

Jones has a substantial collection of bound scores that covers the vast majority of his projects to date, some of which have been copied and are included within the archive at Leeds. Sketches, short scores and compositional ideas are bound in with the full-score for several projects, and some volumes also include additional materials that contextualise the score and/or the film. The score for *Angel Heart* (1987), which is bound into a single volume with Jones's other score for Alan Parker, *Mississippi Burning* (1988), includes a typed breakdown of the narrative and both hand-written and typed information on the film's 'toolkits',[1] and *Sea of Love* (1989) includes a draft sketch, three-stave short score and full orchestral score for many of the film's cues. Jones has also retained extensive audio recordings of spotting sessions for many of the projects on which he has worked; at present copies of these materials are not held in the archive to protect the privacy of the film-makers. Mera and Winters (2009) note that film-music archives at UK higher-education institutions, much like those at their US counterparts, consist mainly of musical scores, and the existence of demos and recordings alongside musical and textual artefacts makes the Trevor Jones Archive unusual, if not unique, in the UK. They identify the potential for the collection to 'become one of the most significant collections for the film and television music researcher in the UK' (2009, p. 46), and the richness and variety of resources in the archive offer significant scope for the scholarly examination of both process and product in screen music that Mera (2007) advocates.

Trevor Jones

South African-born Trevor Jones has been writing music for films and television programmes for nearly forty years. He is distinguished by the volume and range of high-profile projects on which he has worked, the directors – including John Boorman, Alan Parker, Ridley Scott, Andrey Konchalovsky, Jim Sheridan, Michael Mann, Mark Herman and Harold Becker – with whom he has collaborated, and his innovative approach to the creation and development of music for the screen. Jones worked throughout the extended transition from analogue to digital technologies in screen production and post-production that included significant changes to picture editing (which had consequential effects on composers and their teams) and the recording and editing of sound and music.[2] Specific developments impacting directly on the music team in this period also include the introduction of digital synthesisers and other electronic instruments and the widespread adoption of sequencers, digital audio workstations and music-processing software. Jones has always worked at the cutting edge of the industry in terms of his use of technology – for example, the Finn brothers tested their Sibelius music-processing software at his studio, he and his team being integrally involved in its early development (Sapiro 2016, p. 209) – and he has remained in the vanguard throughout his career.

Jones has resisted being pigeonholed as the composer of a specific type of score, and although he may not be a household name he has a very strong international fan base, as evidenced by comments on video-sharing websites and social media. His output includes music for projects in a wide variety of genres, as demonstrated by the following snapshot of his career to date. Fantasy pictures range from Jim Henson's animatronic features *The Dark Crystal* (1982) and *Labyrinth* (1986) through the mini-series *Gulliver's Travels* (1996) and *Merlin* (1998) to the comic-book and graphic-novel adaptations *From Hell* (2001) and *The League of Extraordinary Gentlemen* (2003). He has moved between romantic comedies like *Sweet Lies* (1987), *Molly* (1999), *Crossroads* (2002) and *I'll Be There* (2003); comedy dramas such as *Just Ask for Diamond* (1988) and *Blame It on the Bellboy* (1992); the horror comedy *Arachnophobia* (1990); and more conventional horror films including *The Sender* (1982), *Angel Heart* (1987) and *Hideaway* (1995). Action-adventure films like *Runaway Train* (1985), *The Last of the Mohicans* (1992), *Cliffhanger* (1993) and *Around the World in 80 Days* (2004) contrast with crime dramas, which include *CrissCross* (1992), *Chains of Gold* (1993), *Desperate Measures* (1998) and *How to Steal 2 Million* (2011). Dramas inspired by history and biography range from the ancient Egypt of *Cleopatra* (1999) through the race between Scott and Amundsen to reach the South Pole in *The Last Place on Earth* (1985) and Richard Loncraine's reimagining of Shakespeare's *Richard III* (1998) in 1930s England to the Battle of Gettysburg in *Fields of Freedom* (2006).

Jones has scored films that tackle sensitive topics in British politics, notably *In the Name of the Father* (1993), which examines the wrongful arrest, prosecution, treatment and eventual acquittal of Northern Irishmen Gerry and Patrick 'Giuseppe' Conlon and the other members of the so-called 'Guildford Four' and 'Maguire Seven'. He has similarly written music for pictures dealing with political matters overseas including *Mississippi Burning* (1988), which focuses on the persecution of civil-rights activists and the black community by the Ku Klux Klan in the southern US during the 1960s; *A Private Life* (1989), which is based around the lives of a mixed-race South African couple during the apartheid era; and *Thirteen Days* (2000), a dramatisation of the Cuban Missile Crisis of 1962. He has also composed music for films that have had significant and long-lasting cultural impact, notably the British romantic comedies *Brassed Off* (1996) and *Notting Hill* (1999); indeed, many of the pictures Jones has scored retain currency and continue to appear regularly on British television schedules many years after their theatrical releases.

Screen-music, research and archival materials

The approach to the scholarly investigation of screen music and its composers has developed over time as researchers have gained access to resources that permit more detailed study. Earlier publications were generally of book-chapter or journal-article length and tended to be based around the aural analysis of the music as heard in the theatrical release of a film. The book-length studies of individual film scores, *Max Steiner's 'Now, Voyager': A Film Score Guide* (2000) by Kate Daubney, and David Cooper's *Bernard Herrmann's 'Vertigo': A Film Score Handbook* (2001), both published by Greenwood Press, marked a sea change in the musicological study of film scores. Both authors were able to access additional materials to supplement the soundtrack, notably the composers' manuscript scores, which often showed marked differences between the music as notated and the sound heard in the actual film. The additional contextual and compositional information yielded by these previously untapped resources provided the foundation for other scholars to embark on similar musicological studies of the film score, effectively establishing the use of a manuscript score as a normal expectation for research of this type. Between 2004 and 2017, when the series was published by the Rowman & Littlefield Publishing Group,[3] the manuscript score was a principal resource for nineteen Film Score Guides.

While access to notated scores was a significant development in film musicology, the value of archival resources relating to the processes of screen-score production has more recently been recognised by researchers. These materials can often establish the context of the notated score, enabling scholars to evaluate previous incarnations of musical ideas and structures and to chart the ways that musical and filmic decisions have impacted on the composer's music. Owing to the access difficulties outlined above there are currently only a relatively small number of publications that have drawn extensively on archival film-music sources, with Miguel Mera's *Mychael Danna's 'The Ice Storm': A Film Score Guide* (2007) and *Ilan Eshkeri's 'Stardust': A Film Score Guide* (2013) by Ian Sapiro, both in the Scarecrow series, the two publications to date that draw most significantly on resources from the composition and production processes beyond the manuscript score. Nonetheless, archival film-music studies remains an area of research growth. In 2013 the Arts and Humanities Research Council (AHRC), part of Research Councils UK, awarded a grant of around £570,000 to David Cooper and Ian Sapiro for the three-year project 'The Professional Career and Output of Trevor Jones' (reference: AH/K003828/1) through which the research team – Cooper, Sapiro, post-doctoral research fellow Laura Anderson and doctoral researcher Sarah Hall – undertook a large-scale investigation into the resources in the Trevor Jones Archive. The project featured three annual international conferences on music for audio-visual media, each of which included scholarly presentations that utilised archival resources, with the second conference held at the British Library in London and focused explicitly on the topic of 'Audio-Visual Archives'.[4] Over the last five years presentations given by scholars at other conferences (including those by the project team) have drawn on material from screen and screen-music archives, and in the summer of 2017 scholars using archival resources to work in a range of audio-visual areas and aesthetics were brought together for a successful symposium held at the University of Huddersfield. Just as it has become easier for researchers to obtain copies of manuscript scores as studios and producers have become more aware of developments in scholarship, so it may be hoped that increased use of archival materials may lead to corresponding improvements in retention and access.

Metadata for the archival materials digitised in the course of the AHRC-funded project was captured and logged using an innovative schema designed by the project team (see Figure 0.1) and first presented in the article 'Digitizing, Organizing and Managing an Audio-Visual Archive: The Trevor Jones Archive at the University of Leeds' (Cooper, Sapiro, Anderson and Hall 2016, p. 106), along with discussion of the processes concerning the creation and curation of the digital archive. Over time all of the metadata – there are more than 100,000 pieces of information across the whole collection – will be uploaded into the website www.screenmusic.leeds.ac.uk, from where they may be publicly browsed and searched. However, in accordance with the agreement made between the University of Leeds and Trevor Jones, the materials themselves are only available for research and teaching purposes and are therefore not directly accessible via the ScreenMusic website.

Although the availability of resources such as those in the Trevor Jones Archive and the additional information provided by accompanying metadata of the sort outlined in Figure 0.1 can augment the study of screen music, the use of archival materials can also bring difficulties and complexities to the study of screen music. A particular issue is projects from which resources are missing, ranging from occasional items of paperwork to almost everything, with *The Last of the Mohicans*, perhaps Jones's best-known film score, being a case in point. The archival holdings for this picture comprise a small number of VHS tapes, 5.1 surround sound mixes for some cues, stereo mixes for the soundtrack CD, and a Sibelius score of the concert suite. However, despite the prevalence of audio recordings in the archive more broadly, there are none from any of the sessions for *The Last of the Mohicans*, nor are there any items of paperwork for the project. These absences limit substantially the extent to which the score can be explored from the perspectives of technology, process or production. By contrast, the holdings for the lesser-known 1989 film *Sea of Love* include two sets of spotting notes, eight-track audio demos and

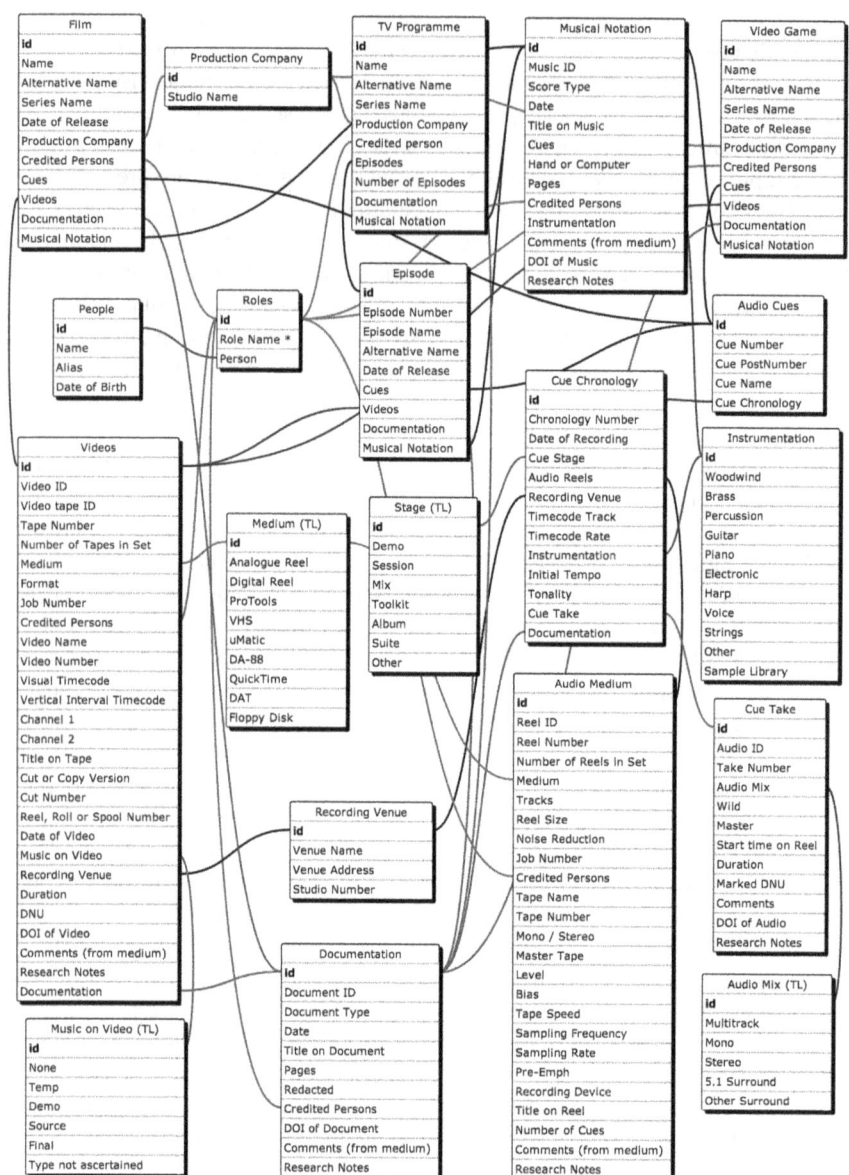

Figure 0.1 Graphical representation of the metadata schema for the Trevor Jones Archive[5]

twenty-four-track multitrack recordings, hand-annotated track sheets for almost all of these recordings, three VHS tapes from different points in the production process and a digitised copy of the score (which, as already noted, includes some drafts and sketches). Whereas *The Last of the Mohicans* frustrates through the absence of evidence, the vast amount of material for *Sea of Love* provides information about and evidence of the absence of sources that must have existed – both known and unknown unknowns – for other films but are now lost. These matters are raised where relevant in the book and in Chapter 4 in particular, which includes contrasting consideration of the archival materials for *The Last of the Mohicans* and *Arachnophobia*.

Another key issue that relates closely to the availability of archival sources is the choice of which of Jones's ninety-plus projects should be included, let alone made the subject of more detailed scrutiny within this book. Such decisions have been informed by considering multiple criteria:

> the quality or success of a film; the perceived aesthetic quality or success of a score; the amount of materials relating to a particular film or programme held in the collection; or a particular research need. [. . .] The picture becomes more complex still if one takes into account the interests and expectation of the broader user community, such as members of the public who might engage with publications arising from the research.
>
> (Cooper, Sapiro, Anderson and Hall 2016, pp. 108–109)

A flexible approach has been taken across this volume, with each of the above possible criteria responsible (either in whole or in part) for the inclusion of several screen projects. To a large extent the scores that are highlighted as case studies in each chapter have been selected through a combination of the availability of archival sources and the particular research imperatives that form the focus of the specific chapter. Notwithstanding this, however, most chapters also draw on a wide range of projects to contextualise the case studies, support discussion of the continuous development of Jones's working practices and the impact of relevant technological advances, and demonstrate the breadth of the composer's output across his career. More than seventy of Jones's scores are discussed in varying degrees of depth and detail in an effort to avoid the accidental prioritisation, valorisation or – worse – canonisation of any of the composer's works. While such a challenge can never be overcome entirely, not least because as David Neumeyer has observed, 'the canonization process itself is not taking place among scholars [. . .] but among fans and others with an interest in promotion' (Buhler et al. 2003, p. 90), it is hoped that discussion of so much of Jones's screen-music output might mitigate any sense of canonisation inferred by readers.

Technology, process, production

This monograph arises from the AHRC research project discussed above and utilises the resources of the Trevor Jones Archive in a critical investigation of the composer's career and output from his time at the National Film School (now the

National Film and Television School) to the present. Indeed, this is the first publication in the area of screen music to use archival materials of this sort within an investigation of the career of a single composer, with texts such as those previously identified focused principally on a single film score. The development of Jones's working practices over time is analysed, notably with respect to technological advances, evaluating key phases in his career within the context of changes in both the British and global screen-music industries.

The book's subtitle – Technology, Process, Production – identifies three key angles of enquiry that permeate its text. Advances in technology, musical process and industrial production are related through what might be conceived as a virtuous triangle, with change in any one area influencing a positive development in at least one of the other two. In this study Jones's process is interrogated within the context of the changing industrial climate and against a background of rapid advances in technology, thereby positioning him clearly within the mainstream Anglo-American film-music industry. Jones's specific background and training (which are detailed in Chapter 1) are, of course, critical to understanding some of his more individual approaches and working practices. However, the length and variety of his career coupled with the availability of archival materials from the film-score production process makes Jones an ideal subject for an investigation of this type and supports the extrapolation of some of the findings of this study beyond the individual composer and across the industry (in and beyond the UK) as a whole.

The book is in four sections and in the main moves chronologically through Jones's career. Projects are occasionally considered out of strict sequential order when a broader discussion – of Jones's music for narrative television programmes or video games, for instance – facilitates greater understanding of his working processes and the impact of technology. The first part, 'Jones's early career (1978–87)', comprises two chapters that provide an overview of Jones's training and entry into the industry. Chapter 1 begins with an outline of Jones's biography, not simply to provide the practical details of his formative education but because he references explicitly his South African heritage and early educational experiences in the UK in interviews, and these matters resonate in both his compositional language and his motivation for choosing to work on certain projects. This exploration also illuminates the extent to which Jones's career can be mapped on to parallel developments in technology, and thus connections between biography, a sense of national identity, technology and his ongoing transatlantic professional relationships underpin Jones's entire career. The second part of the chapter considers his time at National Film School (NFS), which he attended having completed undergraduate study at the Royal Academy of Music and a postgraduate Masters course at the University of York. While attending the film-making course and learning about direction, cinematography, lighting, editing and the other filmic arts, he also delivered the first classes at the NFS in composition for film, and in his dual role as student and teacher he worked with other film-makers on a number of short pictures. Most notably he provided scores for the George Lucas-backed *The Black Angel* (1980), which was created as the pre-film short for the UK opening of *The Empire Strikes Back* and the Academy Award-winning *The Dollar Bottom* (1981). These film scores demonstrate the influence of Jones's diverse musical training through his undergraduate and postgraduate degrees and the start of a process through which he began to find his own filmic 'voice'.

Jones's early years as a professional in the film industry revolve mainly around his work on John Boorman's *Excalibur* (1981) and the animatronic films of Jim Henson – *The Dark Crystal* and *Labyrinth* – while the most substantial of his early television scores are for the mini-series *The Last Days of Pompeii* (1984) and *The Last Place on Earth* (1985), which were produced in the years between the two Henson projects. These pictures form the spine of Chapter 2. For *Excalibur* Jones crafted a score that combined original material with extracts from works by Wagner and Orff to create a coherent and powerful musical tapestry for Boorman's presentation of the Arthurian legend. By contrast, the music for *The Dark Crystal* fuses symphonic writing with the experimental sounds of the world on which the narrative is set. The archival materials for *The Dark Crystal* include a large number of reels of multitrack tape from recording sessions and offer significant insight into Jones's working methods and practices at the outset of his career. *Labyrinth* starred David Bowie, who performs on the film's soundtrack, and this picture marks Jones's first of many collaborations with an established pop star on a film. The two miniseries were his initial engagement with a programme type that he acknowledges to be his preferred small-screen format and to which he returned later in his career.

Towards the end of the 1980s Jones entered what we have termed 'The "toolkit" years (1987–93)', during which he drew on an experimental compositional approach he called 'toolkits' that he had first developed while studying at York. Chapter 3 explores Jones's toolkit scores for director Alan Parker, who commissioned him to compose the music for *Angel Heart* having heard his score for Konchalovsky's *Runaway Train*. Both Jones and Parker were keen for the director to have an active involvement in the sound of the picture, so Jones constructed a series of toolkits for the film, each of which was a bank of twenty-four sounds recorded onto a multitrack tape, that could be employed as and when desired by the director to generate atmosphere within the film. Jones refined the idea further on Parker's next picture, *Mississippi Burning*, creating layers of sound that could be played alone or stacked to thicken the texture. His use of toolkits marks him out as an innovator in both compositional approach, and also in his relationship with Parker as a musically-aware director, enabling the composer to retain some control over the score while simultaneously permitting the director to exert a strong authorial influence over the sound of his film. Jones's development of the toolkit idea across the following five years is discussed in Chapter 4. He drew on aspects of this approach over a dozen film and television projects including *Sea of Love*, *Bad Influence* (1990), *Arachnophobia* and *Detonator* (1993), developing the concept and changing its focus from a directorial device to a creative compositional tool, before beginning to cultivate a more mainstream sound and approach to scoring in the early 1990s in films such as *Cliffhanger*.

For around a decade Jones worked with a number of leading directors and actors, scoring numerous Hollywood blockbusters in an era of 'Mainstream scoring (1993–2004)'. Chapters 5 and 6 consider the pictures from the late 1990s and early 2000s respectively, noting the development of Jones's approach and techniques across a period of significant technological change. *Brassed Off* and *Notting Hill* are possibly the two most commercially successful films for which Jones has provided scores, but in both cases his original contributions are somewhat overshadowed by pre-existing material; brass band music in *Brassed Off* and pop songs in *Notting Hill*, particularly the Elvis Costello cover of 'She'. However, Jones played a key role in devising the sound of both pictures, being involved in the production of the brass band music for the former and creating and coordinating arrangements of songs for the latter, including 'She'. Having established a strong reputation in the industry, at the start of his third decade as a film composer Jones provided scores for pictures starring Kevin Costner (*Thirteen Days*), Johnny Depp (*From Hell*), Sean Connery (*The League of Extraordinary Gentlemen*) and Steve Coogan/Jackie Chan (*Around the World in 80 Days*). In contrast to the films considered in the previous chapter, his scores took centre stage musically in these pictures, offering opportunities to evaluate his sound and style on productions with significant budgets, as well as considering the impact on Jones's approach and practice of changing technologies in this period.

This section of the book also contains Chapter 7, an overview of Jones's work in television, since the scores he composed in this period for the two- and three-part Hallmark mini-series *Gulliver's Travels*, *Merlin*, *Cleopatra* and *Dinotopia* (2002) are the most well-documented television works in the Trevor Jones Archive. While some of his television scores are discussed in other parts of the book, this chapter provides a significant opportunity for exploration of his compositional approaches and working practices in this related medium, and to analyse consistencies and developments in his practice over time both within the area of television music and with respect to his parallel work in film. This chapter is based on material from Sarah Hall's doctoral thesis, 'The Television Music of Trevor Jones: Using an Audio-Visual Archive to Explore Scoring Processes' (2017), which she undertook as part of the AHRC-funded project.

The final section of the book examines 'Recent projects (2004–)', beginning in Chapter 8 with Jones's limited work in composing music for video games. In 2005 he created the score for EA Games's *Marvel Nemesis: Rise of the Imperfects*, and the chapter evaluates his approach to working in this (for him) new area of audio-visual scoring. There is also consideration of the limited materials that exist in the Trevor Jones Archive relating to his only other video-game project, music for a demo for an aborted game in the *Zelda* series, dating from 2007. Chapter 9 considers Jones's output since 2004, when he completed the Hollywood feature film *Around the World in 80 Days* and the low-budget animated short *The Unsteady Chough*. Subsequent projects have seen him working in more geographically diverse regions of the global film industry, providing scores for projects including the Japanese film *Aegis* (2005), the Canadian and South African co-produced television series *Jozi-H* (2006–7), and a number of South African pictures including the drama *How to Steal 2 Million* and the documentary *My Hunter's Heart* (2011). After spending over thirty years in the screen-music industry, Jones found himself in a position to choose the projects on which he wished to work, and this most recent period is the most varied in his career in this respect. While the number of scores produced in the last twelve years is relatively low for Jones, the range of project types makes interrogation of his approaches and processes invaluable for consideration of his continuing stylistic and practical development and for understanding of the range of working practices employed by composers in the contemporary industry. This section, and the book as a whole, ends with conclusions, which start with discussion of Jones's most recently completed substantial project – the two-part television mini-series *Labyrinth* (2012) – before offering a summary analysis of his musical and production processes and the impact of technology across his whole career to date.

Notes

1 See Chapter 3 for a full discussion of 'toolkits' and the role of this compositional device in these pictures.
2 For consideration of the impact of video-editing technologies on the creation of music for the screen see Sapiro (2016, pp. 84–92).
3 The first fifteen books in the series (up to 2013) were published under the group's Scarecrow Press imprint, with the final four (2015–17) published as Rowman & Littlefield books.
4 A special edition of the *Journal of Film Music* arising from the conference (volume 6, no. 2) was co-edited by Ian Sapiro and Laura Anderson and published in 2016.
5 Tables with names containing the abbreviation (TL) show term lists rather than additional metadata fields.

Part I
Jones's early career (1978–87)

1 Musical education and the National Film School

As outlined in the introduction to this book, echoes of Jones's South African heritage and his musical training in the UK can be heard across his career, and the country of his birth has always been an important part of his personal and professional life. Accordingly, this chapter begins with a brief summary of Jones's early years in South Africa before exploring his education in the UK at the Royal Academy of Music and the University of York. His years at York are shown to be particularly important in his increasing ease with technological affordances and understanding of how new developments could be harnessed in his scores, something that is particularly apparent in the toolkit scores of the late 1980s that are discussed in Chapter 3. The second part of this chapter focuses on Jones's engagement with student film projects and his work with other students at the National Film School (now the National Film and Television School) in London and takes *The Black Angel* (1980) and *The Dollar Bottom* (1981) as case studies. These projects gesture towards the development of a compositional voice that can be seen to anticipate two broad trends in Jones's use of musical language: the creation of atmospheric soundscapes including film music toolkits and his large symphonic scores with clear melodic themes. They also mark the beginning of Jones's lifelong engagement with new technologies, particularly the synthesiser, and throughout this book the influence of technological developments and the connections that he made in his student years and early graduate work are shown to have shaped Jones's career development.

Early life and musical education

Trevor Jones was born in Cape Town, South Africa in 1949 and grew up in the inner-city District Six area, a neighbourhood that had a tough reputation. Music and film provided a means of escape from a harsh environment for him, and as a child he was a keen cinema-goer, sometimes skipping school to go to his local cinema. Even at the age of six he knew that he wanted to compose music for film (Carte Blanche 2014). Jones's mother worked as a machinist at Rex Trueform but could not afford to pay school fees for her three children; fortunately, Jones won a scholarship that allowed him to attend high school. His grandmother's piano provided an introduction to the instrument, and at seventeen he auditioned for the

Royal Academy of Music in London and was awarded a scholarship for one year. Following a long boat journey from South Africa to Southampton, Jones's suitcase fell into the harbour while being unloaded, and he began his new life in Britain with minimal possessions.

At the Royal Academy of Music Jones was able to develop as a performer in a conservatoire environment, taking piano lessons with Harry Isaacs (1902–72) and composition classes with John Gardner (1917–2011) between 1969 and 1970. Subsequently he worked in reviewing, cataloguing and recording services at the BBC for a further four years, where he developed strong technical skills in tandem with continuing part-time studies at the Academy. Jones was initially employed as a record filer at the BBC and, following promotion, became a classical cataloguer in the Gramophone Library. He orchestrated popular music in his spare time for commercial purposes and composed a children's school mass. Thus he was developing experience of orchestration from an early age, a skill that would prove invaluable in his future career (Sorrell 2015). While at the BBC, he applied to study on an undergraduate programme at the University of York, a decision that was shaped by a meeting at the BBC with Wilfrid Mellers, a founding member of the department of music at York. Mellers was impressed with Jones's musicality and recommended him for their degree programme. Jones described the significance of York in his education:

> The course at York was designed really to fill in gaps in my musical education which the Academy hadn't dealt with: ethnic music, rock, jazz, pop, avant-garde, 20th century, electronic, all kinds of music.
> (Fox and Cooper 2008, p. 1)

During his degree studies from 1974 to 1977, it was apparent that Jones, who was registered as a mature student, was already an outstanding pianist and had a high-profile teacher in Yonty Solomon. While an undergraduate Jones studied open form with Richard Orton (who had introduced the electronic studio to the university), producing a realisation of Cardew's *Octet 61*. On the musicology course he completed a Beethoven string quartet module led by the composer David Blake, a Bach and Beethoven module led by Mellers, and engaged with ethnomusicology with Neil Sorrell. He also performed a solo piano recital and undertook studies in acoustics. While he appears to have been regarded by his tutors at York principally as a talented pianist, the university's distinctive degree structure allowed him to shape his course according to his interests. The University of York's undergraduate programme in Music was atypical at its inception for three main reasons: firstly, it had no final examinations; secondly, its practical project system allowed students to focus on in-depth topics of their choosing provided that there was adequate supervision available; and thirdly, the music history syllabus did not follow a traditional linear chronology from the Middle Ages to the present day. Jones worked on two practical projects that enabled him to draw together various strands of history, composition, and technology: one was a Chinese Revolutionary Opera led by David Blake, and the other was a production of Satie's *Relâche* led by David

Kershaw (Sorrell 2015). Jones's technical knowhow and practical skills were praised by Kershaw, and Jones expressed an interest in further research in aspects of film following his degree (Sorrell 2015). Engagement with Satie also seems to have had an early impact on his creative approach; in recent interviews, he has highlighted the influence of this composer on his musical style, noting the impact of recurring motifs in a cyclical pattern without a discernible melody that an audience may respond to subliminally (Jones 2014b). Jones's interest in film and television scoring also shaped his decision to investigate this area in his solo project during the spring term of 1977. For this independent research module, he worked on a film about the department of music at York and wrote an essay about the differences between television and film as media.

The degree programme equipped Jones with an understanding of a broad range of styles and further experience of the use of electronics. Indeed, York had a reputation for being at the cutting edge of contemporary composition at this time with a number of high-profile composers on the staff or in visiting roles. They included English-American Bernard Rands, who had studied with Pierre Boulez and was known for his modernist style; David Blake, who had studied with Hanns Eisler; David Kershaw who taught composition with a particular interest in film; and Elizabeth Lutyens (1906–83) who became composer in residence in 1976. Rands had interviewed Jones for his place at York in February 1974 and noted his maturity and obvious talent with potential for development at York (Sorrell 2015). While Jones had varying levels of contact with these composers, he particularly recalled the impact of conversations with Lutyens and how they afforded him rich insights into the world of film scoring (Fox and Cooper 2008). Musically influenced by Webern, Lutyens scored for film and television extensively and is best known in this regard for her work in the horror genre, notably the *Hammer Horror* films. Traces of her influence can be found in Jones's work from the late 1980s and early 1990s on films such as *Angel Heart* and *Freejack*, where he created atmospheric horror/thriller scores using 'toolkits' of synthesised sounds.[1]

The National Film School

From the autumn of 1977, following his graduation from York, Jones began both to study and to work as a teacher at the UK National Film School (now the National Film and Television School, or NFTS) in Beaconsfield, and he became involved with scoring student films there. The NFTS encouraged its students to create companies to facilitate individual film projects, which allowed them to experience real-world film-making conditions within a supportive environment, and Jones has highlighted how this approach facilitated his move into the industry:

> The importance of the film school for me was that the transition to the industry was almost imperceptible. It didn't matter to us whether we were working on film-school projects or on small commercial projects. [. . .] We would set up a company specifically for a particular short-film project and try to raise money to make it. The company would be disbanded after the film was made.

So whenever anyone had a project they'd start a company and find likeminded film-makers to join them in order to complete the project.

(Jones 2014b)

The NFTS has preserved records of its student films from this period, and those for which Jones was credited as composer are listed in Table 1.1 along with their different narrative themes and the festivals at which they were exhibited. In addition, Jones recalls using the NFTS library to access a number of short films made by former students that he used as compositional exercises, noting that:

> the scores were written but at best only realized as piano versions. The exercises not only served to develop my compositional ideas about themes and how they could be varied to pertain to scenes in an on-going narrative, but also to developing a writing style and sound for a particular genre and how these themes could be varied in the context of the narrative.
>
> (Jones 2018)

Jones occupied more than the role of composer on several of the projects that he scored for his contemporaries, helping the lighting team, operating the camera and getting involved during both the pre-production and post-production stages. This knowledge of all aspects of film-making would support his later working relationships, equipping him with a shared language and understanding that he has used in discussions with film-makers and production teams across his career. His development of toolkits to enable Alan Parker to make musical decisions about the sound worlds of his films (see Chapter 3), the process of discussing the director's vision for *Notting Hill* (see Chapter 5) and Jones's pivotal relationship with the music editor on *Thirteen Days* (see Chapter 6) are all cases in point. Films of this early period notable for their musical content include *Smile Until I Tell You to Stop* (1979) and *The Stranger* (1980), the scores for both of which include stylistic elements that anticipate his work on later films. *Smile Until I Tell You to Stop*, for instance, employs sounds including chimes and what is described in the Jones Archive as a 'synth bong', while *The Stranger* combines a string quartet and electronic sounds, a common combination for Jones and one found in his first professional project after film school, *The Black Angel*.

The Black Angel (1980)

Jones met Roger Christian at the National Film School and would go on to collaborate with him on advertisements and on three films: his directorial debut *The Black Angel*, the Oscar-winning short film *The Dollar Bottom* (1981) and *The Sender* (1982). Christian was best known for his work in the art department for *Star Wars: A New Hope* (1977) and garnered the financial support of George Lucas for *The Black Angel*, which was planned for exhibition before *Star Wars: The Empire Strikes Back* (1980) in selected UK cinemas. Jones enjoyed his collaboration with

Table 1.1 Student films scored by Jones at the National Film School

Title and Medium	Running Time	Director	Year	NFTS Plot Summary	Exhibition
The Night of the Captain (16mm)	35 mins	Luis Mora del Solar	1978	A captain of the Chilean Navy comes to London for a training course to find out he is suspected of treason. He has a crisis of conscience, as he has been instrumental in a murder, and he deserts.	Edinburgh 1978 Bilbao 1978
The Beneficiary (16mm)	47 mins	Carlo Gebler	1979	An adaptation of a Chekov short story, *The Beneficiary* is set in the west of Ireland at the turn of the century. A poor dowry-less girl is married into the family of a prosperous local shopkeeper. Denied her inheritance, she takes her revenge.	Edinburgh/ London 1979 Berlio (Celtic) 1980 Mannheim 1980
Smile Until I Tell You to Stop (16mm)	20 mins	Stephen Bayly	1979	A group of stage kids refuse to jump the hoops at a film audition. Using the paraphernalia of the film studio as toy weapons, they bring the auditions to a chaotic close.	Special Mention Lille 1980 Cape Town 1981
The Stranger (35mm)[2]	18 mins	Ian Knox	1980	On Christmas Eve, a self-assured young woman confronts an old friend whose impassiveness has threatening implications for her comfortable existence. She is forced to re-interpret events in this psychological game in which questions are answered by silence.	Thessaloniki 1981 London 1981 Chicago Certificate of Merit 1981
A Stolen Portrait (16mm)	39 mins	Brian Ward	1981	An actress and a painter meet again, four years after a traumatic break-up. In an isolated cottage in the West Highlands, their memories of a past life together in London begin to illuminate the tensions of their present situation.	

Christian and recalled the creative freedom afforded to him by the director's open brief for the music on projects:

> Roger was very exciting to work with because he allowed me to suggest styles of music, or he left pretty much the kind of stylistic decisions about the score, and in fact where to put music on the film, he left that pretty much to me; it was quite an open brief.
>
> (Jones 2014b)

The Black Angel is the tale of Sir Maddox, a knight who returns from the Crusades to discover that his family have died as a result of disease and his estates have been destroyed. Lost and bereft, he stops by a lake with his horse and accidentally falls in, dragged down by a mysterious current. His death is prevented by the intervention of a young woman (played by Christian's wife Patricia) who begs Death to allow her to take Sir Maddox's place. Saved, the knight wishes to repay the woman by saving her from her master, the eponymous black angel. The rest of the film charts his quest to find the black angel and do battle with him. Ultimately, the knight succeeds in freeing the maiden, though he pays for it with his own life.

Jones was provided with a screenplay and a rough cut of the film to aid his composition, and owing to the small scale of the project, he called on friends to participate in the realisation of the orchestral parts. This perhaps explains the slightly idiosyncratic ensemble employed in the film – voices, piccolo/flute, trumpet theorbo/guitar, strings, keyboard and percussion – as outlined on the track sheet in Figure 1.1. Jones was also involved in the post-production phase of the project, contributing to the balancing of the music with the other elements in the soundscape when the film was dubbed (Jones 2014b).

The Trevor Jones Archive contains audio files from the recording sessions and paperwork relating to the film. There are 48kHz 24-bit recordings, stereo transfers of the final mix, and three two-inch sixteen-track transfer tapes, the contents of which are outlined in Table 1.2.

One of the most interesting aspects these cues is the insight that they provide into the recording process. It is evident that most of those involved are learning about the process while carrying it out, and there are several dialogues between Jones and the musicians about how best to achieve the intended effects with their instruments. This is particularly notable in relation to cue 2M5 in which the string players discuss with Jones how to tackle the bowing most effectively during a fast-paced sequence; as indicated in Table 1.2, two takes of this cue were recorded with the strings played 'wild', without any form of click track or timing aid. This close involvement with the recording sessions would remain typical of many of Jones's subsequent projects, with similar engagement in *Excalibur* (1981), *Labyrinth* (1986), *Brassed Off* (1996) and *Notting Hill* (1999), notably with regard to the recording of pre-existing music in these pictures.

Studying the archival paperwork in conjunction with listening to the audio files exposes the fact that some of Jones's music was placed at different narrative points from those originally intended by the composer. For example, Jones wrote

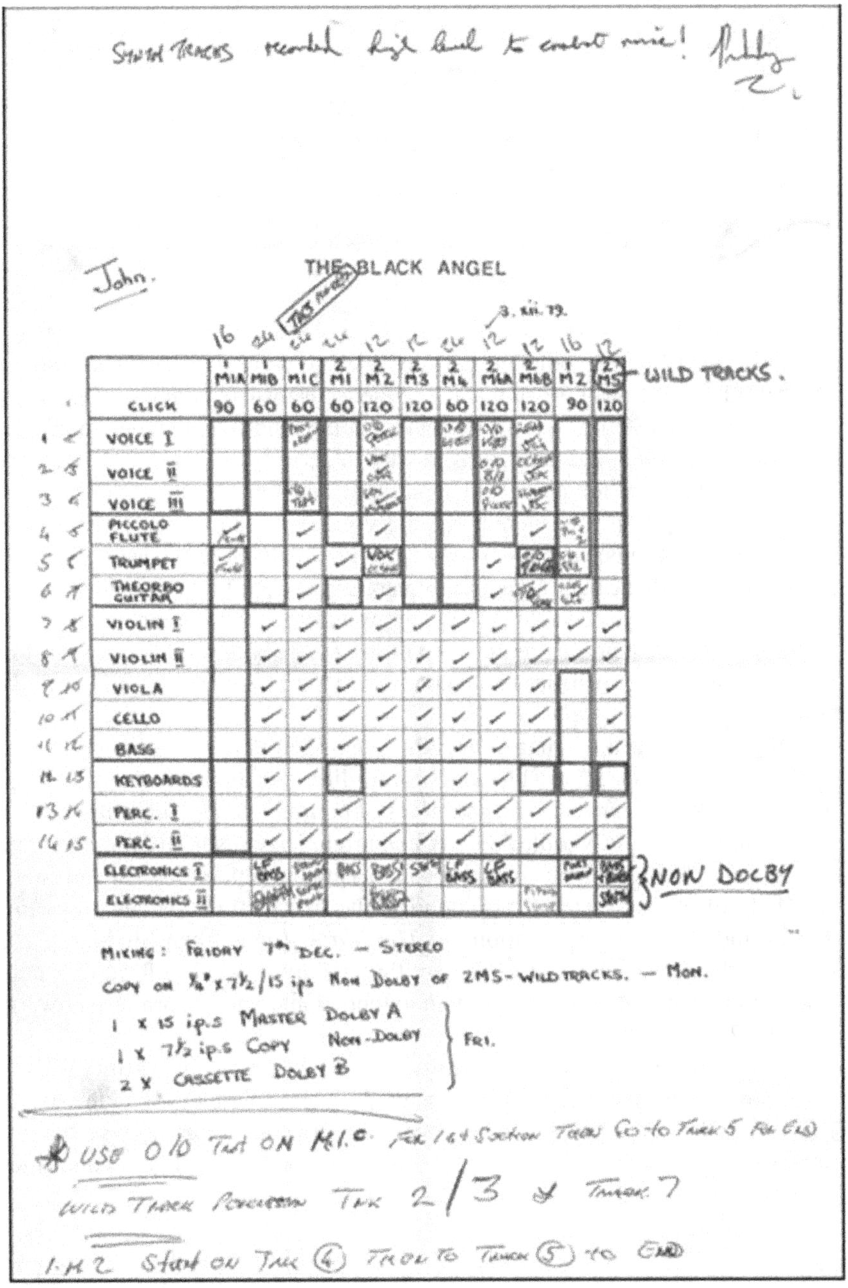

Figure 1.1 Track sheet showing the breakdown of instrumentation for each cue of *The Black Angel*

Table 1.2 Breakdown of audio recordings across the three sixteen-track two-inch tapes for *The Black Angel*

Tape	Audio Recordings
One	M1B; M1C; 2M1; 2M5
Two	2M3 takes 1 and 4; 2M4 take 1; 2M6B takes 1–5
Three	1M2 takes 1–2; 2M5 takes 1 and 3; wild track strings only 2M5 takes 1–2; wild track 4 take 1; M1A takes 1–2 and 4–12; wind chimes, crotales on timps, timps and bass drum take 1; mark 3 take 1

a cue for the climactic battle scene between the black angel and Sir Maddox, but the music heard at this point in the final picture comprises electronic sound effects and a low drone note so that the sequence is instead largely accompanied by sound design (Stemp 2015b). It seems that the music he intended to accompany the fight scene, cue 2M5, was moved to accompany a journey sequence after Sir Maddox has left his ruined homestead, and Jones notes that this change and the resulting sequence were particularly influential in his understanding of the power of film music to suggest what may not be visible onscreen. He recalls a child in the audience at a Leicester Square screening of the film, drawing her father's attention to Sir Maddox travelling through the forest even though he was not onscreen. The combination of the editing of the shots and the presence of Jones's transplanted music implied a continuous journey, enhancing the narrative (Jones 2014b).

In terms of musical language, the influence of *The Black Angel* can be traced forward to *Excalibur* (1981), which was directed by John Boorman and released the following year. The narratives of both *The Black Angel* and *Excalibur* are situated in the Middle Ages, which might have inspired Jones to create similar musical atmospheres for scenes involving the supernatural and mysterious 'lady of the lake' characters found in the two pictures. He employs low drones under choral vocalisations in *The Black Angel* when Sir Maddox is saved by the mysterious water maiden, the melody taking the form of a five-note phrase that is then repeated in an extended and varied form as shown in Figure 1.2.

This can be compared to the scene in *Excalibur* in which King Arthur dishonestly defeats Lancelot in battle by calling on the supernatural power of the sword. This causes the sword to break in half, and the distraught Arthur throws it into the stream. The lady of the lake repairs the sword and returns it to him accompanied

Figure 1.2 Aural transcription of the main theme from *The Black Angel*

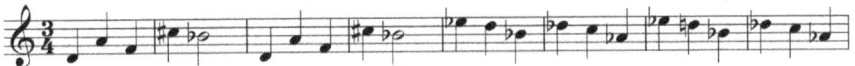

Figure 1.3 Lady of the Lake theme from *Excalibur*

by an eerie cue, the melody of which is shown in Figure 1.3. While the theme from *Excalibur* is undoubtedly more chromatically adventurous, there are some similarities, including beginning with a five-note phrase that ends with a descending minor third/augmented second. Equally, from the point of view of timbre, the scene is characterised in a similar way to *The Black Angel* by the use of a low drone with the melody presented vocally.

The Black Angel's influence can also be heard in a much later project in Jones's career, *War Paint*, a short film made in 2011.[3] Jones took the falling chromatic motif that appears during the knight's drowning scene and developed it in this later film for a scene of psychological anguish suffered by the leading character. While the characters and specific contexts vary considerably between *The Black Angel* and *War Paint*, in both cases the material accompanies a sequence highlighting the distress of the picture's protagonist, demonstrating Jones's understanding of the ways in which music can be inflected and adapted to support similar situations within different filmic genres and narratives.

The Dollar Bottom (1981)

Directed by Roger Christian and produced by Lloyd Phillips, *The Dollar Bottom* won an Academy Award for best live action short film and was nominated for a BAFTA award. It is the tale of a Scottish schoolboy, Taylor, who decides to set up an insurance company to compensate his fellow boarding schoolboys when they are subjected to caning. Each boy takes out an insurance policy for sixpence and if beaten is awarded ten shillings. The venture proves to be such a remarkable success that children in other Scottish schools wish to follow suit and take out similar policies. Taylor is somewhat dismayed by some of the boys' attempts to disrupt classes to provoke punishment, thereby securing the accompanying compensation, the decision of other pupils to float the business on a student stock market, and the repeated attempts of the schoolteachers to quash his fledgling business. The company is finally wound down when they mistakenly issue insurance to prefects who cannot be beaten and thus overstretch themselves financially as soon as the teachers spot the weakness and threaten to beat the prefects to bust the business. Not to be outwitted, Taylor finds a neat solution to this dilemma, encouraging all the boys involved to spend their capital at the school tuck shop, moving the money beyond the reach of the teachers.

The screenplay for *The Dollar Bottom* was written by Shane Connaughton, who adapted James Kennaway's short story of the same name. Roger Pratt was the lighting cameraman, and Richard Trevor was the editor. Jones composed and conducted the score, which was recorded at Trevor Pyke Sound Ltd in London, with post-production carried out at The Production Village in Cricklewood, London. The music recordist was John Richards from the Wembley Music Centre. The film contains original music by Jones and some pre-existing music, including one piece of source music, the song 'Isn't it Romantic?' sung by Ella Fitzgerald, which places the film musically into the 1950s. The track sheet for the film, which has a similar basic layout to that of *The Black Angel*, is shown in Figure 1.4 and reveals the required instrumentation for Jones's cues.

Jones employed three recorders, two violins, viola, cello, percussion, and keyboards which, while still a relatively unusual ensemble, is perhaps more timbrally coherent than that for *The Black Angel*. As with the earlier picture, the score is based around one main theme, but the soundscape of *The Dollar Bottom* is very different to the previous film. Musical signifiers for Scottishness imbue the score and reflect the narrative setting. Thus, the theme can be heard as evocative of traditional Scottish music owing to its modal sound and the frequent use of the Scotch snap (inverted dotted) rhythm. The modality, stepwise movement and open fifths in the harmony could also be linked to Jones's later composition of a melody

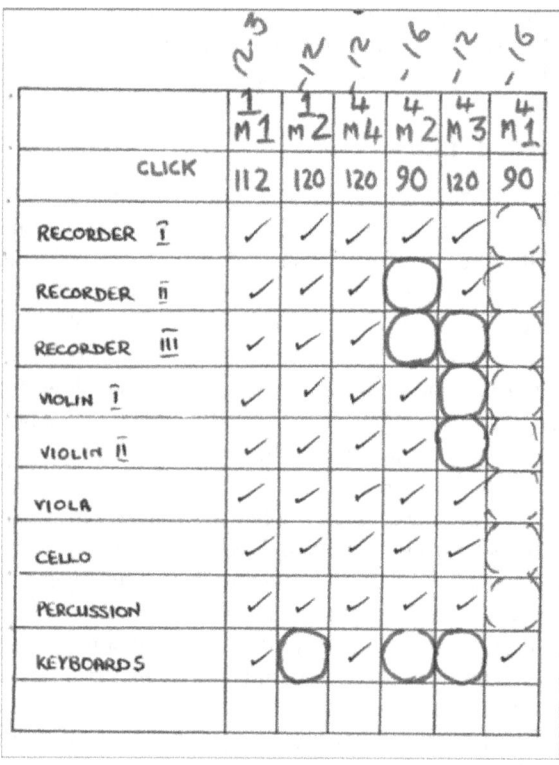

Figure 1.4 Extract from a track sheet for *The Dollar Bottom* showing the required instrumentation

for Igrayne's dance sequence in *Excalibur*, which is likewise based on a stepwise modal melody and indeed to what Rebecca Fülöp has called 'the Celtic Old-World European musical flavour' (2017, p. 463) of his main title theme for *The Last of the Mohicans* (1992). The theme and its variations provide the basis for the six main cues in *The Dollar Bottom*: 1M1 'Opening Titles'; 1M2 'Knox Celebrates'; 4M1 'Boys in Classroom'; 4M2 'Walk to the Gymnasium'; 4M3 'Taylor Leads Company'; and 4M4 'End Sequence and End Credits'.

As their names indicate, the cues are used at the key narrative points in the film, heightening the excitement once the boys launch their company and increasing the tension when it is threatened. Further reinforcing the markers of Scottishness, Jones used bagpipes at two instances in the film, firstly when Mr Cuddlestone complains to the Housemaster about Taylor's scheme and secondly when Taylor tells his friends that they are temporarily in the clear after a meeting with the Headmaster. The pipes are recorded at a much lower volume than the six cues listed above, and their effect could be described as reinforcing the setting for the events rather than moving the narrative forward.

Development of a distinctive filmic voice

Comparing *The Black Angel* and *The Dollar Bottom*, it becomes apparent that they present contrasting compositional voices. While it would be overly simplistic to suggest that Jones's musical approach can be neatly categorised into different styles, broadly speaking his musical language in these early films anticipates two approaches that he would go on to develop in many of his subsequent projects. There are very clear links between *The Black Angel* and *Excalibur*, but more generally the earlier film foreshadows Jones's development of atmospheric soundscapes, his interest in film sound design, and his toolkits for films such as *Angel Heart* (1987), *Mississippi Burning* (1988) and *Sea of Love* (1989). By contrast, *The Dollar Bottom*, with its clear, singable melody, folk-tune style and richer orchestration, can be situated as a forerunner of Jones's large symphonic scores for films such as *Cliffhanger* (1993) and *Loch Ness* (1996), as well as anticipating the use of folksongs and folk styles in a range of scores across Jones's career.

These films sit at a pivotal point for Jones, marking his transition from student to professional film composer, and his early compositional experiences at the University of York and the National Film School can be heard through the recording sessions and in the resulting film soundscapes. The dialogue with musicians reveals a young composer finding his way in the industry and polishing his idiomatic use of instruments, and his musical language at this point clearly foreshadows elements of the style that he would develop in his subsequent scores. Perhaps most significantly, *The Black Angel* and *The Dollar Bottom* nurtured collaborative and creative connections between Jones and professionals who would go on to become leaders in the industry. Through the working relationship with Christian, Jones came to collaborate with Roger Pratt (known for being the director of photography on Tim Burton's *Batman* (1989) and two *Harry Potter* films [2002, 2005]) and Gary Kurtz. Jones and Pratt worked together again on *The Sender* (1982), and Kurtz, who was the producer for *Star Wars: A New Hope* (1977), introduced the composer to Jim Henson, leading to their collaboration on *The Dark Crystal* and *Labyrinth*. Indeed, as Jones has stated, these early collaborations and projects facilitated 'a very smooth transition into the industry' (Fox and Cooper 2008, p. 2).

Notes

1 Toolkits are discussed in detail in Chapters 3 and 4.
2 The NFTS records that Jones was responsible for composing, conducting and sound design.
3 *War Paint* is considered in Chapter 9, during an examination of Jones's more recent projects.

2 Breaking into the industry

The previous chapter outlined Jones's formative education at the University of York and the National Film and Television School, exploring his first professional screen compositions for the short films *The Black Angel* (1980) and *The Dollar Bottom* (1981). Employing the earliest materials in the archive relating to professional work in the film and television industries proper, this chapter shows how his composition for student films provided a solid foundation for his scores of the early to mid-1980s. Concurrent developments such as the advent of digital sampling technologies and MIDI supported Jones's interest in experimental approaches to film music; he was already well versed in using the VCS3 and Prophet 5 synthesisers (as heard in *The Black Angel*), and he continued engaging with emerging technologies in his breakthrough scores.

This chapter considers his approach and his musical language for John Boorman's *Excalibur* (1981), the animatronic films of Jim Henson – *The Dark Crystal* (1982) and *Labyrinth* (1986) – and the television mini-series *The Last Days of Pompeii* (1984) and *The Last Place on Earth* (1985). For *Excalibur*, Jones crafted a score that combined original material with extracts from works by Richard Wagner and Carl Orff, creating a coherent and powerful musical tapestry for Boorman's presentation of the Arthurian legend. By contrast, the music for *The Dark Crystal* fused symphonic writing with experimental sounds representing the fictional and fantastical world in which the narrative is set. The archival materials for *Excalibur* and *The Dark Crystal* include a large number of reels of multitrack tape from recording sessions and offer significant insight into Jones's working methods and practices at the outset of his career. The music for *The Last Days of Pompeii* and *The Last Place on Earth* shows the continued maturing of Jones's compositional approach and sonic style as these larger television projects afforded him opportunities to develop his strategy for television scoring and adopt more of his filmic practices when writing for the small screen. By contrast, *Labyrinth* presented Jones with the chance to work in a popular-music idiom for the first time in his scoring career. The picture starred David Bowie, who performs on the film's soundtrack, and this project marked the first time that Jones collaborated with an established pop star on a film, something that he has done many times since across his career. Through exploration of these scores, this chapter establishes compositional approaches and uses of technology that Jones developed across his first decade in the industry and that became a distinctive part of his method.

Breakthrough scores: *Excalibur* (1981) and *The Dark Crystal* (1982)

Directed and produced by John Boorman and based on the fifteenth-century story *Le Morte d'Arthur* by Sir Thomas Malory, *Excalibur* was Boorman's eighth project and is generally considered to be Jones's breakthrough film. The film was shot on location in Ireland and released by Orion Pictures in 1981. Boorman had a long fascination with Arthurian legend prior to making this film and stated in interview that he felt that, 'we are attracted to the legend of the Grail because it speaks to us of a period when nature was unsullied and man in harmony with it' (Ciment 1986, p. 188). Revolving around the eponymous sword, the film's plot charts its acquisition by a young Arthur and the subsequent adventures of the Knights of the Round Table. The central romance between Arthur's wife Guinevere and the champion knight Lancelot is the catalyst for a period of sickness in the kingdom, which can only be cured when Perceval finds the Holy Grail.

As already noted, *Excalibur* combines pre-existing music by Wagner and Orff with Jones's original score. Music from Wagner's operas is used very heavily throughout the film, the Prelude to *Parsifal*, the Prelude to *Tristan and Isolde*, and 'Siegfried's Funeral March' from *Götterdämmerung*, the final part of *The Ring*, being specially recorded for the soundtrack by The London Philharmonic Orchestra under the baton of Norman Del Mar. In particular, the *Tristan* Prelude is used to underscore Lancelot and Guinevere's love for each other, as might be expected given its context in Wagner's opera. A 1937 recording of the Leipzig Radio Symphony Orchestra and Chorus conducted by Herbert Kegel performing 'O Fortuna' from Orff's *Carmina Burana* accompanies key plot points where Arthur marshals his knights to ride into battle. These scenes mark significant plot developments for which 'O Fortuna', with its theme of fate and power, seems eminently suitable. The film's mixture of pre-existing music with Jones's original score may have been shaped by Boorman's attitude to the historical setting of the legend, for as he remarked:

> What is at stake is the myth. The other dilemma is that much of the legend is associated with a twelfth-century setting, with knights in armour and jousting and so on; the poets who wrote about it incorporated the values of their own period. [. . .] I don't think one can go against that – the context is too deep-rooted, too familiar. What I had to do – with my set designer, Tony Pratt – was include the iconography and, at the same time, play with it by creating a 'Middle-earth', and in the sense intended by Tolkien in *The Lord of the Rings*: which is to say, a parallel world, similar to our own but somehow different, with numerous allusions to the Middle Ages. [. . .] What is essential, then, is not to refute the myth, but to refresh it.
>
> (Ciment 1986, p. 196)

The director noted how Wagner's music was a strong influence on the work from the early stages but that the decision to use extracts from his operas for certain scenes in the film was taken with Jones's full agreement:

I saw *The Ring* at Bayreuth in Patrice Chéreau's production and was deeply impressed by it; my impressions have stayed with me undiminished, ever since. Wagner's music served as a guide in the early stages of my work. I didn't think of actually using it at the beginning but, little by little, in agreement with Trevor Jones, I decided that it would be suitable for certain passages; it was very well integrated into Jones's own score. Together we selected extracts from 'Siegfried's Death' in *Götterdämmerung*, the prelude to *Tristan and Isolde*, for the love story, and the prelude to *Parsifal*, which I've always adored, with those ineffable chords that raise the spirit up and, in the film, become the motif of the quest for the Grail.

(Ciment 1986, p. 200)

Manfred Giampietro suggests that the placement of the Wagner extracts marks the timeline of the story into death, love, and rebirth; 'Siegfried's Funeral March' bookends the film and appears for scenes of death, while extracts from *Parsifal* are, as Boorman notes, used for the search for the Grail (Giampietro 2014). Giampietro argues that, 'Boorman is thus able to maximise the use of his means insofar as the musical pieces within the film are used as "concentrated" references from a multitude of worlds'. His argument highlights the extent to which pre-existing music was used to imbue the film with layers of meaning and even to elevate and canonise this representation of the myth. Boorman's other intention was to 'refresh' the myth, and Jones's music can be heard to fulfil this aim. Jones's engagement with new technologies to create innovative and unusual timbres displays the influence of the avant-garde, and his employment of extended techniques for selected woodwind and string parts recasts recognisable and understood sounds in new and interesting ways.

Before exploring Jones's musical language in more detail, it is helpful to consider the balance and placement of his music in relation to the borrowings from Wagner and Orff. Table 2.1 outlines the music utilised at important plot points in the film, highlighting the heavy use of pre-existing music. It demonstrates that, broadly speaking, Jones's music tends to be reserved for scenes of music making within the film and those that explore the power of the supernatural. The titles of the Wagner extracts in Table 2.1 have been abbreviated to Siegfried (for the Funeral March), *Parsifal* and *Tristan* (for the respective preludes) for clarity.

The archive contains forty-seven original cues in addition to the recordings of 'Siegfried's Funeral March', the Prelude to *Parsifal*, the Prelude to *Tristan*, and sound effects recorded on a Fairlight workstation.[1] The recording and mixing sessions took place between March 1980 and February 1981, with music for the dance sequences recorded earliest (March and April 1980), presumably to be used during the shooting of those scenes. The paperwork relating to the film includes lists of samples to be recorded, both of sound effects and of scales and chords played by guitarist Michael Lewin, which are used heavily in cue 1M3 ('Ygrayne's Dance'). Creating samples and using the Fairlight to record sound effects in this way was highly innovative, and it emphasises Jones's experimental approach to compositional practice. It permitted the composer to manipulate and mix the samples once they had been recorded, resulting in him producing complex dance sequences for the film.

Table 2.1 Music used at key plot points in *Excalibur*

Key Plot Point	Music (Pre-existing; Jones)
Opening credits and battle between Uther and the Duke of Cornwall	Wagner: Siegfried, b. 9–25 dovetailed with b. 36–49
Merlin summons the sword out of the lake	Wagner: Siegfried, b. 19–25
Ygrayne's dance at Cornwall's party	Jones: Ygrayne's dance
Merlin casts the Charm of Making	Jones: Synthesiser
Uther rides to Cornwall's Castle	Jones: Lady of the Lake theme
Uther drives Excalibur into the stone	Wagner: Siegfried, b. 16–21
Joust	Jones: Female voice with crumhorn
Arthur pulls the sword out of the stone first time	Wagner: Siegfried, b. 16–17
Arthur pulls the sword out of the stone second time	Wagner: Siegfried, b. 42–44
Arthur chases Merlin	Jones: Wordless voice, strings, and synth
Arthur and the Knights ride to Leondegrance's aid	Orff: 'O Fortuna'
Arthur is knighted	Wagner: Siegfried, b. 23–30
Party at which Arthur falls in love with Guinevere	Jones: Music derived from Ygrayne's Dance
Lady of the Lake mends Excalibur	Jones: Lady of the Lake theme
Arthur forms the round table	Wagner: Siegfried, b. 36–44
Guinevere sees Lancelot for the first time	Wagner: *Tristan*, b. 8–11
Lancelot declares 'While you live I will love no other'	Wagner: *Tristan*, b. 16–17
Arthur and Guinevere's wedding	Jones: Choral music with a Latin text
First sight of Camelot	Wagner: Siegfried, b. 41–44
Lancelot sees Guinevere on the stairs with Morgana	Wagner: *Tristan*, b. 16–21
Guinevere asks why Arthur can't defend her	Wagner: *Tristan*, b. 51–63
Gawain and Percy prepare for battle	Sound Effects – Drum rolls
Lancelot leaves for the forest, followed by Guinevere	Wagner: *Tristan*, b. 71–86
Merlin declares that the world is done for him	Wagner: Siegfried, b. 4–12
Shows Morgana the cave, intercut with scene of Lancelot and Guinevere	Wagner: *Tristan*, b. 45–55; Wagner: *Tristan*, b. 64–83
Morgana traps Merlin with the charm of making	Jones: High Pitch Synthesiser
Beam of light from the Grail	Jones: Lady of the Lake theme
Mordred gets ready	Jones: Percussive music
People despair	Jones: Lady of the Lake theme
Perceval drowning, finds the Grail and restores Arthur	Wagner: *Parsifal*, b. 6–12 dovetailed into b. 20–38
Arthur recovered and moves to battle	Orff: 'O Fortuna'
Guinevere returns Excalibur to Arthur	Wagner: Siegfried, b. 24–30
Arthur calls on Merlin's help at Stonehenge	Wagner: *Parsifal*, b. 1–16
Arthur and his Knights attack Morgana's army	Orff: 'O Fortuna'
Arthur and Lancelot are reconciled	Wagner: *Parsifal*, b. 1–7
Final battle between Arthur and Mordred	Wagner: Siegfried, b. 4–12
Arthur instructs Perceval to throw Excalibur into the lake	Wagner: Siegfried, b. 18–81 (end of the march)

As noted above, the influence of Jones's earlier work can be heard in *Excalibur*, particularly in the theme for the Lady of the Lake. This melody recurs throughout the film in scenes of supernatural activity, as can be seen in Table 2.1, and is the most prevalent part of Jones's original score. Harmonically it is modal and evocative of 'ancient' music, but it is presented in different ways texturally when it reappears in the picture. For example, the descending scalar figures that accompany the theme in cue 1M2C1 (the first occasion on which the material from 1M2 is heard in the film) echo the use of similar features in the drowning scene from *The Black Angel*, but its next occurrence, 1M2C2, is quite different texturally, being homophonic with repeated open fifths accompanying a wordless high-pitched choir singing the modal melody. The diegetic music in the film mixes musical codes and instruments associated with medieval dance music with modern timbres, an element of Jones's stylistic approach that recalls his musical training at York, where there was an emphasis on electronic music and a pervasive interest in both medieval and non-Western instrumentation. Of course, the Early Music revival of the late 1960s and 1970s had seen musicians such as Christopher Hogwood and David Munrow performing regularly and broadcasting on the radio, so the sonority of instruments from the medieval and renaissance periods may already have been familiar to at least some members of the listening public.

All of the dance sequences in the film are derived from Jones's material for 'Ygrayne's Dance'. In triple time, the melody is played on flute with guitar accompaniment, ending with repeated ascending scalar figures as the dance reaches its climax with a double-speed rendition of the theme. The cue, 1M3, was recorded wild – with no reference to the picture, which had not yet been shot, and without clicks or audible timing aids – perhaps in order to capture a freer performance and style that would be more appropriate for a diegetic dance sequence than something kept rigidly in time. The crumhorn features heavily in cue 3M2, which underscores Arthur's search for a sword in the joust scene, perhaps reinforcing the film's twelfth-century context, but although Jones employs instruments associated with medieval music (including the lute, crumhorn and recorder) for these sequences, he often combines them with extended techniques, taking them out of their normal environments. For example, in 1M4 he combines a drone with *sul ponticello* violins playing out of their usual register, while 2M1 features overblown flutes combined with a wordless choir and synthesiser, all of which show Jones adhering to Boorman's idea of 'refreshing' the myth through his musical score.

Considering the relationship between pre-existing music and original score for *Excalibur*, it is clear that Jones does not attempt to emulate or integrate his material with Wagner's or Orff's musical language, and his cues are audibly distinctive from the well-known operas and cantata. Yet, on a stylistic level he adopts a similar approach to scoring a legendary text: in the same way that Wagner's and Orff's compositions carry their own musical codes of ancient myths and poetry refreshed by the contemporary musical language of their respective composers, Jones's cues also allude to an earlier period – the Middle Ages – rejuvenated through the use of twentieth-century extended techniques and emerging technologies. Crucially for his development as a film composer, it is clear that Jones succeeded in delivering a score that addressed the director's wishes for the film, playing with and reinvigorating the myth without refuting or unsettling the twelfth-century setting. His ability to accurately represent a director's vision of a world through an original score was again highlighted the following year, though Jim Henson's world for *The Dark Crystal* was in no way related to any era of Earth's history, actual or mythologised.

The initial development of *The Dark Crystal* paralleled Jones's studies at the National Film and Television School, and his work with Gary Kurtz on *The Black Angel* led to an introduction to Jim Henson in September 1980. Kurtz would become Henson's producer on the film, and the associate producer, Duncan Kenworthy, arranged for Jones to have another meeting with Henson, which led to his employment on this project (Benitez 2004a). At that time Henson was best known for *The Muppet Show* television series, and *The Dark Crystal* was to be his first major animatronic feature film. Set on an unnamed fictional planet, the film's narrative concerns a battle between good and evil characters, the gentle Mystics and the cruel Skeksis, respectively. The Skeksis derive their power from the life-giving dark crystal, which has been broken and is in their possession. In a similar manner to *The Lord of the Rings* and, perhaps more pertinently in this case, *Star Wars*, the film charts the quest of an unlikely hero. Jen, a young elf-like creature known as a Gelfling, who has been raised by the Mystics, embarks on an adventure to repair the broken crystal, thus restoring the power of the Mystics and defeating the Skeksis. Along the way he befriends another orphan Gelfling, Kira, who joins his quest and becomes the principal love interest.

Henson started with the visual world of the film and let the story grow around it. He happened to see the printed work of fantasy illustrator Brian Froud in 1976 and invited him to be the conceptual designer on the film, a role that involved Froud providing the production designers with illustrations for the world and its characters, which they then realised in their workshops. The Henson Production Company was founded in London in 1978 for the purposes of developing the project, but it took a further three years to work out the plot, write the screenplay and secure the necessary funding from Paramount to allow filming to begin in April 1981 for a period of six months. Relative to industry norms, Jones was involved early in the project, attending a week of meetings with the team in February 1981 and developing the music in parallel with filming. Jones drew inspiration from Henson's early sketches, the script and the puppet workshop and planned initially to create a score that would be as innovative as the images and would involve experimentation with sound. However, Kurtz suggested strongly that the music should adopt the symphonic sound of Classic Hollywood films, a style with which audiences would already be familiar (Larson 1986/1987).

Jones recalled in interview that Henson liked the music intended for the Mystics and Skeksis characters so much that he used it while shooting the scenes, playing it back on set (Benitez 2004a). The composer worked for eighteen months on the music for *The Dark Crystal*, an exceptionally long time to spend on a film project, recording ambient music for use when shooting and then rescoring the movie as needed to fit the final cut from the editing room (Benitez 2004a). As with *Excalibur*, it appears that some of the first musical cues recorded were those intended for scenes of music making within the film. This was particularly necessary given the puppetry in the film since it would have been more complicated to compose music for such scenes later in the process. The archive reflects this long working process with recording sessions from March, April, and May 1981 and January and February 1982 when the London Symphony Orchestra were employed to record the final score. Evidently, the work on this film dovetailed with finishing work on the previous project, and Jones also appears to have worked on other smaller projects in this period including *The Appointment* (1981), *The Sender* (1982) and the television programme *Joni Jones* (1982).

The musical style of *The Dark Crystal* can be considered within the broader context of film scoring of this period, which has often been characterised as marking a return to a traditional symphonic style for science fiction, most notably through the work of John Williams for the original *Star Wars* trilogy (1977–83). The comparison seems particularly apt given the setting of both *Star Wars* and *The Dark Crystal* in the distant past on far-away planets. Emilio Audissino argues that by the time Williams started to compose music for *Return of the Jedi* (1983) the 'classical' sound was accepted as one of the principal options for scoring a film (2014, p. 83). Yet, whereas Williams's *Star Wars* scores occupy a separate sonic space to the cutting-edge sound effects of sound designer Ben Burtt, Jones combines his orchestra with Fairlight and Synclavier synthesisers[2] and selected period instruments to evoke the sense that while the Gelflings, Mystic and Skeksis share human emotions, unlike many of the main characters in *Star Wars*, they are alien species.

In describing the process behind his composition of the score, Jones recalls how the experimental nature of the project as a whole gave him stylistic license to employ more unusual instruments (Jones 2016b). As was the case in *Excalibur*, he drew on period instruments for scenes of music making, choosing instruments that approximate the appearance of those played by characters in the film. For instance, Jen frequently plays an instrument with two pipes that Jones reflects in his use of either the double flageolet or recorders, an instrumentation exemplified in the melody Jones identifies as the 'Love Theme', which is first heard as Jen and Kira sail on the Black River. When Jen starts to play the theme it is initially presented on the recorder, before being taken up by the orchestra with the melody in the strings now being decorated with short figures on the recorder. The first iteration of the love theme concludes with repeated falling figures on the synthesiser reminding the audience that despite the bucolic character of the scene, the action is firmly rooted in an extra-terrestrial setting.

The effectiveness of the film's combination of futuristic timbres with those that evoke the Middle Ages for the fantasy world of *The Dark Crystal* lies in the sense of familiarity and shared memory evoked through the individually readily recognisable sounds of the orchestra, the keyboard synthesisers and the medieval instruments. It is the combination of all three that renders the score simultaneously strange yet familiar to the audience, as Kurtz advised. Arguably this instrumentation allowed Jones to succeed in his aim for the score, which was to 'bridge the gap between that world that wasn't real and the audience, giving a sense of a real world to something that is totally unreal' (Benitez 2004a). The combination is used to great effect in the scene of the dance at the Podling party. The archive allows the development of this 'pod dance' cue to be traced, revealing the changes that took place from its initial composition through to the final cut and exemplifying the iterative nature of the collaboration between director and composer. The pod dance occurs relatively early in the film, shortly after Jen has met Kira, and she introduces him to her surrogate family, the Podlings. The Podlings are observed throwing a party and the sequence includes several images of them playing instruments and dancing. The close synchronisation of the music with the images is evident in the sequence, with particular instruments coming to the forefront of the texture when the camera focuses on the musicians. Jones recalled that 'the main objective of that piece of music was to make it strange instrumentally but also to be very upbeat, to be very celebratory' (Jones 2016b). Accordingly, although the melody has a jig-like feel, it is actually written in the unusual time signature of 5/4 rather than the 6/8 usually employed for jigs, a conscious decision on the composer's part to suggest the intelligent character of the Podlings and again present the familiar and the strange simultaneously (Jones 2016b).

Table 2.2 shows the development of the pod dance cue as evidenced by recordings held in the Jones Archive. Close observation demonstrates the flexible approach adopted by Jones, changing his instrumentation and even the melody of the cue until a version was finalised that worked with the scene. The earliest version of the music for this scene in the archive is dated 26 March 1981 and is scored for an ensemble comprised of recorders, racket, finger cymbals, cello, hurdy-gurdy, vibes, drums, claves, vibraslap, tambourine and ocarina. There is no archival material that documents the directors' and producers' views of this version, but based on the changes made in the next recording it can be hypothesised that they may have found it too evocative of classical music because the version of 6 April 1981 has a stronger folk-like quality owing to the addition of a guitar and the replacement of finger cymbals with clapping and drums. In addition, the cello part is less prominent and is changed to be mainly pizzicato. However, just two days later, on 8 April, a stripped-back version of the cue was recorded with no clapping or excessive percussion, and somewhat unexpectedly a four-track mix was created that reinstated the hand claps and percussion just five days after that.

On 7 May Jones's original melody line was replaced with that which is heard in the film sequence. For this stage of the project, the archive includes mixes recorded with guide tracks for ocarina, racket and mandolin (cittern), and the track sheet for the recording session on 13 May includes a guide track for the recorders. This indicates the instrumentation used in the film, but there are three versions of the double flageolet (Jen's solo) in the recording. The first runs throughout the cue, the second is timed correctly but has the wrong feel, and the third (marked as Master) is what is actually heard in the film itself. Also on 13 May a corrected section of the cittern part was recorded on track 20 for later overdub of track 13, and five days later, on 18 May, an erroneous part of the cittern recording and the unused versions of Jen's double flageolet solo were removed from the mix, leaving the corrected sound. The final mix dates to almost a year later, 22 February 1982, and comprises five music tracks combining to form the whole cue, indicating strongly that the compositional development and recording of the cue in 1981 enabled it to

Table 2.2 Development of the pod dance from *The Dark Crystal* based on audio recordings in the archive

Date	Recordings in the Archive
26 March 1981	TDC_A_POD-DANCE_S24_C1_T1: 1:20 music TDC_A_POD-DANCE_S24_C1_T2: 1:50 music with a corresponding modal section TDC_A_POD-DANCE_S24_C1_T3: 1:10 music abruptly cut off TDC_A_POD-DANCE_S24_C1_T4: 3:05 music (complete cue). Obbligato high-pitched recorder and prominent percussion TDC_A_POD-DANCE_M4_C1_T4: Four-track mix of T4
6 April 1981	TDC_A_POD-DANCE-REMAKE-1_S24_C1_T1: Cue with string introduction and thicker textures owing to overdubbed stings and the addition of guitar and *pizzicato* cello. Finger cymbals replaced by clapping and drums. TDC_A_POD-DANCE-END-SECTION_S24_C1_T1
8 April 1981	TDC_A_POD-DANCE-REMAKE-1-DRY_M4_C1_T1: Cue in stereo mix. No clapping or excessive percussion. TDC_A_POD-DANCE-REMAKE-1-ECHO_M4_C1_T1: Cue with echo.
13 April 1981	TDC_A_POD-DANCE-MASTER-MIX_M4_C1_T1: Cue with hand claps and percussion reinstated.
7 May 1981	TDC_A_POD-DANCE-SNAKE-RANCH-STUDIOS_M4_C1_T1: Cue with melody used in film. Mix recorded with guide tracks for ocarina, racket, mandolin (cittern) and bass drum but not claves or tambourine. Guide tracks for claves and tambourine recorded at Snake Ranch Studios ahead of the next session.
13 May 1981	TDC_A_POD-DANCE-SNAKE-RANCH-STUDIOS_S24_C2_T1: The instrumentation used in the film but with three versions of the double flageolet. Corrected section of cittern part recorded on track 20 for later overdub of track 13.
18 May 1981	TDC_A_POD-DANCE-ROUGH-MONO-MIX_M4_C1_T1: Four-track mix removes the erroneous cittern part (replaces with overdubbed cittern) and also omits the unused versions of Jen's double flageolet solo.
22 Feb 1982	TDC_A_POD-DANCE-MIX-ONE_M16_C1_T1: Five tracks containing the whole cue plus count and sync, with other tracks silent.

be used alongside the filming of the sequence, with the final soundtrack captured in 1982 once the shooting and editing of the picture were complete. Tracing this cue through the archive demonstrates Jones's musical responses to feedback from his collaborators and his willingness to edit and even change completely aspects of his cues to fit a given scene better.

It is apparent from the information contained in the archive that Jones adopted similar approaches to his role on both *Excalibur* and *The Dark Crystal*, preparing diegetic music before recording the underscore and mixing medieval and orchestral instruments with electronic timbres. Yet in contrast to *Excalibur*, *The Dark Crystal* allowed him to develop an original score that did not need to be integrated with pre-existing music, and thus it challenged him to expand the scope and style of his composition. This development of skills as a film composer naturally shaped his approach to scoring television programmes, although the different medium resulted in some key differences in terms of process and musical continuity. Both film and television have played a role in his development as a composer from early in Jones's career, and he has often undertaken film and television projects at the same time – as was the case with *The Dark Crystal* and *Joni Jones* – necessitating effective compositional multi-tasking and facilitating a transfer of practices and approaches between big- and small-screen compositional projects.

Developing a filmic voice through television scoring: *The Last Days of Pompeii* (1984) and *The Last Place on Earth* (1985)

Jones embarked on his first projects for television in the late 1970s with *Britannia* and *Ripping Yarns* (both 1979), and by the mid-1980s he completed the mini-series *Joni Jones* (1982) and the made-for-television films *Those Glory, Glory Days* and *One of Ourselves* (both 1983), which are considered in more detail in Chapter 7. As with his engagement on *The Dark Crystal*, it is likely that the relationships Jones developed while at the National Film and Television School facilitated his employment as a composer for television – for example, the director of *Britannia* was one of his fellow students, John Samson – and it is also likely that his work experience at the BBC doing radio reviews developed his understanding of the corporation, supporting his transition to employment on their productions. Jones completed several television scores between his two film projects for Jim Henson, with two major mini-series – *The Last Days of Pompeii* (1984) and *The Last Place on Earth* (1985) – standing out in terms of their scale and the opportunities they afforded the composer to continue developing his style and sound.

The Last Days of Pompeii is a three-part mini-series, co-produced by Italian company Radiotelevisione Italiane and the American companies David Gerber Productions and Columbia Pictures Television and in association with Centerpoint Productions. Directed by Peter R. Hunt, it had an A-list cast including Brian Blessed, Olivia Hussey, Ned Beatty and Ernest Borgnine and featured a special appearance by Laurence Olivier. The mini-series was initially broadcast by ABC-TV in the US and later by ITV in the UK, condensed into two parts and presented on adjacent days (part one on 29 December and part two on 30 December 1984), and it has been re-run in several countries since, including on the American channel *True Stories*. It was Jones's first television project to be produced and broadcast in America (every other project up to this point had been British-made and broadcast), and was apparently the first (and, to this point, only) project of his career for which he did not meet the director, only one of the producers. They spoke on the telephone, and Jones remembers the producer's positive reaction to the opening titles: 'that's not lollipop music, that's not bubble gum music, that's music with integrity and taste' (Larson 1986/1987). This response was perhaps partly a consequence of the music being performed and recorded by the London Symphony Orchestra under the baton of Marcus Dods, as had been the case for *The Dark Crystal*, though the lack of direct communication with the director necessarily restricted the degree to which other aspects of Jones's filmic practice could be transferred directly to this television project. The three parts total five and a half hours of programming (without adverts), requiring considerable underscoring, but there is no evidence that any spotting sessions took place or that any temp tracks were provided for Jones (Hall 2017). Similarly, Jones did not attend any of the dubbing sessions as a result of the fast process of television production (Larson 1986/1987), which contrasted with his typical working methods:

> The amount of input I usually put in a dubbing session is quite considerable; I try not to harass the dubbing mixer, but the score's cues are designed to fit into the soundtrack spectrum at various levels. Sometimes they need to be up front, sometimes they are designed only to work behind dialog and behind effects, and it's critical, I feel, that I instruct the dubbing mixer as to exactly where I envisaged it in the first place, and it's up to him to find out whether that works best, if he feels it works in other contexts that's fine. But I have an idea, it's like tailoring a suit; you know how it's got to hang, and if I can be of help then I am, and usually it works. Usually they're happy with it.
>
> (Larson 1986/1987)

The archive illuminates the large number of cues required of Jones to score the mini-series, with thirty-five individual cues, some chants, and a selection of bumpers to be placed before and after commercial breaks (Hall 2017).[3] However, despite the scale of the project, Jones still approached it as 'a conventional score' (Larson 1986/1987) and undertook considerable research into the sound and setting of the ancient Roman city of Pompeii before beginning writing, reflecting his process for scoring a film. For example, he wrote a theme for the character Isis based on music heard in temples of Isis that exist today, reflecting their use of percussion in his score (Larson 1986/1987). Track sheets reveal that Jones also retained the approach to instrumentation cultivated through his film scores from the preceding years, combining ancient instruments such as the shawm and dulcimer with a symphony orchestra, electronics, and percussion instruments such as claves and chimes to form a score that reflects the setting of Ancient Rome but is still grounded in Western film underscoring technique (Hall 2017). In order to distinguish the many characters who appear over the course of the mini-series Jones wrote specific themes for each couple that had an important narrative role,

Figure 2.1 Aural transcription of the main theme from *The Last Days of Pompeii*[4]

a device that supported continuity over the episodes. However, as with his early film work, the score for *The Last Days of Pompeii* is underpinned by a main theme, shown in Figure 2.1.

The harmonic language employed for *The Last Days of Pompeii* is more conventional than that found in *Excalibur* and *The Dark Crystal*, reflecting the historical – rather than mythical or fantastical – setting of the narrative. However, as Sarah Hall observes, although Jones employs the circle of fifths in this score, his use of this progression shows a development in his handling of harmony since his earliest television scores that betrays the influence of his more harmonically adventurous film scores of the early 1980s:

> Firstly, a fanfare-style figure on strings and brass is presented over a sustained tonic pedal, underpinned by prominent timpani alternating between A and E to reinforce the A minor tonal centre, with the circle of fifths coming to the fore only in the second half of the theme. A layer of complexity is added to the harmony in this section, however, with Jones substituting the expected F–B° in bars 13–14 of the theme for F#°–Bb, pushing the music a significant distance away from A minor before abruptly returning to an extended dominant chord in bar 15.
>
> (Hall 2017, p. 120)

Hall identifies notable differences between the structure and sound of the main themes for *The Last Days of Pompeii* and Jones's previous mini-series score, *Joni Jones*, suggesting that whereas the circle-of-fifths harmony is heard at the very start of the earlier score, in *Pompeii* it is delayed by the opening fanfare and developed towards the end of the phrase. Indeed, while the theme for *Joni Jones* ends with a perfect cadence and a tonic chord in the final bar of the phrase, the return to the tonic is delayed in *Pompeii*, with the dominant chord sustained through to the end of the 16th bar and the harmony only returning to A minor at the start of the next phrase. This subtle distinction, alongside the rather more noticeable difference in instrumentation between the two scores – *Joni Jones* is not scored for orchestra – helps each to set an appropriate tone for its picture, with the folk-like feel of the first score becoming more strident and dramatic in style in the second. Furthermore, while the main theme is a critical part of the score for *The Last Days of Pompeii*, it shares the soundscape with the separate themes Jones crafted for each principal couple in the narrative. While this is a change of strategy relative to his earlier television projects, it is entirely in keeping with the approach to thematic writing found in *The Dark Crystal* and which he continued the following year in *The Last Place on Earth*.

The seven-part television mini-series *The Last Place on Earth* was produced in the UK for Central Independent Television and Renegade Productions. Directed by Ferdinand Fairfax, with a screenplay by Trevor Griffiths based on Roland Huntford's controversial *Scott and Amundsen*, and produced by Robert Buckler (executive producer) and Tim Van Rellim, it was originally broadcast in a one-and-a-half hour opening episode (including advertisements) on 18 February 1985 and six subsequent one-hour instalments in successive weeks. The mini-series, much of which was shot on location in Canada, narrates the race to the South Pole between rival teams led by the British explorer Captain Robert Falcon Scott (Martin Shaw) and the Norwegian Roald Amundsen (Sverre Anker Ousdal) in the Antarctic summer of 1911–12. It takes a critical view of Scott's leadership, strategy and preparedness for the expedition and presents the British team's failure to reach the Pole first and the ultimate death of the five members of the polar team on their return to the base camp as the result of his strategic incompetence and poor planning.

As one of the largest-budget television programmes of the year, eventually costing £6.7 million and involving seven months filming in 1984, it brought the narrative developed in the book published by the Thatcherite Huntford in 1979 to a worldwide audience through a screenplay written by the Marxist dramatist, Griffiths. Max Jones notes how Griffiths's response to the Falklands War of 1982 and, in particular, the development of jingoistic public sentiment in Britain at the time was influential in his interpretation of Huntford's text and how the series 'powerfully reveals the collision of debunking and declinism in the 1980s' (2014, p. 858). Broadcast seven decades after the onset of World War I, Britain's more recent conflict cast its shadow over the production, and this reading could not have been lost on the contemporary audience.

Among its holdings, the Jones Archive contains seventeen sequentially numbered twenty-four-track tapes of Jones's cues used in the series, as well as recordings of the opening movement of Beethoven's *Moonlight Sonata* (op. 27 no. 2) and Schumann's 'Vom fremden Ländern und Menschen' from *Kinderszenen*, both of which are played diegetically in the first episode. This set of tapes includes one further recording that is not used in the series, associated with the death of Evans in Episode 6 and employing a Penderecki-like texture of string harmonics that are played as glissandos crossing each other. In addition to the seventeen core reels, there are two other twenty-four-track tapes, stereo recordings of all dubbed cues, and album masters, as well as a promotional video recording.

Jones's score continues the development of his distinctive sound, being written for full orchestra with a large percussion section and integrating electronic sounds through the use of the Synclavier. Indeed, the very first sounds heard against the opening titles are synthesised, employing the pitches of a diminished seventh chord (G#–D–F–B) in an ethereal timbre that, like the opening notes of the theme to the original *Star Trek* television series, suggest the emptiness of space.[5] Eighty-six cues numbered from 1M1 to 44M2 (two of which are alternatives) and eight 'bumpers' were recorded for the series, though the cues are distributed unevenly across the seven episodes. The largest number (twenty) appear in the longer first episode, with thirteen in the second and sixteen in the third (excluding the repetition of opening titles and closing credits music). Thereafter the density of cues diminishes somewhat, with nine, eight, twelve and eight respectively in the final four episodes.

As with *The Last Days of Pompeii*, Jones utilises a number of themes across the mini-series, but in this project he also exploits sets of musical codes that appear to distinguish the British and Norwegian teams of explorers. Perhaps unsurprisingly, given the polemical thrust of Griffiths's screenplay, much of the material associated with Scott and the British team invokes the musical language of Elgar, though without slavishly reproducing it. Cue 25M1 from Episode 4, 'Scott's Departure', which is heard as the British team set off from their base camp like a military operation, has a clear model in the trios of Elgar's *Pomp and Circumstance* marches. Its martial opening gambit rapidly moves into an elegiac melody that seems to bind Scott to an imperialist project, though arguably one that is already tinged with a sense of heroic failure. This theme is subsequently heard again, now much more subdued, when Scott's team arrives at the South Pole after Amundsen (cue 36M1 'Second at the Pole') and reaches its apotheosis in Episode 7 when it is converted into a symphonic adagio. Here it is absorbed into the central part of the beautiful and deeply affecting cue 42M2 'Message for the Public' that accompanies the reading of Scott's journal entry explaining the failure of the expedition.

The melody of the 'main theme' (as it is described in the concert suite), which features in the opening titles, end credits and in numerous other cues, might also be taken to have some Elgarian aspects. It comprises two elements: the first elaborates an underlying four-note figure (C–D–F–E) as shown in Figure 2.2, and the second involves a descending passage built from a five-note falling pattern (A–G–F–E–D). In the first four episodes this theme appears to be exclusively associated with the British team, and the circularity of the first element and overall downward trajectory of the second along with the jittery accompaniment seem to be indicative of challenge, hardship and frustration, hinting at the eventual failure of the British expedition to reach the Pole first. That it should be so construed appears to be reinforced by cue 15M2 from Episode Three, which is titled 'Heroes Dream of

Figure 2.2 Main theme from *The Last Place on Earth*

Failure', picking up a line of Scott's wife Kathleen in response to Scott's confession that 'lately I've been thinking I might not [come back]'.

However, if this theme is assumed to relate specifically to Scott and his team rather than more generally encoding the race for the Pole, it is less immediately obvious why it appears in two later cues concerning the Norwegians in Episodes Five and Six. The anachronistic application of a big band style redolent of Les Reed's score for Jack Cardiff's *The Girl on a Motorcycle* (1968) in the first of these cues, 27M3 ('Axel Heiberg – The Norwegian'), as Amundsen's team makes rapid progress on their dog sledges over what they feared would be very difficult terrain, seems in the first instance quite out of place in the score. However, this unbuttoned and jazzed-up version can perhaps be understood to mock the sense of difficulty and of Britishness that the theme encapsulates. Reflecting a comment earlier in the episode that 'mountains could be a lot of fun', the hitherto laboured main theme (in its earlier proposed link with the British team) is leavened in this (literally) up-beat treatment, its pervasive feeling of anxiety being replaced with optimism, even joy. In the following episode, as the final part of the outward journey is traversed on skis by Amundsen, it appears once more as part of cue 35M2 ('The Last Half Mile') but with no suggestion of parody, ending with a long-held top A on the trumpet.

Two themes are unambiguously related to Amundsen and the Norwegian team. The first is initially found in cue 1M2 ('Prelude – Snow Mistress') where it develops from the repetition of the three pitches E_5–D_5–A_5, a motif later heard in the episode as Frederick Cook (the discredited American explorer who claimed to be the first to reach the North Pole in 1908) describes 'The Great Nail' – the Inuit name for the North Pole – as 'cold' to Amundsen. This conversation is reciprocated towards the end of the final episode as Amundsen uses the same word to Cook about the temperatures in the Antarctic. A simple hymn-like idea forming the final part of the 'prelude' to the first episode and heard as Amundsen is seen receiving a carving from an arctic Inuit man, it insinuates a close physical connectedness to the autochthonous people and by extension to the Polar Regions themselves. Through the simple structure and slow pace, a timbre that is redolent of a church organ and a tendency to plagal progressions, the material seems to imply a spiritual and idealistic dimension to Amundsen's quest. The cue is restated at the end of the first episode as Amundsen reveals to his brother Leon his plan to go to the South Pole, and it reappears as the final cue in the mini-series, 44M2 'The South Pole Remembered', musically closing the narrative as it had opened it, though now accompanying first Scott's and then Amundsen's memories.[6]

The second, explicitly designated, Norwegian theme (it is described thus in the concert suite) is heard in cue 8M1B ('Going South') at the close of the first episode, immediately after Amundsen and Leon have concluded their discussion about going for the South Pole. This jovial theme in A major suggests through its hemiola pattern (alternating 3/4 and 6/8) the Norwegian folk dance music form called Gangar or 'walking dance'. Grieg had used such dance tunes on several occasions: as the second of the *Six Lyric Pieces* Op. 54 ('Gangar: Norwegian March') and in *Norwegian Peasant Dances* Op. 72 as the sixth ('Myallarguten's Gangar'), fourteenth ('Tussebrureferda på Vossevangen. Gangar'), fifteenth

('Skuldalsbrura. Gangar') and seventeenth ('Kivlemøyane. Gangar') numbers. Equally the eleventh piece of this set (Knut Luråsens halling II') exhibits the same rhythmic device. Grieg's application of the hemiola in his gangar and halling tune settings is perhaps a touch subtler than Jones's – he tends to retain the compound duple metre throughout as a cross rhythm. Nevertheless Jones's cue seems to insinuate an optimism, dynamism, adaptability and self-confidence in Amundsen that contrasts with Scott's uptight, reserved and inflexible character. One further cue deserving mention in relation to Amundsen and his team is heard near the start of Episode Five, as they emerge from their tent after the storm and see the mountains for the first time. In a similar vein to the prelude to Bartók's ballet *The Wooden Prince* and parts of Strauss's *Eine Alpensinfonie*, the majestic theme in E flat major (27M2 'First Sight of the Mountains') sweeps out, brilliantly reinforcing the beauty of the scene, while again suggesting a connectedness between the Norwegian explorers and the natural world.

As well as thematic cues related to the principal characters and the nations they represent (though these are hardly used in a leitmotivic fashion), and set-pieces like the elegant salon music heard at Mabel Beardsley's party and again at the reception for Shackleton, a number of the cues are more texturally conceived. Examples of this textural technique include the use of repeated formulae such as the falling chromatic sequence in perfect fifth dyads in 19M2 ('Ponies Founder') and 19M4 ('Ponies Collapse') and the reiteration of slurred couplets B–C and E–F in 7M2 ('Amundsen Avoids Journalists'). This approach is also evident in cue 29M1 ('The Devil's Ballroom'), heard in Episode Five as the Norwegians struggle through a blizzard, and here Jones foreshadows a style that would come to the fore in a few years' time in his music for *Angel Heart*. Overall, the score for *The Last Place on Earth* balances cues that are 'characterising' in a thematic sense and those that are more neutral, 'mood-setting' ones.

The cue numbering of material held in the archive reveals a small if significant change in the ordering of events in the first episode, which apparently occurred in post-production. Cues 2M1 ('Mabel Beardsley Party') and 2M2 ('Kathleen's Room') were clearly originally intended for scenes which preceded those in which Scott recruited Wilson and the latter persuaded Shackleton not to compete with Scott, for they are followed by the three cues 3M2 ('Scott Recruits Wilson'), 3M3 ('Wilson Walks with Shackleton') and 3M4 ('Shackleton Signs Letter'). Whether this change resulted from a correction of faulty chronology or, more likely, an improvement to narrative flow, is not clear from the evidence of the archive. It does, however, have the effect of closely aligning the main theme with the British team and of bringing the two related cues 2M1 ('Mabel Beardsley Party') and 6M2 ('Ensemble – Shackleton's Reception') rather closer together than originally intended.

Crafting a rock score: *Labyrinth* (1986)

The last project to be discussed in this chapter is Jim Henson's film *Labyrinth*, a magic fantasy tale that combines action adventure and puppetry. It was Jones's first score in a popular-music idiom, although there are clear connections to his previous film and television projects: it was his second project with Henson, and, as had been the case for Boorman's *Excalibur* and with the Elgarian stylings of parts of *The Last Place on Earth*, *Labyrinth* required Jones to integrate his score with pre-existing music and fashion his material to coalesce with the recognisable sound of another composer. Filmed in both the UK and USA, the film was produced by Henson Associates and Lucas Film and was released on 27 June 1986 in the US. Written by Henson, Dennis Lee and Terry Jones, the film stars David Bowie and includes several of his original songs including 'Underground', 'Magic Dance', 'Chilly Down', 'Within You' and 'As the World Falls Down'. Bowie plays a Goblin King who steals away Toby, the baby brother of bored teenager Sarah (Jennifer Connolly), who must find her way through a labyrinth filled with monsters, decoys such as the Junkwoman, and swamps, in a race against time to rescue her sibling. Along the way, Sarah learns some valuable lessons about friendship and selflessness, befriending numerous puppet characters. She finally faces the Goblin King alone when she arrives at his castle and manages to defeat him, enabling her and Toby's safe return home. The film was not a commercial success on its initial release, but it has since become a cult classic and is regularly featured at film festivals and David Bowie retrospectives. Jones's previous work with Henson resulted in his involvement in the project at a much earlier stage than would be usual for a film composer. Indeed, in the composer's description of the project's inception, he comments:

> Sitting in Atlanta airport with Jim Henson after we did *Dark Crystal* – we were on a publicity tour of America, I think, we had thirty cities in thirty days or something – and Jim said 'you know, we've done this picture, what should we do next?' And I said, 'well we should do another picture, and this time, [since] I've done an orchestral score, why don't we do a rock score with someone famous like Bowie or Mick Jagger or someone?' So he said 'with animatronics', and I said 'well pretty much along the lines of *Dark Crystal*, but if we had someone like Mick Jagger or Bowie then it would be a very good excuse to put a rock score to it.' So anyway that's how *Labyrinth* came into being.
> (Fox and Cooper 2008: p. 6)

Once Bowie was on board the production team decided on the scenes that were appropriate for his songs. Jones and Henson met with him to talk about the ideas for the songs; then, once he had recorded them, the film was shot using them as playback on set (Jones 2016b). Subsequently, Jones received the film on Umatic tape and, following a number of edits, he scored it in a similar style to Bowie's songs so that the overall sound of the music would be consistent across the whole film. This contrasts with Jones's approach to *Excalibur* where he did not attempt to merge his music with the Wagner and Orff, instead providing the source music for dance scenes and setting his underscore music apart by the combination of early instruments with twentieth-century electronics.

Labyrinth is heavily scored throughout – Jones composed seventy cues for the film, though not all are held in the archive – and his music dovetails effectively

Figure 2.3 Pitches of the labyrinth motif from *Labyrinth*

with Bowie's songs, both employing the same core instrumentation of drum kit, synthesiser, electric guitar, and saxophone. Jones made extensive use of the synthesiser in his score, drawing on a wide range of electronic sound effects for the film (shard, tinkles, raindrops, cymbal fx, stab fx, etc.) in addition to some sounds that would become established favourites in his later 'toolkit' scores,[7] notably the bourdon, Synclavier brass, and percussive 'chomping' cello. The labyrinth is, unsurprisingly, central to the plot of the film, and Jones reflects this through the presentation of a short motif that symbolises it in cue 2M4. This four-note motif constitutes two pairs of notes – a rising perfect fifth followed by a rising minor sixth, shown in Figure 2.3 – and is heard played by brass when the labyrinth appears on screen for the first time. As Sarah sets off towards the labyrinth to begin her quest, the sun rises, the maze becomes clearly visible and a decorated version of the motif is heard in cue 2M5, suggesting Sarah's acceptance that she must enter the labyrinth to undertake her quest. The labyrinth motif reappears at several points during her journey, and Jones supported continuity across the picture by providing musical signposting to help viewers navigate the labyrinth sonically, weaving its motif into other musical cues such as fight and chase sequences as a constant reminder that all of the action takes place within the confines of the maze.

The motif is used as a musical clue in the scene in which Sarah has lost her memory and is led by a 'Junkwoman' into a false version of her own bedroom. The two cues in this sequence, 7M6 'Bedroom in Junkyard' and 7M7 'Junkwoman in Bedroom', feature a variety of atmospheric and unsettling timbres, with Jones combining high strings with synthesised trumpets, French horn, high harp, cymbals, bourdon, 'weird vox', 'shock waterphone' and shard mobile effects. Sarah struggles to remember her mission, but on noticing her storybook, *The Labyrinth*, the labyrinth motif is heard at a low volume and she realises that the false bedroom is another trick by the Goblin King designed to prevent her reaching the castle in time to save her brother. As she and her friends finally arrive at the castle, cue 9M2 presents a highly decorated elaboration of the labyrinth motif in a major key, and at the film's dénouement, when Sarah faces the Goblin King for the last time, the stripped-back four-note motif is heard on brass, indicating that the quest has come to a close and she will return to her own world very shortly.

The central importance of Bowie to the project is reflected by the placement of his songs and the manner in which Jones built his score around them. Bowie's song 'Underground' bookends the film: it is used in the film's opening titles and returns again at the end as Sarah dances around her bedroom with her new friends. The song was also used as part of the promotion for the film, shots from which appear in its music video. However, the film's opening titles actually begin with Jones's decorated 'labyrinth motif', as heard in cue 2M5 (though at this stage it is impossible for audiences to associate it with the maze itself), which dovetails into 'Underground' through shared instrumentation, and this transition is typical of Jones's approach to developing his score around the pre-existing songs. The four other pop songs are spaced throughout the film, with three of the four occurring in the second half, and the strategic placement of Jones's cues is apparent on examination of the complete cue list in the archive.[8] In order to integrate the songs smoothly into the film's soundscape, Jones composed short 'lead in' cues such as 3M1 'Introduction to Magic Dance' and 5M6 'Rhythmic Intro to "Chilly Down"' that blend into Bowie's song just as the labyrinth motif does at the start of the opening credit music. The cue 7M2 'Sarah's Hallucination' exemplifies the style of these brief cues, employing electric guitars, drums, and saxophone, to accompany Sarah eating a poisoned peach, and building the sound as the action moves to her hallucination of a masked ball so as to ensure that the transition from Jones's cue to Bowie's song is entirely imperceptible.

The archive contains recording sessions for some of the later cues in the film, but the majority of the collection relates to the mix sessions for both the film and the soundtrack album, the latter being co-written and produced with Bowie and released on 23 June 1986. The extensive paperwork includes details of the technical settings for the Lexicon 224XL – a highly popular studio reverb unit and a relatively recent development – to be used for various cues. Its forerunner, the Lexicon 224, was introduced in 1978 and became quickly known for its capacity for long delays; indeed, film composer Vangelis was a pioneer in using the unit's extra-long delays on the science fiction classic, *Blade Runner* (1982) (Vintage Digital 2015). Jones employed the unit on his cues in the mixing sessions, and he also used the Lexicon PCM 70 digital effects processor, utilising its 'rich chamber' and 'concert hall' settings extensively on this project, and it is clear that he was entirely comfortable harnessing cutting-edge technology to create a distinctively modern soundscape.

Conclusions

The archival materials help to trace the development of Jones's industrial and creative processes across the early years of his professional career, enhancing understanding of his approach to conceptualising, composition, recording and mixing music for films and television. The 1980s were a period of considerable technological change, and Jones was at the forefront in engaging with cutting-edge technology such as state of the art synthesisers and reverb units in his preparation of both symphonic and rock-influenced big- and small-screen scores. This engagement was rooted in his formative student experiences, and it shaped the diverse musical language employed in these early scores and the development of his later musical voice. The film and television projects discussed in this chapter illustrate Jones's command of both traditional musical codes, as seen in *The Last Place on Earth* with its musical characterisation of British and Norwegian explorers, and experimental sounds, as heard in the extended techniques and electronics used in *Excalibur*. He worked with pre-existing music in *Excalibur* and *Labyrinth*, adopting different approaches to each one to forge an integrated, convincing film soundscape and showed his ability to integrate the sonic stylings of other musicians in his own work, in particular in his scores for *The Last Place on Earth* and *Labyrinth*. The latter film also facilitated his development of a rock score, utilising sound palettes and textures that would shape his creation of atmospheric toolkits in the scores of the late 1980s and early 1990s. Perhaps most importantly of all, these breakthrough scores established Jones as a flexible film and television composer who could collaborate with film directors and producers to deliver high-quality scores in a range of styles at the service of the picture. This quality, coupled with his continued commitment to using technology to create innovative and unique scores and sounds, would lead him to work with director Alan Parker and his development of new compositional devices to foster even closer director-composer involvement.

Notes

1 The Australian Fairlight company produced music workstations that included samplers. A composer could create and manipulate an image of a sound wave onscreen, which the Fairlight could play back instantly. Fairlight workstations were pioneered in the late 1970s and used widely by pop musicians throughout the 1980s. The choice of a Fairlight for *Excalibur*'s soundscape therefore situates the film at the cutting edge of technological developments in the industry.
2 Developed in the United States in the late 1970s, the Synclavier comprised a sampler, digital synthesiser and workstation. It is likely that Jones worked with the Synclavier II, which was developed in the early 1980s. Synclavier II had a 'partial timbre' sound editing feature in addition to 64-voice polyphony that afforded the possibility of sounding several channels simultaneously to produce a richer harmony.
3 Bumpers are short pieces of music designed to separate the programme from the sounds of adverts and are considered in more detail in Chapter 7.
4 Taken from Hall (2017, p. 120).
5 The theme for *Star Trek*, which first aired in 1966, was written by Alexander Courage. See IMDb.com (2017d).
6 A version of the cue recorded as 33M2 'Waiting for the Sun' in Episode 6 is not used in the final dub.
7 The toolkit scores are discussed in Chapters 3 and 4.
8 'Cue List', *Labyrinth* (Trevor Jones Archive, University of Leeds, 1986).

Part II
The 'toolkit' years (1987–93)

3 Alan Parker and the development of the toolkit

Jones's work with Boorman and Henson established him as a professional film composer, and his profile continued to rise through the late 1980s. He was approached by Andriy Konchalovsky to score his action thriller *Runaway Train* (1985), and it was his music for that picture that brought Jones to the attention of director Alan Parker. He scored two films for Parker in quick succession, *Angel Heart* (1987) and *Mississippi Burning* (1988), being drafted as a late replacement for the latter when Bruce Broughton's score was rejected. It was through the Alan Parker projects that Jones developed what he terms 'toolkits', collections of sounds that could be used both within and in place of specific cues to maintain and develop a film's sonic environment. Jones outlined the origins of the toolkit concept in a 2007 interview, noting that:

> It started out when I wanted to do a piece of music and I was at York and I had a 24-track tape [recorder] at the BBC and I had access to certain synthesisers so I set off a metronomic beat and I would use certain sounds. [. . .] I would do a track of, say, a rhythm, or a track of the sound [. . .] and so you ended up with 24 different sounds on 24 tracks at different intervals.
>
> (Jones 2007)

As noted in Chapter 1, Jones studied at York University, and he has previously said that the degree course there broadened his musical horizons, exposing him to 'ethnic music, rock, jazz, pop, avant-garde, 20th-century, electronic, all kinds of music' (Fox and Cooper 2008, p. 1). It seems apparent that it was a certain sense of compositional experimentation that led to the basic toolkit idea, which also speaks to his strong interest in music technology and an enduring desire to work at the forefront of technological development. Jones's continual development of the toolkit idea across his scores of the late 1980s and early 1990s emphasises his ongoing engagement with compositional and technological experimentation and also highlights two other key aspects of his industrial practice. The toolkit scores of 1987–8 in particular show the various ways that Jones used this device to respond to the specific needs of these projects, with toolkits employed in different ways as part of the compositional process in this period. More broadly, the shifting function and purpose of the toolkit can be related to the different relationships Jones had with the directors with whom he worked, and in particular the balance of musical creativity and decision making on the two films he scored for Alan Parker in the late 1980s.

Runaway Train (1985) and *Angel Heart* (1987)

When Parker approached Jones in 1986 to score *Angel Heart*, the composer returned to the toolkit idea, refining it to suit the needs of this complex horror-thriller. The film, an adaptation of William Hjortsberg's 1978 novel *Falling Angel*, stars Mickey Rourke as Harry Angel, a private detective who is hired by the wealthy and mysterious Louis Cyphre (Robert De Niro) to track down a former singer, Johnny Favorite. Angel's task becomes harder and more dangerous as his investigation continues since each time he uncovers a new lead the contact is brutally killed in often quite bloody circumstances, and he finds himself trapped in the world of voodoo and the occult. The film, with a screenplay by Parker, stays close to the plot of Hjortsberg's book; indeed contributors to several online book-club sites come close to criticising the film for retaining, and therefore revealing, the significant plot-twist at the culmination of the narrative.[1] The story itself focuses mainly on Angel's investigation and the growing sense of the supernatural that accompanies his enquiries as he progresses with his search for Favorite, and Jones's score supports the tension and darkness of the piece, both of which seem to grow inexorably as Angel's journey continues.

On the cover notes to the LP release of the *Angel Heart* soundtrack, Parker (1987) claims that it was Jones's score to the recently released *Runaway Train* that persuaded him that he was the right composer for his project. Konchalovsky's film opened in US cinemas in January 1986, while Parker would have been writing if not already shooting his picture, and Jones's work on *Runaway Train* therefore actually predates his involvement with Jim Henson on *Labyrinth* (1986), notwithstanding his early contribution to establishing the animatronic fantasy film. Like *Labyrinth*, the music for *Runaway Train* draws largely on popular music influences, with Jones using an instrumental line-up based around electric guitar, bass, drums and percussion for the most part, supplemented with sustained strings and electronic sounds and effects of the sort that had by this stage already become a signature of his sound and style. Contrast is provided most markedly by the use of the shakuhachi, the haunting tone of which is heard most prominently in 'Reflections', where it acts as a foil for the unrelenting bass drones and low dissonant harmonies. Indeed, 'Reflections' utilises two sonic strategies that are important in Jones's compositional style and recur across his output: the employment of non-Western instruments for timbral variety rather than geographic signposting and the use of extremely low bass pedal notes. The only surviving materials in the archive for *Runaway Train* relate to the soundtrack CD and take the form of a dozen stereo mixes and an accompanying list of tracks for the album release. However, these tracks provide some insight into Parker's thinking behind commissioning Jones for *Angel Heart* and also reveal the musical elements that underpinned the composer's first filmic toolkits.

The main theme for *Runaway Train* is presented on electric guitar in the track 'Moving On'. The melody, shown in Figure 3.1, is a simple repeated pattern of one

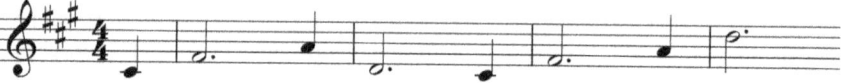

Figure 3.1 Aural transcription of the melody of 'Moving On' from *Runaway Train*

beat pick-ups and three-beat sustained notes that oscillates back and forth harmonically between the related tonal areas of F# minor and D major over a repetitive bassline that draws almost exclusively on F# and A, the two pitches common to the tonic arpeggios of both keys. However, Jones does not really make use of the apparent tonal ambiguity offered by this material, the omission of the note D from the bass riff preventing the music from ever moving properly away from F# minor, and the prominent ascending perfect fourths at the beginning and mid-point of the melody acting almost like pre-emptive perfect cadences and asserting unambiguously the minor tendencies of the theme. The music is extremely repetitive – over the entirety of the track's duration of 3 minutes and 40 seconds, the theme is heard three times without any variation or development at all – and although rhythmic repetition is a feature of Jones's compositional approach (as discussed below), the unvarying recurrence of melodic material marks this cue as unusual in his output.

There is greater uncertainty and unease in 'Reflections', despite the whole of this cue being grounded by a held low C# drone and a similar lack of musical development. The melody adds G# to the pitches of the film's main theme, creating a minor-key pentatonic set (F#–G#–A–C#–D), and most of the melodic content in 'Reflections' is built from a slow-moving A_5–$G\#_5$–$F\#_5$–$G\#_5$ motif heard variously in strings, shakuhachi and electronics. In combination with the drone this creates an implied oscillation between second-inversion tonic and root-position dominant chords in F# minor (Ic – V) with the whole cue being based on a dominant pedal note, a reading reinforced by clearly audible D naturals (rather than D#s) within the texture, and the resolute F# minor tonality of the film's main theme. This typically Western pre-cadence progression seems at odds with the pentatonicism of the melodic pitch set and the timbre of the shakuhachi (which, by its nature, is slightly out of tune with the electronics and strings), though the resulting internal musical incongruity helps maintain a level of tension across the cue. A reviewer on the blog *ScreenSounds* sums up the score most succinctly, noting that:

> *Runaway Train* being a Cannon production, there was probably pressure to produce something good, but cheap. What results, though undoubtedly suitably rhythmic and propulsive in the main, I just find largely irritating and very dated indeed; and, I would imagine, under different circumstances Jones would not have chosen to go down that path.
>
> (Hall 2009)

The reviewer's suggestion that the score sounds dated perhaps overlooks the fact that it was written in the mid-1980s, and indeed its rock and electronic stylings echo Jones's work on *Labyrinth*, which also dates from this period. However, the material is doubtless employed relatively simplistically in *Runaway Train*, and Parker's *Angel Heart* arguably provided Jones with an alternative and more interesting 'path' that bears some distinct echoes of his score for Konchalovsky.

Angel Heart diverges sonically from what Lee Barron and Ian Inglis call 'the allegiance between the horror film and heavy metal' (2009, p. 191) in the 1980s, with Parker favouring a composed score featuring strings, percussion and electronics over a popular-music-influenced soundtrack. In the cover notes for the LP release of the

Angel Heart soundtrack, Parker (1987) remarks that he 'pinched a couple of tracks [from *Runaway Train*] to use on [the] rough mix whilst editing the film', and five of *Angel Heart*'s music cues have accompanying comments that make reference to 'Reflections', with 'We would need a new piece to replace "Reflections"' being typical of this correspondence. A track sheet for cue 5M1 from *Runaway Train* is bound in with the hand-written *Angel Heart* score, and the instrumentation listed for this cue includes bourdons, (synth) strings, a Fairlight panpipe, and, most notably, the shakuhachi, indicating strongly that the document relates to 'Reflections'. This connection can be verified through exploration of the audio recordings for *Angel Heart*, one of which indicates explicitly that it is '5M1 *Runaway Train* 1st part of "Reflections"'. The opening cue of *Angel Heart*, 1M1 New York Alleyway, provides a good example of the influence Jones's score for Konchalovsky had on the sound of Parker's film. The short score for the cue has 'Reflections (1)' written at the top (there are four other such markings across the *Angel Heart* score), and like the *Runaway Train* cue the music is rooted on a resolute low C# drone played on bourdons and synthesised low strings. The A_5–$G\#_5$–$F\#_5$–$G\#_5$ motif is also retained, albeit with a significantly faster and more regular rhythmic profile, but developments in the supporting music means that in this score the harmony sounds more like a minor-key plagal cadence (IVc–I), with the drone as the tonic pitch. The melodic range is also expanded, moving beyond the original's pentatonic set, and chromaticism is introduced through the free-sounding saxophone line, performed by Courtney Pine, that gives 1M1 a different sound to 'Reflections' while retaining a 'similar mood, similar power' as demanded by the production notes.[2]

Parker is a musically sophisticated director, and he has talked in interviews about playing music on the set while shooting some of his films and also about being actively involved in the selection of music for use while editing a picture, as this instance demonstrates. Jones (2007) noted that for *Angel Heart* Parker requested 'a basic toolkit for one of the cues', and Parker (1987) describes in the LP cover notes how 'Trevor had laid down the separate tracks in what we called our "toolkit" method allowing the greatest freedom when doing the final film mix at Warner Hollywood Studios'. Papers bound in with the handwritten score for the film show that only fourteen 'scenes for scored music' were identified in the whole film, each of which was then properly spotted resulting in the allocation of cue numbers and indications concerning start and end times for individual cues. There are, however, more than fourteen points in the film where music is heard, and there is a document from 11 November 1986 headed 'Music Notes: *Angel Heart* Toolkit', summarised in Table 3.1, which identifies 16 distinct sound sets or pieces of music that could be dropped into the picture to capture particular moods or effects and in several cases to create whole cues in addition to the fourteen identified for scoring.

Jones (2007) notes that:

> Alan loved the idea of being able to be told by a dubbing mixer 'the composer's not around, you play this track with that track, what do you think of that? And watch it with your image and see what you're doing'. And you're giving him, to a great extent, the idea that he's playing music to his picture.

Table 3.1 A list of toolkits and descriptions for *Angel Heart* as described in the 'Music Notes'

No.	Toolkit Name	Description from Music Notes (11 November 1986)
1	Anatomy	Continued drone and occasional hellish groan. It would be nice to have an orchestral version of this plus other similar drones. It's an easy way to get tension, I know, but it always works.
2	Lounge Lizard	It would be nice to have a similar moody plaintive sax piece to put us in our period and to create a raw portentous (sic.) atmosphere.
3	Extinction	Classic piano chords for chase and scary situations.
4	Point of Contact	Conventional 'sting'.
5	Morricone A [to which has been added in pencil: 'Gumbo Nightmare Tracks 13–19']	Use on run up to smashing vase with dog tags. New piece to be scored to picture.
6	Morricone B	Weird pipes similar to 'Reflections' handy to lay over for scary atmos. Perhaps saxophone? Perhaps re-iteration of 'theme' 'Girl of My Dreams'.
7	Alex 2	Gentle marimbas and drone. Portentous (sic.) without intruding. Something like this, perhaps on real instrument with some variation would be nice.
8	Alex 3	Scary higher pitched drone – we have used quite effectively on the trailer (plus other layers).
9	Alex 6	Fast rhythmic chimes to give excitement to chases. Not good or exciting enough. It would be nice if we could improve on this. This could be scored to picture (see video).
10	Alex S.3	Drone and marimbas. We did this as an alternate to Alex 2 to perform a similar function; it gives energy to the scene without intruding.
11	Fauré's Requiem	Works most effectively.
12	Moodpiece	Stringed underscore. Most useful. Any variations on this would be appreciated.
13	Chimes and Vivaldi	We should replace, but it works very well.
14	Girl of My Dreams	Actual recording.
15	Girl of My Dreams Piano	Slow piano one finder we have used most effectively. I have also versions with two hands and up tempo. However it would be nice to have other versions, e.g. plaintive sax and weird 'nightmarish' rendition or any others you could suggest.
16	Electric Scream	Effective scream – it would be nice to have a musical version.

Accordingly, although initially created as a compositional tool detached from anything related to film scoring, at its inception into film music the toolkit became a directorial device, created to enable Parker to assert some control over the sound of the music in his picture.[3] There are 36 multitrack reels for *Angel Heart* in the archive, and they reveal the nature of the toolkits. While not all of them take quite the form that Jones described, several do comprise of multiple sounds layered on top of each other and offer opportunities for shifting textures and balances. As indicated by the comments alongside some of the toolkits in this list, in many cases variations or alternative sounds were suggested, and the archive enables a closer exploration of the timbres used to create some of these toolkits. The first toolkit on the list, 'Anatomy', has been superseded by sounds labelled 'New Anatomy' in the archive. The elements that comprise this toolkit are voices, low bourdons in both 'light' and 'heavy' recordings, 'Reflection' (presumably a reference to *Runaway Train*), and tam-tam, and they are brought together in two configurations – 'regular' and the much fuller and louder 'shebang' – each of which runs to over five minutes. In a similar vein, the toolkit Alex 2 exists as five largely percussive recordings identified as passes 1 to 5 and two mixes labelled as pass 6 and pass 7.[4] Pass 6 is labelled as 'compshebang building' and introduces each of passes 1 to 5 in turn, gradually increasing the rhythmic complexity and tension, whereas pass 7 features all five rhythmic passes at the same time across its full duration and is named 'compshebang full blast'. Further consultation of the surviving materials reveals that a toolkit such as Alex 2 conforms to Jones's original structure almost exactly, with twenty-three tracks recorded and then used in different configurations across the first 5 passes.

As can be seen from Figure 3.2, there is considerable duplication of sound types across this toolkit, with six tracks of bourdons – one of Jones's signature sounds in this period – being the most obvious.[5] However, the audio recordings reveal that with the exception of tracks 3 and 4, which are a stereo pair, each of these tracks is an individual layer of sound. The only track within the 24 that does not contain a toolkit sound is number 23, which is timecode, and is therefore the only track not to feature in one of the first five passes of Alex 2. Each of these passes presents a different rhythmic and stylistic feel owing to the individual sounds used to create them; as Table 3.2 shows, each of the 23 toolkit tracks is used in just one of the passes, which vary considerably as a result.

Not all of the toolkits are based on rhythmical elements, however. 'Morricone B', for instance, comprises melodic motifs and shifting sustained harmonies that can be used to develop a tense atmosphere that unfolds gradually over a period

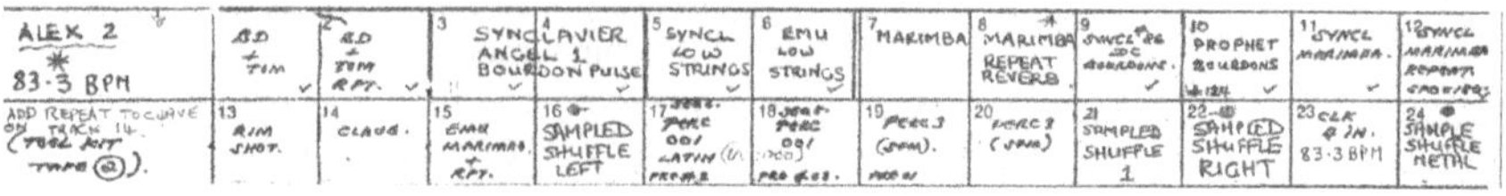

Figure 3.2 Twenty-four-track breakdown of the toolkit Alex 2 from *Angel Heart*

Table 3.2 Construction of passes 1 to 5 of toolkit Alex 2 from *Angel Heart*

Pass	Tracks	Sounds
1	3–6, 9–12	Bourdons FX x 6; Marimba FX x 2
2	13–14	Rim Shot; Claves
3	7–8, 15	Marimba x 3
4	1–2, 17, 19–20	Bass Drum and Tom x 2; Latin Percussion; Percussion 3 SFM x 2
5	16, 18, 21–22, 24	Sampled Shuffle x 4; Percussion

of several minutes. The name of this toolkit might be construed to come from the prominent use of the blown bottle sound that perhaps recalls the bass ocarina of Ennio Morricone's score for *The Good, the Bad and the Ugly* (1966), though the documentation reveals the presence of the shakuhachi alongside this timbre, linking it rather more closely to *Runaway Train*. Pass 1 comprises four tracks of a sound called 'EMU Girl's Voice' used to create a sustained sound that falls away at various points as the recording progresses, with the tracks seeming to shadow each other resulting in a semi-echo effect and an almost uncomfortable thickness of sound at times. The use of strings and string clusters in pass 2 works similarly, though here harmonic clusters are unfurled and withdrawn again slowly across the duration of the pass. The blown bottle sound of pass 3 offers the most melodic material found in the toolkit – indeed the passage heard is named in the documentation as the 'Bottle motif', and a separate recording of the motif is present on another of the multitrack tapes. There is also a percussive effect that sounds like flutter-tonguing across the top of a bottle that provides contrast within this pass. The final pass contains the most timbral variety, with two bass drum effects, a shakuhachi and voice combination that has been dropped onto a bass register to anchor the pass and a short mournful motif for shakuhachi in its lower register. The four passes are combined in a composite recording labelled 'Morricone B 2M2/4M2/4M3', which is the only indication in any of the toolkit recording names of specific places within the film where the material might be used. However, the title is ultimately misleading since the cues that feature this recording are 2M2, 4M1 and 4M2, perhaps indicating a slight change to the picture after the pass was named that necessitated cues being brought forward in reel 4 of the film.

Notwithstanding this single instance of a pass name including cue numbers, the presence of multiple passes for each toolkit links directly to the notion outlined above that Parker retained a degree of control over the sound of *Angel Heart*, since he could choose when to deploy which pass of which toolkit without necessarily needing to gain Jones's approval or assistance. Indeed, the importance of the toolkits to the sound of *Angel Heart* is revealed through a grid appended to the end of the hand-written score, which breaks down all of the musical cues and cross references them with the film's toolkits. There are thirteen instances of music shown on the first page of the document, only four of which are composed cues – 1M1, 3M2, 4M3 and 4M4 – but the toolkits even infiltrate these parts of the score, generating additional sonic connections between them. For example, the first two of these cues draw on the 'Reflections' toolkit, 3M2 and 4M3 use elements from 'Extinction', and 4M3 and 4M4 are both cross-referenced with 'Anatomy', while elements from the 'Girl of My Dreams', 'Point of Contact', 'Fauré', 'Alex 3' and 'Gumbo Nightmare' can also be found in one or other of the two cues from reel 4 of the film. The remaining nine cues on the first sheet of the grid are comprised entirely from toolkits, with 'Alex 2' appearing six times – indeed, 1M2, 1M3 and 1M4 are made up exclusively of this toolkit – 'Anatomy' and/or 'Morricone B' featuring 7 times, and another seven toolkits appearing at least once. While it is not possible to determine the precise pass of each toolkit featured within each cue from the surviving documentation, the number of possible sound combinations offered by there being multiple passes of several toolkits enabled Parker to give each constructed cue an individual identity if he so desired, with the use of shared sounds across cues supporting the overall cohesion of the score.

Dominick and Eugene (1988) and *Just Ask for Diamond* (1988)

Jones returned to work for Parker again a year later, but despite these projects following in relatively quick succession he provided music for three further films and the television movie *Coppers* (1988) in the interim. The archival documentation for the first of these pictures, *Sweet Lies* (1987) is quite limited, but there is no evidence of the use of toolkits on what has been retained. Indeed, there seems to be relatively little music in this picture at all based on the audio recordings, a trait that is common to *Coppers* and perhaps offers an explanation as to why Jones avoided toolkits in both scores. The *Angel Heart* toolkits were created to enable the director to fill out the musical environment both within and between scored cues, a strategy that would have been inappropriate in such lightly-scored pictures as these two. By contrast, the documentation for both of the 1988 films *Dominick and Eugene* and *Just Ask for Diamond* (also known variously as *Diamond's Edge* and *The Falcon's Malteser*, the latter being the name of the book on which the film is based) makes explicit reference to toolkits.

Dominick and Eugene, directed by Robert M. Young, is a drama about the titular twins. Eugene (Ray Liotta) is a high achiever who is close to finishing medical school, while Dominick (Tom Hulce), who has impaired mental capacities owing to a childhood accident, works as a bin man to support them. Eugene finds himself caught between a need to look after his brother and a desire to complete his medical training at Stanford, away from their Pittsburgh home, leading to rising tension in their relationship as Dominick struggles to come to terms with changes in their everyday lives.

Three toolkits were created for this film, all of which were recorded on a single twenty-four-track multitrack tape, though they are not all readily traceable through the film score, raising questions as to why Jones employed this approach, and about the function of these musical materials. TK1 is constructed in a similar way to the *Angel Heart* toolkits, with electronic and blown-bottle sounds used to create cellular, repeating lines that produce a composite texture. There is a heartbeat pattern that underpins the toolkit, and on track 4 something that sounds like either a combination of a ringing bell and escaping gas, or a clichéd 'flying saucer' taking off. Unusually, rather than having a repeated pattern this track runs continuously, growing in intensity across the 3:13 duration of the toolkit until it is close to overwhelming all of the other elements in the mix. The sound of the toolkit is extremely eerie, which feels quite out of place in the context of the story, so it is perhaps unsurprising that TK1 does not seem to feature anywhere in the final score for the picture at all. TK3, which is subtitled 'percussion', is a rhythmic toolkit comparable to 'Alex 2' from *Angel Heart*. The toolkit seems clearly designed to build tension, but the generally slow narrative arc of the film runs counter to the sort of fast-paced, rapid build that TK3 offers, and like TK1 it is conspicuous by its absence from the theatrical release.

By contrast, TK2 is subtitled 'main theme', and this melody appears at several points in the picture as well as over the opening credits. Jones often employs the main theme at points where the closeness of the brothers' relationship is presented in the story, particularly when Dominick is talking with Eugene about their past and his accident and when Eugene is trying to lift his brother's spirits and self-esteem. However, the sounds used in TK2 are clearly electronic rather than acoustic, differentiating the toolkit markedly from the cues recorded on the other multitrack reels and that are used in the actual picture, and it is therefore unclear precisely what function TK2 has in the score. Indeed, like the other toolkits, TK2 is not actually used in the picture at all. The Jones Archive includes two video tapes of complete cuts of the film dating from 13 and 27 July 1987, each of which differs from the final picture in small ways, though these resources do not help to clarify the reason for the existence of the three toolkits. The first video contains no music at all, and although the second has music over the opening and closing sequences (the former footage being quite different to the final theatrical release), none of it corresponds with any of the toolkits or indeed any part of Jones's score.

This is not the only puzzling thing about the development of *Dominick and Eugene* revealed by the archive. There appears to have been an unusual length of time between the score being recorded and the film being released. Indeed, as Table 3.3 shows, the trailer was only released in 1988, over two months after the score was recorded, permitting Jones's main theme to be used.[6] This is not the only significant time gap, however, with a period of around ten weeks between the date of the second video cut of the picture and the recording of multitrack tape 3. Since multitrack tapes 2 to 4 all feature acoustic recordings of cues from the film there is an implication that they were recorded around the same time, but the toolkits could have been written and recorded much earlier, at any point after Jones received the first video cut of the picture. It is possible, therefore, that the toolkits were created as placeholders that could be used by Jones to demonstrate particular ideas or, in the case of TK2, the proposed main melody for the film, and that they

58 The 'toolkit' years (1987–93)

Table 3.3 Sources and dates (where known) relating to *Dominick and Eugene*

Item/Source	Date
First cut of picture in archive	13 July 1987
Second cut of picture in archive	27 July 1987
Multitrack reel 1 (electronically-produced toolkits)	Undated
Multitrack reel 2 (acoustic recordings)	Undated
Multitrack reel 3 (acoustic recordings)	7 October 1987
Multitrack reel 4 (acoustic recordings)	Undated
Eight-track mixes (acoustic)	27–29 October 1987
Theatrical trailer	Copyright 1988
Theatrical release (US premiere)	18 March 1988

are labelled as toolkits because they could be used in various different places to give an impression of how the score would work, rather than being precursors to specific numbered cues. While there is no concrete evidence in the archive to support this hypothesis explicitly, the combination of missing information (such as the recording date of multitrack tape 1) and the long periods of time outlined in Table 3.3 do lend support to such a reading. Accordingly, while it is clear that the toolkits did not play any sort of substantial role in the final film score, and that the presence of toolkits in *Dominick and Eugene* is not at all comparable to their use and function in *Angel Heart*, this picture nonetheless demonstrates the versatility of the toolkit as a creative device and of Jones's application of this device within his practice.

In some respects the situation is similar in *Just Ask for Diamond*, based on Anthony Horowitz's book *The Falcon's Malteser* and directed by Stephen Bayly, with whom Jones had worked previously on the television mini-series *Joni Jones* for the Welsh channel S4C. The film follows inept private investigator Tim Diamond and his rather more capable younger brother, Nick, as they attempt to outwit gangsters and the police and decipher the clues to locate the Falcon's diamonds. This is the only comedy for which Jones created toolkits, preferring generally to associate the device with action thrillers and horror films.[7] In their discussion of film music and its relationship to film genre, Karlin and Wright (2004) note that the 'dramatic elements' of action scores include 'strong propulsive rhythms' (p. 179) and that 'in a horror film [. . .] the scenes of terror are often ones with kinetic action and energy' (p. 185), their thoughts mirroring the rhythmic and textural nature of many of Jones's filmic toolkits. Although it is not an action film, *Just Ask for Diamond* fits within a strand of comedy pictures identified by Karlin and Wright as 'fast-paced adventure[s] with thrills and fun, with music that underscores the sense of suspense and action' (p. 180), a bracket into which they place films such as *Ghostbusters* and *Indiana Jones and the Temple of Doom* (both 1984). While *Just Ask for Diamond* perhaps lacks some of the intensity of these examples, this nonetheless explains why Jones may have chosen to employ toolkits as part of his compositional process on this project. However, although two

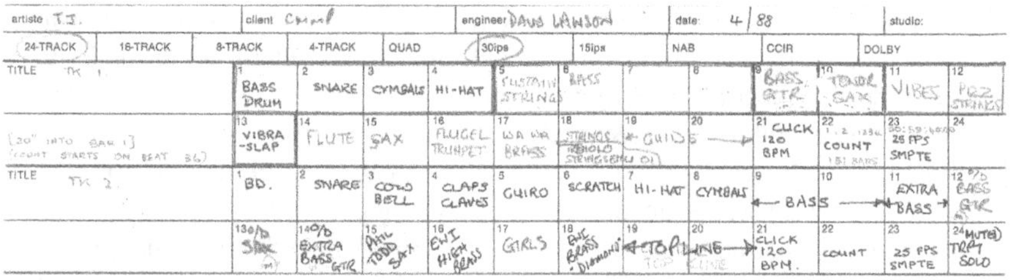

Figure 3.3 Twenty-four-track breakdown of TK1 and TK2 from *Just Ask for Diamond*

toolkits were recorded for the picture neither appears in the theatrical release, and as with *Dominick and Eugene* these toolkits are extended pieces of music. In this case each toolkit lasts around four minutes, and they are through composed rather than being created as multi-layered musical sound sets.

The breakdown of tracks in TK1 and TK2 is shown in Figure 3.3 and emphasises a key point of difference between the toolkits in these two pictures: the presence of live sound in those for *Just Ask for Diamond*. While there is undoubtedly a significant amount of computer-generated material in TK1 and TK2, it is evident from the multitrack recordings that the tenor saxophone on track 10 of the former, and the two saxophone lines, overdubbed bass guitars and three-part women's voices on tracks 12–15 and 17 (and also tracks 21–22, though this is not marked on the track sheet) of the latter are acoustic recordings. This is perhaps particularly surprising when it is considered that there are other lines in both toolkits named for similar acoustic instruments – the sax on track 15 of TK1 and the basses on tracks 9–11 of TK2 for instance – but perhaps speaks to the status of these toolkits as dynamic and developing pieces of music, a further development of the approach. It is notable that whereas the electronic saxophone in toolkit 1 is a functional and fairly repetitive part, the live saxophone sounds quasi-improvised and bears no relation at all to its synthetic equivalent. Similarly, the presence of overdubbed ('O/D' on the track sheet) lines in toolkit 2 indicates strongly that changes were made to the music on the scoring stage rather than the whole toolkit being pre-formed. The overdubbed bass guitar parts reinforce the electronic material, but the audible presence of the sound of fingers sliding on strings and an occasional tuning glitch give the sound much more body. Phil Todd's saxophone part interacts with the electronic elements, giving way to the synthesised muted trumpet solo (track 24) around halfway through the piece before returning to lead through to the end of the toolkit, but the overdubbed saxophone is far more akin to its equivalent in TK1 and sounds rather freely improvised over the other elements of the toolkit. Another notable feature of these toolkits is the presence of guide tracks (19 and 20), which other track sheets and recordings note explicitly as an electric piano sound. While these are the only toolkits to feature this sort of material, it is common to nearly all of the cues in *Just Ask for Diamond*, and therefore appears to be part of the process of creating this score, rather than being specifically related to Jones's use of toolkits.

As already noted, neither of the toolkits appears in the final theatrical release of *Just Ask for Diamond*, though their presence is felt across the film. TK2 bears a marked similarity to the film's opening and closing credits in terms of the underlying musical style and material, and although both credit sequences are shorter than TK2's four minutes, the toolkit can be seen as a structural and compositional model for these 'book-end' cues. By contrast, TK1 contains the basic musical material for a large number of cues from across the film. Its 12/8 lazy swing style with repetitive bassline, 'wa wa brass', hi-hat pattern and saxophone lead permeate the film, though as the action draws nearer to the climactic reveal the presence of the toolkit material is reduced. However, while this perhaps implies that TK1 was used as a constituent element of some of the film's cues in a similar manner to the way toolkits were employed in *Angel Heart*, the track sheets for the multitrack recordings show that this was not actually the case, with all of the musical elements recorded live for each cue of the film. Unlike *Just Ask for Diamond*, the archival materials show that the toolkits were recorded at the same session as some of the film's musical cues, so it seems much less likely that they were used as placeholders while the score was developed. Ultimately it seems that the purpose of TK1 and TK2 remains unclear, with insufficient evidence surviving in the archive for their function to even be properly theorised, a circumstance far removed from that of the next toolkit picture.

Mississippi Burning (1988)

Jones enhanced the toolkit concept significantly for his and Alan Parker's next film, *Mississippi Burning*. Since it was a replacement score it seems likely that he did not have much time to compose the music,[8] and after the somewhat unclear application of the toolkits in *Dominick and Eugene* and *Just Ask for Diamond*, Jones returned it somewhat to first principles in order to expand its potential contribution to the musical sound world for this next picture. The film is based on true events that took place in Mississippi in 1964 and focuses on two FBI agents, Ward (Willem Dafoe) and Anderson (Gene Hackman), who travel to the state to investigate the disappearance of three civil rights activists. Their work is hampered significantly by a lack of co-operation from the local Sherriff's office, and even when it becomes apparent that the three men were murdered, the local black community refuses to talk to them about the matter. It rapidly becomes clear that their silence results from fear of the Ku Klux Klan, who torture and firebomb the African-American population across the course of the narrative. When it transpires that local law enforcement are in league with the Klan, the FBI are forced to step outside the law themselves to try and bring the offenders to justice. Considering the use of toolkits in the film, Jones recalls that:

> on *Mississippi Burning* it then grew into a huge number because fundamentally we had a rhythm that was twelve notes as I recall, and this rhythm was played on different instruments with different combinations of sounds. And you could have a very basic [sound] and it would become more and more complex the more tracks you brought up. And so you had what we referred to as a simple, medium, and 'shebang'.
>
> (Jones 2007)

The archival documentation for *Mississippi Burning* enables closer evaluation of the construction and potential uses of the toolkit elements that permeate the score. There are thirty-seven track sheets for the film, each of which shows the breakdown of sound across two sets of stereo film sounds (left-centre-right), plus a pulse for synchronisation, and the timecode, for a total of eight tracks per cue. The instruments listed on these sheets include 'chomping cellos', 'Herman [*sic.*] strings', various descriptions of marimbas, prepared piano, metallic surging atmos[phere], Miami synths, bourdon, and a range of untuned percussion sounds, with some cues containing amalgamations of others. For instance, cue 1 on multitrack reel 1 is listed as 'TK1A (Pass 1)', the first pass at toolkit 1A, and features left- and right-panned chomping cellos, a centre-panned prepared piano, left- and right-panned snares, and a centre-panned bass drum. The second cue on the reel is 'TK1A (Pass 2)', which provides some rhythmic bass drum slaps, a drum kit bass drum, marimba mobiles in low and high registers, and the aforementioned metallic surging atmosphere sound. The first cue on multitrack tape 3, 'TK1A (Pass 3) Composite' combines these two elements, enabling all twelve sounds to be heard on a single eight-track mix. However, this is only half of the story. Alongside the sound and the record of what is on each track, Jones also provides notes on possible ways of combining and balancing the various elements, and instructions for their use. For pass 1, he states:

> These elements could be heard in the following way. 1. Bass drum followed by snares followed by chomping cellos introduced very quietly then gradually getting louder, finally adding prepared piano to give the chomping cellos a more aggressive edge.[9]

He goes on to note that 'All TK1, TK1A, TK1B and TK1C elements can be played together as they have a common tempo. Whether all the marimba elements should be used simultaneously', and unfortunately he stops mid-sentence so it is unclear whether he is suggesting this is a good thing, or whether he is expressing caution about using all the marimbas together in the way one's voice might tail off when speaking.[10] He simply confirms the various elements for pass 2, though he lists them as marimbas, bass drum slaps, drum kit bass drum, metallic surging atmosphere, which is not track order and might therefore indicate an order of addition much like the guidance for pass 1. When it comes to the composite pass 3, however, Jones's instructions are technical rather than musical. He informs the reader that 'This TK1A (Pass 3) is the full version of TK1A (Pass 1) and TK1A (Pass 2) over 6 tracks – please refer to TK1A (Pass 1) and TK1A (Pass 2) in order to access separate elements'. While this may be obvious, his guidance serves to remind the director of the options available to him when mixing the sound since he can return to the individual passes if he does not like the composite balance inherent in pass 3.

The various layers and sounds of the toolkits are made explicit in the naming of cues found on multitrack reels 8 and 9, relating to toolkit 5, 'New Alex 3'. Toolkit 5 uses some similar sounds to Toolkit 1A – chomping cellos, prepared piano, marimbas and bass drum again comprise pass 1, as well as marimba and kit bass drum in pass 2, though here they are joined by 'tension Herman strings' and a fast hi-hat pattern. Where TK1A (pass 3) was a composite recording, TK5 (pass 3) introduces more new sounds, (stereo talking drums and a slap rhythm on bass drum, also as a stereo pair), and there is nothing on the two centre-panned channels. The three passes are subtitled 'Light to Medium', 'Medium to Driving' and 'Driving to Shebang', indicating the level of complexity and tension that arises through their addition. A six-track pass 4 is included, which Jones notes is a 'composite shebang mix running for 5 minutes approx. in length', a suitable duration for Parker to make use of as much or as little as is needed in the film, and the composer also advises that the individual passes can be layered as a twenty-four-track mix should greater control over the volume of the individual elements be desired than is possible in the composite mix. Of particular interest is an instruction written specifically for Alan Parker by Jones on the sheet for 'TK5 (Pass 1)', where he remarks on the way these sounds might be heard:

Note for AP

NB As you know the panning 'Left, Right + Centre' of any of these tracks is assigned by the dubbing mixer. The assignment I have given just works as a musical balance as a whole so that you may want to pan Trk 2 'Chomp cello' in the centre if you were using it at the start of a cue on its own.

Jones also notes on this sheet that the tracks may need additional EQ and reverb, emphasising how much musical control the toolkits were designed to hand the director. Indeed, in this respect *Mississippi Burning* marks the apotheosis of the toolkit as a directorial device and perhaps singles out Parker among all of the directors with whom Jones has worked in his long career as the most musically minded. While Parker's need for control over the film's score does not strictly align him with Claudia Gorbman's (2007) idea of the *mélomane* director, or sonic auteurs such as Kubrick, Tarantino and Lynch (ed. Wierzbicki 2012), it seems nonetheless that his relationship with Jones was such that the composer was happy to hand him substantial control over the film's musical soundscape.

All in all, there are fourteen toolkits in *Mississippi Burning*, numbered 1 to 10, 12, and 1A, 1B and 1C (it's unclear why there is no TK11). Like those discussed already, most contain a range of musical elements, but there are two that comprise musical effects or sounds – TK12 is a set of four dramatic stings, and TK10 is nine stereo atmosphere tracks spread across three passes. Toolkit elements come to the fore at several points in the film, perhaps most notably in two car-chases: one towards the start of the picture, and one near the end. The film begins with a simple shot of 'white' and 'coloured' drinking fountains, emphasising the segregation that is fundamental to the storyline, and the opening credits that follow establish visually the burning of Mississippi to the sound of Mahalia Jackson singing 'Take My Hand, Precious Lord', a gospel song intrinsically linked with the Civil Rights Movement and Martin Luther King Jr.[11] The narrative proper begins with the first car sequence, as the civil rights activists whose disappearance provides the narrative impetus for the story are seen driving a Mississippi road at nightfall. Jones's music, an orchestral bass drum sound followed by a three-semiquaver rhythm on snare drum – the first two elements of TK1A pass 1 in the order suggested by the composer – starts as the camera cuts to a shot of three other vehicles following behind the activists and makes it apparent immediately that the appearance of these other vehicles is ominous for the activists. As the pursuers catch up with their prey a looped guitar riff is added into the sonic mix, and the frequency at which the various sounds are repeated is increased, thickening the texture and raising the tension to match the increased anxiety of those in the lead car. The toolkit sounds are employed here solely to build suspense, particularly since it is unclear what is happening on screen, and this approach is utilised across the picture, notably in the second car sequence.

As the plot reaches its climax one of the white supremacists, Lester, who has been tricked into revealing some details of anti-civil-rights activity to the FBI agents, is apparently set upon by his comrades. He attempts to flee in his truck, a vehicle that is by this point in the narrative known to be one of those involved in the opening pursuit, and is chased down by aggressors in a truck of their own. The music again begins with single, repeated orchestral bass drum hits, but since Lester is entirely aware of the fate that awaits him if he is caught, several other toolkit elements are added at the same time when he starts his truck and tries to escape. Multiple unpitched percussion rhythms build a dense layer of sound, which is placed between sustained strings in a mid-high register and a repeating bass line, and further sounds such as the chomping cellos can also be heard within the mix. At the end of the sequence the whole situation is revealed to the audience as a set-up designed to convince Lester that he is in danger so that he will work with the FBI, but the use of Jones's toolkit sounds ensures that the sequence is equated with the car chase to that from the start of the film, which ended with the murder of those being pursued. Most of the toolkits *were* created with particular scenes or scenarios in mind, but the nature of the material enabled Parker to use what he wanted when he wanted it, in a manner more akin to the use of Michael Nyman's music by Peter Greenaway in his independent films, than a mainstream Hollywood picture (cf. Cooper and Sapiro 2011; Sapiro 2012). It is also clear from Jones's notes on the track sheets that the primary intention behind the toolkits was indeed to enable the director to have this freedom to shape the music, emphasising the composer's musical respect for Parker and the strength and nature of their working relationship across both of the pictures on which they worked.

Conclusion

Jones's most extensive use of toolkits is in the scores for the Alan Parker films *Angel Heart* and *Mississippi Burning*, and these projects are also those in which he used toolkits to give the director the greatest degree of compositional power. Indeed, it seems that Jones's primary reason for utilising the toolkit approach on these pictures was to afford Parker a high degree of autonomy in dictating their musical landscapes, and that his notes and comments to the director provided sufficient information for Parker to select, combine and place his desired toolkit elements and passes in his films. Jones's active engagement with this somewhat unusual approach to film scoring and Parker's considered and respectful use of Jones's material speak clearly to the strong mutual respect between the composer and director and their close working relationship across *Angel Heart* and *Mississippi Burning*. Toolkits remain a striking feature of Jones's approach through into the early 1990s, permeating both his film and television work in this period, though the function of the toolkits and the ways in which they interact with the rest of the score changes somewhat across this period, and in these subsequent projects no other director was handed the level of musical control that had been afforded to Parker. In some respects the hypothesis suggested for the toolkits in *Dominick and Eugene* and *Just Ask for Diamond* – that they provide an idea of a sound world for the picture – starts to come to the fore more prominently towards the end of the toolkit period. This is particularly the case in pictures with 'dark' narratives, a score type that continued to be something of a specialty for Jones in the years post-Parker.

Notes

1. See, for instance, reader reviews and comments on the *Good Reads* website.
2. 'Scenes for Scored Music', *Angel Heart*, 1986. Trevor Jones Archive, University of Leeds.
3. Laura Anderson notes that Parker was still using a development of the toolkit idea as part of his film-making process over a decade after *Angel Heart*, citing the application of the technique in the director's creation of a temp track for *Angela's Ashes* in 1999 (2018, pp. 282–283).
4. A 'pass' in this context is a sequence to be recorded. In this instance each pass is a recording of a specific set of tracks from a toolkit; Jones uses the same term on *Mississippi Burning* to designate an eight-track recordings that can be combined to create a composite sixteen- and twenty-four-track recordings.
5. Bourdon is a stop (sound) on the pipe organ. Jones uses the sound of the bourdon played on the 64ft (the longest) pipe, which is an extremely low sound.
6. It is unusual for a trailer to include music from a film's original score, since film music is usually recorded very close to the film's release date, and as a result the trailer is usually produced before the score has been written.
7. Jones's score for the horror-comedy *Arachnophobia*, discussed in Chapter 4, does include some toolkits, though this inclusion is readily explained by the horror aspects of the picture.
8. Jones's music replaced a score by Bruce Broughton. See Boggan (2014).
9. 'Track Sheet for Tape 1, Cue 1: Notes', *Mississippi Burning*, 1988. Trevor Jones Archive, University of Leeds. All quotes from track sheets are from the Trevor Jones Archive.
10. Jones was unable to recall his thoughts on the matter when asked about this comment.
11. King had asked musician Ben Branch to play the song, which was his favourite, at a rally later that evening in the moments before he was shot and killed in April 1968. It was sung at King's funeral by Mahalia Jackson. See Pilkington (2008) and Werner (2000, p. 9).

4 Towards a mainstream sound

Jones's development of the toolkit technique can be scrutinised further through consideration of his approach to the large number of projects scored in the five years following *Mississippi Burning*, a period during which he composed at a prodigious rate. Such exploration is, of course, restricted at times by the availability of evidence from within the Trevor Jones Archive, and in particular the archive contains very little material from the production process for one of the best-known pictures on which Jones worked – *The Last of the Mohicans* (1992) – limiting detailed analysis of his scoring practice on that project. Similarly, there is no material at all for the documentary telefilm *Guns: A Day in the Death of America* (1990), though a range of audio, video and textual resources are held for each of the other projects from this part of his career. As identified in the Introduction to this book, the lack of materials for these projects highlights a difficulty in archival research into screen music. However, even as the Jones Archive frustrates with the relative absence of evidence for *The Last of the Mohicans*, so it also provides evidence for other projects of the absence of audio, video, textual and musical resources about which researchers may otherwise have been ignorant, as is the case for *Arachnophobia*. It also enables greater understanding of the technologies and processes that underpinned the creation and production of a large number of the composer's scores.

As noted in Chapter 3, given the frequent use of percussion, bass drones, synthesised sounds and rhythmic cells and effects within Jones's toolkits, the technique was ideally suited to the dark narratives of several of the theatrical and television films on which he worked in this period. Indeed, there is a strong correlation between the use of toolkits and pictures that might be regarded as thrillers, dramas or horrors, and it is notable that this approach is effectively absent from the most light-hearted picture from this time, *Blame It on the Bellboy* (1992). A relative abundance of archival materials for Jones's scores from 1989–93 – with the exception of the two projects identified above – enables a wide investigation of his use and development of toolkits and his general scoring practice across this period and exploration of how he began to cultivate a more mainstream sound and approach to scoring as the mid-1990s beckoned. Notwithstanding this, the chapter revolves around four principal nodes – *Sea of Love* (1989), *Bad Influence* (1990), *Blame It on the Bellboy* (1992) and *Detonator* (1993) – detailed analysis of which supports the addressing of the main themes of this chapter, with reference made to other scores to reinforce arguments and offer points of contrast. Importantly, the projects are considered in the order in which the scores were created, which is not always the same as that in which they were released.

Sea of Love (1989)

Although Jones's next film project subsequent to *Mississippi Burning* was director Hal Becker's erotic thriller *Sea of Love*, in the intervening period he scored two telefilms: *A Private Life*, which was episode six of the seventh season of the BBC's Screen Two series,[1] and the sci-fi mystery *Murder on the Moon* (also known as *Murder by Moonlight*).[2] *A Private Life* 'tells the emotional story of Jack and Stella Dupont who meet, fall in love and live in defiance of the apartheid laws in South Africa' (BBC 1991), a subject that is likely to have had considerable resonance for Jones given his own South African roots. Indeed, while Jones has worked on scores for a number of South African and South African-themed films and television programmes since the turn of the twenty-first century, this was his first professional scoring project with an explicitly South African subject. Dates on the track sheets in the archive show that the score was recorded on 29 September 1988, indicating that unless Jones was given an extremely short time in which to write his score, he must have begun working on it concurrently with completing *Mississippi Burning*, the recording sessions for which had been held only three weeks previously, on 5–10 September 1988. Such an undertaking is particularly remarkable since Jones wrote twenty-six cues for *A Private Life*, and the durations of the multitrack audio recordings indicate that music was composed for around half of the telefilm's 95-minute run-time.

Although none of the cues are labelled explicitly as toolkits – something that is particularly surprising given the proximity of this score to *Mississippi Burning* – the cue 'Bourdons' has all the hallmarks of such a device. Its twenty-four tracks comprise twelve pairs, each of which has been created from a sound generated using a Prophet synthesiser – sounds 121 and 122 – the latter of which has been mixed with something termed 'Matrix D50', which seems most likely to be a patch on the Roland D50 synthesiser. This near-eight-minute cue therefore provided Jones with two versions of each of twelve bourdon pitches, marked as 'feathery' and 'square' respectively, and established a new use of the toolkit that is also found in *Sea of Love*. The twenty-four tracks of that picture's 'TK Bourdons' are split similarly into twelve pairs with the odd tracks containing just the bourdon and the even tracks mixing the sound with low strings; the chromatic pitch set covered by the toolkit from A to G# ensured that a suitable bass note could always be sourced regardless of the prevailing key of the score.

Two cues from *Murder by Moonlight* are designated specifically as toolkits, the first of which is an old version of the opening cue that Jones notes on the track sheet could be used as a toolkit. There is a version of this material titled 'Main Theme – Long Version – Toolkit' that provides a greater body of material for such use and consists of three synthesised elements as stereo pairs within the eight-track mix: 'high register' (bells, guitar and strings), 'low register' (strings and bass guitar), and 'lead melody lines' (sax, guitar, strings and voice). The other designated toolkit is a long version of the next cue, 1M2 'Elazar Falling Down Shaft', and brings an additional key sonic element into the mix – a (synthesised) bass drum sound. Track sheets indicate that the 'militaristic rhythm' of the snare and bass drums in 1M4 'You Will Leave Immediately', and the whole of 3M3 'Killer's Hand' might also be used as toolkits, but while elements from the two named toolkits are heard in numerous cues across the picture, the material from 1M4 and 3M3 is largely overlooked in the rest of the score. The toolkit approach proved to be ideal for these two television scores, which largely eschew melody in favour of a broad soundscape, and these projects start to show Jones taking greater ownership of decisions regarding the use of toolkits in the sound of the film. As well as marking a reduction in the number and variety of toolkits associated with a single project, they also emphasise their value as compositional rather than purely directorial devices, a change in approach that is fundamental to their application in *Sea of Love*.

Whereas Alan Parker had wanted to exert a strong degree of musical influence within his films, there was a more conventional director-composer relationship between Becker and Jones in *Sea of Love*. This stars Al Pacino as veteran Detective Frank Keller, who is investigating a series of murders that seem to be linked to rhyming adverts placed in a lonely-hearts column of a New York magazine. After posting their own poem Frank and his team meet up with all the women who respond to the ad, with Frank becoming personally involved with one of the respondents, Helen (Ellen Barker), who becomes the main suspect in the case. Jones formulated seven toolkits for use across the film – more than in the preceding television scores but far fewer than for *Mississippi Burning* – as well as conceiving a series of cues that were sketched, orchestrated and recorded. TKM1 and TKM2 are collections of largely percussive sounds including 'metal krang', 'Tinkles', various marimba patterns, a heartbeat, and 'skulls'; notably in TKM1 some sounds have three channels devoted to them, one each being left, right and centre panned. TKM2 offers bass drum hits every two bars, as a repeated note, on the off-beat and as a cross rhythm, and both of these constructions indicate that the toolkits were designed to offer significant versatility to the composer when using them within the score.

An examination of one cue from the film, 5M4/6M0 'Set Up', allows a detailed analysis of the ways in which Jones employs the toolkit elements in *Sea of Love*. The final master recording of the cue is on two linked multitrack tapes, a master and slave, the latter of which contains the acoustic elements – strings, brass, and a solo sax – and the former featuring a range of sounds drawn from some of the film-score's toolkits. The opening cue on multitrack tape 4, 'Iranian Fiasco/Suspense Master', is the first complete construction of the pre-recorded elements for this cue, a sound set that is largely common to three other cues in the film, 2M5 'Who Gives a Shit', 3M1 'Iranian Fiasco' and 7M2 'Toy Gun'. These cues are all employed at tense dramatic points in the narrative, often where the protagonist believes he is in danger, and it is therefore understandable that they should share a common soundscape. In addition to the usual click and timecode tracks, the twenty-four-track recording includes two heartbeat patterns (one each for cues 3M1 and 7M2) and 20 tracks drawn from a number of the toolkit sets, as shown in Figure 4.1.

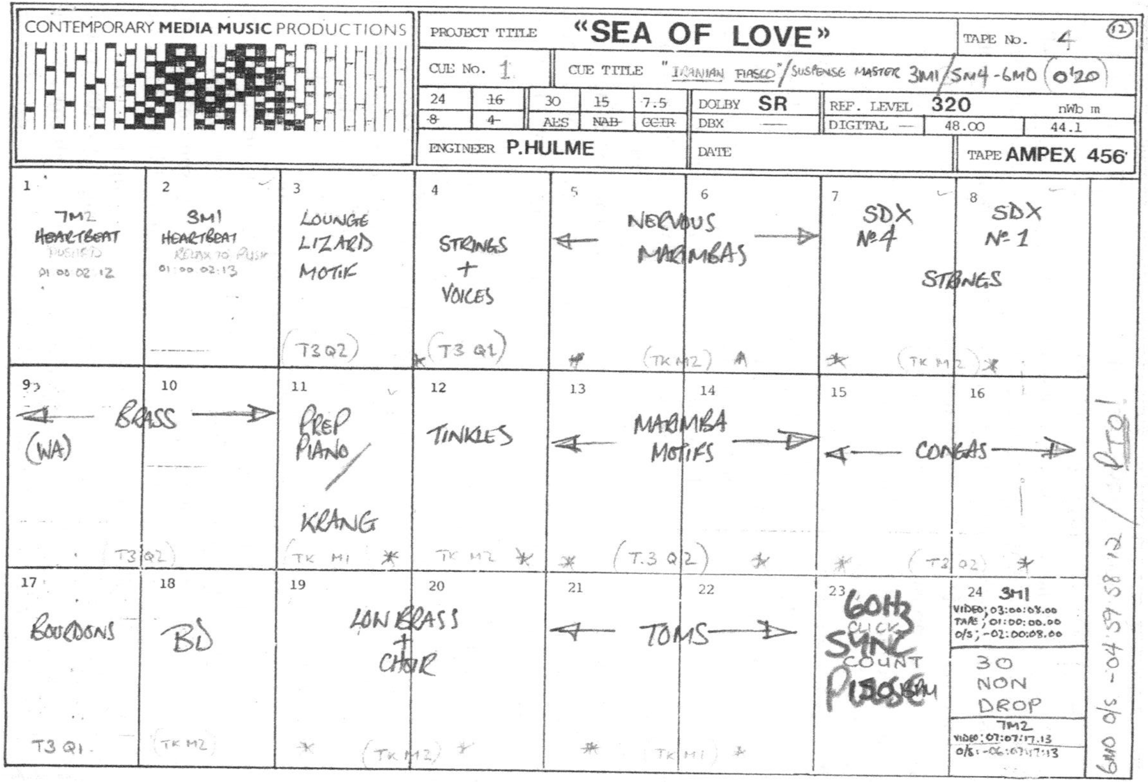

Figure 4.1 Twenty-four-track breakdown of the 'Iranian Fiasco/Suspense Master' from *Sea of Love*

The indications on the track sheet enable the source for each of the tracks to be identified from among the session recordings. The 'Lounge Lizard motif', brass, marimbas and congas are all taken from cue 2 on multitrack tape 3, the 'Iranian Fiasco Toolkit' (Figure 4.2) – these tracks are all marked as 'T 3 Q [cue] 2' on the master track sheet – with more marimbas, strings, 'tinkles', the low brass and choir, and the bass drum taken from TKM2 (Figure 4.3). Elements are similarly taken from TKM1 and TKM3 (which is multitrack tape 3, cue 1) to complete the sound set.

Some sub-mixing occurs during the creation of this multitrack recording, with the four tracks of the 'Lounge Lizard motif' from the Iranian Fiasco Toolkit combined into a single track for the 'Iranian Fiasco/Suspense Master' and retained as a single element in the mix thereafter. In using the toolkits in this fashion, Jones treats them like compositional scrap books; he combines ideas from a number of toolkits to create cues in a similar way to taking existing harmonies, melodies and/or countermelodies from a film score and refashioning them into other cues. This approach contrasts markedly with that employed on the Parker films in the preceding years and shows a significant development in the function of toolkits in Jones's output. It also demonstrates a remarkable flexibility of approach to the use of material given the era in which he was working, with such a process perhaps closer in concept to the twenty-first century strategy of Hans Zimmer's 'evolving score-in-progress' (Hexel 2016, p. 41) than to conventional practice in the late 1980s. Interestingly, there is a possible link between *Angel Heart* and *Sea of Love* through the toolkits, with both film scores including the 'Lounge Lizard motif' within one of their toolkits. The motif includes a distinctive 3+3+3+3+2+2 rhythmic pattern created by a combination of the accented bass line in the piano and bass and pulsing notes on guitar that create a sort of composed reverb sound. The *Angel Heart* material features a strident, repetitive bass riff under light, jazz-influenced harmonies – perhaps explaining the origins of the motif's name – with the bassline borrowed and developed in *Sea of Love* minus the chordal overlay. Their use in this score emphasises the ongoing influence of this motif and of the syncopated rhythmic profile in particular across Jones's output.

While the toolkits play a prominent role in defining the sound of *Sea of Love*, the difference in the composer-director relationship in this film relative to the Parker projects impacts significantly on the way in which they are used in the score. Accordingly, this project marks a shift in the underlying functional purpose of toolkits from directorial to compositional tools, with Jones retaining greater creative control over the sound of the musical score despite the continued use of toolkits within his process.

Bad Influence (1990)

Following the completion of *Sea of Love* in the summer of 1989, Jones appears to have had several months without any screen-composition work before starting on the thriller *Bad Influence* towards the end of the year. Directed by Curtis Hanson, who would go on to direct *The Hand that Rocks the Cradle* (1992) and *LA Confidential* (1997) later in the decade, *Bad Influence* stars James Spader as Michael, a spineless young executive who is befriended by Alex (Rob Lowe), a confident

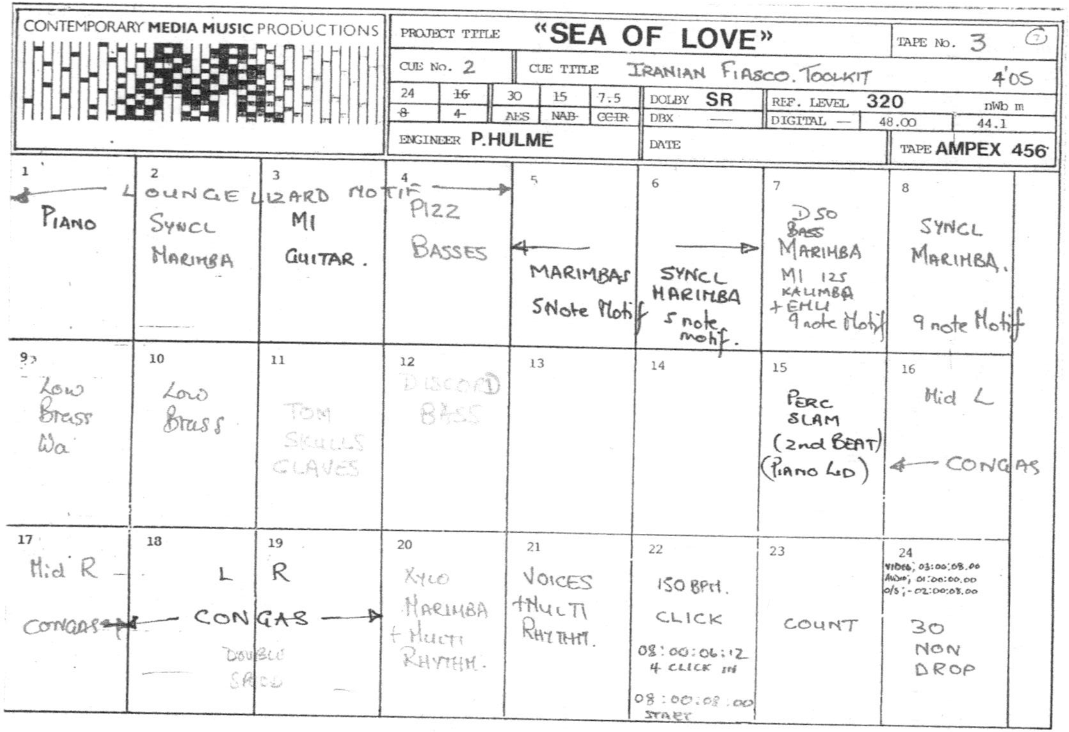

CONTEMPORARY MEDIA MUSIC PRODUCTIONS	PROJECT TITLE "SEA OF LOVE"		CUE No. 2	CUE TITLE IRANIAN FIASCO TOOLKIT		TAPE No. 3 4'05
	24 16 30 15 7.5		DOLBY SR	REF. LEVEL 320		19db m
	8 4 AES NAB GEFR		DBX DIGITAL	48.00		44.1
	ENGINEER P. HULME		DATE			TAPE AMPEX 456

1 PIANO	2 LOUNGE LIZARD MOTIF SYNCL MARIMBA	3 MI GUITAR	4 PIZZ BASSES →	5 MARIMBAS 5note Motif ↓	6 SYNCL MARIMBA 5 note motif.	7 DSO BASS MARIMBA MI 125 MARIMBA + EFFU 9note Motif	8 SYNCL MARIMBA. 9 note Motif
9 LOW BRASS Wa	10 LOW BRASS	11 TOM SKULLS CLAVES	12 DISCORD BASS	13	14	15 PERC SLAM (2nd BEAT) (PIANO LD)	16 Mid L ← CONGAS
17 Mid R CONGAS→	18 L CONGAS DOUBLE SAGO	19 R	20 XYLO MARIMBA +MULTI RHYTHM.	21 VOICES +MULTI RHYTHM.	22 150 BPH CLICK 08:00:04:12 4 CLICK IN 08:00:00:00 START	23 COUNT	24 VIDEO: 03:00:08.00 AUDIO: 01:00:00.00 OBS: 01:00:03.00 30 NON DROP

Figure 4.2 Twenty-four-track breakdown of the Iranian Fiasco Toolkit from *Sea of Love*

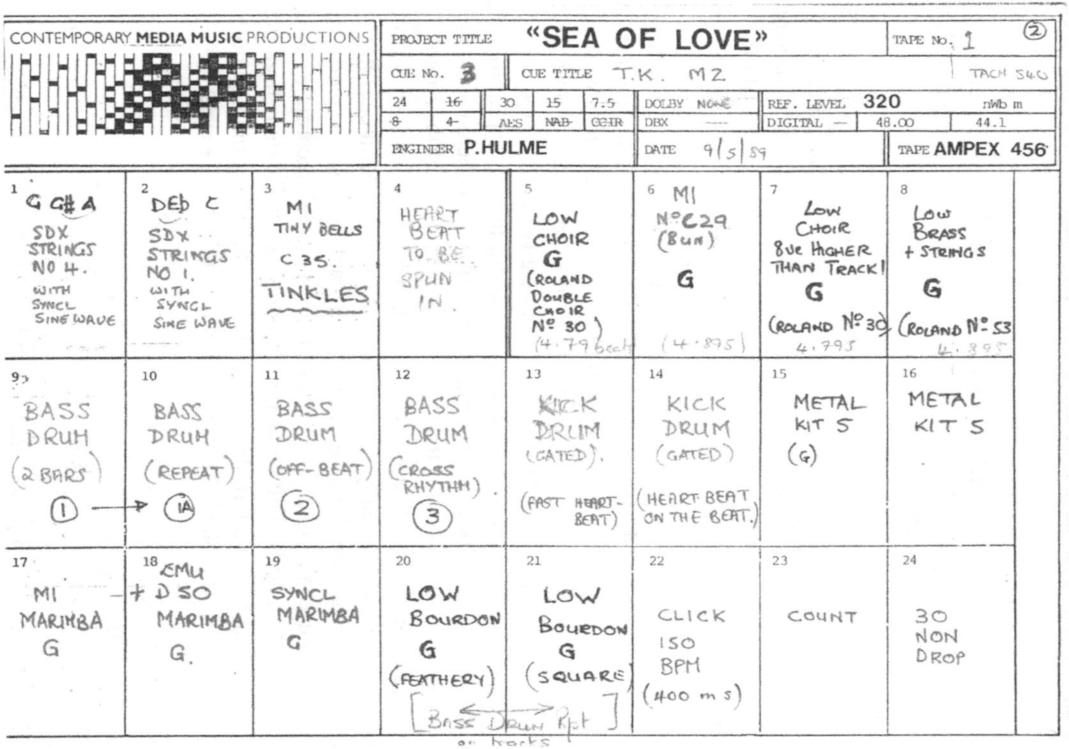
CONTEMPORARY MEDIA MUSIC PRODUCTIONS

PROJECT TITLE "SEA OF LOVE" TAPE No. 1 ②

CUE No. 3 CUE TITLE T.K. M2 TACH 540

24 16 30 15 7.5 DOLBY NONE REF. LEVEL 320 nWb m

8 4 AES NAB CCIR DBX DIGITAL — 48.00 44.1

ENGINEER P.HULME DATE 9/5/89 TAPE AMPEX 456

1 G G# A SDX STRINGS NO 4. WITH SYNCL SINE WAVE	2 DE♭ C SDX STRINGS NO 1. WITH SYNCL SINE WAVE	3 MI TINY BELLS C 35. TINKLES	4 HEART BEAT TO BE SPUN IN.	5 LOW CHOIR G (ROLAND DOUBLE CHOIR Nº 30) (4.79 beat)	6 MI NºC29 (8UN) G (4.895)	7 LOW CHOIR 8ve HIGHER THAN TRACK! G (ROLAND Nº 30) 4.795	8 LOW BRASS + STRINGS G (ROLAND Nº 53) 4.895
9 BASS DRUM (2 BARS) ① →	10 BASS DRUM (REPEAT) 1A	11 BASS DRUM (OFF-BEAT) ②	12 BASS DRUM (CROSS RHYTHM) ③	13 KICK DRUM (GATED). (FAST HEART-BEAT)	14 KICK DRUM (GATED) (HEART BEAT ON THE BEAT.)	15 METAL KIT 5 (G)	16 METAL KIT 5
17 MI MARIMBA G	18 EMU + D 50 MARIMBA G.	19 SYNCL MARIMBA G	20 LOW BOURDON G (FEATHERY)	21 LOW BOURDON G (SQUARE) [Bass Drum Rpt on tracks]	22 CLICK 150 BPM (400 ms)	23 COUNT	24 30 NON DROP

Figure 4.3 Twenty-four-track breakdown of toolkit TKM2 from *Sea of Love*

stranger who encourages Michael to stand up for himself more. While things improve for him in the short term, Michael only comes to the realisation that he is being manipulated by a dangerous sociopath after Alex has infiltrated and taken control of almost every aspect of his life.

Jones's score includes 'Rhythm Toolkit' 1A, Toolkit 1B and 'Atmos Toolkit', and the archival materials indicate that toolkits 1A and 1B were the first sounds recorded by Jones for the film, in January 1990. The Atmos Toolkit followed, along with numbered cues later in the month. The twenty-four-track mixes of each toolkit situate them in a similar sonic space to those of *Sea of Love* and the other toolkit projects, with a range of unpitched percussion instruments sitting alongside recognisable sounds such as 'chomping cellos', marimba and bourdon. Indeed, the Atmos Toolkit – presumably shorthand for 'atmosphere toolkit' – includes four bourdon pitches (A, C, Eb and F) on separate tracks, recalling the strategy employed in *A Private Life* and *Sea of Love*, and the distinctive 3+3+3+3+2+2 rhythm is hinted at in two of the toolkits, though the accents are omitted from the second half of the pattern on this occasion. Toolkit 1B is rather under-used relative to Jones's previous projects, although the Rhythm Toolkit 1A and Atmos Toolkit permeate the score somewhat through a combination of individual elements and a stereo mix of the latter cropping up in numerous cues.

The track sheets for *Bad Influence* are less explicit than those from *Sea of Love* in terms of signposting the use of the toolkits within and across the film's cues. While track 4 of the Atmos Toolkit, 'Industrial Noise', indicates that it is taken directly from TK1B, it does not identify the source as track 8 from that toolkit specifically, and the labelling therefore lacks the detail of Jones's preceding project in this respect. Furthermore, although sounds from the toolkits appear routinely on the track sheets for multitrack recordings of the film's numbered cues, the most direct reference to the toolkit sources is when a stereo mix of the Atmos Toolkit features in a cue and is labelled as such. Instead, indications that sounds have been taken from the toolkits usually take two forms. Firstly, several cues have offset timings hand-written on the reverse of the relevant track sheet, presumably to enable synchronised playback of the tracks from the toolkit recordings along with the live sound. Cue 8M1 'Oil Well', for example, includes sounds from both the Atmos Toolkit and Rhythm Toolkit 1A and has the following timing information relating to two of the toolkits written on the back of the track sheet:[3]

Offset for ATMOS TOOLKIT 07:01:17:13
Bar 39 08:01:30.12
O/S FOR TK1 00:00:19:18.76

The other indication that sounds have been taken from the film's toolkits is the inclusion on track sheets of numbers that appear to imply changes to the input level, presumably to balance the mix of the resulting cue. The track sheet for cue 9M1 'Brother Helps', shown in Figure 4.4, combines recorded sounds with elements from the Atmos Toolkit, and listings for the latter are accompanied by figures of some sort. The 'wind piano', bourdons and bass drums (BD's) are all shown with

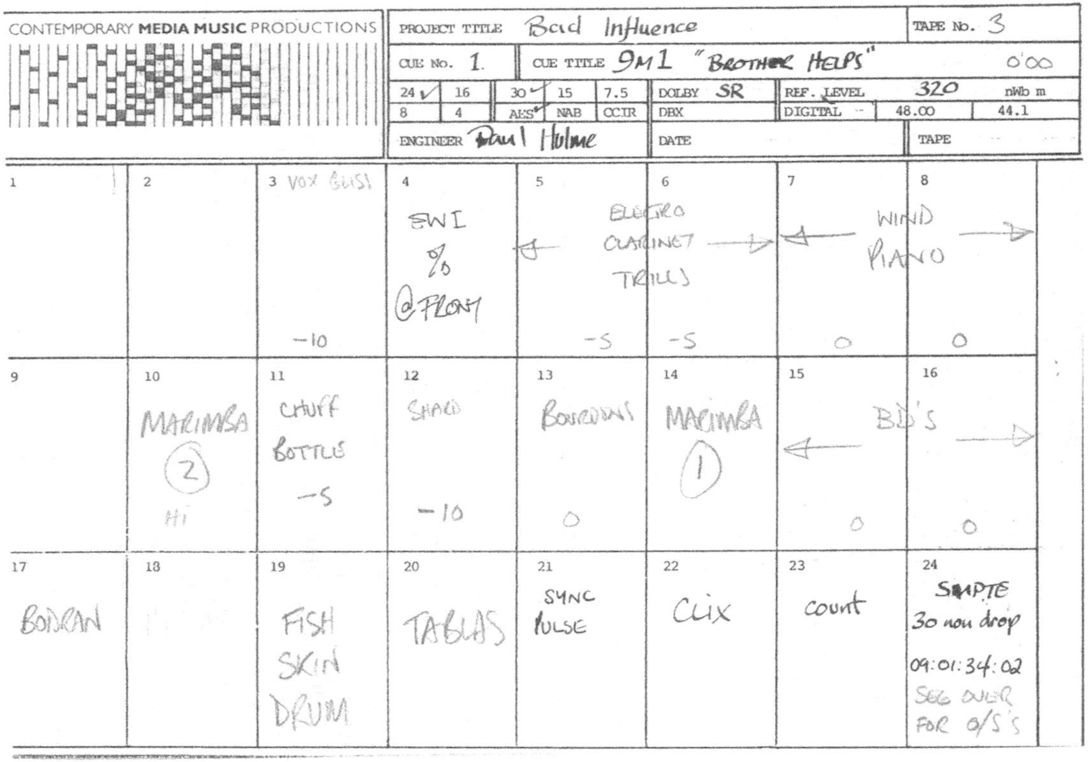

CONTEMPORARY **MEDIA MUSIC** PRODUCTIONS

PROJECT TITLE Bad Influence | TAPE No. 3

CUE No. 1. | CUE TITLE 9M1 "BROTHER HELPS" 0'00

24 ✓	16	30 ✓	15	7.5	DOLBY SR	REF. LEVEL	320	nWb m
8	4	AES	NAB	CCIR	DBX	DIGITAL	48.00	44.1

ENGINEER Paul Holme | DATE | TAPE

1	2	3 VOX GLISS -10	4 EWI % @FRONT	5 ← ELECTRO CLARINET TRILLS -5	6 ELECTRO CLARINET TRILLS → -5	7 ← WIND PIANO 0	8 WIND PIANO → 0
9	10 MARIMBA (2) Hi	11 CHUFF BOTTLES -5	12 SHAD -10	13 BOURDONS 0	14 MARIMBA (1)	15 ← BD'S 0	16 BD'S → 0
17 BODRAN	18	19 FISH SKIN DRUM	20 TABLAS	21 SYNC PULSE	22 CLIX	23 count	24 SMPTE 30 non drop 09:01:34:02 SEE OVER FOR O/S'S

Figure 4.4 Track sheet for the twenty-four track mix of cue 9M1 'Brother Helps' from *Bad Influence*, showing the level adjustments for sounds drawn from the Atmos Toolkit

'0' at the bottom of their respective track boxes, indicating that no change is required from their toolkit level for use in this cue, but the 'electro clarinet trills' and 'chuff bottle' are both shown with a -5 marking and 'vox gliss' and 'shard' carry -10. By contrast, the EWI, marimbas, bodhrán (shown incorrectly as 'bodran' on track 17 of Figure 4.4), hi-hat (which appears to have been erased from track 18 of the track sheet but is nonetheless present on the recording), fish-skin drum and tablas – those parts of the cue not drawn from one of the film's toolkits – have no such markings since they would have been balanced live during the recording session.

The inclusion of track-sheet references to timings and input levels emphasises Jones's active role in determining the sonic profile of the score and also demonstrates the value of the archival materials for enhancing understanding of how the musical material was conceived and produced. It is apparent that the toolkit elements were a constituent part of the musical materials created for directorial approval, rather than existing to enable Hanson to mould the film's soundscape himself, and overall, *Bad Influence* stabilises rather than develops the toolkit approach, reinforcing the idea found in *Sea of Love* that they have become composer- rather than director-facing tools. Indeed, in terms of Jones's processes the score is probably most notable for being the first to feature the term 'atmos', an idea to which he returns in the following years.

Jones's early 1990s scores

In the course of the following two years Jones completed two television scores – HBO's *By Dawn's Early Light* (1990, also called *The Grand Tour*) and *The Object of Beauty* (1990) – and three scores for cinema – *Chains of Gold*, the comedy horror *Arachnophobia* (both 1990) and *True Colors* (1991), the latter of which featured *Bad Influence* star James Spader in another leading role. With the exception of *The Object of Beauty*, the score for which consists exclusively of numbered cues mainly in a light swing-jazz idiom (featuring acoustic guitar played by virtuoso John Williams), Jones drew on toolkits across these projects, in each case utilising the technique to support the musical representation of the dark narratives. Indeed, it is notable that Jones's music for *The Object of Beauty*, his third score for director Michael Lindsay-Hogg, was rejected after recording with Tom Bähler providing a replacement. While the archive does not contain any indication of the reason for this rejection, Jones's change of style and approach relative to his other work of the period – and to his previous score for Lindsay-Hogg, *Murder on the Moon* – may have been a contributory factor.

The scores for *By Dawn's Early Light* and *Chains of Gold* are structured in a similar way to those of *Sea of Love* and *Bad Influence*, combining a small number of toolkits (three in each case) with a series of numbered cues. The two pictures are both action dramas – the former revolves around a power struggle between the US and the Soviet Union and focuses on a military operation to prevent the outbreak of World War III,[4] and the latter follows social worker and unlikely hero Scott Barnes (John Travolta) as he attempts to save a young boy from the clutches of a violent gang of drug-dealers. Despite one project being for television and the other for cinema Jones adopted similar working practices across the two commissions, particularly as regards the toolkits. The archival materials help explain this consistency of approach, despite *Chains of Gold* being released in cinemas in April 1991, a year after *By Dawn's Early Light* was broadcast on television. The earliest VHS tape in the archive for the big-screen picture, which seems likely to be the first resource sent to the composer, includes a note dated 29 December 1989, and there are two further video tapes from mid-February 1990, so it is very likely that outline compositional work on *Chains of Gold* overlapped with the final editing and recording of *By Dawn's Early Light*.

Each of the toolkits for *By Dawn's Early Light* appears to fulfil a different function within the sound world of the picture, with Toolkit TK1 the most varied timbrally. It contains a mix of percussion, bass, strings and brass, though the track sheet, shown in Figure 4.5, does not reveal the full nuance of the recording.[5] While the strings on tracks 7–8 and brass chords on tracks 9–11 are augmented and complemented by tracks 15–16 and 13–14, respectively, the same is not true of the multiple drum and bass sounds in the toolkit. Instead, tracks 17–19 are sub-mixes of 1–2 (bass drums and timpani), 3–4 (basses) and 5–6 (snare drums), meaning that individual and composite sound elements can be taken from the toolkit for use elsewhere without the need for further sub-mixing, as had been required on *Sea of Love*. A similar strategy is employed in Toolkit 3 'High Pulse', which includes 'Trombones Bounce' on tracks 15–16, a mix of four other trombone recordings across tracks 9–12, and is taken to its limit in Toolkit 2 'Long Strings', which has a stereo mix of the full toolkit on tracks 19–20.

Chains of Gold's TK1, the recording of which runs to over seven minutes in duration, consists of three low drones, a series of unpitched percussion rhythms that outline a slow three-beat pattern, and electronic-sounding bass notes that are so low in frequency that they are virtually unpitched. TK2 has more elements than TK1 and contrasts with the first toolkit in numerous ways. It is anchored by a single looped bassline in a brisk four time and an occasional electronic-sounding high-pitched cell but is otherwise made up of unpitched, rhythmic percussion including a range of 'skins', woods and metals, as well as cymbals and shaker sounds. TK3 utilises pitch rather than percussion, combining held drones and pulses usually quite high in register, with a range of musical cells that tend to fall away in a sort of Doppler effect before silencing and restarting. The sustained sounds provide continuity while the other elements create a wave-like effect and a feeling of consistent and constant falling away across the duration of the toolkit.

The respective Toolkit 2s play key roles in the construction of each of these scores. The track sheets for the thirty-seven cues of *By Dawn's Early Light* show extensive use of this material across the score including occurrences of a complete stereo mix of the toolkit being used as a key component of a cue, and *Chains of Gold* employs percussive elements from TK2 at various points, including under the end credits, to give the music energy and drive. Exclusive use of the other toolkits is far less common in both pictures, though this is perhaps unsurprising given the relative lack of melodic material in each of these sound sets. Instead they tend to be used as backgrounds onto which melodies can be overlaid or they are

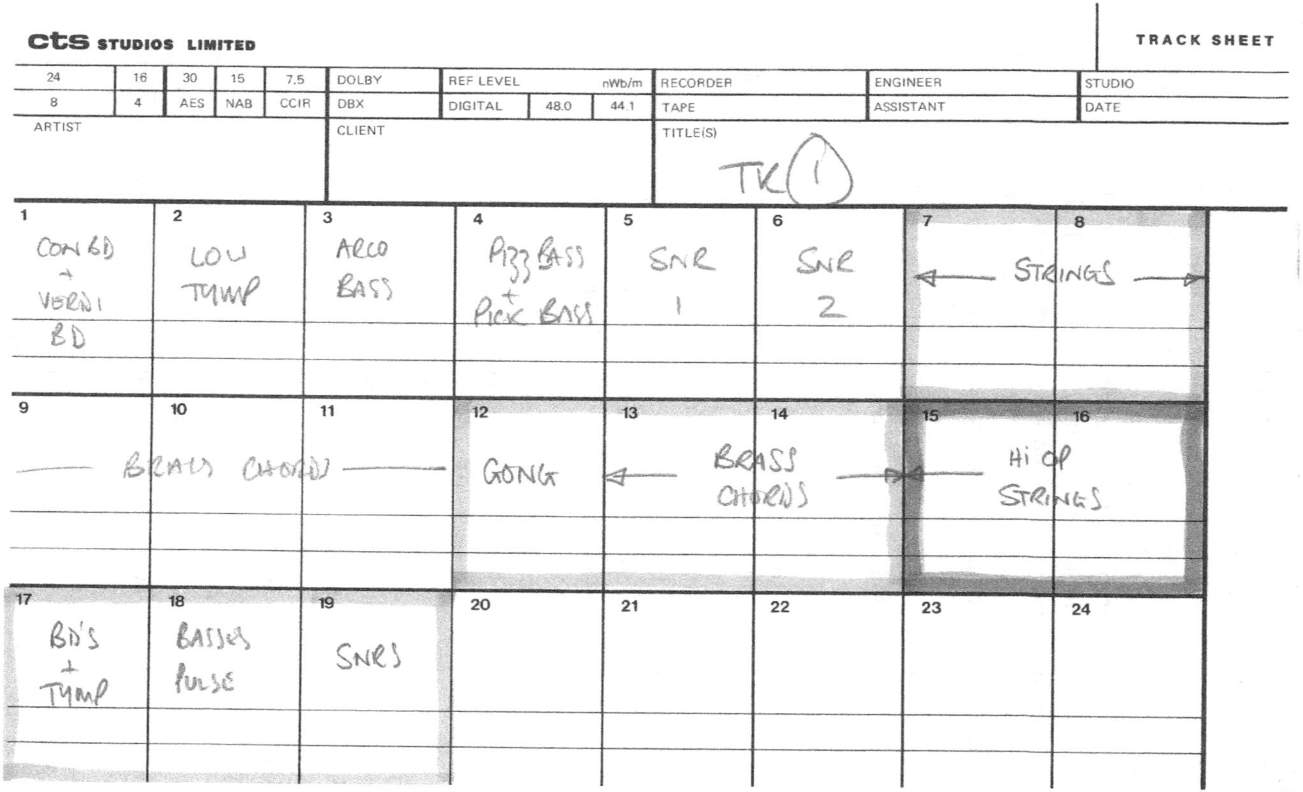

Figure 4.5 Twenty-four-track breakdown of toolkit TK1 from *By Dawn's Early Light*

combined to create composite effects, such as when rhythms from TK2 and some of the Doppler effect phrases from TK3 are used in *Chains of Gold* (1991) for scenes in which Barnes observes the boys being used to transfer cash between gang members. *Chains of Gold* contains two further sonic elements of note, and although they are not drawn from the toolkits they relate closely to some of Jones's other scores. The first is a derivative of the *Angel Heart/Sea of Love* 'Lounge Lizard motif' that brings the distinctive 3+3+3+3+2+2 rhythm into the score in a variation that is modified so that the end of the phrase ascends. While it is not as prominent in this score as it is in the earlier pictures, its presence is nonetheless significant given Jones's frequent use of this rhythmic pattern in scores of this period in particular. Rather than recalling previous work, the second element is a brief passage heard towards the end of the film as Barnes hangs from cables in a lift shaft to avoid dropping into a pit of alligators (*Chains of Gold*, 1991 at 1:21:00) that foreshadows one of Jones's later scores. The melody is quite innocuous in the context of the film – this is its only appearance, and it is entirely undeveloped in this single cue – but Jones would bring this musical idea to its full potential a few years later as the main theme to Hallmark's 1996 television mini-series *Gulliver's Travels*.

The construction of the score for the horror-comedy film *Arachnophobia* aligns broadly with the strategies employed in the two preceding pictures, but alongside five toolkits and a series of numbered musical cues there is some material labelled as 'Spider "Atmos" Master'. The recording includes 'pitched elements' in a stereo pair, 'light percussion' and a gong and is the first instance in the archive of a sound set being labelled specifically as an atmos[phere] rather than a toolkit.[6] *Arachnophobia*'s toolkits consist mainly of electronic sounds, drones and percussive patterns and do not represent a significant advancement of the technique, but the 'Spider "Atmos" Master' is referenced on track sheets for several cues, including functioning as a guide track on early recordings. Indeed, as its name indicates, the sound set provides a consistent 'atmosphere' onto and around which cues can be composed and developed, meaning that they retain a sense of individuality and specificity for their narrative contexts but nonetheless remain connected within the overall sound world of the picture. This strategy connects with the ways in which the rhythmic toolkits of *By Dawn's Early Light* and *Chains of Gold* were utilised and establishes properly the start of a new direction for the ways in which these resources are employed in Jones's scores.

By contrast, the final score of this period, *True Colors*, represents both a forward and backward step in Jones's development of the toolkit method. The information on the boxes for the analogue multitrack reels includes mention of two toolkits, numbered 1 and 2, and makes specific reference to three cues in this regard; the cue number and name for 1M2A 'Main Title' and 5M4A 'Peter Slashes Tyre' are both followed by 'Toolkit 1', with the second half of the main title, 1M2B, succeeded by 'Toolkit 2'. The labelling of these materials is somewhat unclear, however, since taking the track sheets for 1M2A and 1M2B together indicates that the 1M2A is both a cue and a toolkit, with a complete stereo mix of that cue found on tracks 1 and 2 of 1M2B, mimicking the occasional use of Toolkit 2 from *By Dawn's Early Light*. Confusingly this means that in *True Colors* Toolkit 2 comprises the whole of Toolkit 1 plus melodic material for electric guitars and flute/panpipe, bass guitar, an introductory fanfare on synths and a little additional percussion, though some of these elements are already present in 1M2A. The other cue referenced as a toolkit, 5M4A was spotted for a later scene in the picture but does not actually appear in the cinematic release of the film, meaning that despite the complex use of toolkits in 1M2A and 1M2B, because this opening title material is used only in the first few scenes of the film, the toolkits ultimately play a much more limited role than would normally be expected in a Jones score from this period.

Archival materials are key to understanding the construction and use of the toolkits and cues in *True Colors* and exploring similar resources for *Arachnophobia* equally reveals the value of archival research into music for screen media. In this case knowledge of the existing archival materials highlights the absence of other artefacts, with the collection including documentation for twenty-four-track mixes of the film's cues on 'Mix Reel 1' and 'Mix Reel 2', but these physical tapes and the audio materials they contain are missing from the archival holdings. Another notable aspect of *Arachnophobia* as an archival resource is that in addition to being marked with recording dates, some of the boxes for the multitrack reels offer very specific information that supports detailed understanding of the chronology of the audio materials. This is particularly important when other materials and data in the archive are unclear or open to interpretation, and the information also helps to rationalise the absence of some pieces of documentation. For example, slave material for cue 1M2 appears twice in the archival audio recordings, on multitrack reels 2 and 4, which are dated 'May 1990' and 'May/June 1990', respectively.[7] Given the lack of specificity in these dates, the implication is that the latter reel probably contains the later iteration of 1M2, but additional notes are given for this cue only on the boxes. The recording on reel 2 is labelled as 'Tepui Trek (1.6.90) revised', meaning that although recording on the physical tape seems to have begun in May (based on the main date listed for reel 2), this cue is a revision from 1 June. Furthermore, the iteration of the cue on reel 4 is marked 'Tepui Trek ((Original Version) Pre June 1990)', indicating that although the reel is dated 'May/June 1990' and therefore appears to post-date the other recording, this is an earlier version of the cue and is therefore superseded by that on reel 2.

1M2 poses an additional problem since the archive contains a single track sheet for the slave elements of the cue, shown in Figure 4.6, and the document does not indicate the recording to which it corresponds. Comparison of the audio recordings on reels 2 and 4 reveals that Jones made just two small changes when revising the cue, removing a 'pan flute' note in bars 17–19 and repeating the log drum's rhythmic pattern from bar 5 in bars 34 and 37. While normally these changes would not be substantial enough to be discernible from the track sheet (since no instruments have been added or omitted), as can be seen in Figure 4.6, tracks 3 and 11 have been marked up to show the entries of the log drum and pan flute respectively. The inclusion of '34+37' in the former and omission of '17' in the latter thus confirm that the document relates to the later version, on multitrack reel 2. The track sheet for reel 4 is missing from the archive, and it seems likely that it may have been destroyed to avoid confusion, given that the changes made were very small.

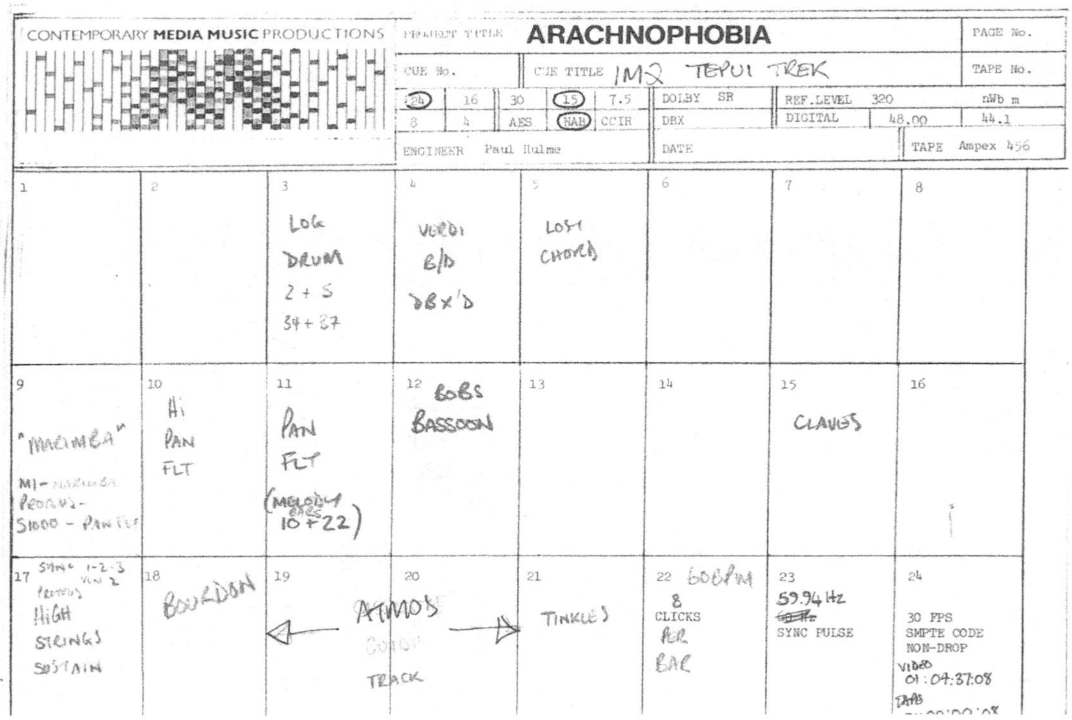

							TAPE No.
CONTEMPORARY **MEDIA MUSIC** PRODUCTIONS		**ARACHNOPHOBIA**					TAPE No.
PROJECT TITLE		CUE TITLE 1M2 TERUI TREK					dBb m
CUE No. 16 30 15 7.5 DOLBY SR REF. LEVEL 320							44.1
8 4 ASS CAB CCIR DBX DIGITAL 48.00							
ENGINEER Paul Hulme			DATE			TAPE Ampex 456	

1	2	3	4	5	6	7	8
"MARIMBA" MI-MARIMBA PEDAL- SLIDO - PAN FLT		LO6 DRUM 2+5 34+37	VERB1 B/B 28x'D	LOST CHORD			

9	10	11	12	13	14	15	16
	Hi PAN FLT	PAN FLT (MELODY 10+22)	12 BOBS BASSOON			CLAVES	

17	18	19	20	21	22	23	24
SYN6 1-2-3 (INTRO) VERS 2 HIGH STRINGS SUSTAIN	BOURDON		ATMOS GUIDE TRACK	TINKLE	60 BPM 8 CLICKS per BAR	59.94 Hz SYNC PULSE	30 FPS SMPTE CODE NON-DROP VIDEO 01:04:37:08

Figure 4.6 Track sheet for the recording of 1M2 from *Arachnophobia*

Blame It on the Bellboy (1992)

Blame It on the Bellboy is the most light-hearted of all the projects scored by Jones in this period and revolves around the similarly named Melvyn Orton (inspecting a villa for purchase by his boss), Maurice Horton (on a blind 'Medi-Date' for middle-aged singles) and Michael Lawton (a contract hitman), all of whom are guests at the Hotel Gabrielli in Venice. The hapless bellboy's limited English means he cannot distinguish between the three surnames, and he mixes up their post, resulting in Orton endeavouring to buy the home of Scarpa, the local Mafia boss; Horton attempting to sleep with estate agent Caroline Wright; and Lawton trying to kill Patricia Fulford, a lady from Huddersfield who is looking for love. The various plotlines are resolved following a number of comedic misunderstandings, most of which involve the bellboy trying to work out which guest is which. A strong correlation has been shown between darker, grittier narratives and the employment of compositional toolkits, so it is perhaps unsurprising to find that there is no mention of this device among the archival materials for this picture. However, in addition to numbered cues the audio resources contain multitrack recordings of six Venetian Dances composed by Jones that can be viewed through a similar lens to the toolkits of his other scores of the early 1990s and show continuous development of his practice in this period.

While they vary in terms of character, key, time signature and tempo, as shown in Table 4.1, the six Venetian Dances are all scored for strings, harpsichord and guitar and seem crafted to evoke a Vivaldian sound world that relates strongly to the film's geographic setting. With running times of around three minutes and structures that draw extensively on repeated phrases and patterns – as might be expected given the Baroque modelling – these dances appear to provide ample material from which Jones could draw to create individual cues and themes for the film. Such a strategy would, in effect, mimic that employed in the early toolkit films, rendering the Venetian dances as toolkits in all but name, but this does not appear to have been the approach taken. Indeed, the only use of the dances within *Blame It on the Bellboy* is as short extracts that act as diegetic background music within the Hotel Gabrielli, as outlined in Table 4.2.[8]

As Table 4.2 shows, despite the total duration of the audio recordings in the archive, the longest uninterrupted use of any Dance, when two of the characters first check into the hotel, is just over one minute. The multitrack reels in the

Table 4.1 The six Venetian Dances from *Blame It on the Bellboy*

Dance	Initial Key	Time Signature	Tempo (bpm)	Duration
1	D minor	4/4	120	3:30
2	G major	3/4	150	2:50
3	D major	4/4	92	3:40
4	D minor	3/4	127	3:10
5	D major	4/4	60	3:20
6	D minor	4/4	60	2:50

Table 4.2 Placement of extracts from the six Venetian Dances in *Blame It on the Bellboy*

Start Time	Dance	Duration	Scene	Interruptions
0:07:10	2	1:02	Horton and Orton check into the hotel	
0:33:56	1	0:34	Orton checks out of the hotel then checks back in	Brief stop for mafia music mid-cue
0:35:50	1	0:10	Bellboy and Mrs Horton exit the lift	
0:37:29	1	0:31	Bellboy and Mrs Horton back in the lift, and exiting again	Gap for short dialogue scene halfway through extract
0:44:02	2	0:20	Lawton and Fulford discuss his pseudonym in the lift	
0:51:37	3	1:30	Horton receives his suitcase and checks it into hotel security	Break in the middle for mafia music
0:54:33	4	0:40	Lawton and Fulford sit in reception and discuss his future	
0:56:23	5	0:58	Orton retrieves his briefcase from the hotel reception	
1:05:02	5	0:45	Orton returns to the hotel and receives a message	Short burst of suspense music early in the cue

archive indicate that some pieces identified as source music – for scenes such as the aeroplane to Venice taking off and Maurice having dinner on the first night – were recorded on 22 and 24 July 1991, with the first two Venetian Dances also listed under the latter date, reinforcing the impression that they were created to be used diegetically. However, the track sheets for these two dances offer a conflicting date of 20 August 1991, when the remaining four Dances were recorded according to both the track sheets and multitrack reel boxes. Seven numbered cues were also brought to the recording studio at the end of that month, with the remainder of the music reaching the scoring stage in early October. The role played by the Venetian Dances 1 and 2 in the development of Jones's score may vary depending on when they were recorded, and the archival evidence enables a compelling case to be made for each of the two possible dates. An argument can be made that the presence of Venetian Dances 1 and 2 on tape W2 alongside the early source material indicates the recording date of 24 July is more likely to be correct. Alternatively, consideration of the printed layout of the track sheets for these Dances, which matches those used for the other Dances but differs from the paperwork for the other cues recorded in July, suggests an August recording date is more credible. Depending on which interpretation is accurate, it is possible that Jones may have originally employed Dances 1 and 2 in all of the places outlined in Table 4.2, with some occurrences changed to other Dances later in the process, or that they were used as placeholders while he worked on the score – in a similar manner to the toolkits of *Dominick and Eugene*, as discussed in Chapter 3 – being replaced with cues once they had been written and recorded. Such a reading is only plausible if the music was recorded on the earlier date since this results in a period of about a month between each set of recording sessions in which Jones could write cues to replace the Venetian Dance 'placeholders'. However, the ambiguity of the archival materials mean that the date of recording cannot be proven, and accordingly this hypothesis cannot be properly corroborated.[9]

There are two VHS tapes for *Blame It on the Bellboy*, and although neither is dated it is most likely that they predate the first of Jones's recording sessions since none of his source music is used on either of them. Each video is a complete rough cut of the film, though they differ from each other and from the final cinematic release. The first has dialogue and sound effects but no music, but the second, which is closer to the final cut, has a complete temp score and therefore reveals more about the film-makers' musical intentions. In this respect, the most notable thing about the temp is its use of music by Italian composers. The arrival of the various characters in Venice is underscored by the title track from Nino Rota's music for *Amarcord* (1973), and part of his score for *Le Notti di Cabiria* (1957) features over the shots of each morning in Venice and as a motif for the speedboat desired by Caroline Wright. Similarly, Orton is chased through Venice by Scarpa's thugs to the sound of Ennio Morricone's main theme from *Le Marginal* (1983), and Lawton and Fulford's elevator conversation about the merits of his false name is backed by the opening of the finale from Concerto for Two Mandolins in G RV532 by Antonio Vivaldi. There is also some Italian-sounding music – notably Georges Delerue's 'Le Grand Choral' from *La Nuit Américaine* (also known as *Day for Night*, 1973), which has a distinctly Vivaldian presence – as well as material such as Bernard Herrmann's *The Twilight Zone* theme, which has clearly been chosen for its aural impact rather than any geographic implication. The closing music is The Christians' track 'The Perfect Moment', presumably chosen because it is the title of the book Fulford is seen reading and to which reference is made within the picture, and the song is retained in this position in the final release. There are two other pieces of music used prominently on the temp that it has not been possible to identify from the available materials. The first is a short motif for the mafia boss, Scarpa, and his men that features a clarinet tremolo and staccato interjection on timpani followed by dissonant leaps on strings and xylophone; the other is a pulsing D minor track in 7/4 (occasionally dropping briefly into 4/4) with repeated timpani crotchets on the tonic and a one-bar quaver motif played repetitively by bassoon and low strings under alternating brass fanfare-type figures and a short oboe melody. While the first track is very short and is heard numerous times across the film, the second appears only once but runs almost continuously for five-and-a-half minutes from the three parties boarding their respective boats until the explosion of Scarpa's bomb, as Orton, Horton and Lawton's narrative paths finally collide.

Like his Venetian Dances, Jones's main theme presents an approximation of a Vivaldian piece of music in terms of melodic and harmonic structure, though it also incorporates a trumpet lead that draws parallels with Delerue's 'Le Grand Choral'. The Baroque illusion is somewhat shattered, however, by the overlaying of a drum pattern, and the track sheet for the cue also reveals the presence in the mix of a Jonesian hallmark, the bourdon. When the theme returns at the end of the film it also features a solo saxophone line, another distinctive fingerprint of Jones's music of this period. Jones's main theme is in D major – the same key as 'Le Grand Choral' – and it is possible that the tonality of the temp score restricted the composer somewhat when he first started work on the score. Indeed, as Table 4.3 shows, with the exception of the material from *Amarcord* and *The Twilight Zone*, each of which is heard only once, all of the main musical elements of the temp track are in D major, D minor or G major, the three keys in which Jones composed his Venetian dances.

Ultimately, however, Jones was able to break away from the influence of the temp, and aside from the instrumental and stylistic relationship to Delerue's theme in Jones's main title (which is arguably as indebted to Vivaldi as it is to Delerue) the score stands well apart from the temp material. Indeed, while there are no toolkits the score nonetheless connects sonically to other Jones scores from this period, notably through the short theme for Scarpa and the mafia that derives sonically from *Sea of Love*'s 'shark signal motif'. The film was a critical and commercial failure, with Hal Hinton commenting in his *Washington Post* review that the picture's setting on Venice's Grand Canal 'is pretty much the sum total of what is grand about it' (Hinton 1992). However, while the picture was poorly received, the project was Jones's first with writer and director Mark Herman, a partnership that would demonstrate its proper potential four years later with *Brassed Off*.[10] The stylistic role played by the Venetian dances can also be viewed as an intimation of Jones's development of 'atmospheres' as part of his scoring process, something that becomes more apparent through his other scores from 1992.

Table 4.3 Key relationships between the temp score and Jones's early material for *Blame It on the Bellboy*

Key	Temp Score	Jones's Early Material
D major	'Le Grand Choral'	Venetian Dance 3 Venetian Dance 5 (Main title theme)
D minor	*Le Notti di Cabiria* *Le Marginal* Mafia motif 7/4 material at filmic climax	Venetian Dance 1 Venetian Dance 4 Venetian Dance 6
G major	Vivaldi concerto 'The Perfect Moment'	Venetian Dance 2

1992: from toolkits to atmospheres

The significant time that elapsed between the recording sessions for *Blame It on the Bellboy* in July 1991 and its theatrical release in January 1992 meant that Jones was able to write and record the complete score to the science-fiction thriller *Freejack* after finishing the other project.[11] *Freejack* was released in cinemas a week before *Blame It on the Bellboy* but was also generally received poorly by critics.[12] Indeed, the film struggled to recoup its estimated $30 million budget despite the novel plotline and an all-star cast that included Emilio Estevez, Anthony Hopkins, Rene Russo and Mick Jagger.

As was the case for *Blame It on the Bellboy*, there is no mention of toolkits in any of the documentation for *Freejack*, but there are references to 'atmospheres' on track sheets and in the musical score. For example, cue 3M1 'Switchboard Ambience' contains a stereo pair of tracks labelled 'Synth Atmos', with a note on the sheet that these tracks along with the bourdon, bass drum and low gong 'are the spiritual switchboard atmosphere'. Similarly, tracks 1 and 3 of cue 4M1 'Brad's Place' are described on the track sheet as 'sinister atmos sounds in stereo', as shown in Figure 4.7. The designation 'Synth Atmos' also appears in other cues, and while the supporting notes sometimes indicate a repetition of a previous sound, for the most part these atmospheres seem to be largely cue specific.

The archival materials for *CrissCross*, which date from the spring following Jones's completion of *Blame It on the Bellboy* and *Freejack*, include a twenty-four-track recording of cue 10M2 dated 12 April 1992 and titled 'The Bust (Toolkit)', though the final eight-track mix of the cue created little over a fortnight later removes this reference, leaving only the cue number and name. The 'toolkit' in question seems to be a reference to the collection of sounds employed in the cue, which include 'hi electric' and 'lo electric', 'sheer', 'Mr. Eno 1', 'Itopia', 'shards' and a 'bottles' sound produced using the Synclavier, though these timbres are by no means unique to 10M2, so it is unclear why the label has been attached only to this specific cue. Indeed, track sheets for the multitrack and mix recordings for other cues from the film show that, as is the case in *Freejack*, atmosphere is more widely used as a catch-all term for this sort of sound set. For example, cues 6M1 'Drug Revelations' and 6M3 'Chris Cuts Cocaine' include all of the unusual sounds found in 10M2 plus 'Inferno' and 'Spacey Vox', and although the term is not used explicitly on the multitrack documentation, these sounds are clearly grouped under the heading 'atmosphere' on the first left and right channels of the dual left-centre-right (L-C-R) of the eight-track mixes, as shown in Figure 4.8.

The relative absence of toolkits in the score is particularly notable given that it was written very quickly to replace music by Michael Convertino.[13] Gergely Hubai notes that 'Convertino's score was dropped shortly before the movie's premiere, and Trevor Jones was hired to write a new one in only one week's time' (Hubai 2012, p. 255), though the dates on materials in the archive indicate that the timeframe was not quite this compressed. Nonetheless, the fact that this was a replacement score may have led to Jones terming 10M2 a toolkit as he was crafting it – toolkits were fundamental to the construction of his previous replacement

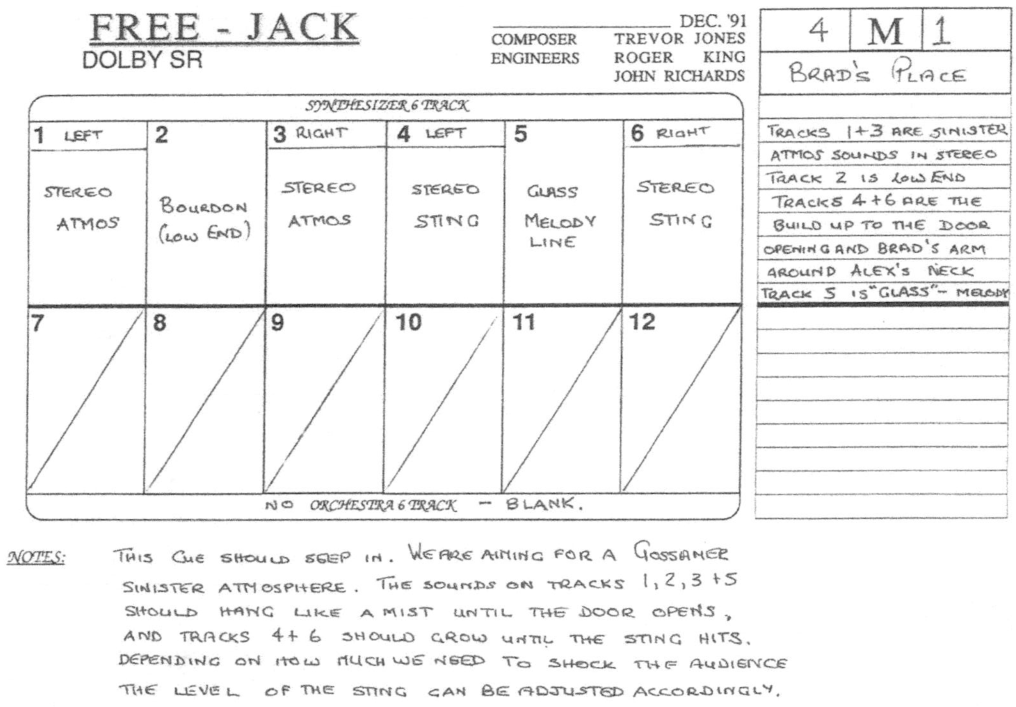

FREE - JACK
DOLBY SR

COMPOSER: TREVOR JONES
ENGINEERS: ROGER KING, JOHN RICHARDS
DEC. '91

4 | M | 1
BRAD'S PLACE

SYNTHESIZER 6 TRACK

1 LEFT	2	3 RIGHT	4 LEFT	5	6 RIGHT
STEREO ATMOS	BOURDON (LOW END)	STEREO ATMOS	STEREO STING	GLASS MELODY LINE	STEREO STING
7	8	9	10	11	12

NO ORCHESTRA 6 TRACK - BLANK.

Track descriptions:
- TRACKS 1 + 3 ARE SINISTER ATMOS SOUNDS IN STEREO
- TRACK 2 IS LOW END
- TRACKS 4 + 6 ARE THE BUILD UP TO THE DOOR OPENING AND BRAD'S ARM AROUND ALEX'S NECK
- TRACK 5 IS "GLASS" - MELODY

NOTES: THIS CUE SHOULD SEEP IN. WE ARE AITING FOR A GOSSAMER SINISTER ATMOSPHERE. THE SOUNDS ON TRACKS 1, 2, 3 + 5 SHOULD HANG LIKE A MIST UNTIL THE DOOR OPENS, AND TRACKS 4 + 6 SHOULD GROW UNTIL THE STING HITS. DEPENDING ON HOW MUCH WE NEED TO SHOCK THE AUDIENCE THE LEVEL OF THE STING CAN BE ADJUSTED ACCORDINGLY.

Figure 4.7 Track sheet for the six-track mix of cue 4M1 from *Freejack*, showing descriptions of the tracks

CONTEMPORARY MEDIA MUSIC PRODUCTIONS LTD	PROJECT TITLE: **CRISS CROSS**			T.AC Jones	PASS No. 2/8
	CUE No. 6M1	CUE TITLE: DRUG REVELATION			TAPE No. MIX 1
	24 | 16 | 30 | (15) | 7.5	DOLBY S R	REF.LEVEL 320		nWbm
	(8) | 4 | AES | (NAB) | CCIR	DBX	DIGITAL	48.00	44.1
	ENGINEER: R. King		DATE: 28th April 1991		TAPE: AMPEX 456

1 (9) LEFT	2 (10) CENTRE	3 (11) RIGHT	4 (12) LEFT	5 (13) CENTRE	6 (14) RIGHT	7 (15)	8 (16)
ATMOSPHERE LEFT	BOURDON (OPTIONAL)	ATMOSPHERE RIGHT		BOTTLE		PILOT 50 hz	EBU 25

FOOTAGE START: 62'+12
VIDEO START: 06:00:41:22
MIX TAPE TIME: 24–30
SYNC BLIP: (Tracks 9–14) 50'+00
06:00:33:09

Figure 4.8 Track sheet for the eight-track mix of cue 6M1 from *CrissCross*

score, for *Mississippi Burning* (1988) as discussed in Chapter 3 – but the abandonment of that terminology in favour of atmospheres shows a continuity of development across *Freejack* and *CrissCross* in terms of Jones's underlying compositional method. Firstly, rather than creating banks of sounds for use across a score the atmospheres in these two pictures are often bespoke sound mixes for individual film cues, meaning that a score might include a larger number of atmospheres than was common with toolkits, each of which is used less often. Related to this, given that the atmospheres usually appear in *Freejack*'s cues as a pair of stereo tracks, something that is also often found in *CrissCross*, they are more likely to be heard and used as full mixes rather than individual elements or submixes as was frequently the case in the earlier toolkit scores. This final consideration begins to 'normalise' the atmosphere sounds *as* instruments, rather than as *collections of* instruments, indicating a significant change in Jones's creative process.

Toolkits do not feature in Jones's final two scores from 1992, Michael Mann's *The Last of the Mohicans* and HBO's *Barbarians at the Gate*, though the 'normalisation' of electronic atmospheres *as* sounds is realised in the latter picture. Indeed, this might have been the circumstance in the former film as well, with numerous sources reflecting Harris's (2018) suggestion that 'Mann hired Jones to create an electronic score', and Susman (2017) going further in claiming that 'in postproduction, Mann scrapped composer Trevor Jones' electronic score and decided he wanted a more traditional orchestral score. Jones reworked his score but didn't have time to finish it, and Mann had to hire composer Randy Edelman to complete the music'.[14] As already noted, there are few items in the archive relating to the creative and production processes for *The Last of the Mohicans*. However, a video tape dated 27 March 1992, six months before the film's Los Angeles premiere, includes a temp tack made up mainly of cues from recent cinematic releases, twentieth-century Western art music, and pieces that draw on traditional folk influences, the acoustic nature of all of these works calling into question just how late a decision to change to an orchestral score might actually have been made. The works in the temp score that it has been possible to identify are outlined in Table 4.4, along with descriptions of the scenes with which they are heard.

The lack of any audio resources or supporting paperwork in the Trevor Jones Archive prevents a detailed exploration of the development from an electronic to orchestral soundscape, but the role of the temp in the sound of the final score (at least as far as Jones's cues are concerned) is relatively apparent.[15] There are rhythmic and motivic echoes of 'O Fortuna' in the track 'Massacre/Canoes', with prominent four-note brass motifs often comprising two sets of repeated notes a semitone apart or variants on this structure. Likewise elements of Horner's 'Charging Fort Wagner' (which itself draws heavily on *Carmina Burana*) are evident in the 'Fort Battle', though arguably the relentless percussion that underpins Jones's music owes more to Holst's 'Mars' than to Horner's cue. Two tracks – Phil Cunningham's *The House in Rose Valley* and Duncan MacLean's *The Gael* – are retained in these locations in the cinematic release, and while the former is a very short cue the latter plays a key role in the harmonic and structural profile of Jones's score. Indeed, the climactic 'The Promentory' (sic), which starts as Duncan is taken to be executed

Table 4.4 Temp track information for *The Last of the Mohicans*

Temp Track Music	Description of Scene
Arvo Pärt, *Cantus in Memoriam Benjamin Britten*	Opening establishing shots.
Richard Thompson, *Andalus/Radio Marrakesh*	First shots of Hawkeye and the Mohicans.
Phil Cunningham, *The House in Rose Valley*	The colonists engage in sport.
Carl Orff, 'O Fortuna' from *Carmina Burana*	Major Duncan Howard and his British troops taking General Munro's daughters, Cora and Alice, to Fort William Henry are ambushed by Magua and his Huron warriors, with Hawkeye and the Mohicans coming to the rescue.
James Horner, 'Charging Fort Wagner' from *Glory* (1989)	The French army attack General Munro's encampment at Fort William Henry.
Anon., *Te Deum*	Diegetic music during a ceremony in the French commander's tent.
Georges Delerue, 'Chomina Decides to Go Back' from *Black Robe* (1991)	Scene between Hawkeye and Cora in the infirmary at the fort.
Richard Thompson, *Andalus/Radio Marrakesh*	The British attack the French and Huron soldiers as a distraction while a messenger attempts to leave the fort [the attack parts of the scene are not in the final cut of the film].
Duncan MacLean, *The Gael*	Hawkeye and Cora kiss.
Ennio Morricone, 'Climb' from *The Mission* (1986)	Scene between Hawkeye and Cora after he is arrested for helping the colonists desert the fort.
Moving Hearts, *May Morning Dew*	The British abandon the fort having surrendered it to the French.
Carl Orff, 'O Fortuna' from *Carmina Burana*	The British are ambushed and massacred by Magua and his Huron warriors. Hawkeye, the Mohicans, Duncan and the Munro sisters escape and flee down the river, chased by Magua and the Hurons.
John Barry, 'The Death of Timmons' and 'Pawnee Attack' from *Dances with Wolves* (1990)	Magua and the Hurons close in on their prey behind the waterfall. Hawkeye and the Mohicans escape, before the Hurons arrive and take Duncan and the Munro sisters prisoner.
Clannad, theme from *Harry's Game* (1982)	Hawkeye and the Mohicans track Magua, the Hurons and their prisoners north to the Huron settlement.
Duncan MacLean, *The Gael*	Music runs from Duncan's execution at the Huron settlement and the release of Hawkeye and Cora through the chase of Magua's rogue Huron band to try and rescue Alice, and the deaths of Uncas and Alice, only finishing as Magua is killed by Chingachgook.

by the Hurons and continues uninterrupted for over eight minutes, layers *The Gael* with Jones's main theme for the film to bring the narrative to its climactic ending, thereby imposing the harmonic structure and tempo of MacLean's piece on the most memorable of Jones's melodies from the score.

Michael Mann's decision to switch from an electronic to an orchestral score (regardless of when that decision was taken) had an unexpected benefit for Jones, who has stated that for *Cliffhanger*, director Renny Harlin asked him to 'write some music like in *The Last of the Mohicans*' (Benitez 2004b). Indeed, this score marks another step – albeit perhaps not a pre-planned step in this instance – in Jones's move away from the use of toolkits, something that he continued to do despite returning to a more electronic soundscape for his next project, *Barbarians at the Gate*, a humorous dramatisation of a failed attempt by the chief executive officer of RJR Nabisco, F. Ross Johnson (James Garner), to buy out the company. There are no references to toolkits or atmospheres in the archival documentation for the project, and Hubai has described Jones's score as 'primarily synthesiser music enlivened by woodwind overdubs'. Although this is something of an over-simplification – the track sheets show the scoring included a significant number of acoustic instruments – the prominent use of electronic sounds and synthesisers as specific timbres within the ensemble continues the approach taken in *CrissCross*. However, while the score may have shown the continual development of Jones's creative practice, Hubai suggests that it 'didn't suit the producers' tastes and expectations' and was rejected, with a new score provided by Richard Gibbs that was 'more lighthearted and funky, with a definite comedic edge' (2012, p. 404). Such an outcome seems quite puzzling given the broadly similar style of Jones's and Gibbs's main themes, both of which utilise similar instrumentation and tempo, and have a light swing feel that captures the essence of the opening shots of the 1940s. More pertinently, however, these similarities highlight Jones's continual movement towards a more mainstream style that incorporated 'toolkit sounds' within an overall sonic profile but was not driven or explicitly characterised by these elements, a progression that marks the beginning of the end of the toolkit method.

Detonator (1993)

The 1993 US made-for-television movie *Detonator*, also known as *Death Train*, is an action thriller starring Pierce Brosnan, Patrick Stewart, Alexandra Paul and Christopher Lee that hit screens in the UK a few years later, in 1996. The film is about United Nations field operatives attempting to retrieve a stolen Russian nuclear device from a train as it passes through Eastern Europe before it arrives at its journey's end in Iraq and causes the Russian military to invade and force its recovery, thus sparking a war. The outline plot has some resonance with the Cold War narrative of *By Dawn's Early Light*, though in this case the terrorists who stole the device want to start a war in order to reinvigorate the former Soviet Union as a military superpower. Surprisingly, given the developing terminology used in Jones's previous projects, the cue list in the archive indicates that there are two toolkits in this score, though they are used in quite different ways.

Toolkit 1 is mentioned explicitly in the descriptions of four cues in a set of spotting notes for the project but is actually heard widely across the picture. Indeed, the audio resources connect elements of Toolkit 1 to around 50% of the thirty-two musical cues in the movie, and in this respect it behaves and sounds much like a 'traditional' Jones toolkit as found in his scores of the late 1980s (albeit with the composer, rather than the director, making decisions about the use of the toolkit sounds). The core elements are flutes, shakers, anvils, a hi-hat, kick drum, tom toms, a sound referred to as 'spun glass' and, of course, the obligatory bourdon, and there is also often a short musical cell included on cello and low piano that sounds like it has been borrowed directly from the *Angel Heart/Sea of Love* 'Lounge Lizard motif'. Interestingly, however, there seems to be no recording of the toolkit as a set of 'raw' sounds as there was in earlier projects. Instead, each of the cues that makes use of it appears to have had the relevant parts of the toolkit re-recorded afresh as part of the twenty-four-track mix. Accordingly, while the sounds from Toolkit 1 can be found across a range of cues these elements are, to some extent, moulded on almost a cue-by-cue basis, linking the sound set more closely with the way that Jones used the Spider Atmos Master in *Arachnophobia* and the Synth Atmos in *Freejack*. By contrast, Toolkit 2 is referenced only in a single cue, 6M1, and is crafted specifically for that musical point. This identifies the designation 'Toolkit' as a misnomer since the material aligns fully with the atmospheres of *Freejack* and *CrissCross*, with the toolkit/atmosphere treated not as a sound set but as a single complex instrument that can be used to extend the timbral palette available to the composer.

Conclusion

Cliffhanger (1993) and *In the Name of the Father* (1993) effectively mark the end of toolkits as a device in Jones's scores. The former, directed by Renny Harlin and starring Sylvester Stallone, revolves around the recovery of stolen cases containing $100 million that have fallen into the Rocky Mountains following the failed hijacking of a treasury plane, while Jim Sheridan's *In the Name of the Father* is the story of the so-called Guildford Four, Irish nationals including Gerry and Giuseppe Conlon (Daniel Day-Lewis and Pete Postlethwaite) wrongly arrested and imprisoned for the bombing of the Guildford pub in London by the IRA in 1974. There is no evidence of toolkits or atmospheres at all in *Cliffhanger*, and while the film's cues contain sounds akin to the electronic and synthesised timbres of the toolkit period, it is apparent from the archival resources that the score was conceived and produced as a series of individual cues, with no consideration of broader or cross-cue sound sets, reinforcing the idea that Jones had moved towards a practice whereby complex synthesised sounds were simply another possible timbral option.

In the Name of the Father was produced six months after *Cliffhanger* and a year after *Detonator*, but despite this it retains an echo of the atmosphere approach. The documentation for *In the Name of the Father* shows that most cues have their own specific synthesised sound palette that forms a bass onto which live, acoustic instruments are overlaid. The synthetic sounds were captured onto master twenty-four-track tapes on 27 October 1993, with the live sounds recorded onto corresponding slave tapes at a recording session one week later on 3 November. These forty-eight tracks were then mixed to two left-centre-right film stereo sets for the film just under a week later, on 9 November. Interestingly, the L-C-R mixes are one for pitched elements and one for percussion rather than one for synthesised sounds and one for live, emphasising that the electronic sounds were treated in the same way as the acoustic when mixing the score and reinforcing the idea that although the score's construction bears some relation to the idea of atmospheres, it is actually best thought of as a hybrid live-electronic score. While there are significant synthesised elements in the score for *In the Name of the Father*, the cue-specific nature of the electronic materials and the way they are mixed for the film marks the final point of departure for the toolkit concept, with the synthesised elements functioning more like sweeteners than sound sets. Indeed, the film's soundtrack is more notable for the way in which Jones's music operates alongside material written by the members of the pop group U2 and a number of pre-existing songs, an aspect of the score that is considered in Chapter 5. Jones has commented on the change of direction and style embodied in his scores from 1993, observing that:

> The studios were going demented because [they were thinking] 'what the hell, who's Trevor Jones, what's he doing and can we categorise and pigeonhole him?' So they discovered that really you can't do that because he's just done a picture called *In the Name of the Father* which has got this weird score using those sounds and samples and synthesisers, and then he's done this very conventional *Cliffhanger* thing.
>
> (Jones 2007)

Indeed, in terms of sound these two projects could scarcely be more different, since *Cliffhanger* is an orchestral score and departs completely from the electronic-infused aural environment of *In the Name of the Father* and the preceding toolkit/atmosphere scores. Jones tended to favour the orchestra as the principal ensemble for his music in the following years, although he continued to experiment with his sound to some extent and both *Hideaway* (1995) and *Kiss of Death* (1995) combine the orchestra with echoes of earlier scores in their instrumental combinations. The horror film *Hideaway* adds an extended percussion section and some electronics to the symphony orchestra and recalls some of the toolkit scores through the integration of sounds such as the bourdon, marimba, and 'krang' into an otherwise acoustic score. Similarly, the thriller *Kiss of Death* (1995) augments the orchestra with rock instruments (notably electric guitar), the Synclavier and extended percussion to create a driving, energetic score, designed to match what was described at the spotting session for the film as the narrative's 'high-energy level'.[16] Such versatility and diversity of sound enabled Jones to continue to advance his career as the 1990s progressed, working in a range of genres and scoring several Hollywood blockbusters.

Notes

1. Although the programme did not air until 24 February 1991, *A Private Life* premiered fifteen months earlier at the 1989 London Film Festival, as was often the case with this sort of production.
2. Jones would return to this eclectic combination of genres nearly a decade later when scoring Alex Proyas's sci-fi *noir*, *Dark City* (1998), which is discussed in Chapter 5.
3. This text highlights an issue with the use of archival materials for research into the processes of screen-music since it is in three different hands and does not read properly or consistently. Firstly the offset for TK1 – which must actually be toolkit 1A based on the sounds – contains too many digits for the SMPTE system (usually displayed as hh:mm:ss:ff – hours, minutes, seconds and frames). Everything on that line of text prior to '19' is in a lighter, blunter pencil, so it is possible that the first two sets of '00:' were written before the offset timing was known and that one should have been removed when the timing was inserted, giving an offset of 00:19:18.76. This reads properly as a timing in hundredths of a second, but calls into question whether the Atmos Toolkit offset should match the format of the other timings and end '.13' (thirteen hundredths of a second) rather than ':13' (thirteen frames), which is a difference of nearly a third of a second at 30 frames per minute.
4. The telefilm is based on William Prochnau's novel *Trinity Child* (1983) and is one of the last films to depict such a scenario made before the collapse of the Soviet Union and the end of the Cold War in 1991.
5. Additionally, although they are not shown on the track sheet, the audio recording includes a click and count, sync pulse and SMPTE time code on tracks 22–24 respectively.
6. Although *Bad Influence* includes a sound set called the Atmos Toolkit, in that case 'atmos' is used as a description of the toolkit much as 'bourdons' is on *Sea of Love*, rather than to identify the material an 'atmosphere'.
7. In another example of evidence for the absence of materials, there are slave tapes but no corresponding masters for *Arachnophobia*, but the archive does contain track sheets for the master recordings. Additionally, in this case a version of the missing resources – the master tapes – can still be accessed since a stereo mix of each cue's master recording is included as a synchronisation guide in the corresponding multitrack slave recording.
8. Although no sound source is ever shown for the music, it plays at a volume that indicates it is meant to be interpreted as diegetic background music playing in public areas of the hotel such as reception and the lifts. Timings are taken from the DVD release of the film (1992).
9. Owing to the time that has elapsed since this project Jones was unable to clarify either the recording date or the initial use of the recordings.
10. *Brassed Off* is discussed in detail in Chapter 5.
11. David Cooper (2009) has discussed elsewhere some of the ways in which materials from the Trevor Jones Archive enable detailed investigation of the scoring of *Freejack*.
12. *Freejack* has a critics score of 14% on website Rotten Tomatoes (2017).
13. As discussed in Chapter 3, Jones drew extensively on toolkits when he replaced Bruce Broughton's score for *Mississippi Burning*, though this might have owed more to the film's proximity to *Angel Heart*, also for director Alan Parker, than because the music was composed in a compressed time-frame.
14. Jones and Randy Edelman are credited as co-composers for *The Last of the Mohicans*, though both claim barely to have met, let alone worked collaboratively on the project (Goldwasser 2001; Melcher 2001). The discussion in this chapter focuses on Jones's material, which is distinguished from Edelman's on the official soundtrack album released by Morgan Creek.
15. In lieu of cue names track names from the soundtrack album are used in the following discussion.
16. 'Spotting Session' [Transcript], *Kiss of Death*, 1995. Trevor Jones Archive. University of Leeds.

Part III
Mainstream scoring (1993–2004)

5 Hollywood blockbusters part one

The mid-1990s marked the beginning of Jones's most prolific period of composition, with eighteen feature film scores produced between 1993 and 2003. In addition to large-scale Hollywood films such as *GI Jane* (1997), *Dark City* (1998) and *Notting Hill* (1999), Jones worked in a variety of genres, including a film adaptation of Shakespeare's *Richard III* (1995); politically and socially engaged projects *In the Name of the Father* (1993), *Titanic Town* (1998) and *Molly* (1999); and smaller-scale pictures such as *Loch Ness* (1996) and *Lawn Dogs* (1997). Commonalities of approach and style shaped by the genres in question and the nature of Jones's involvement can be traced across projects produced in this period, with the necessity to prepare an original score around pre-existing music as one of the most recurrent challenges. As will be discussed in both Chapters 5 and 6, Jones enjoyed varying levels of engagement with pre-existing songs in many of the mainstream films on which he worked during this decade, and he shaped his original scores accordingly, moulding appropriate musical styles to ensure a blended soundscape.

These two chapters also illuminate how closely filmic genre and musical style are intertwined and develop arguments made in Chapter 3 that Jones tends to reserve his atmosphere-based scores for dramatic and often tense films rather than comedies or romantic pictures. Indeed, the first focus score of this chapter, *In the Name of the Father*, demonstrates the way that Jones incorporated some of the ideas that had underpinned the toolkit and atmosphere scores of the previous few years in a more mainstream approach to film-score composition. By contrast, the other two key films considered in this chapter, *Brassed Off* (1996) and *Notting Hill* – possibly the two most commercially successful films for which Jones has provided scores – required him to compose material that blended with popular-music styles. In both of these latter cases his original contributions are somewhat overshadowed by pre-existing material – brass band music in *Brassed Off* and pop songs in *Notting Hill*, particularly the Elvis Costello cover of 'She' – though Jones played a key role in devising the sound of both pictures, being involved in the production of the brass band music for the former and creating and coordinating arrangements of songs for the latter, including 'She'. Before exploring these three scores in detail, however, it is necessary to establish the industrial context within which they were created and produced, notably the impact of the change from analogue to digital recording and related developments in technology on Jones's working practices, and on the industry more broadly.

The film-music industry in the mid- to late 1990s

Innovations in film-sound technology continued to shape Jones's work throughout this period, and the volume of projects he produced was undoubtedly supported by the benefits of emerging technologies. Most notably, the mid-1990s marked the wider scale use of digital audio workstations (DAWs), which have become the principal means of score creation for composers working in the contemporary film industry (Sapiro 2016, p. 204). Logic had been released in 1993, the addition of Virtual Studio Technologies (VSTs) to Cubase in 1996 added DAW capabilities to Steinberg's powerful sequencer, and a new version of ProTools had been produced nearly every year since version 1.0 had been launched in 1991 (Sapiro 2016, pp. 204–206). These new technologies made a profound impression on the wider industrial context, impacting on both the compositional process and the resulting sound quality. The non-linear nature of editing on DAWs permitted smoother and faster composition (Salzman 2015, p. 233), and the various software packages enabled composers to layer dialogue, music and sound effects without losing quality or building up noise (Whittington 2007, p. 1). William Whittington observes that DAWs also simplified previously cumbersome methods of handling sound effects:

> During the classical Hollywood period, sound departments established vast libraries of sound effects. These effects were placed on records and tapes for perusal by sound supervisors and editors then transferred to another medium, such as optical or magnetic film stock for editorial purposes. The sound libraries housed sounds ranging from gunshots to birdcalls. Categories were established and catalogued for easy retrieval. Today, this process continues on digital audio workstations and is assisted by computer databases with the capacity of string searches and relational searches as well as instantaneous retrieval and performance of sounds.
>
> (Whittington 2007, p. 112)

Although the improvements were unquestionable, composing during this period of rapid change could be demanding for technical as well as creative reasons. Jones recalled having to 're-train' himself in the evolving digital technology and highlighted the improvements available once ProTools became the de-facto standard across the industry:

> It kept changing. New software would come out on a weekly basis, developments technologically were remarkable and dependent on the constant increase in computational power. [. . .] And even with the analogue tape we had Dolby SR, Dolby A; all the different formats of noise reduction and capacity of tracks on tape used to drive us all crazy! But not as much as when you had to go into a recording studio and find out that you were working in the analogue domain and the next day a new digital desk would be brought in for trials and your tapes would be transferred to digital! The whole thing was a bit of a technological nightmare until we settled on ProTools and working in

5.1 [surround sound], and this has now become industry standard internationally. So it has settled down and makes life a lot easier.

(Jones 2016b)

ProTools removed the physicality of composing since it was relatively simple to make edits to pre-existing material and there were few restrictions on the number of different versions of a sketch that could be stored. For example, a combination of picture changes and musical amendments resulted in Jones composing sixty-four versions of one cue for *Notting Hill*, and all of these subtly different versions were retained throughout the production process with minimal effort. ProTools also offered the composers the opportunity to be more experimental in their approach to scoring since it afforded the option of copying and pasting material without needing to rewrite it from scratch every time (Jones 2016b). With edits being stored digitally, it was also simple to undo changes or revert quickly to earlier versions of music. Alongside these developments in music technology there were also changes in film sound exhibition, with Dolby becoming the leading producer of film sound processors in cinema theatres by 1998. Impacting on home exhibition, the DVD arrived in the U.S. in 1997 and offered the possibility of cinema-style 5.1 surround sound to audiences watching films from the comfort of their own sofas.

Although the evolution of digital technology enabled Jones to be more experimental in scoring, as discussed in Chapter 4, *The Last of the Mohicans* (1992) and *Cliffhanger* (1993) marked a turning point in his adoption of the symphony-orchestra sound for many of these 1990s projects, a move that aligned him with the typical soundscape for most big-budget Hollywood films of the period. Indeed, this broad trend can be traced to the return of the Classical sound with New Hollywood during the 1970s, when composers such as John Williams and Jerry Goldsmith composed scores with memorable melodic themes for symphony orchestras, often supplemented with additional instruments and electronics. Jones is acutely aware of the expectations of Hollywood film studios and their influence on the scoring process, which can even dictate the quantity and role of music to be composed. In reference to *Cliffhanger*, he noted that the film 'has fifteen more minutes' music than there is footage because of the titles and end credits. There's very little silence because they [producers] feel that the music should dictate to an audience what they should be feeling at any given time' (Fox and Cooper 2008, p. 10). Somewhat paradoxically, in addition to the development of a symphonic sound, Jones's films of the 1990s are notable for the increased prominence of popular songs in the soundscape. Jeff Smith observes that the cross-promotion of film and music has always been attractive to production companies, describing how during the 1980s cross-marketing strategies that benefitted both the film and record industries were identified as providing 'synergy':

> for a film company, sales of soundtrack albums could amortize production costs while radio airplay of film themes served as a cheap and practical form of advertising. For a record company, on the other hand, the link to a film gave a soundtrack album needed name recognition in a highly competitive market.
> (Smith 1998, p. 27)

The strategy is most frequently used when films feature popular songs or highly recognisable film themes, and promotional success during the 1980s and 1990s fuelled the ever-increasing tendency to exploit popular music in film soundtracks. Kevin Donnelly suggests that 'the norm for film music by the 1990s was that there would be a selection of pop songs as well as an orchestral underscore' (2001, p. 153), and he identifies the difference in function between these musical elements. The orchestral underscore follows film-music conventions, highlighting emotion or action, while the pop songs are an attraction, operating either diegetically or non-diegetically in a film and providing an additional revenue stream through popular soundtrack albums (Donnelly 2001). Naturally, the inclusion of pre-existing songs impacts on the composer's process, which Jones acknowledged in an interview with Christopher Fox and David Cooper:

> Ninety percent of the time the politics of music on film dictate how the soundtrack is going to turn out. If, for instance, the production hasn't enough money to fund the budget they would go to a record company and say 'please could you advance us X amount of money for recording the music for the underscore and you could put on X amount of songs'. So this serves as a package. They get to put on songs from their catalogue which they've been dying to dust off and revive and you're stuck there with a bunch of songs which you have to put in the film somewhere to pay for the score that needs to be recorded. So, you know, the trouble with film is that it always has to walk this knife edge between art and commerce.
>
> (Fox and Cooper 2008, p. 11)

Given this delicate balancing act, it is unsurprising that Jones's relationship with pre-existing music varies from film to film, particularly since he is often not aware at the beginning of a project precisely which popular songs will be used. This is not unusual, and much can depend on when a composer joins a project and whether a popular song is explicitly written into the script. Once a song is selected for a film, the composer is usually told where it is to be placed (Jones 2014b), but in some cases, decisions about which songs are used and where they will feature can develop over time and with the composer's input:

> Other projects evolve and develop, like *Notting Hill*. Then you say 'you know what there's another song that's a bit more pertinent to this scene then that' and they suggest this artist or that, so you're part of a compilation of a bunch of commercial songs that come together with the end product being the soundtrack, which is focused towards a particular demographic. [. . .] So the end result is always the commercial [benefit], how much money is this soundtrack going to make? And the more loaded it becomes with the right material, the more people will want to go out and buy it. It's very cynical but that's the bottom line.
>
> (Jones 2014b)

Jones provided original music for several Hollywood films of the late 1990s and early 2000s that employed pre-existing music, such as *Lawn Dogs*, *Molly*, and *Crossroads* (2002). As already noted, two of the most financially successful films in his oeuvre, *Brassed Off* and *Notting Hill*, also fall into this category, although the pre-existing material functions quite differently in each production. Additionally, these two films carry significant cultural relevance and represent contrasting aspects of British life, and this is reflected in both the type of music that is interpolated into each soundtrack, and the sound of Jones's score. Julie Hubbert highlights that in more recent films, 'filmic space is not so rigidly reinforced by the soundtrack. The musical selections instead often move fluidly between diegetic, nondiegetic, and extradiegetic space, generating a host of narrative effects' (2013, p. 308), and this idea applies to the relationship between original and pre-existing music in both pictures. *Brassed Off*'s pre-existing material is drawn from the canon of brass-band works, and leaving aside the opening-credit music, twelve of the thirteen tracks heard in the film have some source anchoring. By contrast, the vast majority of the pop songs in *Notting Hill* are part of the non-diegetic underscore and frequently accompany montage sequences that indicate the passage of time, a circumstance more in keeping with 1980s and 1990s industry practice. Furthermore, the varying nature of the pre-existing music in these two films results in different impacts on Jones's overall musical involvement in each production. He is credited with producing the brass band music and with composing, orchestrating (in conjunction with long-time collaborator Geoff Alexander) and conducting the orchestral music for *Brassed Off*, while for *Notting Hill* he composed the underscore music, performed synthesisers and orchestrated the original music (along with Geoff Alexander and Julian Kershaw). He was also involved with the preparation of some of the pre-existing songs for the film, for example, working with Mutt Lange to create the 5.1 surround-sound mix of Shania Twain's 'You've Got a Way'.

This chapter proceeds with a consideration of the interaction between Jones's original music, pre-existing material, and songs written by others in *In the Name of the Father*, which establishes some of the ground for the discussion of these matters in Jones's scores of the late 1990s. The main focus of the rest of the chapter is on *Brassed Off* and *Notting Hill*, though the integration of original and pre-existing music affected film composition widely in this period and other Jones projects – notably *Richard III* (1995), which was produced a year before *Brassed Off* – are therefore also touched on in the course of the chapter. In particular, *Brassed Off* and *Notting Hill* enable consideration of how Jones's composition of the original underscores developed in relation to the planned pre-existing music. Music's ability to create a sense of place or character sonically is a recurring theme across both of these films and in several of the other projects discussed in less detail, such as *Titanic Town*, *Dark City*, *GI Jane* and *Lawn Dogs*. The archival materials provide an insight into the process in each case, shedding new light on previously hidden aspects of the creation and production of these scores.[1]

In the Name of the Father (1993)[2]

In the Name of the Father was directed by Jim Sheridan and first released in Ireland in December 1993. As noted briefly in Chapter 4, the film is an account of Gerry Conlon (one of the so-called Guildford Four) and his father Patrick 'Giuseppe' Conlon, who were mistakenly arrested and imprisoned through an infamous miscarriage of justice of the British legal system. In Gerry Conlon's case, this was for his supposed involvement (along with Paul Hill, Patrick Armstrong and Carole Richardson) in the Provisional IRA's bombing of the Horse and Groom pub in Guildford in September 1974; his father and members of the Maguire family (and a family friend) were convicted of explosives offences. The convictions of the Guildford Four were reversed in 1989 and those of the Maguire Seven in 1991, though Giuseppe Conlon had died in 1980 while still in prison. Although marketed as a 'true story' a degree of artistic licence was employed, and some key facts were either ignored or glossed over. Despite this it was a critical success and was short-listed for seven Academy Awards in 1994.

Access to the primary materials in the Trevor Jones Archive, such as the sequencer short score, orchestral score, working tapes, session recordings and mix documentation, allows the ways in which Jones elaborates and develops his musical ideas in response to the film's narrative to be observed more clearly. There are seven reels of tape with documentation related to *In the Name of the Father* in the Trevor Jones Archive. Tapes 3 and 4 are working tapes, tape 6 is devoted to several string effects some of which are alluded to on pages at the back of the musical score and tapes 5 and 7 form a complete pair of music mix tapes (by and large the final mixes that appear on the film). Tape 2 contains remixes and final credits and tape 1 has the album mix constructions. All of the cues recorded on the two-inch analogue tapes and the various dates on documentation are itemised in Table 5.1.

The film elides conventional and compilation score by combining Jones's electronic and acoustic music, with the diegetic and non-diegetic use of popular songs; Table 5.2 lists both the popular music sources and cues specially composed for the film in sequence including several cues which were not eventually used.[3] Jones's original score for *In the Name of the Father* holds a very significant and prominent place in the film's narrative: it is often dark and disturbing, apparently including the musical language of Krzysztof Penderecki as one of its points of reference, a page of his composition *Threnody for the Victims of Hiroshima* being included in the full score along with four additional pages of aleatoric string notations. While the electronic writing perhaps suggests the Nono of *Ricorda cosa ti hanno fatto in Auschwitz*, the score also involves some very simple diatonic writing including a modal melody associated with the relationship between Gerry and his father, which is first heard in cue 5M3 'Gerry & Father Embrace' and gradually moves to the foreground from cue 10M1 'Snow'.

As well as transmitting the specific messages encoded within lyrics, musical structure and processes, and through its genre and instrumentation, popular music lets those with the relevant knowledge and experience (or to adopt Stefani's term,

Table 5.1 Contents of the six two-inch multitrack tapes for *In the Name of the Father* held in the Trevor Jones Archive

Tape	Track Sheet Date	Box Back Date	Box Side Date	Contents
1/7	20/11/93	20/11/93	22/11/93	Album mix constructions. Three cues: 'Interrogation'; 'Walking the Circle'; 'Passage of Time'
2/7 Music Cues	19/11/93	19/11/93	21/11/93	Music Cues Mixes: 9M1/3 sweetener; 1M1; 14M1 'End Credits'; 14M1 'End Extended'; 14M1 'End Credits'*
3/7 W1	No track sheets	27/10/93	None	Working Tape 1: 2M1 'Ferry Farewell'; 3M5 'Gerry's Arrest'; 4M1 'Bomb Photo'; 4M3 'Interrogation'; 5M1 'I'm Gonna Shoot Your Da'; 5M2 'Da in Remand Prison'; 5M3 'Embrace in Remand Cell'; 6M1 'Motorcade'; 7M1 '30 Years'; 7M2 'Prison Arrival'
4/7 W2	No track sheets	29/10/93	None	Working Tape 2: 7M3 '3 Minutes'; 8M3 'Promise Me'; 8M4 'Headbutt'; 9M1/3 'Confrontation'; 10M1 'Snow'; 10M2 'Film Show'; 10M5 'Torching'; 10M6 'Gerry Joins Campaign'; 11M1 'Hold My Hand'; 11M2 'Guiseppe [sic] Collapses'; 13M1 'Gerard'; 13M2 'Passage of Time'; 14M1 'Dismissed'
5/7 Music cues	14–17/11/93	15/11/93	21/11/93	Music Cues Mixes Reel 2: 7M2; 8M3; 8M4; 9M1/3; 9M1; 9M1/3 for editing; 10M1; 10M2; 10M5; 10M6; 11M1; 11M2; 12M1; 13M1; 13M2
6/7 String FX	No track sheets	3/11/93	None	String effects: Penderecski [sic]; E string trem[olo]; Cello A string; Violin trem[olo] gliss[ando]; Unison B$\cong$, A, C note everyone
7/7	9–12/11/93 & 14–15/11/93	9/11/93	9/11/93	Music Cues Mixes Reel 1: 2M1; 3M5; 4M1; 4M3; 5M1; 5M2; 5M3 alt version; 5M3; 5M3; 6M1; 7M1; 2M1 remix

Table 5.2 Musical cues by Trevor Jones listed in the score and source popular music used in the film *In the Name of the Father*

Cue	Title	Duration of Jones's Cues	Orchestration of Jones's Cues (from Score)
1M1	'In the Name of the Father'; Bono; non-diegetic. On tapes but not score		
Source	'Voodoo Child (slight return)'; Jimi Hendrix Experience; non-diegetic		
Source	'Like a Rolling Stone'; Bob Dylan; diegetic		
2M1	'FERRY FAREWELL' – Not Used	1'26"	Synthesised
Source	'Tiger Feet'; Mud; non-diegetic		
Source	'Billy Boola'; Bono, Gavin Friday; non-diegetic		
Source	'Dedicated Follower of Fashion'; The Kinks; non-diegetic		
Source	'Leader of the Gang'; Gary Glitter; diegetic (brief snatch sung by Gerry)		
3M5	'GERRY'S ARREST'	1'03"	3 alto flutes, 4 horns, 8 celli, 6 c'bass, synths, [wailing guitar]
4M1	'BOMB PHOTOS'	33"	3 alto flutes, 4 horns, 8 celli, 6 c'bass, congas, synths
Source	'Happy Birthday'; sung by police; diegetic		
4M3	'GERRY'S INTERROGATION'	4'36"	3 alto flutes, strings, synth
5M1	'I'M GONNA SHOOT YOUR DA'	1'59"	4 horns, EWI, harp, strings, synth
5M2	'DA IN PRISON'	42"	Harp, strings, synth
5M3	'GERRY & FATHER EMBRACE'	38"	2 alto flutes, 3 horns, baritone sax, EWI, strings, piano, synth
6M1	'MOTORCADE'	1'09"	3 alto flutes, 4 horns, strings, synth, drums, [guitar]
7M1	'30 YEARS'	1'55"	Strings
7M2	'PRISON ARRIVAL'	43"	Contrabass clarinet in Bb, strings (12-10-8-8-6), EWI
Source	'Is This Love?; Bob Marley; diegetic		

Cue	Title	Duration of Jones's Cues	Orchestration of Jones's Cues (from Score)
7M3	'3 MINUTES' – Not Used	3'10"	Bass clar, bassoon, baritone sax, 3 horns, harp, strings, synth
8M3	'PROMISE ME' (reference to 'You Made Me the Thief of Your Heart' not in score)	42"	Contrabass clarinet in Bb, strings, EWI
8M4	'HEAD BUTT'	44"	Cellos, basses, synth, [guitar]
9Ml/3	'CONFRONTATION'	2'31"	3 alto flutes, strings, synth, [guitar]
Source	'In the Name of the Blues'; Pete Cummins and John Fitzgibbons		
10M1	'SNOW'	2'40"	Baritone sax, strings, harp, piano, EWI
10M2	'FILM SHOW'	1'08"	1 alto flute, 1 bass flute, 1 bass clarinet, 2 horns, strings, guitar
Source	'The Godfather'; Nino Rota		
10M5	'TORCHING'	2'35"	Contrabass clarinet in Bb, contrabassoon (optional), 4 horns (can be done with 2), baritone sax (optional), strings, synth, guitar
10M6	'GERRY JOINS CAMPAIGN'	1'57"	Baritone sax, strings, piano harp, synth
11M1	'HOLD MY HAND' – Not Used	57"	Strings, piano, synth
11M2	'GUISEPPE [sic] COLLAPSES'; No score; based on 'You Made Me the Thief of Your Heart'	55"	Strings (plus overdubbed violins and violas)
12M1	'GUISEPPE'S [sic] DEAD'; 'In the name of the Father'	1'27"	No score
13M1	'GERARD' – Not Used	36"	Contrabass clarinet, 4 horns, strings (0-0-8-8-6)
	'Whiskey in the Jar'; Thin Lizzy; diegetic		
13M2	'PASSAGE OF TIME'	2'19"	3 alto flutes, contrabass clarinet, 4 horns, harp, strings, piano
14M1	'DISMISSED'	1'35"	Baritone sax, strings, piano, pipes
14M2	'END CREDITS'; 'You Made Me the Thief of Your Heart'; Sinéad O'Connor	c4'00"	No score

competence) to locate the film's narrative within relevant cultural times and spaces. As an example, satire is consciously inscribed on The Kinks' 1966 single 'Dedicated Follower of Fashion', the first two verses of which are heard non-diegetically as Gerry arrives back in Belfast on the proceeds of his break-in of the London prostitute's flat, dressed hippie-style in Afghan coat and John Lennon glasses to the amusement of troops and local children who mockingly bleat at him. In the context of the narrative, the upbeat mood and musical characteristics of the song – a vamping accompaniment, community sing-along quality and parodic upper-crust English accent – provide a moment of light relief that, by contrast, makes the emotional impact of his arrest soon after even more powerful. The allusions to the cultural geography of London and, in particular, Carnaby Street offer a further semantic twist which is reinforced by the song lyrics' allusions to the foppish, but heroic, Scarlet Pimpernel ('They seek him here/they seek him there'); the famous references to the 'Carnabetian army' that appear later in the song but are not played in the film neatly support Sheridan's reading (and Day-Lewis's performance) of Conlon as vain, foolish and easily led astray but not an active Republican terrorist. When he sings the first line of the chorus of Gary Glitter's 'I'm the Leader of the Gang' to his sisters as he enters the family house in the Falls Road area of Belfast, this is a direct reference to a contemporary song (released in 1973) as well as taking on ironic significance given that 'his gang' will be deemed to be the Provisional IRA by the Royal Ulster Constabulary.

Of the popular music cues specially written for the film, the two numbers that frame the narrative by accompanying its introduction and conclusion are perhaps the most significant. 'In the Name of the Father' (cue 1M1), composed by Irish musicians Paul David Hewson (Bono), Martin Fionán Hanvey (Gavin Friday) and Maurice Roycroft (Maurice Seezer), and performed by Bono and Gavin Friday, appears at the beginning of the film. While this has subsequently developed an autonomous musical identity outside the film, it is largely obedient to standard film-compositional practices both in its establishment of mood and the employment of signifying elements. It is organised in a kind of loose arch structure with introductory drums, a freely sung melody against a regular martial rhythm, a spoken text with dissonant interjections of a tritone in guitar, and an abbreviated reprise of the vocal melody and concluding drumbeat on fade out. Insistent and martial percussive rhythms (both the Lambeg drum and bodhrán, drums that represent the two traditions of Ireland) at the start of the song become a key element of Jones's non-diegetic score. A vocal line with Mixolydian inflection that emerges and speaks of love (which we will later discover is Giuseppe's parental agapē) is almost plainsong like; it sits in a very different rhythmic, and symbolically speaking moral, space to that of the drums – metrically free and floating above them. The hammered out riff based on the pitches of an F# Dorian/Aeolian tetrachord (F#–G#–A–B) with lower subtonic (E) in a biting, largely dactylic rhythm (see Figure 5.1) is first heard synchronised with the explosion in the Horse and Groom

Figure 5.1 Aural transcription of the riff from the title cue from *In the Name of the Father*

pub, and this gesture draws on an underlying double-tonic scheme that can be seen as a classic marker of both Ireland and Scotland (recalling, for example, the double-tonic of 'Brian Boru's March'). Its musical characteristics (reiterative rhythm, narrow pitch content) can be read as implying relentlessness and, by association with the other musical characteristics, suggests intransigence. The religious insinuation of the film's title is reinforced by the invocatory quality of the performance and the spoken lines, at once incantation and poetic recitation: 'In the name of reason/In the name of hope/In the name of religion/In the name of dope'.

Of course, Bono is himself also part of the signifying system of the music and the film. Many viewers of the film will be aware of the band U2 and of their very successful protest song 'Sunday Bloody Sunday' from the album *War*, released in February 1983, which looks back to the events of 'Bloody Sunday', 30 January 1972, when thirteen people were shot dead by British troops in Derry. Equally, Bono's own 'mixed' religious affiliation – his mother was Protestant and his father Catholic, and he was brought up attending the Church of Ireland – places him in a rather special place in Irish society, South and North. There is only one further direct reference to the material from the song 'In the Name of the Father' in the rest of the score. This is in cue 9M1/3 'Confrontation', which is heard in the scene of the prison sit-in. Whereas in Jones's written score there is a reference to a semi-improvised lead guitar solo at the point where the riot squad enter to break up the protest, and this appears in the mock-ups on reel 4, in the session recordings the riff with its original bass line is heard at this juncture.

The final pair of cues of the score, 14M1 'Dismissed' and 14M2 'End Credits', begin at the point that the judge strikes down his gavel to dismiss the case, and they subsume the second song written by Bono, Friday and Seezer. The version on the second working tape (4/7) is fundamentally a mock-up of the cue as it appears in the score. Written in Bb minor and in 4/4, the score has three main elements: an ostinato based on the alternation of a thirdless Bb^7 and Bb^7 sus 4 chords in the piano, a reiterated bodhrán rhythm that spans six beats (♩♫♫ ♫♫ ♫♫ ♫♫ | ♫♫♫ ♫♫♫) and the melody of 'You Made me the Thief of Your Heart' played on the Uilleann pipe chanter (without drones or regulators).[4] One further element that is recorded on the working tapes but does not appear at all in the score is a repeated one-bar Dorian/Aeolian figure played by violins in the style of a traditional Irish fiddle, notated in Figure 5.2.

The elements found in the mock up are all present in the various versions of the final mixed cue, but the new and defining element is undoubtedly Sinéad O'Connor's voice, a remarkably impassioned performance, the intensity of which is clearly revealed by the unprocessed recording which forms track 5 of cue 14M1 'End Credits' on Tape 2. The pipe melody, piano and fiddle ostinati are still

Figure 5.2 'Traditional' fiddle rhythm from cue 14M1 of *In the Name of the Father* as heard on working tape 4/7

Figure 5.3 The 'Giuseppe' motif from *In the Name of the Father*

important parts of the fabric of the cue, but this is a more sophisticated arrangement than that found on the working tapes, and the Irish markers are even more prominent, the cue finishing with a traditional fiddler playing an energetic (and authentic sounding) reel double-tracked across left and right speakers.

Although the underlying melody is found in the working tape for this cue it does not feature in the rest of the score or in any of the other cues in the working tapes. Rather, a simple diatonic melody whose basic configuration is shown in Figure 5.3 is one of the key signifying elements – a musical figure that denotes Giuseppe's paternal love for Gerry (hereafter called the 'Giuseppe' motif). In arranging the music mixes Jones took the opportunity to rework several earlier cues by introducing a melodic element from 'You Made Me the Thief of Your Heart' (arguably a musical token for Gerry) and changing the role of the 'Giuseppe' motif in the process. Table 5.3 indicates the progress of the two motifs from score to final mixdown. In two cases the cues that were scored and mocked up were not used in the film, and a third, 'Hold My Hand', was mixed but not dubbed. Given that the two ideas have melodic and harmonic configurations that permit them to readily substitute for each other, or even to be played in counterpoint (as in cue 8M3), this provided several advantages to the composer:

1. It allowed him to integrate more closely into the score the musical characteristics of the concluding song and generate a greater overall sense of coherence and consistency to the score;
2. It provided a means of both differentiating and connecting musically the two main characters of the film;
3. It offered a greater semantic potential, through the additional musical token.

Despite its composite sources, and considerable stylistic diversity, from avantgarde techniques to Gary Glitter, and Mud to Thin Lizzy, the music track for *In the Name of the Father* does sound remarkably well integrated. It is Jones's particular skill that he is able to compose music that is both unobtrusive (in that it rarely draws unnecessary attention to itself), highly integrated and effective in supporting the narrative while dovetailing with popular source cues, an attribute he employed extensively across his scores over the following decade.

Brassed Off (1996)

As discussed in Chapter 1, Jones spent a number of years as a student at the University of York and had first-hand experience of the brass-band tradition in Yorkshire, an interest that he developed further by attending performances at Kneller

Table 5.3 Use of the 'Giuseppe' and 'Thief of Your Heart' melodies in *In the Name of the Father*

Cue	Score	Working Tapes	Mix Tapes
2M1 'Ferry Farewell'	Not present	'Giuseppe' motif in guitar solo as father walks away	Cue not used in film
5M3 'Gerry and Father Embrace'	'Giuseppe' motif in EWI bars 5–11, C minor	As score	'Thief of Your Heart' motif, C minor
7M3 'Three Minutes'	'Giuseppe' motif in EWI from bar 17 *passim*, A minor	As score	Cue not used in film
8M3 'Promise me'	'Giuseppe' motif in EWI from bar 2, A minor	As score	'Giuseppe' and 'Thief of Your Heart' motifs played in counterpoint
10M1 'Snow'	'Giuseppe' in EWI from bar 8, A minor	As score	As score
10M6 'Gerry Joins Campaign'	'Giuseppe' in EWI from bar 8, A minor.	As score	Bars 9–16 'Thief of Your Heart', 'Giuseppe' on repeat (25–32)
11M1 'Hold My Hand'	'Giuseppe' in EWI from bar 2, EWI, A minor	As score	'Thief of Your Heart' from bar 2. Cue not used in film
12M1 'Giuseppe's Dead'	No score	No mock-up	'Thief of Your Heart' motif against atmos tracks until near the end. Finishes with O'Connor singing 'Are you lost?'

Hall in London (Fox and Cooper 2008). This musical engagement became key to Jones's involvement in the conception of the *Brassed Off* project, as he described in interview with Christopher Fox and David Cooper. He felt very close to this film, which deals with the demise of brass-band heritage as a result of the coal pit closures in the North of England during the time when Margaret Thatcher was the British Prime Minister. Jones recalls a discussion with his friend, writer and director, Mark Herman:

> He said to me: 'you've done orchestral scores and rock scores and pop scores and all sorts of types of music – what would you like to do?' And I said, 'a type of music that's very close to my heart is brass band', because when I was at York you'd have all these wonderful competitions and see the most phenomenal bands the standard of which was absolutely extraordinarily high. [. . .] We just asked the barman for a piece of paper and started jotting down a one page story of some characters who were part of this brass band, and that's how *Brassed Off* came into being.
>
> (Fox and Cooper 2008, p. 6)

The film is based on the true story of the Grimethorpe Colliery Brass Band – renamed as Grimley Colliery Band in the film – and the impact of the closure of the coal pit on a whole community, albeit with suitable narrative license. While the star of the piece is arguably the band itself, the principal characters are the band leader, Danny (Pete Postlethwaite); his son, Phil (Stephen Tomkinson), who is struggling to support his young family; Andy (Ewan McGregor), a young miner and tenor horn player whose career is one of those threatened by the pit closure; and Gloria (Tara Fitzgerald) who joins the band as a flugelhorn player but is actually surveying the viability of the pit for the management company. The film follows a dual narrative, tracking the band's progress through local and regional festivals to the national brass-band competition at the Royal Albert Hall in London, set against a background of the forced closure of the pit, which threatens the livelihood of the whole town and the continuation of the colliery band itself. Music making is central to the plot, and the film features many performances by the Grimethorpe Colliery Band supplemented by actors in the film. Indeed, the ratio of pre-existing music to Jones's original underscore is evident in the cue list shown in example 5.1, which is divided into band, source, and score music. The cue list elucidates the degree to which Jones's music is evenly interspersed throughout the film, whereas the band music is generally grouped together, being heard in rehearsals, at festivals and in performances as demanded by the film's diegesis. The band cues are all selections from the standard repertoire, which were not modified for the film (Barraclough 2014), and several works are heard in full as evidenced from the durations shown in Figure 5.4. Indeed, such is the importance of music making to the film's characters and the concept of the picture itself that brass band material makes up nearly 30% of the total running time of the film and totals more than double the duration of Jones's original underscore.

As already noted, Jones is credited with producing the brass band recordings used in *Brassed Off*, and the archival materials highlight his involvement in this part of the soundscape. There is mix documentation for the band recording sessions, as well as numerous sketches of the band's seating arrangements for these sessions, such as that shown in Figure 5.5, which demonstrate how Jones brought his experience of recording film music to bear on the ensemble. In a traditional brass band setup the cornet section is seated to the conductor's left with the solo players on the front row and the back row progressing from the soprano to the repiano and then the second and third cornets. The B-flat and E-flat basses are positioned on the back row directly in front of the conductor, and the trombones occupy a similar position but to the conductor's right, opposite the cornets. Thus far this matches the layout shown in Figure 5.5, but Jones adapts the seating positions of the remaining instruments to enable recording and subsequent mixing to take place more efficiently. The document appears to be the recording setup for *En Aranjuez con tu amor*, a brass band work based on the slow second movement of Joaquín Rodrigo's *Concerto d'Aranjuez* and humorously referred to by the characters as 'Concerto d'Orange Juice'. While there is nothing shown explicitly on the seating plan to prove this, moving the baritones and euphoniums from their traditional position in front of the trombones to a new middle row in front of the conductor, and the placement of the flugelhorn in the resulting space indicates

11/2/96

Brassed Off
Music Cues

Cue No.	Title	Band	Source	Score	Clix	BPM	Dur	SMPTE Start	SMPTE Stop	Footage Start	Footage Stop	Pip SMPTE	Pip Footage	SMPTE Start Bar 1
1M1	Brassed Off - Main Titles	●●●			-	-	2:47:10	01:00:13:08	01:03:00:18	0019+15	0271+00	01:01:54:13	0171+12	
1M2s	Source In Pub / Bedroom 1		●		8	129.34	1:15:19	01:02:41:00	01:03:56:19	0241+07	0355+01			01:01:59:06
1M3	You Get Used To It			●	4	58	0:45:13	01:04:26:04	01:05:11:17	0399+03	0467+09			
1M4	Waking Up In Casualty			●	4	58	0:28:24	01:05:51:23	01:06:20:22	0527+13	0571+04			
1M5	Danny And Phil On Bike (Floral Dance Humming)		●		-	-	0:25:21	01:08:55:04	01:09:21:00	0802+11	0841+08			
1M6	Floral Dance	●●●			-	-	1:02:8	01:09:16:00	01:10:18:08	0834+00	0927+08			
2M1	Concerto D'Orange Juice	●●●			-	-	4:02:5	02:05:12:20	02:09:15:00	0469+02	0832+08			
3M1	Danny's First Cough			●	5	58.39	0:33:23	03:00:05:03	03:00:39:01	0008+05	0050+01			
3M2s	Children's T V Source		●		8	200	0:36:21	03:04:14:24	03:04:51:20	0350+01	0405+06			
3M3A	Source In Pub / Bedroom 2		●		-	-	0:26:10	03:04:51:21	03:05:18:06	0437+12	0477+06			
3M3B	Gloria Gets Her Coat		●		-	-	0:08:3	03:05:01:00	03:05:09:03	0451+07	0463+10			
3M3C	Gloria In The Mirror		●		-	-	0:15:19	03:05:28:19	03:05:44:13	0493+01	0516+12			
3M3D	Pool Room		●		-	-	0:50:12	03:06:29:03	03:07:19:15	0538+10	0659+05			
3M3s	Pub Source 2 (Total Of Above 4 Cues)		●		8	105	2:27:19	03:04:51:21	03:07:19:15	0437+12	0659+05			03:04:33:14
3M4s	Source On Bus		●	●	8	120	2:11:19	03:08:34:01	03:10:45:20	0771+00	0968+10			
4M1	Source On Bus Cont...		●	●	-	120	0:44:7	04:00:00:01	04:00:44:08	0000+00	0066+07			
4M2s	* March Of The Cobblers *	●	●●		-	-	3:06:24	04:00:44:00	04:03:50:24	0065+15	0346+06			
4M2A	Effects Track For" March Of The Cobblers"		●	●	8	120 V	0:53:15	04:02:57:20	04:03:51:10	0266+10	0347+02			
4M3	What's That On Your Hanky ?			●	4	51	1:44:13	04:07:09:04	04:08:53:17	0643+12	0800+07			
4M4s	Jukebox In Fish Shop 1		●	●	8	100	0:05:14	04:08:53:17	04:08:58:21	0800+07	0808+03			04:05:44:11
4M5s	Jukebox In Fish Shop 2		●		8	113/84	1:37:24	04:09:37:05	04:11:15:04	0865+12	1012+11			04:08:44:06
5M1	* Cross Of Honour *	●	●●		-	-	2:11:1	05:03:31:00	05:05:42:11	0316+07	0513+11			
5M2s	Pub Source 3		●		8	95	0:44:21	05:08:01:03	05:08:45:24	0721+11	0788+15			05:07:38:10
6M1	Hairdressing Source (Excerpt - Jerusalem)	●	●●		-	-	0:31:23	06:04:40:13	06:05:12:11	0420+12	0468+10	FULL VERSION ON MISCELLANEOUS TRACKS 7+8 STEREO FOR TRANSISTOR RADIO		
6M2	* Florentina March *	●	●●		-	-	4:44:22	06:06:34:09	06:11:19:06	0591+08	1018+14			
7M1	* Danny Boy *	●	●●		-	-	3:06:0	07:05:25:00	07:08:31:00	0487+08	0766+08			
8M1	Phil's Breakdown			●	4	45.59	3:22:22	08:05:41:23	08:09:04:20	0512+14	0817+03			
9M1s	Pot Black " (Pub Source 4)		●		8	96.29	0:30:19	09:04:59:06	09:05:30:00	0448+13	0494+15	09:04:40:09	0420+08	09:04:41:20
9M2s	Headphone Source (Clog Dance)	-	●●		-	-	0:11:21	09:05:49:16	09:06:01:12	0524+07	0542+03	TRACKS 7+8 FOR HEADPHONE		
9M3	* Clog Dance*	●	●●		-	-	1:25:12	09:06:01:12	09:07:28:24	0542+03	0670+06			
10M1	* Colonel Bogey *	●	●●		-	-	0:31:22	10:00:08:10	10:00:40:07	0012+08	0060+07			
10M2	* All Things Bright And Beautiful *	●	●●		-/		0:32:8	10:00:40:07	10:01:12:15	0060+07	0108+13			
10M3	* William Tell*	●	●●		-	-	3:21:5	10:01:18:03	10:04:39:08	0117+02	0418+15			
10M4	* Land Of Hope And Glory *	●	●●		-	-	3:01:17	10:08:38:00	10:11:39:17	0776+15	1049+07	INTRO VERSE 1 VERSE 3	① WET DRY WET	② DRY DRY DRY	③ WET WET WET
10M5A	Brassed Off - End Credits Long Version			●	6	120	1:35:6	10:11:52:00	10:13:27:06	1076+09				
10M5B	Brassed Off - End Credits Short Version			●	6	125	1:00:12	10:11:52:00	10:12:52:12	1076+09				
10M6	Wild Cue Of Wrong Notes			●										

Figure 5.4 Cue list for *Brassed Off*

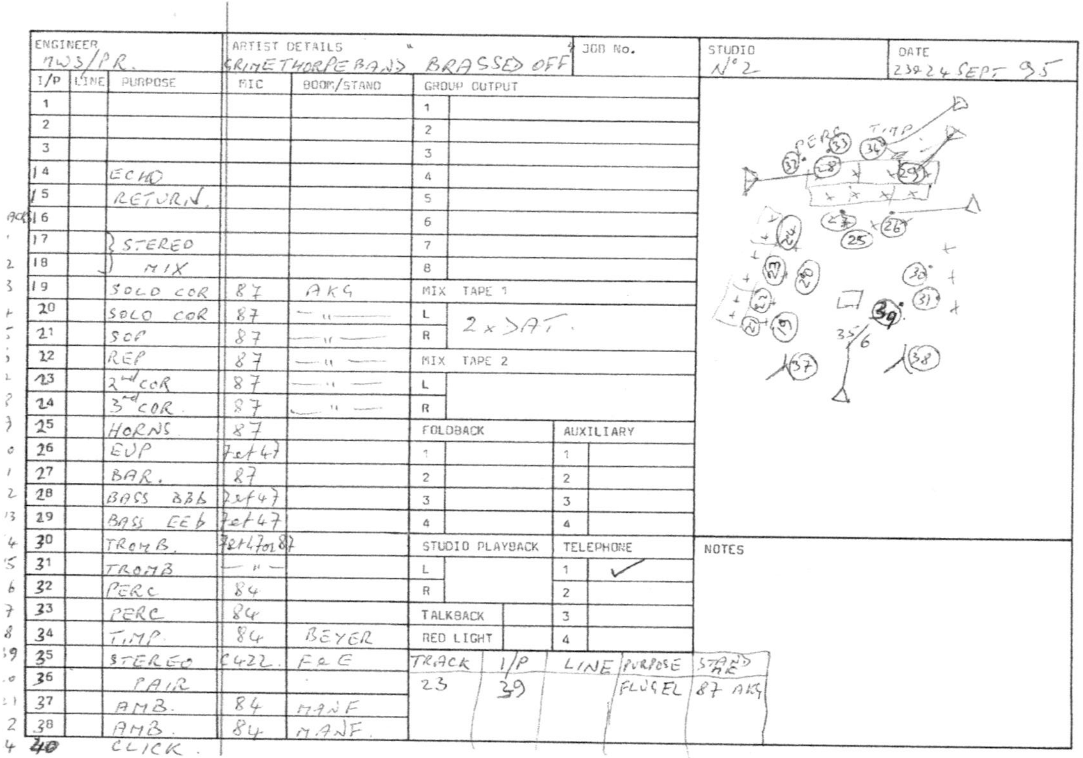

ENGINEER: MWS/PR. | ARTIST DETAILS: GRIMETHORPE BAND "BRASSED OFF" | JOB No. | STUDIO: N° 2 | DATE: 23 & 24 SEPT 95

I/P	LINE	PURPOSE	MIC	BOOM/STAND
1				
2				
3				
14		ECHO		
15		RETURN		
16				
17		STEREO		
18		MIX		
19		SOLO COR	87	AKG
20		SOLO COR	87	"
21		SOP	87	"
12		REP	87	"
23		2nd COR	87	"
24		3rd COR	87	"
25		HORNS	87	
26		EUP	7 or 47	
27		BAR.	87	
28		BASS BBb	2 of 47	
29		BASS EEb	7 of 47	
30		TROMB.	7 of 47 or 87	
31		TROMB	"	
32		PERC	84	
33		PERC	84	
34		TIMP.	84	BEYER
35		STEREO	C422.	F & E
36		PAIR		
37		AMB.	84	MANF
38		AMB.	84	MANF.
40		CLICK.		

MIX TAPE 1: 2 x DAT.

TELEPHONE 1: ✓

TRACK	I/P	LINE	PURPOSE	STAND MIC
23	39		FLUGEL	87 AKG

Figure 5.5 Seating plan for Grimethorpe Colliery Band

strongly that Jones was attempting to isolate the soloist (Paul Hughes) from the rest of the ensemble for recording, without adversely affecting the band's performance or having to record the flugelhorn separately.

Further evidence of Jones's role as a producer is held in the archive in the form of lead sheets for some of the brass band pieces. These sheets of music, usually the solo Bb cornet part, are annotated with markings that show the start and end of each take as well as some indications about which parts of which takes will be used when mixing the final cues for the film. The extract from the overture to Rossini's *William Tell* shown in Figure 5.6 indicates that recording take 3 began with the pick-up to rehearsal mark Q and included some changes to the printed dynamics following rehearsal mark R, and hand-written text across the top of the page noted that an edit should be made from take 1 to take 3 at rehearsal mark R when cutting together the final mix of the piece. Despite all of this, however, Jones's personal involvement with the band appears to have been limited to being on the other side of the glass at recording sessions, and although he did speak with their conductor, John Anderson, he did not actually meet the band members themselves, and none of the band were involved with recording the original score (Barraclough 2014).

Indeed, the recording sessions for the Grimethorpe Band pre-date creation of Jones's original material by several months, with documents in the Jones Archive confirming that the band was recorded at Abbey Road Studios on 23 and 24 September 1995, whereas the original score was not captured until February 1996. It is most likely that the reason for this gap is that the brass band recordings were required before the scenes featuring the band in rehearsal and performance could be shot so that the actors (and band members, who appear in the film) could mime to the recordings. Jones's underscore, by contrast, will have been added in post-production. One of the impacts of this break in Jones's active work on *Brassed Off* is that he was able to undertake other projects during the film's production phase, one of which was an adaptation of Shakespeare's *Richard III* starring Ian McKellen in the title role. This project is of particular note since some of the scoring practices and requirements found within it resonate with Jones's work on *Brassed Off*, notably in terms of the need for the original score to connect or allude to existing musical styles and the relationship of music to the protagonist and the narrative world.

There are connections to pre-existing materials and ideas of time and place in Jones's score for Richard Loncraine's film, which is set in a 1930s fascist Britain. The first is to Jones's own earlier scores, the use of saxophone accompanied by sustained harmonies and pulsing bass-lines recalling the sound of his late 1980s and early 1990s scores *Sea of Love* and *Bad Influence*, but he also captures the stylings of 1930s jazz in his setting of the poem 'Come Live With Me' by Christopher Marlowe, for performance within the film by singer Stacey Kent. This cue recurs in several scenes, and frequently traverses into the non-diegetic realm. Indeed, this material often seems to be controlled by the protagonist, which both complicates the music's role in the narrative space and bestows it with a function as musical characterisation. This material plays in a scene in which Richard talks to the camera as he leaves the mortuary (he frequently breaks the 'fourth wall' during the film by speaking directly to the audience), and culminates in him 'catching' the last note of the cue with a corresponding

Figure 5.6 Extract from the lead sheet for Rossini's overture to *William Tell* with editing annotations

visual action – he literally cues the end of the track with his hand. This calls the music into question, since it seems that Richard can hear the jazz track despite the absence of any sort of sound source, and it becomes clear that the music belongs to and represents him specifically, and indeed might even be playing in his head. There is a similar sort of 'diegetic bleeding' in an early scene in *Brassed Off*, as Danny's humming of 'Floral Dance' blends with the non-diegetic sound of the band as he cycles to rehearsal. While the transfer of the music from the diegetic to the non-diegetic space is much clearer in the latter picture, in both cases the blurring of narrative boundaries serves to highlight the importance of music to a principal character.

This association between music and character is reinforced in *Richard III* in two further scenes featuring 'Come Live with Me'. In the first, the song is heard as Richard receives physiotherapy on his shoulder, and as he rises to leave the room he turns the music off. This is a quite a surprising action in the context of the scene since the impression is given initially that the song is non-diegetic underscoring and the characters have previously given no indication that it is actually playing in the room. The second scene, from later in the film, features Richard in his throne room, and the music, which plays throughout the scene, has been mixed so that it sounds like it is coming from an old-fashioned radio (it is quite tinny and there is a level of noise in the sound typical of analogue radio). However, no source for the sound is seen, and it is left ambiguous as to whether it is actually playing in the room and therefore audible to Richard and the other character, whether it is there purely for the audience watching the film, or if it might be playing in Richard's head much as it seems to have been as he left the mortuary. Jazz has often been used in films for characters who are mentally unstable or sit on the margins or outside of mainstream societal norms (Barham 2017), and as the film progresses these are certainly traits that could be deemed characteristic of Richard.

Jones's score also refers to English orchestral music in characterising both sides in the War of the Roses, nodding to the militarism of Holst's 'Mars' from *The Planets* in the scenes where Richard, now king, prepares to battle Henry Tudor, the future King Henry VII, who despite fleeing to France holds a claim to the English throne. Jones evokes 'Nimrod' from Elgar's *Enigma Variations* in scenes where Henry is portrayed in a positive light, thereby encouraging the audience to associate this solemn, noble and very English-sounding music with the invader rather than the incumbent monarch, calling into questions aspects of patriotism and allegiance. Although there is no actual pre-existing music used in the film, Jones's significant allusions to pre-existing musical styles and, in the case of the Holst and the Elgar, specific works, capitalises on audiences' associations and understanding to give his original music maximum effect within the film. Likewise, the adoption of specific stylistic traits enabled Jones to engage with a different English musical tradition in *Brassed Off* and to develop a score that would blend with very well-known popular repertoire.

The track sheets for Jones's original music for *Brassed Off* such as that shown in Figure 5.7 contain comments indicating that the composer had the track

ARTIST: Brassed Off
TITLE: 1M3/1M4/3M1/4M3/8M1/10M5A/10M5B

#			#		
1	} Trcc.		25	} CD Mix	
2			26		
3			27		L
4	} O/R.		28		C
5			29	} Film mix	R
6	Vl		30		Ls
7	Vl		31		Rs
8	V2		32		
9	Celli		33		
10	Celli		34		
11	Bass Vla.		35	} AF1 Amb Odub	
12	Bass		36		
13	Harp.		37		
14	Fl		38		
15	Tpr/Flug.		39		
16	Euph		40		
17	Perc		41		
18	Timp.		42		
19	} Amb.		43		
20			44		
21	Euph Correction -8M1		45		
22	AF1 ODub		46		
23			47		
24			48		

REMARKS

Figure 5.7 Track sheet for multiple cues in *Brassed Off*, showing the breakdown of instrumentation

sheets for the band music in addition to those relating to his underscore, which suggests that the band material may have played a part in Jones's creative process and in decisions he made about the instrumentation and balances in his original score. Indeed, it is clear that Jones's personal interest in brass-band music influenced the creation of his underscore, which foregrounds brass instruments alongside strings and percussion. He composed seven cues that all feature brass and are also linked by being based around the intervals of a rising fifth and descending minor third, and these cues generally accompany poignant moments in the film, particularly those connected with Danny's ill health and his time in hospital.

The melody lines are always carried by the brass, notably euphonium and flugelhorn, which move the sound somewhat away from a standard orchestral palette and provide a clear timbral link with the brass band music in the story, though the other featured solo instrument, the trumpet, is something of a misnomer in this regard. Alongside this strong connection to the brass band, the slow pace and accompaniment by strings and harp (and percussion for the climax of 'Phil's Breakdown') ensure that Jones's cues also relate to the orchestral language common to underscoring in mid-1990s films, but the melodies situate the music in a third sonic realm, that of English folk-songs. While Jones does not actually quote any existing folk material in his score, there are echoes of the Yorkshire folk song, 'Scarborough Fair' – perhaps best-known by the film-watching public in a version by Simon and Garfunkel that featured in *The Graduate* (1967) – notably the final phrase of the melody with its prominent modal flattened 7th. Jones also composed two source music cues that are totally distinct from the rest of the score – a tuning up sequence for the players on the bus, and music for the jukebox in the fish shop (scored for orchestra with guitar, bass guitar, Rhodes piano, and 'Latino' percussion) – the diegetic nature of both pieces removing them somewhat from the sonic world of the rest of his underscore.

The relationship between Jones's original musical score and the source music can be fluid at times, suggesting close sharing of space in the soundscape. For example, as Danny travels to band practice the cue 'You Get Used to It' begins and the band leader is seen singing and humming the 'Floral Dance' to himself, as noted above. The cue 'Waking Up in Casualty' soon picks up on the melody from 'You Get Used to It' and underscores the conversation between band members Ernie and Jim with cuts to Danny's simultaneous journey to practice. In the following scene, the volume of the 'Floral Dance', now played by the band, increases steadily to support the foregrounding of the performance in rehearsal. Consideration of two versions of the cue list, dated 9 and 11 February 1996 (the latter of which is shown in Figure 5.4), reveals that 'Waking Up in Casualty' and Danny's humming of the 'Floral Dance' were initially distinct sonic elements, cues 1M3 and 1M5. However, later in the editing process it was decided to layer one over the other. Furthermore, the 'Floral Dance' played by the band as cue 1M6 was moved two minutes earlier so that it could be placed under the journey sequence and dovetailed with Danny's humming rather than following on from it, strengthening the connection between music and character.

While Jones's music remains non-diegetic, at times this space is also occupied by the brass-band music, blurring the boundary in a similar (though reversed) way to 'Come Live with Me' in *Richard III*. Brass-band material functions as underscore in scenes such as the montage of the miners and Gloria at work that is accompanied by the band playing 'Cross of Honour', although this is something of an exception. Other band-underscored montages such as the Saddleworth and Halifax competitions, the latter of which is accompanied by the 'Florentina March' and intercut with scenes of vote counting following the ballot of the colliery workers, are supported by shots of the band playing, anchoring the music within the diegesis. Notwithstanding this, the idea that at times the brass-band repertoire functions in a manner very close to conventional underscoring is supported further by the timbral connections between the pre-existing and original music, all of the band material is purely instrumental with no sung lyrics, and the common evocation of Britain through the chosen repertoire and allusions to folk music. In short, Jones' score for *Brassed Off* closely shares the soundscape with the brass-band music, with both score and band cues fluidly traversing into each other's traditional domains, enabled by the musical coherence established by the composer in sculpting his cues to complement the pre-existing music.

GI Jane (1997) and *Lawn Dogs* (1997)

These two pictures contrast sharply in terms of their narratives and musical sound worlds, but both make some use of pre-existing music as part of the filmic soundtrack. Jones provided a score for *GI Jane* (1997) that ramps up the action in this high-octane action adventure, directed by Ridley Scott and based on a story by Danielle Alexandra. The film's plot centres on its leading character Jordan O'Neil (Demi Moore), a topographic analyst in the United States Navy who is selected as a test case to undertake a gruelling Navy Seal training programme. Initiated by a Texan senator who is concerned that the Navy is not gender-neutral, the test case programme is designed to assess whether women can complete the same tasks as men. If successful, women will be integrated into all roles in the Navy. Jordan faces physical, emotional and political obstacles as part of her training, quickly learning that there are multiple stakeholders who do not wish to see her complete her course successfully. Yet, following successful completion of the programme and a terrifying mission in Libya, Jordan earns the respect of her cohort and is awarded her medals.

The film is heavily scored, few scenes being without music, and as in *Richard III* Jones's score draws on elements from his previous projects, most notably the qualities of a rock score and the relentless energy of his toolkit scores. The music for *GI Jane* combines orchestral, electronic and rock instruments and is characterised by its driving rhythms, increasing the tension felt by the audience. The influence of Jones's percussive toolkits can be heard in the opening credits where a steady rhythm on a synthesised metal beat and chomping strings introduce the film's main theme on brass, setting the tone for the rest of the picture. The melodies tend to be performed by brass and strings throughout the film with the trumpet prominent, and many cues incorporate musical codes associated with the United States Armed Forces. For example, cue 2M1, which accompanies Jordan's arrival at the Naval Base, features a solo trumpet playing a simple arpeggiated melody that recalls 'Taps', a piece indelibly associated with the American military. 'Taps' was first played at Harrison's Landing, Virginia in July 1862, a strategically important site during the American Civil War, and from 1891 the melody was incorporated into American military funerals. The second section of the cue is a march on strings, brass, and percussion, with snare drums prominent in the mix, again drawing on established musical codes for militarism and heroism. There are also echoes of an earlier Jones-scored American-themed film in cue 2M4 'Pain is Your Friend', which accompanies a training scene. The soaring theme on brass, strings, and electric guitar recalls the main melody of *The Last of the Mohicans* (1992), and Jones's continued affection for the EWI can be heard in the close of the cue, where its high-pitched solo melody is combined with helicopter rotor noise as the trainees reach the end of their session.

Alongside orchestral and electronic resources, Jones draws on additional instrumentalists to contribute distinctive timbres to specific scenes. Clem Clempson (formerly of the bands Colosseum and Humble Pie) performs the electric guitar in selected cues, giving a harder edge to otherwise orchestral material, and 'ethnic percussion' was provided by Paul Clarvis for the scenes set in Libya, indicating to the audience the foreign territory both geographically and emotionally for Jordan, who is challenged by a real mission. Belinda Sykes, a London-based theatre musician and 'ethnic' session singer provided vocals for these cues, and it is very likely that she also performed the shawm, which can be heard in the cue accompanying the recruits' arrival in Libya.[5] While *GI Jane* features some pre-existing popular songs for montage scenes of training or travel, Jones's score occupies the majority of the sonic space, and like *Richard III* it is more often Jones's own previous scores that leave traces of influence on *GI Jane*. The score draws the audience into the visceral and often terrifying challenges of Jordan's training and effectively highlights the tension caused by the high stakes for both her career and all women aspiring to join the US military.

Released later in the same year *Lawn Dogs* (1997), like the subsequent *Notting Hill*, was produced by Duncan Kenworthy, with whom Jones had worked previously on both *The Dark Crystal* and the TV mini-series, *Gulliver's Travels* (1996). Directed by John Duigan, written by Naomi Wallace and set in Kentucky, the film's plot deals sensitively with the unlikely relationship between the ten-year-old middle-class schoolgirl Devon Stockyard (Mischa Barton), who is scarred from serious thoracic surgery and lives in a world of her imagination fuelled by the Russian folktales of Baba Yaga, and twenty-two-year old, trailer-dwelling Trent Burns (Sam Rockwell), who as a 'lawn dog' mows the family's garden. The relatively modest score makes more use of pre-existing music than Jones's preceding projects and integrates popular sources ranging from Bill Monroe to Bruce Springsteen with original material by Jones. A characteristic sound of the bespoke music is that of the Dobro resonator guitar played by Clem Clempson, which makes its first appearance in the opening titles (cue 1M1). Associated with bluegrass in the hands of performers such as Leroy Mack of The Kentucky Colonels, the distinctive sound of the Dobro acts as a convenient means of encoding the film's locale while also connecting the film's two main protagonists – both misfits sharing physical and emotional scars – who are introduced during the opening title sequence. As well as invoking bluegrass (for example in the scene in which a chicken is rustled by the pair), Jones engages a more classically influenced style (with shades of Mussorgsky) for references to Baba Yaga. In the final sequence of the film, as Devon imagines Trent's escape chased by the ogre Baba Yaga (now clearly understood to be her father), a repetitive folk-like theme in 12/8 played by a solo violin takes the ascendant and completes the film's narrative with a sense of the magical. Musical closure is achieved over the end credits with the resumption of the Dobro theme rather than, as might have been more conventional, the use of a further popular source. Overall, it is a film that uses music sparingly and subtly, many scenes being allowed to speak for themselves without the unnecessary intrusion of hyper-explicative underscore. Indeed, while *Lawn Dogs* does little in the way of progressing Jones's musical voice or practice it can be situated within a body of works in his output – from his earliest television scores such as *Joni Jones* and *One of Ourselves* through blockbusters including *The Last of the Mohicans* and *Brassed Off* and onwards to take in *Titanic Town* and the television mini-series *Merlin* (both 1998) and some of his most recent scores – that draw on the stylistic influence of folk music as a fundamental element of their musical identity.

Titanic Town (1998) and *Dark City* (1998)

Directed by Roger Michell, who would work with Jones again the following year on *Notting Hill*, *Titanic Town* is an outlier among Jones's scores of this period, being a sparsely scored political film with pre-existing songs. Set during the Northern Ireland Troubles, the film centres on a peace movement lead by Bernie McPhelimy (Julie Walters). Most of the pre-existing songs are by singer-songwriter John Martyn, who was popular during the 1970s (the time in which the picture is set), although the film also includes some Irish traditional music performed within the story. As with *Brassed Off*, Jones's original cues, which were composed for acoustic guitar and were arranged and performed by Grammy-winning performer and music producer Kipper, share the film soundscape neatly with these songs owing to the use of similar instrumentation, in this instance supported by the fusion of folk, rock and jazz styles in Jones's music. It is crucial for the story that the time and place of the action are established clearly and quickly in order that an audience can engage meaningfully with the characters, and Bernie in particular, from the outset, and the pre-existing music – notably the choice of songs such as 'Solid Air' – supports the narrative setting and plays a key role in achieving this aim. As was the case for *Brassed Off*, the archive reveals that Jones was involved with recording the pre-existing music, including the diegetic performances on tin whistle and of 'Danny Boy', and with remixing the songs by Martyn, and this doubtless helped him to forge a coherent musical soundscape for the picture.

Identification of character is also a significant part of the use of pre-existing material in *Dark City*, though in this science-fiction thriller it is sound rather than music that is used to forge this connection. Released just over a year before *The Matrix* (1999) showcased the idea of people living in an imagined reality, *Dark City* centres around an alien race, the Strangers, and their experiments on humans. The mise-en-scène and double-level detective story give the picture an air of film noir, albeit one crossed with an alien invasion. Each night at 12 o'clock the Strangers stop time for what they call 'the tuning', during which the humans fall asleep and the Strangers use the power of the mind to change the city and alter reality for its inhabitants. They are assisted by Dr Schreber (Kiefer Sutherland), a human who uses his knowledge of psychology and medicine to implant memories into selected individuals. The Strangers can then observe their behaviour and actions when the population awakens on completion of the tuning. During one tuning John Murdoch (Rufus Sewell) wakes up unexpectedly while time is stopped, setting in motion a chain of events and a journey of self-discovery. The archive contains numerous cuts of the film on VHS tapes, some of which include temp music that gives an idea of how the narrative and its sound world developed as the picture was edited and refined. Extracts from Maurice Jarre's score for *Jacob's Ladder* (1990), Jerry Goldsmith's music for *Alien* (1979), cues from David Arnold's *Stargate* (1994) score and Eric Serra's music for *Léon* (1994) feature alongside material by Howard Shore and a raft of other composers in a patchwork temp that, according to the spotting notes, director Alex Proyas never felt captured the uniqueness of his film properly. Indeed, while the temp often tries to delineate the two races – humans and Strangers – Jones avoids a strict binary representation, and although there are particular sounds in his score that characterise the Strangers, in general he encapsulates all of the inhabitants of the titular dark city within a percussive and often heavily rhythmic score.

Jones features a low wordless choir in those parts of the score that actively relate to the Strangers, but the aliens are more often identified by pre-existing electronic sound that sits alongside the underscore within the film's sonic landscape, sharing the space and serving a clear narrative function. Proyas was keen that Jones understood this element of the film's sound design, which is present in the earliest cuts of the film in the archive, and suggested that the composer could explore similar unusual sounds in his original score. Jones was advised to listen to some tracks by the English experimental-music group Coil, notably their 'Homage to Sewage', which utilises synthesised and heavily manipulated electronic sounds, though ultimately neither the score nor sound design reflect this intensive level of signal processing. Jones's score is dominated by strings, brass and percussion, although there are also electronic elements in the music in keeping with his preferred musical voice, and this provides a subtle link with the sound design in which such sonic elements are more prominent. At the spotting session Jones suggested to Proyas that 'the orchestrations could lend themselves more to what the electronics are doing to fuse more integrally with them. And at other times it would be orchestral FX out of the range of Sound FX and electronics', an approach that the director was keen for him to pursue.[6] Duncan Williams (2016) considers the 'innovative combination of electronic and orchestral textures' to be one of the score's 'acoustic fingerprints' and that the influence of Jones's music can be heard in Hans Zimmer's score for Christopher Nolan's science-fiction thriller *Inception* (2011). He suggests further that:

> The shared musical frame [between *Dark City* and *Inception*] extends to many striking audio cues including the use of distinctive signal-processing techniques such as sampling, time-stretching, and reversing electronic sounds to create multi-modal 'dream-like' sequences in both films.
>
> (Williams 2016)

Nolan has stated that he was influenced by films including *Dark City* when conceiving the narrative of *Inception* (Jagernauth 2010), and Williams's identification of 'a shared musical frame' shows Jones's score as having a parallel impact, notably in terms of the use of technology and aspects of the creative process. In his review of the *Dark City* soundtrack, Bennett Dobbins (2013) observes similarly the influence of Jones's music on Don Davis's score for *The Matrix*, and Luke Goljan identifies that these two films have 'some similar sound qualities during chase sequences' (2003). Goljan also suggests that *Dark City* could have been used to temp parts of *The Matrix*, but he does not offer any evidence to support this idea beyond the sonic connection already noted. Jones's sensitivity to the potential in the orchestra/electronic relationship emphasises not only his comfort with the technology with which he was working but also demonstrates that he held a significant position in the industry in terms of creative experimentation and the use of technology as key elements of film scoring.

While the sound worlds are vastly different, *Dark City*'s sharing of the soundscape between original music and pre-existing electronics is the closest comparator to the relationship between the brass band and underscore material found in *Brassed Off*. These contrast markedly with the relationship between original and pre-existing music in Jones's next film, *Notting Hill*, in which the pre-existing pop songs were chosen to stand out in the texture of the soundscape, presenting Jones with different challenges in the course of his compositional process.

Notting Hill (1999)

Written by Richard Curtis and produced by Duncan Kenworthy, *Notting Hill* is the most successful Hollywood blockbuster scored by Jones to date, winning the Audience Award for Most Popular Film at the BAFTAs in 2000. The film, which had a budget of $42m and grossed over $27m on its opening weekend in the US, tells the story of bookshop owner William Thacker (Hugh Grant) and his romance with world-famous actress Anna Scott (Julia Roberts) following a chance encounter in his Notting Hill book shop. The pair fall in love gradually, although their relationship is far from simple with Anna's ex-boyfriend, William's lovable but naïve housemate, and the ubiquitous British press all presenting obstacles.

Jones's score sits alongside pre-existing classic and contemporary pop songs in a film that is firmly situated in the context of British romantic comedy. Guido Heldt (2012) has highlighted the centrality of popular music to Richard Curtis's romantic comedy films and the way in which song choices can be used by characters themselves and at times even ridiculed. Heldt contrasts *Notting Hill* to the earlier film *Four Weddings and a Funeral* (1994), which uses music largely diegetically as part of the wedding celebrations, arguing that in the later film the popular music is used 'to underscore (in the different meanings of the word) the emotionally charged moments' (p. 77). Indeed, several of the pop songs featured in *Notting Hill*, including 'She', 'When You Say Nothing at All', 'How Can You Mend a Broken Heart', and 'Ain't No Sunshine When She's Gone', accompany montage sequences in which the songs are foregrounded by way of increased volume and use of a faster visual editing style.[7] In contrast with the pre-existing music in *Brassed Off*, the presence of lyrics contributes to these songs providing points of stasis, interrupting the temporal flow and highlighting important moments, rather like arias within an opera. Jones recalls that Curtis had several ideas about music in mind when preparing the screenplay for *Notting Hill*, including the use of 'She' as the music for the opening titles (Jones 2016b), although some songs were changed as the film took shape. The archive's Umatic and VHS tapes of the complete film, which were provided for use during the composition process, include pre-existing songs at the points where they were intended to be placed in the film, and reveal that some song choices were different in the earlier stages.[8] For instance, an early cut of the drive to the Ritz sequence from near the end of the film is accompanied by The Beatles' 'Get Back', rather than 'Gimme Some Lovin'', which is used in the final picture. As well as supporting montage sequences as noted above, it seems apparent that some songs were chosen to provide a window into the perspectives of the protagonists. For instance, Anna's date with William is underscored by 'When You Say Nothing at All', indicating her view of him and the normality of his life that attracts her, while Al Green's 'How Can You Mend a Broken Heart' indicates William's sadness on discovering that Anna has a boyfriend (Heldt 2012).

    The relationship of pre-existing to original music was discussed at a meeting between Jones, Curtis, Kenworthy and director Roger Michell, a log of which is contained in the Trevor Jones Archive, where it was noted that two soul songs were likely to be used in the film; indeed, both choices – The Lighthouse Family's 'Ain't No Sunshine When She's Gone' and Al Green's 'How Can You Mend a Broken Heart' – were ultimately included in the picture. The conversation reveals that the choice of soul songs reflected a desire for music that would be both melancholic and enriching or uplifting to listen to and that the same idea was wanted for the original score. The theme of melancholy was highlighted as a key structural device for the film, yet the director and producer, who were evidently 'hands on' in their treatment of pre-existing music, noted that the placement of melancholic music with melancholic moments was problematic. This might have been due to the redundancy that this synchronisation creates for the audience, a pleonastic arrangement that Heldt's study of other Working Title films shows has been largely avoided post-*Four Weddings and a Funeral*. A temp track provided the impetus for much of the discussion, with positive features highlighted, including the waltz feel to convey the sense of time passing and the melancholic note to suggest a slight sadness to William's character. A transcript of the spotting session indicates that Alan Silvestri's score for *Father of the Bride* was used as a temp track in places, and while the notes do not identify exactly where in the film it was placed, there is an acknowledgement that this score 'worked' for the selected scenes to some extent. However, it was felt to be too sentimental for *Notting Hill* and perhaps too direct in manipulating the audience to feel specific emotions. Indeed, Silvestri's music is more obviously comic in its deliberate references to Wagner's and Mendelssohn's wedding marches, and to Hollywood (the film is even set in Los Angeles), which Michell clearly wanted to avoid.

The spotting notes reveal some concerns expressed about the potential danger of repetition within the music neutralising the linearity of the story, though Jones reassured his colleagues by instead observing the potential of music to suggest an evolution. He resisted the idea of any clear-cut identification of a musical theme with the character of William Thacker, and the director, picking up on this notion, indicated that the music should be about the world of Notting Hill rather than one character. The idea of having different musical styles emanating from different shops on Portobello Road was mooted as a way of achieving this but was dismissed owing to the potential sonic conflicts between musical genres. Unsurprisingly, the team paid very close attention to the plans for cue 1M2, the first time Jones's music is heard following the opening song, 'She'. The cue accompanies the first appearance of William as he walks the audience through the streets of Notting Hill, establishing the setting and style of the whole film, as well as presenting the character's rather sad backstory. Jones noted key words for the music here included 'waltz feeling', 'Le Ronde', 'fairy story', 'pleasant paralysis', 'new tone', 'different texture', 'enchanted', 'surprising', 'occasional note of melancholy', 'romantic', 'sad guy thinks he's happy', 'complicated', 'busy', 'futile', and 'particular place' and endeavoured to reflect these ideas in the cue. The resulting music for 1M2 is a simple acoustic guitar melody shown in Figure 5.8, which can be seen as a decoration of a broken A major chord rising and oscillating around the third and fifth degrees, though there are some minor inflections in the supporting harmonies played by keyboards. The cue is kept quite low in the mix relative to both the voiceover narration and the sound effects of the market on Portobello Road, preventing any form of musical association with Thacker and meeting the film-makers' desire for the music to relate to and almost seem a part of life in Notting Hill.

Perhaps surprisingly given the prominence accorded to the popular songs in the film's soundscape, Jones composed thirty-eight original cues for the film, several of which are interlinked and based on similar melodies with varying

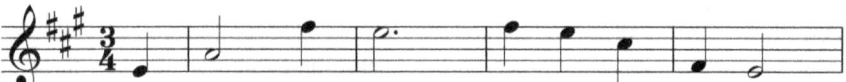

Figure 5.8 Acoustic guitar melody from cue 1M2 of *In the Name of the Father*, taken from the Sibelius file 'Notting Hill – Will and Anna edit' in the Trevor Jones Archive

instrumentations. His long enthusiasm for the synthesiser continues to be evident in the instrumentation of these cues, which usually involves acoustic and electric guitars, bass, drums, saxophone, and Hammond and Rhodes keyboards. According to the engineer on the film, Gareth Cousins, the decision to use guitars and pianos in the underscore was due to the wishes of the director and producer, although this decision raised issues about the balance of sonic elements competing in the soundscape since, as Cousins notes, dialogue usually occupies the same frequency range as the selected instruments. Nonetheless, Jones's careful handling of the instrumentation meant that he was able to meet the needs of the director and producer while also allowing him to create a soundscape that bridges the pop songs and the classical Hollywood score. The spotting notes reveal that all four professionals paid close attention to the music, and that when describing what they were hoping for in the score for *Notting Hill*, Michell, Kenworthy and Curtis made numerous references to other film scores that they admired. *The Graduate* and *Manhattan* (1979) were both noted by Curtis as having idiosyncratic sounds, who suggested that *Notting Hill* could set a new tone instrumentally and thus invoke a similar reaction from audiences, who would observe that this would be a film of a different texture. Both of the films referenced are well known for their heavy use of pre-existing music, which is a major contributing factor in their sonic textures. Michell, by contrast, highlighted that despite there being comic elements in *Notting Hill*, the original music should not be comedic and that the germ of the romantic melody for the whole film needed to be found within the opening theme.

Federico Fellini's *Amarcord* (1973) was mentioned alongside *Manhattan* as a film that has a strong sense of place, an important feature of the intended project (being named for an area of West London), and the film-makers also articulated a desire for *Notting Hill* to sound European rather than American or, as had been the case in *Richard III*, English. This may also have been a key consideration in the selection of a non-orchestral ensemble for the film, actively rejecting the established sound of classical Hollywood and the English twentieth-century music of Elgar, Vaughan Williams and their contemporaries in favour of something that would relate more closely to that found in British and European popular music. Aligned with this, the creators clearly aimed to choose pop songs for the film performed by artists associated with the British market including The Spencer Davis Group ('Gimme Some Lovin''), Ronan Keating ('When You Say Nothing at All'), Texas ('Once in a Lifetime') and The Lighthouse Family ('Ain't No Sunshine When She's Gone').[9] The archive includes track sheets for pre-laid tracks and from the recording sessions, cue lists and spotting notes for *Notting Hill*, and the paperwork shows that Jones and his team were involved with the preparation, remixing and transferring of the pre-existing pop music.[10]

The track sheets illuminate the intertwined relationships between the timelines for composition, remixing and transferring music for the film, showing that Jones's original score was recorded between 3 and 8 January 1999 at Abbey Road. The composer had received five Umatic tapes with a rough cut of the film dated 20 December, before the recording period, and a further two tapes on 5 and 7 January, respectively, suggesting that he may have composed some music without any images or that he was composing based on viewing the picture at, and discussions from, an earlier spotting session. The use of digital software means that films continue to be edited late in post-production, which can result in such changes to the music requirements very late in the process. Indeed, Jones composed some music for *Notting Hill* that was not used in the final cut, notably a jazz arrangement of his music for the cue 'Gramercy Park' for the film within the film scene, which was ultimately rejected for an orchestral version of the same material. He also wrote music to accompany a shot of a poster of Anna on the side of a bus, but that was replaced with a snippet of the pop song 'Once in a Lifetime' in the final picture. This latter example indicates that Jones did not necessarily have a complete idea of where pop songs would be used while he was composing his score and that the film's soundscape remained fluid until close to the release date. The pop songs for the film were all recorded or transferred over three months from January to April 1999, with 'She' being re-mixed last of all, just one month before the premiere.

'She' is used for the opening credit sequence, which is a series of images demonstrating Anna's fame, and for the final montage sequence that closes the picture, presenting significant moments in Anna and Will's new life together. The song, composed by Charles Aznavour with lyrics by Herbert Kretzmer, was written in 1974 for the BBC television series *Seven Faces of a Woman* (Herbert Kretzmer 2013) and was released as a single performed by Aznavour in the same year. The notes from the early sketch meeting for *Notting Hill* indicate that this version was favoured initially by the film-makers, and a video file in the archive dated 5 January 1999 that includes the Aznavour recording in the soundtrack shows that it was still being used at this relatively late stage. However, the final picture instead features a re-recording by the British singer Elvis Costello, with Jones suggesting that there was a very practical reason for this change of soloist:

> We wanted to use the original but it was difficult trying to communicate with the copyright owners and publishers. We had contacted them in France and we had a dialogue with them until the eleventh hour but they were unable to lock into whether they would allow us to use it or not, and at the eleventh hour I suggested we re-record it. We looked around for an artist to re-record and settled on Elvis Costello who was going off on tour and came into Abbey Road for a couple of hours before he caught a plane, and so we just managed to record 'She' using Elvis Costello.
>
> (Jones 2016b)

However, it also appears that despite the film-makers' stated desire for a European sound, there may have been a strong aesthetic reason for the change. Jones was concerned that the choice of Aznavour's recording of 'She' as the music for the opening titles might lead to the picture being mistaken as 'French' in sound at the outset, undermining the British feel of the film, and Aznavour's performance is indeed quite incongruous with the sound of the other pop songs in the picture. Jones produced a new arrangement of the song for Costello, though the track sheet for the recording shown in Figure 5.9 indicates clearly that the Aznavour original

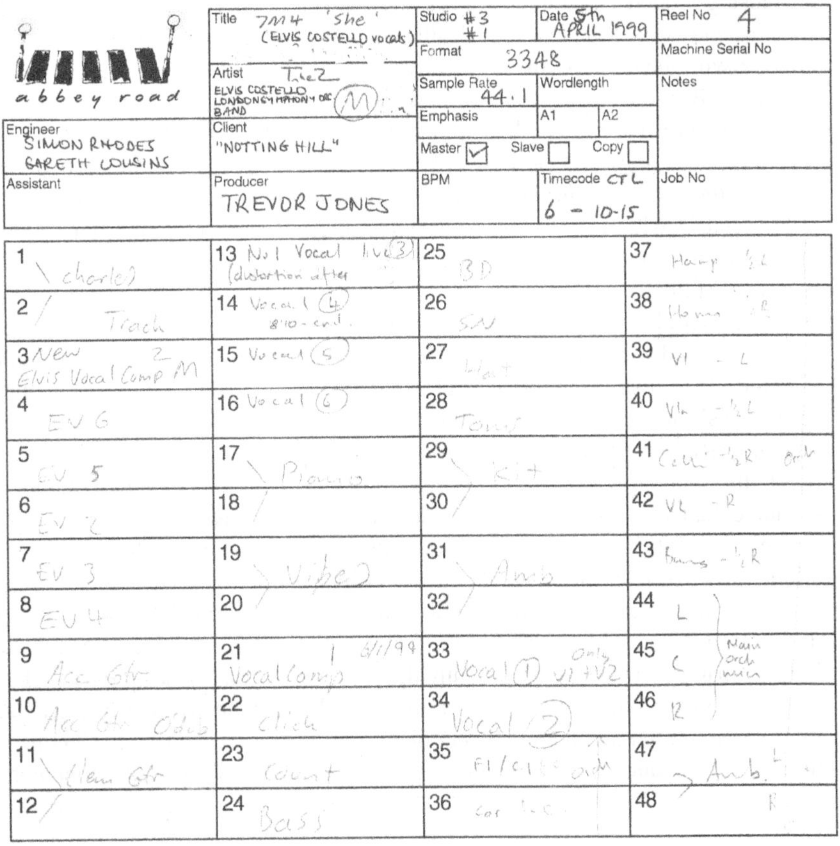

Title	7M4 'She' (ELVIS COSTELLO vocals)	Studio #3 #1		Date 5th APRIL 1999		Reel No	4
		Format	3348			Machine Serial No	
Artist	T.L.2 ELVIS COSTELLO LONDON SYMPHONY ORC BAND (M)	Sample Rate	44.1	Wordlength		Notes	
		Emphasis		A1	A2		
Engineer SIMON RHODES GARETH COUSINS	Client "NOTTING HILL"	Master ☑		Slave ☐	Copy ☐		
Assistant	Producer TREVOR JONES	BPM		Timecode CTL 6 - 10-15		Job No	

1 Charles	13 N.1 Vocal live (3) (distortion after)	25 B.D	37 Harp
2 Track	14 Vocal (4) 8'10-end.	26 S.N	38 16 mm R
3 NEW 2 Elvis Vocal Comp M	15 Vocal (5)	27 Hat	39 V1 - L
4 EV 6	16 Vocal (6)	28 Toms	40 V1 - ½L
5 EV 5	17 Piano	29 K+	41 Celli ½R only
6 EV 2	18	30	42 VC - R
7 EV 3	19 Vibes	31 Amp	43 trans - ½R
8 EV 4	20	32	44 L
9 Acc Gtr	21 3/1/99 Vocal Comp	33 Vocal (1) V1+V2 only	45 C Main orch mics
10 Acc Gtr O.dub	22 click	34 Vocal (2)	46 R
11 Clean Gtr	23 count	35 F1/c1 orch	47 Amb.
12	24 Bass	36 cor...	48 R

Figure 5.9 Track sheet for 7M4 'She', with Elvis Costello's vocals

functioned as a guide track for recording the new version, perhaps unsurprising given the short time-frame for recording the song outlined by Jones, above.

The archival materials also show that several different cuts of Aznavour's 'She' were tried over the film's closing sequence since the song was too short for the amount of visual footage required in the montage to move from Anna's press conference through the wedding celebrations to the red carpet and finally to Anna and William in the park. The song itself has a short introduction, three verses and a bridge, but the montage requires an additional section to be added into the structure to extend the material. A VHS tape from 5 January 1999 includes three versions of the closing sequence that include the same visual footage with different cuts of the song, as shown in Table 5.4. Musically the first structure is the strongest of these options, with the return to the lyrics of verse 1 in the middle of the song somewhat obscured given the change of visual images, though the opening line, 'She may be the face I can't forget' is perhaps the most memorable of the whole song, and its repetition does draw the ear a little. The immediate repetition of the second verse weakens the song, and moving the bridge away from the red carpet sequence – the only scenario within the montage in which the two characters are not equals – means that the music does not support the visual footage as well as in the other two iterations of the song. Re-arranging and re-recording the song offered a solution to all of these problems, with Jones crafting a string instrumental to be interpolated after the second verse, thus providing the missing fifth musical section and enabling Costello's 'She' to meet the durational requirement of the sequence. Although musically Jones's arrangement for Costello is identical to structures 1 and 2, above, the lack of lyrical repetition and the contrast provided by the instrumental, particularly before the song moves to the bridge, makes it a much more convincing fit with the montage than any of the previous attempts using the Aznavour track.

Jones's creation of a sense of place in *Notting Hill* was achieved through employment of a simple style that leaves room for audience interpretation and allows for a presentation of the Notting Hill area as an English home to multiple different cultures. This is apparent in the track sheets, where many of his cues include string orchestra to accompany the leading 'popular' instruments, and in a similar manner to his re-arrangement of 'She', Jones's melodies frequently 'take off' on strings after an iteration on popular music instruments. Despite meeting the film-makers' request to avoid an American sound in the film, Jones nonetheless

Table 5.4 Different structures of 'She' for the closing sequence of *Notting Hill* on the VHS tape from 5 January 1999

Visual Footage	Press Conference	Press Conference to Wedding	Wedding	Red Carpet Walk	Park
Structure 1	Verse 1	Verse 2	Verse 1	Bridge	Verse 3
Structure 2	Verse 1	Verse 2	Verse 2	Bridge	Verse 3
Structure 3	Verse 1	Verse 2	Bridge	Verse 2	Verse 3

manages to marry a popular-music sound world with elements of traditional symphonic scoring through his choice of instrumentation and use of orchestration and a lack of reliance on clear melodic or thematic writing in his underscore. His involvement as arranger and producer of the soundtrack's pop songs also results in a coherent partnership between the original and pre-existing material that enables them to share the film's sonic space.

Conclusion

Despite the different relationships between pre-existing and original material, it appears that there was an impact on Jones's approach on projects that included some form of pre-existing music or sound, notably in terms of instrumentation and musical style. Adopting a commonality of ensemble helped Jones's scores for *Brassed Off* (euphonium and flugelhorn), *Dark City* (electronics) and *Notting Hill* (guitars and keyboards) to work alongside their pre-existing counterparts, and references to established musical styles and codes – folk (including bluegrass) in *Brassed Off*, *Lawn Dogs* and *Titanic Town*, jazz and English orchestral music in *Richard III*, and the avoidance of the orchestra in *Notting Hill* – connect the underscore to the pre-existing tracks further. The flexibility required of the composer in the digital age becomes apparent upon consideration of the archival materials for these projects, which show how closely intertwined the processes of composition, recording, mixing, editing, and transferring can be. While Jones was no stranger to working alongside other artists in the creation and production of scores, having crafted scores around songs by David Bowie in *Labyrinth* (1986) and, as discussed in this chapter, Bono and U2 in *In the Name of the Father*, the increased use of pre-existing music, and popular music in particular, in the 1990s nonetheless challenged composers in the way in which they conceived and developed their original material. Jones would go on to work with two of the leading young female singers of their generation in the coming years – Britney Spears on *Crossroads* and Charlotte Church on *I'll Be There* (2003) – as well as composing scores for a number of further Hollywood films in the early years of the twenty-first century.

Notes

1 There is a considerable body of scholarship on pre-existing pop music in film and compilation soundtracks but little of it considers the compositional approach, partially due to a lack of access to materials from the film-scoring processes.
2 A version of this section of the chapter previously appeared as part of Cooper (2009). Reproduced with permission.
3 The durations of Jones's cues are taken from the source recordings.
4 According to the short score produced from the sequencer, the pipes were recorded on a D set, with the tape speed being set sufficiently fast to cause the guide track to play back a semitone higher than written. Subsequent replay of the tape at normal speed transposed the pitch down a semitone so that the melody appeared in Bb minor.
5 The credits state that she provided ethnic vocals but do not mention the shawm.
6 '*Dark City* Music Spotting Notes, 22 June 1997' [Transcript]. *Dark City*. 1997. Trevor Jones Archive, University of Leeds, p. 2.

7 Hubbert (2013) discusses the advent of such sequences in 1980s compilation scores, and outlines connections between MTV and this audio-visual style.
8 Developed by Sony, the Umatic tape is an analogue recording videocassette, which was used in the film industry from the 1970s. Although similar in appearance to the VHS cassette, the Umatic tape is larger and was never used widely in the consumer market. It was innovative in its placement of the tape reels inside a plastic case.
9 Images from *Notting Hill* appear in the music videos for 'You've Got a Way' and 'When You Say Nothing at All', which were also released in 1999. The video for the former song is intercut with images from the film so that the pop song has a similar function to underscore. The images are structured to reflect the narrative in the film, with the minor key section of the pop song synchronised with scenes of Will and Anna arguing before the conflict is resolved and the final chorus of the song is delivered. In 'When You Say Nothing at All', Keating is seen singing on the same bench that features in the film, sitting next to a girl. This is an unusual mise-en-scène due to the presence of a man with a hand-held video player that is playing scenes from *Notting Hill*. The man is also trying to sell VHS tapes of the film resulting in a sense of self-reflexiveness.
10 While the use of pre-existing pop songs undoubtedly supported the release of a successful soundtrack album, it is also possible that several of the tracks were remixed for licensing reasons.

6 Hollywood blockbusters part two

After the critical and financial successes of the releases of the late 1990s Jones's stock as a composer stood at a high level. In particular, *Notting Hill* had performed extremely strongly at the box office, ranking as the seventh highest worldwide grossing film of 1999 with takings of $363.9m against a budget of $42m. At the start of the first decade of the new millennium he was contracted to score a sequence of films starring leading 'A-list' actors Kevin Costner (*Thirteen Days*, 2000), Johnny Depp (*From Hell*, 2001), Sean Connery (*The League of Extraordinary Gentlemen*, 2003) and Jackie Chan (*Around the World in 80 Days*, 2004), as well as the singers Britney Spears (*Crossroads*, 2002) and Charlotte Church (*I'll Be There*, 2003). However, these six films would have much more variable outcomes, both in terms of box office receipts and reviews.

As a group they place into direct relief a number of the issues revealed by the archive that are addressed in the course of this volume, including: the modes of communication and collaboration between the production and music teams within and across continents (in *Thirteen Days* and *Crossroads*); the employment of temp tracks (in *Around the World in 80 Days*); the use of pre-existing popular music (in *Crossroads* and *I'll Be There*); thematicism and musical identity (in *The League of Extraordinary Gentlemen* and *From Hell*); as well as Jones's personal identity and motivations (in the South African production *The Long Run*). The linear approach to the discussion of the scores in this chapter is in part taken to demonstrate the level and scale of Jones's achievements over the period of just five years and the diversity of the projects he scored. At the same time the continuities and discontinuities of his working practices and network of collaborators across a range of genres and industrial contexts are highlighted by considering them in chronological order.

By this stage in his career, the computer-based technologies discussed in Chapter 5 dominated virtually every aspect of Jones's work. The majority of Hollywood films were now offline-edited on non-linear systems (primarily Avid's Media Composer), which enabled multiple new cuts of films to be created relatively easily. This was a double-edged sword, benefitting directors and producers in refining and honing their product, but placing composers, including Jones, in the position of having to respond increasingly rapidly to recut versions of a film in which their carefully planned cues had to be replaced. Most of the films considered in this chapter bear the traces of this development to some extent.

The extent of the materials held in the archive for each of these films is variable. For instance, *Thirteen Days* and *Crossroads* are particularly rich in terms of spotting notes which are helpful in determining the development timeline of the score, whereas *From Hell* and *Around the World in 80 Days* retain much less written documentary evidence about how and why individual decisions may have been taken. Nevertheless, much can still be inferred from the extant audiovisual data even when some archival material is absent and all the films scored over the period have been included to enable a comprehensive overview of Jones's output.

Thirteen Days (2000)

Directed by Roger Donaldson, *Thirteen Days* depicts the events of October 1962 when Soviet missiles were planted in Cuba, forcing the Kennedy administration to develop a response that would avoid nuclear war. Drawing on Robert F. Kennedy's *Thirteen Days: A Memoir of the Cuban Missile Crisis* and Ernest R. May and Philip D. Zeiklow's *The Kennedy Tapes: Inside the White House During the Cuban Missile Crisis* (which involves transcripts of the conversations that took place among the members of the 'Ex Comm' – the Executive Committee of the National Security Council formed to manage the crisis), David Self's screenplay focuses particularly on the characters of John F. Kennedy, his brother Robert, and Kenny O'Donnell, the president's long-time friend and White House appointments secretary. The role of the Irish-American O'Donnell was taken by Kevin Costner (who also acted as one of the film's producers). O'Donnell was apparently a much less influential figure in the crisis than he is made out to be in the narrative, and more generally *Thirteen Days* has been criticised for the lack of accuracy in its portrayal of both individuals and events (cf. Nelson 2001).

Costner had taken the starring role as district attorney Jim Garrison in Oliver Stone's film about John F Kennedy's assassination, *JFK* (1991), the score for which was written by John Williams. The selection of Jones as the composer for the ostensibly 'patriotic' film *Thirteen Days* (arguably a kind of prequel to *JFK*) seems notable on at least two counts: firstly that he had not previously worked with Costner or any other of the creative leads, and the only senior figure with whom he had collaborated hitherto was executive producer Michael De Luca of New Line Cinema (who had also held this role for *Dark City*) and secondly that an American composer had not been given the job. Of course, the Australian director Donaldson had worked with a range of composers, his three previous films having scores by John Frizell (*Dante's Peak*, 1997), Christopher Young (*Species*, 1995) and Mark Isham (*The Getaway*, 1994), and Jones had gained a significant reputation for scoring politically charged drama with *Mississippi Burning* (1988) and *In the Name of the Father* (1993).

Materials in the archive for *Thirteen Days* provide an interesting case study of the exigencies and pitfalls in the development of a score across two continents. The film editor Conrad Buff and music editor Alex Gibson (assisted by Jeremy Raub) were based in Los Angeles while Jones and most of his collaborators in the music department, who included Steve Price (assistant music recordist) and Gareth Cousins (credited as synthesiser programmer and performer), corresponded from London. Table 6.1 outlines the key dates in the development of

Table 6.1 Outline of the schedule for the production of the score for *Thirteen Days* from material in the Trevor Jones Archive

Date	Archival Material
8 May 2000	Early correspondence between music editor Alex Gibson and Trevor Jones's assistant Steve Price regarding personnel for sound department. Correspondence continues through May regarding the format by which picture and audio will be presented to the composer (Umatic tapes, CUE posting notes, DA88s with the temp dub).
6 June 2000	Updated spotting notes with breakdowns from Gibson to Jones.
12 June 2000	Post-production schedule indicates that the recording and mixing will take place 16–21 July 2000.
13 June 2000	Jones writes to the director Roger Donaldson to outline his working method: to sketch entire score before recording, and to confine recording and mixing to when the director is in London in order to take his thoughts into account. Jones plans to provide Gibson with 5.1 mixes and the stems.
17 June 2000	Tapes sent to London for at least the first half of the film.
Mid-late June 2000	Updated CUE files sent from Gibson and assistant music editor Jeremy Raub to Jones and team. Change sheet outlines changes between old and new versions.
5 July 2000	Potential picture changes flagged up by Gibson and Raub.
Early July 2000	Transfer of Jones's music and updated CUE files and timings sent from music editors.
12 July 2000	Decision to recut, recording and mixing dates in July cancelled.
4 August 2000	New tapes locked for the 4th preview and temp. Jones receives tapes on 7 August.
17 August 2000	CUE breakdowns sent to Jones.
21 August 2000	New version of film cut with new timings. Discussion of final shipment of tapes from Gibson to Jones: 2 copies of Umatics for each reel, 2 copies of VHS for each reel, 2 sets eight-tracks.
22 August 2000	Gibson sends Jones a 'Red/Green list', which indicates the cues that Donaldson is happy with as they stand (green) and which ones require changes (red). Plan to send new tapes and CUE updates.
6 September 2000	Cue timings list.
7 September 2000	Raub writes that the 'cue bible' (approval list, spotting notes, Trevor's log, changes from last version, Cues with tempos and clicks) is on its way to Abbey Road.
8–10 September 2000	Recording Schedule (London Symphony Orchestra).
11–15 September 2000	Mix Schedule.

the film, as indicated by the archival materials. The earliest communication that is held in the Jones Archive dates from May 2000, when the composer received details of the sound department personnel from Alex Gibson and a complete breakdown of the cues for the film. Jones received regular updates from Gibson regarding the views of the director Donaldson.

A note from Jones to the director in mid-June regarding the plans for music recording and mixing reveals his proposed working method: he planned to sketch the entire score for the director before recording it in a mocked-up version. Recording and mixing was to be confined to the period when Donaldson was due to be in London that July. In addition to six-track mixes, the composer and his team would provide the music editor with the stems, and the director's feedback on the sketches would be noted by the music editor so that Jones could respond to it. Despite this careful preparation, the process did not run smoothly. The film was cut, Jones composed his score and then a decision was made to significantly re-cut the picture very close to the planned dates for the recording and mixing sessions in mid-July 2000, which therefore had to be postponed. Subsequently, the film was further radically re-cut on 21 August and was subject to a second spotting session in which the picture was synchronised with Jones's already composed score. He had to respond to a series of changes, some minor and some more substantial, requiring new music for selected cues in order to work with the updated cut and adjusted timings for scenes, and the recording sessions with the London Symphony Orchestra did not finally take place until 8–10 September, conducted by the film's orchestrator, Geoff Alexander. It appears that the original aim was for release on Labour Day (4 September 2000), but this was delayed owing to the significant re-cutting and the film premiered in selected New York and Los Angeles theatres on 22 December 2000, with the general release on 12 January 2001. The outcome of this was much poorer attendance figures than anticipated, with the $80m production budget yielding worldwide receipts of under $67m, and a US domestic gross of only $34.5m (Box Office Mojo 2017b).

As to the score itself, the approved cue list indicates one hour and fifty-two minutes of specially composed music (plus three minutes of source music) in a film lasting two hours and twenty-five minutes. In contrast to John Williams's use of Copland-like tropes in contemporary patriotic pictures *JFK* and *Saving Private Ryan* (1998) (Brown 2009, p. 210), and indeed to Jones's own invocation of American military musical signifiers for *GI Jane* (1997) three years previously, he did not pursue such a style on *Thirteen Days*, opting instead to integrate a diversity of sampled or synthesised sounds into a large orchestral palette. Taking cue 1M1 ('Thirteen Days – Opening Titles Part 1') as an example, the samples used are identified by individual parts in the full score and include lines for 'Deep Pad', 'Ballistic Low hi octave', 'Krang', 'LSO Perc FX', 'Cymscrape 18', 'Serated Brass Rod', '50p CymScrape', 'Synth Snares', 'Timpani', 'Miro BDs', 'Gtr Harmonics', 'Subliminal Low', 'LD String FX', 'Pizz Strings', 'Gran Cassa', 'Sus Cymbs', 'Gong (and rumble FX)', 'Rusty Spoke', 'Hollow Pipe', 'Pit Hit' and 'Soft Vibes'. The music notes for the film reveal that Jones had been asked by the director to generate a signature sound for the missiles that suggested their awfulness, and he

Figure 6.1 Missiles theme from cue 1M2 from *Thirteen Days*

responded by creating a composite of seven sonic elements ('Ballistic Low – Drone', 'Rusty Spoke – Metallic Oil Can', 'Pit Hit – Front Sound', 'Hollow pipe', 'Doom Drum', 'Deep Kettle Drum + Bass Drum Rolls' and 'Gong Fx + Tam Tam metallic rumble and scrapes'). In a comparable mode to the toolkit approach he used extensively in the late 1980s and early 1990s, it was Jones's intention that although a composite sound resulted from their combination, these elements could be used in different permutations and the final combinations would be decided at the mix in order to ensure that they were integrated properly with the sound effects.

As well as these timbres, Jones invented a motif loosely reminiscent of the plainsong 'Dies Irae' melody to represent the missiles; this theme, shown in Figure 6.1, can be heard played by Wagner tubas, trombones and tuba in cue 1M2 '*Thirteen Days*, Opening Titles Part 2'. As a counterfoil to the missiles theme, a much lighter and brisker syncopated derivative picked up by the first flute and oboe in octaves in the same cue, is apparently intended to suggest the 'happy-go-lucky' character of Kenny O'Donnell. Much of Jones's music for the rest of the film underscores the general grittiness and edginess of the narrative and makes strong use of the electronic resources. It is not until the broadly configured and self-enclosed penultimate cue 8M5 'It's a Beautiful Morning', which eschews electronics completely, that the resplendent, majestic and almost Elgarian main theme (in contrast to Williams's rather more Copland-like counterpart in *JFK*), with its poignant suspensions, emerges from the opening trumpet call. Indeed, unusually, the theme only makes its first appearance at the very end of the movie proper, immediately before the suite that accompanies the closing credit 'crawl'.

The Long Run (2001) and *From Hell* (2001)

Jones's homeland formed the location for the following film, *The Long Run* (2001), produced by the South African company Distant Horizon and directed by Jean Stewart, who had previously worked on UK television series such as *EastEnders*, *The Bill*, *Cracker* and *Born to Run* and the TV film *Butterfly Collectors* (1999). Understated and often beautiful, the film's plot concerns a young Namibian illegal immigrant and amateur runner called Christine Moyo (Mthati Moshesh), who is taken up by the white German *ex pat* 'Barry' Bohmer (Armin Mueller-Strahl). Having been pensioned off early against his will from his job as a brick maker, Barry decides to train Christine to take part in the fifty-four mile Comrades Marathon between Durban and Pietermaritzburg.

Ostensibly about marathon running, the narrative is equally, or perhaps more, concerned with post-apartheid issues in the Rainbow Nation, a theme which was particularly important to Jones, who as a member of the 'Coloured' population (as so classified in apartheid South Africa) had closely followed the developments in his native land from his new home in Britain. During the race the dictatorial if well-meaning Barry, who has previously felt the perpetual need to bark out instructions to her about every aspect of her training and diet, passes on the message via his daughter that Christine should run it her own way, to 'enjoy it and forget everything he told [her]'. It is this comment, as much as any, that encourages the reading of the film as a fable about contemporary South Africa.

Music is used much more sparsely than in *Thirteen Days*, and a substantial proportion of it is source (some of which was composed by Jones), comprising twelve out of thirty-one cues. Samples of African instruments employed in the orchestral score (played again by the LSO) include talking-, log- and slit-drums; marimbas; balafon; kalimba; berimbau; and djembe, and Jones's usual filmic language can be heard to absorb the sounds and rhythms of South African music. The majestic main theme, prefigured in the titles music and heard in fully fledged AABA song form at the climax of the race, subtly hints at the South African national anthem 'Nkosi Sikelel' iAfrika' by employing the harmonic pattern I–IIb–Ic–V7–I in A major over a turn-like melodic figure (C#–B–A–G#–B–A) that is similar to the phrase that sets 'South Africa' in the anthem. Indeed, the whole of the A section can be seen as an elaboration of the 3–2–1–L7–1 figure. The male voice a cappella group Ladysmith Black Mambazo, who had appeared on Paul Simon's *Graceland* (1986) and employ a style of singing known as isicathamiya, are featured in the score performing 'Old Barber's Chair' which forms the first half of the closing credits music.

From Hell is ostensibly a gory horror picture concerning the investigation of the 'Jack the Ripper' murders in Victorian London by the clairvoyant opium addict and absinthe drinker, Inspector Frederick Abberline (played by Johnny Depp). It was released on 19 October 2001 and could not be further removed from either *Thirteen Days* or *The Long Run*. Directed by twins Albert and Allen Hughes, it fared rather better at the box office than *Thirteen Days* had done, with a budget of $35m and a worldwide gross of nearly $75m. The movie received qualified plaudits, including those of Elvis Mitchell in *The New York Times*, where he commented that:

> the movie succeeds, but it does have its faults – the attempt to weld social melodrama and suspense creaks at some of the joints. But the Hughes Brothers' goal here is to make an epic of savagery, and they are brilliant at ambience and details.
>
> (2001)

In a keynote interview conducted in 2005, in response to a question from the audience about who chose him for a particular film, Jones described his first meeting with the Hughes twins:

> They called and said they were coming to London to meet with me and talk about me scoring their film and I said I was very flattered and so on and met

them at this hotel. And they brought along what was a roll of wallpaper on which [. . .] was a lot of knights and blood and gore: it was a medieval battle very much like the Bayeux Tapestry. [. . .] I was absolutely dumbstruck by this and I said 'This is fantastic' and they said 'It's for you'. And I said 'Well, you know, what is it?' and they said 'Well we saw *Excalibur* and we wanted to work with the composer who'd written, who'd worked on *Excalibur*', because the dance things and the dance cues they liked very much. They knew about the Wagner but they wanted to work with me on one of their first pictures.

(Fox and Cooper 2008, p. 13)

Of course, both Jones's filmic language and the entire field of music technology had moved on considerably since *Excalibur* (1981), but it is notable that this aspect of his work (rather than, say, *Angel Heart* (1987)) should have attracted the Hughes brothers to him. Equally, it is of interest that their gift should be a depiction of a gory scene, given that the roots of *From Hell* lay in the eponymous graphic novel written by Alan Moore with illustrations by Eddie Campbell that appeared serially in *Taboo* from 1989 to 1996, before being published in a collected edition in 1999.

Surprisingly, given that for most of his films it generally holds a deep level of material, the Trevor Jones Archive contains relatively little related to *From Hell*, other than the two-track mixdowns of all the cues, the CD album tracks and a set of Umatic videos. The non-availability of the notated score, track sheets, cue lists and spotting notes undoubtedly makes it rather more difficult to reconstruct the process by which the music was composed or to evidence the specific resources employed. However, such absences are characteristic of many archives, and the evidence provided in this case by the extant material (including the cinematic release), other available sources, and Jones's standard practices allow the archival scholar to make informed judgements about process and output.

The music editor of *From Hell* was again Alex Gibson, with whom Jones had worked closely on *Thirteen Days* and who had previously been assistant music editor on *Freejack* (1992). Other members of Jones's regular team involved on the project included orchestrator and conductor Geoff Alexander (in this case directing the Academy of St Martin-in-the-Fields rather than the London Symphony Orchestra), orchestrator Julian Kershaw (who had worked with Jones since *Kiss of Death* in 1995) and music recordist Gareth Cousins (who joined the 'team' for *Dark City* in 1998). One might reasonably infer from this continuity within the music department that scoring was likely to have followed a well-established approach.

From Hell, like *Thirteen Days*, uses underscore for much of its duration (in this case, of just over two hours), and Jones's music creates an aural ambience that seems in keeping for a film that was described by Roger Ebert (2001) as 'a Guignol about a cross section of a thoroughly rotten society, corrupted from the top down'. The cue 1M4 'Martha's Murder', which accompanies the sequence of Inspector Abberline's opium-induced dream of the death of Martha Tabram, is an early instance in the narrative of the movie's *Grand Guignol* character. Here an electronic soundscape, which brings to the foreground irregular heartbeat-like sounds and filtered vocals, coalesces with elements on the dialogue and effects tracks to produce an effective sonic correlate to the visuals, accentuating the hyper-reality of the narcotic dream state. While much of the score, in common with cue 1M4, might be described as being 'atmospheric' in tone, with relatively little overtly thematic music as conventionally conceived beyond the source music, the original scheme would appear to have been to strategically place such thematic cues at the beginning, middle and end of the film. 1M2 'Packers Rent Girls' is heard after the night-time prologue, as the prostitutes wash themselves at the drinking fountain and as Ann Crook arrives with her baby. For this, Jones composed a two-and-a-half minute cue in four broad phrases, warmly orchestrated for strings. However, in the dubbed version, a melody that appeared to have the potential to develop as the film's main theme is truncated to its first phrase alone, mixed quietly in the background of the soundtrack. The cue 4M6 'Anne's Cell', heard as Abberline and Mary Kelly visit Ann in the asylum, and against their subsequent discussion as they walk along the road, develops from a melody shown in Figure 6.2 that is heard at the end of the first phrase of 1M2, A_4–[E_5–G_5–]F_5–D_5–E_5–C_5–A_4, transformed into a slow waltz in A minor with the bracketed pitches omitted. A further lushly scored triple-time cue (4M7 'Portrait of a Prince') follows immediately, for the scene at the art gallery during which Abberline shows Mary the portrait of Queen Victoria's son, the Duke of Clarence, and she recognises him to be Ann's husband. Finally, in 7M8 'Abberline's Sacrifice' (a title that indicates his death in fact resulted from suicide, something that must be inferred from the action), which cuts between the London police station and Mary's new home, the music swells out empathetically as we observe Mary and her adopted daughter before briefly returning to a more textural approach; the cue closes the narrative through three expressive *mezza di voce* chords that finish with the tonic D minor.

From Hell may be seen to encapsulate several of the characteristics of Jones's mature approach, with on one hand a tonal (often modally articulated) musical language that draws particularly on early-twentieth-century British models and on the other a refined sensitivity to electronically generated or treated sound, either integrated within the orchestral score or with other elements of the sound track. In *Thirteen Days*, music editor Alex Gibson had played a pivotal role in the creation of the score, and his creativity in the role of mediator between Jones and Donaldson was evident in his development of a practical method to smooth the editing process late in the course of the film when time and financial pressures were most intense. Points of similarity and divergence can be found when examining the composer-music editor relationship on the teen road movie *Crossroads*, directed by Tamra Davis, co-produced by MTV and starring the pop singer Britney Spears.

Figure 6.2 Aural transcription of the melody at the end of the first phrase of cue 1M2 from *From Hell*. The bracketed pitches are omitted when this material is turned into a slow waltz in cue 4M6

Crossroads (2002) and *I'll Be There* (2003)

If the ratio of box office income to budget is taken as one criterion of the success of a film, then *Crossroads*' worldwide takings of $61m against a budget of only $12m must be deemed an extremely positive outcome for the production company. However, despite Spears's strong fan base, which presumably gave rise to the solid attendance figures for the opening weekend (accounting for almost 40% of the US gross), it fared poorly with critics. In the words of Peter Travers, writing in *Rolling Stone* on 15 February 2002:

> *Crossroads* boasts a director, Tamra Davis, who once showed promise (*Guncrazy*) and a screenwriter, Shonda Rhimes, with a prime HBO credit (*Introducing Dorothy Dandridge*). But what's onscreen has all the passion of a balance sheet. No wonder. The powers behind *Crossroads* aren't out to do something creative; they're protecting an investment in a pitchwoman.
>
> (2002)

By 2000 the South African businessman Clive Calder had acquired an extensive range of companies as part of the Zomba Group, including Segue Music (the music editing company); Ingenuity Entertainment (the successor to Zomba Screen Music, the composer management company that represented Jones); and Britney Spears's record company, Jive Records. According to Jones, Calder:

> put together a film in which he wanted to showcase Britney Spears. She's a music artist rather than an actress so the songs were pre-ordained and I was just brought in as a film composer to underscore the action. So it was under one umbrella so to speak.
>
> (Jones 2016b)

He went on to explain that:

> my management had said, you have to do this film, the owners of our company have insisted on your scoring it, and that was it. So it was kind of dictated from on high. When you're in a management company you just accept the fact that your management is not going to leave you vulnerable to some disreputable project. [. . .] It was a commercial project for commercial reasons and you can see how the power of ownership can exert its influence across the board, whether it's artistic or not. You find yourself in a personal situation where you have no control over what you're working on.
>
> (Jones 2016b)

Crossroads appears under two other names in the archive, *Scrabble with Nutmeg* and *What Are Friends For* and it seems that at the beginning of the project there was a degree of secrecy about the movie and the plot and identity of the star were not initially disclosed widely; these obscure or low-key alternative working titles were intended to help maintain this confidentiality. The archive contains six extensive sets of spotting notes dated from July to September 2001, and subsequent correspondence between the US-based production company and Jones in October considers further the music and the recording plans. Spotting notes for *Crossroads* are attributed to Jones and the supervising music editor, Jim Harrison, and much of the communication comes to Jones via Harrison. Indeed, there is a memo from music supervisor Dan Carlin that summarises key points but remarks that Harrison will be emailing his notes from the session, suggesting that it was the supervising music editor's responsibility to handle the more extensive feedback on behalf of the group.

Harrison recorded the director's comments about the individual cues as well as offering his own suggestions. It appears that he performed less of a mediating function than Gibson had done for *Thirteen Days*, and in many cases he simply notified Jones that Davis intended to speak to him directly with her feedback on his music. It is possible that owing to her experience of directing music videos for MTV, Davis had more specific musical ideas than other directors and was able to express them more clearly and succinctly, although the comments attributed to her are fairly terse and not particularly musically technical. Overall the development of *Crossroads* appears to have been much smoother than that of *Thirteen Days*, with a generally linear process from the provision of the temp through Jones's composition of his score to the recording and mixing for the final cut. Given the number of pre-existing pop songs planned for the film from its conception, Jones's music can perhaps be construed to play a mediating role in itself. His score frequently provides a similar sound to the songs used in the film, much as his music for *Labyrinth* (1986) had blended sonically with the songs of David Bowie some fifteen years earlier.

According to the earliest set of spotting notes in the archive for *Scrabble with Nutmeg*, dated 24 July 2001, just over one hour and six minutes of music was originally agreed for the film, of which twenty-nine minutes was to be underscore, the remainder being a mixture of song score (7:19), visual instrumental source (2:56), visual vocal source (20:45), non-visual vocal (4:05) and non-visual instrumental source (2:31). Exactly two months later, the total music slated for the second version of the picture had been reduced to one hour, with a four-minute cut to Jones's original score. Notwithstanding this cut, there remains a reasonable amount of underscore, reserved and subdued as it is, and the project recalls *Notting Hill* both in this respect and in its employment of a simple melodic idea for guitar and strings as the main theme. Indeed, Jones was encouraged to reuse this theme in cues 1M9, heard as the girls are seen digging up the box they buried as children, and 3M5, which accompanies Mimi's revelation that she had been raped. Despite the role played by the Zomba Group in the production of the film, clearance could not be agreed for Jones to make use of, or even allude to, the melody of Spears's core song ('I'm Not a Girl') in his score – a demonstration of the complex rights issues in the film industry – with the result that several cues had to be rewritten for scenes where its use had originally been spotted.

Like *Crossroads*, Morgan Creek Productions' 2003 picture *I'll Be There* aimed to capitalise on the popularity of a young female singer. In this case the film starred the teenage Welsh soprano Charlotte Church, who had originally come to public attention in the UK in 1997 at the age of eleven through her performance of the 'Pie Jesu' from Andrew Lloyd Webber's *Requiem*. Written by the actor, musician and comedian Craig Ferguson, *I'll Be There* was his directorial debut, a role he has not to this point repeated. The plot places Ferguson as the ageing rock star Paul Kerr who, unbeknownst to himself, fathered Church's character Olivia Edmonds to a former girlfriend during a weekend affair. After a motorcycle accident, which is treated as a suicide attempt and results in him being sectioned, he meets his daughter and inspires her to become a musician. Described by Neil Smith (2003) as 'an ill-advised vanity project' for Ferguson, the film generally fared poorly with critics. The only executive common to Jones's previous work was the producer James G. Robinson, the influential CEO of Morgan Creek Productions, the studio that had produced *Freejack* and *The Last of the Mohicans*. Jones's music editor was Jeremy Raub, with whom he had worked on both *Thirteen Days* and *From Hell*, although *I'll Be There* was a very different project in scale and intention and, indeed, original compositional content to either of these.

The Four Tops' 1966 hit 'Reach Out I'll Be There', written by Lamont Dozier and Brian and Eddie Holland (the source of the film's title), forms an important strand of the soundtrack, being (the audience is told narratively) Olivia's mother's favourite song. It is heard sung by Olivia accompanied by an acoustic guitar in the first part of the film, soon after she has met Paul, and in the closing scene of the film at her farewell party in the Stag & Huntsman pub an ensemble rendition led by Olivia and Paul spills over into a highly produced version sung by Church under the first half of the credits. At the conclusion of this version of the song, Jones's main theme appears one last time, demonstrating the care with which he has integrated his original material with the popular source music. The rising perfect fourth and falling perfect fifth (G–C–F) that underpins the hook of the chorus of 'Reach Out I'll Be There' (setting the words 'I'll be there') is loosely mirrored by the opening falling major third and rising perfect fourth (C#–A–D) of Jones's melody, set with a similar rhythm. A balancing figure moves up through a fifth before dropping to the tonic, A (E–B–A), and the combined phrase lies at the centre of a simple though elegant theme that places a solo acoustic guitar in the limelight and is intended to underscore the developing relationship between father and daughter (and is explicitly labelled as 'Paul & Olivia theme' in cue 6M4Re).[1] Among the files in the archive is a version of the cue that was not used in the final mix, involving a vocal duet between Church and Ferguson set to a rather gauche text beginning 'All my life/I've thought of you'. Presumably felt to be unnecessary after the closing rendition of 'Reach Out I'll Be There' (and after most of the audience would, in any case, have left the auditorium), the orchestral version performed by the London Symphony Orchestra provides a cleaner conclusion to the credit sequence.

As was the case with *Crossroads*, the soundtrack relies heavily on pre-composed pop music, although Jones's main theme forms a substantial part of five of the more extended cues. One of his primary tasks with the score was to construct the musical persona of Paul, particularly through the cue heard on his jukebox at the opening of the film that crosscuts with Olivia's performance of the macaronic Gaelic/English song collected by Marjory Kennedy-Fraser, 'In Hebrid Seas', and the song 'All My Life' played non-diegetically as the pair ride his motorcycle across the grounds of his mansion. Although *I'll Be There* might be construed to be little more than a potboiler, Jones's attitude to the scoring of the film was as serious and professional, and indeed, courteous to the cast and crew, as any of his other work. The absence of an album for a film with a successful singer as its star may be seen as an index of its relative commercial and critical failure, but it is unfortunate that Jones's music, and in particular the main theme, has not had another vehicle for its wider dissemination.

The League of Extraordinary Gentlemen (2003)

Jones's other film of 2003 was on a very different scale and was intended to attract a much larger global audience. *The League of Extraordinary Gentlemen*, loosely based on the graphic novel of the same name written by Alan Moore (author of *From Hell*) and illustrated by Kevin O'Neill, was directed by Stephen Norrington and starred Sean Connery. Released on 11 July 2003, it was another weak performer at the US box office: its production budget was estimated as $78m, but its gross takings by 7 November were just over $66m despite an opening weekend in the US generating $23m (IMDb.com 2017a). Its worldwide gross has been estimated at over $179m, and it fared best in the UK, Spain, Germany and Japan (Box Office Mojo 2017a). The complex plot combines a number of characters drawn from, or referencing, a range of sources from literature including Allan Quatermain (*King Solomon's Mines*), Captain Nemo (*Twenty Thousand Leagues under the Sea*), Rodney Skinner (*The Invisible Man*),[2] Henry Jekyll/Edward Hyde (*Dr Jekyll and Mr Hyde*), Dorian Gray (*The Picture of Dorian Gray*), the vampire Mina Harker (*Dracula*) and a US secret agent called Tom Sawyer (presumably the grown-up version of Mark Twain's character). Collectively they form the eponymous League, which is brought together in 1899 by 'M' to do battle against 'the Fantom', who is wreaking havoc in order to foster world war. The denouement of the film reveals that M is both James Moriarty (Sherlock Holmes's nemesis) and, in a bizarre twist of the plot, the Fantom himself.

According to Elvis Mitchell, reviewing *The League of Extraordinary Gentlemen* in *The New York Times* in July 2003:

> The film's screenplay by James Dale Robinson – who toiled in comic books for some time himself – takes pains to get the spirit of Mr. Moore's tale right. It's a formidable task, bringing the comics' dank, coruscating vision to the screen – an abiding interest of the producer Don Murphy. Mr. Murphy was also responsible for a previous Moore adaptation, *From Hell*, featuring another Victorian misfit, Jack the Ripper. Mr. Moore's melancholic and apocalyptic

stories have a dour, murderous humour drizzling through the depressive clouds. No one in comics is his equal at conjuring the end of the world, and in his stories – from *The Watchmen* and *V for Vendetta* through *League* – the world is awash in brutality and ugliness, deserving of doom. Mr. Moore's pleasure comes in serving up Old Testament balance.

(Mitchell 2003)

From Hell (producer Don Murphy's previous film) had certainly been profitable for its producers – principally Twentieth Century Fox – and the presence of Connery (in his final film role) suggested that *The League of Extraordinary Gentlemen* was a fairly safe investment for the five companies that shared the risk. However, it proved a critical disaster, and its potential strengths and actual weaknesses were tersely summarised by Roger Ebert:

The League of Extraordinary Gentlemen assembles a splendid team of heroes to battle a plan for world domination, and then, just when it seems about to become a real corker of an adventure movie, plunges into incomprehensible action, idiotic dialogue, inexplicable motivations, causes without effects, effects without causes, and general lunacy. What a mess.

(Ebert 2003)

Jones's score for *The League of Extraordinary Gentlemen* (often abbreviated to *LXG* in production materials) is very substantial in scale, running to more than 600 pages of full score and consisting of 41 cues. As he had done a couple of years earlier in *The Long Run*, Jones recorded Ladysmith Black Mambazo to provide music referencing Africa – in 1M4 'Kenya, May 1899' and the penultimate cue 7M4 'Burial in Africa' – though in this picture it is the Kenya of 1899 where Quatermain has made his home, rather than Jones's native South Africa.[3] Beyond this, the original score and almost all of the source music was composed by Jones and orchestrated by Geoff Alexander, who also conducted the London Symphony Orchestra in the recording. However, some of this material was omitted, moved around or dubbed so low in the mix that it is nearly inaudible above the overpowering sound effects track. In his review of the score, Jonathan Broxton comments that:

Eschewing the leitmotif method of endowing individual characters with small, defining themes, Jones instead scores the League as a whole with a single style, cornerstoned by an ascending brass fanfare that acts as the score's central theme. [. . .] However by using the broad-brush approach, Jones has left his score with very little individual personality: the theme is not strong enough on its own to act successfully as an all-encompassing heroic motif, and eventually the action music tends to meld together.

(Broxton 2003)

The broadly paced theme alluded to by Broxton makes its first appearance in bars 33–35 of cue 1M6 'Fight in the Britannia Club' as a rising chain of interlocking perfect fifths terminated by a perfect fourth (see Figure 6.3a) and played by brass and upper strings over a pedal C#, but viewers may struggle to hear it over the dominating effects. Patterns of such interlaced intervals are by no means unusual within twentieth-century practice, and conspicuous examples can be found in both Bartók's and Berg's violin concertos. Here the assertive rising fifths – commonplace codes for the heroic – are connected through a shape that combines the tritonally related C# minor and G major, culminating on a dissonant chord containing the pitches C#–E–B–C. The motif – which, as gradually becomes apparent, encodes the league – appears prominently in around twelve further cues in the course of the film, its plastic nature permitting it to be subtly reconfigured in length and modality on each occurrence. For example, in 2M1 ('Introducing Nemo's Car'), heard several scenes later, the motif appears diatonically organised in F minor and has been extended by one permutation as shown in Figure 6.3b; the tonality has shifted again, to C minor, in the middle part of 2M3 ('Library Fight'), set in Dorian Gray's library, and a more compact version of the theme shown in Figure 6.3c is heard with a descending diminished triad at its tail; in 2M6 ('The Nautilus Arrives') it is compressed once more into a diatonic format (see Figure 6.3d) against gently rocking patterns, insinuating the lapping of waves as the submarine is introduced. It is late in the film, close to its climax, that the rationale for the shape of the theme becomes apparent, being heard as the members of the league place their hands over each other.[4]

Clearly if Jones had supplied each of the main protagonists with their own independent thematic identity that was referenced on every appearance, this would likely have resulted in a highly fragmented score – indeed one which might have been considered to draw too much attention away from the action. However, it would be inaccurate to suggest that the score is entirely monothematic, for several other themes reappear in the course of the film with apparent signifying functions.

Figure 6.3 Jones's theme for the league in *The League of Extraordinary Gentlemen*: (a) The initial statement in bars 33–35 of cue 1M6 'Fight in the Britannia Club'; (b) extended by one permutation in cue 2M1; (c) more compact version from cue 2M3; (d) compressed version from cue 2M6

The opening cue supporting the prologue to the film, 1M1–3, presents an idea that will be important for the unfolding of the plot in musical terms in reference to 'the Fantom' or his alter ego 'M'. This is a powerful and sustained idea counterposing a Dorian-inflected D minor and F# minor that emerges in the trombones from bar 63 (F–D–F–D/C#–F#–C#); at its core is an almost Bartókian motif that grows outwards (F–D–C#–F#).[5] In the mysterious and darkly comical cue 1M8 ('Meeting "M"') that betokens the influence of Saint-Saëns – a theme built around oscillations between chords of F minor and a French Sixth on D flat that is subsequently heard when Skinner is alluded to – Jones subtly hints at M's duplicitous nature through the inversion of the orientation of the major third relationship between the final pair of chords, F minor falling to what is effectively C# minor dissonantly placed over the tonic F.

At the same time, cue 1M1–3 includes a further idea related in contour to this motif – the 'Quatermain theme' – first heard exactly as Sean Connery's name appears in the opening credits. Played powerfully by three horns, and in D minor, it pushes upwards sequentially through the pitches F–D–G/A–F–Bb. The first three pitches, transposed into A minor, are subsequently heard in the Britannia Club, in cue 1M6, just before the fight breaks out and immediately after Quatermain has remarked 'and I'm not the man I once was'.[6] The motif reappears in the following cue, 1M7 ('English Summer/Quatermain') after Quatermain has conceded that he is now 'in', played elegiacally by the strings as he surveys the crosses in the graveyard (including that of his son) and then over the jump cut to the scene in London preliminary to his meeting with 'M'. It is now extended by six notes that rise and fall to create the full version of the theme shown in Figure 6.4, and if this seems to set a vaguely Edwardian tone, this may in part arise from the shared contour with the opening three pitches of the theme of Elgar's *Enigma Variations* (Bb$_4$–G$_4$–C$_5$–[A$_4$]). In Jones's score the idea is found in a further eight cues,[7] generally suggesting a positive spirit through the opening two rising figures but one which is tempered by the Phrygian flattened ninth on Bb and the final broken chord ending on the dominant, which ends with a sense of incompleteness.

Some of the other thematic material is relatively generic in structure, such as the chromatically rising and falling broken chords played in triplets (D–F–A/Eb–Gb–Bb/A–F–D/Ab–F–Db) first heard in 2M7 'Hunting Mr Hyde', which is later brought to the foreground in 5M3 'Sinking Hyde Rescues'. Inevitably, given the number of extended action sequences in the film there is considerable use of ostinati to accompany these scenes, and a number of Jones's fingerprints can be found in them, such as the application of an $F^{maj7(\#11)}$ chord near the start (bars 14–28) and at the end (bars 68–75) of cue 1M6 'Fight in the Britannia Club'. The employment of this harmony in his output can be traced back at least as far as *The*

Figure 6.4 The Quatermain theme from *The League of Extraordinary Gentlemen*

Last Place on Earth (1985) nearly twenty years earlier. As had become his standard practice, Jones supplements the large orchestra (including eight horns) and chorus in a number of cues with a panoply of synthesised sounds which are fully notated in the conductor's score. Thus, for example, 2M3 'Library Fight', includes patches called 'UltTimp', 'Wood Hits', 'Fox Drum', 'Ash Choir', 'Sub Low Pizz', 'Glasses', 'Harmonious' and 'Probes'.

In Jack Smith's (2003) review of the soundtrack CD on the BBC website he remarks that the score 'adds up to a rare thing a soundtrack that works much better without the film'. While this may be true, it is in fact difficult to form a reasonable judgement of Jones's intentions from either film or CD, the former being substantially modified in post-production and often mixed at a very low level, and the latter omitting many of the forty odd cues. Two instances of changes made in the film can be found in the cues supporting the voyage to Mongolia and the closing scene depicting Quatermain's funeral. In the former (5M5), the full score reveals that Jones had intended to place the Quatermain theme discussed above into the limelight. Instead, this is replaced by completely new material with a lyrical quality that appears in the full score as 'LXG–7M5 EndIngredientsSP2' (and as the title suggests, is used as part of the closing credits suite); this has been intercut in post-production with a segment of the original cue. For the final scene he had recorded the Ladysmith Black Mambazo choir, supplemented by the overdubbed orchestra, but the choral music was removed entirely from the scene and instead placed in the middle of the credits suite. Many more detailed and gross changes were made to action sequences in which, for much of the time, the score is almost drowned out under the dominant effect and dialogue tracks, presumably in deference to the comic book source.

Undoubtedly music editor Jeremy Raub, who had been the assistant music editor on *Thirteen Days* and *From Hell*, acted in the best interests of Jones and the integrity of the score, though whether in its original configuration it might have helped to retrieve a film that has been regarded as a critical failure is a moot point. Of course, the picture may itself have been the victim of some misunderstanding – an attempt to emulate and reproduce a comic book approach has been judged by many by the standards of an adventure film and criticised for its illogicality (such as the streets in Venice that can accommodate a car). However, like *Dark City* and to some extent *From Hell*, *The League of Extraordinary Gentlemen* presents an imagined world and creates its own internal logic. There is no doubt that Jones's score cannot always be heard at its best and its many virtues are often obscured, though the materials and recordings that are held in the archive make manifest the coherence of his musical vision, the quality of his realisation of this vision (ably supported by orchestrator Geoff Alexander), and the excellent performances by one of the world's leading orchestras, the LSO.

Around the World in 80 Days (2004)

The final large-scale film considered in this chapter is *Around the World in 80 Days*, a co-production between Walden Media – whose tagline is 'we tell stories that recapture the imagination, rekindle curiosity, and demonstrate the rewards of virtue' (Walden Media 2012) – and Disney, which was directed by Frank Coraci and released on 16 June 2004. A 'family film' based extremely loosely on the Jules Verne novel, it was principally a vehicle for the actor and martial arts specialist Jackie Chan who plays Passepartout, the valet to Phileas Fogg (Steve Coogan), in his attempt to circumnavigate the world to satisfy a bet with the head of the Royal Society. The critical response, though generally poor, was not entirely negative, Stephen Holden noting in *The New York Times* that:

> Sometimes nonsense makes good sense. The latest remake of Jules Verne's 1873 globe-trotting fantasy, *Around the World in 80 Days*, is a deliriously silly caper that goes out of its way to thumb its nose at logic. [. . .] Despite its contemporary touches *Around the World in 80 Days* is a satisfying slice of old-fashioned storybook entertainment. It proudly insists on its own innocence.
>
> (Holden 2004)

The film had an estimated budget of $110 million, but notwithstanding the presence of Chan, its lifetime takings at the box office were around $72 million, representing a major loss for its investors including Walden Media's owner, the billionaire Philip Anschutz. Roger Ebert (2004) comments that 'the director, Frank Coraci, takes advantage of Verne's structure to avoid the need for any real continuity' and this no doubt introduced a problem for Jones in maintaining musical coherence. Several reviewers of the soundtrack felt that the score, while often brilliantly written and orchestrated, was derivative of a group of other film composers, with names such as Harry Gregson-Williams, James Newton Howard, James Horner and John Williams being identified (Filmtracks 2011). For Peter Simons (2004) it was 'a wonderfully lush and varied score', but he argues that it 'suffers from one of the worst cases of "temp track love" in recent memory', and he questions whether brickbats or plaudits should be accorded to Jones 'for his efforts to adapt all these influences and incorporate them into what ultimately is a highly enjoyable work'. The anonymous reviewer on the Filmtracks site (2011) goes as far as suggesting that Jones's title theme is a 'variation' on Gregson-Williams's main idea for *Sinbad: Legend of the Seven Seas* (released by DreamWorks in 2003).[8] 'Temp love', the situation in which a director becomes so enamoured with the temp track that he or she finds it difficult to accept the original score, is a not uncommon experience for a film composer. Jones remarked that:

> the biggest danger with temping is that the cutting room falls in love with it because the editor sees it so many times, that the director sees those images with that music on it, and even if it's the most trite piece of music they become wedded to it, they become, 'oh the temp used to this' or 'the temp used to do that', and you say 'but the temp was wrong to do that, that's not what you really want the audience to feel at that point'.
>
> (Jones 2014a)

In 2016, Jones commented that after scoring *The Last of the Mohicans* he decided to

> ask the cutting room on all of the projects that I worked on subsequently to keep the temp track separate, and I would not listen to the temp track until I had conceived what I thought to be the right style and got the bare bones of the musical identity together, and only then would I turn on the temp track and see what the scene had been temped with.
>
> (2016b)

This suggests that, at the least, his first ideas for the theme were unlikely to have been influenced by the temp track. However, the archive does not contain any spotting notes or other correspondence relating to *Around the World in 80 Days*, and there is thus insufficient evidence to trace out the process of the development of the score in as fine detail as can be done for many other films. As far as the relationship between his main theme and that of Gregson-Williams in *Sinbad: Legend of the Seven Seas* goes, it seems to be considerably stretching a point to describe it as a 'variation', though there is some family likeness between the ideas, both of which employ a Mixolydian modality. In Jones's case, the upwardly spiralling line forming the antecedent (G_4–D_4–C_5–A_4/B_4–G_4–B_4–D_5) of the first phrase has a cognate contour to that of the motif associated with the league in *The League of Extraordinary Gentlemen*, and it does not particularly resemble the much simpler elaboration of a rising fifth of Gregson-Williams's theme (G_4–D_5–C_5–D_5–D_5–E_5). However, rather than suggesting direct imitation of any specific theme, it might be proposed that Jones is simply drawing here, with considerable skill and élan, on a particular late-twentieth-century Hollywood film-music archetype.

Jones's score is very substantial in scale, with more than sixty discrete cues (five of which are used as source and several others are brief stingers) forming the original music for the film. Some of the settings call for original or specially composed music reflecting the culture of the locale, and for these Jones displays a considerable degree of sensitivity in both the selection of instrumental resources and approach to the cues' musical organisation. As with the other scores of this period it is brilliantly conceived orchestrally, its fine details being realised by the extremely experienced team of orchestrators led by Geoff Alexander and including Julian Kershaw and David Butterworth. Given the enormous effort in writing the music it must have been deeply frustrating for Jones that the film fared so poorly with critics and public – particularly since his commitment to it meant he had reluctantly had to turn down the chance to score Alex Proyas's *I, Robot*, which was a huge commercial success (Benitez 2004b) – though at least his score did receive fair treatment in the final mix.

Conclusions

Jones completed one other project in 2004, a five-minute animated short for Terry Jones, the budget for which was estimated to be a minuscule (by the standards of *Around the World in 80 Days*) ten thousand pounds. *The Unsteady Chough* tells in verse the zany tale of a drunken bird among the spires and bars of Oxford

University and offers some interesting insights into the process and technology of score production that was fully embedded in Jones's working methods by this stage. The files held in the archive show the progression from his very detailed MIDI file (which drove the mock-up orchestra and formed the input to the music processor) through Alexander's orchestration in Sibelius to Andrew Dudman's recordings of the London Symphony Orchestra and the choir of the Chapel Royal, Hampton Court Palace, using the digital audio workstation ProTools. Jones commented in 2014 that for his scores the 'instrumentation is very pedantically, specifically laid out [in the MIDI score] and people like Geoff Alexander, you know, those people who wrote with me for years, they explode the scores out' (2014a). He sat at the heart of a creative team for which, after music, technology was the primary mediator.

The five years from 2000 to 2004 had been a time of intense activity for Jones and one in which he was arguably working at the peak of his power. The musical range displayed by the scores, which also included the three-episode television mini-series *Dinotopia* (2002) and an identically named six-episode spin-off series (2002–3), is quite extraordinary and testament to his remarkable versatility and energy.[9] However, it was also a period that must have generated some disappointment, for whatever their strengths, none of the mainstream Hollywood projects achieved the public and critical success that films such as *Notting Hill* or *Brassed Off* had done. The following years would see some retrenchment as well as forays into new areas of activity.

Notes

1 The Re at the end of this cue number indicates it is a revised version of the cue.
2 It seems that the film's character was called 'an' rather 'the' invisible man to avoid a potential copyright infringement.
3 The first of these cues was not eventually used in the dubbed film.
4 However, the score has been altered in the mix to the extent that it is difficult to determine what was Jones's intention and what was that of the director.
5 This motif is also found in a variant form in which F rises to Ab (F–D–F–D–F–Ab).
6 It should be noted that the middle part of this cue has been significantly edited: Jones had originally made conspicuous use of the motif in the course of the fight, but this has been replaced by much more generic material that Mickey Mouses the action without offering much in the way of thematic commentary (the score at this point in any case being largely submerged under the thunderous effects).
7 3M2 'The league is set', 3M5 'Pull', 4M1 'Arriving in Venice', 4M3 'Venice explodes', 4M5 'The Cemetery/Fantom', 5M4 'Rebuilding', 5M5 'To Mongolia', and 6M3 'Tom Sawyer Fight'.
8 Transposed to the same tonal level as Jones's theme.
9 In 2002 Jones also scored the telefilm *The Gathering Storm*, also known as *The Lonely War*, a dramatisation of the marriage of Winston and Clementine Churchill (Albert Finney and Vanessa Redgrave) in the years before the outbreak of World War II. The project was Jones's third engagement for HBO and second with director Richard Loncraine following *Richard III* (1995). The track sheets in the archive show that the score was composed for strings, woodwind, horns, two harps, percussion and EWI and was recorded in early April 2002, about three weeks before the scheduled broadcast date. However, the music was rejected following recording and replaced by a new score by Howard Goodall.

7 Music for television[1]

While the majority of Trevor Jones's professional life has been devoted to scoring films, he has also enjoyed a successful career creating music for television. He has composed original scores for programmes produced predominantly by the American and British television industries, which have been transmitted by both commercial and non-commercial broadcasters operating within these industries. Furthermore, Jones has written scores for a range of programme forms, including stand-alone telefilms and multi-episodic mini-series and series.[2] While television music clearly shares traits with its filmic counterpart, there are also many differences between the two media that affect their musical practices and that arise in terms of both the production and function of the music. Kevin Donnelly (2005, p. 111) summarises television music as falling into three categories: underscore (specifically-written music for television programmes such as dramas and wildlife documentaries); 'reiterated blocks of music' written for a series but not a particular episode (for example, game shows such as *Who Wants to Be a Millionaire?*); and pre-existing stock music hired for a show but not written specifically for it (e.g. popular music utilised for reality television shows). He goes on to explain how television is not dominated by the convention of scoring music to action and that the available technology and lower budgets imply that 'television music should not be simply film music for a small screen' (p. 112). These ideas are particularly pertinent when considering Jones's work, especially since the vast majority of his television output can be categorised as music scored to action.

Jones has noted in interview that the mini-series is his preferred television programme format since he can approach it like a film for cinema:

> I imagine that I haven't actually experienced television scoring the way most composers do. I might have at the start of my career when working on projects for the BBC or one-off ITV plays but I tend to be asked to work on television to create film-type scores for mini-series projects, like an extended film with all that production value where one uses similar kinds of forces, orchestra with electronic sounds.
>
> (Jones 2014a)

This quote reveals much about the development of Jones's television career and his practice when writing music for television, in particular that the scores for some of his projects might justifiably be thought of as 'film music for a small screen', in direct contrast to Donnelly's comments. Indeed, Jones's ability to adopt this approach seems to stem from many of his later scores being for high-budget 'quality' television productions, and these projects enable close consideration of the similarities between his processes for television and film scoring. His observation that he has moved from stand-alone telefilms to mini-series might be deemed a slight over-simplification, however, and Sarah Hall has demonstrated that Jones's scores for narrative television projects[3] can be grouped into four distinct periods: the 'Early Career Era', which includes telefilms and mini-series scored in 1982 to 1985; the 'Telefilm Era' between 1988 and 1993, in which Jones's television work is focused mainly on this programme format; the 'Hallmark Era', between 1996 and 2002, in which he scored four mini-series for the company; and the 'Recent Career Era' that contains series and mini-series scored between 2002 and 2012.[4] The Trevor Jones Archive contains materials relating to twenty-two scores for Jones's narrative television projects across these eras, which are outlined in Table 7.1; projects for commercial broadcasters are indicated by asterisks.

The history of the US television industry has been categorised into three broad periods that align with and cut across these portions of Jones's television-scoring career. There is broad agreement in the scholarship that the first of these, the 'network' or 'classical network' era, ran from the start of television in the 1950s to the 1980s, meaning that this period was ending around the time that Jones began working in television. Amanda Lotz (2007) identifies the period that followed, between the mid-1980s and the mid-2000s, as the 'multi-channel transition' (p. 7), during which television went through various developments, and Curtin and Shattuc (2009) adopt this terminology in their introduction to the American industry, summarising this period as the time when programmes with 'mass audiences and high ratings during the classical network era gave way to an expanding number of channels featuring shows that targeted niche audiences' (p. 31). During the multi-channel transition in the 1980s, the status quo was challenged by the launch of a fourth major broadcaster in both the US (Fox) and UK (Channel Four), and the rise of cable network HBO in this decade (having launched in 1972) led to the birth of what some scholars have dubbed 'quality TV'. The most recent era in television history has been defined as 'matrix' by Curtin and Shattuc and 'post-network' by Lotz, who suggests it began in the mid-2000s and was still current by the time her book was published in 2007. There is no strong agreement in the literature about precisely when the 'matrix' era began, although Curtin and Shattuc express a common view that in this most recent period television is 'a leading component of a media matrix that is comprised of broadcast services [. . .] as well as a large and growing number of media services available via the Internet and other telecommunication technologies' (2009, p. 11), offering viewers an extremely broad range of viewing possibilities. The crossover between the 'post-network' and 'matrix' eras in the early years of the twenty-first century is of particular relevance to this consideration of Jones's music for television since the Hallmark Era straddles this significant change in the industrial landscape. Indeed, it is the only part of Jones's television-scoring career that does not fall entirely into one of these broadly defined eras of television production.

Table 7.1 Jones's television projects in chronological order, showing era, programme form, industry and broadcaster (asterisked when commercial)

Era	Year	Programme Title	Programme Form	Industry	Broadcaster
Early Career	1982	Joni Jones	Mini-series	UK	S4C*
	1983	Those Glory, Glory Days	Telefilm	UK	C4*
		One of Ourselves	Telefilm	UK	BBC1
	1984	The Last Days of Pompeii	Mini-series	US	ABC*
		Dr Fischer of Geneva	Telefilm	UK	BBC2
		This Office Life	Telefilm	UK	BBC1
		Aderyn Papur	Telefilm	UK	S4C*
	1985	The Last Place on Earth	Mini-series	UK	ITV*
Telefilm	1988	Coppers	Telefilm	UK	BBC1
	1989	A Private Life	Series episode	UK	BBC2
		Murder on the Moon	Telefilm	UK	ITV*
		A Clydeside Carol	Short telefilm	UK	BBC1 Scotland
	1990	By Dawn's Early Light	Telefilm	US	HBO*
	1993	Detonator	Telefilm	US	USA Network*
Hallmark	1996	Gulliver's Travels	Mini-series	US/UK	NBC/C4*
	1998	Merlin	Mini-series	US	NBC*
	1999	Cleopatra	Mini-series	US	ABC*
	2002	Dinotopia [mini-series]	Mini-series	US	ABC*
	2002–3	Dinotopia [series]	Series	US	ABC*
Recent Career	2006–7	Jozi-H	Series	Canada	CBC*
	2009	Blood and Oil	Mini-series	UK	BBC2
	2012	Labyrinth	Mini-series	Canada	Showcase*

Accordingly, in this chapter the groupings of Jones's career are underpinned by the chronological periods of television in order to explore his small-screen music in detail. The chapter discusses the industrial processes that have impacted on Jones over his thirty-year television-scoring career to date and how he has adapted his methods to account for the changing requirements and limitations to and within which he is required to work. Some of these, such as matters of budgets, schedules and the materials and activities of the production process, are closely related to those encountered in film scoring, and the chapter therefore enables close evaluation of the connection and disjunction between Jones's film and television work in an industrial context. The chapter also examines the composer's musical processes for television scoring and considers the development of Jones's creative approach to a project after the industrial conditions have been met or in order to meet these requirements, as well as the cross-influence of his big- and small-screen scores over the course of his career. The final part of the chapter is devoted to two matters – one an industrial process and the other a musical practice – that are not restricted to a single period of Jones's television career. The former, the creation of 'bumpers' as part of a programme's score, reflects developments in the commercial branding of television programmes over time and across the eras of the television industry as outlined by scholars and summarised above. The latter relates to Jones's cue-numbering conventions when working on multi-episodic programme forms and serves as another point of reference for considering the ways in which he views the composition of music for film and television. As with his film scores, the quantity of surviving archival materials for Jones's televisual output varies from project to project, with the effect that some works can be explored in greater depth and detail than others. Similarly, although the composer retains copies of the notated musical scores for most of his television work, the only one digitised to date is that for *Merlin* (1998); musical examples from all other television scores in this chapter have therefore been transcribed aurally.

Jones's 'Early Career Era'

As shown in Table 7.1, during the period 1982–5 Jones scored eight narrative television projects in the form of three mini-series and five telefilms, mainly for British broadcasters (both commercial and non-commercial), as well as one for the American television industry. Jones's first engagement with music for television grew out of his friendship with Stephen Bayly, with whom he had worked on a number of short films while both were students at the NFTS (Jones 2016b). The pair collaborated on the five-part mini-series *Joni Jones*, which was produced by Bayly and Linda James through their production company Red Rooster Films,[5] and the programme aired on 4 November 1982 on the newly launched Welsh channel *Sianel Pedwar Cymru* (S4C) – the first dedicated Welsh-language television channel – just four days after it began transmitting.[6] The mini-series has been hailed as 'one of S4C's flagship productions in 1982' (BBC no date), lending it particular cultural significance, and it became 'the first ever Welsh-language series' shown on BBC2 when it was transmitted with subtitles in 1986 (Woodward 2013, p. 170). It is based on a semi-autobiographical novel by Robert Gerallt Jones[7] and follows the titular character, a young boy, growing up in North Wales during World War II. The score is monothematic, based largely around a melody shown in Figure 7.1 that is played by recorder and accompanied by strings in the style of a folk tune. The theme is rooted in A minor and based harmonically on the circle of fifths, and its combination

Figure 7.1 Aural transcription of the main theme from *Joni Jones*

Figure 7.2 Aural transcription of the main theme from *Those Glory, Glory Days*

of simple instrumentation, structure and harmonic language evokes a pastoralism that reflects the rural surroundings of the protagonist's home.

This theme links all five episodes, not only through consistent use in the opening and closing credits but also during the underscoring, establishing a musical approach utilised repeatedly by Jones in this part of his television-scoring career. The theme is manipulated in several ways to reflect different situations and moods in the narrative, such as a slower version of the melody accompanied by minor-key harmonies and ending with an interrupted cadence in cue 1M2, and some changes in instrumentation, such as in 1M8 when strings take over the melody normally played by the recorder and Jones adds a layer of percussion.

Jones's earliest telefilm, *Those Glory, Glory Days* (1983), continues the musical strategy employed in *Joni Jones* with the score based around a central main theme, shown in Figure 7.2. Directed by Philip Saville and produced by David Puttnam for Channel Four's *First Love* film series, the picture is a comedy that follows a group of teenage girls obsessed with Tottenham Hotspur Football Club in London and was one of a few selected Channel Four telefilms to be released cinematically a year after its television premiere.[8] This dual release was always Puttnam's intention, and since neither the picture nor the music was edited for the film version, Jones had no further input into the project after its televisual airing. The main theme for *Those Glory, Glory Days* is in G major with the melody played by brass accompanied by strings and percussion, and the descending walking bass line and brass-band nature of the main theme evoke a football atmosphere, driven forward by upbeat and cheerful dotted rhythms. Annette Davison (2013, p. 147) suggests that 'title sequences pitch, or make desirable, the show that follows' and that 'signifiers that suggest the show's genre are often incorporated', and although her consideration focuses on HBO series from the late 1990s and early 2000s, these general principles nonetheless relate closely to Jones's approach to the main theme for *Those Glory, Glory Days*. It draws parallels with musical features recurrent in several well-known themes for television and radio sports programmes from the era, notably those on the BBC, drawing attention to and reinforcing the telefilm's credentials as a sports piece. The prominent use of brass reflects the instrumentation of the opening title music for the Saturday evening football television programme *Match of the Day* and the weekly Saturday afternoon radio show *Sports Report*, and the syncopated percussion rhythms that sit beneath the melody call to mind similar patterns in both television's *Sports Night* and the cricket radio show *Test Match Special*.

Jones's next telefilm, Pat O'Connor's *One of Ourselves*, is an adaptation of a short story about the coming of age of a teenage boy in an Irish provincial town,[9] and as was the case with *Joni Jones* the main melody draws on a folk-music style. In this case it is an Irish jig, as befits the geographic setting, with the rural environment suggested by an Irish whistle heard over pedal notes and drones that evoke the sound of pipes. *One of Ourselves* was broadcast on BBC1 on 22 November 1983, just five days after the television premiere of *Those Glory, Glory Days* on Channel Four, though the archival materials indicate that Jones did not work on the two projects simultaneously, with *One of Ourselves* dating from August 1983 and most of the recordings for *Those Glory, Glory Days* taking place on 11 October that year. However, both television scores do appear to have been composed while Jones was writing music for the film *Savage Islands* (1983, also known as *Nate and Hayes*), the surviving materials for which show a range of dates from March to November 1983. While there is little to connect these scores in terms of their main themes, aural links can nonetheless be made through the secondary musical material in each project. *Those Glory, Glory Days* includes dreamy atmospheric cues without any sort of distinctive melody that are reserved for imaginary or flashback scenes, and a slow variation of the main theme for *One of Ourselves*, heard during scenes in which the protagonist fantasises about an older woman to whom he is attracted, is accompanied by a dreamy atmospheric soundscape that is harmonically static. Both of these 'fantasy' cues draw clearly on the harmonic and timbral profile of Jones's score for *The Dark Crystal* (1982), released the previous year, and these musical elements are also found throughout the underscore for *Savage Islands*. Indeed, the music for *Savage Islands* resonates with echoes of *The Dark Crystal* through the shaping of melodic phrases and its consistency of harmonic language, though the influence is less pronounced in the television scores, perhaps owing to these projects featuring less music and being of shorter duration.

The three remaining telefilms from this part of Jones's career – *Aderyn Papur* for S4C, again directed by Stephen Bayly, and the BBC productions *Dr Fischer of Geneva* and *This Office Life*, directed by Michael Lindsay-Hogg and Ian Keill, respectively – all date from 1984. *Aderyn Papur* is set in an under-developed Welsh village and concerns a young boy whose hopes for a brighter future are raised after meeting two Japanese businessmen whose intention is to build a factory there. Jones's use of the koto in the instrumental ensemble links the score to the Japanese elements of the story. An allusion to Japanese music may also be detected in the opening flute melody of *This Office Life*, although the rationale for the use of this sound world is unclear in this picture, which is 'about a man who is completely satisfied with his life as a filing clerk' (Dear and Davalle 1984). The opening theme of Keill's comedy-drama is suddenly displaced by a jazz-style section featuring a saxophone, providing stylistic development from Jones's earlier scores. Indeed, although this musical material is something of an anomaly in Jones's repertoire up to this point, it foreshadows two notable stylistic approaches to which the composer would return at the end of the decade. The saxophone features in a number of Jones's film scores in the years following *Angel Heart* (1987) and became something of a musical hallmark in that period. Similarly, some of Jones's cues for the toolkit scores of the late 1980s and early 1990s draw on jazz-influenced harmonies and chord progressions, with this style reaching its apotheosis in his jazz-infused score for *Richard III* (1995). *Dr Fischer of Geneva*, which is based on Graham Greene's novel of the same name and follows the development of the protagonist's relationship with his fiancé's estranged father, the eponymous Dr Fischer,[10] has the most chromatically adventurous of Jones's Early Career Era main themes. While the score is largely tonal, the theme moves frequently between A minor and F minor harmonies, creating numerous false relations, preventing the music from settling or resolving and reflecting the telefilm's dark narrative and somewhat unstable and unpredictable characters.

All three of these scores utilise similar approaches to those found in *Joni Jones*, *Those Glory, Glory Days* and *One of Ourselves*, being based around main themes with predominantly minor-key harmonies and often making use of the circle of fifths chord progression, and it is apparent that there is some consistency of musical approach across all of Jones's television work in the Early Career Era. He has a clear preference for acoustic scores based mainly around the string section, a strong sense of tonality (with occasional use of modality), and a thematic approach to score construction, and his use of folk- or traditional-music styles marks the start of an approach that permeates his career across film and television. However, the relative simplicity of Jones's musical language in these early television scores contrasts markedly with his film work at the time, notably the large and sometimes chromatically dense music for *The Dark Crystal*. This perhaps reflects the rather different scales of these projects since Henson's fantasy film offered sufficient resources for Jones to use the London Symphony Orchestra and the narrative space for an expansively orchestrated score with long flowing melodies and a number of key themes, whereas most of the composer's early television projects were much more limited in scope. Not only did he have to work within greater budgetary constraints, but the small-screen nature of both the stories and the cinematography may also have contributed to his utilisation of simpler, less adventurous harmonic and structural approaches.

This point is emphasised by the two outliers in this part of Jones's television career, the mini-series *The Last Days of Pompeii* (1984) and *The Last Place on Earth* (1985). These projects are considered in detail in Chapter 2 within the context of Jones's early professional screen-music career but are also touched on briefly here since they are part of a bridge between the first two periods of Jones's television work and between his approaches to scoring for television and film in the early- to mid-1980s. Both shows embody the ideas of 'quality TV', including substantial budgets (Erickson 2017) and well-known casts, and were scheduled in primetime slots to maximise viewing figures. The more expansive narratives in these mini-series are reflected by a corresponding expansion in Jones's musical strategy, with the thematicism adopted in most of the composer's early television scores growing into a quasi-leitmotivic approach in which themes are altered structurally, harmonically and melodically to reflect the developing narrative, an increased harmonic and chromatic palette, and the use of a large orchestra with a wider range of available timbral combinations. Indeed, while Jones's early television scores are relatively simple musically, with most being largely monothematic and the material being adapted to reflect the action, the strategy employed to some extent in *Dr Fischer of Geneva* and more overtly in the two mini-series from the mid-1980s begins to move away from this approach towards what could perhaps be considered a more filmic way of scoring the visuals. There is also some noticeable development of Jones's harmonic language in these scores that demonstrates an increased maturity in his compositional voice, as well as his growing confidence in, and more sophisticated understanding of, the television environment in which he was working. Bearing in mind Jones's own claim stated above that the mini-series is his television programme type of preference owing to its filmic nature, it is perhaps unsurprising that his most film-like scores from this early period are found in this type of programme and that musically these are the scores that relate most closely to his corresponding film work. However, changes in the television industry in the late 1980s meant that he would not score another mini-series for over a decade after *The Last Place on Earth*, with telefilms dominating the intervening period.

Jones's 'Telefilm Era'

Jones's Telefilm Era spans the period 1988 to 1993 and corresponds with the midpoint of the multi-channel transition in the television industry when the number of broadcasters in both the US and UK was increasing. It also overlaps almost exactly with the period of Jones's film-scoring career in which he used 'toolkits' prominently in his work.[11] Indeed of the five telefilms he scored in this period – *Coppers* (1988), *Murder on the Moon* (1989), *A Clydeside Carol* (1989), *By Dawn's Early Light* (1990) and *Detonator* (1993) – the archival materials indicate that three – *Murder on the Moon*, *By Dawn's Early Light* and *Detonator* – made use of toolkits. These toolkit scores, which are discussed in more detail in Chapter 4 alongside consideration of Jones's toolkit films, are effectively connected by genre, all being thrillers of some sort, and while they all include aspects of US/Soviet tension, *Murder on the Moon* is quite different to the other two in terms of narrative, being a crime mystery rather than an action film. The other two telefilms from this period, both of which were BBC productions, are rather more light-hearted in tone, reflecting a general trend of Jones reserving toolkits for projects with dark narratives. Directed by Ted Clisby and produced by Andrée Molyneux, *Coppers* is a black comedy about two men who feign being policemen, while the made-for-television short film *A Clydeside Carol*, directed by Kees Ryninks and produced by Tom Busby, is an adaptation of Charles Dickens's classic story, *A Christmas Carol* (1843). Of these five telefilms, only *Murder on the Moon* has a reported production budget, an estimated £3.5 million (IMDb.com 2017c), which was put towards securing Brigitte Nielsen and Julian Sands in the lead roles and a number of special effects as befits its sci-fi setting. Given that *By Dawn's Early Light* features James Earl Jones, Rebecca De Mornay and Powers Boothe and *Detonator* stars Christopher Lee, Patrick Stewart and Pierce Brosnan, it is unlikely that either of these programmes was produced on a small budget, and the production values of all three telefilms evince the concept of 'quality TV' that Jones encountered previously through *The Last Days of Pompeii* and *The Last Place on Earth*. Indeed, most of the shows Jones scored in his Telefilm Era were scheduled in primetime weekend evening slots, with *A Clydeside Carol* broadcast at 4pm on Christmas Eve 1989 (by BBC1 Scotland).

The archival materials for these projects are relatively limited, but they do offer insight into parts of the timelines for some of the telefilms. The dates on the video tapes and audio recordings for *By Dawn's Early Light* and *Detonator* show that the composer was afforded six to eight weeks to write each score, a time-frame that relates closely to that generally allotted for the creation of film music in that era. Dates on various archival materials confirm that Jones received the video tapes for *Coppers* more than two months before the music was recorded, giving him slightly more time than he might normally have anticipated, but none of the materials explain why another year elapsed after the music was recorded before the film was broadcast on television. There are no video tapes in the archive relating to the remaining two telefilms from this era, but other evidence from the archive indicates that they ran on quite different schedules. The recording sessions for *Murder on the Moon* were on 4 and 5 April 1989, over twenty weeks before the broadcast premiere, whereas the music for *A Clydeside Carol* was recorded in December 1989 (exact date unknown), the same month as its television debut. While this may be a relatively small sample, the contrasting time periods from receipt of video through recording of the score to televisual broadcast highlight the inconsistencies of the industry through the multichannel transition. The extended period between the recording of Jones's score and the broadcasting of both *Coppers* and *Murder on the Moon* is particularly surprising since these telefilms were created before the widespread use of digital editing technologies and CGI – both of which can delay the completion of film and television productions – and Jones will have received a locked picture on which to work.

The only instance in the archive of spotting notes for a television production relates to a telefilm from this era – *Detonator* – though information provided by Jones shows that some form of similar documentation was also prepared for the four Hallmark mini-series that are considered later in this chapter.[12] Jeannie Pool and Stephen Wright suggest that television programmes are not always spotted, owing to the short time-frames within which they are often produced (2011, p. 43), but the existence of these documents suggests that these programmes were spotted in much the same way as big-screen films would be. The spotting notes for *Detonator*, an extract of which is shown in Figure 7.3, also offer a rare insight into the

① ✓ 1m1 Opening Titles	01:00:00:01	01:01:01:08	3.01	Ominous, trepidatious. Low breathy Flute; woof-woof 16va Gigantic, breathing, awe-inspiring. Rhythmic pattern.
Laboratory				Mystery, tension. Building to sustain climax. Pulse. Continue pulse from 1m1 (since they join).
② ✓ 1m2 Irradiation	01:03:01:08	01:03:42:00	0.41	Under dial. More urgency in pulsing. Low strings, brass. Where is end? Ref. 4m1. NB Sheer needs less attack when spinning out.
③ 1m3 Rail Yard	01:03:42:00	01:06:41:19	3.00	Drama. Toolkit 1 with melody and harmony shaped.
④ 1m4 Sting	01:08:09:08	01:08:20:10	0.11	Sting on insert"Bremen"NB end reel 1 EXTRA 22 FRAMES WHERE is this cue situated?
⑤ 2m1 Eurorail Control	02:00:07:01	02:02:36:07	2.36	Toolkit 1. Fade over cut to UN building. Out by cut to Philpot. NB ROGER, OLD BEAN We need a Doppler effect when trains avoid eachother.
⑥ ✓ 2m2 Fat Man	02:04:09:24	02:06:32:18	2.23	Toolkit 1. Out cut to Philpot

Figure 7.3 Excerpt from the spotting notes for *Detonator*

level of musical detail discussed in a spotting session, with the document including references to the use of Toolkit 1 in cues 1M3 'Rail Yard', 2M1 'Eurorail Control' and 2M2 'Fat Man'. It is perhaps notable that the television projects for which it is certain that spotting was undertaken were a telefilm and four mini-series, the latter programme type being considered by Jones as an extended film and the former being a made-for-television movie. In this respect it is perhaps unsurprising that Jones would have adopted a filmic practice at the start of his musical process since (as already noted) he did not differentiate between film and television projects in terms of his compositional approach. Additionally, it must be considered that none of these commissions required him to work within the sort of restricted schedule that is usually found when writing music for a television series, what Fred Karlin and Rayburn Wright (2004, p. 425) refer to as 'a one-week turnaround [...] that includes making changes, mixing down and allowing enough time for the music editor to prepare for dubbing'. Indeed, Jones's television-scoring career is notable for the relative absence of series, with the *Dinotopia* spin-off series (2002–3) and *Jozi-H* (2006–7) the only such titles in his portfolio.

The scores for Jones's Telefilm Era relate closely to those he wrote for films in this period, notably through the use of toolkits in *Murder on the Moon*, *By Dawn's Early Light* and *Detonator*, which create a consistency of compositional strategy and sonic environment across the big- and small-screen projects from the late 1980s and early 1990s. It also appears that the industrial process for these projects aligned quite closely with that for cinematic productions, with Jones focusing on the 'filmic' aspects of the made-for-television movies and utilising a similar approach when scoring to that found in his cinematic projects from this period such as *Sea of Love* (1989) and *Bad Influence* (1990). Although the television industry underwent significant development through the multi-channel transition, much of this related to the number and range of broadcasters, and there seems to have been some reasonable stability of process across the late 1980s and early 1990s, during this phase of Jones's television-music career. However, the landscape had changed somewhat by the time Jones returned to television in the final years of the twentieth century.

Jones's 'Hallmark Era'

In the late 1990s and early 2000s, a period that straddles the crossover between the multi-channel transition and the matrix era in the television industry, Jones scored four mini-series and one spin-off series for Hallmark Entertainment, which was led at that time by Robert Halmi Sr. These shows were primarily American productions (with the exception of *Gulliver's Travels*, which was a US/UK collaboration) and were produced for commercial broadcasters who screened the episodes on consecutive evenings. The first of these, *Gulliver's Travels* (1996), is a two-part mini-series directed by Charles Sturridge and is based on Jonathan Swift's (1726) classic satirical novel of the same name. The story follows the Englishman Lemuel Gulliver (Ted Danson) who, having been presumed lost at sea, returns from his travels with strange tales that are allegories of the real world. It was a co-production by NBC and the British Channel Four and was first broadcast by NBC in February

1996.[13] Two years later, Steve Barron directed the mini-series *Merlin* (1998), Jones's second score for a story based on the Arthurian legend,[14] which was again broadcast by NBC, and a third Hallmark two-part mini-series, *Cleopatra* (1999), aired the following year, though this time on a rival network, ABC. Directed by Franc Roddam, *Cleopatra* is based on the story of the titular Queen of Egypt and her struggles to protect her country from the Romans through her relationships with Julius Caesar and, after Caesar's death, Marc Antony. The final Hallmark mini-series, *Dinotopia* (2002), directed by Marco Brambilla, was also broadcast by ABC. Based on a book by James Gurney (1992), *Dinotopia* follows two brothers who crash-land on an island inhabited by humans and intelligent dinosaurs, and the mini-series gave rise to a thirteen-episode spin-off series of the same name (2002–3), also broadcast by ABC.

Jones was introduced to Hallmark through his friend Duncan Kenworthy, who was co-producer for *Gulliver's Travels* and whom he had first met on *The Dark Crystal* (1982).[15] Jones recalls Kenworthy asking him 'to do this television project. I think it was two parts, and the budget was sufficient to write an orchestral score in addition to electronics, with synthesisers' (Jones 2014a). The larger-budget Hallmark mini-series afforded Jones bigger instrumental ensembles – something he clearly prized – and more space for thematic development, reflecting his comments from the start of this chapter regarding his preference to work on more substantial projects with high production values. Indeed, it is notable that during the Hallmark Era the only small-screen commissions Jones accepted were for multi-episodic programmes, and while this could be a reflection of the change in the industrial landscape at this time, it is perhaps more likely that with the growth of his reputation as a screen composer Jones became more selective in the projects that he scored.

All of the Hallmark programmes were multi-million-dollar productions and featured well-known actors and substantial special effects. *Gulliver's Travels* enjoyed a budget of $28 million and showcased actors such as Ted Danson, Mary Steenburgen, Omar Sharif and Kristin Scott Thomas; *Merlin*, with a budget of $30 million, starred Sam Neill, Helena Bonham Carter, Rutger Hauer and Miranda Richardson; and *Dinotopia*'s record budget of around $80 million[16] led Don Kaplan (2000), writing in the *New York Post*, to suggest that it 'could be the most expensive made-for-TV-movie of all time'. Kaplan's description of this television mini-series as a 'movie' is particularly pertinent here, given Jones's conceptualisation of this programme type as an extended film, and reinforces the composer's perspective. All of the Hallmark mini-series featured special effects, which impacted on the way Jones worked. In his foreword to the published *Merlin* shooting script, Robert Halmi Sr. notes that there were 125 special effects in *Gulliver's Travels* and that *Merlin* had nearly triple this number (1999, p. viii), with *Merlin*'s director, Steve Barron, suggesting that whereas feature films in the late 1990s tended to have around 150 special effects, the mini-series had 'almost 500' (1999, p. 223). Indeed, there were so many effects in *Merlin* and particularly in *Dinotopia* that Jones had to start composing his scores before the visuals had been completed. Early video tapes in the archive for *Dinotopia* contain pre-CGI footage, some black screens with text describing the final effect, and occasional messages simply stating 'Shot missing', leaving the composer to try and predict the scale and impact of the final effects in order to score them appropriately. Visually reproducing the dinosaurs and locations of Gurney's book in *Dinotopia* pushed the limit of contemporary technological possibilities, and Jones's score was just as integral to bringing these creatures to life as John Williams's music for *Jurassic Park* had been when that film was released in 1993. Tim E. Scheurer (1997) observes that Williams's score is designed to 'capture and articulate what the audience sees – or better, what the audience wants to see – [. . .] and find once again in our modern world a place for these noble beasts' (p. 67), and a similar sentiment can be applied to Jones's musical construction of the mysterious island of Dinotopia and the creatures that live there.

The budgets, well-known actors and notable special effects found in these miniseries arguably reflect the change in attitude at the time to the 'value' of television in relation to film. These four Hallmark productions were scheduled in similar ways to attract the largest possible audience share, with the first episodes all broadcast on Sunday evenings and the remaining parts screened on successive nights. Additionally, they were all released around the time of the sweep stakes in spring, something noted by Elizabeth Jenson in an *LA Times* article on the release of *Dinotopia*:

> The mini-series comes at a time when other networks have cut back on or abandoned the genre after audiences seemed to lose interest. But ABC, which is owned by Walt Disney Co., is giving the six-hour 'Dinotopia' three consecutive nights beginning Sunday, in the middle of the important May ratings sweeps, on which stations depend to set future ad rates.
>
> (Jensen 2002)

Jensen's observation that many networks had stopped producing mini-series emphasises the overlap between Jones's Hallmark Era and the industrial change from the multi-channel transition to the matrix era that brought with it a corresponding difference of approach among many producers of television programming. Indeed, while the first three mini-series – all of which were created in the late 1990s – were well received, *Dinotopia* fared poorly, particularly considering its huge cost. Matt Bacon notes that *Gulliver's Travels* was 'a huge success around the world, attracting 56 million viewers in the US' (1997, p. 151), but episode one of *Dinotopia* was only nineteenth in the Prime Time Nielsen Ratings for the sweeps in May 2002 with an audience of 8.8 million (around half that of the number one ranked programme, an episode of NBC's drama series *ER*), and audience figures continued to decline across the second and third parts of the mini-series (Associated Press 2002a, 2002b). However, while the televisual climate may have been changing, the industrial and musical processes that underpinned the Hallmark mini-series were generally quite stable. All four were spotted, and video tapes in the archive show that the last three were temped, and while there is no evidence of a temp for *Gulliver's Travels* the consistency of process across these projects indicates it is more likely that these materials are missing from the archive than that the process did not happen. As discussed above, the presence of spotting notes

Music for television   161

for these projects may be considered unusual, and the fact that they were temped only serves to emphasise the similarity of industrial process between these mini-series and feature films.

All of Jones's scores for these mini-series are multi-thematic with a defining main theme and a number of secondary themes, developing the approach used by the composer in his mini-series from the mid-1980s, *The Last Days of Pompeii* and *The Last Place on Earth*. There are inconsistencies, however, as Jones shapes his structure to best suit the needs of each project. While the main themes to *Gulliver's Travels*, *Cleopatra* and *Dinotopia* are used frequently throughout all parts, *Merlin*'s main melody is heard regularly during the opening episode, but its influence wanes in the second. Indeed, this score is more overtly leitmotivic, with over thirty themes heard across the two episodes.[17] Jones's use of thematicism as the foundation for these scores contrasts markedly with much of his film work from this period, with pictures such as *Brassed Off* (1996), *Notting Hill* (1999) and *Crossroads* (2002) all featuring substantial use of pre-existing material alongside (and in some cases almost overwhelming) his original music.[18] This perhaps goes some way to explaining his active engagement with the Hallmark mini-series, and indeed his conceptualisation of them as extended films for the purposes of scoring, since they offered him opportunities to express himself musically in a way that was not always possible in his contemporaneous work for cinema.

The main themes for these mini-series also show the development of Jones's musical practice and compositional approach, especially bearing in mind the reliance on short melodic ideas and simple harmonies found in his early television scores. The opening credit music for *Gulliver's Travels* features a strong, tonic pedal bass that often takes the form of repeated quavers pulsing under a slower, sweeping melody line, offering a sense of groundedness and consistency that contrasts with Gulliver's fantastical journey and apparent state of delusion. The melody, shown in Figure 7.4, appears to grow organically from the first two-bar cell to the second with an increased range, and it is then expanded into a four-bar phrase through the falling pattern being extended.[19] This development is reflected in a relatively simple harmonic language, though the added sixths, sevenths and other dissonances created by the melody against the harmony prevent the chord pattern from becoming boring or predictable and support the more fantastical elements of Lemuel Gulliver's story, which combines the comprehensible and the incomprehensible.

Figure 7.4 Aural transcription of the main theme from *Gulliver's Travels*

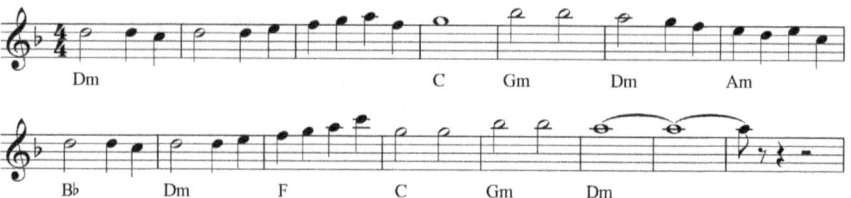

Figure 7.5 Main theme from *Merlin*

Figure 7.6 Aural transcription of the main theme from *Cleopatra*

The apparent tonal simplicity of the theme is clouded by its avoidance of the leading note, rooting it in the Aeolian mode, and Jones draws on its modality to progress the narrative by avoiding the sense of closure that would be granted by the use of conventional perfect cadences. Modality is highlighted in precisely the opposite way in the main theme to *Merlin*, shown in Figure 7.5, which moves from an opening D minor harmony to a strong C major chord, emphasising rather than avoiding the seventh degree of the scale. The mid-melody interrupted cadence, with the theme briefly landing on a chord of Bb major before reaching the tonic, also heightens the modal nature of the music, with the interruption also causing some irregularity in the phrase length that creates something of a restless quality despite the flowing melody. Jones's harmonic language recalls his use of folk styles to evoke ideas of the pastoral in some of his earliest television scores, although the simple woodwind instrumentation of those works is replaced here with full brass, reflecting the role of royalty and authority in the narrative.

Jones uses the ambiguity of the seventh degree of the scale in a similar manner in the main theme to *Cleopatra* (Figure 7.6), with the opening D minor harmony again followed by C major as it was in *Merlin*. However, when the phrase moves to the dominant chord in the fourth bar it is a resolute A major, the sharpened leading note sounding prominently in the harmony and asserting the minor-key tonality of the material in contrast to the modal centres of the previous Hallmark scores. This pattern is repeated, and Jones continues to develop the harmonic language in the third phrase of the theme, momentarily following an excursion around the circle of fifths from F–Bb–Eb before shifting by a diminished fifth to the dominant to end the melody. This brief inclusion of harmony based on the circle of fifths shows not only less reliance on this established chord progression than in his early television scores but also a stronger sense of harmonic confidence, with the conventional VI–ii°–V–i progression found in Jones's previous scores replaced by the more progressive and resolutely major VII–III–bVI–bII–V–i. Indeed, *Cleopatra* draws together harmonic and structural elements from Jones's earlier television scores, with the 4+4+8 bar phrasing of the main theme mimicking that of *Gulliver's Travels*, albeit with the phrase lengths doubled.

The main theme for *Dinotopia* breaks away somewhat from the ideas found in these preceding Hallmark mini-series, lacking some of the tonal and modal ambiguity of *Gulliver's Travels* and *Cleopatra* but retaining some of the added dissonances between the melody and the underlying harmony. These pitches serve to fractionally destabilise the music and add an element of exoticism, with the prominent D# in the second bar of the theme particularly notable in this regard, functioning as an added sharp sixth over the F# minor harmony. Overall, however, *Dinotopia* is more harmonically conservative than *Merlin* and *Cleopatra*, with the theme rooted on an oscillating pattern of two chords – A major and F# minor – with the brief excursions to C# minor and D major in the fifth and sixth bars of each eight-bar phrase acting merely as chord substitutions for the tonic and relative minor (Figure 7.7). In contrast with this reserved harmonic language, the theme receives a substantial orchestration when it is first heard, replete with running inner lines on woodwind and harp, a strident French horn countermelody and the melody itself proclaimed by strings and trumpets. The scale of the music thereby reflects the grandeur of the narrative setting and its pre-historic characters, while the simple repetitive harmony keeps the score grounded and accessible.

Jones's scores from the Hallmark Era contrast with those from the Telefilm Era through his use of a symphonic scoring style cultivated through his mid-1990 films such as *The Last of the Mohicans* (1992), *Cliffhanger* (1993) and *Loch Ness* (1996), though as has already been noted, many of his cinematic projects concurrent with the Hallmark Era make substantial use of interpolated songs, often at the expense of an orchestral score. Jones's use of thematicism, notably the dominance of the main theme in the score for *Gulliver's Travels*, recalls the principal compositional strategy of his Early Career Era, and the way in which he uses harmony and controlled dissonance is also similar to his earliest television scores, reserving highly chromatic or atonal material for narrative moments of inflated peril.

Figure 7.7 Aural transcription of the main theme from the *Dinotopia* mini-series

Notably, however, the ensembles are more substantial for the Hallmark mini-series than for his previous television projects – a result of the larger budgets – consisting of an orchestra of up to ninety players mixed with 'a fair bit of electronic fusion but not so that you would notice' (Jones 2006). Jones explains that:

> I tend to write for big, orchestral sounds basically because I think they don't age the film as much as synthesisers do. There are some electronics but they're there to extend the orchestral palette, they're not in the score for their own sake. Synthesisers come and go; you can listen to scores and you know that they spell out the 60s, 70s, 80s, 90s and they tend to age a film. They tend to date films whereas the big symphonic scores technically sit behind the picture much more effectively I think. You can have a great, big orchestral texture and lots of dialogue without it clashing.
>
> (Jones 2006)

Three performers known for their film-music work feature in Jones's scores for *Merlin* and *Cleopatra*. Andy Findon plays flute and Phil Todd the Electronic Wind Instrument (EWI) in the former, Todd's involvement connecting the score to Jones's long-standing practice of integrating the EWI into his music, while the vocals of Belinda Sykes alongside the Arabic shawm imbue the score for the latter with 'ethnic' touches that enable Jones to emulate an Egyptian feel. The combination of acoustic and electronic instruments is a distinctive element of Jones's musical style that is found across his scores for film and (where budget allowed it) television, and the EWI in particular is a feature of many of his scores from the late 1980s through to the turn of the millennium. Indeed, Jones's musical style and instrumentation strategy across these mini-series is largely consistent with his work for cinema in the years leading up to the Hallmark Era, reflecting a consistency of musical approach and process despite the differences of media. It also reinforces the idea that Jones saw these mini-series as extended films and used them as a means of continuing to write orchestral/electronic 'film' music at a time when this approach was often unavailable to him in his actual cinema-scoring projects.

Jones's 'Recent Career Era'

Jones composed music for three final television projects contained in the archive, which represent his Recent Career Era. These are the thirteen-episode series *Jozi-H* (2006–7), the two-part mini-series *Blood and Oil* (2010) and *Labyrinth* (2012), which was also a two-part mini-series.[20] Aspects of the underlying industrial and musical processes affecting these projects as a body of work are considered here, within the context of Jones's television-scoring career, and specific musical features are discussed in Chapter 9 alongside the rest of Jones's output from the last decade or so. It is relatively difficult to judge the industrial processes and their effect on Jones for these projects since there is very little relevant information in the archive or broader literature. There is no evidence of spotting or temping, and although this does not necessarily indicate that these processes did not take place it is worth recalling Karlin and Wright's observation made above about the rapid turnaround time for projects of this type. Jones's assistant, Neil Stemp, illuminated the work schedule on these recent television scores, his recollections relating closely to the views of Karlin and Wright:

> In my experience, with the TV stuff, especially *Jozi-H* which was thirteen episodes, [...] we had I think between a week and two weeks on each episode. And each episode was one-hour long, so basically, maybe ten days ... let's say ten days per episode. So they don't get much time to throw cues out and get you to re-write them; unless there's something really, really wrong with it then they just say 'great, great, keep it coming!'
>
> (Stemp 2015a)

Stemp's comments are reinforced by the archival materials for *Jozi-H* and *Labyrinth*, both of which include examples of Jones preparing alternative versions of some cues. Given the short turnaround for each episode, it seems likely that Jones created this additional material to provide the programme-makers with options when the visual and musical elements were combined, rather than them needing to return to the composer at that point for replacement music. Stemp also highlights a notable difference between composing music for a two- or three-episode mini-series and for a long-running multi-episode series:

> With something like *Jozi-H* obviously they just deliver you an episode every week and you score what's there and you've no idea what's coming next. [...] Every week another episode is coming up and we just sat down and watched as the audience would [...] we had no synopsis of what the overall arc of the plot was going to be. [...] I think most of the TV projects of Trevor's have been mini-series, which are like films in the sense that you would know the whole story before you start.
>
> (Stemp 2015a)

This notion of mini-series being akin to extended films closely mirrors Jones's own perspective on the programme format, and this is particularly important because it demonstrates a consistency of mind-set between Jones and the closest members of his music team and supports the view that their musical processes would be consistent across film and television projects. The idea that the complete narrative arc is known by the composer before starting work on scoring a mini-series and the greater time afforded for these sorts of televisual projects also perhaps indicate a greater likelihood of spotting and temping taking place on projects of this type. While this hypothesis cannot be substantiated by the archival materials for *Blood and Oil* and *Labyrinth*, the fact that mini-series relate quite strongly to films in terms of conception and narrative structuring indicates that the underlying industrial practices might also be reasonably closely connected.

Bumpers

As noted at the start of this chapter, although Jones's narrative television projects can be deemed to break down into four clear eras, one specifically televisual industrial consideration cuts across all of these periods and is therefore best addressed separately. Television programmes transmitted by commercial broadcasters include regular, scheduled breaks in the narrative to allow for adverts and therefore present a scenario that is unique for composers. They are usually made aware of where these breaks will lie in advance of scoring to ensure that their surrounding music cues will not be cut off abruptly, with the cues heard immediately before and after the advertisement break often referred to as act-outs and act-ins respectively. While consideration of whether or not a cue will be an act-out or an act-in helps the composer shape their score, some programmes transmitted by commercial broadcasters also require music to accompany visual placeholders separating the programme sections from the adverts – commercial bumpers. Figure 7.8 shows Hall's (2017, p. 62) simplified representation of where these different sorts of cues are placed.

In interview, Jones has referred to bumpers as 'guzintos' and 'guzoutos' – music that 'goes-into' the advert break and 'goes-out' of the break and back into the programme – noting that he adopted this terminology having heard it being used by his music editors.[21] He explains how these cues are usually derived musically from a show's main theme or motif and that they:

> signal to an audience that this was the end of the 'Act', and that you were into a commercial break; similarly, that it was the end of the commercial break and that the programme was resuming. So basically, they were little musical idents that made the transition into or out of the commercial breaks.
>
> (Jones 2016a)

Jones's long-time orchestrator, Geoff Alexander, notes that although the bumpers could have been captured by extracting a section from a recording of a particular cue, their normal practice was to:

> [record] them separately because it's easier than crashing in with an edit. It's just as quick to tell everyone to play from bar 60 or something and do the last six bars of something, [. . .] it would sound nicer than if someone chops in from bar 60.
>
> (2016)

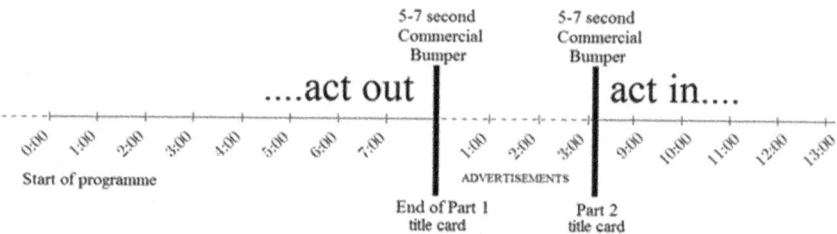

Figure 7.8 Simplified representation of where commercial bumpers and act-ins/outs lie in a television programme with advert breaks

Table 7.2 Names and durations of bumpers for *The Last Days of Pompeii*

Name	Duration
Bumper One Long	8 seconds
Bumper One Short	5 seconds
Bumper Two Long	8 seconds
Bumper Two Short	5 seconds
Bumper Three Long	8 seconds
Bumper Three Short	5 seconds
Bumper Four	5 seconds

The Last Days of Pompeii is the first programme for which these specialised cues exist in the Jones Archive, with the audio recordings found within the set of two-track cues for the mini-series. There are seven musical bumpers for this project, which are listed in Table 7.2 alongside their durations, using their names as they are given on the boxes for the analogue sound recordings. The bumpers are all short musical extracts relating to themes from the mini-series, and as Table 7.2 demonstrates, they are either five or eight seconds in length. Jones's material is roughly consistent with Karlin and Wright's description of bumpers in *On the Track*, in which they suggest that 'bumpers are short musical signatures used in conjunction with the graphic title card for a show. They are usually based on a short phrase or motif derived from the theme and are typically either five or seven seconds long, including the reverb "ring off" after the orchestra cuts off their last note' (2004, p. 436). The archival recordings reveal that the respective 'short' and 'long' bumpers feature the same audio material played at different tempi, increasing the choice of material available to the director, editor and dubbing mixer. This practice again tallies closely with Karlin and Wright's advice to composers:

> it is a good idea to create a softer and louder version of the bumper for movies and mini-series to provide a choice in dubbing, in case the producer might like the idea of matching the outgoing mood of a scene with the incoming bumper.
>
> (p. 436)

Given Jones's filmic conception of the mini-series programme type it is quite surprising to discover that both the industrial and musical processes conform to the norms of the business as far as bumpers are concerned. Indeed, while some aspects of Jones's practice have been shown to diverge from general expectations regarding television music, the bumpers for *The Last Days of Pompeii* act as textbook examples of this sort of cue.

The archive also contains seven bumpers for *The Last Place on Earth* that are located similarly in the archive within the two-track cues for the project. Rather than existing as alternate versions of a smaller number of bumpers, they number

Table 7.3 Names and durations of bumpers for *The Last Place on Earth*

Name	Duration
Bumper No. 1	5 seconds
Bumper No. 2	4 seconds
Bumper No. 3	5 seconds
Bumper No. 5	4 seconds
Bumper No. 6	4 seconds
Bumper No. 7	5 seconds
Bumper No. 8	4 seconds

sequentially and, as Table 7.3 indicates, are much more consistent in terms of duration. Based on the naming convention there is a missing audio file – Bumper No. 4 – which serves as a reminder of the incompleteness of the archive. An additional indication that there was originally an eighth bumper is that each of the existing bumpers is related to one of the musical themes heard in the mini-series, of which there are eight. While it seems likely that Jones was aware of the location of advert breaks in advance of scoring programmes for commercial broadcasters, the archive only contains evidence of this for one project, *The Last Days of Pompeii*. There is a single VHS tape of an early, rough cut of reels 33–34 in the final part of the mini-series that includes two visual place-cards situated about ten minutes apart, showing the words 'COMMERCIAL BREAK'. The tape is labelled as a viewing copy for the composer and would have enabled Jones to devise his score around these breaks, albeit that the precise timings may have changed as the programme moved from a rough to a fine cut. Further evidence of where the advert breaks were situated can be found on the DVD releases of *The Last Days of Pompeii* and *The Last Place on Earth*, both of which include some hangovers from their respective original television productions. The latter contains 'End of Part ___' and 'Part ___' place-cards throughout, clearly defining the programme sections and advert breaks, and while the former is not so explicit, the visual action pauses and fades to black approximately every thirty minutes throughout each episode, indicating strongly that the advert breaks fell at these positions.

There would necessarily have been advert breaks throughout *Murder on the Moon* and *Detonator*, both of which were broadcast on commercial channels, although the archive only contains bumper music for the former project, ordered sequentially from 'Commercial Bumper 1' to 'Commercial Bumper 12'. Like those for the earlier projects, they are all derived from cues heard throughout the film and range from five to seven seconds in duration, and they appear to have been recorded as individual pieces of music rather than being cropped from other recorded cues. It is unclear why there are no archival materials of this nature for *Detonator*, although this is the only programme Jones scored for the USA Network, and it is therefore possible that instead of requesting this music from the programme makers, the broadcaster had its own musical material, such as an audible channel ident, that it used for this purpose.

Jones wrote bumper music for the two Hallmark mini-series transmitted by NBC (*Gulliver's Travels* and *Merlin*) but not for the latter two mini-series despite them being aired on ABC, also a commercial channel. However, this may relate to the changing industrial landscape at the time, which was shifting from the multi-channel transition to the matrix era. In particular, the lack of music for commercial bumpers might relate to the ways in which commercial channels and programming were beginning to generate revenue in the late 1990s, as the following two examples from the British industry detail. In 1992 the broadcaster Sky began to screen live English Premier League football matches on its dedicated sports channel, but rather than separating the programme content from the interceding adverts with a traditional commercial bumper, the programme was instead sponsored by a commercial partner – in this case the car manufacturer, Ford – who provided visual and aural content for this buffer (Thinkbox 2015). Four years later, in March 1996, Cadbury paid £10 million to sponsor ITV's flagship soap, *Coronation Street*, in a deal that 'allowed the name of the confectionary and drinks giant to appear with the opening and closing credits' (Campaign 2011). As these examples demonstrate, the bumper spaces became lucrative opportunities for broadcasters and programme makers to gain revenue rather than having to pay more to produce additional video and musical footage. While there is no evidence in the archive that this was the reason for a lack of bumper music on both the *Cleopatra* and *Dinotopia* mini-series (or even, perhaps, on *Detonator*), such a development would not be out of keeping with changes in the industrial environment at the time of their release. However, perhaps surprisingly the archive does include musical bumpers written by Jones for the spin-off *Dinotopia* series (2002–3). These may have been created to help strengthen the 'brand' identity of the show to help ensure consistent weekly viewing over a longer time period than for the mini-series and to provide 'an auditory cue, a boundary in the "flow" of television's continuous programming' (Davison 2013, p. 148). However it is also possible that the critical and financial failure of the *Dinotopia* mini-series meant that a suitable sponsor could not be secured for the series, thus necessitating the creation of musical bumpers. Indeed, poor ratings led to the cancellation of the series after only half of the episodes had aired despite the complete series being finished and ready for broadcast.

The final project for which the archive contains musical bumpers is *Jozi-H*. Unlike most of the earlier projects for which bumpers exist, these cues are not numbered or listed separately to the rest of the music for the series, and the digital audio files are only distinguishable from the rest of the underscore because the filenames include the word 'bumper' after the cue number. The naming of the files indicates that the bumpers were composed for specific places within each episode, but if this is indeed the case then it appears that the advert breaks were spaced inconsistently across the series – there are no bumpers listed under the tracks for episode 3, but five bumper cues in each of episodes 4 and 6, for instance – which seems unlikely. Indeed, several of the bumpers sound identical despite being stored as separate files, indicating that they were probably not crafted for specific individual locations within the series' narrative.

Cue numbering

Just as the industrial process of bumper music spans Jones's career, so too consideration of one of his musical processes is best served by investigating his televisual output as a whole. Film-music cues are usually numbered using one of two conventions: cues are ordered sequentially within each reel of film so that 1M5 is followed by 2M1, or they are numbered continuously across all reels, with 1M5 followed by 2M6. For the most part, Jones's scores for multi-episodic programmes utilise a combination of these naming conventions, with reel numbers substituted for episode numbers, and cues then numbered in continuous ascending order without regard for the reel of film in which they appear within that episode. Table 7.4 shows the cues for the five episodes of *Joni Jones*, the earliest of Jones's television scores, which are organised using this method, and the same approach is found across the archive including in the three most recent television projects, *Jozi-H*, *Blood and Oil* and *Labyrinth*.[22]

The first three Hallmark mini-series adopt a variant of this structure, whereby the cue number encodes both the episode and reel number as well as the cue order. For *Gulliver's Travels* the cues in the archive run from 1M1 to 8M0 and 11M1 to 18M0,[23] but rather than indicating some missing material, the apparent gap in the sequence shows that there are two sets of eight reels' worth of music, one for each episode of the mini-series. The cues for *Merlin* and *Cleopatra* cues are numbered similarly, although with the end credits being 8M1 and 18M1 in each case. At thirteen episodes, the cue numbers for the later parts of the *Dinotopia* series would be quite confusing if this system was used for the project (episode 13 would begin with cue 121M1), so the digital audio files instead include an abbreviation of the episode name followed by a conventional cue number: for example, the music for episodes 2 and 3, 'Making Good' and 'Handful of Dust', are labelled MG1M1–4M7 and HOD1M1–4M3, respectively.

The remaining Hallmark programme, the *Dinotopia* mini-series, is an outlier in this group and reverts to a numbering convention Jones employed on the two mini-series from the mid-1980s, *The Last Days of Pompeii* and *The Last Place on Earth*. All three of these scores utilise the filmic convention of continuous cue numbering across reels, running from 1M1 to 21M3, 35M2 and 44M2, respectively, with no regard for the episode within which a cue falls. There is no indication in the archive

Table 7.4 The cues for *Joni Jones*, with the cue numbers indicating the episode to which they belong

Episode No. and Title [Translated]	Cues
1. Y Hanner Goron [The Half Crown]	1M1–1M10
2. Y Chewing Gum [The Chewing Gum]	2M1–2M6
3. Y Faciwis [The Evacuees]	3M1–3M9
4. Y Ffoadur [The Refugee]	4M1–4M11
5. Y Llythyr [The Letter]	5M1–5M6

as to why Jones used different numbering conventions for these various projects. It is possible that since all of his television scores around the time he wrote *The Last Days of Pompeii* and *The Last Place on Earth* were for telefilms (given that *Joni Jones* predates the first telefilm), Jones simply continued to use the same numbering system for all of his television projects at that time. By contrast, the archival materials show that Jones received videos for the Hallmark projects, with each reel of each episode on a separately numbered VHS or Umatic tape, so linking the cue numbers directly to the reels of film would likely have been the most efficient way of keeping track of the vast amount of music required for each project. It is unclear, however, why this strategy was not employed for the *Dinotopia* mini-series. It might be speculated that Jones perceived this six-hour production as an extended film in keeping with his overall conception of the mini-series programme type and chose to number his cues accordingly. While such a theory might be compromised by the use of a different numbering system for the other Hallmark scores, the significant budget and scale of *Dinotopia* sets this mini-series apart from the rest and emphasises its filmic credentials more overtly, which might explain the use of a more filmic cue numbering system.

Conclusions

While Jones's television career spans two of the main eras of television as outlined in the prevailing scholarship, it is better viewed as four non-continuous periods of activity. Three of these sit clearly within the industrial eras, but the other – Jones's Hallmark Era – straddles the transition from the multi-channel transition era to the matrix era. This is perhaps the most interesting period from an industrial perspective, owing to large shifts in the priorities and approaches of television production companies and channels at that time. Indeed, although there is a high degree of consistency of process across the Hallmark Era projects, there are small but significant differences – such as the disappearance of bumpers – that indicate shifts in the way that broadcasters wished to present headline productions such as these mini-series to the public. Notwithstanding this, however, in broad terms there seems to have been relatively little change to Jones's musical practices across his career to date despite the changing industrial environment.

Musically, it is possible to draw some conclusions regarding Jones's use of thematicism and instrumentation across his television-music career to date. Most of the Early Career Era projects were monothematic, and while *The Last Days of Pompeii* and *The Last Place on Earth* are exceptions to this pattern, both scores are highly thematic and feature strong main themes. All of the scores written in this period employed acoustic instruments, and most tended to use smaller ensembles, but at the start of his Telefilm Era Jones turned towards fully synthesised scores. The music of these programmes generally takes the form of functional, atmospheric soundscapes, and melodies are far less critical to the structure of the scores, and these shifts in instrumentation and musical structuring reflect parallel developments in Jones's film-scoring practice, notably the development and use of compositional toolkits at this time. The Hallmark Era began in the years following Jones's more regular engagement with symphonic, orchestral film scoring, albeit with the inclusion of some electronics, and saw Jones utilise this approach when scoring television mini-series despite often having to deviate from it in his parallel film work. Jones's most recent projects feature contrasts that in some respects encapsulate his television career to date. *Labyrinth* is monothematic, harking back to his earliest television work, while both *Jozi-H* and *Blood and Oil* avoid a thematic approach; similarly, the score for *Labyrinth* combines synthesised material with acoustic cues performed by the London Symphony Orchestra, whereas the other two projects employ exclusively electronic scores.

Jones's television projects can be usefully studied in relation to his film work, revealing distinctive musical features of his television scores. These include the development of various thematic approaches for different programme forms, the creation of specific types of cues such as bumpers, act-ins and act-outs, recaps and teasers, and multi-episode opening and closing title sequences, as well as the development of musical material to help facilitate a change of broadcast format for film and television hybrid productions. There are also numerous similarities between his filmic and televisual processes, including industrial concerns such as the potential need to meet with a director or other programme-maker for a spotting session and working with a temp track, and musical considerations. The latter include the application of similar compositional techniques such as the use of toolkits in the Telefilm Era projects, consistency of compositional software setup (ProTools and Sibelius) and musical team, the creation of alternate versions of cues to offer the production team options after his work has concluded on a project, and the use not only of click tracks but also a bar count to make recording sessions easier and more efficient. Jones has tended to prefer commissions for large, primetime television productions with budgets more akin to cinema and experienced production teams since these have usually allowed him to compose more complex, thematic scores and to write for a full orchestra (most often the London Symphony Orchestra), which is always his preference, and this reflects his conceptualisation of mini-series as extended films. In general Jones's approach to scoring for television is, in many ways, very similar to his approach for film, but he is creative and flexible in modifying his musical approach to accommodate successfully the medium's rather different industrial demands.

Notes

1 This chapter is based on material from Hall (2017).
2 Following Hall's (2017, p. 43) definitions: 'mini-series' indicates a unique television series consisting of fewer than eleven episodes with a narrative that runs throughout, akin to an extended film; 'series' means a sequence of related television programmes, since sometimes narratives run over entire series as well as within stand-alone episodes; 'serial' is a drama series consisting of sequential episodes of an ongoing narrative that is not always predetermined at conception; a 'telefilm' is a feature-length film originally produced for television broadcast.
3 Jones has written music for adverts, scored a small number of documentaries, and had his music used in 'making of' programmes about films for which he has provided the score, such as *The World of The Dark Crystal* (1983) and *Inside the Labyrinth* (1986). These scores are not particularly well represented in the archive – indeed, there are no

materials at all for some of them – and are not considered in Hall's doctoral thesis or in this chapter, which focuses on his music for narrative television programmes.

4   Jones remains active as a composer for the screen but has not (to date) written for television since the series *Labyrinth* in 2012. The IMDB lists *Frankie & Emma* as a 2017 television series, but the official Facebook page for the show describes it as a 'Web-series', for distribution online via YouTube rather than on television (Frankie and Emma 2018).
5   The IMDB (2017b) incorrectly lists the director of *Joni Jones* as British design critic and journalist Stephen Bayley, an inaccuracy that persists on numerous other websites that include information on *Joni Jones* that have presumably taken their information from the IMDB. The fact that the mini-series was produced by Bayly and James's Red Rooster Films, and that information on Bayly on the website for Sly Fox Films (2015), his current company, lists him as the director of *Joni Jones* provide compelling evidence that it was Bayly rather than Bayley with whom Jones worked on this project.
6   S4C is a sister channel of Channel Four. They are both commercial channels, and S4C shares much of its programming.
7   Entitled *Gwared y Gwirion* (translated *The Lost Innocence*), which was published in 1966.
8   In 1984 it was released in cinemas as a double bill with another *First Love* film for Channel Four, *P'tang, Yang, Kipperbang* (1982).
9   William Trevor's 'An Evening with John Joe Dempsey' from *The Ballroom of Romance and Other Stories* (1972).
10 English novelist Graham Greene's *Doctor Fischer of Geneva or The Bomb Party* (1980).
11 See Chapters 3 and 4 for full consideration of Jones's use of toolkits in this period.
12 These materials have been retained by Jones, and are therefore not currently in the archive.
13 It aired on Channel Four in the UK two months later, in April 1996.
14 Jones's score for Boorman's *Excalibur* (1981) is discussed in Chapter 2.
15 Jones and Kenworthy would continue to work together over the following years on the films *Lawn Dogs* (1997) and *Notting Hill* (1999).
16 Different sources give different amounts ranging from $70–85 million.
17 Hall presents a detailed analysis of *Merlin*'s industrial and musical processes and structures in her doctoral thesis (2017).
18 See Chapters 5 and 6 for discussion of these scores.
19 As noted in Chapter 4, a hint of this melodic outline can actually be heard towards the end of Jones's score for *Chains of Gold* (1991), though it is vastly expanded and developed in *Gulliver's Travels*.
20 These mini-series should not be confused with, and are unrelated to, the 2015 US television series *Blood & Oil*, with music by Mark Isham, and the 1986 film *Labyrinth*, scored by Jones. *Blood and Oil* is also incorrectly listed as a TV movie on the IMDB.
21 Most of his music editors were supplied by Dan Carlin Sr.'s Segue Music Company.
22 *Blood and Oil* uses a slight variation on this system whereby the first part of the cue number identifies the episode, but the final part increases sequentially across the whole of the mini-series.
23 Cues 8M0X and 18M0X also exist and are variants of 8M0 and 18M0 of different durations. These are the closing credit music for the Channel 4 rather than the NBC broadcasts of the mini-series. Similarly, cue 18M1 is a third variation of the closing credit music for the composite telefilm version of *Gulliver's Travels*.

Part IV
Recent projects (2004–)

8 A brief foray into video games

While the vast majority of Jones's career has seen him score films and television programmes, he has also worked in the 'third arm' of the screen-media industry, video games. His initial entry into this part of the business was the Electronic Arts game *Marvel Nemesis: Rise of the Imperfects* (2005), with further work on an aborted game for the *Zelda* series in 2007. The archive holds relatively few items for either of these projects – in the case of *Zelda* the materials are limited to little more than a single piece of music – but they nonetheless enable a brief exploration of Jones's approach to scoring this type of audio-visual work, and the ways in which he adapted his process and style for this arena. The appendix of Tim Summers's book, *Understanding Video Game Music* (2016), is titled 'How to Hear a Video Game: An Outline' and is based around a similar 'how to' guide for film created originally by Royal S. Brown (1994). Summers suggests that his outline is 'an effort to illustrate the possibilities and systematic avenues for reading video game music' (2016, p. 208), and it functions as an effective framework within which Jones's first video-game score may be examined.[1]

Marvel Nemesis: Rise of the Imperfects (2005)

Marvel Nemesis was the first game to arise out of a partnership between Marvel and Electronic Arts (EA) that had begun the previous year. In an article for *Variety*, Ben Fritz (2004) reported that '[the] deal between the no. 1 vid[eo]game publisher and one of the top comicbook publishers will bring the two companies together to create a new line of fighting games' and that 'EA [has] an exclusive license to develop and distribute fighting games featuring Marvel characters'. It seems that a long-term relationship was envisaged by both companies, but *Rise of the Imperfects* was the only game to be released before the partnership was dissolved in 2008, despite a second game being under development at the time (Kohler 2008). The negative reception of *Marvel Nemesis* may well have been a significant factor in the breakdown between Marvel and EA, with criticism of the graphics, story, lack of variety, and 'its horrible looks, non-existent gameplay and shallow controls' (Anon 2005).[2]

Marvel had entered the realm of video gaming in 1982 when *Spider-Man* was published for the Atari 2600 by the toy and game manufacturer Parker Brothers.

178   *Recent projects (2004–)*

Since then, all of Marvel's leading characters have appeared in games for a variety of platforms published by a wide range of companies. By the time *Rise of the Imperfects* was released, Spider-Man, the X-Men, The Hulk and The Punisher were well established as video-game properties, and the inclusion of Spider-Man and two of the X-Men – Wolverine and Storm – in the game was probably designed to enhance its appeal to regular players of games of this genre. Electronic Arts was well established as a video-game producer at the time it entered into the agreement with Marvel, though *Rise of the Imperfects* sat outside what was at that time its main area of production – sports. Notwithstanding this, EA had been producing James Bond-branded games since 1997's *Tomorrow Never Dies*, with several of these taking the form of 'third-person shooters', the same perspective adopted for *Marvel Nemesis*. The intention behind the game was to introduce a set of six newly created characters into the Marvel universe. These 'imperfects' are the results of experiments carried out by the character Niles Van Roekel, an alien who has been attempting to manufacture a perfect warrior to save his home planet from impending invasion and conquest. Van Roekel also takes control of several Marvel superheroes during parts of the game's narrative conceit, meaning that in addition to battles between the imperfects and established characters such as The Thing, Daredevil, Electra and Spider-Man, there are also opportunities for two of these heroes to face off against each other. As is common in fighting games, playable scenarios are linked by cut scenes that progress the story, move the action from location to location, and explain some of the motivations of the various characters.

Despite his long and successful career, Jones had not previously scored a video game when he was commissioned to create music for *Rise of the Imperfects*, although he did have experience of writing for conversions of graphic novels and for comic-book heroes with unusual special abilities, having composed the scores for *From Hell* (2001) and *The League of Extraordinary Gentlemen* (2003) in the previous four years. He recalls that the main attraction of this project was its:

> technical challenge to the craft of scoring [. . .] music that has a particular dramatic potency that you're trying to imbue in a scene, [when] one doesn't know how long a novice of the game will be spending on level one.
>
> (Jones 2016b)

Perhaps surprisingly, a snapshot of Marvel video games from the three years leading up to the release of *Rise of the Imperfects* shows that very few of the composers who worked on these projects had significant experience of working in this area of scoring, with some having little in the way of any screenography at all. As can be seen from Table 8.1, Michael McCuistion and Rik Schaffer are notable as the only composers to feature more than once in this list (though neither had scored for Marvel before 2002), but no-one had a level of screen-composition experience remotely close to Jones's. Indeed, although Christopher Lennertz could boast a reasonable screenography, *The Punisher* (2005) was only his second video game score, and Kevin Manthei's back catalogue of thirty game scores is dominated by

Table 8.1 Principal Marvel video games produced in the three years leading up to *Rise of the Imperfects*, showing the composers and their screen-composition experience

Year	Game Title	Composer(s)	Screen Composition Experience
2002	Spider-Man	Michael McCuistion	Six television projects over ten years including the series *The New Batman Adventures*, *Superman* and *Batman Beyond*, but no previous video game scores.
	X-Men: Next Dimension	Keith Arem	Significant experience in game sound, including on Marvel's *Spider-Man*. Wrote five video game scores and four film projects in previous nine years.
		Michael Cohen	Several short films over five years, but only one video game score.
	Blade II	Martin Oliver	Two video game scores in the previous three years, both for Muddy Foot Productions, who co-produced *Blade II*.
2003	Hulk	Graig Robertson	Only previous score was a video game from 2000 for Radical Entertainment, who co-produced *Hulk*.
	X2: Wolverine's Revenge	Ian Livingstone	Five video game scores over four years, including *Lego Creator: Harry Potter*, distributed by Electronic Arts.
2004	Spider-Man 2	Michael McCuistion	Retained after scoring *Spider-Man* two years previously. Scored the DC Comics *Justice League* TV series between these projects.
		Noel Gabriel	Two video game projects, both in the previous year.
	X-Men Legends	Rik Schaffer	Three video game projects in the previous two years.
2005	X-Men Legends II: Rise of Apocalypse	Gregor Narholz	Twelve documentaries, seven films and a small number of other projects over eight years, but no previous video game scores.
	Fantastic Four	Rik Schaffer	Retained after scoring *X-Men Legends* the previous year. Scored one further video game between these projects.
	Ultimate Spider-Man	Kevin Manthei	Thirty video game scores over nine years, including *Championship Bass* for Electronic Arts in 2000.
	The Punisher	Christopher Lennertz	Thirty-five projects, mainly for television and short films, over nine years. Only previous video game score was *Medal of Honor: Pacific Assault* for Electronic Arts in 2004.
		Tim Wynn	Eleven projects, a mix of films, television programmes and shorts, over eight years, but no previous video game scores.
	The Incredible Hulk: Ultimate Destruction	Bill Brown	Sixteen video game scores over seven years, including two *Command and Conquer* titles for EA in 2003.
	Marvel Nemesis: Rise of the Imperfects	Trevor Jones	Seventy-four film and television projects over twenty-five years, but no previous video game scores.

mysteries involving the teenage detective Nancy Drew, with nothing specific in his résumé to suggest an aptitude for scoring a superhero-themed third-person shooter.

As the title implies, *Rise of the Imperfects* focuses on the Imperfects, the new EA-created characters, meaning that Jones was able to compose an original score without being constrained by any requirement to use themes already associated with any of the existing Marvel superheroes. Although the score is entirely synthesised with no live recording, something that is in itself unusual in Jones's portfolio, it retains several elements of his signature sound and style. The digital audio materials in the archive indicate that there are nine basic timbral areas in the score – brass, choir, drums, metallics, pizz[icato], strings, synths, violin solos and woodwind – and the music seems to be conceived as choral-orchestral with added effects in the form of metallics and synths, although neither of these elements are unusual in Jones's output. Also, despite being composed for samples Jones clearly wrote the score with the properties of the real instruments in mind. The ensemble is likewise used quite idiomatically even though technology would allow unrealistic effects and balances to be implemented successfully, emphasising that Jones thought of this project like any other audio-visual commission despite the lack of live performance. This consistency of practice across different forms of screen media is emphasised by the composer's tendency to describe his approach to video-game scoring as analogous to scoring for cinema:

> The segues to make the levels join up from one to the next seamlessly was the [same] challenge to writing that one has on most films, especially where there are songs involved, where you have to segue from one pre-ordained key, tempo, rhythm or instrumentation into another cue that has another dramatic purpose.
>
> (Jones 2016b)

There are fifty-seven cues in Jones's score, a complete list of which is contained within the archive and is reproduced in Figure 8.1. In addition to revealing how the cues break down into the different elements of the game environment, this list provides information regarding the duration and the start and end tonalities and tempos for each piece of music. The tonalities used across the score are quite limited, with all of the cues except those identified as 'Doom' or 'Tension Build' beginning in A minor, D minor or E minor. Indeed, of these forty-seven cues, only four fail to end in one of these keys, with excursions to F minor ('Peon Fight 5'), G minor and C# minor ('Boss Fight 2' and 'Boss Fight 3') and A major ('Johnny Ohm's back-story') being the only occasions when the score moves any real distance from its A minor base. The seven 'Tension Build' cues are listed as atonal, and each is based around a dense cluster chord presented on strings. These short pieces of music are differentiated instrumentally by the elements of the ensemble that are used to supplement the expanding string cluster, and by the presence or absence of additional percussive effects. The information in Figure 8.1 also shows some differences in the duration

Cue No.	Title	Duration	SMPTE Start	SMPTE Stop		Start key	Stop key	Start tempo	Stop tempo	Free Clix
M01	Front End Music: Imperfects Theme Revised	04:07:00	00:00:00:00	00:04:07:00		A MINOR	A MINOR	76	120	4
M02	Front End Music: Imperfects Sketch Idea	04:20:00	00:00:00:00	00:04:20:00		A MINOR	A MINOR	76	114	4
M03	Front End Music: Superheroes Revised	03:35:00	00:00:00:00	00:03:35:00		D MINOR	D MINOR	150	150	8
M04	PEON FIGHT 1	02:10:00	00:00:00:00	00:02:10:00	'CORE X'	D MINOR	D MINOR	138	138	8
M05	PEON FIGHT 2	03:03:00	00:00:00:00	00:03:03:00	'NIS'	D MINOR	D MINOR	128	128	8
M06	PEON FIGHT 3	02:12:00	00:00:00:00	00:02:12:00		D MINOR	D MINOR	146	146	8
M07	PEON FIGHT 4	02:50:00	00:00:00:00	00:02:50:00		D MINOR	D MINOR	140	140	8
M08	PEON FIGHT 5	03:02:00	00:00:00:00	00:03:02:00		E MINOR	F MINOR	150	150	8
M09	PEON FIGHT 6	02:35:00	00:00:00:00	00:02:35:00		A MINOR	A MINOR	145	145	8
M10	PEON FIGHT 7	02:45:00	00:00:00:00	00:02:45:00		D MINOR	D MINOR	150	150	8
M11	RAGE MODE 1	00:45:00	00:00:00:00	00:00:45:00		D MINOR	D MINOR	138	138	8
M12	RAGE MODE 2	00:40:00	00:00:00:00	00:00:40:00		A MINOR	A MINOR	140	140	8
M13	BOSS FIGHT 1	03:03:00	00:00:00:00	00:03:03:00		E MINOR	E MINOR	150	150	8
M14	BOSS FIGHT 2	03:04:00	00:00:00:00	00:03:04:00		E MINOR	G MINOR	150	150	8
M15	BOSS FIGHT 3	02:53:00	00:00:00:00	00:02:53:00		E MINOR	C#MINOR	165	165	8
M16	BOSS FIGHT 4	02:50:00	00:00:00:00	00:02:50:00		A MINOR	D MINOR	150	150	8
M17	BOSS FIGHT 5	02:53:00	00:00:00:00	00:02:53:00		D MINOR	D MINOR	160	160	8
M18	BOSS FIGHT 6	02:45:00	00:00:00:00	00:02:45:00		D MINOR	D MINOR	160	160	8
M19	BOSS FIGHT 7	02:30:00	00:00:00:00	00:02:30:00		A MINOR	A MINOR	150	150	8
M20	FINAL CONFRONTATION VR's LAB - PEON	03:00:00	00:00:00:00	00:03:00:00		E MINOR	E MINOR	150	150	8
M21	FINAL CONFRONTATION VR's LAB - BOSS	02:42:00	00:00:00:00	00:02:42:00		E MINOR	E MINOR	165	165	8
M22	NIS Score 1	00:32:00	01:00:05:24	01:00:37:24	AM_4_Wol3 Intro	A MINOR	A MINOR	138	138	6
M23	NIS Score 2	00:30:00	01:00:00:00	01:00:30:00	AM_5_Wol3extro	A MINOR	A MINOR	127	128	8
M24	NIS Score 3	00:37:00	01:00:04:03	01:00:41:03	DB_7_Elektra 3 Intro	A MINOR	A MINOR	138	132	8
M25	NIS Score 4	00:28:00	01:00:00:00	01:00:28:00	DB_30_Spiderman3 Intro 3	A MINOR	A MINOR	149	143	8
M26	NIS Score 5	00:38:00	01:00:09:07	01:00:47:07	BB_19	A MINOR	A MINOR	143	138	8
M27	NIS Score 6	00:45:00	00:00:08:03	00:00:53:03	GC_15	A MINOR	A MINOR	81	79	4
M28	NIS Score 7	00:27:00	00:00:08:00	00:00:35:00	GC_16	A MINOR	A MINOR	63	69	6
M29	NIS Score 8	00:52:00	00:00:08:00	00:01:00:00	GC_46	A MINOR	A MINOR	145	140	8
M30	NIS Score 9	00:26:00	00:00:08:03	00:00:34:03	MOV_46	A MINOR	A MINOR	58	58	5
M31	NIS Score 10	00:51:00	00:00:08:06	00:00:59:06	PP_26	A MINOR	A MINOR	90	94	3
M32	NIS Score 11	00:27:00	00:00:08:03	00:00:35:03	PP_39	A MINOR	A MINOR	144	146	
M33	NIS Score 12	00:30:00	00:00:08:00	00:00:38:00	RT_35	A MINOR	A MINOR	131	134	8
M34	Credit Screen	00:30:00	00:00:00:00	00:00:30:00	Jeff Mair used part of Boss Fight 3					
M35	Doom 1	01:30:00	00:00:00:00	00:01:30:00	IMPERFECTS THEME REVISED (FRONT PORTION)	ATONAL	ATONAL	76	76	4
M36	Doom 2	01:30:00	00:00:00:00	00:01:30:00		ATONAL	ATONAL	120	120	8
M37	Doom 3	01:25:00	00:00:00:00	00:01:25:00		ATONAL	ATONAL	75	75	4
M38	Short Intro 1	00:12:00	00:00:00:00	00:00:12:00		A MINOR	A MINOR	100	100	8
M39	Short Intro 2	00:18:00	00:00:00:00	00:00:18:00		E MINOR	E MINOR	100	100	8
M40	Short Intro 3	00:22:00	00:00:00:00	00:00:22:00		D MINOR	D MINOR	92	92	4
M41	Death Piece 1	00:12:00	00:00:00:00	00:00:12:00		D MINOR	D MINOR	120	120	8
M42	Death Piece 2	00:10:00	00:00:00:00	00:00:10:00		A MINOR	A MINOR	120	120	8
M43	Death Piece 3	00:12:00	00:00:00:00	00:00:12:00		E MINOR	E MINOR	120	120	8
M44	Tension Build 1	00:18:00	00:00:00:00	00:00:18:00		ATONAL	ATONAL	120	120	8
M45	Tension Build 2	00:21:00	00:00:00:00	00:00:21:00		ATONAL	ATONAL	100	100	8
M46	Tension Build 3	00:20:00	00:00:00:00	00:00:20:00		ATONAL	ATONAL	150	150	8
M47	Tension Build 4	00:19:00	00:00:00:00	00:00:19:00		ATONAL	ATONAL	92	92	4
M48	Tension Build 5	00:17:00	00:00:00:00	00:00:17:00		ATONAL	ATONAL	70	70	4
M49	Tension Build 6	00:25:00	00:00:00:00	00:00:25:00		ATONAL	ATONAL	95	95	4
M50	Tension Build 7	00:19:00	00:00:00:00	00:00:19:00		ATONAL	ATONAL	120	120	8
M51	Faultzone Backstory	01:18:00	00:00:00:00	00:01:18:00	FZ_edit2	A MINOR	A MINOR	97	97	8
M52	Brigade Backstory	01:17:00	01:00:00:00	01:01:17:00	B_cut1	A MINOR	A MINOR	61	60	3
M53	The Wink Backstory	01:56:00	01:00:00:00	01:01:56:00	TW_cut3	A MINOR	A MINOR	115	114	6
M54	Johnny Ohm Backstory	01:54:00	00:00:00:00	00:01:54:00	JO_mars_cut	A MINOR	A MAJOR	90	87	4
M55	Solera Backstory	01:39:00	01:00:00:00	01:01:39:00	S_cut_2	A MINOR	A MINOR	60	91	3
M56	Hazmat Backstory	01:32:00	00:00:00:00	00:01:32:00	HM_cut3	A MINOR	A MINOR	59	60	5
M57	Outro Animatic	02:03:00	01:00:00:00	01:02:03:00	outro_animatic	A MINOR	A MINOR	72	144	4

Figure 8.1 Complete cue list from *Rise of the Imperfects*

and tempo of these seven cues, which seem to be used to accompany the low-action scenes in the game that precede fighting sequences.

Atonal elements aside, the tonality of the score is relatively consistent, but the need for music to support different parts of the gameplay results in Jones using quite a wide range of tempi, with M56 'Hazmat Backstory' the slowest at an initial speed of 59 bpm and M15 'Boss Fight 3' and M21, the final boss confrontation at Van Roeklel's lab, the quickest at 165 bpm. Indeed, the eighteen fighting cues – M04 to M21, which break down as seven 'Peon Fights', two 'Rage Modes', seven 'Boss Fights' and two 'Final Confrontation' pieces – all play at between 128 and 165 bpm, with the boss and final confrontation cues all at least 150 bpm. In his discussion of Nobuo Uematsu's music for the combat sequences in another contemporary third-person game, *Final Fantasy VII*, Summers observes that:

> The standard battle cue is a driving *allegro-vivace* piece that uses a synthesized orchestra in a heroic-military topic based primarily on brass *marcato* interjections and fanfare gestures (accompanied by snare drum, cymbal, tambourine and other percussion). The musical cue stimulates my psychological arousal – I am primed to react and I am aware that it is down to my personal skill whether the heroes' party will defeat the enemy.
> (Summers 2016, p. 166)

While Jones's fighting cues do not particularly feature synthesised brass as a prominent sound, his use of 'a driving *allegro-vivace*' and 'marcato interjections and fanfare gestures' demonstrates the similarity of his approach to that outlined by Summers. Much of the material for these cues is drawn from the two longest cues in the score: M01 and M03, the main themes for the imperfects and the superheroes, respectively.[3] Both are labelled in Figure 8.1 as 'Front End Music', indicating use at the opening of the game and menu sequences, and perhaps unsurprisingly given their names and the nature of the game, each of these pieces of music presents a thematic idea that recurs melodically and rhythmically across Jones's score.

M01 opens with a slow, dissonant, sustained high-string chord around which sporadic woodwind, percussion and metallic effects are heard, generating an air of uncertainty and mystery. After about a minute and a half a melody enters at the bottom of the texture, a winding line alternating between dotted minims and crotchets as it gradually ascends from tonic to dominant by way of the Gypsy/Hungarian scale often employed by Jones (Figure 8.2a). This melody bears an aural resemblance to a slow creeping bass theme from Jones's score to *Dark City* (1998), which uses a hybrid of the Gypsy/Hungarian and octatonic scales – notably the flattened third and sharpened fourth degrees that are common to both – to encapsulate the oppressive darkness of Alex Proyas's sci-fi *noir*. A similar environment is found in *Rise of the Imperfects*, the narrative for which begins with The Thing walking across a New York City bridge under black skies when he is attacked by aliens, and every subsequent scenario appears to take place at night or in a similar *noir*-influenced darkness. The bass material gives way to the main Imperfects theme, shown in Figure 8.2b, a pulsing 3/2 rhythm in strings and percussion that moves between harmonies of

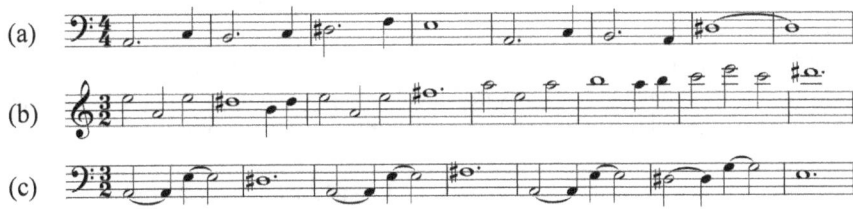

Figure 8.2 The three main melodic elements of M01 from *Rise of the Imperfects*: (a) The initial ascending melody drawing on the Gypsy/Hungarian scale that bears a similarity to the opening bass theme of *Dark City* (1998); (b) the Imperfects theme; (c) variant bass melody with echoes of Holst's 'Mars'

Figure 8.3 The three main melodic elements of M03 from *Rise of the Imperfects*: (a) The Superhero theme; (b) angular melody that recalls a second theme from *Dark City* (1998); (c) third melodic idea from M03

Am–Gaug–Am–B. When the low brass return with a variant of the bass melody (Figure 8.2c), the effect is reminiscent of Holst's irrepressible 'Mars' from *The Planets*.

By contrast, M03 is in a fast 4/4 throughout and opens with the Superhero theme, a spiky melodic cell on flute and strings shown in Figure 8.3a. This is supported by two further thematic ideas, Figures 8.3b and c, which operate within similar harmonic and rhythmic frameworks to complement the main theme and generate additional material for Jones to use in the rest of the game score. The second theme bears an aural resemblance to another melody from *Dark City* this time an angular, staccato motif for strings and high woodwind that emerges stridently from the texture to highlight moments of tension in the film.

The music in *Rise of the Imperfects* can be understood as what Karen Collins terms 'adaptive' since it 'reacts to the game states, responding to various in-game parameters such as time-ins, time-outs, player health, enemy health, and so on' (2008, p. 4). Despite his lack of prior experience in scoring for video games, Jones was nonetheless alert to the ways in which gameplay could potentially shape the music on a macro-level when he approached the project, noting:

> Instead of scoring in two dimensions linearly from start to finish, you are actually looking at it as though you are looking at a plan of the entire game and trying to put together four consecutive pieces of music depending on the levels, and then making the transitions to each level as seamless as possible. At the same time you are hyping the musical intent – the drive, the rhythm, the tempo – and modulating and moving into a different instrumentation very quickly after a transition from one level to the next.
>
> (Jones 2016b)

The main examples of this influence within the game are the abrupt triggering of a victory cue on the successful completion of a level, or a death cue if a player fails to do so, although there is otherwise relatively little in the way of 'dynamic audio' (Collins 2008, p. 4). Indeed, the automatic cueing of victory music actually provides a strong example of the way that Jones's score is underexploited in the game, particularly bearing in mind the strong thematic identification afforded to the imperfects and the superheroes through the musical material in cues M01 and M03, respectively. As already identified, in order to complete the game a player must control a mix of superheroes and imperfects, fighting several generic alien foot-soldiers, other imperfects and superheroes, and finally Van Roekel himself. However, when a scenario is completed successfully the victory is always accompanied by a fragment of the main Superhero theme regardless of which character was used in the level; given that several battles require the player to control an imperfect and defeat a superhero, the Imperfects theme would be a more logical music choice on these occasions.

The intensity of the sound effects and the relatively low level of the music in the final product mean that it is often not possible to fully hear the score during the combat sequences in any case, but where the music is audible it seems that other cues are applied in a similarly indiscriminate manner. For example, there is no obvious pattern to the employment of the various Peon Fight and Boss Fight materials, even though some of these cues are based around the Imperfects theme and others on the Superheroes theme. Indeed, as can sometimes happen in films, the subtlety exercised by Jones to ensure that his score differentiated between the two groups of characters while retaining underlying musical connections between the themes through their harmonic profiles was completely negated by the use of the material in the game itself. Such problematic use of the musical material perhaps hints at a degree of naivety on the part of both the composer and the game's producers. Indeed, between them the senior producer David McCarthy and the five producers – Daniel Ayoub, Terry Coleman, Joel Manners, Tony Rushton and Brandie Stephens – had a total of six production credits prior to *Rise of the Imperfects*, while Jones brought to the project a much greater level of screen-scoring experience than any of the previous composers for Marvel games, as shown in Table 8.1. Although Jones was mindful of some of the specific requirements of video-game music, he conceived and crafted his music using similar practices and approaches to his feature-film work without necessarily accounting for all of the peculiarities of the medium, a situation that may have been exacerbated by a lack of realisation on the part of the producers that the score might contain filmic markers of narrative and characterisation that could enhance the gameplay.

As noted at the start of this chapter, Jones's score for *Marvel Nemesis: Rise of the Imperfects* can be considered through the lens of Tim Summers's outline for reading a game score. Summers breaks his consideration down into five broad areas – 'origins of music'; 'original scores: types of music'; 'the function of music in the game'; 'the use and nonuse (*sic*.) of music in the game', and; 'miscellaneous' (2016, pp. 208–214) – each of which contains a number of sub-sections and sub-questions that support detailed exploration of a game score. Table 8.2 draws on relevant parts of Summers's outline to offer a summary reading of Jones's first video-game project. Responses to points and questions posed in the outline are shown in italics for clarity.

Zelda Ruin (2007)

Jones's only other engagement with video-game music to date came two years after *Rise of the Imperfects*, when he created a demo for a game in the long-running *Legend of Zelda* series (Seale 2017), which the digital files in the archive refer to as *Zelda Ruin*. The production company wanted music for an animated sequence from the game – which would have been the fourteenth *Zelda* title, sitting between *Phantom Hourglass* (2007) and *Spirit Tracks* (2009) – to present to other company members for support (Jones 2016b), but their efforts failed, and the project was abandoned. There is a MIDI file included within the archival digital materials, and although the only sound in the file is a twenty-eight-second long sustained low A natural that runs from the start of the music, when opened in Sibelius it reveals a sequence of hit points, shown in Table 8.3, that detail the narrative of the game demo. Jones wrote a single piece of music for this *Zelda* demo, and it is apparent from the digital audio files that, like his score for *Rise of the Imperfects*, this material was conceived in much the same way as Jones's other narrative projects. Indeed, while Jones doubtless learned much about the specifics of video-game scoring from his experience on *Marvel Nemesis*, it is apparent that where possible he maintained a similar approach to screen-scoring projects regardless of the medium. The *Zelda* materials include ProTools files labelled as sketches as well as balanced mixes of the final demo in both stereo and 5.1 surround-sound mixes. Like the music for the Marvel/EA game, the *Zelda* cue is a sampled choral-orchestral piece – this time with stems for strings, brass, percussion, choir and 'hits and stings' – and is written

Table 8.2 Summary of Trevor Jones's score for *Marvel Nemesis: Rise of the Imperfects* using Tim Summers's outline 'How to Hear a Video Game' (2016, pp. 208–214) as a structural framework

---

I. *Origins of music*

A. Score composed originally for the game?
   Yes. There was no need for Jones to reuse existing music.

II. *Original scores: types of music*

A. Classical
   2. Instrumentation
      a. Full orchestra *albeit sampled*
   4. Individual style: does the music quickly revel itself as the creation of its composer?
      Yes, through aspects of rhythm, timbre, and texture.

III. *The function of music in the game*

B. The style(s) used within the particular genre(s)
   1. What elements of the music are stressed and how does this relate to the game?
      b. Short motifs: 'Final Fantasy VII'

V. *The use and nonuse of music in the game*

A. Points at which music is used in the game: relationship to narrative structure
   2. Musical [. . .] motifs seem to have [. . .] a general, mood-producing function?
      Yes, despite Jones's intentions there is no specific linking of motifs to characters or other aspects of the narrative.
C. The introduction of music into the game
   1. Non-diegetic music
E. The overall musical profile of the score
   There are 57 cues in total, using a range of tempi and tonalities.

VI. *Miscellaneous*

A. The relationship of the composer to the game
   1. Whether the score was done after the game was largely finished?
      Yes, Jones joined the project late in the timeline as usual for this sort of score.
   7. And how many composers worked on the project?
      1, just Jones.
C. The composer's profile
   1. Is he or she principally a game composer?
      No, despite a substantial screenography this is Jones's first game score.
D. The involvement or noninvolvement of an orchestrator and/or an arranger and/or an audio designer
   As a purely electronic score this is something of an outlier in Jones's oeuvre, so the noninvolvement of an orchestrator is very unusual.
G. Documentation: availability of resources
   Some materials are held in the Trevor Jones Archive at the University of Leeds. The game has vanished from the records of both EA and Marvel based on their websites, however.

Table 8.3 Hit points in the MIDI file from *Zelda Ruin*

Time (mm:ss:ff)	Bar.Beat.100th	Description of Visual Action
01:00:03:00	02.4.60	In – Camera starts to move
01:00:10:19	07.3.98	CUT – Overhead shot ruin
01:00:13:04	09.3.30	CUT – Knight on horseback looking around
01:00:17:14	12.1.98	CUT – Zelda carrying box
01:00:19:22	13.3.92	Hears something!
01:00:21:04	14.3.04	CUT – Bats
01:00:22:11	15.2.27	CUT – Knights convoy
01:00:24:01	16.2.23	CUT – Blurred shot horses' heads
01:00:26:10	17.4.07	CUT – Behind shot knight on horseback
01:00:28:08	18.2.32	CUT – Gargoyles attack
01:00:28:20	18.2.73	CUT – Knights defending
01:00:30:08	19.3.97	CUT – Carriage
01:00:30:18	19.4.98	Man hits ground
01:00:31:16	20.3.25	CUT – Zelda in carriage
01:00:33:13	21.3.72	CUT – Gargoyle coming through roof
01:00:34:11	22.2.06	CUT – Horses leap over rock
01:00:35:15	22.4.91	CUT – Gargoyle growling at Zelda
01:00:36:13	23.3.14	Magical sting!
01:00:36:20	23.3.86	CUT – Carriage on two wheels
01:00:37:10	24.1.22	CUT – Carriage careering down hill
01:00:38:10	24.3.72	CUT – CU [Close up] Granite
01:00:42:04	26.4.87	CUT – Marauding baddies
01:00:44:21	28.3.48	CUT – Back shot of Zelda in cloak
01:00:46:15	29.3.75	Zelda turns
01:00:47:04	29.4.98	CUT – Behind shot Zelda
01:00:47:13	30.1.98	EVIL STING!
01:00:48:17	30.4.83	CUT – CU Zelda
01:00:49:16	31.2.93	SWORD STING!
01:00:50:08	31.4.80	CUT – Marauding baddies close in on Zelda
01:00:52:23	33.3.43	Explosions
01:00:53:18	34.1.51	CUT – Zelda unsheaths sword
01:00:56:08	35.4.15	Figure on horseback – HERO THEME
01:00:57:10	36.3.04	CUT – CU Link firing arrows
01:00:58:22	37.3.04	CUT – Gargoyles facing onslaught
01:01:00:16	38.3.68	CUT – Huge rocks
01:01:01:10	39.1.68	Link lands
01:01:04:04	41.1.00	CUT – Whole army advancing
01:01:05:15	41.4.70	CUT – 2-shot Link and Zelda
01:01:07:00	42.4.19	CUT – Tall knight advancing
01:01:09:07	44.2.00	CUT – Link and Zelda look on
01:01:10:18	45.4.70	CUT – Green faced evil knight sneering with his evil army in background
01:01:12:14	46.2.35	All swords fully lifted
01:01:14:10	47.3.01	CUT – Link looking over at Zelda
01:01:18:10	50.1.00	CUT – Extreme close up Link
01:01:20:12	50.1.00	Last frame

with the balances and capabilities of real instruments in mind despite the likelihood that the score would ultimately be realised electronically.

The storyboard must have developed from the timings in the MIDI sketch over the course of the project, with the final sound file having a duration of 1:33 minutes, thirteen seconds longer than indicated by the hit points in the MIDI file. Unfortunately there is no visual footage for this project in the archive – indeed, no trace of this project exists at all on any *Zelda* website, official or otherwise – so a precise correlation cannot be made between Jones's music and the listed narrative events. However, listening to the sound indicates that some parts of the action must have been allocated more time in the final visual footage, with Jones's music moving from a mysterious if sedate opening to faster more dramatic material after thirty seconds, somewhat later than the 19:22 seconds listed in the MIDI file. There is a second injection of fast music around forty-four seconds into the track, perhaps aligning visually with the dramatic shot of Zelda's carriage on two wheels, but given the lack of synchronicity between the archival sources it is impossible to know precisely why Jones's score is structured in the way it is.

Conclusion

Jones's brief excursion into video-game music was, ultimately, undermined by the projects he was approached to score. *Rise of the Imperfects* was the flagship product for Marvel and Electronic Arts and the game that launched what should have become the leading partnership in superhero games, given the prominence of the two companies in their respective fields. Instead it heralded an 'imperfect' relationship. Given the number of different composers who had scored Marvel superhero games prior to *Rise of the Imperfects* it is almost impossible to even speculate whether or not they would have retained Jones for any further titles featuring the game's new characters, but the strong negative critical reaction to *Marvel Nemesis* makes such thoughts moot in any case. Similarly the failure of *Zelda Ruin* at the demo stage means it is unknown if Jones would have been considered as the composer for the main game had it been made, a job that would have made him the first non-Japanese composer to work on the series. While this may seem unlikely, it might not have been out of the question given that Jones had won the Japan Academy Prize for his score for the Japanese film *Aegis* (2005) only two years earlier.[4]

Notes

1 A breakdown of the score for *Rise of the Imperfects* with respect to Summers's outline is shown in Table 8.2.
2 This review is cited on the website Metacritic along with others that offer similar criticisms. *Rise of the Imperfects* has an aggregated score of 53 out of 100 from 30 critic reviews on Metacritic; the lowest score awarded is 20.
3 The longest cue is actually M02 Front End Music: Imperfects Sketch Idea. The function of this cue is unclear, given the use of the word 'sketch' in the cue name and the fact that this material is very similar to M01, and if it does appear in the game it is indistinguishable from M01. Accordingly, it is not considered in this discussion of the score.
4 Jones's score for *Aegis* is considered in Chapter 9.

9 Work in diverse areas of screen programming

Jones's workload in the previous decade had been principally concentrated around the composition of film and television scores for major Hollywood and UK studios – it had been a time of frantic activity with most years involving at least three major projects. The period from 2005 up to the present has seen some gradual diminution in the number of productions he has taken on (having become increasingly absorbed in other musical and educational interests) but also diversification, with several being for his native South African industry, including the Canadian co-produced TV series *Jozi-H* (2006–7), the Zulu language feature film *How to Steal 2 Million* (2011), the two-part TV film *Blood and Oil* (2009 – an Anglo-South African co-production) and the feature length documentary *My Hunter's Heart* (2010).

The three other films of the period were Japanese (*Aegis*, 2005), Canadian/British (*Chaos*, 2005) and British (*Three and Out*, 2008, also known as *A Deal is a Deal*). Jones's two scores for video games, which also date from this period, were considered in Chapter 8, and his work for television also included the two-part *Labyrinth* (2012 – discussed in the book's conclusions), an international co-production involving companies from the UK, Germany, the Czech Republic and South Africa. Two smaller projects were produced for exclusive performance at specific sites in 2006, *Fields of Freedom* (Gateway Theater in Gettysburg) and *We Fight to Be Free* (Mount Vernon Museum and Education Center). Perhaps closest to his heart, in 2011 Jones scored *War Paint*, a fifteen-minute short film starring his daughter, Emily Seale-Jones.

While considering the musical and narrative characteristics of the outputs in chronological sequence, this chapter explores a range of themes supported by evidence from the Trevor Jones Archive. In contrast to the five years surveyed in Chapter 6, Jones's work in this period lay outside Hollywood and involved new creative collaborators. What remained consistent was the involvement of a tried and trusted team to support the development of the score. The scoring of films and TV programmes for the African industry, following on from *The Long Run* of 2001, can be seen as a deliberate and strategic engagement with the continent that had shaped him as a young man before he settled in England. They bring with them issues of the sensitive encoding and projection of Africanness within a primarily European/American musical vernacular. Although relatively small in scale, the pair of scores written for patriotic short films for the American heritage industry, which bring together documentary, re-enactment and fictional account, illustrate his approach to composition for this niche genre. And finally, and for perhaps the first time since the beginning of his career, the digital technologies he employed and engaged with had largely stabilised to the point that they did not form a potential distraction from the creative activity of composition, and require little further comment.

Aegis (2005)

The Japanese film *Aegis* (Bōkoku no ījisu) placed Jones into a rather different industrial context to his more familiar one. Produced by Cross Media, the director Junji Sakamoto, the cast and many of the crew were Japanese, whereas the producer (post production) and post producer, the film and picture editors, and most of the members of the sound and music teams were not. Although it was little understood by, or familiar to, Western critics, it received nominations in the 29th Japan Academy Prize in twelve of the fourteen relevant categories including outstanding achievement in music, and Jones won the Japan prize for his score. He notes that:

> it was the only film culture that I've encountered where the music seemed to be celebrated over and above any of the other film-making disciplines, so that the composer, editor and other technical people were regarded more highly than the actors, director or producers – a phenomenon that I've not experienced before or after working in Japan.
>
> (Jones 2017)

Based on the novel of the same name by Harutoshi Fukui, an author described in 2005 by Norimitsu Onishi in *The New York Times* as 'a Japanese Tom Clancy', its title translates as 'Aimless Aegis' (2005). According to Norimitsu, Fukui

> has to his name a handful of best sellers whose common themes – post-war Japan's mistaken path, its wounded pride, the sense of stagnation today and the need for a virile military – resonate in a country shedding its pacifism and rearming itself. [. . .] The novels and movies, not to mention Mr Fukui himself, have been embraced by conservatives eager to revise Japan's war-renouncing constitution and transform the Self-Defense Forces into a fully-fledged military.
>
> (Onishi 2015)

The book is a complex thriller set on the Japanese military destroyer Isokaze in which the crew is infiltrated by a foreign (either North Korean or Chinese) terrorist called Pao Yeung Fan who has smuggled chemical weapons on board, the day being saved by the vessel's Chief Petty Officer, Hisashi Senguku. The word 'Aegis', of the film's English title, relates to the ship's impenetrable defence system. Jones recollects that:

> the project was the result of various Japanese captains of Industry and Commerce wanting to finance a film about the North Korean threat to Japan [. . .] to draw the attention of the West to their plight (in particular the US, who they

felt were more concerned with Middle East issues) [and] employed their leading Japanese film company and stellar actors to make a film showing what would happen if North Korea became aggressive.

(Jones 2017)

Because of the need to attract Western interest it seems the film's producers looked first to Los Angeles to hire their editor and composer but ended up taking on the Northern Irish editor William M. Anderson (a regular collaborator with Peter Weir and best known for films such as *Dead Poet's Society* (1989) and the *Truman Show* (1998)), who was then based in Sydney, and Jones, who lived in London. When the entourage of twelve Japanese film executives came hotfoot from Los Angeles to discuss the project, Jones (2017) recalls that 'a great deal of bowing ensued on first meeting and throughout the remainder of the project'. The executives also recruited the Western sound department and Jones presumed that the non-Japanese members of the crew 'were employed to present a film to the outside world which would be paced and scored like a "Hollywood" film of its genre' (2017). He did not find the language caused him particular problems and remarked that 'as long as the dialogue was subtitled both Bill Anderson and I were happy to have a verbal account, qualifying the action and the dramatic intent of the scenes, from the translators' (2017).

No separate music editor was employed, although Jones indicates that this was not unusual for the Japanese industry. As was by now his standard approach, the score was performed by the LSO and recorded at Abbey Road (in one day, with the orchestra sight reading to reduce the costs) and the 'final music mixes were in 5.1 surround sound and time-coded as ProTools sessions, which the delegation hand-luggaged – after a thirty-six hour (all night) mixing session – back to Tokyo' (Jones 2017). Musically the score for *Aegis* inhabits a space not far removed from that for *Thirteen Days* (2000) or *The League of Extraordinary Gentlemen* (2003), although it is rather less densely spotted and with fewer cues than its US-produced counterparts. It is principally scored for three variant orchestras labelled respectively: A – two flutes, two clarinets, four horns, two trumpets, three trombones, tuba, percussion, electronics and strings; B – as orchestra A but excluding woodwinds; and S – two horns, electronics and strings. Only occasionally are oboes and bassoons introduced to specific cues, and the brass and percussion take a prominent role.

Jones had been explicitly requested not to use Japanese instruments such as the koto or shakuhachi in case these were to alienate a Western audience, and although he largely avoids overt employment of Western musical codes for Japan and Japaneseness, a characteristic of the score is the use of drums (actual and synthesised) and syncopated rhythmic ostinati (a regular feature of his scoring practice), which may have resonated with Japanese audiences through a connection to Taiko drumming. Figure 9.1 demonstrates four such figures taken from different sections of cue 1M2. While most of the themes are diatonic in nature, one in particular does have a pentatonic aspect, interestingly that heard in cue 5M4 'Yeung-Fan Flashback', associated with the terrorist Yeung Fan. Thus the most explicit orientalist code is reserved for those who threaten Japan, implicitly orienting Japan ideologically to the West.

192 Recent projects (2004–)

Figure 9.1 Syncopated rhythmic ostinati from different sections of cue 1M2 from *Aegis*

Three of the principal musical themes of the film are set into clear relief in cue 7M4, the suite composed by Jones for the end credits. The first is warmly lyrical and in Mixolydian D major with an elegiac melody taken by the violas, and this is followed by the theme associated with Yeung Fan in a pentatonically inflected D minor over a tonic pedal. The film's main theme (as so described in the two-track sketches held in the archive) ensues, played as a stately sarabande in D minor. It has the feeling of an anthem, creating a curiously muted ending after the high drama but helping to highlight the political issues embodied by the picture. Looking back on his experience of scoring *Aegis*, Jones observed that:

> The fact that's most memorable for me was that it was the first true 'international' project that I was creatively involved in, because we would have online meetings with Bill Anderson in Sydney, the director Junji Sakamoto in Tokyo, me in London and my management in L.A. – there was always one of us who would be trying to have a creative conversation at 4am.
>
> (Jones 2017)

Chaos (2005)

Jones's second film released in 2005 was *Chaos*, written and directed by Tony Giglio and starring Jason Statham, Ryan Phillippe and Wesley Snipes. Set in Seattle, it is a crime thriller with a twist in its tail, focussing on a bank raid in which no money has been stolen, but as later becomes apparent, a virus somehow employing chaos theory has been implanted in the bank's computer. Only much later in the narrative are we made aware that one of the detectives, Quentin Connors (played by Statham), and his former disgraced colleague Jason York (Snipes), are responsible for the crime.

Once again, *Chaos* involved a new set of studio relationships, Jones not having previously worked with either Giglio or the film's producers, although this seems to have had little impact on his working methods, which followed their customary course. Along with his established music team (including Geoff Alexander, the LSO and Neil Stemp), he was joined by music editor Graham Sutton, who had collaborated with him on *Talk of Angels* (1998), and recording engineer Andrew Dudman of Abbey Road Studios, who had been assistant engineer on *Thirteen Days* and *I'll Be There* (2003). Jones appears to have completed the score by 23 December 2004, the cues being noted as 'locked' between 7 and 23 December at the head of the individual Sibelius files created by Alexander (more than one third of them being on the later date). The creation/modification dates of the Sibelius files suggest that, apart from one file (1M5) which was completed on 15 December, the orchestration and music processing of the rest of the score took place between 22 and 31 December, with Alexander only taking a break on Christmas Day. The cues were not provided, nor were the orchestrations completed, in sequential order, and indeed 1M1 (which actually encapsulates 1M1 and 1M2) is one of the latest-dated cues.

This opening cue, which accompanies the film's preamble depicting the shooting of a criminal called Curtis and his hostage on a bridge in Seattle and its aftermath, as well as the opening credits and titles, offers an interesting case study of Jones's mature style along with the resources that go to make up the score. Material from around the start of the millennium has been passed on directly by Jones in native digital formats on hard disk, and thus the archive holds all of the recordings of the London Symphony Orchestra and electronic instruments as well as the mixes, mix data and score. To imagine the Sibelius file of the cue as a comprehensive record of its musical content would, of course, be entirely inappropriate, for it encodes only the first of the two equally important fundamental components – orchestral and electronic – in any detail. These are kept separate in the stereo and 5.1 stems and combined in the full mixes. One of the most aurally compelling electronic sounds used in 1M1 was generated by the Propellerhead program Reason and is labelled 'sonar'. Using an almost sinusoidal sound and digital delay with feedback, it is heard particularly prominently as the title card appears, doubling the melody in lower strings and trombones. In its simultaneous purity and instability, perhaps it can be taken as a musical symbol of chaotic mathematical systems in which a small cause can have a large effect.

The cue falls loosely into three sections which are separated by the absence, or attenuation, of music. In the first, in E minor, a solo horn and the cellos elaborate a slow-moving melody against a tonic drone that begins with a pattern of interlocking fifths (shown in Figure 9.2) loosely recalling the motif from *The League of*

Figure 9.2 Melody from the first section of cue 1M1 from *Chaos*

Extraordinary Gentlemen described in Chapter 6 (see Figure 6.3). This melody is extended through an alternative strategy of infilling the rising minor seventh, passing through the sharp submediant before being completed by a further rising fifth that drops chromatically back to the tonic. In its second phase it moves to, and oscillates around, the dominant (B–A–C–A–B). With a cut to a car speeding through the rain the modality changes to E Phrygian and strings and brass rise through the pitches of a modified pentatonic scale (A–B–D–E–F) to create an extended musical upbeat to the crash. The music is subsequently attenuated before returning at the *Chaos* title, the slow syncopations of the melodic line gently spiralling down through an E minor arpeggio. It is gradually submerged beneath metallic percussive sounds and a driving rhythm, and a subtle recall of Jones's use of electronics in *In the Name of the Father* (1993) may perhaps be detected. The orchestra returns to the texture as Curtis points his gun at the police.

The next new material of the cue is found at the credit montage as a news report is heard. A figure in the cellos subdivides pairs of 4/4 bars to create a vigorously syncopated 3+3+3+3+2+2 pattern that has been shown to be something of a fingerprint of Jones's style across his career, and it will be suggested later in this chapter that this additive rhythm may derive from, or allude to, African musical practices. The recall of the cantabile melody from the opening of the cue played by the cellos gives way to a further repetition of this rapid syncopated material, and it is heard once more after the screen fades to black and the tonality shifts up a minor third to G minor against the close-up of Connors in newspaper cuttings of the incident. Jones subsequently restates the slower melody shown in Figure 9.3 that had originally accompanied the *Chaos* title card, which decorates a linear descent from the submediant to the new tonic of G minor. These two basic elements are then repeated (in varying proportions) to finish the cue. Overall, the change of tonality from E minor to G minor can perhaps be taken to both mirror and denote the movement from the narrative past to the present.

In summary, cue 1M1 serves several functions: to suggest the overall mood of the film; to support the specific action of the opening scenes; to indicate the passage of time inherent in the narrative; to intimate the chaos of the title; and to create a convincing and coherent musical structure that does not distract from the visuals. Necessarily, the cue provides the seeds for much of what will follow, and although its components are in themselves quite simple, their combined impact is complex. Throughout the score, musical units of the type presented in 1M1 are integrated with rock- and jazz-influenced bass guitar riffs and electronic sounds in what, despite the disparate sources, is remarkably coherent. Many of the carefully wrought subtleties of the score are hidden beneath sound effects in the final mix, and while from the perspective of the audience expecting a visceral cinematic experience this

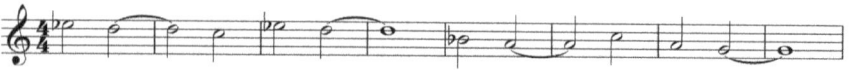

Figure 9.3 Decorated linear descent to the tonic from the final part of cue 1M1 from *Chaos*

may not be a problem, it remains an undoubted frustration for the composer whose conception of the balance between the various audio elements, which underpinned the construction of a cue, is at odds with those of the director.

Although *Chaos* premiered on 15 December 2005 in the United Arab Emirates and was subsequently released in parts of Europe, it did not appear in the Anglophone world until August 2006 (in Australia). It was not until the first quarter of 2008 that it reached US and UK audiences when it was released on DVD and as a result received little mainstream critical attention.

Fields of Freedom (2005–6) and *We Fight to Be Free* (2006)

In 2005–6 Jones scored a couple of bespoke films for heritage centres: *Fields of Freedom*, which concerned the 1863 Battle of Gettysburg, the turning point of the American Civil War; and *We Fight to Be Free*, dealing with the life of US President George Washington. Given their patriotic themes and the fact that they were written for very specific venues and audiences (with funding from the commercial world), Jones's brief seems to have been slightly more constrained than was usual in the feature films he scored. For such outputs, however, they had relatively generous budgets, and while the musical canvas may have been a little more restricted, the technical quality of the performances and recordings of the score is absolutely on a par with his usual work.

Fields of Freedom was a thirty-minute large-screen-format picture commissioned for the multiplex Gateway Movie Theater in Gettysburg, Pennsylvania, by the Washington real estate developer Robert J. Monahan Jr. and was premiered on 19 April 2006, with an estimated budget of $3.2 million. It was written and directed by David de Vries and designed for visitors to the battlefield. Focussing on 'Pickett's Charge', the failed Confederate assault ordered by General Robert E. Lee on 3 July 1863, the short film narrated the battle from the perspective of two of its protagonists, one Confederate, the other Unionist. Jones was working on *Fields of Freedom* by October 2005, and the archival materials show he had sketched both the main theme and a secondary theme labelled 'angsty idea' by 7 October. Evidently activity on the project was relatively swift, a sketch mock-up having the file date of 21 October, and recording (of the London Symphony Orchestra) and mixing taking place at Abbey Road on 30–31 October. A CD album was compiled by the middle of November.

Although the film is only thirty minutes in length, the score consists of thirteen cues and plays almost continuously – for more than twenty-nine minutes of the total duration. As well as Jones's original music he draws on several traditional tunes including 'John Brown's Body' (popular among the Unionists in the Civil War), 'Dixie' (effectively the Confederate anthem), 'Shenandoah' (forming the basis of cue 1M11 'Aftermath of Battle' where it functions as a lament) and an Irish jig called 'The Gobby O' (also known as 'Jefferson and Liberty'), which is used in 1M2 ('Confederates March In'). In the titles overture, Jones makes reference to both participants in the conflict by interlacing sections of 'John Brown's Body' and 'Dixie' performed by piccolos (in lieu of fifes) before neatly superimposing the second halves of the melodies contrapuntally. This source music forms a preface to the main theme which is all but in a pentatonic D minor, and employs a broadly paced folk-like melody in an ABA'B'B"A' structure, heard on the cut to the opening battlefield scene. It subsequently recurs in 1M6 ('Confederates and Unionists Regroup') in the minor mode, heroically in the major in 1M10 ('Charge of Armistead') and elegiacally in 1M12 ('Epilogue–Three Days after the Battle'). This plaintive mood continues in the closing titles music where it betokens pathos, and this sentiment is reinforced by the reprise of 'Shenandoah' at the heart of a simple ternary structure. The secondary 'angst' theme is first presented in 1M4 ('Build Up to Final Battle') and is also in D minor; it is structured in four-bar phrases, each of the four successively varying the previous one in a stepwise descending sequence.

A prototypical melodic trait of Jones's writing can be seen in 1M5 ('Cannonade') in the fall from the dominant to sharpened subdominant in a minor context, and this feature returns in the battle sequence accompanied by 1M8 ('Confeds Cont. to Advance') and in 1M9 ('Unionists Start to Fire'). In this latter cue, Jones's tendency to work in harmonic blocks which connect the chromatic fall from fifth to sharpened fourth is also manifest; here the repeating sequence follows the pattern Dm^9–Fm^9–Cm^9–Dm^9, the ninth being voiced close to the tonic at the bottom of the chord to intensify the dissonance. While *Fields of Freedom* was a relative lightweight by comparison with his mainstream film work, Jones clearly treated the commission with due respect and sensitivity to its subject. He produced a score replete with his musical fingerprints that subtly integrated traditional and original material without particularly compromising either and was sonically of a very high quality.

We Fight to Be Free, the other commission for an important American historic site – George Washington's ancestral home of Mount Vernon in Virginia – was slightly briefer, running to twenty-four minutes, and had an estimated budget of $5 million. Presented by 'The Mount Vernon Ladies' Association' with funding from Ford Motor Company and private sponsors Donald and Nancy de Laski, it was produced by Greystone Communications and directed and filmed by Kees Van Oostrum, who had also been the cinematographer for *Fields of Freedom*. Sebastian Roché, who plays Washington, had a previous connection with Jones, having been a member of the cast of both *The Last of the Mohicans* (1992) and the television mini-series *Merlin* (1998).

Depicting key moments in Washington's life, the film also has thirteen cues, but Jones's input was somewhat slighter. Two were of keyboard music by Scarlatti, two of military drum beats, and a further pair (1M2 and 1M3) were eighteenth-century pastiche composed by Jones, suggesting Cherubino's canzona 'Voi, che sapete' from Mozart's *Le Nozze di Figaro*. Only in the overture (1M1), the extended cue 'Forest battle' (1M9) and the closing credits (1M13) does he really get the opportunity to flex his compositional muscles, and 1M9 in particular, although relatively restricted in melodic terms, is conceived extremely effectively orchestrally.

These three cues make considerable use of the score's main theme, an expressive idea in the horns presented at the beginning of 1M1 and shown in Figure 9.4, that in its invocation of an American musical archetype would not have seemed out of place in the score for *Thirteen Days*. In a modally mobile D, it assertively

Figure 9.4 Main theme from *We Fight to Be Free*

rises through an octave and a minor third largely by way of open intervals before curling down to the dominant, the consequent phrase ending on the tonic. The figure can be seen to have its forebears in the vernacular tradition that Cecil Sharp captured in the Appalachians in the early years of the twentieth century – a tradition that links back to the early Ulster Scot, Scottish and English immigrants to America and indeed one with which Washington himself (who was of English ancestry) would probably have been familiar.[1]

Jozi-H (2006–7)

Jones's other project between 2006–7 was the TV hospital Drama *Jozi-H* co-produced by Toronto-based Inner City Films Inc. in association with CBC and Morula Pictures from Johannesburg in association with the South African Broadcasting Corporation. The thirteen-part series of one-hour episodes was originally shown on CBC between 13 October 2006 and 2 February 2007 before being aired in South Africa between 26 April and 19 July 2007. According to the synopsis on TVSA's mini-site devoted to the series:

> Ancient custom and modern cutting edge medicine square up for a head-on collision in Jozi-H.
>
> Set in Johannesburg's world renowned trauma department at Johannesburg Metropolitan Hospital, Jozi-H is set in the new post-apartheid South Africa and looks at the personal and professional struggles faced by an eclectic, international band of doctors, nurses and surgeons from South Africa, Canada, the US and Britain.
>
> Their stories take place on a frontier, where modern medicine meets traditional African healing, where groundbreaking HIV/AIDS research leads the way in the search for a cure, where diseases no longer found in the first world remain a deadly challenge and the volume of violent crime forces interns to become world experts on trauma in weeks instead of years.
>
> (TVSA 2017)

The creation of South African producer and writer, Mfundi Vundla, direction of the series was farmed out to a team of eight (four of whom were responsible for more than one episode each), and several editors were similarly employed for the cutting of the shows. Jones's signing up as the composer was noted as something of a coup at the time, and Vundla was quoted in the announcement in the trade newsletter *SCREENAFRICA* on 11 July 2006 as commenting that 'it is a great honour for us to have a composer in the league of Trevor Jones, and more importantly, he is South African' (2006). In the same article the Canadian producer Amos Adetuyi remarked that 'music is a key feature of JOZI H thanks to Trevor Jones insightful style and approach', and Jones responded that he:

> love[d] the opportunity of working at home, being back home is amazing. It's exciting to work on a show that will be aired within a few months and that the public can experience in a short while, I am excited and grateful having been asked to work here.
>
> (2006)

Although Jones was entirely assimilated to England by the start of the millennium, having lived, studied and worked there for most of his adult life, he retained an enormous affection for his native land. Like many who have experienced two very different cultures and a transformative relocation in their late adolescence, his personal and musical identity can be seen to draw on both to varying degrees. Several of his film and television outputs from 2006 onwards reflected a post-apartheid 'return' to South Africa, including *Jozi-H*, *Blood and Oil*, *My Hunter's Heart* and *How to Steal 2 Million*. A number of explanations can be posited for this: a desire on his part to help the burgeoning industry in South Africa, particularly in the field of music production and post-production; a feeling of responsibility in the area of education to develop the kinds of opportunity he had as a young man; an urge to withdraw somewhat from the frenetic pace of Hollywood production; and a realisation within the South African industry of the significant value he could bring through his craft, reputation and influence.

In scoring *Jozi-H*, Jones collaborated once more with music editor Jeremy Raub (who several years later would give up his career in the film industry to become a full time brewer), and programming and mixing of the synthesised score was undertaken by Neil Stemp at Jones's studio, CMMP. Given the absence of a single overall point of directorial control for the series and the need for musical continuity, Raub's role as intermediary with the production company was vitally important. Resources held in the archive permit the inference of some details of the score production process. Three main folders, the substructure of each of which is organised by episode, embrace the ProTools sessions and audio files, the audio stems for Raub (though only nine episodes are included for these) and stereo versions of mixes of the cues. Although the audio stems, which contain the unmixed individual synthesised tracks for each cue, are indexed in the usual manner, several features are designed to help in the dub. Individual tracks are given filenames which indicate their source sound (for example, 'bass', 'kalim', 'lo str', 'melod', 'pads', 'rhythm' and 'strings'), and the folders containing the stems for each cue are labelled by tonality and tempo in beats per minutes (thus the second cue of episode one is '1M02 Am 100bpm').

Unusually, the ProTools files for the first episode distinguish material by its function in the drama rather than by cue numbers, with tracks marked as 'Main Title', 'End Credits', 'Underscore' by 'acts' (numbered from one to five, the show having four advertising breaks) and 'bumpers' (leading into or out of the breaks, as discussed in Chapter 7). Later episodes also have files marked 'recalls' scoring passages that are intended to remind the viewer of the key narrative developments of the previous episode. File dates indicate that Jones was working on the score during most of the period of four months from mid-August until mid-December 2006, and as the files for *We Fight to Be Free* are dated at the end of September and early October 2006, it appears that some work was done in parallel for the two projects, a circumstance that has permeated his career.

The individual episodes vary considerably in the quantity of cues used, ranging from fifteen in the fifth to thirty in the final one, although there is considerable duplication and many brief cues. This was Jones's first explicitly South African score since *The Long Run* (allowing for the elements of *The League of Extraordinary Gentlemen*), and he draws on such musical markers of Africanness as the kalimba (or mbira, the pan-African so-called 'thumb piano') and the marimba in his core synthesised/sampled ensemble. Despite the more restricted palette, the score – which is characterised by the tendency towards restlessness and edginess that might be expected of the genre of hospital drama, albeit with moments of tenderness and introspection – conforms by and large to his usual approach. Perhaps in so doing it draws attention to those aspects of his mature style which may reflect his early musical experiences growing up in South Africa.

Three and Out (2008)

Jones returned to the familiar territory of the British film industry for his subsequent project, *Three and Out* (also known as *A Deal is a Deal*), directed by Jonathan Gershfield, starring Mackenzie Crook, Colm Meaney, Imelda Staunton and Gemma Arterton, and released on 25 April 2008. A black comedy, its narrative concerns tube driver and budding author Paul Callow (Crook) who over the previous month has had the misfortune of two people committing suicide by throwing themselves in front of his train. He is convinced by fellow London Underground workers that if a third person commits suicide in the same way within the month he will receive a large pay-off. In the hope of being able to set himself up as a writer in the highlands of Scotland on the proceeds, he seeks out an individual who wishes to die. Discovering Tommy Cassidy (Meaney), a terminally ill Irish tramp, Callow cuts a deal that involves him helping Cassidy to find his estranged wife Rosemary (Staunton) and his daughter Frances (Arterton) and to meet up with them for one final time over the weekend. In the course of the subsequent madcap road trip the two men bond, and Callow finds himself unwilling to carry out his part of the bargain but is eventually persuaded by Cassidy that 'a deal is a deal'.

Perhaps unsurprisingly, given its subject matter, the film garnered considerable controversy and a protest from the train drivers' union ASLEF, a number of whose members picketed the premiere. ASLEF executive Simon Weller commented that 'It's a very serious subject for us. It destroys lives. The drivers are never the same again. The film trivialises it. They are saying they have dealt with it sensitively. We don't think they have' (Byrne 2008). The picture did not perform well at the box office, and despite what was seen as a strong cast it received generally poor reviews from critics.

The archive holds the Sibelius score along with 5.1 stems by reel, and stereo tracks for the film cues and soundtrack CD, the audio material all being in native digital format. At the heart of the score and forming its musical matrix is an English folk melody in the Aeolian mode, which is traditionally set to the ballad 'The Grenadier and the Lady', and in this respect the score can be seen as part of a subset of Jones's output stretching back over thirty years to his earliest television scores, which draws on traditional music and musical styles. This particular folk melody was adopted by Barry Taylor in his 1998 song 'An Emigrant's Daughter', which tells the story of one of his distant ancestors who died on the passage from Ireland to Canada in 1842 (*Rootsweb* 2006–7), and this is sung diegetically by Imelda Staunton (herself the daughter of Irish immigrant parents) during the course of the film. Coincidentally, and perhaps fittingly, there is a related tune in the Irish tradition called 'Paddy's Return', which appears in the nineteenth-century collection *O'Farrell's Pocket Companion for the Irish or Union Pipes*.

As well as Staunton's rendition, several of Jones's cues use the tune of 'An Emigrant's Daughter' directly, and a secondary theme that is heard on a number of occasions in relation to Paul's aspiration to set himself up as an author in a cottage in Scotland has some correspondence to it. In fact, more of Jones's score was conceived to employ 'An Emigrant's Daughter' than appears in the final dub, and the inventive cue he wrote for the end credits converts it to a rhythmically mobile jig spiced up with hemiolas. However, this was supplanted by Carole King's 'You've Got a Friend' and The Spencer Davis Group's 'Somebody Help Me', both covered by actor Lee Mead.[2] The other element that bookends the film is Elvis Costello singing 'Accidents will Happen' for the establishing scenes at the opening, and as he had done on many previous occasions (most recently in *Crossroads* and *I'll Be There*), Jones found himself required to accommodate popular source with his original music.

Overall, by comparison with Jones's scores for Hollywood films the score is relatively modest in terms of material employed, and beyond the two previously mentioned ideas, a third gently syncopated idea elaborating the underlying figure G#–A–B–A–G# is brought to the fore as the narrative moves to the Lake District, in particular in the scene in which Tommy chases Paul having discovered that he has slept with his daughter. Arguably this pattern is also derived from 'An Emigrant's Daughter', picking up the rising and falling melodic characteristics from the third strain, and it should have reached its apotheosis in the second part of the closing titles music had this not been replaced by 'Somebody Help Me'. A familiar shape from earlier scores makes an appearance at the film's climax in 6M3 ('Paul kills Tommy') as Paul watches Tommy walking onto the track, in the melody that loops upwards through interlocking intervals in bassoon and cellos, as shown in Figure 9.5.

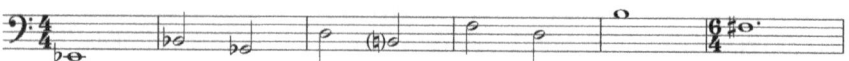

Figure 9.5 Melody from cue 6M3 from *Three and Out*

Unlike many of his other recent projects Jones's music was recorded by the English Sinfonia, restricted to clarinet, bassoon and strings and conducted by its Artistic Director Janice Graham. Curiously, the score explicitly indicates the performer of just one instrument (beyond a fleeting reference to Graham herself in an ossia marking), Andy Findon of The Michael Nyman Band – who had played for Jones on *Merlin* and is one of the most active session musicians in London – who plays the whistle and associated flutes on this score and contributes significantly to the putative Irish and Scottish aspects of the soundtrack. Although there are additional parts for acoustic and bass guitars, fiddle, Celtic harp, piano and drum kit, none of the performers of these are identified, and Findon receives no mention in the closing credits.

Blood and Oil (2010)

The two-part thriller *Blood and Oil* (which had alternate titles during production of *Sweet Delta* and *Troubled Water*), a co-production between the British company Tiger Aspect Productions Film and the South African company Afrika Worldwide, was directed by David Attwood and first broadcast on BBC 2 on 29–30 March 2010, running for a total of two hours and forty minutes. Written by Guy Hibbert, it is set in Nigeria and ostensibly deals with the kidnapping of four workers from an oil installation in the Niger Delta, written from the perspective of Claire, the wife of kidnap victim Mark Unwin, and Alice Omuka, a PR executive for the oil company who investigate the men's murder. At a deeper level, it is concerned with the illegal practice of oil bunkering, the theft of crude from pipelines that has proved a disaster for the region, as well as a host of other social and political issues facing Nigeria.

The archive holds two important resources relating to Jones's largely electronically mediated score for the film: Sibelius files for cues numbered from 1M1_2 to 1M27 (Episode One) and from 2M28a to 2M55_6 (Episode Two) which are dated May 2009, though Jones's frontispiece indicates it was written in March 2009; and stereo audio files in wav format dated 29 June 2009, with those for the first episode labelled 'FullMix' and those for the second episode marked 'Full Mix Respot'. Sibelius files indicate patch and sample names, and the ensemble employs a number of indigenous African instruments, including Nigerian udu (a kind of clay water jug with a hole cut into the body), kalimba, marimba, Ugandan low drum, darbuka and a range of other African percussion. However, traditional instruments from very different cultures are also used, such as the south-east Asian Gendang or kendang.

The music that opens the first episode sets the tone for much of the rest of the score. Although unmistakably Jones's idiolect it draws on several rhythmic and melodic markers of African music beyond the sounds themselves. A two-bar ostinato using the pitch set $F\#_3-C\#_4-D_4-G\#_4$ is played by a bass udu to form a simple 'timeline' consisting of quavers in a 3+3+3+3+2+2 pattern recognisable from Jones's score for *Chaos* as well as several of the 'toolkit' projects of the late 1980s and early 1990s.[3] This is articulated rhythmically by the reversed sample of a celeste with delay, which acts as a kind of surrogate for the bell patterns of sub-Saharan music. Against this the chord progression of Cm–B–Cm–G#m is established, with each chord lasting for the two bars of the ostinato and the Eb/D# acting as a pivot tone. Gradually the sounds of a kalimba, harp and lute harmonics join in, and almost by stealth a fragmentary melodic line appears built around chains of descending diatonically infilled thirds that pick up the prevailing harmony, now a double tonic oscillation between C minor and B major/minor. In the second half of the cue the melody becomes more highly developed and a favourite device of Jones, the use of the sharpened fourth in the minor context, comes to the fore in the figure G_3–Eb_4–C_4–$F\#_4$.

Given the film's dual Nigerian and British perspectives, Jones's score takes a hybridised approach that coalesces elements from both cultures. This is heard strikingly in cue 1M10_11 'Arrival at Airport', where the scenes featuring the white British woman Claire are accompanied by music suggesting African culture at its most frenetic (and for Claire extremely threatening), whereas black British-Nigerian Alice is insulated in her chauffeur-driven limousine and is bathed in gentle euphony that almost intimates Muzak. Cues 1M12a ('Journey to Collect Mark') and 1M12 ('Mark's Hanging Body') largely eschew musical codes for Africa for scenes which focus on Claire and her response to the discovery of her husband's body.

At the end of Episode Two, the closing credits music provides a sense of musical resolution and hope for the future, taking on the character of an anthem, in which an African choir closes with the words 'It is our right to live in peace'. Although it may not necessarily attempt to reproduce an indigenous musical style, it is an ending that intimates authenticity and sensitivity to the culture of Nigeria and to Africa more broadly.

My Hunter's Heart (2010)

Jones's next project was *My Hunter's Heart*, an eighty-three-minute documentary produced by Videovision Entertainment for The South African Broadcasting Corporation and premiered on 30 July 2010. An exploration of the shamanic culture of the Khomani San of the Southern Kalahari – said to be the 'oldest living indigenous tribe in the world' (My Hunter's Heart Movie 2013), it was filmed over three and a half years and directed by brothers Damon and Craig Foster. The latter explained that 'In *My Hunter's Heart*, Orogap "Toppies" Kruiper and two fellow bushmen, who have seen their clan marginalised and decimated by modern civilisation, go on a personal odyssey to re-ignite their culture' (Sterkowicz 2010, p. 42). The film-makers were approached by Orogap and members of his community to film this odyssey, and they commented that:

> A question that always seems to emerge is, 'when will the Bushmen die out, when will the bow and arrow disappear . . .' Our desire is that this film will address this and give hope to many of the grand cultures of the world who are also under threat.
>
> (Foster and Foster 2013)

While acknowledging the technical quality and beauty of the documentary and the coherence of its basic narrative, Kavish Chetty (2011) drew attention to the problem of 'the compassionate anthropologist who wishes to romanticise the native past that we can't access'. Chetty cites Marxist theorist Masao Miyoshi's comment that 'once dragged out of their precolonial state, the indigenes of peripheries have to deal with knowledge of the outside world, irrespective of their own wishes and inclinations' (2011). For Martin Botha, however, *My Hunter's Heart* forms a kind of requiem, 'a sad portrait of marginal characters, somewhere stuck between memories of a rich past and modernisation' (2014, p. 36).

To record the score for *My Hunter's Heart* Jones used the Stellenbosch University Camerata (consisting of professional musicians and their students) and conducted it himself, allowing the project to have an educational benefit. Pre-production and production of music were well established in South Africa by this stage, but Jones could see significant opportunities in film-music post-production in South Africa, noting in a piece published in *Cape Town Magazine* that:

> I'd like people to realise that post-production in its entirety can be carried out here. It should work on two levels. You should be able to come here, as foreigners, with a proper budget and agenda and get a very serviceable score. That's being part of a service industry. I'm also talking about the cultivation of a S[outh]A[frican] film like *District 9* and NOT posting it in New Zealand, but completing it here. I want people to say 'why are we paying to fly abroad here, staying in expensive hotels, paying for expensive dubbing, when we've got that aspect at home?'
>
> (Henson 2010)

The live music for *My Hunter's Heart* is written for a limited selection of woodwinds (piccolo, flute, alto flute, oboe d'amore and cor Anglais), brass, harps and strings and in general places less severe technical demands on its performers than many of the scores composed by Jones for orchestras such as the LSO. Samples of similar African instruments to those found in *Blood and Oil* (most notably kalimbas, marimbas, and a large array of shakers and drums) are fully integrated into the ensemble, providing both textural and rhythmic reinforcement. Indeed, cue 1M19 specifically indicates the use of the udu patch which featured in 2M45 of what is referred to as *Sweet Delta* in the Sibelius file, showing a conscious linking of these scores through the use of specific African instrumental timbres.

The score consists of 19 cues (1M1 to 1M27) completed in mid-June 2010 and in total lasts for just over fifty-nine minutes; it was recorded and mixed in the Stellenbosch University Studios by Andrew Dudman from Abbey Road. Since there was no orchestration budget, the Sibelius score was constructed from Jones's demo sequencer files by Neil Stemp, and, in line with their usual practice, it includes the electronic/sampled elements on reduced-size staves at the top and the orchestral instruments in standard-size staves immediately below.

This is a dignified, reflective and often tender response to the visual images and narrative. The opening titles music sets the scene in a steadily paced cue that, after the ethereal sound of bowed vibraphone, begins with a spiky sub-Saharan rhythmic pattern (♪♩♩♫♩♪♩♩♫♩♪♩♪♩) similar to the 3+3+3+3+2+2 figure used in numerous other Jones scores, alternating between idiophones (marimba and vibraphone) and a pair of kalimbas. The primary thematic material of the cue, in F minor, is a slow-paced and sustained homophonic idea that soon modulates to A minor, and it is in that tonality that a vestigial figure appears in the first violins prefacing a near doubling of the underlying pulse and rapid figurations in live and sampled harps. Two types of motion are now overlaid, the fast moving arpeggiations of harps and percussion against slowly evolving chords in the orchestra. As this dissipates, much more dissonant sounds are briefly heard before a resumption of the stately material.

Subsequent cues pick up various of these characteristics – rhythmic, thematic and textural: in 1M7 ('Into the Cave') a rising figure played by the strings in pairs of repeated semiquavers from tonic to dominant in A minor hockets with the familiar sixteen-quaver timeline pattern in the sampled marimba; in 1M11 ('Journey to Namibia') a new expressive theme in D major with a Lydian fourth is built around the progression $D-E^7-E^{\varnothing 7}-D$ over a tonic pedal; and in 1M17 ('Orogap visions') a luminous cluster slowly builds up, Penderecki-like, via chromatic motion outwards from E_4. At the climax of the film comes the hunt and slaughter of a giraffe, and this is accompanied by the sequence of cues 1M20 ('Following Giraffe'), 1M21 ('Conclusion of Hunt'), 1M22 ('A Proud hunter') and 1M25 ('Honouring the Giraffe'). Jones carefully balances and coalesces what might be seen as alternative African and European/North American musical tropes and sonorities throughout these cues.

How to Steal 2 Million (2010)

New York-born director Charlie Vundla's film *How to Steal 2 Million* represented a move from what he felt was the typical South African film by avoiding conventional subjects (what he describes as the 'three As' – Aids, abject poverty and apartheid) and adopting the aesthetics of *film noir* for a crime thriller (SIFF News 2012). In the Zulu language (interspersed within English), according to distributor Indigenousfilm it runs to 109 minutes (though the DVD lasts only 82 minutes) and was co-produced by DV8 Films and Morula Pictures, which had also been responsible for *Jozi-H*. It went on to win three awards in 2012 from the African Movie Academy, including that for best director.

Set in Johannesburg, it is the story of ex-convict Jack (played by Menzi Ngubane) whose partner in crime Twala (Rapulana Seiphemo) – who was not arrested for their previous heist – has married Jack's former fiancée Kim. Wishing to go straight and form a construction company, Jack needs capital and, failing to get a bank loan, is persuaded by Twala to take part in one more robbery, of two million Rand, from Twala's father, Julius. Jack's partner is tough-woman Olive (Terry Pheto), and the narrative plays out the failure of the attempted robbery and its aftermath.

Jones's previous foray into *film noir* had been *Dark City* (1998), although that had been a hybrid genre with science fiction and both picture and score were on a very much larger scale. His largely synthesised/sampled score for *How to Steal 2 Million* is relatively modest in dimensions, running to just fifteen cues and lasting for around thirty minutes. The Sibelius files (dated 4 September 2010) consist only of parts for clarinet and soprano and alto saxophones, which in the main play sustained lines written in unison, and there is no attempt to notate the sequenced material (as had been done in *Blood and Oil*). Almost entirely subdued in tone, and in a style that could be characterised as 'moody' or 'atmospheric', overtly 'African' elements are kept much more in the background than in *Jozi-H*, *Blood and Oil* and *My Hunter's Heart*.

War Paint (2011)

The last project to be considered in this chapter had a strong personal connection for Jones. The fifteen minute dialogue-less film *War Paint*, starring his daughter Emily Seale-Jones, was produced in 2011. The storyline concerns a young woman who feels unable to leave her apartment because of a skin condition that affects her face, and the 'war paint' of the title is the make-up she applies to try to hide it. Discovering that the young man in a neighbouring flat suffers from vitiligo and is equally incapable of facing the world, she decides to try to help him. The film movingly deals with her failed attempt to disguise his unpigmented patches and their eventual, mutually supported facing down of their fears.

Given the absence of dialogue, considerable emotional weight is placed on Jones's electronic score. A falling chromatic figure derived from *The Black Angel* (1980), one of Jones's own apprentice works, is heard as we observe the girl's first attempt to open the front door of the apartment block. In its manifestation in *The Black Angel* it had first appeared as the knight, Sir Maddox, came close to drowning, being rescued by the woman who was prisoner of the eponymous Black Angel; it was repeated on his death at the end of the film. Here it indicates the psychological trauma suffered by the panic-stricken girl as she proves powerless to turn the door handle.

Conclusion

Although the films and TV programmes that Jones worked on in the period between 2005 and 2011 tended to have a lower profile in the US and Europe than those of earlier decades, he continued to work at the forefront of his profession as a composer. In combination with the video games considered in Chapter 8, these bear witness to both the range and scope of his accomplishments, and his ability to appeal to global audiences.

In an interview conducted in 2016 Jones commented that his 'commercial work [. . .] has eased off recently – because I'm doing something less commercial, more altruistic and hopefully beneficial' (2016b). These educational activities included the promotion of Maria Botha and Joseph Machiah's Violin Project in Khayelitsha (the so-called murder capital of South Africa) and the Christel House School in Ottery. He also instituted a film scholarship in conjunction with the National Film and Video Foundation for South African students who are talented in any aspect of film to study at the UK National Film and Television School. As a mentor to the final eight contestants, he took part in the ninth series of the reality-TV talent show

South African Idols which was broadcast between June and November 2013. He remarked in May 2016 that:

> My interest is in better educating the next generation because they are the South Africa of the near future. I want to rekindle the dream, which I think we're in danger of losing, and we need to inspire the young to have the courage to dare to realise their own individual dreams and ambitions. [. . .] 'It always seems impossible until it's done' – I've lived by that. When I'm talking to pupils and students, I love to remember this particular Madiba quote: 'We ask ourselves, "who am I, trying to be brilliant, gorgeous, handsome, talented and fabulous? Actually, who are you *not* to be"?'
>
> (Abarder 2016)

Notes

1 One might compare, for instance, the melody of 'The Mermaid' that Sharp recorded from Eliza Pace in Leslie County, Kentucky in 1917 (cf. Yates, Bradtke and Taylor 2004, p. 86).
2 Mead had won the role of Joseph in Andrew Lloyd Webber's musical *Joseph and the Amazing Technicolor Dreamcoat* as a result of the television series *Any Dream Will Do*.
3 See Chapters 3 and 4 for discussion of the toolkit scores.

Conclusions

Since scoring his first picture at the National Film School in the late 1970s, Jones has written music for over 100 screen projects. This final chapter begins with his most recent completed project for which materials exist in the archive, the television mini-series *Labyrinth* (2012), a score that embodies several musical features that are characteristic of Jones's compositional voice. This is followed by a broader discussion of his style and his career to date and consideration of the ways in which this detailed investigation of Trevor Jones may have greater resonance in the field of screen-music studies.

Labyrinth (2012)

The two-part TV mini-series *Labyrinth* was a co-production between Scott Free Productions, Tandem Communications and Film Afrika Worldwide, in association with Universal Production Partners. Lasting in total for three-and-a-quarter hours and broadcast in 2012, *Labyrinth* was adapted by Adrian Hodges from Kate Mosse's eponymous bestseller and directed by Christopher Smith, its headline star being John Hurt. Entirely unrelated to the film *Labyrinth* (1986) scored by Jones over twenty-five years earlier, it tells a version of the grail story that lies in the tradition of Michael Baigent, Richard Leigh and Henry Lincoln's *The Holy Blood and the Holy Grail*; Umberto Eco's satirical novel on conspiracy theories, *Foucault's Pendulum*; and Dan Brown's blockbuster *The Da Vinci Code*. The film's narrative focusses on two women – the thirteenth-century Carcassonne-dwelling Cathar, Alaïs Pelletier du Mas (played by Jessica Brown Findlay) and her twenty-first century descendent, Alice Tanner (Vanessa Kirby) – and criss-crosses between the two eras they inhabit as the plot develops.

The archive holds Jones's score for the film, which consists of fifty-eight cues in Sibelius format, including an arrangement of Puccini's aria 'E lucevan le stelle' from *Tosca*, which acts as a CD source for the second episode. It was noted in Chapter 9 that a figure from *The Black Angel* (1980) was reused in *War Paint* (2011) to indicate the trauma suffered by the female protagonist, and in *Labyrinth* Jones reconfigures the main theme of *The Black Angel* as the principal idea of the score. The fifteen-bar melody – which was originally written in a duple-time Bb minor and played on the alto flute as the first part of cue 1M1A of *The Black Angel*

– now appears in triple time (as it did in the closing cue for the earlier film) and in D minor. An associated figure that functions as a counterpoint in a quartus paeon (short-short-short-long) metre and based on the repetition of the pattern D–C–Bb–A/Bb–A–G–D is also re-appropriated, and collectively this material may be construed to connect the world of the returning crusader of *The Black Angel* with that of the Albigensian Crusade (1209–29), which effectively wiped out the Cathars and forms a major narrative thread of *Labyrinth*.

The mini-series provides a useful conspectus and summary of Jones's scoring technique in the latter part of his career. It is composed for an orchestra consisting of full brass and strings with additional parts for flute, clarinet and acoustic guitar, chorus, and a large array of electronic and sampled resources. The London Symphony Orchestra was engaged to perform the score and choral parts were taken by the Pro Cantu Choir (which would later change its name to the Cape Town Youth Choir) conducted by Leon Starker. The orchestra was recorded in Abbey Road and engineered by Andrew Dudman, and the choir recorded in the Stellenbosch University Studios, a further example of Jones finding a way to create an educational opportunity from his work. Unusually for a large-scale project, Jones is credited himself as orchestrator, though Geoff Alexander (who conducted the LSO in the recording) is described as having supervised the orchestration, and Neil Stemp took the significant role of synthesiser programmer; no music editor is identified. Of course, Jones's approach had for many years involved the production of detailed sequencer files that enabled accurate mock-ups of his scores to be prepared in advance of the final recordings, and without underestimating the creativity and professionalism of Alexander's contribution, an important element of the work of Jones's orchestrators was the notation of the nuances of individual voices and the provision of detailed performance markings from such mock-ups. In his overall conception of the score for *Labyrinth*, Jones appears to be acting in accord with the comment he made in 2005 that:

> what a good composer is trying to do is to optimise, to maximise the effect of a score, of music, on a particular scene, to give it the emotional depth and weight that is required to fulfil the director's vision of what the film is about.
> (Fox and Cooper 2008, pp. 4–5)

The score is substantial in scale – the stereo cue files in the archive have a combined duration of two hours and forty-five minutes – and thus nearly eighty-five percent of the film has musical accompaniment, an approach that is consistent with typical contemporary mainstream Hollywood practice.

Although his language is fundamentally tonal (often expressed modally) the resources employed range from pure diatonicism to highly chromatic writing. D minor appears to act as the tonic for twenty-one of the twenty-eight cues of the first episode, although the final cue – the Latin setting of Psalm 23 – is in A minor, suggesting plagal closure at a higher structural level. Through the course of the second episode A minor becomes increasingly evident as the score's overall tonality, and in the penultimate cue, 2M28 ('Alice Visits Montsegur'), which makes

Figure 10.1 Some of Jones's harmonic fingerprints as heard in cue 1M1A from *Labyrinth*

passing reference to Wagner's *Parsifal* in its restrained ecstasy, it is fully and firmly revealed. A characteristic melodic and harmonic resource found throughout Jones's output is the minor scale with a sharpened fourth, a form sometimes labelled as the Gypsy or Hungarian scale. This is first heard in the very opening thematic statement of *Labyrinth* as the camera descends to Audric Baillard's house in Los Seres. Several other of Jones's fingerprints can be distinguished in the harmonisation of the principal thematic material of cue 1M1A 'Episode 1–Opening Titles Pt 1', as shown in Figure 10.1: it is underpinned by a tonic pedal or drone (here of D and played by the electronic instruments) and involves pairs of chords that progress through small steps against the pedal tone.

At the same time it is supported by a set of delicate rhythmic ostinati played by sampled harps that collectively articulate the pitches D–E–F–A–Bb as a background wash of sound. And in the harmonisation of the main theme as it appears in bars 12–28 of 1M1C 'Episode 1–Opening Titles Pt 3', Jones restricts the harmonic palette to effectively two chords, a tonic D minor and supertonic seventh (E–G–Bb–D), which alternate against the held pedal D. Triads are frequently intensified by dissonances – often closely voiced minor seconds – and examples of this can be found throughout the setting of Psalm 23 that ends both episodes. The final sonority of 1M1C is a complex chord ($F\#_2$–A_3–$C\#_4$–F_4–A_4–Bb_5) that takes this approach a degree further by forming a major-minor triad with major seventh on F#. And in the terminal chord of 2M28, the sense of closure in A minor is tempered by the presence of a B a major ninth above the tonic.

As well as the staple fare of ostinati, a particular rhythmic idea found in several of Jones's previous scores reappears in various guises in *Labyrinth*. This is a pattern consisting of sixteen beats divided 3+3+3+3+2+2 that has been compared to the timelines of some sub-Saharan African musics. A striking example of its use is found in 2M23 'Alais and Guilhem Confront Oriane' where it moves into the forefront of the texture from bar 36, notated across pairs of 4/4 bars, driving the cue towards its climax. On the whole, Jones's language tends to integrate rhythms and melodic structures more commonly associated with popular and vernacular genres with those of Western classical music, and this strategy sometimes results from the need to ensure that the original score is able to coexist coherently with source music. Only one such piece of source music is used in *Labyrinth* (Puccini's 'E lucevan le stelle'), and thus he is not required to make allowance for extraneous material in his original score on this occasion. However, several subtle intertextual allusions to other music can be heard, including the brief *Parsifal*-like figure already discussed (in which a large-scale suspension and resolution onto a C major triad is immediately followed by a subtonic chord of Bb major), and the Gregorian plainsong melody 'Dies Irae' (that forms a sequence of the Requiem Mass) which, although not cited directly, is suggested through a similar melodic contour.

Major aspects of Jones's style

While there is no doubt that Jones's musical voice has continued to mature across the nearly forty years since he scored his first pictures at the National Film and Television School, this detailed exploration of his output has nonetheless revealed a number of musical features, strategies and approaches that may be considered hallmarks of a Jones score. Some aspects – such as the use of compositional toolkits – are quite time-limited, but others are more long-lasting, appearing consistently or recurring largely unchanged or in a developed form after a period of absence. Technology and people have always played significant yet contrasting roles in Jones's career, with the experimentation and opportunities generated by constant changes in the former set against the establishment of repeatable processes enabled by consistency in the latter. Accordingly, Jones's style is considered here under four broad headings – musical fingerprints, creative approaches, the music team and technology – followed by reflections on his career at present, and on the value of this investigation of a single composer's oeuvre for the field of screen-music studies.

Musical fingerprints

Rhythm is perhaps the most readily recognisable 'Jonesian' characteristic, none more so than the 'timelines' 3+3+3+3+2+2 pattern that permeates much of his output. The first notable instance of this accented syncopated cell being foregrounded is in *Angel Heart* (1987), where it acts as the basis for the 'Lounge Lizard motif' and is the fundamental rhythm of some of the marimba 'mobiles' found in the film's toolkits. The recurrence of the lounge lizard motif and its derivations across other toolkit pictures kept this distinctive rhythm at the forefront of Jones's musical voice across the late 1980s and early 1990s, and although its presence faded somewhat as he moved away from toolkits, the pattern can nonetheless still be found clearly in later Jones scores. For example, one of the musical ideas in the training montage from *GI Jane* (1997) utilises woodwind playing a staccato 3+3+3+3+2+2 pattern while the intervening quavers are 'filled in' by the strings; after teasing the listener with varying combinations of 3-beat and 2-beat pulses under growing chromatic chord swells, the full 'timelines' pattern then drives much of the music for the chase in *Desperate Measures* (1998), played prominently by the full orchestra; this rhythm is presented forcefully by strings as they underpin the main theme to *The League of Extraordinary Gentlemen* (2003); woodwind flourishes in the video-game score for *Rise of the Imperfects* (2005) are structured as 3+3+3+3+2+2; and it is also heard clearly in the scores for *Chaos* (2005), *My Hunter's Heart* (2010) and, as identified above, *Labyrinth*. Jones's scores are full of repeated rhythmic cells such as the 'timelines' pattern, and although other ostinati may not be so widely used, pulsing and pressing patterns and sequences have always been, and continue to be, one his key stylistic markers.

Linked quite closely to this is Jones's use of bass and sub-bass pitches within his music. Rhythmic basslines and drones feature commonly in his output and can be traced all the way back to the scores composed at film school and in his early professional career. The sound of the 64-foot bourdon organ stop is highly characteristic of Jones's music from the first half of his career to date, and the depth of sound in some of his scores can be attributed to the particular way in which he employs this timbre:

> on *Angel Heart* and *Mississippi Burning* I started using it in what I thought was an interesting way, because you could clash an A and a B flat, [so] instead of having a thing which is in A minor I had an A and Bb clashing at the low end, and this would just be very unnerving for an audience and they didn't know why. So I was conceiving a lot of the low end almost subliminally, below the audience's [range of actual hearing].
>
> (Jones 2007)

The idea that the very lowest sounds in the texture are felt rather than heard, and that they can be particularly disquieting for an audience if they clash harmonically, is a feature of many of Jones's scores for darker narratives, extending beyond the two Parker films he mentions through *Sea of Love* (1989), *Bad Influence* (1990) and other toolkit pictures. While he has moved away from the bourdon, Jones has continued to utilise technology to generate these very low sounds in later scores, such as the horrors *Hideaway* (1994) and *From Hell* (2001) and the sci-fi noir *Dark City* (1998). Indeed, Jones can be seen as something of a pioneer in the use of this sort of sound and pitch range for haptic impact, with Duncan Williams (2016) suggesting that this and other techniques found in the score for *Dark City* have had a strong influence on contemporary scores, including those of Hans Zimmer.

Semitone relationships such as that in the clash identified by Jones are also a key component of his approach to harmony, with many of his scores making use of parallel or near parallel progressions such as A minor–Bb major, A minor–Bb minor or A minor–Ab augmented. This does not seem to have been Jones's practice at the very start of his career, however, his earliest television scores instead showing something of a reliance on the circle of fifths, which seems to be almost the antithesis of these highly chromatic progressions. However, considering this change through the analytical lens of Neo-Riemannian theory shows a subtler development in Jones's harmonic language than might be apparent at first glance.[1] Movement around the circle of fifths such as that heard in the opening two bars of the main theme for *Joni Jones* (1981) (see Figure 7.1) requires a number of compound transformations in Neo-Riemannian terms: Am–(LR)–Dm–(LRP)–G–(RL)–C. The first two chromatic progressions outlined above, which are typical of those found in Jones's later works, can also be represented using Neo-Riemannian transformations – Am–(LRL)–Bb major; Am–(PS)–Bb major – while the third exhibits similar properties, with the A minor and Ab augmented triads sharing two common pitches, and the third altered by just a semitone to move from one to the other.[2] In each case these transformations are little more complicated that those found in the circle-of-fifths movement, and the harmonic progressions can therefore be interpreted simply as slightly more distant than, rather than radically different to, those found in Jones's early works. Indeed, despite moving towards a more chromatic harmonic language as his career has progressed, most of Jones's music still has a strong tonal or sometimes modal foundation and often betrays the influence of folk styles or hymn tunes.[3] While he does depart from this approach at times – to capture a specific effect such as the Penderecki-style string writing in *In the Name of the Father* (1993) – Jones avoids atonality, even when other sonic elements like the electronic effects in *Dark City* seem to push the soundtrack in that direction. This is not to imply that Jones is immune to the musical characteristics of other parts of a picture's aural environment when composing, and a feature of some of the scores he has written that also include pre-existing pieces of music is the appropriate incorporation of harmonic profiles and structures from those pieces within his own original material. The smooth transfer from Jones's cue to David Bowie's song 'As the World Falls Down' in the film *Labyrinth* (1986); the references to Bono, Gavin Friday and Maurice Seezer's title track in Jones's cue 'Giuseppe's Dead' from *In the Name of the Father*; and the subtle transition from the title song of *I'll Be There* (2003) into Jones's main theme, for instance, all attest to his skill at connecting the harmonic profile of his score with that of source material.

Similarly, throughout his career Jones has often drawn on the instrumentation of a film's source music when determining the ensemble for his score. The addition of the main instruments found in Bowie's songs – drum kit, synthesiser, electric guitar, and saxophone – to the orchestra for *Labyrinth* (1986) is a case in point, and along with the use of similar harmonic progressions (as identified above) facilitates the integration of score and songs in a coherent and unified soundtrack. Jones has also drawn on what could be termed 'ethnic' resources in a good number of his scores. Live and sampled percussion sounds, particularly the kalimba, are a feature of several of his South African pictures such as *Blood and Oil* (2010) and *My Hunter's Heart*, and Jones collaborated with vocal group Ladysmith Black Mambazo to evoke the sounds of Africa in both *The Long Run* (2001) and the opening of *The League of Extraordinary Gentlemen*. 'Ethnic percussion' was played by Paul Clarvis for *GI Jane*'s scenes in Libya, with London-based theatre musician and 'ethnic' session singer Belinda Sykes providing vocals for these cues and singing on the score for the Egypt-based television mini-series *Cleopatra* (1999). Jones adopts a similar instrumental strategy in the Irish and Irish-themed films *In the Name of the Father*, *Titanic Town* (1998) and *Three and Out* (2008), although as noted in Chapter 9, Japanese instruments are conspicuous by their absence from his score for *Aegis* (2005).

However, it is apparent that Jones selects timbres based on their sonic contribution to the ensemble, and accordingly non-Western instruments are not reserved purely as geographic markers. For example, the sound of the shakuhachi plays such a prominent and distinctive role in his score for *Runaway Train* (1985) that he retained the instrument (and the performer, Paul Hirsh) for both *Angel Heart* and *Mississippi Burning* (1988), despite none of these films having any connection to Japan. Indeed, this perhaps supports the notion that Jones has an interest in the use of solo woodwind timbres, particularly given that flute and pipe-type sounds feature in several of his scores throughout the toolkit era, and are also heard clearly in *In the Name of the Father* (played by Phil Todd), *Loch Ness* (1996), *I'll Be There* and *Three and Out* (all performed by Andy Findon). Similarly, the sound of a solo saxophone heard in the *Labyrinth* film returns in *Angel Heart* and *Sea of Love* courtesy of Courtney Pine, and Jones has employed this timbre several times in his career when dealing with darker, grittier narratives.

Electronics are a key aspect of Jones's approach to instrumentation, and there are some periods in his career – notably the toolkit era – in which he is almost synonymous with specific samples and sounds. The bourdon, metal 'krang', 'chomping cellos', marimbas, brass swells and prepared piano sound, a combination of electronic and synthesised sounds, are mainstays of the toolkit scores and imbue them with a highly distinctive sonic personality. Similarly, the use of the Electronic Wind Instrument (EWI) as a solo timbre across several scores in the late 1980s and 1990s marks them out as being by Jones. However, perhaps the most widespread way in which Jones has used electronic sounds is to expand the palette of the symphony orchestra, which has occupied a central position in his approach to scoring since around the time of *The Last of the Mohicans* (1992) and *Cliffhanger* (1993), and remains his ensemble of choice.

Jones's melodies are often deceptively simple and relatively unassuming, and they are sometimes subservient to the more rhythmic elements of his scores. Notwithstanding this, there are some characteristics that link several of his main themes, and can be seen as stylistic features of Jones's scoring style, albeit that they are not necessarily found across the whole of his career. The most prominent of these is the use of interlocking intervals to construct a melodic idea, first heard in the Eb_3–D_4–Bb_3–Eb_4–C_4 horn countermelody at the start of *The Dark Crystal* (1982), and more prominently in the insistent $C\#_4$–$F\#_4$–A_4–D_4 of *Runaway Train*'s main theme. However, this strategy largely disappears with the introduction of toolkits for Jones's following picture, *Angel Heart*, and it lies dormant for a significant time before being resurrected in the early 2000s. Scores such as *The League of Extraordinary Gentlemen* and *Chaos* and *Three and Out* all feature melodies that comprise rising chains of fifths (with the last three pitches repeated in *Three and Out*), a technique that can be seen as deriving from the earlier practice of using interlocking intervals. The approach is simplified in the *Labyrinth* mini-series, with its A_4–F_4–$G\#_4$–C_5 somewhat closer in construction to *Runaway Train* than any of its more recent counterparts. Several themes make use of the sharpened fourth degree of the scale in a minor or modal context, sometimes using the semitone interval created between this raised pitch and the fifth degree of the scale, and a variant of this idea appears in some of the scores from the late 1990s such as *Loch Ness* and *Dark City*, in which the melodies centre around the semitone relationship between the fifth and flat sixth notes of the harmonic minor scale. Thematicism does come to the fore in some scores, notably the television mini-series *Merlin* (1998), in which Jones employs a leitmotivic technique with themes for most of the protagonists, and some characters in *The League of Extraordinary Gentlemen* are similarly given their own motifs. However, melody is probably the least distinctive and the most inconsistent element of Jones's style, perhaps because it is the aspect of a score most likely to be impacted directly by the demands of the picture.

Creative approaches

Jones has always maintained that his aim when scoring a film, television programme or video game is to write the music needed by that specific picture, and throughout his career he has been flexible in his creative approach in order to achieve this objective. The toolkits he developed and used between 1987 and 1993 are an example of this, the technique arising out of the particular demands of Alan Parker's *Angel Heart* and then being moulded on a project-by-project basis to ensure that the resulting musical material was suitable for the picture. Indeed, the fact that some of Jones's scores in that period do not use toolkits demonstrates that the needs of the picture were paramount in his thinking when conceptualising the score.

He has engaged with pre-existing sources and collaborated with high-profile popular musicians including David Bowie, Sinéad O'Connor, Bono, Charlotte Church, Elvis Costello and Britney Spears to fulfil a film's dramatic aim. While the nature of these relationships has varied from project to project depending on the film or television programme's required musical style, Jones has demonstrated a constant and consistent ability to shape his compositional style and musical language to ensure that both original score and pre-existing materials are contained within a coherent musical soundscape. In the case of films that incorporate popular songs, Jones tends to embed their characteristic features in his original score. The dovetailing of score and songs in *Labyrinth* (1986) has already been discussed, and on projects such as *Brassed Off* (1996), *Titanic Town* and *Notting Hill* (1999), for which he was involved with the recording or production of the pre-existing music, aspects of instrumentation, style, form and structure are smoothly transferred from source to score.

In many cases Jones's allusions to pre-existing musical styles include subtle references to traditional folk tunes or styles. Elements of traditional music are evident in film and television scores ranging from *Joni Jones* and *One of Ourselves* (1983) through *Lawn Dogs* (1997) and *Merlin* to *Three and Out*, as well as the Irish-themed pictures already identified in this chapter and several of the South African productions discussed in Chapter 9. Notable examples of this practice are Jones's scores for *The Last of the Mohicans*, which features and also draws on the harmonic profile of Dougie MacLean's 1990 folk-style work 'The Gael', and *Brassed Off*, which evokes an English folk-music style by echoing the traditional song 'Scarborough Fair' in the original cues. This idea is taken further in *Fields of Freedom* (2006), for which Jones drew on traditional tunes more overtly associated with the opposing Unionist and Confederate sides of the American Civil War, superimposing the melodies in a manner that suggests the narrative conflict and introduces his original main theme. In a similar way, he sometimes references broader musical styles, such as the music of Holst and Elgar in *Richard III* (1995) and 'Taps' – a brass melody inextricably bound up with American military identity – in *GI Jane*, as he searches for the appropriate creative approach and sound for a given project.

The music team

Like many other composers of music for screen media, Jones appears to have developed multi-project working relationships with people taking key roles in his music team as shown in Figure 10.2. While there are some significant gaps in Figure 10.2 – perhaps most notably the lack of any credited orchestrators in the five years from *Runaway Train* to *By Dawn's Early Light* (1990) – it highlights the importance of continuity to Jones's working methods. Victoria Seale, Jones's wife, has taken on the role of music co-ordinator across the majority of his career to date, working on behalf of Jones's studio, Contemporary Music Media Productions (CMMP), and long-running relationships with the London Symphony Orchestra (20 projects), orchestrators Geoff Alexander and Julian Kershaw (23 and 22 projects, respectively), copyist Tony Stanton (19 projects) and recording engineers and mixers Simon Rhodes and Gareth Cousins (both 16 projects) have enabled the composer to establish efficient and reliable processes for score creation and production.

Despite this broad continuity, Jones has ensured that his team remains flexible enough to adapt to the demands of the changing industry and the opportunities afforded by technological developments, something illustrated by the addition of Sibelius editor Costas Fotopoulos on four projects in the 2000s and of synth programmers in the early 1990s. Between them Roger King, John Whynot and Kirsty Whalley took on the role of programmer for ten different projects between 1992 and 1997, and since the turn of the twenty-first century programming has usually been handled by one of Jones's assistants: first by future Academy Award-winning composer Steven Price and then by the current incumbent of the role, Neil Stemp.[4] These five programmers also attest to the fluidity of responsibilities within the team, since each of them has also worked for Jones in other capacities – King, Whynot, Whalley and Price as engineers and mixers, Price as a guitarist, and Stemp as a music editor.

While perhaps not technically part of the composer's team, close relationships with music editors have nonetheless been important to Jones's practice. In the late 1980s and early 1990s Jones wrote scores for projects on which both Dan Carlin Sr. and his son, Daniel Allan Carlin, were music editors, although a music editor does not always appear to have been employed for projects. Having worked with Jones in 1992 on *Freejack*, Alex Gibson returned to this role eight years later for *Thirteen Days* (2000), assisted by Jeremy Raub, leading to the only notable period of continuity in this area. This small music editing team completed three more Jones projects in the following years, with Raub adding another three without Gibson.

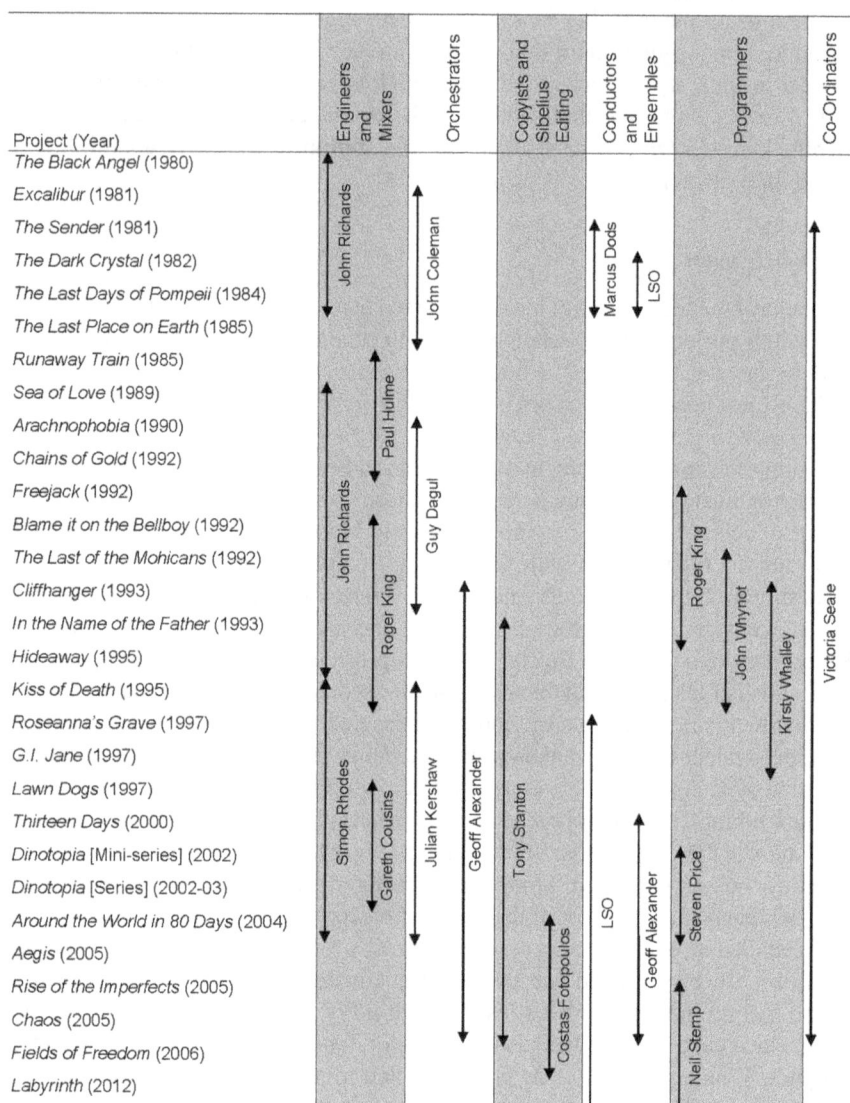

Figure 10.2 Main members of Jones's music team across multiple projects[5]

Jones has worked with several performing ensembles to record film scores including the English Chamber Orchestra (*The Sender*, 1982), London Philharmonic Orchestra (*In the Name of the Father*), The Academy of St Martin in the Fields (*From Hell*) and, of course, the Grimethorpe Colliery Band (*Brassed Off*), but by far the most commonly employed ensemble is the London Symphony Orchestra. The LSO recorded three of Jones's scores in the early 1980s including his first completely original professional score, *The Dark Crystal*, but he did not use the orchestra through the 'toolkit era' in the late 1980s and early 1990s, when his material was less symphonic in construction and sound. However, starting with *Roseanna's Grave* in 1997, the LSO has recorded the majority of his scores over the last twenty years, often with Geoff Alexander conducting, giving a consistency of sound and tone to Jones's output across this period.

Individual credited musicians on Jones's projects, several of whom have already been mentioned in this discussion, also bear testament to the quality of performers who have worked on his scores. Virtuoso guitarist John Williams performed the solos on *Dominick and Eugene* (1988), *The Object of Beauty* (1990), *Blame It on the Bellboy* (1992) and *CrissCross* (1992); Dave Arch, nowadays probably best-known as the conductor, arranger and musical director for the BBC television series *Strictly Come Dancing*, played piano on five occasions for Jones, including *Notting Hill*; international flautist Andy Findon demonstrated his expertise on fife and penny whistle as well as flute across *Loch Ness*, *I'll Be There* and *Three and Out*; and Courtney Pine and Catherine Bott provided saxophone and soprano voice solos, respectively, for *Angel Heart*. Highly respected and experienced session violinists Gavyn Wright and Mark Berrow receive individual credits for several projects, and specialist Phil Todd played solos on EWI, saxophone and flute on a number of scores across the 1990s.

It seems apparent that the employment of regular collaborators across key parts of his music team has enabled Jones to establish consistent working methods and practices, and he must have had a very high level of professional trust and confidence in long-term colleagues such as Rhodes, Cousins, Stanton, Alexander, Kershaw, the LSO and, of course, Victoria Seale. Figure 10.2 shows that in general as Jones's career has progressed transitions in personnel have occurred gradually and often with some degree of overlap, facilitating continuity of approach even as new members have joined the team and old members have left. It seems likely, given the length of some working relationships, that the engineers, orchestrators, performers and other role holders who worked on one or only a small number of projects were managed by their more established colleagues. Indeed, it may well have been people such as Rhodes and Alexander rather than Jones himself who selected these personnel,[6] and they would probably therefore have approached people who they believed would fit well into the team's working methods.

Technology

The utilisation of new audio technologies and the concomitant accommodation of an unprecedented level of technological change have been vital aspects of Jones's approach to film composition since his earliest scores. His career began at the tail end of the analogue era, when magnetic tape was still the primary medium for sound recording, and film for the picture. The domestic video format VHS became available in 1976, heralding a revolution in home entertainment but also providing a convenient medium for the film composer to work with in home studios. As with all things technological, Jones embraced developments in visual media, and the presence of Betacam, VHS and various types of Umatic tapes, in both PAL and NTSC formats, indicates that he must have maintained a broad array of playback devices in order to work with whatever materials were provided for him by film-makers.

While the analogue EMI VCS3 synthesiser, which was used to good effect in *The Black Angel* (1980), had been available since 1969 and could be found in electronic studios such as that of the University of York where Jones studied, the 1970s saw the development of the more powerful if expensive Synclavier (1977) and Fairlight (1979) digital synthesisers. Sequential Circuits' Prophet 5 (1978) offered five-note polyphony at a much lower cost and was adopted rapidly by pop musicians and film composers alike, including Jones. All three of these instruments are referenced directly in paperwork for some of Jones's earliest professional scores, indicating that he was acutely aware of the strengths of and opportunities for experimentation offered by each synthesiser and locating him at the cutting edge of the industry in his use of these digital tools from the very start of his career. As well as the Yamaha DX7 sixteen-voice polyphonic digital synthesiser (1983) and the Akai S1000 sampler, the following decade saw the introduction of the compact disc in 1982, the Apple Macintosh computer in 1984 and the digital audio tape in 1987. As the millennium approached, film studios gradually began the move towards the digital recording of picture and sound with a bewildering array of formats appearing and disappearing, some more quickly than others. This period of change is reflected by the physical holdings of the Trevor Jones Archive, which also bear testament to Jones's ability to work effectively with whatever type of audio-visual material was supplied or required by producers.

Although all of these, and many other, developments were undoubtedly significant for him, the creation of the sequencing programmes Notator (1988) and Cubase (1989) and of the music-notation program Sibelius (1993) would perhaps have the most substantial impact on Jones's day-to-day working methods. As noted in the introduction to this book, Jones and his music team tested Sibelius as it was developed, working with the Finn brothers to ensure it was both a useful and usable tool for film-score creation, and Jones's rapid adoption of these pieces of software moved him (and those working for him) from manuscript paper and pencil to a largely computer-mediated modus operandi while such a transition was still in its infancy. A further element in Jones's personal creative desktop was provided by the release in 1989 of ProTools, Avid's digital audio workstation.

In the course of his career digital technologies have come to dominate almost every aspect of the score-production process. As well as the obvious practical advantages they confer, such as the ability to produce rapidly a high-quality mock-up of the score, these tools have been beneficial to Jones in the realisation of his particular musical vision: one in which acoustic and electronic instruments can be combined in novel ways to produce a kind of hyper-orchestra with an expanded range of colour. At the same time, the toolkit approach he devised in the late 1980s demonstrates a concern for forms of sonic polyphony that extend beyond the conventional to an aesthetic more closely aligned to that of electro-acoustic music. That these characteristics are now more commonplace in film and television music may be seen, in part at least, as testament to the influence Jones has had on the profession.

Looking forward

Several of the more recent scores composed by Jones have been for productions created by and/or starring members of his family. He provided music for the short films *Run* (2009) and *Sitting Man* (2010), written and directed by his son Caspar Seale-Jones, whose debut feature film, *To Tokyo*, was scored by Jones in 2018. Interestingly Neil Stemp, Jones's assistant, is credited as composer of the music for *To Tokyo*'s teaser trailer (ToTokyoTheFilm 2013), the sound world for which not only reflects the Japanese setting but also hints strongly at Jones's own musical language (and presumably his actual score for the picture) through the incorporation of electronics and African vocal chants. *To Tokyo* stars Jones's daughter Emily Seale-Jones, who wrote and directed two other recent projects that he has scored – the short film *Husk* (2017) and the web series *Frankie and Emma* (2018). He also scored the short film *Phoenix* (2016), which was directed by Josh Trigg – who was editor and assistant director on *Frankie & Emma* – and stars Florence Kosky, who plays opposite Emily Seale-Jones in *To Tokyo*, and it seems clear that all of these projects have strong personal meaning for Jones. South Africa also retains a significant place in Jones's life, with his new theme tune and closing credit music for the soap opera *Generations* (2013) – created by Mfundi Vundla, father of Charlie Vundla, the director of *How to Steal 2 Million* (2011) – the latest scoring project he has undertaken in the country. Given how recently these projects were completed there is no material for any of them in the Trevor Jones Archive at present beyond stereo mixes for *Run* and *Sitting Man*, but the collection is dynamic, and discussions are ongoing with Jones with regard to adding new scores to the holdings and keeping the archive as complete as it can be, bearing in mind that he is still an active composer for the screen.

The professional career and output of Trevor Jones

This large-scale study of the screen music of Trevor Jones aimed to use archival materials to explore four key questions regarding his career and output – concerning the development of his career and working practices, the relationship of processes and archival materials, the impact of technology, and the wider application of the study within and beyond the British screen-music industry – all of which are addressed in this book. The exploration of his near-forty-year career has enabled consideration of the ways in which Jones has developed and adapted his approach to the creation and production of screen music within the context of broader practices and changes in the British and global screen and screen-music industries, and has established beyond doubt his position as a technological innovator in the field (cf. Williams 2016).

Close interrogation of the archival materials of screen-music production relating to a large number of his scoring projects has facilitated detailed investigation of the creative and interpretative processes by which Jones and other members of the production team conceived, composed and realised specific scores. As has been emphasised numerous times across this volume, the additional information and context beyond a manuscript score that is afforded by the use of a collection such as the Trevor Jones Archive enriches substantially the degree to which matters of process can be understood, and enables greater engagement with and appreciation for the screen music created through these processes. In a similar way, the scope and depth of the archive has permitted what is effectively a longitudinal study of the ways that technological changes have affected Jones's scoring practices and impacted the various archival sources and their interactions. By approaching his career chronologically (for the most part), this study has traced the close relationship between Jones's working methods and the available technologies and shown how this bond is manifest in the archival materials created in the course of producing each score. As observed in the introduction to this book, including consideration of a large number of Jones's scores was intended to mitigate any sense of prioritisation or canonisation within his output, and although some projects have received much more detailed attention than others, this should not be taken to show a hierarchy or to indicate the relative importance or merit of individual scores.

This study has placed Jones at the forefront of the profession and in doing so identifies him as an exemplar of the industry both in Britain and, through the broad geographic spread of the projects that he has scored, beyond the UK. No two composers are the same, and each doubtless crafts an individual approach to the creative and interpretative practices of screen composition, and engages with technologies as their (and their team's) skillset permits. However, Jones's film and television work across a wide range of genres, and his ability to constantly reinvent himself while retaining the essence of his signature sound, suggest that the specific findings of this case study may indeed have broader applicability within and beyond the UK industry. This relates closely to the first of two specific impacts intended to arise from this investigation of Jones: to demonstrate the ways in which the study of music for the screen can be enriched and extended by the critical and methodological tools derived from the use of archival materials. Indeed, just as it is hoped that the findings of this investigation may be applied beyond the case study of Jones, so too the methodology and processes utilised in the analysis and discussion of his scores may be transplanted for use in the study of other composers and works, and, in adapted form, other areas of the creative arts.

Lastly, the repository framework developed for and employed in this project for the secure storage and retrieval of the digital and digitised archival materials, and the metadata schema that underpins the searchable database behind the ScreenMusic website, may have application and value for both scholars and practitioners of screen music. The schema, which was designed through the analysis of the archival materials across the research project, is the first of its kind and may be of significant use to those studying and curating other audio-visual collections. The combination of the schema, website and repository supports access to metadata without compromising the security of the archival sources and serves as a model for similar collections of screen-music materials, and those in related areas of the creative and visual arts. These structures could be utilised effectively by those working in the screen and screen-music industries for the archiving of projects, enabling studios, producers, composers and other personnel to access materials from past projects easily and efficiently. Such a development might assist the process of creating a spin-off television series or video game from a feature film (or vice versa), the revival or creation of a new series of a television programme, or the gathering of footage or music to be interpolated in a new screen production, saving time and money, perhaps the two most valuable commodities in the industry.

A case in point is the re-release of *The Black Angel* in 2015, thirty-five years after it was first screened, following the discovery of the original negative in the Universal Studios archive in December 2011 (Mattise 2012). Jones was able to access the session recordings from 1980 in the Trevor Jones Archive, with the metadata helping to identify the nature and content of each audio file. Looking forward, the teaser trailer for the forthcoming Netflix series, *The Dark Crystal: Age of Resistance* (2018) – which will be a prequel to the 1982 film – shows many of the puppets being created and is accompanied throughout by extracts from Jones's original score for *The Dark Crystal*.[7] While it is currently unclear what role (if any) his music will play in the series – his main theme might be used for the opening title sequence but this is still under discussion – the captured metadata relating to the vast amount of audio material in the archive for this film score is helping Jones and Stemp to understand what recordings exist and might be suitable for reuse or remastering. These examples demonstrate the rich and otherwise potentially unrecoverable metadata and materials that may be saved using the schema and repository, offering professionals and organisations the ability to capture information relating to facets of creative projects like the screen-music scores of Trevor Jones: technology, process and product.

Notes

1 In basic terms, Neo-Riemannian theory relates chords that share two pitches, and identifies transformations between chords. Frank Lehman outlines the four transformations used here – parallel (P), leading tone (L), relative (R) and slide (S) – in detail in his article advocating this analytical approach to film music (2014).
2 This property places A minor in the Weitzmann Region based on the pitches of an Ab augmented triad, making them closely related (Cohn 2012, p. 57).
3 Jones was an altar boy and then a church organist and was brought up in what he describes as 'a very high English church' (Jones 2007).
4 Price won for *Gravity* in 2014. He recalls that when he worked for Jones he 'started off as the tea boy and then by the end of it I would do the programming by the side of him as he wrote' (Price 2016).
5 This data has been drawn from a combination of the IMDB listings for Jones's projects and references on the archival materials.
6 Supervising orchestrators will usually take responsibility for engaging the rest of an orchestration team (cf. Sapiro 2016, pp. 158–161).
7 The teaser trailer is online at Netflix (2017).

Trevor Jones's filmography

The following list includes all projects for which Jones composed music with the exception of 'making of' documentaries that used Jones's music from the main project and did not involve any additional composition. Projects are listed in chronological order by date of theatrical release or first television broadcast, whichever is sooner, and all projects are feature films unless otherwise stated. The list is subdivided according to the broad structure of this book for ease of reference, although it should be borne in mind that a large number of Jones's television scores are considered in Chapter 7 and the video-game scores are the focus of Chapter 8 and not all projects are discussed in this book. Where relevant, the list contains three further pieces of information alongside the filmographic details:

- If Jones is credited with a role in addition to composition, or with the composition of a specific musical element, this is shown in parenthesis at the end of an entry.
- A project title is preceded by an asterisk if Jones's score was rejected. Although asterisked in this list owing to Jones's material not appearing in the picture, *I, Robot* is an exception since Jones started work on the score then withdrew from the project owing to a scheduling clash with *Around the World in 80 Days*.
- When the Trevor Jones Archive contains no materials or only stereo mixes for a project, the entry is enclosed in curly brackets.

Chapter 1: Musical education and the National Film School

The Night of the Captain. 1979. [Student Film]. Luis Mora del Solar.
Brittania: The First of the Last. 1979. [Documentary short]. John Samson.
The Beneficiary. 1979. [Student Film]. Carlo Gebler.
Smile Until I Tell You to Stop. 1979. [Student Film]. Stephen Bayly.
'Golden Gordon'. 1979. [Television Series Episode]. Season 2 Episode 2 of *Ripping Yarns*. Alan J.W. Bell. Composed by David Howman, André Jacquemin and Trevor Jones (Also arranger: incidental music, and conductor).
The Stranger. 1980. [Student Film]. Ian Knox.
The Black Angel. 1980. [Short]. Roger Christian.

Brothers and Sisters. 1980. Richard Woolley (Also conductor).
A Stolen Portrait. 1981. [Student Film]. Brian Ward.
The Dollar Bottom. [Short]. 1981. Roger Christian (Also musical director).

Chapter 2: Breaking into the industry

Excalibur. 1981. John Boorman (Also conductor: original music).
The Appointment. 1981. Lindsey C. Vickers (Also conductor).
The Sender. 1982. Roger Christian.
Joni Jones. 1982. [Television Mini-Series]. Stephen Bayly.
The Dark Crystal. 1982. Jim Henson and Frank Oz (Also synthesised electronic sounds).
Those Glory, Glory Days. 1983. [Telefilm]. Philip Saville.
Savage Islands (also known as *Nate and Hayes*). 1983. Ferdinand Fairfax.
One of Ourselves. 1983. [Telefilm]. Pat O'Connor.
Aderyn Papur . . . and Pigs Might Fly. 1984. [Telefilm]. Stephen Bayly.
The Last Days of Pompeii. 1984. [Television Mini-Series]. Peter R. Hunt.
This Office Life. 1984. [Telefilm]. Ian Keill.
The Last Place on Earth. 1985. [Television Mini-Series]. Ferdinand Fairfax (Also conductor).
{*From an Immigrant's Notebook*. 1985. [Television Documentary Series Episode]. Part of *Arena*. Laura Hastings-Smith.}
Dr Fischer of Geneva. 1985. [Telefilm]. Michael Lindsay-Hogg.
Runaway Train. 1985. Andrey Konchalovskiy (Also conductor).
Labyrinth. 1986. Jim Henson.

Chapter 3: Alan Parker and the development of the toolkit

Angel Heart. 1987. Alan Parker.
Just Ask for Diamond. 1988. Stephen Bayly.
Sweet Lies. 1988. Nathalie Delon.
Dominick and Eugene. 1988. Robert M. Young (Also conductor).
Coppers. 1988. [Telefilm]. Ted Clisby.
The Lone Rider Rides Again. 1988. Unknown.
Mississippi Burning. 1988. Alan Parker.

Chapter 4: Towards a mainstream sound

A Private Life. 1989. [Television Series Episode]. Part of *Screen Two*. Francis Gerard (Also music arranger).
Murder on the Moon (also known as *Murder by Moonlight*). 1989. [Telefilm]. Michael Lindsay-Hogg.
Sea of Love. 1989. Harold Becker.
A Clydeside Carol. 1989. [Short Telefilm]. Kees Ryninks.
Bad Influence. 1990. Curtis Hanson.
By Dawn's Early Light. 1990. [Telefilm]. Jack Sholder.

{*Guns: A Day in the Death of America.* 1990. [Television documentary]. Malcolm Clarke and Lorenz Knauer.}
Arachnophobia. 1990. Frank Marshall.
* *The Object of Beauty.* 1991. Michael Lindsay-Hogg.
True Colors. 1991. Herbert Ross.
Chains of Gold. 1991. Rod Holcomb.
Freejack. 1992. Geoff Murphy.
Blame It on the Bellboy. 1992. Mark Herman (Also orchestrator and performer: synthesiser).
CrissCross. 1992. Chris Benges (Also orchestrator, conductor and performer: synthesiser).
The Last of the Mohicans. 1992. Michael Mann.
* *Barbarians at the Gate.* 1993. Glenn Jordan.
Detonator. 1993. [Telefilm]. David Jackson.
Cliffhanger. 1993. Renny Harlin (Also orchestrator).
In the Name of the Father. 1993. Jim Sheridan (Also orchestrator and performer: synthesiser).
{*De baby huilt.* 1994. [Short]. Mijke de Jong.}
Hideaway. 1995. Brett Leonard (Also conductor).
Kiss of Death. 1995. Barbet Schroeder (Also orchestrator and conductor).

Chapter 5: Hollywood blockbusters part one

Richard III. 1995. Richard Loncraine.
Gulliver's Travels. 1996. [Television Mini-Series]. Charles Sturridge.
Loch Ness. 1996. John Henderson (Also orchestrator).
Brassed Off. 1996. Mark Herman (Also orchestrator, conductor and music producer: brass band).
Roseanna's Grave. 1997. Paul Weiland (Also orchestrator and music arranger: songs).
GI Jane. 1997. Ridley Scott (Also orchestrator).
Lawn Dogs. 1997. John Duigan (Also orchestrator).
Desperate Measures. 1998. Barbet Schroeder (Also orchestrator).
Dark City. 1998. Alex Proyas (Also orchestrator and performer: synthesiser).
Merlin. 1998. [Television Mini-Series]. Steve Barron (Also orchestrator).
The Mighty. 1998. Peter Chelsom (Also orchestrator and performer: synthesiser).
Titanic Town. 1998. Roger Michell (Also music producer).
Talk of Angels. 1998. Nick Hamm.
Notting Hill. 1999. Roger Michell (Also orchestrator and performer: synthesiser).

Chapter 6: Hollywood blockbusters part two

Cleopatra. 1999. [Television Mini-Series]. Franc Roddam (Also orchestrator and performer: synthesiser).

Molly. 1999. John Duigan.
Thirteen Days. 2000. Roger Donaldson (Also orchestrator and performer: synthesiser).
The Long Run. 2001. Jean Stewart.
From Hell. 2001. Albert Hughes and Allen Hughes (Also orchestrator and performer: synthesiser).
Crossroads (also known as *Scrabble with Nutmeg*, and *What Are Friends For*). 2002. Tamra Davis (Also orchestrator).
* *The Gathering Storm*. 2002. Richard Loncraine.
Dinotopia. 2002. [Television Mini-Series]. Marco Brambilla.
Dinotopia. 2002–3. [Television Series]. Various.
I'll Be There. 2003. Craig Ferguson (Also orchestrator and performer: synthesiser).
The League of Extraordinary Gentlemen. 2003. Stephen Norrington (Also orchestrator).
* *I, Robot*. 2004. Alex Proyas.
Around the World in 80 Days. 2004. Frank Coraci (Also orchestrator and performer: synthesiser).
The Unsteady Chough. 2004. [Short]. Sam Leifer and Jonathan van Tulleken.

Chapter 9: Work in diverse areas of screen programming

Aegis. 2005. Junji Sakamoto.
Marvel Nemesis: Rise of the Imperfects. 2005. [Video Game].
Chaos. 2005. Tony Giglio (Also orchestrator and performer: synthesiser).
Fields of Freedom. 2005–6. David de Vries.
We Fight to Be Free. 2006. [Short]. Kees Van Oostrum.
* *Alex Rider: Operation Stormbreaker*. 2006. Geoffrey Sax.
Jozi-H. 2006–7. [Television Series]. Thabang Meleya.
Zelda Ruin. 2007. [Video Game].
Three and Out (also known as *A Deal's a Deal*). 2008. Jonathan Gershfield.
{*Run*. 2009. [Short]. Caspar Seale-Jones.}
Blood and Oil. 2010. [Telefilm]. David Attwood.
{*Sitting Man*. 2010. [Short]. Caspar Seale-Jones.}
My Hunter's Heart. 2010. [Documentary Film]. Craig Foster and Damon Foster.
War Paint. 2011. [Short]. Marcus Liberski.
How to Steal 2 Million. 2011. Charlie Vundla.

Conclusions

Labyrinth. 2012. [Television Mini-Series]. Christopher Smith (Also orchestrator).
{*Generations*. 2013. [TV Series – new title and end credit music]. Created by Mfundi Vundla.}

{*Phoenix*. 2016. [Short]. Josh Trigg.}
{*Husk*. 2017. [Short]. Emily Seale-Jones.}
{*Frankie & Emma*. 2018. [Webseries]. Emily Seale-Jones.}
{*To Tokyo*. 2018. Caspar Seale-Jones.}

Jones has also written music for advertising; recent work in this area includes *KFC* in South Africa (2014) and the launch of the Coca-Cola Company-made sports drink Aquarius in Spain (2014). These projects are not contained in the archive, although the holdings do include recordings for some of Jones's older music for commercials.

Bibliography

Abarder, G. 2016. Trevor's Life Is an Original Soundtrack. *IOL*. 20 May. [Accessed 3 December 2018]. Available from: www.iol.co.za/capeargus/trevors-life-is-an-original-soundtrack-2024239

Anderson, L. 2018. Sounding an Irish Childhood: John Williams's Score for *Angela's Ashes*. In: Audissino, E. ed. *John Williams: Music for Films, Television and the Concert Stage*. Turnhout: Brepols, pp. 277–292.

Anon. 2005. Review of Marvel Nemesis: Rise of the Imperfects. *Official Playstation II Magazine UK*. December. [Accessed 3 December 2018]. Available from: www.metacritic.com/game/playstation-2/marvel-nemesis-rise-of-the-imperfects/critic-reviews

Associated Press. 2002a. Prime Time Nielsen Ratings. *Entertainment News*. 14 May. Available from: Nexis.com.

Associated Press. 2002b. Prime Time Nielsen Ratings. *Entertainment News*. 21 May. Available from: Nexis.com.

Audissino, E. 2014. *John Williams's Film Music: 'Jaws', 'Star Wars', 'Raiders of the Lost Ark' and the Return of the Classical Hollywood Musical Style*. Madison: University of Wisconsin Press.

Bacon, M. 1997. *No Strings Attached: The Inside Story of Jim Henson's Creature Shop*. London: MacMillan Publishing Company.

Barham, J. 2017. Birth and Death of Cool: The Glorious Afflictions of Jazz on Screen. In: Sadoff, R., Mera, M. and Winters, B. eds. *The Routledge Companion to Screen Music and Sound*. New York: Routledge, pp. 375–387.

Barron, L. and Inglis, I. 2009. Scary Movies, Scary Music: Uses and Unities of Heavy Metal in the Contemporary Horror Film. In: Hayward, P. ed. *Terror Tracks: Music, Sound and Horror Cinema*. London: Equinox Publishing Limited, pp. 186–197.

Barron, S. 1999. A Conversation with Steve Barron. In: *'Merlin': Shooting Script*. New York: Newmarket Press.

BBC. [no date]. Lle aeth Pawb?: 'Joni Jones'. *BBC*. [Accessed 3 December 2018]. Available from: www.bbc.co.uk/programmes/p02z166y

BBC. 1991. A Private Life. *BBC*. [Accessed 3 December 2018]. Available from: www.bbc.co.uk/programmes/p032kjgd

Benitez, S. 2004a. Two Days with Trevor Jones at the Phone (First Day). *BSO Spirit*. [Accessed 3 December 2018]. Available from: www.bsospirit.com/entrevistas/tjones_e.php

Benitez, S. 2004b. Two Days with Trevor Jones at the Phone (Second Day). *BSO Spirit*. [Accessed 3 December 2018]. Available from: www.bsospirit.com/entrevistas/tjones2_e.php

Blame It on the Bellboy. 1992. [DVD] Mark Herman. dir. USA: Walt Disney Studios.

Boggan, J. 2014. Rejected Film and TV Scores. *Rejected Film Scores*. [Accessed 3 December 2018]. Available from: http://archive.is/hdOFA

Botha, M. 2014. Speaking with Earth and Sky: Oral Storytelling in the Cinema of Craig and Damon Foster. *Rebeca: Revista Brasiliera de Estudos de Cinema e Audiovisual*. 3(5), pp. 17–44.

Box Office Mojo. 2017a. *The League of Extraordinary Gentlemen*. [Accessed 3 December 2018]. Available from: www.boxofficemojo.com/movies/?id=leagueofextraordinarygentlemen.htm

Box Office Mojo. 2017b. *Thirteen Days*. [Accessed 3 December 2018]. Available from: www.boxofficemojo.com/movies/?id=thirteendays.htm

Brown, J. 2009. Music in Film and Television. In: Harper-Scott, J.P.E. and Samson, J. eds. *An Introduction to Music Studies*. Cambridge: Cambridge University Press, pp. 201–214.

Brown, R.S. 1994. *Overtones and Undertones: Reading Film Music*. Berkeley: University of California Press.

Broxton, J. 2003. The League of Extraordinary Gentlemen; Trevor Jones. *Movie Music UK*. 11 July. [Accessed 3 December 2018]. Available from: https://moviemusicuk.us/2003/07/11/the-league-of-extraordinary-gentlemen-trevor-jones/#more-4091

Buhler, J., Kassabian, A., Neumeyer, D., Stilwell, R., Barnett, K., Bowman, S.L. and BoaVentura, A. 2003. Panel Discussion on Film Sound/Film Music: Jim Buhler, Anahid Kassabian, David Neumeyer, and Robynn Stilwell. *The Velvet Light Trap*. 51, pp. 73–91. Available from: *Project MUSE*. DOI:10.1353/vlt.2003.0003.

Byrne, C. 2008. Train Drivers Protest at Premiere of Film 'That Trivialises Railway Deaths'. *Independent*. 22 April. [Accessed 3 December 2018]. Available from: www.independent.co.uk/arts-entertainment/films/news/train-drivers-protest-at-premiere-of-film-that-trivialises-railway-deaths-813327.html

Campaign. 2011. *The History of Advertising 14: Cadbury's 'Coronation Street' Idents*. 13 May. [Accessed 3 December 2018]. Available from: www.campaignlive.co.uk/article/historyu-advertising-14-cadburys-coronation-street-idents/1069743

Carte Blanche. 2014. Interview with Trevor Jones. *YouTube*. [Accessed 3 December 2018]. Available from: www.youtube.com/watch?v=ufk2V2HOAIA

Chains of Gold. 1991. [DVD] Rod Holcomb. dir. USA: MGM.

Chetty, K. 2011. My Hunter's Heart. *Mahala*. 6 July. [Accessed 3 December 2018]. Available from: www.mahala.co.za/movies/my-hunter's-heart/

Ciment, M. 1986. *John Boorman*. Adair, G. (trans.). London and Boston: Faber and Faber Ltd.

Cohn, R. 2012. *Audacious Euphony: Chromatic Harmony and the Triad's Second Nature*. New York: Oxford University Press.

Collins, K. 2008. *Game Sound: An Introduction to the History, Theory, and Practice of Video Game Music and Sound Design*. Cambridge, MA: MIT Press.

Cooper, D. 2001. *Bernard Herrmann's 'Vertigo': A Film Score Handbook*. Westport, CT: Greenwood Press.

Cooper, D. 2009. Trevor Jones's Score for In the Name of the Father. In: Scott, D. ed. *The Ashgate Research Companion to Popular Musicology*. Ashgate Research Companion. Aldershot: Ashgate, pp. 25–42.

Cooper, D. and Sapiro, I. 2011. A Source-Studies Approach to Michael Nyman's Score for *The Draughtsman's Contract*. *Journal of Film Music*. 3(2), pp. 155–170.

Cooper, D., Sapiro, I., Anderson, L. and Hall, S. 2016. Digitizing, Organizing and Managing an Audio-Visual Archive: The Trevor Jones Archive at the University of Leeds. *Journal of Film Music*. 6(2), pp. 101–110.

Curtin, M. and Shattuc, J. 2009. *The American Television Industry*. London: Palgrave Macmillan.

Daubney, K. 2000. *'Now, Voyager': A Film Score Guide*. Westport, CT: Greenwood Press.

Davison, A. 2013. Title Sequences in Contemporary Television Serials. In: Richardson, J., Gorbman, C. and Vernallis, C. eds. *The Oxford Handbook of New Audiovisual Aesthetics*. New York: Oxford University Press, pp. 146–167.

Dear, P. and Davalle, P. 1984. Television Listings for 29 December. *The Times*. [Online]. 29 December. [Accessed 3 December 2018]. Available from: The Times Digital Archive.

Dobbins, B. 2013. Dark City Review. *Soundtrack Universe*. 8 June. [Accessed 3 December 2018]. Available from: https://soundtrack-universe.blogspot.com/2013/06/dark-city-review.html

Donnelly, K.J. 2001. *Film Music: Critical Approaches*. Edinburgh: Edinburgh University Press.

Donnelly, K.J. 2005. *The Spectre of Sound: Music in Film and Television*. London: BFI.

Ebert, R. 2001. From Hell. *RogerEbert.com*. 19 October. [Accessed 3 December 2018]. Available from: www.rogerebert.com/reviews/from-hell-2001

Ebert, R. 2003. The League of Extraordinary Gentlemen. *RogerEbert.com*. 11 July. [Accessed 3 December 2018]. Available from: www.rogerebert.com/reviews/the-league-of-extraordinary-gentlemen-2003

Ebert, R. 2004. Around the World in 80 Days. *RogerEbert.com*. 16 June. [Accessed 3 December 2018]. Available from: www.rogerebert.com/reviews/around-the-world-in-80-days-2004

Erickson, H. 2017. The Last Days of Pompeii. *All Movie*. [Accessed 3 December 2018]. Available from: www.allmovie.com/movie/the-last-days-of-pompeii-v126910

Filmtracks. 2011. Around the World in 80 Days. *Filmtracks*. 7 October. [Accessed 3 December 2018]. Available from: www.filmtracks.com/titles/around_world.html

Foster, D. and Foster, C. 2013. Directors' Statement. *My Hunter's Heart*. [Accessed 3 December 2018]. Available from: www.myhuntersheartmovie.com/production/directors-statement.html

Fox, C. and Cooper, D. 2008. 11th Bradford Film Festival, Film & Music Conference, 2005: Keynote Interview with Trevor Jones. In: Cooper, D., Fox, C. and Sapiro, I. eds. *Cinemusic? Constructing the Film Score*. Newcastle-upon-Tyne: Cambridge Scholars Publishing, pp. 1–14.

Frankie and Emma. 2018. Frankie and Emma. *Facebook*. 30 January. [Accessed 3 December 2018]. Available from: www.facebook.com/Frankie-and-Emma-736722666455564/

Fritz, B. 2004. Marvel, EA Tag Team for Fighting Games. *Variety*. [Online]. 5 February 2004. [Accessed 3 December 2018]. Available from: http://variety.com/2004/biz/news/marvel-ea-tag-team-for-fighting-games-1117899621/

Fülöp, R. 2017. Music, Whiteness, and Masculinity in Michael Mann's *The Last of the Mohicans*. In: Sadoff, R., Mera, M. and Winters, B. eds. *The Routledge Companion to Screen Music and Sound*. New York: Routledge, pp. 463–476.

Giampietro, M. 2014. *Excalibur*: Death, Love and Rebirth in an Original Score. *Music and Audio-Visual Media Conference*. 4–6 September. University of Leeds.

Goldwasser, D. 2001. Interview. *Soundtrack.net*. 23 October. [Accessed 2 December 2018]. Available from: www.soundtrack.net/content/article/?id=87

Goljan, L. 2003. The Return of the Temp Score Extravaganza: Part 3/4. *Film Score Monthly*. 25 November. [Accessed 3 December 2018]. Available from: www.filmscoremonthly.com/articles/2003/26_Nov---Temp_Score_Extravaganza_3.asp

Gorbman, C. 2007. Auteur Music. In: Goldmark, D. and Kramer, L. eds. *Beyond the Soundtrack: Representing Music in Cinema*. Berkeley: University of California Press, pp. 149–162.

Greene, G. 1980. *Doctor Fischer of Geneva or The Bomb Party*. London: The Bodley Head.

Gurney, J. 1992. *Dinotopia: A Land Apart from Time*. Nashville: Turner Publishing Inc.

Hall, J. 2009. *CD Review: Runaway Train. ScreenSounds.* 20 August. [Accessed 3 December 2018]. Available from: http://screensounds.blogspot.co.uk/2009/08/cd-review-runaway-train-runaway-train.html

Hall, S. 2017. *The Television Music of Trevor Jones: Using an Audio-Visual Archive to Explore Scoring Processes.* Ph.D thesis, University of Leeds.

Halmi Sr., R. 1999. Foreword. In: *'Merlin': Shooting Script.* New York: Newmarket Press.

Harris, D. 2018. Revisit: *The Last of the Mohicans*: Original Motion Picture Soundtrack. *Spectrum Culture.* 26 February. [Accessed 3 December 2018]. Available from: https://spectrumculture.com/2018/02/26/revisit-last-mohicans-original-motion-picture-soundtrack/

Heldt, G. 2012. '. . . There's No Music Playing, and It's Not Snowing': Songs and Self-Reflexivity in Curtisland. *Music, Sound and the Moving Image.* 6(1), pp. 73–91.

Henson, J. 2010. Trevor Jones and the First Fully Local Soundtrack. *The Capetown Magazine.* [Accessed 3 December 2018]. Available from: www.capetownmagazine.com/interviews/trevor-jones-and-the-first-fully-local-soundtrack/146_22_17417

Herbert Kretzmer. 2013. History. *Herbert Kretzmer Lyricist.* [Accessed 3 December 2018]. Available from: www.herbertkretzmer.com/history.html

Hexel, V. 2016. *Hans Zimmer and James Newton Howard's 'The Dark Knight': A Film Score Guide.* Lanham, MD: Scarecrow Press.

Hinton, H. 1992. Blame It on the Bellboy. *Washington Post.* 6 March. [Accessed 3 December 2018]. Available from: www.washingtonpost.com/wp-srv/style/longterm/movies/videos/blameitonthebellboypg13hinson_a0a750.htm

Holden, S. 2004. Film Review; Jackie Chan Dives in to Rough Up Jules Verne. *The New York Times.* 16 June. [Accessed 3 December 2018]. Available from: www.nytimes.com/2004/06/16/movies/film-review-jackie-chan-dives-in-to-rough-up-jules-verne.html

Hubai, G. 2012. *Torn Music: Rejected Film Scores: A Selected History.* Los Angeles: Silman James Press.

Hubbert, J. 2013. The Compilation Score from the 1960s to the Present. In: Neumeyer, D. ed. *The Oxford Handbook of Film Music Studies.* New York: Oxford University Press, pp. 291–318.

IMDb.com. 2017a. Box Office/Business for *The League of Extraordinary Gentlemen. IMDb.* [Accessed 3 December 2018]. Available from: www.imdb.com/title/tt0311429/business?ref_=tt_dt_bus

IMDb.com. 2017b. *Joni Jones:* Full Cast and Crew. *IMDb.* [Accessed 3 December 2018]. Available from: www.imdb.com/title/tt0130404/fullcredits?ref_=tt_ov_st_sm

IMDb.com. 2017c. Murder on the Moon. *IMDb.* [Accessed 3 December 2018]. Available from: www.imdb.com/title/tt0097931/?ref_=nm_flmg_com_62

IMDb.com. 2017d. *Star Trek* (TV Series 1966–1969): Full Cast and Crew. *IMDb.* [Accessed 3 December 2018]. Available from: www.imdb.com/title/tt0060028/fullcredits?ref_=tt_ov_st_sm

Jagernauth, K. 2010. Christopher Nolan Talks More *Inception*, Says Film Is in the Same Ballpark as the Matrix & Dark City. *The Playlist.* 5 April. [Accessed 3 December 2018]. Available from: https://theplaylist.net/christopher-nolan-talks-more-inception-20100405/

Jensen, E. 2002. A Tall Order for ABC's *Dinotopia. Los Angeles Times.* 10 May. [Accessed 24 September 2017]. Available from: http://articles.latimes.com/2002/may/10/entertainment/et-jensen10

Jones, M. 2014. 'The Truth about Captain Scott': *The Last Place on Earth*, Debunking, Sexuality and Decline in the 1980s. *The Journal of Imperial and Commonwealth History.* 42(5), pp. 857–881.

Jones, R.G. 1966. *Gwared y Gwirion*. Llandysul: J.D. Lewis.
Jones, T. 2006. Trevor Jones Talk about *Dinotopia* Music. *YouTube*. 23 August. [Accessed 3 December 2018]. Available from: www.youtube.com/watch?v=CQQ8tSGIMbg
Kaplan, D. 2000. *Dinotopia* Busts Monster Budget: $70M Mini-Series Makes Others Look Prehistoric. *New York Post*. 1 June. [Accessed 3 December 2018]. Available from: https://nypost.com/2000/06/01/dinotopia-busts-monster-budget-70m-miniseries-makes-others-look-prehistoric/
Karlin, F. and Wright, R. 2004. *On the Track: A Guide to Contemporary Film Scoring*. 2nd edition. New York: Routledge.
Kohler, C. 2008. EA, Marvel Cancel Fighting Game. *Wired*. 28 January. [Accessed 3 December 2018]. Available from: www.wired.com/2008/01/ea-marvel-cance/
Larson, R. 1986/1987. An Interview with Trevor Jones. *CinemaScore*. 15. [Accessed 26 July 2014]. Available from: www.runmovies.eu/?p=25
Lehman, F. 2014. Film Music and Neo-Riemannian Theory. *Oxford Handbooks Online*. [Accessed 3 December 2018]. Available from: www.oxfordhandbooks.com/view/10.1093/oxfordhb/9780199935321.001.0001/oxfordhb-9780199935321-e-002
Lotz, A. 2007. *The Television Will Be Revolutionized*. New York: New York University Press.
Mattise, N. 2012. The Sword and Sorcery Precursor to *Empire Strikes Back*. *Wired*. 28 December. [Accessed 3 December 2018]. Available from: www.wired.com/2012/12/20-12-pl_blackangel/
Melcher, S. 2001. MohicanLand Musical Musings: The Music of *The Last of the Mohicans*. *Mohican Press*. [Accessed 3 December 2018]. Available from: www.mohicanpress.com/mo11126.html
Mera, M. 2007. *Mychael Danna's 'The Ice Storm': A Film Score Guide*. Lanham, MD: Scarecrow Press.
Mera, M. and Winters, B. 2009. Film and Television Music Sources in the UK and Ireland: A Scoping Study. *Brio*. 46(2), pp. 37–65.
Mitchell, E. 2001. Film Review: A Conspiracy Shrouded in London Fog. *The New York Times*. 19 October. [Accessed 3 December 2018]. Available from: www.nytimes.com/2001/10/19/movies/film-review-a-conspiracy-shrouded-in-london-fog.html
Mitchell, E. 2003. Film Review: Loner's League to Foil Villainy. *The New York Times*. 11 July. [Accessed 3 December 2018]. Available from: www.nytimes.com/2003/07/11/movies/film-review-loners-league-to-foil-villainy.html
My Hunter's Heart Movie. 2013. Synopsis. *My Hunter's Heart*. [Accessed 3 December 2018]. Available from: www.myhuntersheartmovie.com/production/synopsis.html
Nelson, M. 2001. *Thirteen Days* Doesn't Add Up. *Chronicle of Higher Education*. 2 February. [Accessed 3 December 2018]. Available from: http://historymatters.gmu.edu/d/5428
Netflix. 2017. *The Dark Crystal: Age of Resistance* Teaser [HD]. *YouTube*. 18 May. [Accessed 3 December 2018]. Available from: www.youtube.com/watch?v=OGzVYyV_Jsg
Onishi, N. 2005. For a Hungry Audience, a Japanese Tom Clancy. *New York Times*. 9 July. [Accessed 3 December 2018]. Available from: www.nytimes.com/2005/07/09/world/asia/for-a-hungry-audience-a-japanese-tom-clancy.html?_r=0
Parker, A. 1987. Cover Notes. *Angel Heart*. [LP]. [Accessed 3 December 2018]. Available from: www.cdandlp.com/en/courtney-pine/angel-heart-original-motion-picture-soundtrack/lp/r3083168042/
Pilkington, E. 2008. 40 Years after King's Death, Jackson Hails First Steps Into Promised Land. *The Guardian*. 3 April. [Accessed 3 December 2018]. Available from: www.theguardian.com/world/2008/apr/03/usa.race

Pool, J. and Wright, H.S. 2011. *A Research Guide to Film and Television Music in the United States*. Lanham, MD: Scarecrow Press.

Prochnau, W. 1983. *Trinity Child*. New York: Putnam Publishing Group.

Rootsweb. 2006–7. [Accessed 24 March 2017]. Available from: http://archiver.rootsweb.ancestry.com/th/read/CoTyroneIreland/2006-07/1153596619

Rotten Tomatoes. 2017. *Freejack. Rotten Tomatoes*. [Accessed 3 December 2018]. Available from: www.rottentomatoes.com/m/freejack

Salzman, S. 2015. *Music Editing for Film and Television: The Art and the Process*. New York and London: Focal Press.

Sapiro, I. 2012. The Filmmaker's Contract: Controlling Sonic Space in the Films of Peter Greenaway. In: Wierzbicki, J. ed. *Music, Sound and Filmmakers: Sonic Style in Cinema*. New York: Routledge, pp. 151–164.

Sapiro, I. 2013. *Ilan Eshkeri's 'Stardust': A Film Score Guide*. Lanham, MD: Scarecrow Press.

Sapiro, I. 2016. *Scoring the Score: The Role of the Orchestrator in the Contemporary Film Industry*. New York: Routledge.

Scheurer, T.E. 1997. John Williams and Film Music since 1971. *Popular Music & Society*. 21(1), pp. 59–72.

SCREENAFRICA. 2006. *Jozi-H* Signs Up Top Hollywood Music Composer. *SCREENAFRICA*. 11 July. [Accessed 3 December 2018]. Available from: www.screenafrica.com/2006/07/11/all-news/jozi-h-signs-up-top-hollywod-music-composer/

SIFF News. 2012. SIFF 2012: Filmmaker Interviews: *How to Steal 2 Million* & the *Long Ride Home. YouTube*. 6 June. [Accessed 3 December 2018]. Available from: www.youtube.com/watch?v=pJLiqX3k9fY

Simons, P. 2004. *Around the World in 80 Days:* Trevor Jones. *Movie Music UK*. 18 June. [Accessed 1 February 2017]. Available from: https://moviemusicuk.us/2004/06/18/around-the-world-in-80-days-trevor-jones/

Sly Fox Films. 2015. Stephen Bayly. *Sly Fox Films*. [Accessed 3 December 2018]. Available from: www.slyfoxfilms.com/page3.htm

Smith, J. 1998. *The Sounds of Commerce: Marketing Popular Film Music*. New York: Columbia University Press.

Smith, J. 2003. Trevor Jones: *The League of Extraordinary Gentlemen. BBC Music*. [Accessed 3 December 2018]. Available from: www.bbc.co.uk/music/reviews/3zdp/

Smith, N. 2003. 'I'll Be There'. *BBC*. 16 May. [Accessed 3 December 2018]. Available from: www.bbc.co.uk/films/2003/05/16/ill_be_there_2003_review.shtml

Sterkowicz, J. 2010. Tracking the World's Oldest Culture. *ScreenAfrica Digital Magazine*. May. [Accessed 29 March 2017]. Available from: www.screenafrica.com/download_files/latest_edition/pdfs/SCAF-May10(33-58)_Web.pdf

Summers, T. 2016. *Understanding Video Game Music*. Cambridge: Cambridge University Press.

Susman, G. 2017. 17 Things You Never Knew about *The Last of the Mohicans. Moviefone*. 24 September. [Accessed 3 December 2018]. Available from: www.moviefone.com/2017/09/24/last-of-the-mohicans-movie-facts/

Swift, J. 1726. *Gulliver's Travels*. London: Benjamin Motte.

Thinkbox. 2015. Introduction to TV Sponsorship. *Thinkbox*. 19 November. [Accessed 3 December 2018]. Available from: www.thinkbox.tv/How-to-use-TV/Sponsorship-and-content/TV-Sponsorship/Introduction-to-TV-sponsorship

ToTokyoTheFilm. 2013. *To Tokyo* The Film: Teaser Trailer. *YouTube*. 11 August. [Accessed 3 December 2018]. Available from: www.youtube.com/watch?v=XvjYShp8V_Q

Travers, P. 2002. Crossroads. *Rolling Stone*. 15 February. [Accessed 3 December 2018]. Available from: www.rollingstone.com/movies/reviews/crossroads-20020213

Trevor, W. 1972. An Evening with John Joe Dempsey. In: *The Ballroom of Romance and Other Stories*. New York: The Viking Press.
TVSA. 2017. *Jozi-H. TVSA South Africa's TV Website*. [Accessed 3 December 2018]. Available from: www.tvsa.co.za/shows/viewshow.aspx?showid=202
Vintage Digital. 2015. Lexicon 224 Digital Reverberator. *Vintage Digital*. [Accessed 3 December 2018]. Available from: www.vintagedigital.com.au/lexicon-224-digital-reverberator/
Walden Media. 2012. *Official Website*. [Accessed 3 December 2018]. Available from: www.walden.com
Werner, C. 2000. *A Change Is Gonna Come: Music, Race & the Soul of America*. Edinburgh: Payback.
Whittington, W. 2007. *Sound Design and Science Fiction*. Austin, TX: University of Texas Press.
Wierzbicki, J. ed. 2012. *Music, Sound and Filmmakers: Sonic Style in Cinema*. New York: Routledge.
Williams, D. 2016. Acoustic Fingerprints from Trevor Jones's *Dark City* Found in Hans Zimmer's *Inception*. *Music and Audio-Visual Media II Conference*. 20–22 June. University of Leeds.
Woodward, K. 2013. *Cleddyf ym Mrwydr yr Iaith?: Y Bwrdd Ffilmiau Cymraeg*. Cardiff: University of Wales Press.
Yates, M., Bradtke, E. and Taylor, M. eds. 2004. *Dear Companion: Appalachian Traditional Songs and Singers from the Cecil Sharp Collection*. London: English Folk Dance & Song Society.

Personal communications and interviews

Alexander, G. 2016. *Interview with Sarah Hall*. 4 March. Via Skype.
Barraclough, D. 2014. *Interview with Laura Anderson*. 15 May. Leeds.
Jones, T. 2007. *Interview with Ian Sapiro*. 17 October. London.
Jones, T. 2014a. *Interview with David Cooper and Sarah Hall*. 4 September. Leeds.
Jones, T. 2014b. *Interview with Sarah Hall*. 10 December. London.
Jones, T. 2016a. *Interview with Sarah Hall*. 8 January. Via Skype.
Jones, T. 2016b. *Interview with Laura Anderson*. 6 July. Via Skype.
Jones, T. 2017. *Email to David Cooper*. 6 March.
Jones, T. 2018. *Email to David Cooper and Ian Sapiro*. 5 January.
Price, S. 2016. *Interview with Ian Sapiro*. 15 January. Via Skype.
Seale, V. 2017. *Email to Ian Sapiro*. 23 September.
Sorrell, N. 2015. *Interview with Laura Anderson*. 26 March. York.
Stemp, N. 2015a. *Interview with Sarah Hall*. 19 January. Via Skype.
Stemp, N. 2015b. *Email to Laura Anderson*. 25 February.

Cited materials from the Trevor Jones Archive

Cue List. *Labyrinth*. 1986. Trevor Jones Archive, University of Leeds.
Dark City Music Spotting Notes, 22 June, 1997 [Transcript]. *Dark City*. 1997. Trevor Jones Archive, University of Leeds.
Scenes for Scored Music. *Angel Heart*. 1986. Trevor Jones Archive, University of Leeds.
Spotting Session [Transcript]. *Kiss of Death*. 1995. Trevor Jones Archive, University of Leeds.
Track Sheet for Tape 1, Cue 1: Notes. *Mississippi Burning*. 1988. Trevor Jones Archive, University of Leeds.

Index

Abarder, Gasant 206
Abbey Road Studios 111, 193
ABC *see* American Broadcasting Company
Academy Awards 9, 18, 23, 100, 215
Academy of St Martin-in-the-Fields 135
A Clydeside Carol 150, 155–6, 223
act-outs and act-ins 166, 172
A Deal is a Deal see Three and Out
Aderyn Papur . . . and Pigs Might Fly 150, 153, 223
Aegis 10, 188n4, 189–92, 212, 225
Africa 10, 15, 60, 66, 134, 141, 189, 194, 197, 198–205, 209, 212, 219; *see also* South Africa
African Movie Academy 204
AHRC *see* Arts and Humanities Research Council
Alexander, Geoff 99, 132, 135, 141, 144, 146–7, 166, 193, 208, 215, 216, 217
Alexandra, Danielle 116
Alex Rider: Operation Stormbreaker 225
American Broadcasting Company 36, 159–60, 169
Anderson, John 111
Anderson, Laura 5, 7, 11n4, 64n3
Anderson, William M. 191–2; *Dead Poet's Society* 191; *The Truman Show* 191
Angel Heart 2–3, 9, 17, 25, 42, 49–60, 63–4, 64n3, 69, 77, 90, 92n13, 135, 154, 210–11, 213–14, 217, 223
Anschutz, Philip 145
Any Dream Will Do 206n2
apartheid 4, 66, 133–4, 197–8, 204
The Appointment 223
A Private Life 4, 66, 72, 92n1, 150, 223
Arachnophobia 3, 7, 9, 64n7, 65, 74, 77–8, 90, 92n7, 224
Arch, Dave 217

archival materials 2, 4–5, 7–9, 20, 27, 45, 56, 60–1, 65, 72, 74–5, 78, 80, 82, 84, 89, 92n3, 92n7, 99, 108, 126, 127n3, 132, 151, 153, 155–6, 165, 168, 171, 172n3, 195, 219–21
Arem, Keith 179
Arena 223
Arnold, David 119; *Stargate* 119
Around the World in 80 Days 3, 10, 129–30, 144–6, 222, 225
Arterton, Gemma 199
Arts and Humanities Research Council 5, 7, 10
A Stolen Portrait 19, 223
atmospheres 9, 15, 22, 25, 53–4, 61–2, 72, 77, 83–4, 87, 89–91, 92n3, 92n6, 95, 152–3, 171; *see also* Jones, Trevor, creative approaches; toolkits
Attwood, David 201, 225
Audissino, Emilio 33
avant-garde 49
Ayoub, Daniel 185
Aznavour, Charles 124, 126

Bach, J.S. 16
Bacon, Matt 160
Bad Influence 9, 65, 69, 72–4, 92n6, 111, 158, 211, 223
BAFTA 23, 120
Bähler, Tom 74
Baigent, Michael 207
Barbarians at the Gate 87, 89, 224
Barker, Ellen 67
Barraclough, Dave 108, 111
Barron, Lee 51
Barron, Steve 159, 224
Barry, John 88; *Dances with Wolves* 88
Bartók, Béla 42, 142–3; *The Wooden Prince* 42

Barton, Mischa 117
Batman 25, 179
Bayley, Stephen 173n5
Bayly, Stephen 19, 58, 151, 153, 173n5, 222, 223
BBC *see* British Broadcasting Corporation
The Beatles 121; 'Get Back' 121
Beatty, Ned 36
Becker, Harold 3, 66–7, 223
Beethoven, Ludwig van 16, 39
Beintez, Sergio 32–3, 89, 146
Bell, Alan J.W. 222
The Beneficiary 19, 222
Benges, Chris 224
Berg, Alban 142
Berrow, Mark 217
The Black Angel 8, 15, 18–27, 31–2, 205, 207–8, 218, 221
Blake, David 16–17
Blame It on the Bellboy 3, 65, 80–4, 224; 'The Perfect Moment' 82–3
Blessed, Brian 36
Blood and Oil (2010 TV mini-series) 150, 164–5, 170–2, 173n20, 173n22, 189, 198, 201, 203, 205, 212, 225
bluegrass 118, 127; *see also* Jones, Trevor, creative approaches; Jones, Trevor, influence of folk styles; Jones, Trevor, musical fingerprints
Boggan, Justin 64n8
Bonham Carter, Helena 159
Bono 102–5, 127, 212, 214; *see also* U2
Boorman, John 9, 22, 27–31, 43, 49, 173n14, 223
Boothe, Powers 156
Borgnine, Ernest 36
Botha, Maria 205
Botha, Martin 203
Bott, Catherine 217
Boulez, Pierre 17
Bowie, David 9, 27, 43–5, 127, 138, 212, 214
Brambilla, Marco 159, 225
Branch, Ben 64n10
brass band 10, 95, 99, 106–8, 111, 115–16, 120, 152, 224
Brassed Off 4, 10, 20, 83, 92n10, 95, 99, 106–21, 127, 147, 161, 214, 216, 224; 'Cross of Honour' 116; 'Floral Dance' 113, 115; 'Florentina March' 116; 'Scarborough Fair' 115, 214
British Broadcasting Corporation 16, 36, 49, 66, 124, 144, 148, 151, 153, 155–6, 201, 217

Brittania: The First of the Last 222
Brosnan, Pierce 89, 156
Brothers and Sisters 223
Broughton, Bruce 49, 64n8, 92n13
Brown, Bill 179
Brown, Dan 207
Brown, Julie 132
Brown, Royal S. 177
Brown Findlay, Jessica 207
Broxton, Jonathan 141
Buckler, Robert 39
Buff, Conrad 130
Buhler, James 7
bumpers 40, 46n3, 151, 166–9, 171–2, 199
Burton, Tim 25
Burtt, Ben 33
Busby, Tom 156
Butterworth, David 146
By Dawn's Early Light 74–7, 89, 150, 155–8, 215
Byrne, Ciar 200

C4 *see* Channel Four
Calder, Clive 137
Campbell, Eddie 135
canonisation 7, 220
Cape Town Youth Choir 208
Cardew, Cornelius 16; *Octet 61* 16
Cardiff, Jack 41; *The Girl on a Motorcycle* 41
Carlin, Daniel Allan 215
Carlin, Dan Sr. 138, 173n21, 215
Chains of Gold 3, 74–7, 173n19, 224
Chan, Jackie 10, 129, 145
Channel Four 149, 152–3, 158, 173n6, 173n8, 173n13, 173n23
Chaos 189, 192–5, 201, 211, 213, 225
Chelsom, Peter 224
Chéreau, Patrice 29
Chetty, Kavish 202–3
Christian, Roger 18, 20, 23, 25, 222, 223
The Christians 82
Church, Charlotte 105, 127, 129, 139, 214
Ciment, Michel 28–9
Clannad 88; *Harry's Game* 88
Clarke, Malcolm 224
Clempson, Clem 117
Cleopatra 3, 10, 150, 159, 161–4, 169–70, 212, 224
click track 20, 67, 92n5, 172
Cliffhanger 3, 9, 25, 89–91, 97, 163, 224
Clisby, Ted 155, 223

CMMP *see* Contemporary Music Media Productions
Cohen, Michael 179
Cohn, Richard 221n2
Coil 119; 'Homage to Sewage' 119
Coleman, John 216
Coleman, Terry 185
collaboration 18, 25–6, 34–5, 46, 129, 158, 189, 217
Collins, Karen 184
communication 2, 124, 129, 132, 138
'Concerto d'Orange Juice' *see* Rodrigo, Joaquín, *Concerto d'Aranjuez*
Connaughton, Shane 23
Connery, Sean 10, 129, 140, 143
Connolly, Jennifer 43
Contemporary Music Media Productions 198, 215
Convertino, Michael 84
Coogan, Steve 10, 145
Cooper, David 4–5, 7, 16–17, 26, 43, 49, 63, 92n11, 97–8, 107, 127n2, 135, 208
Copland, Aaron 132–3
Coppers 56, 150, 155–6, 223
copyist *see* Jones, Trevor, music team, music preparation
Coraci, Frank 145, 225
Coronation Street 169
Costello, Elvis 10, 95, 124–6, 200, 214; 'Accidents will Happen' 200
Costner, Kevin 10, 129–30
Courage, Alexander 46n5; *Star Trek* 40, 46n5
Cousins, Gareth 123, 130, 135, 215, 216, 217
CrissCross 3, 84, 87, 89–90, 217, 224
Crook, Mackenzie 199
Crossroads 3, 99, 127–30, 136–9, 161, 200, 225
Cubase 96, 218
cue list 45, 89, 108, 115, 123, 132, 135, 181
Cumming, Pete 103
Cunningham, Phil 87–8; *The House in Rose Valley* 87
Curtin, Michael 149
Curtis, Richard 69, 120–3, 193–4, 223

DA88 131
Dafoe, Willem 60
Dagul, Guy 216
Danson, Ted 158–9
Dark City 92n2, 95, 99, 118–20, 127n6, 130, 135, 144, 182–3, 204, 211–14, 224

The Dark Crystal 3, 9, 26–8, 32–9, 117, 153–4, 159, 172, 213, 216, 221, 223
The Dark Crystal: Age of Resistance 221
Daubney, Kate 4
Davalle, Peter 154
Davis, Don 120; *The Matrix* 119, 120
Davis, Tamra 136–8, 225; *Guncrazy* 137
Davison, Annette 152, 169
DAW *see* digital audio workstation
Day-Lewis, Daniel 90, 104
Death Train see Detonator
De baby huilt 224
de Jong, Mijke 224
de Laski, Donald 196
de Laski, Nancy 196
Delerue, Georges 82–3, 88; *Black Robe* 88; *La Nuit Américaine* 82 ('Le Grand Choral' 82–3)
Del Mar, Norman 28
Delon, Nathalie 223
De Luca, Michael 130
De Mornay, Rebecca 156
demos 2, 5, 10, 105, 185, 188, 203
De Niro, Robert 50
Depp, Johnny 10, 129, 134
Desperate Measures 210, 224
Detonator 9, 65, 89–90, 150, 155–8, 168, 169, 224
de Vries, David 225
diegetic 31, 35, 39, 80–1, 92n8, 98–100, 102–4, 111, 113, 115–16, 118, 121, 140, 186, 200
'Dies Irae' 133, 210
digital audio workstation 96, 147
Dinotopia (TV mini-series) 10, 147, 150, 159–63, 169, 170–1, 225
Dinotopia (TV series) 147, 150, 158, 159, 169, 170, 225
Disney 145, 160
District 9 203
Dobbins, Bennett 120
Dods, Marcus 37, 216
Dolby 96–7
The Dollar Bottom 9, 15, 18, 23–7, 223
Dominick and Eugene 56–60, 64, 82, 217, 223
Donaldson, Roger 130–2, 225
Donnelly, Kevin 98, 148–9
Doppler effect 77
Dozier, Lamont 139
DreamWorks 145
Dr Fischer of Geneva 150, 153–5, 223
Dudman, Andrew 147, 193, 203, 208

Duigan, John 117, 224–5
Dylan, Bob 102; 'Like a Rolling Stone' 102
dynamic audio 184

EA Games 10, 177, 179–80, 188
Ebert, Roger 135, 141, 145
Eco, Umberto 207
Edelman, Randy 87, 92n14
Eisler, Hanns 17
electronic wind instrument 74, 102–3, 107, 117, 147n9, 164, 213, 217
Elgar, Edward 40, 43, 113, 123, 133, 143, 215; *Enigma Variations* 113, 143; *Pomp and Circumstance* 40
En Aranjuez con tu amor see Rodrigo, Joaquín, *Concerto d'Aranjuez*
engineer *see* Jones, Trevor, music team
English Chamber Orchestra 216
English Sinfonia 201
ER 160
Erickson, Hal 155
Estevez, Emilio 84
ethnomusicology 16
EWI *see* electronic wind instrument
Excalibur 9, 20–38, 43, 46n1, 135, 173n14, 223
experimental music 9, 27, 29, 33, 46, 97, 119

Fairfax, Ferdinand 39, 223
The Falcon's Malteser see *Just Ask for Diamond*
fanfare 38, 78, 82, 141, 182
Fellini, Federico 123
Ferguson, Craig 139, 225
Fields of Freedom 3, 189, 195–6, 214, 225; 'Dixie' 195; 'The Gobby O' 195; 'John Brown's Body' 195; 'Shenandoah' 195–6
Findon, Andy 164, 201, 213, 217
Finn brothers 3, 218
Finney, Albert 147n9
Fitzgerald, Ella 24
Fitzgerald, Tara 108
Fitzgibbons, John 103
Foster, Craig 202, 225
Foster, Damon 202, 225
Fotopoulos, Costas 215, 216
The Four Tops 139; 'Reach Out I'll Be There' 139
Four Weddings and a Funeral 121
Fox 141, 144, 149

Fox, Christopher 16–17, 26, 43, 49, 97–8, 107, 135, 208
Frankie & Emma 173n4, 219, 226
Freejack 17, 84–91, 92n11, 92n12, 135, 139, 215, 224
Friday, Gavin 102–5, 212; *see also* U2
Fritz, Ben 177
Frizell, John 130; *Dante's Peak* 130
From an Immigrant's Notebook 223
From Hell 3, 10, 129–30, 133–6, 139–41, 144, 178, 211, 216, 225
Froud, Brian 32
Fukui, Harutoshi 190
Fülöp, Rebecca 25

Gabriel, Noel 179
Gardner, John 16
Garfunkel, Art 115
Garner, James 89
The Gathering Storm 147n9, 225
Gebler, Carlo 19, 222
Generations 219, 225
Gerard, Francis 101, 223
Gershfield, Jonathan 199, 225
Giampietro, Manfred 29
Gibbs, Richard 89
Gibson, Alex 130–2, 135–6, 138, 215
Giglio, Tony 192, 225
GI Jane 95, 99, 116–17, 132, 210, 212, 215, 224; 'Taps' 117, 215
Glitter, Gary 102, 104, 106; 'Leader of the Gang' 102, 104
'Golden Gordon' 222
Goldsmith, Jerry 97, 119; *Alien* 119
Goldwasser, Dan 92n14
Goljan, Luke 120
Goodall, Howard 147n9
Gorbman, Claudia 62
Graceland 134
The Graduate 115, 123
Graham, Janice 201
The Grand Tour see *By Dawn's Early Light*
Grant, Hugh 120
Green, Al 121; 'How Can You Mend a Broken Heart' 121
Greenaway, Peter 63
Greene, Graham 154, 173n10
Gregson-Williams, Harry 145–6; *Sinbad: Legend of the Seven Seas* 145–6
Grieg, Edvard 41–2; *Six Lyric Pieces* 41
Griffiths, Trevor 39
Grimethorpe Band 111

Gulliver's Travels 3, 10, 77, 117, 150, 158–61, 163, 169, 170, 173n19, 173n23, 224
Guns: A Day in the Death of America 224
Gurney, James 159–60
'guzintos' and 'guzoutos' *see* act-outs and act-ins
Gypsy scale *see* Hungarian scale

Hackman, Gene 60
Hall, Jeff 51
Hall, Sarah 5, 7, 10, 37–8, 46n4, 107–8, 149, 159, 166, 172n1, 172n2, 173n3, 173n16
Hallmark 10, 77, 149, 156, 158–64, 169–71
Halmi, Robert Sr. 158–9
Hamm, Nick 224
Hammer Horror 17
Hanson, Curtis 69, 223; *The Hand that Rocks the Cradle* 69; *LA Confidential* 69
'Happy Birthday' 102
Harlin, Renny 89–90, 224
Harris, David 87
Harrison, Jim 117, 138
Harry Potter 25, 179
Hastings-Smith, Laura 223
Hauer, Rutger 159
HBO *see* Home Box Office
Heldt, Guido 120–1
Henderson, John 224
Hendrix, Jimi 102; 'Voodoo Child' 102
Henson, Jim 3, 9, 26–7, 32, 36, 42–3, 49–50, 154, 203, 223; *The Muppet Show* 32
Herman, Mark 3, 83, 107, 224
Herrmann, Bernard 4, 61, 82; *The Twilight Zone* 82–3
Hexel, Vasco 69
Hibbert, Guy 201
Hideaway 3, 91, 211, 224
Hinton, Hal 83
Hirsh, Paul 213
Hjortsberg, William 50
Hodges, Adrian 207
Hogwood, Christopher 31
Holcomb, Rod 224
Holden, Stephen 145
Holland, Eddie 139
Hollywood 1, 9–10, 32, 52, 63, 91, 95–7, 99, 105, 107, 111, 113, 115, 117, 119–23, 127, 129, 135, 137, 139, 141, 143, 145–7, 189, 191, 198, 200, 208, 224

Holst, Gustav 87, 113, 183, 215; 'Mars' 87, 113, 183
Home Box Office 74, 87, 137, 147n9, 149, 153
Hopkins, Anthony 84
Horner, James 87–8, 145; *Glory* 88
Horowitz, Anthony 58
Howman, David 222
How to Steal 2 Million 3, 10, 189, 198, 204, 219, 225
Hubai, Gergely 84, 89
Hubbert, Julie 99, 128n7
Hughes, Albert 134–5, 225
Hughes, Allen 134–5, 225
Hughes, Paul 111
Hulce, Tom 56
Hulme, Paul 216
Hungarian scale 182–3, 209
Hunt, Peter R. 36, 223
Huntford, Robert 39
Hurt, John 207
Husk 219, 226
Hussey, Olivia 36

I'll Be There 3, 127, 129, 137, 139–40, 193, 200, 212–13, 217, 225; 'All My Life' 140
Inglis, Ian 51
instrumentation *see* orchestration
In the Name of the Father 3, 90–1, 95, 99–107, 122, 127, 130, 194, 212–13, 216, 224; 'You Made Me the Thief of Your Heart' 103, 106
Ireland 2, 19, 28, 90, 100, 104–6, 118, 130, 153, 191, 195, 199–201, 212, 214
I, Robot 146, 222, 225
Isaacs, Harry 16
Isham, Mark 130, 173n20; *Blood and Oil* (2015 TV series) 173n20; *The Getaway* 130
ITV 36, 148, 169

Jackson, David 224
Jackson, Mahalia 62, 64n10; 'Take My Hand, Precious Lord' 62
Jacquemin, André 222
Jagernauth, Kevin 120
Jagger, Mick 43, 84
James, Linda 151, 173n5
Japan 10, 140, 153–4, 188–91, 212, 213, 219
Japan Academy Prize 190
Jarre, Maurice 119; *Jacob's Ladder* 119

jazz 16, 41, 49, 69, 74, 89, 111, 113, 118, 124, 127, 154, 194
Jenson, Elizabeth 160
Jones, James Earl 156
Jones, Max 39
Jones, Robert Gerallt 151
Jones, Terry 43, 146
Jones, Trevor: creative approaches 214–15; influence of folk styles 25, 34, 39–41, 87, 115–18, 127, 151–4, 162, 196, 200, 212, 214 (*see also* atmospheres; toolkits); musical fingerprints 119, 143, 196, 209, 210–14 (bourdons 52, 54, 64n5, 72, 92n6; chromaticism 23, 42, 52, 66, 155, 163, 196, 204–5, 208, 210–12; circle-of-fifths harmony 38, 151, 154, 162–3, 211–12; drone 22–3, 31, 38, 50–3, 65, 75, 77, 105, 142, 153, 161, 192–3, 204, 209, 211; electronics 3, 16–18, 22, 31, 36, 40, 44, 49–51, 57, 59, 75, 77, 87–91, 100, 116–20, 133, 136, 148, 164, 172, 186, 193–4, 203, 205, 208–9, 212–13, 218; interlocking intervals 141, 200, 213; modality 24–5, 31, 35, 100, 104, 115, 120, 136, 142–3, 146, 154, 162–3, 192, 194, 196, 208, 212–13; rhythmic 3+3+3+3+2+2 pattern 69, 72, 77, 194, 201, 203, 209–11; sharpened fourth 182, 196, 202, 209, 213; thematicism 129, 142, 151, 155, 161, 163, 171–2); music team 3, 129, 165, 172, 190, 193, 210, 215–17, 218 (engineer 123, 193, 215, 217; mixer 2, 37, 52, 62, 167, 215; music co-ordinator 215; music editor 18, 130–2, 135–6, 138–9, 144, 158, 166, 173, 191, 193, 198, 208, 215; music preparation 215; music supervisor 138; orchestrator 135, 144, 146, 166, 186, 208, 215, 217, 221n6, 224, 225; programmer 37, 130, 169, 173, 189, 191, 193, 195, 197–9, 201, 203, 205, 208, 215, 221n4, 225); technology 15, 29, 49, 96–7, 135, 217–18; television music eras 148–72 ('Early Career Era' 150–5; 'Hallmark Era' 158–64; 'Recent Career Era' 164–5; 'Telefilm Era' 155–8)
Joni Jones 33, 36–9, 58, 118, 150, 151–4, 170–2, 173n5, 211, 214, 223
Jordan, Glenn 224
Jozi-H 10, 150, 158, 164–5, 169–72, 189, 197–8, 204–5, 225
Just Ask for Diamond 3, 56–60, 64, 223

Kaplan, Don 159
Karlin, Fred 58, 158, 165, 167
Keating, Ronan 123, 128n9; 'When You Say Nothing at All' 121, 123, 128n9
Kegel, Herbert 28
Keill, Ian 153–4, 223
Kennaway, James 23
Kennedy-Fraser, Marjory 140; 'In Hebrid Seas' 140
Kent, Stacey 111
Kenworthy, Duncan 117, 120–3, 159, 173n15
Kershaw, David 17
Kershaw, Julian 99, 135, 146, 215
King, Carole 200; 'You've Got a Friend' 200
King, Martin Luther Jr. 22, 43–4, 62, 64n10, 140, 215
King, Roger 215
The Kinks 102, 104; 'Dedicated Follower of Fashion' 102, 104
Kipper 118
Kirby, Vanessa 207
Kiss of Death 91, 92n16, 135, 224
Knauer, Lorenz 224
Knox, Ian 19, 25, 222
Kohler, Chris 177
Konchalovskiy, Andrey 223
Kosky, Florence 219
Kretzmer, Herbert 124
Kubric, Stanley 62
Kurtz, Gary 25, 32–3

Labyrinth (1986 film) 3, 9, 20, 26, 27, 42–5, 46n8, 50–1, 127, 138, 173n10, 207, 212–13, 214, 223
Labyrinth (2012 TV mini-series) 11, 150, 164–5, 170, 172, 173n4, 189, 207–11, 213, 225
Ladysmith Black Mambazo 134, 141, 144, 212
Lange, Mutt 99
Larson, Randall 32, 37
The Last Days of Pompeii 9, 27, 36–40, 150, 154, 156, 167–8, 170–1, 223
The Last of the Mohicans 3, 5, 7, 25, 65, 87–9, 92n14, 97, 117–18, 139, 146, 163, 196, 213–14, 224
The Last Place on Earth 3, 9, 27, 36, 39–46, 150, 154–6, 161, 167–8, 170–1, 223
Lawn Dogs 95, 99, 116–18, 127, 173n15, 214, 224

The League of Extraordinary Gentlemen
    10, 129, 140–4, 178, 191, 210,
    212–14, 225
Lee, Christopher 89, 156
Lee, Dennis 43
Lehman, Frank 221n1
Leifer, Sam 225
Leigh, Richard 207
Lennertz, Christopher 178, 179
Lennon, John 104
Leonard, Brett 224
Lewin, Michael 29
Lexicon 224XL 45
Liberski, Marcus 225
The Lighthouse Family 121, 123; 'Ain't No
    Sunshine When She's Gone' 121, 123
Lincoln, Henry 207
Lindsay-Hogg, Michael 74, 153, 223, 224
Liotta, Ray 56
Livingstone, Ian 179
Lloyd Webber, Andrew 139, 206n2;
    *Joseph and the Amazing Technicolor
    Dreamcoat* 206n2; *Requiem* 139
Loch Ness 25, 95, 163, 213–14, 217, 224
Logic (software) 96
Loncraine, Richard 3, 111, 147n9, 224, 225
London Philharmonic Orchestra 28, 216
London Symphony Orchestra 33, 37,
    131–2, 134, 139, 141, 144, 147, 154,
    172, 191, 193, 195, 203, 208, 215–17
The Lonely War see *The Gathering Storm*
The Lone Rider Rides Again 223
The Long Run 129, 133–4, 141, 189, 199,
    212, 225
Lotz, Amanda 149
Lowe, Rob 69
LSO see London Symphony Orchestra
Lucas, George 8, 18; *The Empire Strikes
    Back* 8, 18; *A New Hope* 18, 26; *Return
    of the Jedi* 33; *Star Wars* 32, 33
Lutyens, Elizabeth 17
LXG see *The League of Extraordinary
    Gentlemen*
Lynch, David 62

Machiah, Joseph 205
Mack, Leroy 118
MacLean, Duncan 87–9, 214; *The Gael*
    87–9, 214
main theme 22, 24, 38–42, 50–1, 57, 66,
    77, 82–3, 89, 116, 133–4, 136, 138–40,
    146, 152–4, 161–3, 166, 171, 182–3,
    192, 195–6, 207, 209–13, 215, 221

Malory, Sir Thomas 28
Manhattan 123
Mann, Michael 3, 87, 89, 224
Manners, Joel 185
Manthei, Kevin 178, 179
marimba 61, 67, 72, 91, 199, 201, 204, 210
Marley, Bob 102; 'Is This Love?' 102
Marlowe, Christopher 111; 'Come Live
    With Me' 111
Marshall, Frank 224
Martyn, John 118
Marvel 10, 177–80, 185–6, 188, 225
Marvel Nemesis: Rise of the Imperfects 10,
    177–86, 188n1, 188n2, 210, 225
Match of the Day 153
Mattise, Nathan 221
May, Ernest R. 130
McCarthy, David 184
McCuistion, Michael 178, 179; *Justice
    League* 179
McGregor, Ewan 108
McKellen, Ian 111
Mead, Lee 200, 206n2
Meaney, Colm 199
Media Composer (software) 129
Melcher, Sarah 92n14
Meleya, Thabang 225
Mellers, Wilfrid 16
mélomane 62
Mendelssohn, Felix 122
Mera, Miguel 1–4
Merlin 3, 10, 30, 118, 150, 151, 159, 161–4,
    169–70, 173n16, 196, 201, 214, 224
metadata 5–6, 11n5, 220–1
The Michael Nyman Band 201
Michell, Roger 118, 121–3, 224
Mickey Mousing 147n6
Middle Ages 16, 22, 28, 31, 33
MIDI see Musical Instrument Digital
    Interface
The Mighty 19, 224
mise-en-scène 128
Mississippi Burning 2, 4, 9, 25, 49, 60–4,
    64n4, 64n9, 65–7, 87, 92n13, 130, 211,
    213, 223
Mitchell, Elvis 134, 140–1
mixer see Jones, Trevor, music team
mixing 1–2, 29, 35, 45, 61, 66, 69, 75, 91,
    100, 108, 111, 127, 128n10, 131–2, 138,
    147n4, 158, 191, 198
mock-ups see demos
Molly 3, 95, 99
Molyneux, Andrée 155

242 *Index*

Monahan, Robert J. Jr. 195
Monroe, Bill 117
Moore, Alan 135, 140–1; *V for Vendetta* 141; *The Watchmen* 141
Moore, Demi 116
Mora del Solar, Luis 19, 222
Morgan Creek Productions 92n14, 139
Morricone, Ennio 53–6, 82, 88; *The Good, the Bad and the Ugly* 55; *Le Marginal* 82–3; *The Mission* 88
Moshesh, Mthati 133
Mosse, Kate 207
motivic writing 23, 29, 41, 44–5, 51–2, 55, 69, 77, 82–3, 87, 90, 106–7, 133, 141–3, 146–7, 166–7, 183, 193, 210
Moving Hearts 88; *May Morning Dew* 88
Mozart, Wolfgang Amadeus 196; *Le Nozze di Figaro* 196
MTV 128n7, 136, 138
Mud 102; 'Tiger Feet' 102
Mueller-Strahl, Armin 133
multitrack recordings 2, 7, 9, 27, 39, 49, 54–61, 64n4, 67, 69, 72, 77–81, 91, 92n7, 100–1
Munrow, David 31
Murder by Moonlight see Murder on the Moon
Murder on the Moon 66, 74, 155–8, 168, 223
Murphy, Don 140, 141
Murphy, Geoff 224
musical codes 31, 40, 45, 117, 191, 202
musical identity 8, 56, 104, 118, 129, 137, 142, 146, 169, 198, 215
Musical Instrument Digital Interface 27, 147, 185–8
musical score 2, 52, 97, 100, 124, 127n4, 131, 132, 141, 144, 188, 195
music editor *see* Jones, Trevor, music team
Mussorgsky, Modest 118
Muzak 202
My Hunter's Heart 10, 189, 198, 202–5, 211–12, 225

Narholz, Gregor 179
Nate and Hayes see Savage Islands
National Broadcasting Company 158–60, 169, 173n23
National Film and Television School 7–8, 15, 17–19, 23, 25, 26n2, 27, 32, 36, 151, 205, 207, 210, 222
NBC *see* National Broadcasting Company
Neill, Sam 159

Nelson, Michael 130
Neo-Riemannian theory 211–12, 221n1; Weitzmann Region 221n2
Netflix 221n7
Neumeyer, David 7
New Line Cinema 130
Newton Howard, James 145
NFTS *see* National Film and Television School
Ngubane, Menzi 204
Nielsen, Brigitte 156, 160
The Night of the Captain 19, 222
'Nkosi Sikelel' iAfrika' 134
noir 92n2, 119, 182, 204, 211
Nolan, Christopher 120; *Inception* 120
Nono, Luigi 100; *Ricorda cosa ti hanno fatto in Auschwitz* 100
Norrington, Stephen 140, 225
Notator 218
Notting Hill 4, 10, 18, 20, 95–9, 117–27, 128n9, 129, 138, 147, 161, 173n15, 214, 217; 'She' 10, 95, 121–6
Nyman, Michael 63

The Object of Beauty 74, 217, 224
O'Connor, Pat 153, 223
O'Connor, Sinéad 103, 105, 214
'Old Barber's Chair' 134
Oliver, Martin 179
Olivier, Laurence 36
One of Ourselves 36, 118, 150, 153–4, 214, 223
O'Neill, Kevin 140
Onishi, Norimitsu 190
orchestra *see* symphonic sound
orchestration 2–3, 16–21, 24–5, 31, 33–40, 43–5, 49–52, 59–61, 67, 72, 78, 80, 87, 89–91, 97, 99–100, 108, 111, 114–18, 123, 126–7, 134, 136, 139, 145, 147, 152–4, 162–4, 168, 171–2, 178, 180, 184, 188, 191, 193, 199, 201, 203, 208–18, 221; hyper-orchestration 218; *see also individual instruments*
orchestrator *see* Jones, Trevor, music team
Orff, Carl 9, 27–31, 43, 88; *Carmina Burana* 28, 30, 87–88
Orton, Richard 16
Oscars *see* Academy Awards
Oz, Frank 223

Pace, Eliza 206n1; 'The Mermaid' 206n1
Pacino, Al 67
Paramount 32

Parker, Alan 2–3, 9, 18, 46, 49–63, 64n3, 67, 69, 92n13, 177, 211, 214, 223; *Angela's Ashes* 64n3
Pärt, Arvo 88; *Cantus in Memoriam Benjamin Britten* 88
Paul, Alexandra 89
pedal *see* Jones, Trevor, musical fingerprints, drone
Penderecki, Krzysztof 39, 100, 204, 212; *Threnody for the Victims of Hiroshima* 100
pentatonicism 51–2, 191, 194, 196
percussion 20, 24, 34–7, 40, 44–5, 50–1, 54–7, 61–7, 72, 75–8, 87, 91, 102, 104, 115–19, 123, 134, 147, 152–3, 180, 182, 185, 191, 194, 201, 203, 212
Pheto, Terry 204
Phillippe, Ryan 192
Phoenix 219, 226
Pilkington, Ed 64n10
Pine, Courtney 52, 213, 217
Pool, Jeannie 156
popular music 10, 16, 27, 42, 45–6, 50–1, 95, 98–100, 102, 104, 120–7, 127n1, 128n9, 128n10, 129, 138–9, 148, 218
Postlethwaite, Pete 90, 108
post-production 3, 18, 20, 24, 42, 124, 144, 198
Pratt, Roger 23, 25
Pratt, Tony 28
pre-existing music 10, 20, 24, 28–31, 36, 43–6, 91, 95–9, 108, 111, 113, 116–23, 127n1, 128n10, 129, 138, 148, 161, 163, 212, 214
pre-production 18
Price, Steve 130–1, 215, 221n4; *Gravity* 221n4
Pro Cantu Choir *see* Cape Town Youth Choir
Prochnau, William 92n4
ProTools 96–7, 147, 172, 185, 198, 218
Proyas, Alex 92n2, 119, 146, 182, 224, 225
P'tang, Yang, Kipperbang 173n8
Puccini, Giacomo 207, 209; *Tosca* 207
Puttnam, David 152

'quality TV' 149, 155–6

Rands, Bernard 17
Raub, Jeremy 130–1, 139, 144, 198, 215
Reason (software) 193
recording sessions 9, 20, 25–7, 33, 45, 66, 82–4, 111, 123, 132, 156, 172

Redgrave, Vanessa 147n9
Reed, Les 41
rejected scores 1, 49, 64n8, 74, 89, 124, 147n9, 222
Rhimes, Shonda 137; *Introducing Dorothy Dandridge* 137
Rhodes, Simon 215, 216, 217
rhythm 24, 42, 49–54, 57–69, 72, 75, 77, 104–5, 116, 119, 139, 180, 182–6, 191–4, 198, 201–4, 209–13
Richard III 3, 95, 99, 111, 113, 116–17, 123, 127, 147n9, 154, 215, 224
Richards, John 24
Richardson, Miranda 159
Ripping Yarns 36, 222
Roberts, Julia 120
Robertson, Graig 179
Robinson, James Dale 140
Robinson, James G. 139
Roché, Sebastian 196
Rockwell, Sam 117
Roddam, Franc 159, 224
Rodrigo, Joaquín 108; *Concerto d'Aranjuez* 108
Roseanna's Grave 217, 224
Ross, Herbert 224
Rossini, Gioachino 111–12; *William Tell* 111–12
Rota, Nino 82, 103; *Amarcord* 83, 123; 'The Godfather' 103; *Le Notti di Cabiria* 82–3
rough cut 20, 82, 123, 168
Rourke, Mickey 50
Royal Academy of Music 8, 16
Run 54, 219, 225
Runaway Train 3, 9, 49–52, 55, 213, 215, 223
Rushton, Tony 185
Russo, Rene 84
Ryninks, Kees 156

S4C *see* Sianel Pedwar Cymru
Saint-Saëns, Camille 143
Sakamoto, Junji 190, 192, 225
Salzman, Steven 96
samples 29, 91, 132, 180, 213
Samson, John 36, 222
Sands, Julian 156
Sapiro, Ian 3–5, 7, 11n2, 11n4, 63, 96, 221n6
Satie, Erik 16–17; *Relâche* 16
Savage Islands 153, 223
Saville, Philip 152, 223

Sax, Geoffrey 225
saxophone 44–5, 52–3, 59–60, 67, 83, 102–3, 111, 123, 154, 212–13, 217
Scarlatti, Domenico 196
Schaffer, Rik 178, 179
Scheurer, Tim E. 160
Schroeder, Barbet 224
Schumann, Robert 39
Scotland 19, 23–5, 105, 156, 197–201
Scott, Ridley 3, 116, 224
Scott Thomas, Kristin 159
Scrabble with Nutmeg see Crossroads
ScreenMusic 5, 220
screenplay 20, 23, 32, 39–40, 50, 121, 130, 140
Screen Two 66, 223
Seale, Victoria 185, 215, 217
Seale-Jones, Caspar 219, 225, 226
Seale-Jones, Emily 189, 205, 219, 226
Sea of Love 2, 7, 9, 25, 65–9, 72, 74–7, 83, 90, 92n6, 111, 158, 211, 213, 223
Seezer, Maurice 104–5, 212; *see also* U2
Seiphemo, Rapulana 204
Self, David 130
The Sender 3, 18, 25, 33, 216, 223
Serra, Eric 119; *Léon* 119
Seven Faces of a Woman 124
Sewell, Rufus 119
Shakespeare, William 3, 95, 111
shakuhachi 50–2, 55, 191, 213
Sharif, Omar 159
Sharp, Cecil 197, 206n1
Shattuc, Jane 149
'shebang' 54, 60, 62
Sheridan, Jim 3, 90, 100, 104, 224
Sholder, Jack 223
Shore, Howard 119
Sianel Pedwar Cymru 58, 151, 153, 173n6
Sibelius (software) 3, 5, 122, 147, 172, 185, 193, 200–4, 207, 215, 218
Silvestri, Alan 122; *Father of the Bride* 122
Simon, Paul 134
Simons, Peter 145
Sitting Man 219, 225
sketch 2, 97, 124, 131, 132, 188n3, 195; *see also* musical score
Smile Until I Tell You to Stop 18, 19, 222
Smith, Christopher 207
Smith, Jack 144
Smith, Jeff 97, 225
Smith, Neil 139
SMPTE *see* timecode

Snipes, Wesley 192
Solomon, Yonty 16
Sorrell, Neil 16–17
sound design 22, 25, 26n2, 33, 119
South Africa 3–4, 8, 10, 15–16, 66, 129, 133–4, 137, 141, 189, 197–206, 212, 214, 219, 226
South African Idols 206
Spader, James 69, 74
Spears, Britney 127, 129, 136–8, 214; 'I'm Not a Girl' 138
The Spencer Davis Group 123, 200; 'Gimme Some Lovin'' 121, 123; 'Somebody Help Me' 123, 200
Sports Night 153
Sports Report 153
spotting 1–2, 5, 37, 52, 78, 91, 92n16, 119, 122–4, 127n6, 131–2, 135, 138, 146, 156, 158, 160, 164–5, 172, 191
Springsteen, Bruce 117
Stallone, Sylvester 90
Stanton, Tony 215, 216, 217
Starker, Leon 208
Statham, Jason 192
Staunton, Imelda 199–200
Steenburgen, Mary 159
Stellenbosch University Camerata 203
Stellenbosch University Studios 203, 208
Stemp, Neil 22, 165, 193, 198, 203, 208, 215, 219, 221
Stephens, Brandie 185
stereo mixes 2, 5, 50, 219, 222
Sterkowicz, Joanna 202
Stewart, Jean 133, 225; *The Bill* 133; *Born to Run* 133; *Butterfly Collectors* 133; *Cracker* 133; *Eastenders* 133
Stewart, Patrick 89, 156
Stone, Oliver 130
The Stranger 18, 19, 119, 222
Strauss, Richard 42; *Eine Alpensinfonie* 42
Strictly Come Dancing 217
student films 15–18, 27, 222
Sturridge, Charles 158, 224
Summers, Tim 177, 182, 185–6, 188n1
surround sound 5, 97, 99, 185, 191
Susman, Gary 87
Sutherland, Kiefer 119
Sutton, Graham 193
Sweet Delta see Blood and Oil (2010 TV mini-series)
Sweet Lies 3, 56, 223
Swift, Jonathan 158
Sykes, Belinda 117, 164, 212

symphonic sound 9, 15, 20, 25, 27, 32–3, 36–7, 39–40, 43, 45, 53, 63, 87, 89, 91, 97–100, 107, 113, 115–20, 123–7, 132, 134, 136, 139, 144, 147, 147n9, 148, 155, 159, 163–4, 172, 180, 182, 185–6, 191, 193–4, 203–4, 208, 212–13, 217

synthesiser 15, 17, 31, 33, 40, 44, 46, 59, 66–7, 89–91, 116, 119, 123, 130, 132, 144, 171, 172, 182, 191, 198–9, 204, 208, 213, 218, 223, 224, 225; Fairlight 29, 33, 46n1, 52, 218; Prophet 5, 27, 66, 218; Roland D50 66; Synclavier 33, 40, 44, 46n2, 218; VCS3 27, 218; Yamaha DX7 218

Taboo 135
Talk of Angels 193, 224
Tarantino, Quentin 62
Taylor, Barry 200; 'An Emigrant's Daughter' 200
Te Deum 88
temp track 37, 64n3, 82–3, 87, 119–22, 129, 131, 138, 145–6, 160, 164–5, 172; 'temp love' 145
Test Match Special 153
Texas (band) 123; 'Once in a Lifetime' 123–4
Thatcher, Margaret 39, 107
Thin Lizzy 106; 'Whiskey in the Jar' 103
Thirteen Days 4, 10, 18, 129–39, 144, 191, 193, 196, 215, 225
This Office Life 150, 153–4, 223
Thompson, Richard 88; *Andalus/Radio Marrakesh* 88
Those Glory, Glory Days 36, 150, 152–4, 223
Three and Out 189, 199–200, 212–14, 217
timecode 54, 61, 67, 92n3, 92n5, 191
timelines pattern *see* Jones, Trevor, musical fingerprints, rhythmic 3+3+3+3+2+2 pattern
Titanic Town 95, 99, 118, 127, 212, 214, 224; 'Danny Boy' 118
Todd, Phil 59, 164, 213, 217
Tolkien, J.R.R. 28; *The Lord of the Rings* 28, 32
Tomkinson, Stephen 108
toolkits 2, 9, 11n1, 15, 17–18, 25, 26n1, 44, 46n7, 47, 49–63, 64n4, 64n7, 65–7, 69, 72, 74–5, 77–8, 80, 82–4, 87, 89–91, 92n3, 92n6, 92n13, 95, 116, 133, 154–5, 158, 171–2, 173n11, 201,

206n3, 210–14, 217–18, 223; *see also* atmospheres; Jones, Trevor, creative approaches
To Tokyo 219, 226
track sheets 1, 7, 20, 24, 34, 52, 59–63, 64n9, 65–6, 69, 72, 74–8, 81–4, 89, 92, 101, 113, 123–6, 135, 147n9
Travers, Peter 137
Travolta, John 74
Trevor Jones Archive 2, 5–7, 10, 18, 20, 27, 34–5, 39, 42–5, 46n8, 50, 54, 57–8, 60, 64n2, 64n9, 65, 74–5, 78, 80, 84, 87, 89, 92n7, 92n11, 92n16, 100–1, 111, 118–24, 127n6, 129–32, 135, 137–9, 144, 146, 147n9, 149, 156, 159–60, 164, 167–72, 180, 185–9, 192–3, 198, 207–8, 218–22, 226
Trevor, Richard 23
Trevor, William 173n9
Trigg, Josh 219, 226
Troubled Water see Blood and Oil (2010 TV mini-series)
True Colors 74, 77–8, 224
Twain, Mark 140
Twain, Shania 99; 'You've Got a Way' 99, 128n8
Twenty Thousand Leagues under the Sea 140

U2 91, 105, 127; 'Billy Boola' 102; 'In the Name of the Blues' 103; *War* 105 ('Sunday Bloody Sunday' 105)
Uematsu, Nobuo 182; *Final Fantasy VII* 182, 186
University of Leeds 2, 5, 46n8, 64n2, 64n9, 92n16, 127n6, 186
University of York 8–9, 15–17, 25, 27, 31, 49, 52, 67, 106–7, 132, 134, 140, 145, 159, 182, 190, 192, 204, 218
The Unsteady Chough 10, 146, 225

Vangelis 45; *Blade Runner* 45
Van Oostrum, Kees 196, 225
Van Rellim, Tim 39
van Tulleken, Jonathan 225
Vaughan Williams, Ralph 123
Verne, Jules 145
Vickers, Lindsey C. 223
video games 1, 8, 10, 177–88, 189, 205, 214, 221; *Blade II* 179; *Championship Bass* 179; *Command and Conquer* 179; *Fantastic Four* 179; *Hulk* 178, 179; *The Incredible Hulk: Ultimate Destruction*

179; *Medal of Honor: Pacific Assault* 179; *Phantom Hourglass* 185; *The Punisher* 178, 179; *Spider-Man* 177, 178, 179; *Spider-Man 2* 179; *Spirit Tracks* 185; *Superman* 179; *Tomorrow Never Dies* 178; *X2: Wolverine's Revenge* 179; *X-Men Legends* 179; *X-Men Legends II: Rise of Apocalypse* 179; *X-Men Next Dimension* 179
video tapes 57, 75, 156, 159–60; Betacam 217; Umatic 43, 121, 123, 128n8, 131, 135, 171, 217; VHS 5, 7, 75, 82, 119, 121, 126, 128n8, 131, 168, 171, 217
Vivaldi, Antonio 53, 80–3; Concerto for Two Mandolins in G 82
Vundla, Charlie 204
Vundla, Mfundi 197, 219, 225

Wagner, Richard 9, 28–31, 43, 88, 122, 135, 209; *Götterdämmerung* 2–9 ('Siegfried's Funeral March' 28–30); *Parsifal* 28–30, 209–10; *The Ring* 28–9; *Tristan and Isolde* 28–30
Walden Media 144–5
Wallace, Naomi 117
Walters, Julie 118
Ward, Brian 223
War Paint 23, 26n3, 189, 205, 207, 225
Webern, Anton 17
We Fight to Be Free 189, 195–9, 225
Weiland, Paul 224

Weir, Peter 191
Weller, Simon 199
Werner, Craig 64n10
Whalley, Kirsty 215
What Are Friends For see Crossroads
Whittington, William 96
Who Wants to Be a Millionaire? 148
Whynot, John 215
Wierzbicki, James 62
'wild' recording 20, 22, 31
Williams, Duncan 120, 211, 219
Williams, John (composer) 33, 97, 130, 132, 145, 160; *JFK* 130, 132–3; *Jurassic Park* 160; *Saving Private Ryan* 132
Williams, John (guitarist) 74, 217
Winters, Ben 1–2
Woodward, Kate 151
Woolley, Richard 223
Working Title 121
Wright, Gavyn 217
Wright, Rayburn 58, 158, 165, 167
Wright, Stephen 156
Wynn, Tim 179

Young, Christopher 130; *Species* 130
Young, Robert M. 56, 223

Zeiklow, Philip D. 130
Zelda Ruin 10, 177, 185–8, 225
Zimmer, Hans 69, 120, 211